DATE		

BOHICA

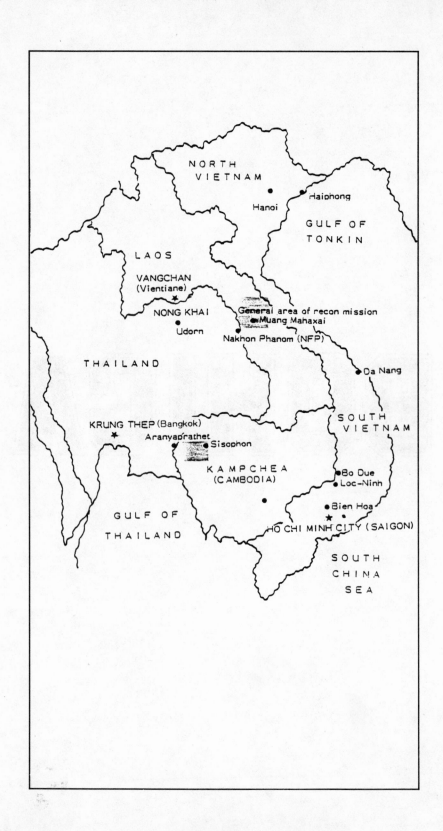

BOHICA

by

Scott Barnes

with

Melva Libb

BOHICA Corporation
Canton • Ohio

Library of Congress Cataloging-in-Publication Data

Barnes, Scott T. (Scott Tracy), 1954-
    Bohica / by Scott T. Barnes with Melva Libb.
       p.   cm.
       Includes index.
       ISBN 0-938936-61-1 : $19.95
       1. Vietnamese Conflict, 1961-1975--Prisoners and prisons,
Lao. 2. Vietnamese Conflict. 1961-175--Missing in action.
3. Prisoners of war--United States. 4. Prisoners of war--Laos.
I. Libb, Melva. II. Title
DS559.4.B37 1987
959.704 '37Z--dc19   87-16497
                                                CIP

This book is dedicated to Lieutenant Colonel Charles E. Shelton, his wife Dorothy M., and their five children, Lea Ann, Charles Jr., John Edward, Michael James and Joan Marie.

Colonel Shelton was born 29 April 1932 in Utica, N.Y. He attended Evansville College, Evansville, Il., receiving a B.S. degree in 1954. Entering active duty with the Air Force in October 1954 he began pilot training. A number of assignments followed after graduation from pilot training and on 4 June 1964 he was assigned to 15 Tac Recon Sq, Kadena AB, Okinawa. On 29 April 1965 while on a mission over Laos, his F-1C1 aircraft was struck by hostile antiaircraft fire. Colonel Shelton was subsequently captured and interned by hostile forces.

The following pictures of the Shelton family are as they were when Colonel Shelton was reported missing and as they are today.

Charles Ervin Shelton, USAF
Born April 29, 1932

As of Aug. 15, 1986 Col. Shelton
is still listed as a prisoner of war.

DATE OF REPORT
10 MAY 65

TO: Director of Military Personnel Headquarters USAF ATTN: Casualty Branch Washington 25, D. C.	THRU: (Command channels) 313 AIR DIVISION APO San Francisco 96239	FROM: 634 CMB SPT APO San Francisco 96239

1. MISSING		2. TYPE OF MISSION	3. DEPARTURE	
a. DATE 29 APR 65	b. TIME 0400Z (1100 Local)	Bomb Damage Assessment	a. TIME Ø 355Z	b. PLACE South Air, Thailand

4. INTENDED DESTINATION OR TARGET	5. INTENDED ROUTE	
Rost 6, near Sam Neva, Laos	Direct	UNCLASSIFIED

6. WEATHER CONDITIONS IF APPLICABLE (Include ceiling, visibility, winds, sea conditions, temperature of water, etc.)	7. LAST KNOWN LOCATION (Give coordinates and name of place)
Sky conditions: Broken;ceiling: 3000 agl feet;visibility: 10 miles	Near Sam Neva, Laos 20 degrees, 23 minutes North 104 degrees, 42 minutes East 2028/10402

PAGE 1 OF 5 PAGES
COPY 1 OF 1 COPIES

COPY ___1___ OF ___1___ COPIES

8.	AIRCRAFT (Check applicable box)		
a. LAST SIGHTED OR SEEN	b. LAST CONTACTED BY RADIO	c. SEEN TO CRASH	d. INFORMATION NOT AVAILABLE

9.			DESCRIPTION OF EQUIPMENT (If missing in aircraft)				
ITEMS	TYPE	MODEL	NAME	SERIAL NUMBERS	WEAPONS OR SPECIAL EQUIPMENT		
					NAME	TYPE	SERIAL NUMBER
ACFT ENGINES							
PROPELLERS							

9. NICKNAME OF AIRCRAFT OR OTHER IDENTIFYING MARKINGS			
RF-101C RC-90 "VOODOO"	ERIC-631-73	#1029	

10.	PERSONNEL AND/OR CREW (If missing in aircraft)			
CREW POSITION	LAST NAME - FIRST NAME - MIDDLE INITIAL	GRADE	SERVICE NUMBER	CURRENT STATUS
PILOT	Shelton, Charles E.	CAPT	AO3054666	SS MILST

AF FORM 484

UNCLASSIFIED

SAVEMER 6002

Apel L

REPORT OF CASUALTY	1. REPORT NUMBER AND TYPE C-7 Corrects Report J-86(1975)	2. DATE PREPARED 15 Apr 86

3. SERVICE IDENTIFICATION *(Name, Social Security Number, Grade or Rate, Component, Branch and Organization),* (MOS/NEC)
SHELTON, Charles Ervin, 401-38-4899FV, Col, Reserve, USAF -
15 Tac Recon Sq, APO San Francisco 96236   AFSC: 1323D

4. CASUALTY STATUS a. ☒ BATTLE ☐ NON-BATTLE   b. CONFIRMED YOUR DATE: 29 May 64

c. STATUS: ☐ DEATH ☐ ILL ☐ MISSING ☐ MISSING IN ACTION ☒ CAPTURED *‡ ☐ OTHER *(Specify)*

6. DATE: 29 Apr 65**   e. PLACE: Laos

7. CAUSE & CIRCUMSTANCES:

5. a. DATE AND PLACE OF BIRTH 29 Apr 32 - Utica, KY	b. RACE Caucasian	c. SEX Male	d. RELIGIOUS PREFERENCE Baptist

6. DATE AND PLACE OF LAST ENTRY ON ACTIVE DUTY IN CURRENT STATUS AND HOME OF RECORD AT TIME
Owensboro, KY

7a. PAY GRADE O-6	b. BASIC PAY	c. INCENTIVE/ADDITIONAL PAY ☒ YES *** ☐ NO	d. CHECK IF APPLICABLE ☒ CREW ☐ PASSENGER

8. DUTY STATUS

Active - On Duty

9. INTERESTED PERSONS *(Name, Address, Relationship)*   DATE OF RECORD OF EMERGENCY DATA FORM:

Mrs Dorothy M. Shelton	5238 Caminito Aruba, San Diego, CA 92124	Wife
Lea A. Shelton	Same	Dau
Charles E. Shelton Jr.	Same	Son
John E. Shelton	Same	Son
Joan M. Shelton	Same	Dau****

10. REPORT FOR VA TO FOLLOW ☐ YES ☒ NO	11. REPORTING COMMAND AGENCY AND DATE REPORT RECEIVED IN DEPARTMENT UDORN AFLD THAILAND - 29 Apr 65

12. PRIOR SERVICE DATA ☒ YES ☐ NO   FV2204666

13. REMARKS
*All previously issued DD Forms 1300 indicating subject as being in an interned status should be corrected to reflect captured.

**Individual was reported missing in action on 29 Apr 65. Sufficient evidence was received on 24 May 65 to warrant placing him in a captured status. A determination under the provisions of Title 50, USC, Missing Persons Act, was made to continue him in a captured status following the expiration of twelve months absence, effective 30 Apr 66.‡

***HOSTILE PAY: Yes
****Michael J. Shelton   Same   Son
FY 86 Fund Cite: Officer 576 3500 326 5781.0* 503725
                    Enlisted 576 3500 326 5881.0* 503725
NOTE: THIS FORM MAY BE USED TO FACILITATE THE CASHING OF BONDS. THE PAYMENT OF COMMERCIAL INSURANCE, OR IN THE SETTLEMENT IF ANY OTHER CLAIM IN WHICH PROOF OF DEATH REQUIRED

FOOTNOTES:
1. Adult next of kin.   ‡Indicates Change
2. Beneficiary for gratuity pay in event there is no surviving wife or child—as designated on record of emergency data.
3. Beneficiary for unpaid pay and allowances—as designated on record of emergency data.

14. DISTRIBUTION NOT USED	15. SIGNATURE ELEMENT *(signature)* DAVID M. O'CONNELL, SMSgt, USAF Chief, Casualty Assistance and Circumstances Branch	OFFICIAL

DD Form 1300, 1 FEB 73   REPLACES DD FORM 1300, 1 MAR 60, WHICH IS OBSOLETE.

Dorothy M. Shelton and daughter Joan, April 18, 1965, Easter Sunday. Charles Shelton left two days later. "We never saw him again."

Col. Charles Shelton and Dorothy M. Shelton, 1964.

*Grandmother Dorothy and
Mikey, November 1985.*

*Dorothy M. Shelton
September 1985.*

1964-65

1987

Lea A. Shelton

1964-65
10½ years old

1986

Capt. Charles E. Shelton Jr.

1964-65
9½ years old

1986

John E. Shelton

1964-65
8½ years old

1987

Michael James Shelton and son Francis Michael Shelton
- Born September 19, 1983, only grandchild of Col. Shelton.

1964-65
16 months old

1987

Joan M. Shelton

U.S. Unaccounted for Personnel

Army	782
Air Force	913
Navy	486
Marines	290
Coast Guard	1
Civilians	42
Total	2,434

U.S. Servicemen Unaccounted for by State

Alabama - 42
Alaska - 3
Arizona - 24
Arkansas - 27
California - 244
Colorado - 41
Connecticut - 39
Delaware - 5
District of Columbia - 9
Florida - 80
Georgia - 48
Hawaii - 11
Idaho - 12
Illinois - 100
Indiana - 70
Iowa - 39
Kansas - 38
Kentucky - 22
Louisiana - 34
Maine - 17
Maryland - 37
Massachusetts - 59
Michigan - 75
Minnesota - 47
Mississippi - 18
Missouri - 51
Montana - 21

Nebraska - 24
Nevada - 10
New Hampshire - 18
New Jersey - 63
New Mexico - 17
New York - 157
North Carolina - 61
North Dakota - 17
Ohio - 128
Oklahoma - 49
Oregon - 46
Pennsylvania - 119
Rhode Island - 18
South Carolina - 10
South Dakota - 9
Tennessee - 44
Texas - 158
Utah - 23
Vermont - 4
Virginia - 61
Washington - 60
West Virginia - 26
Wisconsin - 37
Wyoming - 6
Puerto Rico - 2
Virgin Islands - 1
Other - 7

Table of Contents

Preface

"Scott, you won't believe this new book that's out. It's all wrong!" It was mid-April, 1986 and my dear friend, Marian Shelton, wife of the only recognized POW still alive in Laos, phoned me at my home in Kernville, California, to inform me of a recently published book *The Heroes Who Fell From Grace* written by Army Special Forces Sergeant Charles J. Patterson and G. Lee Tippin, Colonel, (U.S. Army, Retired). As I sat at the desk in my den looking out my picture window at the beautiful view of the Kern River valley, Marian shared the chapter of the *"Heroes"* book that described *Operation Grand Eagle*. This portion of the book was inaccurate and had sadly discredited me.

Not long after Marian's call, Elvus Sasseen, a POW advocate from Oklahoma City, phoned me. He too was upset about *"Heroes"*, published by Daring Books. "I know you, Scott," he lamented, "and the part about you in this book is all wrong!"

CIA counsel Richard Sullivan mailed me excerpts from the book. I felt this was an attempt to intimidate me sufficiently to top me from talking about the POWs I had seen while assigned to *Operation Grand Eagle* in 1981. (*Operation Grand Eagle* was referred to as *Bohica* in secret communications between our team while in Southeast Asia and the Defense Intelligence Agency (DIA), the Central Intelligence Agency (CIA, known as "The Agency"), and the Intelligence Support Activity (ISA, known as "The Activity"). (Document 14 - A,B,C) As I read these excerpts I began to boil internally. Five years of trying to withstand the threats against me and my family, five years of attempts to ridicule me and discredit my name finally erupted in pure rage.

"This is enough! Now I'm really angry!" I shouted to no one in particular. Then I calmed down enough to know I wanted to find out more about this book, so I called Daring Books and ordered a copy.

After reading *The Heroes Who Fell From Grace*, I telephoned Daring Books once again and asked to speak to Dennis Bartow, the publisher. By this time the serenity of the view out my den window disturbed me. I really had no desire to be calmed. As I waited for Mr. Bartow to come to the phone, I turned my back to the window to look at the familiar world map on my wall. For a moment I stared at the highlighted Indochina area, then, almost involuntarily, focused on the POW slogan hinging beside the map: *You'll never be forgotten.* Bartow's "Hello?" interrupted my thoughts.

"This stuff about me in *The Heroes Who Fell From Grace* is an outright lie!" I immediately protested to this man I'd never met.

"Prove to me that it's wrong," he replied calmly.

"In the back of the book, Mr. Bartow, look at the list of persons said to have been involved in *Operation Grand Eagle.*" Quickly I grabbed my copy of the book from my desk and flipped to the list the names of those who had supposedly been involved with *Operation Grand Eagle.*

Operation Grand Eagle

Vinnie Arnone

J.D. Bath

Scott Barnes

"Cranston" (Jerry Koenig)

Congressman Robert Dornan

Ben Dunakoskie

James "Bo" Gritz

Harry Holt

Walter "Butch" Jones

Charles "Chuck" Patterson

Admiral Paulson

"Shipman" (Daniel Johnson)

General Vang Pao

"Vinnie Arnone...He wasn't on our mission at all. Ben Dunakoskie, yes...Colonel Gritz, yes (pronounced Grights)...Walter 'Butch' Jones, yes. Patterson? He wasn't involved. Admiral Paulson? Yes. General Vang Pao? Yes. And where are the others? You don't list Colonel Mike Eiland, or other CIA personnel. Jerry Daniels, who I feel was one of the most important participants, well, he isn't listed, or William Macris. In fact, Macris isn't in your book at all. Neither is CIA Station

Chief Daniel C. Arnold or Robert Moberg who was to be our main helicopter pilot."

"I published the book the way it was written, Mr. Barnes," Bartow explained.

"This other stuff about *Operation Grand Eagle* - you've been taken in! You don't include Dominic Zappone; you don't include Bobby Schwab. It's incomplete."

"Is that all that makes the book incomplete?"

At least this man was willing to listen to me, which was more than I could say for the many government officials I had talked with over the years; so I continued, hoping I wouldn't be told to shut up as I had been told so often in the past. "*Bohica* was the only official government POW reconnaissance operation in Southeast Asia," I said. Bartow agreed. "And it went public. Do you think any normal person is going to risk attempting another mission now that this one's gone public?" Again Bartow agreed.

When I asked Mr. Bartow for the phone number of Charles Patterson, co-author of *The Heroes Who Fell From Grace*, he said he wouldn't tell me, so I did a little research on my own and found out that Patterson didn't live far from me. I called and, talking pretty rough, confronted him with the inaccuracies in his book. Curtly I informed him of the February 21, 1983, *Los Angeles Times* (Document 15) story which he knew nothing about, explaining to him that this *Times* article was the first to publicly identify all who actually were part of the recon team called *Operation Grand Eagle*.

"You wrote a bunch of lies!" I shouted over the phone, still unable to control my feelings of rage and giving him little opportunity to respond. In spite of my verbal attack, Patterson admitted that he'd never met me - although the book made it appear that he had - and also admitted that he had not been involved with *Operation Grand Eagle*.

"But you lied to the publisher!" I accused him. He tried to explain that he had related to co-author Lee Tippin only information that had been given to him about *Grand Eagle* from participants of that mission and then suggested that I talk to Bartow about my complaints, unaware that I already had done so.

"This has to be corrected," I said and hung up.

Disturbed by all my shouting, my wife Donna came into our den and interrupted my series of phone calls. "Look, Scott, you've come to the point where you're going to have to make a decision between the POW issue and your job."

I knew Donna was right, but at that moment my head was swirling with so many things that needed to be done. "Okay Donna," I said. "But this Bartow's wronged me. As soon as I sue him and we own him, then I'll call it quits." The years of denial and loss of material, as well as emotional, well-being had taken their toll. Visions of a financial gain and retaliation brought a feeling of deep satisfaction to me.

Apparently appeased by my response, Donna left the room and once again I dialed the number for Daring Books and asked to talk with Dennis Bartow. "I just spoke to Patterson," I told him. I couldn't keep the smugness out of my voice.

"How'd you find him?" he asked. He was so cordial; he really could have cursed at me instead.

"I'm an investigator," I retorted. "I know how to find people. Look, I'll give you names of five people to contact. They can give you the names of others to check with so you will know I am telling you the truth."

At my recommendation Bartow called David Taylor, Executive Producer of British Broadcasting Corporation (BBC), Washington, D.C. Bureau; Gary Lane of the Christian Broadcasting Network (CBN); Captain Eugene "Red" McDaniel, U.S. Navy Retired, former POW and president of the American Defense Institute; Dr. Chris Gugas, former CIA agent and one of the world's outstanding polygraphists, member of the General Tighe POW Commission; and my good friend Marian Shelton. Several days later he called me back and apologized.

"The more I look into this, the more I believe that the references to you in the book are inaccurate." Eager to discover the truth about the whole matter, he had checked further and found that the Spring, 1983, *Soldier of Fortune* (Document 16) article which was being widely used against me in government circles was purposely set up as disinformation. "What should we do now, Scott?" he asked.

"I'm going to sue you," I told him. "I've already contacted a libel lawyer in Canton, Ohio, recommended by my attorney here in Fresno. I'm going to sue you for everything you've got." I hung up, then phoned Attorney Snow in Canton telling him to proceed with the suit. Next I phoned my lawyer in Fresno who is known to be good in libel and slander cases regarding books.

"I'll get a certified letter out to Bartow immediately," he responded after hearing my story. "We'll have him in court in a week. We'll get an injunction. This guy's over."

"Damn right he is!" I agreed indignantly, feeling very satisfied with his reaction.

Then I remembered that Dennis Bartow had mentioned something about paperback rights to *The Heroes Who Fell From Grace* going to Dell Books, so I warned Dell by phone, "You better not do this book. There are lies in it."

Later that same week Gary Lane, Washington, D.C., correspondent for CBN News who had interviewed me for the 700 Club, called me. "Scott, I just had a phone inquiry about you from a Dennis Bartow of Daring Books." Lane said he told Bartow CBN had investigated me thoroughly and he felt that Pat Robertson*, plus many other credible people, believed my story because none of them had found anyone who could disprove me. He also told Mr. Bartow their interview with me brought out portions of truth which others in the media had not. "We've proved the government isn't telling the whole story." Lane paused, then spoke cautiously, obviously aware of the fragility of my emotional state. "However, Scott...I don't believe the publisher of *Heroes* can be faulted for these lies. I think this Bartow is a...believer."

"A believer?" That was the last thing I wanted to hear.

"A Christian brother, Scott."

---

*Founder and president of Christian Broadcasting Network.

Because I could not reinforce my anger if I accepted Gary's conclusion, I rejected his observation. "I don't believe it! - And I really don't care!"

"Look into it before you take any further legal action, will you?" he suggested. The moment we hung up, my phone rang again. It was David Taylor of BBC telephoning from Washington, D.C.

"Scott, how are you doing?"

"Oh, all right." I'm sure he could tell by my voice how upset I was.

"I've received a copy of the *Heroes* book."

Fearing that he too might try to dissuade my plans to retaliate, I had no desire to talk with him about that book. "It's ignorant," I responded.

"So I've heard. But don't make a big deal. ...Scott, I don't know why, but I feel this Bartow chap might be a religious man." I began to think about the opinions of Lane and Taylor whose support and encouragement I valued. At the same time I remembered seeing something in the Bible that said Christians shouldn't sue Christians. If you have a problem with a brother, the Bible says, you are to take it to the elders of the church.

No sooner had I hung up than my lawyer from Fresno returned a call I had made to his office earlier in the day. "Are you ready? Just sign me a letter of Power of Attorney approval, and we'll take legal action against Mr. Bartow for ten million dollars. We'll put him out of business."

Much of my steam having been vented and the advice of my two friends still fresh in my mind, I hesitated. "...Okay. ...Good," I answered slowly, now troubled and feeling very uneasy about the lawsuit. I had to call Dennis Bartow again.

"Hey, are you a Christian?" I asked bluntly when he came to the phone. "Absolutely. In fact, my father's a well-known pastor."*

"OHHhhh."

---

*Rev. Donald Bartow has been pastor of the Westminster Presbyterian Church, Canton, Ohio, since 1966. He is also the founder/director of The Spiritual Healing Ministry, Inc.

"...And I have a very close relationship with my father," he continued. "In fact, I've told him everything that's been going on. I'm a man who believes in truth, Scott. The truth should get out. ...Why don't we tell your side of the story?"

I'll bet he wondered why such a long silence followed his suggestion. *Hmm*, I thought, *I wouldn't cooperate with the New York publishers - or that Christian company down in Tennessee.* I leafed through the *Heroes* book that was lying on my desk. "Dennis, I'm getting ready to go to Sacramento. I have to give a speech on POWs at the state capital for the Disabled American Veterans. I'll get back with you."

"Why don't I send a letter to anybody you want me to," he offered. "I'm going to clear this whole thing up, Scott. I'm going to put an 'errata' in the front of every copy of the *Heroes* book in our inventory. I'm determined to fix this." His earnestness surprised me.

"You know you could be putting a knife in your own back and in your sales if you did that, Dennis." I was alarmed at my concern for this publisher I had been so angry with. Was I beginning to soften? But the Spirit of God seemed to speak to my heart, *"Wait a minute. Nothing can happen to you as a result of this Heroes book unless I allow it."*

Caring more about truth than the financial success of the book, Dennis Bartow did just what he said he would do. Overnight, he expressed a retraction/errata to Colonel Earl Hopper who was in charge of a POW/MIA group in Arizona, one to Dr. Bruce Adams in New Mexico and another directly to the POW Conference in Sacramento where Colonel Hopper was to be moderator. (Document 17 - A,B)

Everyone at that meeting seemed to have heard of the *Heroes* book, although few had had opportunity to read it. I was relieved to see that when the Colonel stood and read the letter, everyone present was astonished at the publisher's honesty.

In a subsequent official meeting of the National League of Families of American Prisoners and Missing in Southeast Asia (The families of POW/MIA's direct link to the U.S. government) at an Air Force base in New Mexico, Dr. Bruce Adams, relative of a POW, also read the publisher's notice. It was reported to me this upset Ann Mills Griffiths, Executive Director of the National League of Families who had already begun to use the book as evidence to discredit me. She interrupted Dr. Adams, attempting to prevent him from completing the reading of the errata notice.

Lieutenant Colonel Dick Childress of the National Security Council in the White House also interrupted Dr. Adams, saying he was out of order because reading the notice was not on the agenda.

Following the meeting I phoned Dennis and thanked him. "Scott, let's arrange for you to come to Canton as soon as possible and get started with your book." I was eager to begin.

*   *   *   *   *

On the day I was to arrive in Canton, Ohio to begin work on my book, I phoned Dennis Bartow, publisher of Daring Books, from my home in California. "I'm not coming," I told him. "The whole thing's finished. I've had it." Disappointed, Dennis asked for an explanation.

"I just received another threatening phone call, and I can't ignore this one. The voice said, in essence, 'We know where you live...that you have children. We know the vehicles you drive and the schedules you and your wife keep. Yesterday you took your daughter with you and bought her a popsicle at James Market in Kernville. So you'd better keep your mouth *shut*! You shouldn't have testified, Barnes. You'll regret the day you were born!' "

This threat wasn't from some kook. Unlike the other harassing calls I had received, without a doubt this one was serious. I decided I just couldn't leave my family and fly to Ohio, not knowing what might happen to Donna and the two children while I was away. Our home is located the in Sierra Mountain foothills. The closest towns of any significant size where I have close associates are Bakersfield or China Lake, fifty miles away. I wondered why I'd ever become involved in this POW thing and felt it now was best to call the whole thing off. So I had phoned Dennis, hoping that whoever was listening in on my call would say, "Good, the threat worked!" and my family would be safe.

The following day I drove some distance into a town to see someone who wanted to engage my services as a private investigator. Returning home tired and discouraged, I was dreading the emptiness I would find inside, with Donna still at work and Jessica, age three, and Joshua, one, at the babysitter's. As I pulled up into my driveway, something by our front window caught my eye. I dragged myself from my car, walked up the steep hill to my home and found two dead birds tied together with a fishing line around their necks. I picked them up by the string. Their necks had been broken.

Never having seen birds like them in our area, I wasn't sure what they were, so I walked down the road to show them to a friend. He confirmed what I had thought. Turtledoves.

"But we don't have turtledoves around here," I responded in disbelief.

"Not unless somebody's pets got away," he agreed. *Yeh*, I thought, *they do know where I live - whoever 'they' are, and they've actually been to my home!*

As I walked home, I remembered that CIA, Clandestine Section, always said that the dove is a symbol of peace and a dead dove means "Your peace is over." I was mad - mad that somebody had killed two innocent little birds in an attempt to intimidate and threaten me. By the time I arrived home, I was filled with anxiety and fear for my family's safety. Tossing the dead birds far into the brush, vowing not to tell Donna, I immediately checked all the doors and windows for signs of a break-in or of tampering. There weren't any. Then I packaged up all the documents that remained dealing with the *Bohica* mission and all the records of my contacts, put them in my car and drove fourteen miles to the home of a friend. From there I mailed the documents "Certified/Return Receipt" to Daring Books for safekeeping.

It was then that I decided to get a Doberman Pinscher. Now that he stays in the house a lot, I'm not quite so concerned. Yet, every time we go away, I cannot resist checking all the screens, doors and locks and the security system when we come home to see if there are any pry marks. My neighbors have told me that several times they have seen suspicious people they didn't know in cars they did not recognize watching the house with binoculars. Every time I hear a car I get up and look out the window and wonder why *they* are here.

The FBI, the Naval Investigative Services and the State Department have sent personnel to pressure me several times in recent months. Less than two weeks after the threats were made, a Lieutenant Fred Ross from the sheriff's office phoned to inform me that on orders of Sheriff Larry Kleier my firearms permit was to be denied. "It's all because of this POW thing and the *Soldier of Fortune* article," he told me. "You should never have talked." As a private investigator, losing the right to carry a gun caused me to feel extremely vulnerable. And very angry. I was convinced suspicious dealings had to be going on, and that some very powerful people in the government were involved.

Because I knew the sheriff personally, I decided to talk with him. Through his arrangements, I often had taken a lot of my students (I taught a college at the time.) to his buddy Norman Power's security training academy to teach them about firearms. I asked Sheriff Larry Kleier, "Who's pressuring you?"

He'd been under investigation himself by the attorney general of California and the district attorney's office for all kinds of allegations of misdeeds and satanic doings, so he was under a lot of heavy duty scrutiny. "I'm not going into details, Barnes," he told me, "but as chief law enforcement officer of MY county I feel you shouldn't be armed any longer."

"Being without firearms protection makes me quite vulnerable. If you won't grant me a permit, I'll apply for a state permit," I told him.

My permit was renewed by state authorities in Sacramento, which upset Sheriff Kleier. He was even more upset because I supported his political rival John Smith and vowed to get even with me somehow. (Winning the election by a landslide that year, Smith defeated the allegedly most corrupt sheriff in Kern County history.)

I continued to keep in touch with Dennis, but with extreme caution. More than once my phone calls had been interrupted, so I knew my line was tapped.

Bob Dorf of Beverly Hills, who was looking into a case regarding the use of yellow rain in Southeast Asia, called me to discuss the Robert Kelly case, a cocaine bust in northern California which also implicated Daniel Arnold, CIA, and Vang Pao, the Laotian general now living in the States. While we were agreeing that we both disliked the fact that certain members of the CIA were selling drugs in order to finance some of their operations without having to report to Congressional and Agency officials, someone broke in on our conversation.

"You're not supposed to discuss matters like that on the telephone," the voice warned.

The story about Kelly, a CIA man who lived just north of me who had been caught with several hundred pounds of cocaine secretly warehoused at a small ranch in Termo, California, barely made the news. He wasn't in jail even a full day. "Technicalities," was the explanation given by the U.S. Attorney's office for his brief incarceration. No charges were ever filed against him. No trial occurred.

Bob complained to his phone company and I filed a telephone interruption complaint with the sheriff's department and with my phone company. A young man who worked for the phone company did several tests.

"Somebody's definitely monitoring your phone calls," he told me after hours of searching, at an excessive cost to the phone company, "but we can't pinpoint where the tap is located. You're in a rural community and the lines go so far through the desert-mountain area by microwave, it would take weeks - maybe months - to find the source. This kind of interruption is usually done using high frequency equipment and high tech electronic devices, - the kind China Lake (a Naval Weapons Center about 50 miles away) uses. All I can say is that if you're going to make important phone calls, you'd better do it from a phone other than the one in your home."

For a long time I had suspected someone was listening to every phone conversation made from our house and this incident confirmed

my suspicions. If I talked to my lawyer about a new piece of information and he promised to follow up on it, he would later report back
to me, "By the time I got there, somebody else had already talked
to them."

"It's got to be the phone," he had concluded. And so had I. No
doubt about it.

I really felt sorry for Donna. "This is no way to raise a family,"
she complained about the eavesdropping discovery.

During 1985 I learned another phone in the area had been intercepted
by mistake. A woman who gave her agent number and identified herself
as Genevieve Kane from the CIA had been instructed to call me. Immediately I recognized her name. She was a security officer at CIA
headquarters - a "Watch Officer." I wasn't surprised to receive a call
from her.

"We're investigating a report of a break-in on one of your phone
calls to the Agency," she told me. "The tappers were one digit off
and were listening in on someone else's phone conversation about
three miles away." She advised me that I could call back to verify
the information, which I did. Apparently someone had thought they
were listening to my line and had threatened the person on the line.

"Do you know anything about this?" Genevieve asked.

"Yeh! It's your people again!" I accused her.

"You know we don't do things like that anymore, Scott," she quickly
responded. (It's not often that you hear the CIA admit they've made
even a minor mistake.) Wanting to make sure others were aware of
what her section was doing, I asked her if my former agent/handler
Dan Mulqueen was in but was told he was out of town on assignment. I then asked to speak with another agent, Larry Straderman.
He was out of town too. In other words, according to Ms. Kane, all
the personnel I had been told to keep in contact with were suddenly
"out of town." As usual, no one from the Agency wanted to talk with
me any longer.

As I continued to keep Dennis and my attorney informed of any
new developments, I went to great lengths to make sure our phone
conversations were heard only by two of us. Often I loaded all my

fishing gear and my weapon into the car and drove throughout this valley - up the road that follows Kern River or to Ridgecrest - using only pay phones to make my calls and using a scrambler. I screened my automobile for any bugs and watched carefully to make sure no one had followed me, making certain there was *nobody* around when I made my calls. One time I drove in excess of one hundred miles to San Bernadino County, changing cars twice.

"I'll communicate with you by mail from now on, using no return address," I finally told Dennis. I knew and trusted the postmaster who had agreed to give special attention to all my incoming and outgoing mail.

Although I continued to work with BBC on their reports of the POW situation and filed a complaint against a lieutenant commander in the Navy who was harassing me with letters and phone calls, I tried to remain low key - nothing in the media. Yet more and more pressure came from various government agencies and "unofficial" officials.

My experiences while trying to find someone in government to listen to my story have been extremely frustrating. Had I kept my nose clean and told the news people "No, I'm not interested," I probably still could have been living leisurely in Hawaii today. For six years, my life has been tipped over. When I interview for a job I am usually asked, "Hey, aren't you the guy...?" and my opportunity for employment is gone. Or they do a background investigation and run my fingerprints. Even though I have no criminal record, they quickly conclude, "Forget it. We're sorry, but we can't hire you." Constantly I've been turned down for jobs because of the POW issue and the allegations of heavy CIA involvement in cases against Hell's Angels and involvement throughout Indochina and the Mideast.

"You're the guy who went against your government," they often accuse.

"No," I answer. "I love my government and my country. Ours is the greatest country in the world and I've served proudly and honorably. The government hired me to do something and I did it. I reported it. Now the government isn't doing anything about it."

"Well, we believe in the government," they usually respond.

"So do I. Would U.S. Federal Judge Boyle uphold a lawsuit against the President of the United States and the entire U.S. government if there was nothing to it?" I ask. "There's a cover-up. An absolute cover-up."

One day as I was mulling over the whole problem in my mind I thought, *Now that Jerry Daniels* is dead I am now the only living American who can testify about the findings of the Bohica mission, the only known American who has seen live U.S. POWs in Indochina during a government sanctioned mission. Everyone else who was involved is either dead, missing or not talking. You're it, Scott!** The world should have known about this many years ago. It could not continue to be covered up any longer. Dennis had reminded me of this when we last talked.

Although I was tired of the pressures and the hassles, I couldn't forget my experience in Laos. I prayed about this a lot. Surely other citizens of this country have firsthand knowledge of live POWs. Why haven't they come forward?

Mark Waple, attorney for the Smith/McIntyre lawsuit against the government, encouraged me, "Get the truth out, Scott. Then maybe government officials will be pressured into action." I then realized that for my own peace of mind I *must* get the truth about remaining live POWs in Southeast Asia to the public and I recommitted myself to push on at any cost.

---

*The only other American who, with Scott, sighted and photographed live POWs in Laos in October, 1981, *Bohica* mission.

---

*General Robert Robinson, who was connected with Bohica, has committed suicide; Jerry Daniels, CIA, mysteriously died of carbon monoxide poisoning. Michael Hand, a Green Beret who was to be a financial and contact man for the mission and in 1981 briefly met with Scott in a bar in Bangkok, was associated with the Nugan/Hand banking industrial front for the CIA which was exposed in 1982. None of the other Special Forces men who were involved will talk about *Bohica*.

Acknowledgments

Many people have helped me with this book and in my life, especially the past six years. Some I am unable to fully identify due to their sensitive positions, but to all I am deeply and personally indebted for their love, friendship and the risking of their lives and reputations.

I must begin by pouring out my heart to M.A.J., the dearest and truest friend I've ever had. I shall always hold you in my heart. April 27, 1987, the day I lost your friendship and support, was the saddest day of my life, I'll always hold you dear.

Powerful individuals have sought to stop the publication of this book and the safe return of our fellow American POWs/MIAs. For you I pray for God's mercy.

Dr. Steve W., thank you for all your help, for your friendship which goes back to the time we were first school buddies 19 years ago.

A special thank you to David Taylor of BBC, Washington, D.C., for uncovering and reporting the *Bohica* mission. You are a true friend of the POWs and of mine. To H. Ross Perot for your many words of encouragement and your efforts to get our men home.

To Major Mark Smith and Sergeant First Class Melvin McIntyre for your special operations, for your efforts to expose the truth and for not revealing our missions. To Lieutenant General Eugene Tighe for your helpful words and deeds in an attempt to get our POWs home. To Professor Matthew Meselson, Harvard University, for our many conversations concerning the POWs and for your guidance. To Professor Howard Holter, California State University, Dominiguez Hills, for your help and sincere involvement with the POW issue.

To Marian Shelton, Chris and Ann Gugas, Eugene 'Red' McDaniel, General Vang Pao and his staff; to Ralph Moore, Craig Englert and Randy Sanford of Hope Chapel: how can I ever thank you sufficiently for your friendship and your prayers? To Congressmen Robert Smith, Bill Hendon, Robert K. Dornan and former Congressman LeBoutillier; to Senators Strom Thurman, Rockefeller and Cranston; to Zac Mazarian and General David Jones; to those loyal members of ISA, CIA, NSA and DIA who assisted covertly in this entire mission but for security reasons were not able to step forward. In memory of Jerry Daniels, General Robby C. Robinson and General Hunter Harris.

To Mark Waple for spending so much time and effort to right the wrong which has been done. To Senator Deconcini for the many conversations; to Colonel Earl Hopper for your support and kindness.

To Cruse Reynolds, Melvin Belli, Dr. Brian Jenkins of the Rand Corporation, and John Delorean. To David, Barbara, Patty, Gary, Jimmy, Bobby, Dan H., Mark, Becca, Margaret, Jack, Ruby, Doug M., Susie, Laura, Julie and Mary.

To my brother Brian, you have always been there when I've needed you. To those in Kernville who have been supportive because you too want our men home. To the Davy family - Laura, Julie and Mary - thank you for your years of friendship.

My deepest apology to Donna and my children Marc, Jessica and Joshua who have had to suffer so much because of my involvement in this issue. I truly wish you a better life.

To the many at Daring Books who have labored with me to bring this book to reality and to Marjorie Murch Stanley for her editing. *God bless our POWs, MIAs and their families!*

Greater love hath no man than this, that
a man lay down his life for his friends.

John 15:13

Introduction

Most decent Americans would not want to believe this story; frankly, neither did I. However, as I researched Scott Barnes' story, the facts seemed to be overwhelmingly in his favor. *Bohica*, code name for *Operation Grand Eagle* in October of 1981, was a government-sanctioned mission to scout for our POWs in Southeast Asia. Until recently, our government denied that there was ever such a mission. Bill Paul in an August 1986 *Wall Street Journal* article confirmed that a government-sponsored operation did occur.

Bohica is told by the only American survivor of this mission, Scott Barnes. He and another CIA agent - M.J.B., or Michael J. Baldwin, alias Jerry Daniels, actually saw and photographed two caucasian males under heavy guard and heard them speak English with a long-range listening device, in 1981.

After dividing the more than 400 exposures taken of these presumed POWs, Jerry Daniels left to hand-deliver his to the U.S. Embassy in Bangkok. Six months later, he died mysteriously in Thailand of carbon monoxide poisoning in his apartment there. Scott mailed his, as he was directed, to Daniel C. Arnold, CIA. He was later told that all the negatives had accidentally been destroyed in processing. His paid, round trip ticket back to the United States had been canceled by persons unknown and he had to pay a large sum out of his own pocket to get home. He was detained and searched three times.

Back in America, Scott tried to reach his former contacts involved with this mission. Suddenly, no one knew him. Those who did claimed he was crazy, and since 1981, Scott Barnes has been harassed, threatened, called a flake and a liar, lost employment, and spent his meager financial resources on phone calls and travel to search desperately for someone to believe him. Not surprisingly, his family suffered also, and he eventually lost them in his obsessive quest for something to be done about our POWs.

The only supposed "evidence" against Scott was based on a 1983 *Soldier of Fortune* article, which branded him a "flake" but offered no real evidence, only third-hand disinformation. Scott tells his side of that article in *Bohica*.

Interestingly, some of the people who claimed not to know Scott have been included in documents in this book, i.e., personally signed business cards, photographs, and letters.

Even some people in the media were either deliberately duped, or did not research his story completely. Some claimed that his numerous exams; polygraph, psychological, and sodium amytal (truth serum) were scams; when, in fact, they were all administered by recognized experts in their respective fields, and all chosen by other parties; including Ted Koppel and ABC *Nightline*. Each of these experts proclaimed their belief that he was telling the truth.

Fact 1 - At the request of Ted Koppel and ABC *Nightline*, Dr. Chris Gugas, world-reknowned polygrapher who has conducted over 30,000 such tests, many for the government, tested Scott seven or eight times and was so convinced that he was telling the truth, that he became involved in the POW/MIA problem.

Fact 2 - Dr. Frederick Hacker of Beverly Hills, California, who has examined Patty Hearst and others, also tested Scott at the request of the *Nightline* program. He told Bill Redecker, who was then employed with *Nightline,* that Scott was not crazy or a liar. He said he believed Scott was telling the truth.

Fact 3 - Dr. Robert Crummie administered an excessive dose of truth serum in the presence of BBC producer David Taylor, who filmed the entire episode. This event was also documented by two U.S. Federal Court reporters on behalf of Judge Boyle, and that film is now being used as evidence by attorney Mark Waple in his case for the Smith/McIntyre lawsuit against the United States Government for failing to do something to rescue the POWs in Southeast Asia.

Fact 4 - After the Carter Administration declared all of our POWs to be dead, with the exception of Captain (now Colonel) Shelton, Bobby Garwood came home in 1979. He was never debriefed even though he told our government that there were other American POWs still in Southeast Asia. He was labeled a traitor, and fined for the exact amount of money that our government owed him for the years he was held captive.

Fact 5 - Bobby Garwood told of a cistern in Hanoi where he saw a dozen or more American POWs bathing. Our government claimed there was no such place. Several U.S. congressmen went to Hanoi and walked away from their Vietnamese guides and found the cistern Garwood described in the presence of an ABC News *20/20* camera crew. The DIA now admits the cistern does exist.

Fact 6 - A top secret CIA report states that Colonel Shelton was rescued by friendly indiginous personnel, but that he was recaptured on the way to freedom.

Fact 7 - The bones which have been returned to our country and alleged to be those of POWs have been examined by forensic anthropoligist Dr. Michael Charney and found not be those the Pentagon claimed.

These and other events are documented in *Bohica*. It is such a tragic and complicated situation, but there are too many deceptive events and unanswered or ignored problems in this POW/MIA situation. We purposely chose a woman with no military background to write Scott Barnes' story. Melva Libb is a lay minister in the United Church of Christ, and has written curricula for church schools and other projects. She has spent a full year transcribing tapes, documents and videos, plus hours talking to Scott to record his story.

Based on my experiences as a book publisher and as a military officer (13 years in the U.S. Army Special Forces, 101st Airborne Div., and Psychological Operations), I came to the conclusion that with all the names, phone numbers, knowledge of events and connections that Scott Barnes has had plus documents of the same, it is crucial his story be made public. At no point did we find solid evidence to discredit him, rather the evidence continues to confirm his story through events revealed in the media this past year.

Scott Barnes is no hero and never claimed to be, but it seems to those of us who have worked closely with him that even a flake or an opportunist would have quit long ago after six years of seeing no fame or fortune for his efforts. Quite to the contrary, Scott has lost much personally, and even turned down money offered in efforts to quiet him. It seems logical, in fact, to assume that only a man who had actually witnessed something so horrible, something indelibly printed in his memory, could continue in the face of so many trials, to persist in his quest for his story to be believed and acted upon by this great nation. Thus, our decision to publish *Bohica*.

In spite of the fact that efforts to hush and discredit Scott Barnes continue, a new wave of activities has begun. Numerous highly respected United States' citizens intend to restore his credibility. Some of their letters of recommendation and commendation are included in this book. New information confirming various previously debunked details of Scott's testimony has been uncovered. Several seemingly unrelated lawsuits have been filed - unrelated until the names of the people accused in these suits are recognized as those connected with the *Bohica* mission. Scott Barnes' account of *Bohica* is now being heard and believed.

On November 13, 1986, along with seven other highly respected participants, Scott was a speaker at the MIA/POW symposium, *MISSING BUT NOT FORGOTTEN*, held at Colorado State University. (Document 6) Robert Smith, Vietnam veteran and congressman from New Hampshire, said on that day: "In countless numbers of DIA folders in the Pentagon today, if you've flunked the polygraph you're a fabricator - that's a big word for liar. But if you don't flunk it, and you pass it like Scott Barnes did, seven or eight times...Well...polygraphs aren't all that credible."

Dr. Chris Gugas, former Marine and CIA man who polygraphed Scott for ABC, admitted he first became intensely interested in the POW issue because of the results of the polygraph tests he administered to Scott. At the Colorado State Symposium, Dr. Gugas said in part, "What Scott Barnes did not tell you is that he lost his wife; he lost his car; he lost his furniture. He's lost any chance of getting a job in his particular area. Many of us that know him have checked him out. His credentials are impeccable. ...Here's a young man - I guess he's probably thirty-two - thirty-three - who out of his heart went over to try to do a job at the government's request, did the job, came back and was inundated with all types of hearsay and incompetency and was called crazy."

Colonel Earl Hopper, who introduced each of the speakers, said of Scott, "Scott Barnes has been polygraphed seven or eight times, and he has passed every polygraph test. But he's gone a step farther. In December of last year, he took a sodium amytal truth serum test to prove again he was telling the truth. He has an incredible story."

Evidently the CIA files on Scott contain information they don't want even him to know about. His 1982 request for copies was met with a mostly deleted copy. His subsequent inquiries were delayed until early 1987, then refused. (Document 9 - A,B,C,D,E,F,G,H for history of Scott's request.) The basis of the refusal was referred to as (j)(1) and (k)(1) on a sheet of "Explanation of Exemptions." As a result of his appeal, the CIA has recently informed him his request will be referred to either the Deputy Director or the Senior Official of the CIA. To the many who are supporting Scott in his efforts to make the truth known about POWs and his involvement in the *Bohica* mission, this reluctance to comply shows that somebody has something to hide and the referral to higher ups indicates the importance the CIA places upon keeping Scott's records secret from even Scott himself.

Scott's resume includes a list of the organizations to which he belongs: (Document 10,11 - A,B,C,D,E,F,G,H,I,J,K,L,M,N,O, P,Q.) If he is such an undesirable character, wouldn't he have been asked to resign or sever relationships from one, several - all? Yet not one has asked that he step down.

On January 3, 1987, someone in government evidently thought Scott had important and credible information to share. He was subpoenaed to testify before a grand jury in Oklahoma City and deluged with phone calls from U.S. federal officials. (Appendix 12)

The man responsible for the *Soldier of Fortune* magazine article which has damaged Scott's credibility more than any other piece of false information has been busily trying to stop Scott from making mention of his wife, a Drug Enforcement agent, in this book. This publisher, as well as Scott has received numerous warnings. Finally Scott phoned the Drug Enforcement Agency to complain about these threats and to ask whether the man's wife was still in DEA employ.

As a result, Frank Panessa, Senior Inspector for DEA Internal Security from the Office of Professional Responsibility, flew to California to meet with Scott and listen to his story. "These past few years you've been trying to make a point and no one would believe you. I believe you," he told Scott in a March 1987 phone conversation. "Every time you've approached the government they've said you're a flake. I know there's substance to the story you're telling and I would like you to tell me the story so I can pursue it." This was the breakthrough Scott had been looking for for nearly six years - someone with high official government responsibility to hear him out.

David Taylor, Executive Producer for BBC (Document 13) in the United States was told by Mr. Panessa that someone involved with the *Bohica* operation - "a very credible witness" - supports what Scott is saying. The opinion of many, who have voluntarily given hours and prayers to help Scott regain his credibility and discover why government officials refuse to acknowledge *Operation Grand Eagle*, is that Scott had no idea what he was really involved in.

As this book goes to print White House Chief of Staff Howard Baker's aide called David Taylor to ask about *Operation Grand Eagle*, code named *Bohica*. Evidently even the President has now begun to sit up and take notice. As Dr. Chris Gugas admits about himself and others, "Scott woke people up."

Scott has received a letter dated May 27, 1987, from the U.S. Strategic Institute of Washington, D.C.*, stating, "Please find enclosed President Reagan's new Central American policy doctrine. Please review at your earliest convenience for the crisis currently in Central America and forward a response back to us immediately." Regarding this request, Scott comments, "It's uncanny I have been asked to respond to a secret operation at the request of an institute for strategic studies, intelligence and counterintelligence."

---

*The director of this institute is Richard Allen; the president, General Holloway; the vice president, Admiral Moorer.

Scott Barnes' story is full of unanswered questions. Why does the government harass and seek to discredit the first American who, on a government-sponsored mission, did see and photograph two Caucasians who have now been confirmed to be Americans? What was the real purpose of *Bohica*? Was its major purpose to *VERIFY* or *DISCOUNT* the hundreds of reports the U.S. government has received that POWs still exist in Southeast Asia? Was the reconnaissance team expected to actually find POWs? Who gave the order to kill the two men who were sighted and why? Did those who gave the order believe these men in captivity were *PRISONERS OF WAR OR DRUG SMUGGLERS FOR OUR GOVERNMENT* who got caught? Read the account of Scott Barnes' knowledge and experience, examine the documents and photographs and draw your own conclusions. We believe it to be one of the most heinous cover-ups in the annals of American history.

Dennis W. Bartow
Publisher

Dateline of POW Developments

January 23, 1973: America issued official notice that the Vietnam war was over for the U.S.

"A cease-fire internationally supervised will begin at 7:00 p.m. this Saturday, January 27, Washington time. Within 60 days of this Saturday, all Americans held prisoners of war throughout Indochina will be released. There will be the fullest possible accounting for all those who are missing in action." - President Richard Nixon

January 29-31, 1973: Pentagon listed 317 missing or held in Laos. The Vietnamese listed 56 men held, none from Laos.

"American prisoners held in Laos and Vietnam will be returned to us in Hanoi." - Henry Kissinger

March 31-April 1, 1973: *Operation Homecoming*. 591 American POWs came home; 101 remains had been recovered; 2,435 were still missing. Few of the POWs returned in *Operation Homecoming* had been dismembered or brutally beaten. A study has revealed that most of those returned were pilots or ground people, rather than technicians or specialists. None was returned from Laos.

Early April, 1973: The Laotians wanted to negotiate with the United States for the return of prisoners.

April 12, 1973: Someone in the U.S. government announced there were "no prisoners in Southeast Asia. They're all dead." (This pronouncement is being perpetuated by our government to this day.)

April 29, 1975: The fall of Saigon marked the official end of the Vietnamese war. (On April 29, 1965, ten years to the day before the end of the war, Colonel Charles Shelton, photo reconnaissance pilot, was shot down on his birthday. Villagers witnessed the crash and his capture.)

1979: President Carter declared all but one POW (Charles Shelton) dead.

Late 1979: Bobby Garwood, a POW since 1965, was released by the North Vietnamese.
> "I was not and am not the last American live POW in Vietnam." - Garwood.

In 1981, Garwood was court marshaled for collaborating with the enemy, but never seriously debriefed about the others he had seen in captivity. (Since the late '70s, Southeast Asian refugees have reported more the 700 sightings of Americans in captivity to the U.S. government.) (Document 1, 2, 3)

April, 1981: Scott Barnes was contacted by Lieutenant Colonel James 'Bo' Gritz (pronounced 'Grights') to become part of *Operation Grand Eagle*, code-named *Bohica*. Barnes arrived in Bangkok to begin the first phase of his mission on June 15, 1981 and returned to California June 25.

October, 1981: Scott and three other visible team members returned to Bangkok to proceed with the U.S. government-sanctioned reconnaissance mission.

November, 1981: Scott returned to California where he lives alone today.

April, 1982: CIA man Jerry Daniels, who, accompanied by Scott Barnes, had entered Laos and sighted live POWs, died of 'accidental carbon monoxide poisoning,' leaving Barnes the only publicly known American who has actually seen and photographed live Americans in captivity in Southeast Asia during a government-sanctioned mission.

January 28, 1983:
> "The government bureaucracy now understands that these goals are the highest national priority. I pledge to you we

will take decisive action on any live sighting report that can be confirmed." - President Ronald Reagan.

November, 1983: Former New York Congressman John LeBoutillier was offered DEA (Drug Enforcement Administration) monies by Richard Childress, National Security Council official in charge of Asian Affairs, to discredit Republican William Hendon who had just alleged that the Pentagon was covering up information about POWs in Vietnam. Hendon was considering running for his old House seat in North Carolina. (Document 4)

> "I felt that I was definitely set up, because not only did I accomplish nothing towards getting the prisoners out, but I helped attack Hendon in a way that was unnecessary and I got nailed by Childress because they never came forth with any of the DEA support that they had promised me."- Congressman LeBoutillier

September 4, 1985: The Smith/McIntyre lawsuit was brought against the President of the United States under the Hostage Act, accusing the President and other high government officials of neglecting to make every possible effort to bring American POWs home.

January 28, 1986: Scott Barnes and other key people involved in the POW issue testified before the Senate Veterans' Affairs Committee. Scott's testimony was interrupted, then ended when announcement was made that the Space Shuttle Challenger had just exploded.

February, 1986: A delegation of 9 congressmen including Robert Dornan, Bill Hendon, Chris Smith, Frank McClosky, David Drier, John Rollin, and Robert Smith traveled to Hanoi. An ABC news show 20/20 TV report showed these men walking away from their guides to search for a cistern where American prisoners had bathed which Bobby Garwood and others had mentioned but DIA (Defense Intelligence Agency) said did not exist. These men found the cistern.

Early spring, 1986: The Tighe Commission, appointed by President Reagan and headed by General Eugene Tighe, former director of DIA, began to investigate DIA to see if any evidence of reported live sightings (over 1,000 reports by that time) could be confirmed, to evaluate if the Agency was properly investigating the reports of live sightings and to evaluate whether or not the Agency needed assistance, funding or guidance. In late fall of '86, the completed investigation revealed there possibly are live Americans still held in Southeast Asia. (Document 5)

August, 1986: Senate Veterans' Affairs hearings were declared officially closed, with no conclusions. No follow-up has taken place.

Late 1986: H. Ross Perot was appointed by President Reagan to conduct an independent investigation of military and government procedure for handling live sighting reports. Perot, who asked permission to go to Vietnam and was refused, is assisted by a nebulous 'unofficial' committee.

1

Why This Guy?

"Why are you on this mission?" I was asked the first time I met the others whom Bo Gritz, under orders from government and military officials, had handpicked to be part of *Operation Grand Eagle*. That is a question I've been asked by others and have asked myself many times. Some feel my credentials and my experience in covert law enforcement and intelligence, which I have been involved in since high school, were key factors.

When the guys in my high school class of '72 at Redondo Union High School, Redondo Beach, California, took a field trip to the Selective Service Center so we who were getting close to eighteen could consider military service as a career and could learn how to register for the draft, several draft protesters outside the door tried to talk with us. One day, a man named Robert Fry pulled me aside, offered me a beer and told me he could get me all I wanted. This sounded exciting to an obviously underage student, so I accepted the beer. Fry talked excitedly about burning draft cards and the American flag and mentioned things like explosives and bombings. Although I didn't believe any of his big talk, it intrigued me, and so did the free beer he continued to offer me. So I made arrangements to meet him again later that week.

I met him several times to drink his beer and listen to his wild claims. He was very much against the American system. Eventually he invited me to his home in Long Beach where, after several visits, he proudly showed me all kinds of weapons: machine guns, rifles, explosive and rocket launching devices. The display was impressive, but I knew that it must be illegal to have such a large collection of arms in a private home. So one day after spending some time at Fry's home I stopped at the pay phone outside Redondo Union High School and reported his arsenal to the City of Long Beach. Evidently the police officer I talked to did not believe what I was telling him. "If there really is something like what you're describing, kid, you've got to inform the appropriate people." I was told to contact the U.S. Treasury Department, Alcohol, Tobacco and Firearms Bureau.

I phoned the ATF. "Describe some of these explosive devices," the man I talked to asked, and I did. A period of silence followed, then the voice on the phone instructed, "Stay where you are. We'll be right there." I gave him the location of the pay telephone I was calling from.

After what seemed like an eternity to me, a couple of U.S. Treasury ATF Agents met me at the phone booth. After we had talked a good forty minutes, I was thrilled to be asked to go with them to their headquarters in Long Beach to discuss the possibility of my cooperating in exposing this man and to give me instructions. Because I was still just under eighteen, the ATF officials phoned my home and asked my parents' permission to allow me to work with them. Although they couldn't be told much about the case, my parents consented. By continuing my friendship with Fry, eventually I was able to introduce him to an undercover agent who posed as an international explosives expert and arms dealer.

When I turned eighteen the agents I was working with decided that for my safety I should be taken out of the picture gradually so they could file an indictment. "We don't want you caught in the middle," I was told.

Several months later, after I was no longer involved, undercover agents continued to negotiate arms deals with Fry. Soon a search warrant was issued, numerous explosive devices were removed from his home and he was arrested.

In a ceremony at the Federal Building, Wilshire Boulevard, Westwood, Los Angeles, I was presented with a commendation (Document 18) for my service and a college fund was begun on my behalf. One of the agents I had worked with closely indicated, "You handled yourself quite well for a young man." I knew I had learned to like the excitement of this kind of work. But my love for working for justice on behalf of my country went deeper than the intrigue.

During that brief ceremony I remembered Rick Sullivan, my neighbor and childhood hero who had taught me how to play basketball. When Rick entered the military service I had felt lost. I recalled the day in August of 1968, when I watched a green car drive slowly down our street and stop three doors from my home where Rick's family lived. A man in black garb and a little white collar and two military officers were helped from the car. Several neighbors who had been outside stopped visiting and stood still as these gentlemen entered the Sullivan home. I stopped my play.

Moments later, Rick's mother ran from the house, screaming. The neighbors hurried to her only to learn that Rick had been killed in action in Vietnam. His body was unrecoverable, nothing was left. One of the military men presented Rick's mother with his unit's flag. A memorial service was planned.

The pride of having known someone who had served my country so heroically welled up inside me. Although I had been raised to honor my country in the Baptist church I attended as a child, I never really understood the fullness of patriotism until that moment. I will never forget the impact of losing that friend, only three years older than I, had on me that day. It was a turning point in my life.

For a long time following Rick's death, every time I said the Pledge of Allegiance or sang the Star Spangled Banner, I thought of Rick's bravery and longed to make him proud of me. Working with ATF and the ceremony in Los Angeles were only the beginning.

When the time came for my draft classification, I eagerly returned to the Selective Service Center for a battery of tests. After looking over the results, the recruiting officer recommended that I become part of an organization called ASA.

"What's that?" I asked.

"Army Security Agency," he explained. "Not many people even know of its existence. You scored high in that area."

"I'd rather get into law enforcement," I told him.

"Well, we've got 95 Bravo* and 95 Charlie*," he said looking through his list of possible assignments.

"What's that?"

"Military Police, Special Investigations. Transporting military convicts. Things like that."

That sounded good to me, so I enlisted and was sent to Fort Ord, California, for basic training; then to Fort Gordon, Georgia, for advanced training; then to Fort Bragg, North Carolina, for special training.

While at Fort Gordon, my commander, Captain Cherry, called me into his office. "Scott, the FBI and the 525th Military Intelligence group have flagged your orders and assignments," he told me. "There's some suspicion about what you were doing in Saigon, South Vietnam, eight months ago."* (Document 19 - A,B,C)

"I was a civilian then," I explained. "I traveled there as a tourist." They had checked and discovered my trip into South Vietnam had taken me to LBJ (Long Bien Jail), Bien Hoa airbase, An Loc, My Lo, and with a South Vietnamese Army patrol into denied areas.

---

*95 Bravo: Military Police/Intelligence

---

*95 Charlie: Military Police/Corrections

---

*Editor's note: Scott's travels into these countries during this period of his life are highly classified, therefore he will not discuss with anyone what took place.

Their investigation had uncovered the fact that this trip with Joseph Bissett was classified.

"They're a bit nervous," Captain Cherry related. For days I was interviewed about the possibility of Southeast Asia connections with unauthorized intelligence missions. Both the FBI and the 525th suspected that I had been a CIA free lancer in Nam.

"Look," I reminded them, "I was just eighteen at the time."

"But what's a eighteen-year-old kid who's supposedly without a job doing with enough money to go to Southeast Asia - especially to denied areas where not even standard military personnel are permitted because either it's not secured or there's a lot of Viet Cong infiltration?" They were very suspicious but could prove no wrongdoing. (I had been issued a uniform without insignias and had to sign a declaration stating, "I will not involve myself in any political activities or break the Vietnam Current Rules and Regulations during my stay in the Republic of Vietnam. I will leave the Territory of the Republic of Vietnam at expiration of the stay granted." *THIS DECLARATION OF HONOUR* concluded, "It is suggested that this Declaration of Honour duly signed by you be presented to the American and Vietnamese Immigration Authorities on your arrival in Saigon." (Document 20)

My interrogators had a copy of that Declaration and thought it strange for a eighteen-year-old kid to go as a tourist to Vietnam in the middle of a war. They were also concerned about my travels to ten other countries my passport (Document 21) recorded I had traveled in from January 27, 1973, into early spring. Finally my company commander, the FBI and the Military Intelligence got the matter straightened out to their satisfaction, only to learn my assignment had been changed from Europe to Fort Lewis, Washington. Prior to my leaving I was puzzled by my commander, Captain Cherry's words of warning, "Watch out for the CIA."

While stationed at Fort Lewis from the end of 1973 until about June, 1974, I was schooled in narcotics and intelligence to work with CID (Criminal Investigative Division of the Army) and co-work on the military reservation with the Seattle Police Department Narcotics Intelligence. (Document 22)

The Drug Enforcement Administration (DEA) had come to the base several times looking for good personnel prospects and a CIA recruiter came through about once every three months. I asked my commanding officer if I could sit in on one of the briefing sessions with the Agency and he granted me permission to do so. I was impressed and my ever-increasing desire to serve my country through law enforcement and intelligence landed me assignments with Covert Operations at Fort Lewis and with General McFadden on *Operation Boldfire*, a mission to make sure there were no security breaches on the Army post.

Periodically Agency recruiters would come through and want to talk with thirty to forty people at a time, probably handpicked by commanding officers, about available positions within the Agency. I told one recruiter named Hull on his second stop in about four months, "If I ever get the opportunity, I would be willing to be recruited for operations."

He said he'd see what he could do. In 1974, I was sent to Yakima Fire Base, Army Security Agency Center in the eastern part of the state of Washington. For two months I worked on undercover assignments, then received orders to report back to Fort Lewis immediately to meet with Colonel Kannamine, commander of the Military Police Intelligence unit. I was transported to Fort Lewis by helicopter. Besides the pilot and the co-pilot, I was the only one aboard. At Ft. Lewis the Colonel informed me, "We have an offer for you, Scott. Get out of the military service now instead of waiting."

"But I still have a few months left on my hitch," I told him, curious about what he had in mind. "What am I going to be doing?"

"The war's over now, so we don't need so many troops. We have many wounded and a lot more coming back to the States, so we'll be able to process you out early." At first I believed his explanation. Three weeks later I was told, "Here are your papers. (Document 23) Do you want to take this opportunity?" My senior officers were very encouraging.

Impressed with the possibility that I might soon be offered a special assignment from my country and wanting to return to college, I agreed, "Yeh, I'll do it."

"Go back home to Redondo Beach and we'll contact you."

Once home and officially out of the U.S. Army only a matter of weeks, I enrolled at El Camino College part-time to study criminology at their South Bay Reserve Police Academy, and worked for the Inglewood Police Department, becoming heavily involved in gang and narcotics intelligence investigations in this suburb of Los Angeles.

While walking through the college parking lot one day, I saw a guy I had gone to high school with, a Jesus Freak. I never did like the guy and had a strong urge to just walk up and hit him. I remembered how he had always preached to everybody at school. It had turned me off. Unable to, or perhaps unwilling to, control my urge, I began to walk toward the parked car he was standing near. Just as I was ready to raise my hand to strike him across the side of his head, another fellow stood up from behind their automobile. He was bigger than I. My former high school classmate turned and glanced in my direction.

"Scott!" he exclaimed in surprise. "How ya doin'?"

"Oh, hi there, Dave," I answered, trying to appear innocent and casual. "I didn't know you were out of the army. What are you doing tonight? Why don't you come to Bible study?" He and his friend who now stood beside him worked with the Christian campus organization.

"You still at it, huh?" I said with disgust.

"There's always pretty girls..." He knew my weakness too well.

"I'll be there," I decided without further thought. For the next seven or eight months I attended Bible study at First Baptist Church, Manhattan Beach. At that Bible study I met Vickie, the girl I was soon to marry.

I hadn't worked with the Inglewood police long when one of the drug enforcement agents informed me my name was on a list of select people they would like to recruit for a special detail. I would have to attend a school that was beginning shortly.

I received very good training in international narcotics trafficking and weapons intelligence at the U.S. Department of Justice Drug Enforcement Training School. Just before I had completed the training I was told by Gil Mora, DEA Senior Intelligence Recruiter, "As soon as you finish your last semester we'd like you to come down to San Diego to work on special detail in our organized crime unit." I accepted enthusiastically, eager to learn everything I could about the international drug and arms trafficking trade.

While in San Diego I received a letter asking me to take a job with the El Cajon Police Department. Following my acceptance in early 1976, I was sent to the San Diego Sheriff's Academy for continued training. While finishing up my work at the Academy, I was contacted by C. Colbert, an agent with the U.S. Treasury Alcohol, Tobacco and Firearms.

"Nobody knows you in San Diego, Scott. You're brand new; you've got a baby face and a good background, plenty of experience and education. We want you to continue to work for the El Cajon Police Department, then eventually we'll make you look corrupt and we'll go from there."

The DEA wanted to break the Hell's Angels' major stronghold in that area, used especially for the funneling of guns into Mexico and Central America in exchange for drugs. Through prostitutes and drug dealers the DEA filtered information to the Hell's Angels that the Mongols, a rival gang, were taking over the Mexican drug trade as well as the gun plan and the California methamphetamine trafficking. Undercover agents wore phony Mongol jackets with California rockers. The disinformation worked. In 1976-77 a major gang war between the two groups broke out resulting in several murders, bombings and assassinations. Several kidnapings took place during that time.

It was then I began to work extensively with the San Diego District Attorney's Intelligence Unit.

At one point Ed Miller, the D.A. himself, called me into his office. "There's a lot of shady things going on in the Department, so we're going to quietly make you part of the BET." (Bikers' Enforcement Team, which involves the Secret Service; Alcohol, Tobacco and Firearms; numerous federal, state and some local county law enforcement agencies.)

A short time later I was "fired." The newspaper articles, the radio and TV reports began to emerge: *"Corrupt Police Officer..."* to make my severance believable. Hell's Angels bought the story. I became known as a dirty cop and was transferred to Ridgecrest Police Department next to the China Lake Naval Weapons Center. There was a lot of heavy Hell's Angels activity in the area between this rural community and the landing strip in nearby Inyokern. "We'll get you back in uniform again," I was assured by my superiors.

"But if all the papers have said I'm corrupt, how can I become a cop again?" I asked. But somehow they worked it out. The DEA and the FBI visited me quite often while I was on the job, causing Ridgecrest police chief Earl Fike to become uneasy about my covert investigations. Not fully knowing what I was involved with, he frequently called me into his office, pressing me to tell him exactly what was going on. Of course, I didn't tell him but referred him to the FBI.

He threatened, "I'm going to terminate you. I think you're doing something you shouldn't be doing. You're investigating people you have no business investigating."

"That's right," I retorted. "And you're one of them."

Several weeks later, in December, 1977, I was forced to shoot a suspect several times and was wounded myself. (Document 24 - A,B,C) The report of this gunfire exchange brought the District Attorney of Kern County, the Attorney General of the state of California and the county sheriff to look into my activities. Prior to the East Kern Court trial, the bullets lodged in one of the suspect's forearms were removed and kept as evidence.

I was tipped off by an evidence technician that someone had removed the bullets, blood still on them, from the police department
Evidence Room and had thrown them in the garbage. Immediately
I returned to police headquarters and retrieved them from the dump-
ster then turned them in to the D.A.'s office for safekeeping. The only two people who had keys to the Evidence Room were Chief Earl
Fike and Sergeant Ken Vineyard, Detective Intelligence, who had investigated my shooting. Both admitted that somehow someone must
have broken in to steal the evidence.

Chief Earl Fike suddenly resigned his position, taking a medical
retirement. Sergeant Vineyard is no longer with the Department and
the city manager has resigned.

Why this guy - me - for *Operation Grand Eagle* when all the others
involved were prior U.S. Army Green Beret and Delta Force members?
Opinions vary. Some are convinced my credentials, my knowledge
and my experiences were significant factors. Being known in Southeast
Asia is another reason that has been suggested. Many members of
special military units and intelligence teams were very well known
in that area. Communist agents watching for infiltration would have
picked them out immediately. Several of the prior Army Special Forces
team members had had a lot of trouble with the Laotian youngsters
who were connected with the operation. They liked to boss the kids
around which did not make them very popular with the people. Others
have surmised I was selected because I was young, in good health
and my "baby face" would not be as suspect as an old combat veteran.
I had lots of contacts and excellent training in the intelligence and
counterinsurgency field, so I would never be suspected as someone
working with any special military teams or as having ties with General
Vang Pao or with the ISA. (Document 14 - B)

But I have a different opinion as to why I was selected. I believe
the key was my friendship with General Vang Pao, developed while
I worked through Hope Chapel, Hermosa Beach, to resettle Laotian
refugees in the United States in late '79 and the first part of '80. Vang
Pao, 53-year-old leader of the Laotian Hmongs who spends part of

his time at the Laotian center in Orange County, California, and part at his ranch in Montana, was on the outs with the CIA at that time. They had broken some very important promises made to the General and to his Hmong tribes in Laos. Somehow someone found out that he liked me, that he and I had a close friendship, thus I became the pawn in a very powerful game which still has not been completely uncovered.

2

I Became an "Angel"

January, 1978

Only a few days after I was released from the hospital following the shooting incident, Ron Dowan, Oakland Police Organized Crime Intelligence agent in charge of the international drug trafficking case against the Hell's Angels, contacted me. Ron and I had been in touch several times previously to plan my undercover infiltration into the Hell's Angels to share information. "We're going to start the indictments in the Bay area, Scott - where the Hell's Angels are headquartered. We think it would be a good idea for you to come up here." (Document 25)

But soon, these covert investigations of the Hell's Angels became too dangerous to suit me. Somehow the Angels had learned a cop was trying to get into their organization. Cars belonging to undercover cops like Sergeant Joe Crock, San Jose Police Department; and Agent William Zerby, Sonoma County Narcotics Task Force, were bombed. One of the police witnesses against the Angels in Hillsboro, Oregon - Margo Compton - was murdered and her five-year-old twin daughters were shot in the head with .22 stinger bullets. A nineteen-year-old Coast Guard service member who was visiting her was also murdered. All these crimes were suspected to have been done by Hell's Angels.*

Thinking my assignment might be becoming too dangerous, my wife Vickie, who was pregnant, and I decided in the summer of '78 to move north on the Pacific Coast to a little town called Crescent City.

Crescent City seemed like a nice little Christian community. My first thought was, *Look at all these religious people. I'll cater to them.* The government had given me enough money to lie low for a while which I used to start a small business of my own, a little shop called *The Gift Store: Coins and Collectibles.* Deliberately I stocked the shelves of my little shop with a selection of sand candles, posters, and religious "trinkets."

Because the Christian Family Life Center Church, the largest church in the city, was so pleased that a new "Christian" business had come to their community, the gift store was instantly successful. But soon my greedy attitude began to wear at me and an internal battle with my conscience began. It didn't take long for my love of money to win out.

It took even less time for the underworld to locate me. Because Hell's Angels work closely with the Mafia, Barry Tarlow, a criminal defense attorney sent his associate Richard Fanning to see me about one of their clients. "About Angelo Marino* - we're handling his case - what do you know?... What are your connections with BET?*" I refused to talk. "We'll be in touch," he promised.

Later that week, Marino phoned me from Vegas where he was attending a wedding. "Don't talk to the Bureau!" he warned. Obviously he knew what was soon to take place. FBI Agent Nicodemus from the Portland Organized Crime Bureau came to question me about Marino, other syndicate people and their dealings with the Angels.

Evidently word of the success of my business had spread. One day

---

*April 4, '79 *Rolling Stone* Magazine gives a detailed report on the bombings and shootings.

*Marino, owner of the California Cheese Company and reputed to be one of the top California Mafia figures, worked with the Hell's Angels and was a prime suspect in a mob hit.

*Bikers' Enforcement Team.

a heavyset man in his early fifties came to the shop. Introducing himself as Calvin Brown, he proceeded to look over my inventory very methodically and thoroughly. "Nice collectibles," he observed. Finally he commented, "I see you have several Hummel figurines. They're very expensive."

"Yes, they are. I have a direct connection in Germany, so they are shipped frequently."

Abruptly he announced, "I want to buy into your business." His request took me by complete surprise. I had no intention of selling and bluntly told him so. He suggested that I call a couple of banks about his credit and left.

Out of curiosity I immediately followed through on his suggestion and learned that he ran a large contracting company out of Orange County. His assets fell in the high six digit category. The following day Mr. Brown returned with a briefcase full of cash. Again my love for money prevailed. It seemed that whenever the dollar sign was flashed before me I pushed everything else out of the way. So, without investigating too deeply, I sold Calvin Brown 49% of my business and held the controlling interest.

I should have been more cautious about selecting a business partner. It wasn't long until I learned the guy I was in business with was a big time international drug dealer, worked with Hell's Angels and was involved in union syndicate dealings.

While living in Crescent City, Vickie and I rented a home from an elder of the Foursquare church in town. One day while she was visiting in L.A. to show our new son Marc to her mother, I was relaxing on the front porch pondering my next step. Hell's Angels had just been indicted for the first time. There was a rumor that they wanted to talk to me. I was hoping they didn't know where I was living. Yet, if Attorney Tarlow knew, the Angels knew.

Without warning someone fired an automatic weapon at me from a slowly moving car. Having learned long before to always keep a gun on my side, I quickly returned fire as I ran in the house for cover. Within moments the California state highway patrol, the Del Norte County sheriff's department and the Crescent City police arrived on

the scene. More than thirty bullets were removed from the north side
of our home, around the front door and through the water heater inside. No suspects were ever taken into custody.

Within days, criminal defense attorney Al Kriger from Miami
phoned me at my shop. "They're* looking for you in southern California, Scott. They're after files and info on the Hell's Angels, on Santo
Trafficante, Anthony Accardio and on Carmine Galente." These were
three big-name Mafia figures, Trafficante being a former close
associate of Laotian General Vang Pao in his drug dealings. This was
all it took for me to sell my gift shop as quickly as possible and move
to Manhattan Beach where I rekindled a friendship with some old
college buddies who lived in the area. Vickie had decided to remain
with her mother for a while.

One day in early January, 1981, while my buddies and I were visiting
in my apartment on the beach, someone knocked on our door. When
I opened it, an attractive young woman asked, "Is this 2200 B Strand,
Apartment B?"

Being the smart alec I was, I looked closely at my apartment door.
"It says B," I answered innocently.

"I'm looking for Scott Barnes."

I stammered, trying to stall until I could think up a good response.
"I know he lives here," she persisted.

"Oh...well...he'll be back in a little while." It was the best I could
come up with.

"Then I'll stop by later," she said and started down the stairs. I
watched out my side window to see what she would do next. In a
four-door dark blue Cadillac parked on the street were two men dressed
in business suits. The girl talked with them, motioning back and forth.
One of the men showed her what was obviously a photo. She looked
back at my apartment window, nodded her head and the two men
got out of the car and followed her to the apartment house door.

This must be some sort of a hit by the Angels! I thought. I pulled
out my gun, dreading the knock on the door that came moments later.

*Referring to other syndicate lawyers.

One of the two men yelled an introduction through my door and gave me the number of their office so I could phone to verify their identity. I did and also called the police and requested verification. The gentlemen were in fact legitimate attorneys with a San Francisco law firm.

When I opened the door I was served with a subpoena. "The United States of America vs. Hell's Angels subpoenas Scott Tracy Barnes..." (Document 26 - A,B) Having been undercover in what was considered a covert case, I never thought I would have to appear in court. *I'm in trouble* was my only thought. As soon as I could get my belongings together, I headed for Hope Chapel, Hermosa Beach, the first place I always went when I was in trouble.

I first became acquainted with the people at Hope Chapel in early 1979, while still living in northern California. I'd begun to think a lot about my infant son Marc. Vickie had never returned from her visit with her mother, having left me when he was seven weeks old, after only two and a half years of marriage, so I hadn't seen Marc for a long time. I could understand why she'd left me. While going to college, as a reserve police officer, I had been the "All American Boy" - short hair, clean cut. But after I became involved with BET and the Angels it was a whole different world. She couldn't get used to seeing me carry guns, wear long hair and a bulletproof vest and run with weird-looking people. (She didn't know they were federal agents.) Lucky to be home more than five hours a day to sleep, I rarely communicated with her. I was too wrapped up in the excitement of my work and didn't care about much else. I took it for granted that Vickie would always be there.

Although I could understand why my marriage didn't work out, that didn't diminish my loneliness in this uncomfortable time, so I called my mother in Palos Verdes and asked if she had ever heard where Vickie and Marc were living. She said a church in Hermosa Beach was taking care of Marc while Vickie worked. Immediately I drove to Hermosa Beach.

The church, located on the Pacific Highway overlooking the Pacific Ocean, was sandwiched between an office complex and a Lucky

Supermarket. I parked in the supermarket parking lot. As I walked toward the large two-story building that was once a bowling alley, my eyes were drawn to a sign, a dove and an olive branch imposed on a large H, then O - P - E. Hope Chapel.

I found a very kind, polite girl at the reception desk in the church office. Hearing my inquiry, the preacher came out of his study. "We cannot divulge names of the children to strangers," he explained, "but why don't you come to an evening service? The children are always in the nursery." I tried to explain to him that I was Marc's father and had not seen my son since he was seven weeks old, but this had no effect on their nursery policy.

I talked with the lady in the nursery who told me that Vickie used to come there a lot, but that her recent attendance had been very sporadic. At least I found out that both Vickie and Marc were okay.

Although I was well aware of what the pastor was up to - trying to get me to come to church - my loneliness influenced me to attend anyway, hoping the service wouldn't be too inspiring. But it was. And everybody was so friendly. Never before had I attended or heard of a church like this one. "Get away from me," I wanted to shout at first as they welcomed me with warm handshakes, hellos and hugs. Unable to resist their warmth and sincerity I continued to attend the evening services, but only at my own personal convenience.

By late '79, I had learned about the church's refugee ministry and began to help with the resettling of Laotian Hmong refugees in our area. I really liked these people, especially their leader, General Vang Pao. When I first met him, I just thought he was sort of "the leader of the pack." But by our fifth or sixth meeting, when he hinted at who he really was, I remembered hearing of him when I was in 'Nam in '73. I began to see that he was quite wealthy. We became good friends.

Several times we met with Dr. Jane Hamilton Merritt. She was an extreme pacifist who helped with the refugee program and conducted refugee investigations. Dr. Merritt traveled to Southeast Asia to help Vang Pao's people there but would never cross into Laos. Always she insisted they cross the Mekong River away from the gas warfare. Then she would get medical attention for victims and try to relocate them in a neutral country.

By 1980 I was hooked. I had begun to attend Hope Chapel on a regular basis. A young man, Randy Sanford, a recent graduate from Bible school, came on staff as the singles pastor. Randy and I became good friends, and I assisted him with the singles' activities. He was very helpful when I returned to the Chapel after I had been subpoenaed to testify in the Hell's Angels RICO (Racketeering Influence of a Corrupt Organization) trial.

So was Ralph Moore, the young dynamic charismatic founder and senior minister of the church. "I don't care what the consequences are, young man," he counseled me about going to testify. "Even if they do take your life, it's not worth losing your salvation."

Still a self-centered hardhead, I argued, "I'm not interested in salvation, pal. I'm going up against the largest organized crime biker gang in this country. And elements of the Syndicate, the mob." One hundred two members of the Hell's Angels had been indicted including Sonny Barger, president of Hell's Angels.

"I don't care who they are, Scott." He kept repeating how powerful Jesus was, just what I didn't want to hear.

"Aw, I know all about Jesus," I would tell him.

"I'm really worried about this. Go and tell the truth."

"No," I persisted. He gave me a New Testament just before I ran out the door. Reading it sparked a battle inside me. *What should I do?* I cried, lonely and afraid of the outcome and consequences of the trial I faced.

My experience on the witness stand January 12, 1981, was intimidating. Although I had traveled with Hell's Angels since 1975 (mostly via Cadillac rather than a Harley Davidson) none of the Angels had discovered I was an undercover agent until I appeared in court, clean cut, well-groomed, wearing a short beard. I could picture myself being murdered as I left the security of the courtroom. (Most people don't realize that some of the Hell's Angels are business people who have short hair and business suits and drive nice cars. They use their Hell's Angels affiliations as an outlet for laundering money - putting illegal money to legitimate use - from racketeering, drug trade, prostitution and gun smuggling.)

During the trial I was ordered to testify about my covert involvement with the Hell's Angels. Finally the U.S. attorneys asked the judge to stop the trial and called for a conference. The judge consented. I was instructed to accompany two U.S. attorneys and several FBI agents into the judge's chambers where I was debriefed for six hours while they tried to persuade the judge to uphold their decision that I would not have to testify. Eventually the government attorneys succeeded in gaining the conclusion that they couldn't let me continue to testify because what I had to say "was immaterial" but could ruin their case. I knew too much about the illegal activities of law enforcement personnel the government used to get their evidence.

We all returned to the courtroom where all those biker defendants and their associates were lined up, flanked by armed U.S. marshals. My testimony continued for approximately twenty minutes longer before I was released.

All the Hell's Angels were acquitted, thanks to the government's and the prosecutor's own witnesses. The majority of their witnesses were murderers and robbers, placed in the Secret Witness program and paid large quantities of cash to testify.

For example, as the defense attorneys were trying to prove that their clients, the leaders of the Hell's Angels, were set up by a law enforcement conspiracy to target the Angels, one big ugly old witness who took the stand was asked by the defendants' attorneys - some of the top attorneys in the country - "Were you paid to say what you are saying?"

"No, sir," he answered confidently, "but an agent did give me thirty thousand cash last night." It was a reward, he said.

After two and a half years of prosecution, in two trials, the government lost because of a hung jury. All the defendants were acquitted and several government personnel were fired or transferred as a result. A U.S. attorney out of Washington, D.C., announced that this was the longest racketeering trial in American history and the most expensive. "ABC News Closeup," following this case all along and present at the trial, asked to interview me about my involvement with the case for a special that would be aired four or five months later for the purpose of pointing out how the government was more corrupt than those they prosecuted. A movie, *Hell's Angels Forever*, was filmed with Willie Nelson, Johnny Paycheck, Jerry Garcia, Bo Diddley and myself, plus the New York chapter and some of the California chapters of the Hell's Angels.

Thinking I had ended that particular chapter of my life, I was shaken when shortly after the trial one of the chief Hell's Angels called and asked me to join them at the Angels' headquarters in Oakland for a news conference. They wanted to say to the American people, "Look, the government lost their case against us. This undercover cop was one of the main people working with the government. But we're not mad at him. We want the world to know there are no hard feelings. We're nice guys." Feeling it would be wise to cooperate, I agreed to meet with them.

When I walked into their headquarters at 4019 Foothill Boulevard, Oakland, the first person I saw was Sonny. He looked at me, then opened a can of Coors. In his deep voice and cautious manner of speech, he said, "Here, Barnes, take a drink, so all my leaders who are here can see that you and me have buried the hatchet. ...I could have my henchmen hit you - just like that!" The mustached leader snapped his fingers. I was scared. Very scared. "But for some reason, I don't want you killed. You're not exactly a friend, remember, but you will no longer be our enemy either. I want everybody to know I have no desire to have you killed." I breathed a deep breath of relief and humbly accepted his "peace offering."

At Hope Chapel I gave a testimony about my court experience. When nearly everyone had left and I was the only one still in the coffee room, a lady approached me. Looking around to be sure we were alone, she said, "I'd like to speak to you. We have something in common."

"What's that?" I asked.

"One of the Hell's Angels is my nephew - Ralph 'Sonny' Barger, the Godfather." *Is she going to kill me or something?* We stepped outside so we could be certain no one would hear our conversation.

"I don't know why I'm doing this, except that I feel the Lord wants me to," she said nervously. I was baffled until she explained, "In '71, Sonny's father died. At the funeral, the Teamsters, his father's union, presented Sonny with a white leather Bible in a wooden case. Sonny didn't want anything to do with it." She held out a small wooden box. "I feel that I'm to give this to you and that you're to give it to Sonny."

By this time the preacher had come out to go home and, sensing something serious was taking place, joined us.

I protested to the woman, "Oh man! You gotta be crazy! Your nephew must be closer to Satan than anybody." I turned to Pastor Ralph Moore for his support. "Tell God He's got the wrong guy for this job."

"Take it to him, Scott," Ralph insisted. I gave in and agreed to take the box containing the Bible to Sonny, wondering how I would ever give it to him and return alive.

With great reluctance, I flew up to meet with Sonny once again. "Hi, Sonny. Your aunt, Mrs. Newell, and I go to the same church," I explained. "Here, Sonny, she asked me to give this to you." I held out the wooden box.

"So you know my aunt." At first he didn't want the Bible, then he acted as though he did. Finally I gave it to his wife Sharon, a former California beauty queen. She thanked me.

"I'll be praying for you, Sonny," I told him.

"I don't believe in God," he snapped as I was leaving. I understood. He has a lot of peer pressure to deal with. He didn't dare accept his father's Bible in person.

Although several of the Angels have become Christians since the time of my association with them, not one Christian has been among those murdered.

In the spring of 1981, while I was on the first phase of *Operation Grand Eagle*, ABC Closeup aired their special, "When Crime Pays," about the thousands of dollars the government pays to murderers and drug addicts and perjurers to be witnesses. The paid witnesses at the

Hell's Angels trial and my involvement as undercover agent were included. Because I was aware of the possible reverberations from this forthcoming TV publicity, I realized taking the advice given me by a U.S. attorney at the January trial would be wise. He had recommended that I should get out of the country for a while. Again I returned to Hope Chapel to seek the advice of Pastor Ralph Moore.

"We've just started a new church on Maui, Hawaii, Scott. I can arrange to have you hide out there for a while," he suggested.

"That's not going to be a problem?" I didn't want to cause these wonderful people any trouble.

"No. I'll call the pastor there and let him know the situation. He'll keep you low for a while." I figured, *If I stay there six months or so, I can come back stateside under a different name and everything will be all right.* It was a strange feeling. I'd never had to use an alias before, except during covert operations.

I was mostly concerned about my Volvo. "Leave your car with us," some of the men from the church told me. I remembered the bombing of the cars belonging to Crock and Zerby. Too many of the wrong people knew my car and my license number. I was afraid someone from the church would get bombed or killed. "We'll take care of it for you," they insisted. Never before had I met people like this.

Hours before I was to catch the plane to Frisco and split to Hawaii, I was baptized into the Christian faith. When I came up out of that water and looked at all the people who had tolerated me and loved me, I experienced a strange unidentifiable feeling - one I would never forget.

3

The Initial Contact

March, 1981

The Hope Chapel people in Maui, Hawaii, were just as sincere and comfortable to be with as those I'd left behind in Hermosa Beach. For three or four weeks I bummed around on the beach. Then one of the men told me about a possible opening for a security consultant at a Wailea Beach resort where celebrities held big parties and golf classics. Hired to pose as a maintenance man, doing repairs and using a long stick with a nail on the end of it to pick up cigarette butts and trash, I was there to insure that V.I.P. guests were not harassed or disturbed and to keep an eye on company employees making sure they did not disturb the clients. I didn't really need the money at the time; I just wanted something to do.

During my time of employment at the resort, a man named Rewald held a large party. Double security - the resort's and the government's - was ordered. The government security people were pointed out to me so I wouldn't sound an alarm if they were seen snooping around. Little did I realize what a significant part Rewald would play in my own life in the future.

The job wasn't very fulfilling or challenging. I needed to be involved with something more intellectual, more meaningful, so I spent a lot of my time - as much as eighteen or twenty hours a week - helping out at the church.

Helping at the Maui church wasn't the same as it had been in California. Ninety-nine percent of our time was spent telling people about Christ on the beach rather than in a building. With Pastor Craig Englert as my example I learned a lot about how to build up a church, how to care about people and to witness. This man knew exactly how to approach individuals who lived on the beach, well- known areas for derelicts and down-and-outers. He knew exactly what to say to those who had been forgotten by the world. Most were druggies, prostitutes and the old hippies who had stayed in Hawaii. In the few months I spent with Pastor Englert I experienced tremendous spiritual growth.

While I was working with the Maui Hope Chapel, the young assistant pastor, Jason Spence, came down with Hodgkin's disease. Often I would drive him to the cancer center for his treatments. It bothered me to see this handsome man in his mid-twenties, only recently married, lose his hair, lose so much weight and feel so sick all the time, yet continue to affirm the love of God. "God is so good. God is good," he affirmed again and again.

"Here you are dying," I would argue, "sick and throwing up, losing weight. How can you say that?" He even witnessed to the doctor who finally diagnosed his condition as possibly terminal.

One day on our way home, I said to him, "Jason, every time I'm with you, all you talk about is Jesus. Don't you have anything else to talk about? Aren't you mad at God?"

He looked at me and smiled. "How can you be mad at such a loving Father?" *The drugs and other medication must be affecting his brain,* I concluded. *Gosh, he needs to go out and have a good time and forget about his cancer.* I tried to get him involved in more worldly activities, asking him things like didn't he want to go out and have a drink or party. Now, as a more mature Christian, I realize my suggestions were totally selfish and wrong.

Jason, now completely cured of Hodgkins disease, pastors one of the Hope Chapel churches on Maui. When I saw him about three years ago, I couldn't believe it. In perfect health. Muscular. Happy.

"I can't believe you're the same guy!" I exclaimed.

"I told you Jesus is good," he replied. Every time I think about Jason, I'm in awe. He is one of the most inspirational people I've ever met.

For three or four months my life was more relaxing and fulfilling than ever before. But that peaceful time didn't last long. It was broken in late March or early April, 1981, the day I received a phone call while I was working at the church.

"Scott Barnes?" the female voice on the other end of the line asked.

"Yes."

"The Scott Barnes who was involved in the Hell's Angels RICO?"

Oh my gosh, they found me! I thought it was the Angels or the Mob. "...Yes."

"I'm calling from Hughes Aircraft."

I tried to remain casual. "What can I do for you?" I said in my calmest possible tone of voice.

"Are you still friends with General Vang Pao?"

Why would Hughes Aircraft care about my friendship with the General? "...Yes, we still keep in touch."

"A military man from Hughes would like to talk with you. His name is James Gordon Gritz*...Do you know him?"

"James...Gritz? I've never heard of anyone by that name."

She chuckled. "Well, he doesn't know you either, but he wants you to call him. He works for the Advanced Program Development for Overseas Operations Department, Section C-142, Hughes Aircraft, El Segundo," she said slowly so I could write it down. "You can reach him by dialing area code 213-670-1515, extension 6563." Curiosity and love of adventure wouldn't permit me to refuse. My excitement increased some time later when I received a second call from a man at Hughes saying Mr. Gritz would call me the following week, giving me a specific date and time to expect the call.

---

*Pronounced "Grights"

Several times I dialed the secured number* I had been given, but
Mr. Gritz was never in. I decided to wait to see if he really would
try to contact me again. It worked. One day the pastor's associate
said someone from Hughes had called for me and had left the same
213 number.

I returned the call right away and was greeted by a female voice.
"Hughes Aircraft, Advanced Program Development, Overseas Operations, C-142. Secured Line." *Wow! What a long greeting to answer
the phone with!*

"This is Scott Barnes," I responded in my most businesslike manner. "I'm returning Mr. Gritz' call."

"Oh...yes...Just a minute, Mr. Barnes. He just tried to reach you."
I listened to the clicking which evidently transferred my call.

"Mr. Gritz' office." Another female voice. I told her my name and
listened to more clicks.

Finally a deep voice spoke, "This is Bo. I guess we kept missing
one another's calls. We're talking on a secured line, Barnes, so let's
get right to the point. I need your help on a matter of high national
priority and security regarding American POWs in Southeast Asia."

His request was a total surprise. I thought for a few seconds, then
asked, "Where do we have prisoners?"

"Indochina."

"But the war's over. There aren't any more prisoners. They were
all released during *Operation Homecoming*."

Emphatically he asked, "Will you help me?" *This must be a really
important cause*, I thought. *Maybe God is telling me something.* It
would be next to impossible for me to say "no" to any request to serve
my country; and the possibility of travel and intrigue made Gritz'
invitation even more appealing.

Bo interrupted my thoughts. "Are you still friends with General
Vang Pao?"

When I told him we still kept in touch (Often I would send Vang
Pao letters and religious materials.), Bo asked again if I would secretly

---

*A secured phone line is one which electronically scrambles the conversation.

work on a highly classified project regarding POWs, explaining the CIA's connections with General Vang Pao had been cut and previously made promises had been broken when new agents took over. Also the new ambassador to Thailand had discovered Vang Pao's involvement with agent Daniel C. Arnold in dealings with drugs, guns and guerrilla warfare. By this time I was so excited about the opportunity to help fellow Americans and work with my friend Vang Pao, nothing could have stopped me from accepting this assignment.

Yet, I could not help wondering...Did we leave Americans behind? Would our government have done such a thing? If so, we'd certainly better get over there and get them back right away. Now!

"Okay. Then I have to get this packet to you," Bo responded with increased excitement in his voice after I told him I would work with him. "And I can't waste any time getting it there. Is there anyone stateside that you know personally - someone who doesn't have much contact with the government you can trust to deliver it to you immediately? The fewer people who know about this, the better for us."

I thought of my good friend Steve who had been raised in a government family and was in the process of completing his doctorate degree. Steve, a devout atheist, and I had been friends for fifteen or sixteen years. He was very trustworthy and was living in the area Mr. Gritz was calling from.

Not wanting to involve too many ISA people, Bo was pleased with my choice. "Good," he responded. "Send him to my home and I'll have him courier the package to you."

Eager as I was to become a part of this operation, I did not want to jump in blind. "Wait a minute, Bo. I've got to do some checking on this before we begin." He had seemed to take it for granted that I would help him, a complete stranger, without any verification from anyone that the operation was government-sanctioned. But wanting to move forward with his project as quickly as possible, he gave me some phone numbers I could call for verification. I talked to Colonel John Kennedy, DIA, to verify government approval of the operation and Colonel Robert Robinson, DIA (Later he was promoted to General, then committed suicide January 14, 1985, at his home in

Fairfax, Virginia.) I phoned Daniel C. Arnold, CIA Station Chief
mainly in charge of Thailand and Laos; and John Stein, agent in charge
of the Clandestine Operation Division of the CIA; and Gene Wilson
of Litton Industries, Van Nuys, California.

There was a myriad of questions I needed to ask these gentlemen.
Who was Bo Gritz? Who sanctioned this project? Who was calling
the shots? What evidence did we have that suggested the possibility
of POWs still existing? Why were we verifying in this way? Why not
a full scale operation?

Bo also gave me numbers to contact Pat Hurt, Laotian specialist
for Defense Intelligence Agency and Michael Burns, with whom I
talked for a considerable length of time. Both Burns and Hurt confirmed that Bo was "Okay," a big ex-Green Beret. Burns kept
reiterating that the assignment was official. I found through my calls
that all these gentlemen knew someone would be phoning them for
verification, but none knew who that caller would be. Although Bo
was not the one who was really in charge of the whole thing, I had
no doubt that the operation was legitimate.

Through talking to Gritz himself and by doing some research of
my own, I learned that Bo was a retired lieutenant colonel, a U.S.
Army Special Forces (Green Beret) commander and Vietnam War
hero who had been asked through secret papers to retire from his
military career to take part in a secret POW recon mission and a possible rescue attempt. He was working undercover at Hughes and was
hired to train men who had previously served as Green Berets to run
the POW recon missions. It took me a couple of days to contact
everyone, but with my drive to serve God and country, plus the at-
tractively large amount of money Gritz had offered me - he'd even
reassured me there was a place in Hawaii where we could get more
money if we needed it.* I phoned him once again.

---

*A CIA money laundering firm called Bishop, Baldwin, Rewald, Dillingham and Wong. Our
contact men were to be Ron Rewald and CIA Station Chief Jack Rardin or Agent Kindschi,
phone number (808) 536-6009. General Hunter Harris and Braswell would assist.

"Well, are you willing to get involved?" was his greeting when he answered the phone.

"Yes. And Steve is willing to bring the package. But there's a catch."

"What's that?"

"You've got to pay his way over here and back, plus give him a week's paid vacation in Hawaii."

"No problem." The deal was set. I phoned Steve and told him he was to go to 8029 Holy Cross, Westchester, Los Angeles to get the package and that his plane tickets would be waiting at the airport. The following day he called me to say he'd picked up the sealed package from Bo and was on his way to the airport.

It was good to see my friend Steve once again. Going over the contents of the package and thinking about the trip to Bangkok Bo had asked me to make alone was adventuresome, yet a bit scary. In the package for what was to be a classified mission were two documents marked TOP SECRET, one in a code I couldn't understand and the other a directive from General Aaron of DIA directing Gritz and the ISA group to launch a POW reconnaissance mission. There was money for my plane tickets and some other miscellaneous documents with instructions attached as well as a list of the names of people to contact on my trip to Thailand. The most important contact I was instructed to make was with cover agent Robert Moberg, a former Special Forces man who was using his position as DEA pilot as a cover. Moberg had flown several secret missions into Laos and Vietnam, was fluent in a couple of languages and was currently on contract from the CIA to DEA to work the Golden Triangle, making secret deliveries. He was to be the helicopter pilot later for the actual rescue team. I was to build up relationships between certain agents in Southeast Asia and Vang Pao and make sure plans were still in order and that Moberg approved of me.

My instructions spelled out in detail where I was to go, whom I should see, and what I was supposed to say. I was given more in-depth information about Bo. Also included were several area code 202 phone numbers and one 703 number, plus coded Telex numbers which I could call to confirm the additional information I'd received. There was a code book, a Presidential charter sanctifying the mission - *meaning the Executive Branch approved the mission* - and numerous 10 classified documents, maps and code numbers.

As I leafed through the contents, I caught Steve up on what I'd been doing in Hawaii, then told him, "Let's just have a good time scuba diving and partying for a week, because then I'll be leaving for another country." I knew that's what would please him most.

"Another one of those CIA things?" he asked. I had used him more than once as a personal reference, so he was aware of my previous involvements.

I couldn't tell him exactly. "Aw, I don't know," I evaded.

"Scott...I kind of...looked inside the package," he confessed. I told him I'd noticed the seal had been broken, and I understood his curiosity. "I'll stay here and scuba dive for a few days after you leave," he suggested in a helpful tone. Steve had always been a loyal friend.

Jason Spence, my pastor and friend, tried to talk me out of going on the mission. In fact, all the pastors including the music director asked me to come to the church so they could talk with me.

"We believe it is of God that we come together to tell you this, Scott. Don't go," Jason advised me the day we met.

"But it's for God and country," I argued. I didn't want to hear what they were saying.

"No, Scott. It's for Gritz and the CIA," he retorted. For two to three hours my spiritual counselors and friends tried to talk me out of going to Indochina again. Today I would agree with them one hundred percent, but at the time I did not. I had tunnel vision with money, intrigue and adventure at the end. I didn't care what anybody said and somehow enjoyed their looks of dismay when I gave the church gifts of several one hundred dollar bills.

"Where are you getting all this money?" they asked several times.

"From the government. No big deal. It's tax free," I bragged.

Realizing that our discussion had changed nothing, Craig Englert later asked me to go for a walk with him along the beach.

The peaceful sound of the waves was in direct contrast with the tone of deep concern in Craig's voice. "I don't think this mission is of God, Scott. I really feel the Holy Spirit is telling me this," he said as we walked along Kanole's number one park beach. He kept looking up into the stars, saying, "Seek Him, Scott. Seek Him."

"But how can you judge me like this?" I asked.

"I'm not judging you, Scott, I'm telling you what I feel God is telling me in my heart."

But my mind was made up. I refused to listen. I now believe, although I opted for money and excitement over the will of God, the prayers of those caring friends protected me and now I am compelled to tell a side of the POW issue many people are trying to cover up.

4

How I Became Known As A Flake

June 15, 1981

In the wee hours of the morning, I arrived at Don Muang Airport in Bangkok, Thailand, and immediately proceeded through customs in order to report to the Nana Hotel at SOI4 Sukhumvit Road, Bangkok 11, as instructed. But customs had other ideas until I nervously showed them my passport. Then they put me right through, showing no further interest in inspecting my bags. It was as though they were expecting me.

Armed escorts in a waiting Mercedes Benz 450 SEL immediately transported me through unfamiliar back streets to the Nana where I asked at the desk for my first contact, Chanida. Without hesitation the gentleman in charge left the desk and walked to a back room to awaken my official contact person. A nicely dressed Viet/Thai woman emerged smiling.

"Colonel Gritz has already telexed us. I've been expecting you," she said in a charming oriental accent. "We thought you would be here earlier. Your room is ready and has already been secured." I observed that she spoke fluent English. Apparently during the war she'd worked for our government at some time.

Realizing how tired I was, Chanida directed me to my room, telling me not to worry about a thing and explaining that "their" people were in the rooms adjacent to mine. At each end of the corridor agents stood guard day and night the whole time I was there. Although feeling lonely and very uncertain, I was too fatigued from jet lag to lie awake but for a few moments.

Too early the next morning, Chanida called my room from the lobby asking if I was ready for visitors. I told her I was, then rushed to get ready. Moments later, I was introduced to another agent, a Chinese/Thai woman, Marian Nencharoen - "Miss Sorry" for short. (She was always saying how sorry we Americans were.) During my brief stay in Bangkok, I talked with her often. She seemed to be more in tune with the situation and very security conscious, knowing whom to watch out for, where to go; and she was much more progressive in her thinking than the others. No doubt she had been trained in the States. Miss Sorry made arrangements to meet me at daybreak the following morning and asked me all kinds of personal debriefing-type questions. I got the feeling there were some behind-the-scene dealings going on I knew nothing about.

A third agent, Miss Mareekij, we called "S". *How strange*, I thought, *All women. ...and very professional.* I observed they made daily communiques with the U.S. Embassy via courier.

"You must be very careful," Chanida warned. "There are some men who somehow knew you were to arrive. They've already been asking if you're here yet. ...But don't worry, we've got them under surveillance." This alarmed me.

"Who are they?" I asked.

"Robert K. Brown, publisher of *Soldier of Fortune*, a disinformation magazine, and his reporter Jim Coyne. You'd better contact Bo stateside and let him know about this," Chanida advised.

Immediately I phoned Bo from a secured line, but - just my luck - he wasn't in. His wife Claudia answered the phone and assured me he would return my call.

The following day, after my meeting with Miss Sorry, the "girls," in compliance with Moberg's instructions to Chanida, brought to my hotel room Dominic Zappone and Bobby Schwab, two others I had been told to contact. Zappone, a frustrated Green Beret because he had never seen combat, was later captured by Laotian guerrillas in the ill-fated *Operation Lazarus* led by Bo Gritz. Schwab was arrested April 23, 1985, for violating Vietnam's territorial waters and for committing acts "against the sovereignty and security of Vietnam" while allegedly attempting to return to that country in search of the fiancee he had left behind at the end of the war. Schwab was freed in August of '86. (Document 28) Because they were the "disinformation men" for the mission, I was to tell them who I was, what was going on, and show them Bo's orders. Schwab had brought along his buddy Chumo, a contact agent working with the underground Lao resistance fighters - Vang Pao's people.

After I gave them a lengthy introduction and many explanations, Schwab concluded, "Okay. You're the one we've been looking for. What's next?"

I told Schwab he was supposed to continue what he had been doing - running across the southern border to collect bones to ship to the States as alleged remains at approximately two hundred dollars a set to keep peace with Ann Mills Griffiths, head of National League of Families of POW/MIAs, and the League members. This was to be a diversionary tactic to keep the communists' attention in the region while we prepared the real mission up north and to keep Griffiths out of our way. Zappone, a mean looking muscle man who trusted no one, was to check for security leaks in the northern areas.

Schwab, Zappone and I talked about the *Soldier of Fortune* (SOF) men. "The only way you're going to get them off your back is to drink too much so they think you're a drunken bum or tell them a cock-and-bull story," they advised. (Document 16)

After they left my room, I phoned a George Brooks in Stanford, Connecticut, whose son had been declared missing in action. "Why should I call him?" I'd asked Bo when we'd discussed the intructions in my package over the phone.

"Just do it," was the only explanation he would give me. "Tell him you're there working for Bo and things are going along fine." So that's what I did and learned from the call that Mr. Brooks had given Bo twenty thousand dollars to find his son. (Before the *Bohica* team left for Bangkok in October, 1981, Bo purchased a brand new street motorcycle, had his Cadillac and MG repainted and bought a third vehicle. I asked him if he had received an advance for the mission, but he explained that he was spending part of Brooks' money.)

That evening when I finally talked to Bo, he gave me advice about handling the SOF people similar to that given me by Zappone and Schwab by saying certain coded words and phrases. Then I would look them up on a sheet to find their meaning. "They're mercenary-type magazine people," he said in essence. "Tell them an outlandish story. They'll think you're crazier than a loon, a nobody; and they'll leave you alone."

About a day and a half passed before the two SOF men approached me at a poolside bar at the Nana. It was around eleven in the morning.

"We understand you're here on a POW rescue mission," Brown commented confidently.

"No, man. Hey, I just got robbed. I mean, these guys had M-16 guns and everything." As we drank beer continuously - they bought - I rambled on and on about a robbery that had never taken place, dreading the headache I knew I was going to have the rest of the day.

"Barnes, you're a flake. You're nuts," Brown finally concluded. "Tell you what. Here's my American Express. Go charge everything you owe if you got robbed." Although I didn't realize they would write such a destructive article in their magazine, their disgust was exactly what I needed at the time. But I certainly have not needed the damaging effects in the months and years that followed.

As soon as Brown and Coyne left me, I hurried to Chanida's back room office to tell her what I'd said to them and their response. We both laughed. "Use his American Express, then," she said. "I'll give you back all your cash. You just gained $750. I'm glad they're gone, but we'll continue to keep surveillance."

Although I still read my note-filled Bible infrequently, I was no longer walking with the Lord. My Hope Chapel friends' attempts to discourage my coming to Bangkok still returned to my memory from time to time, but I tried to shelve their concerned words of advice along with my Bible.

5

The U.S. Embassy

June 17, 1981

The second morning after my arrival, before I had put on my act for the *Soldier of Fortune* reporters, one of the three female agents told me, "You've got to get to the CIA post at the Embassy."

"You need to see Mr. Moberg," Chanida explained.

"Well..." I hesitated to respond, wondering how much they knew or should know.

"I'll get you there," she said.

At 10:00 a.m. the following morning, using the directions Chanida had given me, I walked around the corner from the Nana and down several side streets to make sure I wasn't being followed. Although we were convinced that the magazine pests had given me up as a waste of time, Chanida thought it was best that I not be seen riding in any of the vehicles that couriered back and forth from various points in the city to the Embassy. Finally I turned down the busy street and approached the large heavily-guarded gates of the United States Embassy, just across the street from the big yellow and red Shell Oil Company building.

Once inside, I was immediately met by an armed Marine guard and escorted to a steel cage surrounded by cameras and additional armed Marines.

"Give them your identification," my escort instructed me. Another guard checked my passport and code number carefully, then examined a list of the names of people who must have been expected on the third floor at the CIA offices that day. Sure enough, my name was on the list. He made a phone call and in moments a large-framed man in civilian clothes came toward me from upstairs.

"I'm Bob Moberg," he said in a businesslike manner. "Let's go down to the cafeteria and grab a cup." We walked together down a long corridor to the Embassy cafeteria and took our place at the end of a line of other cafeteria patrons, mostly Embassy personnel dressed in civilian clothes.

We filled our cups, the smallest coffee cups I'd ever seen, and I followed Moberg to a corner table he selected after looking around for a place where we could get to know more about one another without being easily overheard. A picture of President Nixon hung over our heads.

"I'm to be the main helicopter pilot for *Grand Eagle*," he explained. "We got a communique from Washington that you were to arrive. After we drink this I'll take you up and introduce you to the rest of the men." To me it sounded as though he thought I was to be part of the mission, which surprised me. But I allowed his comment to pass without questioning it, because I knew I was supposed to be there only to make introductions.

We discussed the situation of Vang Pao and his people being on the outs with the new people in the CIA because of their unwillingness to supply him with previously promised weapons, ammunition and medicines. Vang Pao's airline cargo connections were also removed from his control. I was to assure the General and his people this operation would not be CIA, but private and humanitarian, although certain select people from the Embassy were to help. This getting-to-know-you mission was so that Vang Pao could later inform his people, "Co-operate with my friend Scott." We had to be really careful who we were dealing with, and Moberg had a reputation among them of being a civilian pilot.

I told Moberg this time Vang Pao must receive what we promise and asked him what his current position was.

"I'm on contract with DEA as a cover* to fly 'things' into the Golden Triangle region, if you know what I mean." I knew, but let that comment pass too when I saw the alarmed expression on Moberg's face. I looked around. Another guy in civilian garb was walking toward us.

"Scott, keep your head down and don't talk to this guy," Moberg said in muffled tones. "He's *not* one of us."

The man greeted Moberg, then asked, "Who's your friend?"

"Oh, just an old buddy passing through." Moberg's efforts to remain casual became more difficult as their conversation progressed.

The fellow looked at me. "Hey! Wait a minute! Don't I know you?" I didn't recognize him at all.

"I don't know, do you?" I too was straining to maintain a casual attitude.

"...Yeh! ...It was the beard that threw me. Weren't you in the Drug Enforcement Administration class of 1975?"

I looked hopelessly at Moberg. "Yep, sure was," I admitted with a gulp.

"I'll be darned! So was I!" Still I didn't recognize him. There had been approximately forty covert agents in the class. "Then we know the same DEA intelligence people!" he continued. "One of the agents we're dealing with now - Thuy - she's our disinformation gal but she doesn't even know we've been using her." I wondered, *Why is he telling me this kind of stuff?* It was obvious that he was ready to settle in for a long gabfest, but Moberg put an end to that before it was begun.

"We've got to go." Moberg stood up and his look indicated to me that I was expected to do the same. We said goodbye and retraced our walk through the long corridor back to the steel gate where an armed Marine patted me down and ran an electronic device over each of us. I looked questioningly at my new acquaintance.

---

*CIA covert operations.

"For where we're going, they have to do this," Moberg explained. It was okay for him to carry a gun, but no electronic listening devices.

Following the check another armed Marine guard escorted us up a couple flights of stairs to a point on the third floor where a bright red line was painted. There the Marine abruptly stopped. "This is as far as I'm allowed to go."

"Thanks, pal," Moberg told him and led me down a dark, apparently windowless, hall off to the left. When we'd nearly reached the halfway point, he suddenly stopped in front of a door on the left.

"Stand back there a second, will you?" He motioned for me to move to a position where I could not see beyond him to a small box with numbers on it attached to the door. I realized the door was electronically locked. Bob pushed on the numbers, and, bing, the door opened. We entered a small office with concrete walls and no windows.

He sat down behind his cluttered desk. "Have a seat," he invited me and waved his hand toward a plush chair facing him. On the wall behind him was a photograph of a Huey helicopter hovering over hostile territory with several U.S. soldiers climbing down ropes. It was the copter he had piloted during the war, he said. I stared at the file cabinets and the Telex machine as he made a lengthy phone call, talking in upset tones in Vietnamese. I could only recognize "Barnes" in the conversation and a repeated "Thuy, Thuy" in upset tones. (At the time I thought he was saying "Suey.")

"Everything's okay," he told me as he hung up. "It'll be just a few minutes." Before we could talk further, there was a knock on the door and a huge guy with super short hair entered. Moberg introduced him as Marine William Wharton, "one of *our* translators." "Come on," he told the two of us. "We're going down to the CIA office."

We walked farther down the hallway to another door which Moberg opened by pushing more electronic buttons. The only thing I could see as the door opened was a big desk and a man who was not in uniform sitting behind it. The name plate on the desk read, "Lt. Col. Paul Mather, USAF." (Document 29) Moberg introduced him to me as commander of the Joint Casualty Resolution Center, a CIA front which had been there since the end of the war for the purpose of bringing POWs back home. (JCRC seemed to have easy access to Hanoi and was good for intelligence reasons, to see what was going on with the Soviets by effectively using their POW inquiries as a front. They have never brought back one live POW.)

"We've been expecting you." Mather stood and shook my hand. "Have a seat." It was then I could see that Colonel Mather was not alone in the large but dimly lit room with weapons and various military pictures hanging on the walls.

In a brief but silent pause I remembered the phone call Moberg had made from his office. The fact that I could understand only my last name and the repeated name "Thuy," the Vietnamese agent the fellow in the cafeteria had mentioned, concerned me. I thought, *there must be a lot more to this mission than I know about, but I haven't the foggiest idea what it is.*

"Want me to leave during the briefing?" It was Moberg standing next to the closed door who broke the silence.

"Well...not yet," Mather answered. *Briefing???,* I questioned to myself. According to my instructions included in the package Steve had brought to me in Hawaii, I gave Mather a letter from General Aaron, DIA commander; a code book and a map; some biographical and additional coded information, plus some updated info about Bo and Vang Pao. He introduced me to a Jim Tully who worked with him and a couple of other guys whose names I can't remember. Then Mather swiveled his chair past the paper shredder that had caught my eye as I had entered the room toward the locked file cabinets behind him. He opened a drawer labeled *Top Secret*. Moberg excused himself and left. Four files were removed from the *Top Secret* drawer. Mather heaved a sigh and looked at the men seated around the room. "Okay. We know there are live POWs in Laos," he began. "But there's a problem. This man..."

I interrupted. "I'm just here to deliver those papers and to make introductions."

"We know," Mather responded, "but we need to get to know you and you need to have an idea of what we're doing. We can use your services. I understand you have a knack of getting info by talking to people on a friendly basis."

"Okay. Then who are these people?" I motioned toward the files in his hand.

"People we're very concerned about. Our biggest problems right now are with this man." He tossed a file on his desk. The name on the tab read "USMC PFC Robert Garwood" and gave Garwood's Social Security number. I'd never heard of him. "We knew about him in '77 and should have done something then, but we didn't. Now we regret it."

(When I met Garwood for the first time in January, '86, he confirmed that twice in '77 he was moved under heavily armed guard. On at least one occasion he had successfully slipped out a note. Someone must have received that note and did nothing about it.)

"I could have had him taken care of..." Wharton interjected.

Ignoring his comment, Mather continued, "He was the last one to come out alive, after the U.S. government declared there were no other existing POWs, except one - Shelton. But now...well...he could open his big mouth." The other men seated in the room and standing by the files were carefully taking notes. "If people start to listen to him, we've got problems. But no matter, he'll be taken care of."

I was beginning to feel very uneasy. "What do you mean?" I asked.

"Doesn't matter. It's just to our best interest that no live POWs ever come out. *Ever!*" Mather was emphatic.

Now I was really alarmed. "Now wait a minute! I thought we were here to plan a rescue mission!"

"I'll take care of Garwood," Wharton repeated. I was very tense and uncomfortable. *Are they just testing me to see how I will react?* I wondered and, trying to calm myself, asked about the other files.

Mather continued. "There was a guy shot down on mission in Laos - Major Albro Lundy, Jr. That one we've had bad reports about too." He tossed the *Lundy* file on the desk. "He was shot down on a clandestine bombing mission. There have been rumors that he is possibly still alive. And this guy..." He tapped the file marked *Shelton*. "Captain - *Colonel* - Charles Shelton. They've promoted him now.

He was shot down while on secret mission over Laos and captured alive. Not long after he was captured, CIA sent a special team to get him out. They got intelligence regarding other POWs and locations from him under *Operation Duck Soup* but, rather than send him home, arranged to return him to his Laotian captors and monitor him electronically.

I couldn't believe what I was hearing. "But why was he given back?"

"We got the intelligence information we needed out of him and figured that if we knew where he was, we could go back later and get him out again under *Operation Duck Soup*. But we lost track of him. He's still carried as a live POW on the official records, the only live POW the United States recognizes. And we're still receiving reports of him being seen and moved around in this area." He pointed to a map that was open on his desk. "This is the hottest area in Laos. We have reports of more live sightings in this area than any other. (Document 30) That's what this mission is all about. We've got to get a ground confirmation." He pointed to another location. "This is the closest reported live sighting to the free border. The others are too far into communist territory. This is why Moberg's working with us." I thought Moberg should have been there.

"Now this man..." Mather laid the final *Top Secret* file on his desk. "Commander Ronald Dodge. We're going to bring his body back in a few weeks."

"How do you *know* you're going to bring..."

Mather didn't allow me to complete my question. "We know. It's all taken care of. He was shot down, captured alive, tortured and debriefed. He never came out during *Operation Homecoming*, but we have a picture of Dodge alive in captivity - a picture that was published in several U.S. magazines and circulated in publications all over the world after the Paris Peace Accord. Now we're faced with some problems because he didn't come home in '73. The League of Families members and others are starting to pressure the Administration, so we're going to bring his body home next month."

I persisted, "But how do you *know?*" *If they knew he had been captured alive, why hadn't they done something about it then?*

Mather changed the subject. "Barnes, I want you to deliver a package to some of our contacts in Cambodia."

"Cambodia?" I'd read about Cambodia. "Genocide City? Pol Pots' territory?" *Why would he ask me to deliver anything to the Khmer Rouge? I could be killed!*

"Don't worry," he said, realizing my alarm. "We're working with the Khmers and with Task Force 80 and Justmag. (Task Force 80 - Thai military forces guarding the border. Justmag - military group of U.S. and Thai officials.) He gave me the impression that this assignment was just one phase of the whole Gritz operation. I was to be given the package by a covert courier called Tek in the morning. "It'll be a box like this," he said, holding out a shoebox-sized box covered with a black rubberlike substance.

6

Into Cambodia

June 18, 1981

Thoughts and questions raced through my mind as I walked back to my hotel. *Why was this little package so important that it had to be delivered personally? Why me? Was I being tested? If I get caught, who will take the blame?*

I really hadn't wanted to go and had protested to Mather, "There are communists over there. The North Vietnamese have invaded the place. I hear there's a lot of fighting going on."

I could tell he didn't appreciate my resistance. Impatient with having to take time for explanations, he said, "Look, unbeknown to the Americans, we're (the CIA) helping the Khmers. The war hasn't really ended; it's just over as far as the folks back home are concerned.*

"But if this is supposed to be a POW mission...," I reasoned.

"I need to see if we can depend on you." His sharp tone of voice told me I was to question this portion of my assignment no further.

Early the next morning, just as I had been told, an old taxi cab with the steering wheel on the righthand side - #22 - waited in front of my hotel. The driver, slender, wearing tailor-made silk pants and

---

*Refer to 10-10-83 *Newsweek*, (Document 14 - B).

alligator shoes, identified himself as Tek. He handed me a knapsack. Inside was a small shoebox-sized package tightly wrapped in a black rubberlike substance and weighing about two pounds.

For a couple of hours we taxied down a narrow but mostly paved road, then across several dirt roads toward Task Force 80 and Justmag headquarters. Every few miles a group of displaced people had little markets set up along the side of the road to sell ornaments and trinkets.

Tek, probably Thai/Chinese and about forty-two to forty-three years old, spoke very good English. In the course of our travels I learned that he spoke four or five languages. He was to introduce me to another agent, Prasit Saengrunguane, whom he knew personally, then wait at TF-80 headquarters for my return. It was evident that Tek knew exactly where to go and what to do.

Prasit's home, a beautiful little place for being so close to a war zone, was on the outskirts of the town. Prasit and his wife, carrying their new baby, came out to greet us. His wife was very nice, very friendly, in spite of the fact that she couldn't speak a word of English. Their tranquil "home and family" image was marred by tight security. Several little compounds were set up within a thousand yards of the house.

After Tek saw to introductions, Prasit, probably in his 30's, led us to the basement of his home where to my surprise all kinds of electronic devices were set up and maps lined the walls. He made some radio communications in his native tongue. Although I couldn't understand a word he said, I guessed he was confirming my arrival. Then he gave me a pair of unmarked military fatigues and instructed me to wear them the whole time we were in the area so that anyone who saw us would think we were part of a military advisory team. I was given a .45 automatic pistol and a Wingmaster 870 army issue shotgun and Prasit carried an M-16. Still holding tightly to the knapsack Tek had given me back at the Nana, I followed Prasit to his car. He was to take me to a safehouse at #25 Suwaansorn Road, Aranyaprathet, Thailand, on the border of Cambodia. From there we would be taken into Khmer Rouge country.

We traveled probably fifteen miles, past Task Force 80 to the border to a Buddhist monastery which was being used as an underground safehouse. There we met our interpreter and the village chief, a little man in black shorts, who I learned was in constant contact with the Khmer Rouge. Once introductions had been made, Prasit, the interpreter, the chief and I picked up our weapons and took a walk outside.

Through a rice paddy I could see Thai military tanks and artillery only several yards away from the village. Prasit noticed my concern. "That's Task Force 80, Barnes. Don't worry. Justmag has been waiting a couple of days for us." I caused him some uneasy feelings as I snapped some photos with my personal 35mm camera. "Tourist stuff," I told him. Reluctantly he mumbled, "Okay."

Then in the distance we spotted a North Vietnamese army patrol. "We've got to get out of here," Prasit whispered. "If they see us, we'll be wiped out." I stepped out hoping to get a photo, but Prasit grabbed me and pulled me back.

"No!" he rasped. "You'd be nuts to stand out there!" Quickly we returned to the monastery.

In a candlelit area where the aroma of incense was so strong it was difficult to breathe, a monk was kneeling in prayer before several ornate golden ornaments. He sensed our presence, rose to his feet and greeted us with a smile and a bow.

Pointing to the images of Buddha, I said, "That's idolatry."

Prasit, a kind and friendly fellow, couldn't find a word that would translate "idolatry" into their language. The monk motioned for the three of us to be seated on the several mats that lay on the floor, then motioned for us to look up. There was a gaping hole in the ceiling.

"What's that from?" I asked him through our translator Prasit.

"A mortar round during the fighting last night. It blew up on impact, just as it hit the roof, but some of the shrapnel came through." I could see bits and pieces of shrapnel embedded in the wooden floor and asked if anyone had been hurt. Thank goodness no one had been injured.

While waiting for the North Vietnamese patrol to pass, out of curiosity I told Prasit, "Ask him if he's ever heard of the Bible," remembering with a tinge of guilt that I hadn't been using the one that I carried in my luggage.

Before the monk could respond, I told Prasit, "Ask him if he knows about Jesus Christ." I figured, *Here we are, way out in the boonies of Cambodia - war raging around us, bloodshed and death very present - and this guy who looks as old as Abe Lincoln couldn't have...* As soon as I said "Jesus Christ," the monk's eyes lit up with excitement.

"Didda Chi! Didda Chi!" he cried, and began to talk so fast Prasit strained to keep up with him. Alarmed, I asked what I had done wrong.

"He's trying to say 'Jesus Christ' in English. He wants me to tell you that long ago, before these wars, he'd heard that a mighty one whose name was Jesus Christ would come."

Through a lengthy and awkward exchange among the three of us I learned that because this monastery was many miles away from any white men, no Christian missionaries had ever been there. Even during the war no white man except soldiers had come. The predominant religion of the area had always been Buddhist.

"Then who told him about Jesus?" I asked, still in shock.

"Someone told him when he was very young wherever he was training to become a priest." *And he still remembers...* I got the feeling he knew that to follow Buddha left a lot to be desired, but it was the best he had. Again I looked at the mortar hole in the ceiling and thought, *We needed to come into a Buddhist monastery to be protected from communists. Is God saying something to me in all this?* Today, every time I look at this monk's picture, I wonder where he is and how he is doing. We spent the night at this monastery safehouse.

It was raining and muggy early the next morning when the four of us began our trek across the field into Khmer country. Prasit, who knew the area well, carried the knapsack. Every now and then we had to stop off to wait for security reports from the two Thai's who traveled ahead of us to guard against our running into any NVA (North Vietnamese Army) booby traps. I didn't envy their job.

"When we get near the camp area, you are going to have to strip down to your shorts to cross a small river," Prasit advised. "Justmag orders," he explained. By the time we reached the river we would have passed through all the neutral areas where we needed to be seen as military advisors.

Prasit waited for me to cross. It was a good thing I did have to strip, because as I was crossing the barely twenty foot wide Stung Houei Sai River, I slipped off a log, fell in and had to swim the remaining ten to fifteen feet. I panicked, remembering the threat of booby traps that could be anywhere.

After reaching the opposite bank, Prasit tossed me the package we had so carefully protected, then crossed the river himself. Our traveling companions pulled us up the bank. As we walked he continued to warn about booby traps. About sixty yards from the river bank we spotted a clearing. Black communist "pajamas" were drying on a line. Men with guns walked around the perimeter as if they were expecting someone. A large antenna on a pole rose above the roof from the rear of a bamboo hut. I was told by Prasit this was the Khmer Rouge stronghold camp where I was to deliver the rubber-coated box given to me by Mather's agent. I've often wondered why Prasit couldn't have delivered it. Maybe this was a test of my loyalty, to see how much I would risk for my country.

"We're really helping the Khmer Rouge?" I asked him.

"Yeh."

"But why? These are communists."

"The NVA invaded Cambodia. We don't like the Vietnamese, so we help Pol Pots' people fight them."

"Here I am," I complained, "in a communist camp..." I was worried.

"Just deliver your package. They know what it's all about." I certainly didn't know. There wasn't even an address or writing of any kind on it. Prasit's attempt to reassure me wasn't effective.

When the guard spotted us, it was obvious that we were the ones they were looking for, that we were expected, because they didn't shoot us. Evidently our point men had already made contact. We were welcomed, then escorted into a little rundown camouflaged shack built of tin and local wood and bamboo, well-equipped with Soviet and American arms as well as electronic equipment. There we waited until one of the Khmers returned to tell us everything was okay. We had arrived undetected. I removed the package from the knapsack I carried and placed it on a table. The Khmer's eyes lit up. He grabbed it quickly and took it into an underground cell next to the little shack we were in.

During our twenty or thirty minute stay, as I was nosing around and taking photos, I pointed toward a tunnel. Another Khmer translator motioned for me to follow him, took me into the tunnel and proudly showed me an arsenal of American-made weapons. They looked like new. Supposedly they had been left behind in Saigon in 1975 and were airlifted by the CIA into Thailand for safekeeping for future conflicts. Whenever the Khmers needed weapons, some were shipped here and stored in this tunnel to then be delivered to their fighting men.

It was not a pleasant bit of information to receive. We in America believed the war had ended, but actually it was far from over. I snapped a few more pictures in spite of Prasit's looks of disapproval. The Khmers did not like my taking pictures either. Soon we left. Meeting Tek once again, he and I traveled nonstop all the way back to the Nana in Bangkok.

The clean dry sheets on my hotel bed felt good but the night was far too short. In my mind I re-traveled the road, recrossed the river, delivered the package all over again. I thought about Prasit, my translator, his little family and the danger he faced as he worked so loyally for our CIA. How could I know that two weeks later he would be shot to death while on a reconnaissance team, a sad reward for all his efforts.

Early the next morning I returned to the Embassy, passed by the cameras, through the steel cage and up the stairs to report to Mather. He seemed relieved. "One more thing," he said as I turned to leave.

"I want you to go by the Vietnamese Embassy right around the corner and make a contact. ...Don't worry. Everything's been arranged. You are expected."

7

The Vietnamese Embassy

Knowing I was under surveillance, I walked with fear and trembling around the corner to face the big, cold, bluegray steel doors of the communist Vietnamese Embassy. No one responded to my first knock, so I knocked again. A slide built into the top of the door opened and a little face peeked out, but still there was no greeting or warm welcome.

I decided to initiate a possible discourse. "My name is Scott Barnes. I was told to come here."

"Oooh, ta ta..." I couldn't understand a word. What a relief to then hear a greeting in English as the door opened. But that feeling of relief did not last long.

Two men in North Vietnamese uniforms armed with Soviet AK-47 assault rifles stood just inside the door, and my entrance immediately set off the front alarm - two Doberman Pinchers with spiked collars around their necks, lunging and barking ferociously. The two guards struggled to hold tightly to their chains. I stepped back. In Vietnamese one of the guards yelled a command to the dogs and they obeyed.

How do those dogs know to respond to a foreign language, I wondered. It was then I realized how nervous I really was. *What a silly thing to think!* I had to remind myself that just because all the dogs I knew understood only English commands, to these dogs, Vietnamese wasn't foreign. *I must pull myself together. Calm down, Scott,* I told myself.

I was escorted by the two Vietnamese guards through a steel gate, then down a sidewalk to the right toward a large building that reminded me of an old French colonial building. The armed guards, pulled by the two Dobermans, led the way across a large courtyard nearly filled with bushes. A flag flapping in the breeze boasted the Vietnamese communist red star. Reaching the opposite side of the courtyard, I faced another pair of huge doors, beautifully carved of teak wood.

One of my escorts opened the doors. "Go in and sit down," he instructed me in English. A guard and one dog remained posted on each side of the doors.

Several Vietnamese gentlemen were seated around a large teak hand-carved coffee table. A very pleasant man politely stood and welcomed me into the large room with barred windows. He introduced himself as an official from Hanoi. I was seated. The only American in the room.

"So you're here to discuss the release of prisoners of war?" he asked in perfect English, setting a pot of hot tea on a small table nearby.

I was astonished. "Your English is almost better than my own!" Leery of being poisoned, I declined his offer of a cup of tea.

"I was educated in the United States and am now a captain in the North Vietnamese Army," he explained. "You come to admit to the war crimes?"

"I came because a Lieutenant Colonel at the U.S. Embassy told me to come." He seemed to understand that I wasn't really sure why I had been sent.

"You're here because we cannot deal with them without first going through your Washington. But I understand you are a civilian. We can ask you to relay messages unofficially." I still didn't understand why it was necessary for me to be here. What was I supposed to do? What was I supposed to say? (I later learned General Vang Pao had recently renewed his acquaintance with former Vietnamese

Premier Ky who was still involved with people in Hanoi. Since I was a friend of Vang Pao and Vang Pao was a friend of Ky, I could be considered a connection.)

The man from Hanoi removed some pictures from the drawer of a desk and very deliberately placed them in front of me, making sure I had sufficient time to see every detail of one before he displayed another. I cringed as I looked at horrendous scenes of alleged American troops torturing young men, woman and children. *Maybe they did this and are just saying the Americans did it,* I hoped. Looking at each one closely, I could see no clues of touchups, but still I was suspicious. *Why hadn't they taken these pictures to the U.N. or publicized them through world media as they had done with the My Lai massacre?*

"That's pretty horrible!" I didn't know what else to say.

"Right," he affirmed, obviously pleased with my dismay. "This has been going on for many, many years. You Americans...! My Lai was nothing!"

"Oh, the massacre?"

"Yes. ...You admit to the war crimes? You give us three million dollars per prisoner?" He seemed so sure that I had the power to do this and would consent. I was at a loss for words.

He admitted there were living American prisoners of war, but that they are moved across the border through the Mu Gia Pass into Laos when the U.S. begins to pressure for information about reported live sightings. Then they can truthfully say there are none in their country. *You S.O.B.'s!* I wanted to shout. *So that's how you operate!*

"Your Bobby Garwood!" he continued. "He opened his big mouth!" *Garwood!* I remembered what Mather had said. There was that name again! Abruptly he changed the subject. "You going to exchange or not?"

"You think I'm a direct link to the Executive Branch? All I can do is relay what you've told me. I'll report back to Mather. But you've probably already talked to Mather and his people." It was obvious that Paul Mather was not one of his favorite people.*

Our brief conversation, those terrible pictures, filled my thoughts as I returned to the U.S. Embassy. I was escorted to report to Mather, then met once again with Moberg. "The helicopter's ready," Moberg assured me. "We can fly in low and do a pluck with the ISA team. But you guys are going to have to go in on foot first because we need a ground confirmation." We'll be loaded with medical supplies and corpsmen ready for immediate rescue."

Once again I resisted. "The rescue people will need to know all this, but, remember, I'm just here for intelligence and recon information only and to help the relationship with Vang Pao go a little smoother." He seemed very nervous about the possibility of an intelligence leak. We said goodbye and I returned to the hotel.

Evidently Chanida had been watching for me. No sooner had I entered the front doors of the Nana than she hurried toward me. "This Alan Dawson has been asking about you."

Oh no! I remembered that name from a list of people to watch out for which Bo had included in the package that Steve had delivered to me in Hawaii. Dawson had a reputation for being a kind of left-behind free lancer who floated around from bar to bar to see what he could learn. He could be considered a small-time reporter who wrote for the *Bangkok Post* whenever he could to get a buck for a drink. I was to meet him for lunch. Recalling that Bo's advice about dealing with reporters had worked the first time I'd had a run-in, I tried the method again.

"Barnes!" Dawson greeted me as I walked into one of the dumpiest bars I had ever been in. "I heard all about this mission you're on." He was a short, wiry character and very unstable. Possibly intoxicated.

---

*I later learned it was because Mather's Vietnamese wife had been a communist who had defected, and also found out that this fellow I was talking to knew that Thuy was now investigating for U.S. Intelligence drug crimes; the Vang Pao connections going on in the Golden Triangle with former CIA Station Chief Daniel C. Arnold. Oliver North. Tom Clines, Ted Shackley, Dale Duncan, Air America and others involved. (Document 31)

I whipped a map out of my inner jacket pocket. "Good!" I said. "Then maybe you can help me. Where's the road that'll take me over into Laos to this...Sam Nuea POW camp? I've got to get over there."

His look indicated he thought he had a maniac on his hands. "What are you? Crazy? You can't do a thing like that!"

"What do you mean?" I continued as if I hadn't noticed his alarm. "We're going to rent a car, drive over there and pick up a few and..."

"You are crazy. Look, stay here and finish your lunch; I'll pay. See ya." Bo was right. Give them a little bit of crazy information and they don't bother again. He was also right in his evaluation of Dawson who was later fired from the *Bangkok Post* because little of his reporting could be validated. I can believe it; he wrote a fictitious story about me and had never interviewed me. (Document 16 and 32)

That evening I was to meet Moberg at Lucy's Tiger Den, the watering hole for the Special Forces and the CIAs, to discuss the mission and the necessary big money contacts. (Document 33) Michael Hand, who was allegedly laundering drug money for the CIA via the Nugan/Hand banking firm, was also there.

Excited about the thoughts of a rescue mission, Moberg told me, "You'll see, Scott. Things will soon begin to happen in nine to twelve weeks. After the monsoon season's over, they'll do the ground recon. Then we'll go in. Now that you've met the people you need to know, go back and tell Bo everything's fine. Vang Pao's people are cooperating thus far, thanks to you. And we accept you."

I stayed on for a couple of days to make further contacts, supposedly for tourist-type sightseeing, then caught a plane back to California to report to Bo.

Scott's photo of U.S. Embassy in Saigon, taken quickly so as not to be detected. He was instructed to go there for a briefing.

Scott in "Sanitized fatigues standing in front of a communist refuge area, South Vietnam.

U.S. Army Base in South Vietnam.

Top: Scott in Israel

Bottom: Toward the Dead Sea near Masada.

Underground safehouse at Prasit's home.

Prasit.

Into Cambodia

Task Force 80 headquarters within 100 yards of communist territory.

Scott Barnes crossing Stoeng Huoy Sei River into communist Cambodia into Khmer Camp.

"Village Mayor" climbing banks of river. Khmer camp in background.

Looking out of the monastery into Cambodia. Mosquitos flourished.

Cambodian, Khmer soldier on left, with Scott. They have been fighting against V.C. Part of Pol Pot's forces, inside Cambodia. Very dangerous area.

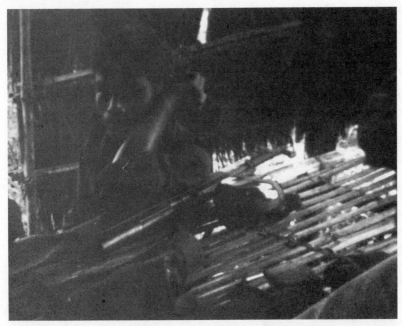

Inside Khmer Rough camp with soldiers, Chinese weapons, taking pictures very difficult and very scary. Many fire fights with N.V.A.

Sitting inside of camp with Khmer troops at fire base. Khmer soldiers trying to get out of the picture. They are very anti-photo.

Scott in Khmer camp in Cambodia.

Scott and Pol Pot's Khmer soldier in Cambodia - young kid who doesn't know his family and must fight V.C. to survive.

Inside Khmer camp. Weapons hidden under leaves on ground. Note the black communist "PJ's" hanging on the line.

The frame is the beginning of the construction of a temporary structure in the Khmer camp.

8

Home Again

June 25, 1981

I was in California once again. One of the first things I did was call Bo Gritz to report on my stay in Thailand and Cambodia. He asked me to meet him by the taco stand on the Strand at Hermosa Beach.

What a busy place! People of all shapes and sizes were walking up and down the pier talking, laughing, enjoying the sunny weather. As I approached the taco stand with its huge statue of a surfer in front, I wondered how Bo would recognize me in the crowd. I certainly didn't know what he looked like. Although I'd talked with him by phone many times, this would be our first meeting face to face. I decided to stand near the door.

Just as I approached the building, a big husky fellow wearing leather pants and vest walked out.

"Scott," he said in a familiar voice. "I'm Bo." We shook hands. "Your photo is a good one."

"What photo?"

"Aw, I got one from...other personnel." He held out his hand. My law enforcement photo lay in his palm. "Come on in. I'll buy you a beer."

Inside the crowded restaurant we managed to find an empty booth. He ordered a light beer for each of us, then leaned across the table so we could hear one another above the laughter and the juke box music.

"Well, tell me about it," he said expectantly. "How'd it go?"

I gave him a run-down on the whole trip, telling him Moberg said the helicopter was ready to go, Vang Pao's people were cooperating, but also told him that I didn't understand why Paul Mather wouldn't want any live POWs to come out of Laos, if indeed there were any still there.

"He was probably just testing you to see what your reactions would be. POWs are just one element of this mission, Barnes," Bo assured me. "They had to know where you stood in this matter." I believed him.

He was pleased when I handed him the code book Moberg had given me. "Everything seems to be a 'Go,' " he said. "The monsoon season will be coming to a close in a couple of months or so."

"Bo, I made a run into Cambodia to do something. I'm not quite sure what it was about."

"Immaterial," was all he said.*

When I related the *Soldier of Fortune* reporters' reaction to my crazy story, he was pleased. "There's got to be a leak somewhere. How did they know?" I asked.

Bo answered, "That's why I had Chanida there - to figure it out. ...How's Dominic?"

"Fine. Just a big dumb Green Beret."

He laughed. "Don't worry about him. He's there to work on some other things. Some follow up. ...Want something to eat?"

"Naw." I sipped my beer.

"Tell me about yourself. Family background and stuff." I did, but had the feeling he knew just about everything there was to know about me and wanted to check it out.

---

*Several months later I read in *The Wall Street Journal* that a team investigating the possibility of yellow rain experimentation found suspicious samples on bits of shrapnel, trees and leaves in that same area. Now it has been proven conclusively what they found was yellow rain, but not the kind spread by the Soviets as the U.S. had alleged.

When I had finished, Bo admitted, "I already had a little bit of bio on you - bet that Hell's Angels thing was pretty scary."

"Yeh."

Bo frowned. "They should all be killed. Did you know the Hell's Angels wrote a letter to President Nixon asking permission to rescue POWs?"

"Yeh," I said. "I read about that."

"It's true. The leader of the Hell's Angels sent a letter to Nixon asking him to let them go to Hanoi to rescue POWs. A lot of those guy are ex-Special Forces from the sixties."

"I didn't know that," I told him.

"Oh, yeh." Bo smiled. "But they weren't needed except for some of their drug connections for secret funding. We're going to do the rescuing." At that time I thought "we" meant Bo and his Special Forces colleagues.

He became edgy when I told him about the photos I had been shown at the Vietnamese Embassy; and when I asked him why everyone was so upset about this fellow Bobby Garwood, he replied in a firm tone of voice, "There's a lot you don't understand, Scott. But that's immaterial. We need you to get to Vang Pao and that's all. Okay?"

"Okay." What else could I say? His response sounded so blunt, so final. Then he invited me to his home. I accepted his invitation, eager to get to know more about this colorful man. We pushed our way through the crowded smoke-filled room to the fresh air outside. Bo hopped on his motorcycle, and I followed in my car to 8029 Holy Cross, Westchester, Los Angeles.

There he introduced me to his wife Claudia who appeared to be fifteen years or so younger than Bo. "This is my third or fourth wife," he said laughing. "I've had so many, I've lost track." When I admired the two framed blackbelt certificates that hung over the fireplace in their living room, Bo explained proudly that one belonged to him and the other to Claudia, who was the daughter of a military officer in Panama.

After a brief moment of chit chat, he led me outside to a room attached to the back of his garage. This was Bo's office, filled with military memorabilia. I scanned the room and noticed antibugging and eavesdropping devices, a nightscope nicknamed Starlight Starbright, a couple of guns and pictures taken in Southeast Asia during the war. Some of the electronic devices were on a small desk along with a couple of phones. Behind the file cabinets was a quiet area furnished with a couch where we sat and talked.

As I reiterated in greater detail some of the happenings of my trip, Bo asked many questions. By the time our conversation ended, he was satisfied he had the full account of my stay in Bangkok and I had the approval and acceptance of the contacts I had been instructed to make. My Bangkok assignment was complete.

"Okay," he said, leaning forward. "Here's the next deal. You've got to get me in to see General Vang Pao. Then after he and I become friends, we'll quietly move you out of the picture. We'll keep in touch. Okay?" Nearly every day he would phone to "keep me up on things."

One particular day when he called he was exceptionally upset.

"Scott, there was a military crash near Nellis Air Force Base outside Las Vegas." Some of the men working with the Activity and training for our mission were killed. A part of the 75th Rangers, and some Special Forces, they had been preparing to make low level night drops for rescue. (The only media report I heard about the crash simply stated that some men working on a classified military training exercise were killed in a plane crash. That was it.)

"Scott," Bo continued somberly, "things will have to be changed. You've got to stay on board."

That was the last thing I wanted to hear! "Wow," I exclaimed. "I think I'm getting in over my head!"

He persisted. "But you're an integral part of this operation now whether you like it or not. We have an investigative assignment you must do right away." He proceeded to tell me he had received an intelligence report about a Catholic priest who was seeking permission from his diocese to go to Laos to work with Catholic relief while he sought information about his father who was said to have been held as a POW. I asked Bo his name.

"Charles Shelton, Jr., Colonel Charles Shelton's son." (Note: Chaplain Shelton is no longer in the USAF.) Colonel Shelton's file and Mather's conversation about him flashed through my mind. Bo continued, "Charles, Jr. is at Our Lady of Guadalupe Church, Hermosa Beach. I understand you're pretty good at interrogation, that you've received training in this field by the U.S. Army, the Department of Justice and the Drug Enforcement Administration. Go up there and pick his brain. See what's really going on. We're afraid he's going to muddy up our mission."

I visited the priest and could see that he was not to be easily swayed. "I am going to go," he kept insisting. He phoned his mother in San Diego several times to find out her opinion and why she thought there was so much resistance to his going. Although she didn't fully understand the reason for the strong resistance either, she finally advised him not to go.

Bo was relieved. "The ISA would break his legs to stop him," he told me in a grave tone of voice when I phoned to inform him that Father Shelton had changed his mind.

"You'd hurt a Catholic priest?" I asked in dismay.

"If... we had to... Look, I need to meet with Vang Pao soon, and also with Congressman Robert K. Dornan." Bo knew by this time that through my church I also had contact with Dornan, then chairman of the POW/MIA Task Force for Congress. I hesitated, not wanting to take advantage of this relationship. "Come on, Scott. We're getting a charter from ISA for this mission. It's official. Besides, there's a lot of money in it for you." There was that word "money" again.

"Oh, Okay. Dornan speaks at our church on occasion and I sort of know his aide. I can probably get you in to see him."

"Well, start arranging things right away."

9

Planning Operation Grand Eagle

Summer, 1981

I couldn't get the names on the files in Mather's office off my mind, especially after I had talked with Father Shelton. The offhand manner in which Mather had talked about sending Dodge's body home bothered me, so I telephoned Mrs. Shelton and in a polite but brief conversation found out how to get in touch with Janice Dodge and phoned her. I told her that her husband's name had been mentioned while I was at the Embassy in Bangkok. The news really upset her. I felt so sorry for her. What agonizing the POWs' loved ones have to suffer, waiting, hoping. Ron Dodge's remains were returned to the U.S.A. *within sixty days* after my return from Indochina. President Reagan telephoned his condolences. It's unfortunate the Dodge family neglected to order an autopsy to find out how long he'd been dead. (Bo suggested to Ted Koppel on an ABC *Nightline* interview in 1982 that Koppel should find out how long Dodge had been dead. Ted cut him off.)

I shared with my pastor/friend Randy Sanford that I could possibly be involved in a second mission. "Don't do it, Scott," he warned, yet reluctantly agreed to accompany me to Congressman Dornan's office. I introduced Randy to aide Stan Mullin, then as instructed, gave Mullin photographs of myself to be used by Dornan later for confirmation in case there was any diplomatic trouble. *No doubt Dornan was one of the men who was calling the shots*, I thought at the time, but later determined he was being used. Through a series of phone calls and contacts, with Randy constantly insisting, "No, no, don't do this," the initial meeting to plan *Operation Grand Eagle* was arranged for August 26, 1981, in Congressman Robert K. Dornan's Los Angeles office. I kept trying to calm Randy's fears by flashing one hundred dollar bills to prove how legitimate this mission was. He said this only added to his concern.

I arrived a bit early at the meeting place just off Century Boulevard next to LAX (Los Angeles International Airport). It wasn't long until Bo came in, then Stan Mullin. Finally General Vang Pao and his entourage arrived, Colonel Vang Gee and another colonel plus several security people. A body guard stayed in the front office where we signed in. A lot of greeting, bowing and saluting official military respect - took place.

After I had introduced Bo to the General, to Colonel Vang Gee and Vang Pao's other people, we went into the Congressman's office. Congressman Dornan was not present at the meeting. After everyone was seated, Mr. Mullin asked if he should leave.

"No," Bo told him. "We need you here." Bo laid his briefcase on Dornan's desk and placed his gun on top of it. "I've got some super-top-secret stuff in there," he explained. I knew he didn't really trust Vang Pao because of the "Emperor in Exile's" feelings toward the CIA at that time.

Formalities complete, Bo began. "General, this mission is strictly humanitarian; it has nothing to do with the United States government or the CIA. A group of individuals who care about their fellow missing Americans want to rescue them." Bo was very convincing.

The General made it known that he was very angry at Daniel C. Arnold of the CIA and why.

"...As a matter of fact, I can show you my retirement card," Bo offered for further assurance. "I've retired from the Special Forces." To be sure Vang Pao was convinced he had nothing to do with the government, Bo handed him the card so he could check its validity. As I listened to their conversation, it became obvious to me the General and his beloved Hmong people had had many problems with the CIA, mainly between the Indochina drug war lords and some personnel within the Agency who were interested only in making millions from the drug trade - Ted Shackley, General Secord, Tom Clines, Carl Jenkins, all involved with Vang Pao and Daniel Arnold in narcotic trafficking with Air America. Apparently after the war nearly everyone had become more concerned with profiteering from narcotics and weapons trade than about those fellow Americans who were left behind.

Cautiously Bo led the discussion into the logistics of various prison camps and numerous reports of POW sightings by the General's Hmong people. Finally he asked, "General, how much?"

The General's response took me by surprise. He was not the least bit interested in receiving money. He repeated Bo's inquiry.

"How much? Radio equipment, weapons, medication - potassium and atropine..."

I was curious. "Atropine?"

"In case of gas," the General explained. "You stick atropine in your leg when you are exposed to gas." I hated to think there was a possibility that chemical/biological warfare was still being used in the jungles.

Immediately Bo changed the subject. "General, I think it would be best for you to leave the room for a few moments. Only Scott and Mr. Mullin should see the document I am about to discuss."

Unshaken by Bo's request, the General smiled knowingly and asked, "Is it a map you will talk about?"

Suspicious, Bo hedged, "What if it is?"

"And does it have various circles drawn in red, marking locations in Laos where known POW camps are located?" The General began to draw on a piece of paper, writing first in Laotian then in English. "Compare this to your secret paper you wish to discuss."

Bo was astonished. "My God! They're the same!"

"That is the information I gave to your government nearly one year ago," he informed Bo in his usual businesslike manner. "They did

nothing!" He told about all the intelligence information he had filtered
back about American prisoners of war being moved frequently through
the Mu Gia Pass to the Na Mara Mahaxay Region from approximately
1978, to late '80, early '81. His last confirmed reports were that the
Mahaxay Region was still a holding area. (Document 30) Now he
had won Bo's complete trust. Bo removed from his briefcase his copy
of the map which revealed the sites of known POW camps in Laos.
It was covered with a transparent film so he could make markings
which could be wiped off. "U.S. Department of Defense" was im-
printed at the top and in red letters "Top Secret."

"The hottest spot has been the Mahaxay region," Vang Pao informed
us. "My men have gone in and out several times - some have lost
their lives. That's where we've had the most live sightings. There is
definitely a camp there. Mahaxay is closest to the border and therefore
safest to reach." Several hours were spent planning and briefing. Vang
Pao was asked to provide underground assistance for the mission in
exchange for weapons, medical supplies and radio equipment. He
agreed.

"I'll dispatch my people to check the camp again. It may take several
weeks."

One CIA document released June 4, 1982, admits "A series of unconfirmed reports...(deleted)...stated that nine American POWs were
held in the vicinity of Mahaxay in September 1973. Mahaxay is in
Central Laos, about 30 miles east of Thakhek and sixty miles south
of Lak Sao. One report said the nine were taken to Hanoi in September,
1973. Another report said the nine were still in the area, at a detention camp near a town called Pha Katao, in March 1974. ...The Mahaxay reports remain unconfirmed in spite of extensive research and
follow-up." I thought there might be some continued CIA activities
down in this area, but I couldn't believe we'd left American soldiers
behind. I didn't want to believe it.

After the meeting, I rode with Bo in his Mustang to his home less
than six miles away. I was nervous and asked a lot of questions. Part
of my jitters stemmed from the fact that Bo had begun to carry a lot

of weapons with him. "I carry so many classified documents," was his explanation.

"But this is the United States..." I reasoned.

"We just need to make sure Vang Pao doesn't know this is an Activity operation. He might turn on us." (Most people in the government didn't even know this secret commando group existed.)

"You would...kill him?" I questioned in unbelief.

"Only *if* we had to." We were both silent for the remainder of the trip to Bo's home.

Once again we talked in Bo's office off his garage. I shared my increased feelings of uneasiness. "I don't like all this deception," I told him, "telling Vang Pao this was not to be a CIA operation when it really was, telling him the Activity wasn't involved. We should get the cooperation the Agency promised and tell the truth." Again Bo explained that, due to new leadership and a new President, policy had been changed and the promises made to Vang Pao and his people could no longer be fulfilled. He gave me more money, at first glance two to three thousand at least.

Still feeling uneasy, I conceded, "I guess if there's a chance we can find out about fellow Americans over there, we must go through with this as is."

That evening Bo talked a lot about Zen Buddha. It seems that he believed in several gods, changing from one to another on the basis of his needs and situations. As he talked I looked around the small room lined with medals and awards. I was impressed by his medals and reminded myself that my training and experience was not nearly as extensive as his.

Again I argued, "All these well-trained people are already working in Thailand on other operations, and I have so little training for this type of mission. I still don't understand why I have to be involved."

"Scott, you're new to the Activity," Bo reiterated. "The communist agents don't know you as a recon man. Besides, you're close to Vang Pao. He trusts you and he believes you're not government any more."

It was getting late. I finished my snack, then Bo took me to spend the night at my parents' home in the Hollywood Riviera Section rather than drive me all the way back to where I parked the truck I had been driving.

The following day Bo phoned to tell me he needed to meet again with General Vang Pao immediately to gather more information on the particular site. I called the General at his ranch in Montana. He suggested we meet at his office at Garden Grove the next morning. It would be a safe and secure place to talk. I hoped he wouldn't be upset, having to return to Garden Grove after just having arrived in Montana.

Bo picked me up at my parents' home in his Mustang and we drove to Orange County to General Vang Pao's Garden Grove office nestled in a shopping center at 14095 Euclid. (Phone (714) 539-1183 or 556-9520) As we waited for the General, we looked over the bulletin board on the wall of his waiting room. It was filled with all kinds of information about the war in Laos. It wasn't long until he came to the door of his office and invited us in. Colonel Vang Gee and another officer were also there. "This room is secure," he assured us. But Bo did not accept Vang Pao's word, and without saying anything, he opened his briefcase, removed an electronic device and began to move it over the clothing of the General and the other two gentlemen, then around the rug, the walls and the desk. "Okay, let's go on," he said as he sat down, satisfied that no electronic eavesdropping devices were present.

I was embarrassed, but General Vang Pao was insulted. "If you're going to do that, let me unbutton your shirts to make sure there's no wires on you." He patted us down, checking our clothes. Bo excused his actions by saying he was only making sure our government would not find out about the mission plans.

I gulped as the General told us in greater detail the problems he'd had with Daniel Arnold of the CIA, because I knew Arnold was working with Bo.

Again Vang Pao pointed out the locations where his people had sighted American POWs, then asked Bo and I to have current black and white photos made of each of us. We dashed out to a nearby quick photo booth, deposited the necessary coins and returned to the General's office and handed him the pictures.

"I'll send these to my men. One or both of you *must* be there on the appointed date to meet my agents," the General told us.

"Wait a minute," I protested. "I'm just supposed to make the contacts, Bo."

"Let's go have a beer. We'll talk." Bo and I left Vang Pao's office and drove to the Marriott Hotel, LAX.

"We'll have to go as Hughes technicians," Bo told me at the Marriott, as if I had never protested. "We'll have red passports... ID as U.S. officials..." He held out a finger for each point. "And a third cover will be, we can say we're working for Robert Dornan as aides."

"Look," I said emphatically, "I got you in to see Vang Pao. This is where Scott Barnes steps out."

"Oh, just hang on for a little longer. The Agency feels you need to work with us just in case we receive more confirmation of sightings and need to get rescue people ready. Without you Vang Pao may not continue to cooperate. ...There'll be a substantial amount of money in it for you." I had grown used to the luxury of being able to buy all the things I'd ever dreamed of - a truck, clothes, rare coins, gold - without worrying about the cost.

Blinded by contradictory feelings of patriotism and greed, I yielded. "...but I'm not going to leave the United States again. Understand?"

Unmoved by my loud pronouncement, Bo gave me further instruction. "Return the phone call from Stan Mullin at Dornan's office. The ISA doesn't want it known that we had that meeting. Have him send you the page we all signed in Dornan's guest ledger the first day we met. If he'll send it to you, make sure it's the original, then destroy it."

Mullin wasn't in when I phoned, so I left a message. When he returned my call he agreed to mail the page for me to destroy. (I'm so thankful I decided it would be wise to keep it instead.) (Document 34 - A,B,C,D)

I spent a lot of time with Bo Gritz as he traveled from place to place throughout southern California making plans for the mission. We became close friends. I respected and admired him, yet was worried about all the fire power he carried with him and the dangerous games of lies and deceit he played with people.

Bo secretly met with Dornan on a Sunday shortly after our initial meeting in his office and they discussed the mission with Bobby Inman of the CIA. Dornan assured Bo he would immediately contact the President if the operation went sour.

In late '79 Bo had used Ann Mills Griffiths of the National League of Families of POW/MIAs to get misinformation out to the advantage of his rescue plans. Although we shared many personal things about ourselves with each other in what seemed to me to be a trusting relationship, he never would tell me exactly whom he was dealing with in Washington beside those he had told me to call to confirm the mission - only that the ISA, a few DIA, CIA and NSA people were involved.

10

Getting the Go Signal

Late September, 1981

Bo phoned late one evening. "I need to see you, Scott. Pronto." His words came so forcefully I knew he was excited. "Come now. Tonight. It'll be worth your while."

When I arrived at Bo's sometime between midnight and one o'clock in the morning, he answered the door wearing only his briefs. "Come on inside." He hurried me toward his living room where he opened a large briefcase filled with cash. Running his fingers to the bottom of the case, he assured me, "It goes all the way down, Barnes. The charter's been approved by the Executive Branch and here's four hundred twenty-six thousand dollars to finance the mission and to be used for bribes, drugs, weapons - whatever we will need. Our operation's been dubbed '*Operation Grand Eagle*,' but the radio code is for us to choose. We'll use '*Bohica**.' " Bo mentioned that an associate who would be working with him - a Colonel Dale Duncan - also had access to large quantities of money through ISA.

"You've got to go with us, Scott. The Activity's cleared you and some others. I'll introduce you to them later."

*An acronym used by military personnel: "Bend Over Here It Comes Again."

Feeling as though I was being forced deeper and deeper into a trap, I again insisted on making phone calls to Washington and Virginia to verify the mission and the fact that I was to be a part of it. Again I called Mike Burns, Colonel Kennedy, Colonel Robinson, all with DIA. The charter was government approved. Official. As an additional incentive Bo grabbed a wad of one hundred dollar bills from the briefcase and handed it to me. "Here. Go have a good time."

The next morning I called my pastor and friend Randy to tell him about my new assignment.

"Hey, I told you not to go on that first mission, and you shouldn't go on this one either. Let me buy your breakfast."

We met in a corner booth at Jo Jo's on Hawthorne Boulevard in Torrance, the spot where the church people frequently met socially after services.

"Look at all these hundreds!" I pulled my thumb across the bills in my wallet.

"Scott, you're basing your decision on the temptation of greed." Realizing the luxury of owning things and greed had taken control of my life long ago, I knew he was right.

"Okay, Randy, I won't go."

"You'll go. I know you will," he said sadly. "Just be careful."

Bo called again the first of October. "Vang Pao's people have just reported back. Monsoons are over, so it's dry over there. Blackbird SR-71* has taken another series of photos proving the camp is still active." Again I drove to Bo's home at his request and again he loaded me with money. He knew my weak spot. I thought, Okay. *I go along for the ride, but only as far as Bangkok.*

"I've got to get this pickup truck back home before I get too involved," I told him. I'd sold my Volvo and had been driving a borrowed truck.

"Butch will take care of returning the truck." Butch Jones was Claudia Gritz' brother-in-law. I spent the night with my parents, then

---

*Blackbird: High altitude U.S. spy plane.
 SR: Strategic Recon.

drove my borrowed truck to Bo's house early the next morning as he had specified. He introduced me to Butch who worked in the electronic division at Hughes and had access to the equipment needed for the mission. "Butch will return the truck. Now come with me and I'll introduce you to the other guys."

After I had given the truck keys to Butch, Bo and I walked next door to a little blue house, the only house in the neighborhood with all the shades drawn. Bo opened the door using a key he'd been holding in his hand and motioned for me to enter. Sitting in the living room were three men, armed but dressed in civilian clothing. Boxes containing medical supplies, binoculars, cameras and all kinds of electronic equipment filled one corner of the room. Even a layman like myself could see that this was far too much equipment for a recon mission.

"Scott, this is J.D. Bath, Special Forces. He's going to be our communications specialist." Bo gestured toward a gentleman sitting on a chair examining a part of a weapon. "This is Ben Dunakoskie, also with Special Forces, Delta, Clandestine Operations." Neither man acknowledged Bo's introductions with more than a grunted "Hi." Ben continued turning the weapon piece over and over, while J.D. Bath practiced aiming one of the listening devices.

Bo turned toward the third man in the room. "All you need to know about this gentleman is...his name is Mac." I reached out to shake Mac's hand, but he refused. I sensed that here was a man with a lot of hostility. Surmising by his gray hair that he was older than the other two, I decided to try again to break the ice. "So you're Gramps?" I teased.

"Shut your mouth!" He glared. "You'll do as I tell you." *This guy must be the boss*, I thought, but soon learned it would be the responsibility of this strong quiet World War II and Vietnam veteran to decipher code out of Washington and the U.S. Embassy in Bangkok for us. I knew he would not be able to be involved in anything too strenuous because he was overweight. I recognized the code Mac was studying as the one I'd delivered to Mather months before.

Bo then explained we would be smuggling the piles of equipment into the country for Vang Pao's Hmong people. I still was impressed that the General would not be bought with money, but rather insisted on equipment needed so desperately by his Hmongs. Most of the cartons in the room were marked "Litton Industries." Some were from Hughes. All the serial numbers had been removed. "In case it's captured, it's 'stolen,' " Bo explained. I was also told that a sixth man involved with the mission was already in Bangkok.

This time it was Bath who glared at me. "You're not Special Forces, are you?"

"No!" I replied. "Intelligence."

"Then why are YOU involved in this mission?"

Bo interrupted. "I told you we'll talk about it later," he said firmly. I didn't quite understand what this friction was all about at the time. "Come on, Scott," Bo said trying to clear the tension, "don't tell them anything."

Ignoring Bath, Bo continued to brief us. "These three are the only people you need to know, Scott. Those who are paying you to go on this mission know who you are, but you don't need to know who is really in charge." It was not until I went on special assignment to Israel in March, 1983, that I learned who some of the behind-the-scenes players were: Tom Clines, Carl Jenkins, Ted Shackley, General Secord, Tom Polgar, Oliver North and many others - all associates of CIA Chief Daniel C. Arnold.

The contrast between Bo's passion for rescuing POWs and the empathy of the other three could not go unnoticed. Constantly Bo referred to the need for our country to risk whatever was necessary to rescue those he was convinced were left behind, but the others seemed indifferent. On occasion they remarked, "So what if they've been left behind? That's what war's all about." *Pretty callous*, I thought.

For several days we met in the little blue safe house* next door to Bo's residence, but I never slept there. Even though we usually talked into the wee hours of the morning, I would be driven to Butch's home, eight or nine miles away in Hawthorne, to sleep. I'm sure a couple of the fellows stayed there to guard the equipment, but I have no way of knowing.

"We will have no problems smuggling this electronic equipment through customs," Bo informed us. "That's all been arranged. Now all we have to do is wait to be told our day of departure and receive our last intelligence briefing. Until then we will be moving from safehouse to safehouse to finalize our plans.

"From now on you will move in two-man teams. We don't even split up to sleep." He assigned me to J.D. Bath, who I later learned was the only one of our team who had been involved in the original planning of the mission in '79, when General Aaron had asked Gritz to step down from his military position to secretly head up the recon and rescue operation.

The whole time Bo was going over information with us, I watched Ben play with some sort of wire he had around his neck under his collar. Once after Bo had finished talking, I asked Ben, "What's that?"

"It'll cut your head off in an instant!" He motioned for me to follow him outside to a rosebush. "Watch." He leaned back then quickly bowed forward. Swish! The rosebush branch was cut off in a split second. With a quick twist and a jerk, he removed the wire from around his neck. "This is called a garrote wire. We cut throats with these. It'll cut spinal cords, neckbones, just as easily as it cut that bush. I can't wait to use it again. ....It's been years..." I shuddered to think of the possibility, wondering how any human could become so cold-blooded.

Ben told a lot of war stories about cutting off ears and body counts. He was in a different world. A world of violence. In fact, all three

---

*Safehouses, where government personnel can safely hide to plan clandestine operations, look like typical upper- to middle-class homes and are scattered throughout the country, usually near major airports. Only certain select government personnel know the locations which change every couple of years.

of these men did a lot of reminiscing about killing, torturing and about working on special operations with the CIA. They talked about SOG (Special Operations Group) and their missions to kill Viet Cong leaders and suspects.

Once J.D. approached me and asked if I would like to go for a ride. I looked at Bo who nodded his approval. J.D. grabbed a set of keys from the rack on the wall near the stairs leading to the second floor and motioned for me to go with him. I followed him to the cars parked outside. (Vehicles are always made available for those who were staying at a safehouse.) As he backed the car out of the driveway and drove down the street away from the safehouse, J.D. was silent. I decided I would let him speak first. Finally he asked, "Now tell me, what's going on between you and Bo?"

"I don't know what you're talking about."

"I worked for Bo in Panama and Nam. Gave up a good career to go on this mission. Now why were you chosen? And what's with you and Vang Pao?"

"I introduced Bo to Vang Pao," I told him.

"You did, huh?" He bristled as he told me Bo had impressed upon him and the others that he was the major contact with this Laotian leader. "I'd like to see the General and confirm that myself."

"I think he's in Orange County right now." A few more moments of silence followed. Then J.D. wheeled the car to the side of the road and nodded toward a nearby phone booth.

"Call him," he ordered. I called the General from the phone booth, and he said it would be all right for us to come to his office; so we drove all the way from Los Angeles to Garden Grove, a 30 mile drive on the freeway.

On the way J.D. discussed his experiences with Bo in Central America. He had been working under his command when Bo had been asked to step down to work with these missions. (Document 35) He had a feeling that Bo hadn't known Vang Pao previously, because while they were together in Central America Bo had never mentioned the General's name. He shared the story about how and why he got involved with this mission. He also asked a lot of questions

about my background. Surprised that I'd had so much training in narcotics, his confidence in me began to build.

When we reached Garden Grove, I directed him to Vang Pao's office, a building in a shopping plaza. He read the sign on the front,
The Lao Community Development Center, then slowly circled the parking lot a couple of times, looking all around as he drove. Finally he
parked the car near a little photo developing booth, and we walked
toward the building.

When I knocked on the door, a little Laotian gal answered. Behind
her stood Colonel Vang Gee and another general who hurried back
to the General's office to tell him I had arrived.

Following introductions, Bath bluntly asked, "General, who do you
know that is involved with this mission?"

"Scott. Why?"

"Bo lied!" J.D. was very upset. He too assured the General that
this operation was not government, thanked him for meeting with us,
and we left. He said little on the way back to the safehouse and continued to remain silent after we arrived.

The other three were anxious to blow their wads of money on drinking and partying, but Bo was very strict. No booze. No women. We
stay together.

After two and a half days of planning, late one evening Bo announced, "We're moving to Vic's house." (None of us knew who Vic
was.) "We'll travel in separate cars."

As we left the little blue house next door to Bo's home, Claudia
joined us. I noticed I was the only guy who did not always carry a
handgun. After we'd begun our move, I asked J.D. the reason for being so heavily armed in our home country. "We want to make sure
we're not compromised," he answered.

"But what if we get stopped and a cop sees those guns?"

"We'll have no problem like that. We have credentials."

Early evening, just before dark, we arrived at Vic's house on Billow
Vista Drive in the ritzy part of Playa del Rey, overlooking Santa Monica
Bay. A blue four-door Mercedes was parked in the driveway and a
Porsche on the street. As I was getting out of the car, Bo came to

me and advised me, "All you need to know is that the name of the man who lives here is Vic. Ask no questions. We're just using his house."

I was intimidated by all the beautiful women of various nationalities who stayed at Vic's for short periods of time, but I do not know whether these high-class visitors were international prostitutes or perhaps agents being moved in and out of the country on assignments.

Vic's was a huge house with sleeping rooms everywhere, even in the basement. The rooms were blah - no pictures, only a couple of beds in each and a closet with all kinds of clothes hanging in it. Some were women's uniforms for various airlines, some were business clothes and some were casual. Of course, I was ordered to stay with J.D. Bath.

We always did our planning around a large table next to a bar. A couple of phones and a communication printer machine were available. Every now and then the printer would automatically print a coded message. A huge plate glass window provided a 180 degree view from the inside, but was coated so that no one could look in from the outside.

Each time we sat around the spacious table planning in typical military fashion the logistics of the operation, Bo would plug in a device with a blue/green computer screen in order to send and receive coded messages. Our covert cargo would be sent via American Transair. The name of Admiral Paulson, DIA, came up a lot in the discussions, also Daniel Arnold who seemed to be a major shot-caller. And a few times a Jerry Daniels was mentioned.

Mac interrupted one of these meetings to complain, "I still want to know why this man is going with us." He nodded toward me.

This time J.D. answered on my behalf. "Let me explain something. Scott is Vang Pao's buddy, not Bo's."

This announcement upset Bo, but finally after an exchange of heated words with the other three, he admitted, "That's why he's going. You must accept him. That's the way it is."

On the second or third day we were at Vic's, during one of our meetings, the phone rang and a man who worked for Vic came into the meeting room to tell Bo the call was for him. Quickly he connected his electronic coding device to the telephone. The coded message he received upset Bo even more. "What??? Damn! ...Why not?" He was devastated. Turning toward us, he announced unbelievingly, "I'm not going with you. Because of the crash I've got to stay stateside to organize another rescue team. ...*Why are they doing this to me?* I'll check this out later."

The following morning Bo returned to Hughes and made vocal contact, confirming that his coding device had been functioning properly. From that time on Bo remained quite subdued. I think he felt he had been set up by someone in Washington, but probably his ego was hurt more than anything else.

At one of our meetings a large sum of the money was divided equally. We were issued red passports* but instructed to use our standard blue passports unless we got into diplomatic problems. Black passports* are used only by diplomats to assure diplomatic immunity if necessary. We were also given business cards identifying each of us as Congressman Dornan's aides. This would also assure us of a cover if needed.

ROBERT K. DORNAN.
UNITED STATES CONGRESSMAN
27TH DISTRICT CALIFORNIA

SCOTT T. BARNES
STAFF ASSISTANT

6151 WEST CENTURY BLVD.
SUITE 1018
LOS ANGELES, CA 90045
(213) 642 5111

---

*Red passports - issued to official people who are employed by the government.

---

*Black passports - issued only to diplomats. Other team members held our black passports which were never used.

"Your last cover will be as Hughes Aircraft Satellite Technicians," Bo informed us, explaining that this would help us gain access to the areas where we could seek information about refugee camps without causing suspicion. "Now, if you are discovered, all anyone can do is slap your fingers and send you back to America."

Finally, after three days or so at Vic's, General Vang Pao phoned to say he'd just received word from his people that the camp was still active and POWs were still there. He was to immediately write a letter of introduction to Col. Soubom for his friend Scott and another companion. Bo told him there was a Special Forces man near him in Montana who would come to his ranch to pick up the letter and Federal Express it to us.

I shared my suspicion with Bo. "How coincidental there's a Green Beret right down the road from Vang Pao's ranch." Bo only smiled.

He then contacted a Lance Trimmer and told him about the letter, then asked me to give Lance instructions to get to the General's Missoula, Montana ranch. Bo concluded the phone conversation by informing Trimmer that the letter had to be marked with the Hmong seal or the mission would be scrapped. Then we phoned Vang Pao to inform him of the arrangements.*

After only nine hours of waiting, the letter arrived. Immediately Bo checked the seal. "The people you will give the letter to will expect to see that seal unbroken, but I'm going to know what this letter says before you deliver it."

I disagreed. "We've lied to Vang Pao enough, telling him we're not U.S. backed. Don't mess us up anymore."

"Don't worry. We have ways of getting into envelopes." Once a gain he used the coding device to inform a contact that the letter had been received. That evening he left for the TRW M-4 building in Redondo Beach, taking the letter with him, and didn't return until the wee hours of the morning.

Somehow he was able to have the letter deciphered without opening it. According to Bo, it was a very good letter of recommendation.

---

*Trimmer was later arrested in Thailand and convicted for smuggling in high-tech radio equipment for the POW mission *Operation Lazarus*. He was returned to the United States.

My name was in it. He gave the letter to Ben for safekeeping. "Take care of this, Ben, until you meet the agent. Then Scott should personally deliver the letter."

Again I protested to Bo about having to be so deeply involved. A small argument followed. "How many times do I have to tell you? You must help us." He laid out another stack of money.

"Okay. But I'm only going as far as Bangkok," I retorted, remembering the vow I had made with myself previously. I'd backed down again. Greed is a terrible affliction. It distorts one's values.

The next morning Bo came in with a couple of guys I didn't know and haven't seen since. "We're ready to leave," he announced. "We each will be driven in a separate car to the Amfac Hotel adjacent to the airport where we'll spend the night. Sleeping arrangements will be different for this one night. Scott, you will spend the night with Mac." We traveled to the LAX airport in Vic's Mercedes, a Volvo and, if I remember correctly, an Audi and a BMW.

Mac was very unhappy about the new sleeping arrangements. "I'll pay to get my own room," he had told Bo.

But Bo's words were sharp and final. "No! Orders are that you two spend the final night planning together." I would guess the Agency wanted to give J.D. and Ben information about the mission that Mac and I were not to know.

My time with Mac was less than pleasant. All evening he stood at the window of our hotel room looking down on the highway. "I feel this would be a good place...It's a good day to die..." The wild comments he made!

"Hey! I've heard stuff like this in the movies," I told him, disgusted with his immature and foolish talk. "Knock it off!" He turned and began to curse at me.

"Why are you even on this mission?" He glared with hatred. I'd never met a more hostile man.

Later in the evening I was shocked when, instead of using the bathroom, Mac defecated in the ice bucket and then wedged the bucket under his bed.*

At the airport, on the morning of October 21, 1981, Bo gave each of us a large envelope containing instructions, the paraphernalia we would need for the mission, and lots of cash. He also gave J.D. Bath, who would be our finance man, a generous amount of extra cash.

"Here's your tickets. Pan Am, Flight One, L.A. to Hong Kong to Bangkok. Once there, you are to split up in pairs again. Mac and Ben, you go the Nana Hotel. Scott and J.D. to the Rah-ja. Then await instructions. There will be six others on your flight who will be security personnel." His eyes began to water. "I should be going..." He kissed Ben and Mac on their left cheeks, then Bath and me on our right, and quoted something that ended with "when it falls, all hell will fall." He gave each of us a code decipher and code sending book which gave instructions for us to send and receive coded messages: "Send:TWX710822001. Subject:BOHICA HQ ComCtr Wash D.C." and 'Ans. back:DOE FRSTAL-WSH. Subject:BOHICA."

"Let's bring our men home!" Bo proclaimed, emotion nearly preventing him from speaking audibly. He took one step back and saluted.

"Bo, we'll see you." J.D. tried to encourage him.

"I hope so," Bo replied, shaking our hands. In silence we entered the boarding area, showed our passports, boarded the waiting Pan Am 747 and were seated four across, right in the middle of the plane.

Each of us carried only one small bag of personal belongings.

Immediately after takeoff, J.D. broke the moody silence. "Let's start drinking."

Mac flared. "Bo said no booze, no women!" Flight time was spent mostly in sleep.

I had known J.D. and Ben were to meet with one of their contact people during our forty-minute layover in Hong Kong. Again I was stuck with Mac, so I spent my time silently recalling my previous

---

*The beds at the Amfac did not have regular metal frames, but frames nailed to the floor. Months later, when Mark Gladstone and Richard Meier of the Los Angeles *Times* went to the hotel to investigate my story, they found the partial remains of the defecation in the bucket still lodged under the bed and sent it to a lab to be analyzed. A psychiatrist explained this bizarre behavior is common for this type of person and proceeded to describe with amazing accuracy this man he'd never seen: eyes deep set and dark, filled with anger, no wife or children, involved in secret operations, dislikes everybody, doesn't drink. The *Times* learned that Mac lived alone, except for his nine cats, in a small apartment above a liquor store in Salisbury, Massachusetts.

stopovers there in '73 and earlier in '81. J.D. and Ben explained they were to meet with an agent to confirm that the special weapons had arrived. Arrived where, I don't know, although I was told there were AR-180's with laser sights and nightscopes. These I knew were very special sophisticated weapons and would be difficult to get in to any country. I remembered that a guy named Silas Hong had been in frequent contact with Bo. Silas was in charge of the ICA cargo office in Hong Kong. I had read some of the correspondence between this Silas and Bo. ICA (International Christian Aid), a very legitimate and well-recognized organization, would make an excellent cover for a contact agent.

J.D. and Ben returned from their meeting quite pleased. There had been some excitement, but they never would explain what it was about. All J.D. would tell me was the weapons were enroute without problem and contact had been made confirming the POW camp was still alive.

I never did find out which of the other passengers on the plane were accompanying us as security personnel to make sure we were not compromised.

11

Arranging For The Recon

October 21 - November 3, 1981*

We arrived in Bangkok in the middle of the night, knowing how dangerous it was to have the radio equipment, maps and the large amounts of undeclared cash we carried with us. We could certainly be jailed. Many countries will search baggage only as persons leave, but Thai customs search upon arrival and departure. Noticing they were carefully searching everyone's bags, we decided to split up as we went through customs. Thinking we might be in deep trouble, we had bribe money ready.

The customs officers looked at our passports, looked at us, then at a piece of paper on the customs table. It was obvious we were expected. Instead of going through customs, we were escorted through a different gate to two waiting cars which traveled from the airport in totally different directions.

J.D. and I arrived at the large Rah-ja Hotel to discover a room had been reserved and secured for us. Sensing an uncanny silence, an emptiness, J.D. walked down the corridor checking for bugging

---

*Publisher's note: During the time of this mission (October 21 - November 3, 1981) Scott traveled almost constantly with only brief periods of sleep, making it difficult for him to pinpoint exact times and days.

devices. It was apparent no one was using the rooms near ours. He checked the equipment we'd brought with us. Satisfied nothing had been damaged in flight, he said, "Let's get a few hours of shuteye before the sun comes up."

Early the next morning we were awakened when Mac called to say we were supposed to meet at the Nana for breakfast. As we walked the approximately three hundred yards to the Nana where Mac and Ben were staying, I recalled from my stay there in June '81 it was known as the place where spies and indigenous agents hang out. Why, I don't know. It's not a bad place, but certainly not swanky either.

Mac and Ben met us in the lobby. Without explanation, plans were changed and we all returned to the Rah-ja for breakfast.

After we had placed our orders, Mac said, "Okay, this is the deal. Colonel Mike Eiland is on his way to make contact with me. He's the CIA man for this mission. Scott, you and Ben sit over there. Read the local rag and drink your coffee. Play tourist. I'll keep him over here." *Why didn't he want Eiland to see us?* I wondered. We did as we were told.

Soon an unmarked U.S. Embassy car pulled up outside the large front window of the coffee shop. Two armed U.S. Marines got out and opened the door for a tall lanky man wearing glasses and in civilian clothes. They accompanied him to the door, where he apparently gave them orders. It seemed as though they were saying "Yes, Sir" and "No, Sir" in response.

As the guards returned to the Embassy car and waited, a lot of why's flashed through my mind. *Why did Eiland need armed escorts? The country wasn't stable, but neither was it at war. If counterintelligence people were around, a meeting at this location would be easily photographed for verification.* It was then I first suspected that our mission might be unauthorized. If it were a secret mission, Eiland couldn't alert the attention of other Embassy personnel by holding this meeting there. Many did not realize he was CIA. Not everybody on the CIA floor knew about the operation. Plus, the Embassy was constantly watched by the communists.

Colonel Eiland made recognition of Mac and J.D. by eye contact only, then walked toward the area where Ben and I were sitting. We tried to raise the newspapers we were "reading" casually. Pausing for only a brief moment, he returned to Mac who stood and greeted him with a hug. "Mac! How're you doing? It's been years!"

"Yeh. Since Nam."

"What brings you down here?" Meaningless shop talk ensued. Finally Eiland asked, "...So how is it?"

"Just like *Operation Cherry* in Saigon, '71," Mac replied.

"That bad, huh?" As Colonel Eiland was watching and moving the whole time they talked, Mac tried to pull him farther away from our table. In tones more quiet than before Eiland continued, "If Scott Barnes is with you, don't tell me. He's hot. Get him to the Northeast Quadron immediately. - And don't ask me any questions."

Mac responded calmly, "If I run across him - whoever he is I'll tell him." After a few more moments of hushed talk they looked around to see if they recognized anyone. Then the two old friends shook hands.

As he turned to leave, Eiland, becoming very serious, said, "By God, I hope it goes."

Mac waited until the car was out of sight before he came to sit with us. "He's *the* one. You heard what he said about Scott?" We nodded. "I don't know what he meant - could be good, could be bad. Scott, you and J. D. are leaving *right now*. As soon as we go to Gem World, you'll take your passports to the main international airport. They'll stamp them as if you were leaving the country on a specific date. Then you will hop a flight to northeast Thailand and set up there. Ben and I will stay here and get things moving."

The four of us walked around the corner from both hotels to a small shop with metal bars on the windows. A neon sign, "Gem World," indicated a jewelry shop was located upstairs. Mac pushed a button and a male voice from a speaker asked, "Who is it?"

"The Team," Mac answered.

"Okay." A buzzer released the lock on the door, but before we could open it, an attractive Oriental girl pushed it open. She greeted us in very good English and bowed and shook hands with each of us. Then, telling us to wait just a moment, she began to deftly run her hands over our clothing, obviously looking for guns or listening devices. "Come upstairs," she invited us after she had completed her search.

We walked up a rather steep flight of steps to another door with several locks. She opened this second door and ushered us in to a world completely different from the clamor of the street below. The carpet was like velvet. There were several circular glass tables with two or three chairs at each and a beverage container in the center. Beautiful gems were on display everywhere. There were no "customers."

The owner of the lavish shop looked me over carefully. "My name's Ken Vest. You must be - him." Obviously I was the youngest and clearly the outcast. He looked at Mac. The tension between Mac and me could not be disguised. I continued to call him Gramps trying to get him to smile, but he didn't like it one bit.

Vest walked to the window that overlooked the street below, watched in silence for a moment, then announced, "I've already talked to the boys at the Embassy. Everything's fine. I just wanted to meet each of you." Once again he looked at me. After he and the others discussed the type of weapons we had smuggled in (AR-180's with silencers, nightscopes and laser sightings; teflon ammunition - all assassination weapons). Vest commented, "For this operation, that type of weapon isn't what you'd want to use." He seemed suspicious.

J.D. argued, "But if a sniper has to take out tower guards from a distance..."

"Well, yes..." It seemed as though Ken was probing, and the guys I was with were playing dumb, except for Ben. He was too interested in the precious stones and the girl to care about what was going on. Vest and J.D. hit it off well. I wondered if they had known each other previously.

I learned bits and pieces from the discussion which followed, although most of it made little sense to me. I'm still not sure why we had to go to that shop. As a front Ken ran a legitimate business, but I suspect he was shipping gems all over the world for CIA people who laundered drug money on the side while he also played the role of contact man to smuggle weapons, medication, food and electronic equipment from Bangkok to the Golden Triangle.

After what to me seemed a fruitless 20 to 30 minute conversation, we returned to the Rah-ja where we went over the code with Mac once more. After making a few scrambled phone calls about the gun shipment and the helicopter rescue pilot, Mac concluded, "Everything's secure. You guys get out of here."

Taking the main set of binoculars, cameras and radio equipment, J.D. and I were driven to the airport by Embassy security officials. I was proceeding without choice into a phase of the mission in which I had vowed not to be involved. Entering the gate we had been told to enter, J.D. informed the man at the flight desk, "We need the next flight to Udorn. (During the war Udorn was the main U.S. air base for Air America secret military flights to and from Laos in the secret war between Laos and North Vietnam.)

"Let me see your papers." He motioned to another man who joined him to inspect our passports. Talking in their native tongue, they both shook their heads and smiled, looking carefully at every page of both passports, even holding them under a special light several times. I noticed that these two were in uniforms unlike those of the police or customs officers.

In clear English one officer asked me, "You've been in Thailand recently?"

"Yes." I wondered what difference that made.

He gave me a strange look, then said, "Awkay," and stamped both passports 'Immigration Division. Departed 24 October, 1981.' "As far as anybody knows you both left country today. Follow me." (Document 23)

He led us to a totally different section of the airport. "No baggage check in!" he warned. "Carry on aircraft everything you are taking with you."

We were flown by Thai Airways nonstop to Udorn. During the flight J.D. looked at the Bible on top of the baggage on my lap. "You believe in that, huh? I *was* a Christian."

Our plane taxied to a section where a number of military cargo planes and three or four F-4 Phantom fighter jets were parked. From a distance we could see an approaching military jeep with an M-60 machine gun mounted on a tripod on the middle. It drove up just as we exited from the plane. "You come with us," the man standing behind the machine gun ordered.

"Oh, god, we're in trouble!" I told J.D.

"No we're not. This is our escort." After loading our cargo, I started around to the passenger side of the jeep but quickly learned that we were walking, not riding, to the next phase of our travel. It would look like we were under armed escort, J.D. explained. Had we been riding, we would have been sitting ducks. By walking, we could quickly dive under or to the side of the vehicle in case of an attack.

With people going busily in all directions, we walked behind the jeep away from the mainstream, the jeep driving in front of us no faster than five miles per hour for fifty to eighty yards or so, the man at the gun and the driver constantly looking around. Our escort vehicle stopped near a second vehicle that was evidently awaiting our arrival, because as soon as we approached, a man in civilian clothes got out and opened the trunk. He helped us load our personal bags and cartons. The trunk was so full that one box had to be placed on the front seat beside the driver.

After helping us into the back seat and settling himself behind the steering wheel, he looked back at us and smiled, exposing a large gold front tooth. He spoke no English. Next he pulled out a gun he'd had concealed in his clothing and placed it on the open door of the glove box. We must have traveled forty-five or fifty minutes through what seemed to be the middle of nowhere. The area was flat, with some dry open spaces, with others green and fertile.

Suddenly the outline of a tiny refugee settlement sprang up before us. Our driver stopped the car in front of a rickety building where a few people - I assumed they were Thai - were standing around. After J.D. and I removed our luggage, our gold-toothed chauffeur smiled again, waved goodbye, then drove away.

As we turned around to walk inside, we were greeted by a small young man carrying two cold beers. "This way, please. You arrive late." We gratefully accepted his gesture of hospitality and followed him.

Our luggage was transferred to a van which could have seated ten to twelve people, yet J.D. and I, plus all of our equipment, were the only passengers. The man who was to be our driver explained, "We must wait for it to get a little darker before we leave, so let's just drive around for a while." Since he was the driver and knew best, we consented. We must have ridden for 4 to 6 hours before we pulled into the town of Nakhon Phanom (NKP) in the late evening.

During the long ride up a mostly paved road except for the holes caused from mortar explosions, through barren flat country then jungle, J.D. and I came to know each other even better. He asked why I was not a part of the Delta Force, the super elite of the Green Berets who worked especially with CIA. I told him I had been more interested in going to college. (None of the others on the team had ever gone to college.) I asked what line of work he was in. He earned a comfortable income in Florida by "raising hay" - he winked - to sell to local "farmers." Hearing his offhand comments about "when his crops came up" I thought, *This guy's not a farmer! The crop he profits from is definitely not regular hay.**

For the first time, he opened up and told me a little about his personal life. His home was Lakeland, Florida; he was married and had children. He had been with Bo in Nam and on two previous tours for the CIA and had worked with Bo on the original planning of *Operation Velvet Hammer*, an aborted mission which was an attempt to say, "Look, the U.S. government is doing something about the POWs" in response to media pressure.

"I didn't know that," I told him.

"Yeh. Remember? I told you that when I was stationed in Panama, Bo was my commander. I was part of the Delta Team. We were working with the CIA at the time, setting up special operations in Central

*Hay frequently means marijuana.

America." While he looked out the window, he related a few war stories, then questioned me to see how much I knew about what was about to take place and asked further information about my background. "Except for knowing General Vang Pao and having an intelligence background, I still don't understand why you're here," he concluded. "What are you going to do with all your money?"

I shared my dreams with him. Another new car...more real estate... when I would someday have all the money I could do anything I wanted. Somewhere in the middle of my dream we both dozed off.

Our rest was interrupted by the driver of our van. "This Nakhon Phanom."

Even at night NKP was a hustling, bustling city. Although there weren't many lights for a city of this size, lots of poor people, some of whom appeared to be refugees, were on the streets. It reminded me of Saigon. We drove around for a few minutes, then pulled up to an area surrounded by a steel fence with big steel gates at both ends. I guessed it was 11:00 p.m. or later.

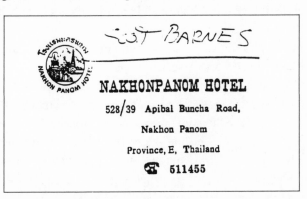

A young boy seated on a nearby chair sauntered over and unlocked the gates for us. I asked my traveling companion, "What kind of hotel has locked gates on both ends?" and was told that the fence was left from the war. This NKP hotel had been one of our intelligence strongholds for NSA. The boy closed and locked the gates behind us. Our van stopped in front of the main entrance.

"I'll help with your luggage," our driver offered.

J.D. sharply refused. "No! We'll take it." I helped him grab our bags and all the cartons and carry them into the hotel.

From behind the desk in the lobby, a young girl greeted us.

"Ah, hello, hello. Oh, Americans!"

"We want the whole top floor," J.D. said.

"Passport, please. Passport." She examined them casually. "Ah, Okay."

"How much?" From the amount of cash J.D. paid her, it must have cost us quite a bit. I hadn't expected to find such a nice hotel so close to the Laotian border.

From the time we left Bangkok we had seen no other Caucasians until now. A man with a gray beard, conspicuous because of his height and light skin color, was seated in the lobby. As we walked up the stairs, I asked J.D., "Is he CIA?"

"What makes you think so?"

"Look at his socks." Although he wore Thai clothing, his socks were black military issue. Those and his military-looking belt buckle gave him away.

"Hmm. That is unusual," my friend commented. I could tell my companion knew he was a security agent.

As J.D. thoroughly combed every room on the top floor, I followed. He removed sheets, looked under mattresses. He really knew how to secure an area. Finally convinced we were alone and without listening devices, he stopped beside the open door of one of the rooms. "This will be your room. If you have to jump out the window, there's a small ledge outside. You can quickly get to the street and boogie. We'll plan more later. Right now you need to write five or six letters to friends. We'll have them dated and mailed to them at different times, so if we need to, we can use them to prove we never left Thailand." (Document 36)

We wrote the letters, then went down to the lobby again. J.D. recognized two local fellows and talked to them in English for a moment. "These two will be our eyes and ears," he informed me. "Now we've got to set up communications." He walked to the hotel desk and asked the girl for our driver. She spoke in her native tongue to our two "lookouts" and within minutes we were in a human-powered rickshaw, zooming toward the requested area. Upon our arrival, J.D. looked around. "Wait a minute. ...Oh, there it is."

I followed him into a cream colored concrete building, with various antennas on the roof and armed personnel standing guard at the entrance and inside. "I want to send communications," J.D. told the girl at the main desk.

"Okay. - You KGB?" She laughed.

"You wish we were!" J.D. joked. KGB were known throughout the area as money throwers. They liked to impress the people by leaving lots of generous tips.

J.D. entered a little soundproof room and closed the door behind him. Through the window I watched him put on headphones and send a message. Then we waited. And waited. And waited.

Finally the girl at the desk announced, "Return message. Return message. Return message."

J.D. read the short communique. "Okay. Let's go," he told me, hurrying toward the exit door. "I've let them know where we are and that we arrived safely." Plans for shipping the medication and weapons as well as making necessary contacts were almost complete. It must have been at least 3:00 a.m. when we finally returned to the hotel for some welcome rest.

In the morning J.D. and I walked around town for a while. He wanted to go to the river to get a feel of the area and hoped to give the impression we were tourists. Walking felt good. I had been cooped up in vehicles and rooms far too long.

I don't know when or where it had been prearranged, but we had to return to a spot about fifty yards from the hotel gate at a specific time for an appointment with a Thai intelligence agent (See insert, photo.) whose name was Sunthorn Chirayos. His nickname was "Southern Chicago." I chuckled to myself when I noticed that he held his cigarette between his pinkie and his ringfinger. I hadn't seen that done since I watched German movies when I was a kid. In very good English, Southern Chicago identified himself and told us he was

working with a firm called SEA/THAI, LTD. owned by Richard Armitage. He asked to see our papers.

"You must be very careful. Move only at night. Round eyes haven't been seen here much since the war, and the only ones who were in the area then were American intelligence or KGB. We'll have our people protecting you, but be very very careful. Now, before you leave, let me buy you a beer." We soon learned Chicago, who worked with Daniel C. Arnold and Richard Armitage, was more feared than respected. Apparently people were aware he was commander for Thai intelligence for the region. As we walked, people - even merchants would look up, see who was coming and immediately get out of his way.

We accompanied him into a dark, sleezebag bar and grill near the Mekong River. Once J.D. and I were seated, our acquaintance looked around the room, spoke sharply to the people sitting around us, and suddenly the place was vacated.

After we were alone, he said softly, "I just returned from across the river. Now I will arrange for the two of you to cross."

J.D. perked up. "How many POWs are there?"

"I can't tell you." He was evasive. "You'll be going to a different area. This has been long overdue. We wanted you to come sooner, but we understand the monsoon season prohibited that. Now that you have a new leader in America, maybe we can accomplish something." He was very knowledgeable, having been sent to the United States in the mid-sixties to be trained. "I'll make sure everything goes smoothly," he assured us, "so you will not be captured or shot by our people or by the communists. Everywhere we've gone along the border there have been heavily armed Thai military looking across. They just sit with their hands on their heads, watching."

"What kind of life is that?" I was alarmed, wishing I hadn't agreed to deliver Vang Pao's letter.

"We get a lot of infiltration," he explained in a matter-of-fact way. "CTs too." (Communist Terrorists) He escorted us back to our hotel and arranged transportation for our 1 to 1½ hour trip from NKP to Ban Pheng.

While traveling along the Mekong River approximately an hour, we had to make several quick stops at military checkpoints along the way. Four to seven heavily armed military personnel with radios were posted at each barricade, checking papers and watching for unusual border activity. Suddenly our vehicle stopped.

"This is it," J.D. announced, hopping out and beginning to unload our gear once again. It was obvious we were the only Americans around. Laotian guerrillas in fatigue uniforms were waiting to help us. Other Laotians were "standing watch." It appeared they suspected we might have been followed by people who were unwanted in this tiny village.

"Hurry, we go." We were ushered aboard a small carriage that resembled a small American travel van and bounced approximately a thousand yards to a dirt road. Two armed Laotians stood guard at a cross bridge over a little creek. "Go," one urged when our vehicle paused.

We traveled only about fifty yards further, to a little Laotian settlement - all Vang Pao's people - on the banks of the Mekong River. We were guided to the rear of a 20 x 15 foot warehouse where a young Laotian began to search all our cargo. As he examined all the equipment we had with us his eyes grew large with pleasure.

To my surprise a lovely Laotian lady wearing a dress, nylons and makeup popped her head from behind a sheet-like curtain which covered one of the openings of the building. As I marveled at the contrast between the appearance of this fine lady and the desolate jungle region which surrounded us, the young man whispered, "That Soubanh's wife."

"Ah-h-h." That explained her dignified dress and gracious manner. She was the wife of the colonel we were supposed to see on orders of Vang Pao. We told our young friend we were also to make contact with Lieutenant Colonel Kham Ouane and Colonel Vang Yee.

"*She* talk to you," the young Hmong insisted.

"We've been waiting for you," she told us following introductions. While some of the uniformed men provided security on the outside, we carried the cartons inside 284 Amphen. The interior of the building was divided into two rooms. We showed her some of the equipment in the hopes of reopening a trust the Agency had destroyed. She was obviously pleased.

I handed her the sealed letter we had brought from Vang Pao. Stepping back, she said fervently, "No,no! No can touch!" She explained that her husband was in Laos confirming the location of a POW camp at the time, but she would introduce us to someone who could accept the letter.

Communications from homes or hotels in this area were unsecured, therefore unsafe for us to use except in utmost emergency. We had a base in NKP from which we could radio in code to the Embassy in order to give or gather intelligence and to order medical supplies, ammunition, more batteries, etc., which were then shipped to us as quickly as possible by special bus or plane, then transported by local agents to our location. Although officially our mission was classified as *"Operation Grand Eagle,"* we never used that name when sending messages back to the States. Instead we used the code name *Bohica*. "Subject: *Bohica,"* we would Telex to the Washington communications center at the Department of Energy. "Please order the following parts." Then we would send our message in "bursts."* As soon as the communications chief in D.C. would see the code name *"Bohica,"* he would know exactly to whom to channel the coded message.

Whenever we needed to contact the CIA in Hawaii, we had been given a classified CIA Telex number 248923 which was used only for secret missions in '80, '81 and '82. We were also given access to a Department of Defense Audovon number, 2244708 or 709, DC-2, where we could contact Pat Hurt or Mike Burns.

While we were there a couple of Vang Pao's guerrillas came to us and gave us an American dog tag (metal identification worn around the necks of military personnel) they claimed to have just found in Laos. Seeing no rust, no scratches on the tag, I was suspicious. It seemed to be in like-new condition. We decided to run a check on the tag by sending a courier to the Telex center in NKP. The communication we received from Washington upon our return from Nong Khai the next day reported that the name on the dog tag was not on the POW/MIA list. (A later L.A. Times article said they were told by the government that this man, who is said to be alive, lost the tag in '71 in a firefight along the border. However, the government would not tell where this person was at that particular time.)*

I don't buy the 1971 firefight story because the tag was in such good condition. If those Hmongs had found it just previous to giving it to J.D. and me, the owner had to have lost it very recently. I wonder if it could have been a "plant" they had been instructed to give us.

---

*We would give a few words in code, wait 10 to 15 seconds, then give a few more words to make it sound like we were ordering parts.

---

*Publisher's Note: The name on the dog tag has been verified. He is living and has received V.A. benefits. The dog tag is in possession of the publisher at this time.

J.D. returned by bus to NKP to make sure the rest of our equipment and the sophisticated weapons and cases of medical supplies for Vang Pao's people had arrived safely, to radio to the others on our team that everything was a green light, and to help bring the rest of our cargo up. No sooner had he left than Ben walked in.

"I thought you guys were in Bangkok," I said, surprised to see him.

"I just got here. Wanted to see the base and know the people - get the feel of the area and check out security, just in case you or J.D. get...taken out." I wondered where Mac was. As if he were reading my mind, Ben continued, "Mac is still setting up communications. Let's go to the river."

As we sat together on the river bank, looking into Laos, a distant low-flying biplane approached. A Laotian soldier ran out of a little hut.* "Spotter plane! Spotter plane! If they spot you, they'll know something's about to happen."

Just as we lay low on the bank we could hear gunfire diagonally across the river, then blue smoke appeared. I looked up at Ben in alarm. "Firefight?"

"Yeh," Ben concurred. "We'd better get out of here." We ran to the little hut.

"This happens a lot in this area," the Laotian scout told us. "Probably some communists spotted a group of indigenous trying to get back to the base. Let's get out of here." The fight continued seven or eight minutes. I had an eerie feeling as we returned to the headquarters.

Ben was quite familiar with this area and, I think, with some of the people. He knew enough bits and pieces of the language to under stand without a translator's help anything that was being said. A couple of times he left for brief periods, saying, "I'll be right back." I wondered if he was sending communications or following someone, but had learned long ago not to ask questions.

Ben was upset when he realized I'd brought my personal camera with me and had snapped pictures along the way. "No pics of the

---

*When the river goes down, the people pull their boats up the bank and put them in little bamboo/grass huts scattered along the river banks.

people," he ordered. "No pics of anything at Ban Pheng. Strictly recon." But I did talk him into taking one picture of me with my shirt off, posing with two of the guerrillas as they pointed across the river toward the direction they would soon be going.

When J.D. returned to Ban Pheng, Ben boarded the same bus and returned to NKP, taking with him the info from the dog tag in the hope that he could get a quicker response than the courier.

"You ready?" J.D. asked me. By that time it was nearly dusk and time for Colonel Soubanh's wife to take us on to Nong Khai, another Hmong stronghold. We caught the next bus going north. I noticed it was contructed from heavy metal and protected by heavy mesh screening surrounding the sides and covering the windows. The crowded bus, full of Laotian village people, mostly Vang Pao's Hmongs traveling to replenish supplies and exchange personnel, and the bumpy unpaved road made the short trip seem to last two to three hours. J.D. and I were advised to crouch low so we couldn't be seen at the check points. Just after dark, about the time I thought I couldn't remain in my cramped position any longer, the bus stopped.

"Wait here," the Colonel's wife told us. Cautiously she looked around the area, then leaning back inside the door of the bus, she motioned for us to exit.

As we stepped off the bus, four men quickly shoved local woven cone-shaped hats on our heads and escorted each of us to a rinkydink kind of carriage to be transported to our destination. J.D. was to ride in one, I in another, a couple of Laotians in another. After talking with and paying each of the four who pulled the carts, Colonel Soubom's wife got in the lead cart and we began the final phase of our journey, a wild goose chase kind of ride to make sure we weren't being followed. Several times we stopped while the Colonel's wife talked to guerrilla people, and once to talk to a woman taking a shower along the street. I learned later she was lining up contact people, telling them that we had arrived, asking them to inform her of any suspicious activity and lining up women to prepare food for the mission.

Finally we arrived at our destination, 1068 Wat Haisoke, Nong Khai, Thailand, right at the northern border of Laos. J.D. and I walked the

short distance to the river bank. "That's Vientiane," he said, pointing across the river. "The capital of Laos." I thought of all the
Americans who may have been missing in action or prisoners. *That's
why we're here,* I felt. For me it was an emotional moment.

To my surprise, J.D. tackled me from the rear and threw me to the
ground.

"Don't move! Don't make a sound!" he warned. I laid motionless,
afraid to breathe.

Br-r-r-r-r-r. We could hear a patrol boat slowly cruising up the river
long before we could see it. Through the brush I could see in the
grayness of sunset the outline of a large machine gun mounted on
the boat and a man behind it. It passed not thirty feet away from where
we were hiding.

"We just can't take chances," J.D. whispered after the boat was out
of sight and the sound of the motor had begun to fade. "Had he seen
us we'd be dead, and the mission too."

One of the guerrillas motioned for us to come back inside. A
gentleman wearing a blue dress shirt greeted us in broken English.
"So glad to meet you. We've been waiting for you. The Colonel is
still across the border. He will return shortly. The letter and papers,
please."

He looked carefully at the seal, stepped to the door of another room
and motioned for someone to come out. A monk in orange garb
responded, bowing toward J.D. and me in silent greeting.

"Meet Luang Pho Phoy Phachon, a former CIA operative. During
war he worked with D.C. Arnold and his associates." This was a
monastery! A cover for all the Laotian guerrilla operations across
the border. And this monk was the local boss.

The first man, Lieutenant Colonel Kham Ouane, held out 2 photos.
"This one you," he said to me.

"Let me see those!" They were the same photos Bo and I had given
General Vang Pao months ago.

Almost reverently he broke open the seal and checked the contents.
He was pleased. "You Mr. Barnes. You stay here tonight."

He then pulled aside a huge picture of Buddha that was hanging on the wall and revealed an indentation where a fully loaded Soviet AK-47 assault rifle hung. *What kind of religious character has machine guns hidden in the wall?* I wondered. *Is he going to wipe us out? Is he a double agent?* Next he pulled out a map.

I was astonished. "That's the exact same map we had in Dornan's office when I met with Bo and Vang Pao in August!" I told J.D.

"Oh, yes. Vang Pao, Vang Pao," the two gentlemen said almost simultaneously. It was obvious they loved the guy.

With the aid of translators, J.D. talked with them about different areas where POWs had been sighted in the past. Pointing to the map, they showed us the area from which the Colonel and his people were returning at that very moment, where the camp closest to the border was located, and numerous other camps many miles inland. The more they talked the more restless J.D. became. "Relax," I told him.

"This is hard to swallow," he answered. "So many POW camps still in operation."

We were served some lousy-tasting tea, then the Lieutenant Colonel took us not even a block away to a one-level concrete building where we could safely stay the night. A Laotian holding a rifle sat by the door. As usual, J.D. thoroughly checked the rooms and the small cubicle about the size of a large jail cell with no windows. Not wanting us to be separated, he insisted we sleep in the same room, one of us in the corner and one by the door. We were given little mats to lie on.

"Don't go out." "Just don't go out on the streets," we were warned again and again by the Hmongs. Not as aware of infiltration as the others on the team, not knowing what they knew, to me the whole sequence of events was spooky.

"Better get some shuteye before this Colonel comes back," J.D. decided. We kept our .45 caliber pistols next to us. In the middle of the night we were awakened by a tremendous roar. A very nervous translator burst into our room.

"Get out of here! They may drop a bomb!" The roar of a Soviet fighter had awakened us. Skirmishes were frequent in the border area but it was rare to have a MIG fly this close.

"It's almost time to leave anyway," J.D. consoled me about our loss of sleep. Moments later Kham Ouane came to our room to give us three letters (Document 37 - A,B), all supposedly the same, to be delivered to Daniel Arnold, General Vang Pao, and to a General Kham Vong whom I'd never heard of when we returned to the States. J.D. told me, "You keep them and deliver them. You're the one who knows Vang Pao."*

Again accompanied by the Colonel's wife we climbed on another bus filled with people and resumed our crouched positions. I wondered where the lady, so neat and unwrinkled, had spent the night. She chattered intimately with the other passengers. Although she was dressed far better than any other woman we had seen, there appeared to be no jealousy or rivalry. She was highly respected by her people and definitely in control.

When we had returned to Ban Pheng, she told J.D. and me, "We wait here for my husband."

"You stay here," J.D. instructed me. "I'm going down to NKP to see how the other two are doing. Radio us when the guerrillas are ready, then I'll be back with the team and the rest of the equipment and we'll get this mission moving."

Moments after he was out of sight, a relatively husky Caucasian man approached me. "Hi, you must be Scott Barnes." Evidently he had been waiting for J.D. to leave so he could talk to me alone.

---

*Supposedly the letters contained confirmation that we had arrived safely, the camps had been located, and that recently the General had come out of a re-educational camp. I have never found anyone who would give me the full translation, not even the Senate Veterans' Affairs Committee where I testified in January, 1986. Surely they could have sent it to a linguistic specialist or taken it to the CIA, but they didn't seem to want to. However, the publisher had the letters translated in June 1987.

12

Infiltration

"I'm Michael J. Baldwin, MJB they call me. Are you ready?" Somewhere between the ages of 39 and 43, this stranger had a dark complexion, dark receding hair and appeared to be in very good physical condition.

"Ready for what?" I asked.

"To do the recon mission." He took me inside the same building J.D. and I had left the equipment in. The women the Colonel's wife had talked to were busily packing food - lots of food - bananas, a fruit that looked like an onion with something rolled up inside it, and hot spicy rice balls, fish and some other kind of meat. The room was filled with guerrillas, guns and equipment. There was an atmosphere of expectancy, as though everyone was ready, waiting for something to begin. A feeling of doom overwhelmed me.

"Wait a minute!" I protested. "One Green Beret just left. He'll be back as soon as possible with the others. In three to six hours at least. If there's any delay, he'll radio. I'm not even supposed to be here!"

MJB smiled. "I was given two photos and instructed that whichever guy showed would be the one who was to go on recon with me." The photos were copies of the ones Bo and I had taken for Vang Pao.

"I'm supposed to cross the border? Without the others? This isn't the way it was supposed to be! I'm not Delta. Intelligence only."

"Look, Barnes, this other guy's not here." He tore Bo's picture in half and threw it down. "So it's you and me. ...You, the indigenous and me. Now, everything's ready. It's getting dusk and that's the time to cross, so let's go."

"I'd better radio the other guys..."

"No. Let's go." His firmness convinced me there was no way out. Having had mostly intelligence experience and only limited combat-type training, I began to prepare for the trip I had tried to avoid and dreaded so intensely. I searched through my small overnight bag, the only luggage I had with me, for my toothbrush and my Right Guard, for my watch and my code book, my dog tags, passport - all my identification.

"No toothbrush, Barnes. No cologne. No shaving gear, soap or toilet paper," MJB instructed. "All that's history. For the first day or two, when you go to the bathroom, you will bury and camouflage it. They can smell whether its local or not. Here, eat this."

He handed me one of the rice balls with red peppers in it. I took a bite. "NASTY!"

"That will begin to clean out your system. Your breath, your excrement, your sweat-everything about you will soon smell like the locals."

"This mission is real stuff, isn't it?" I tried not to let the hot peppers prevent my breathing.

"Of course. You weren't briefed at all?"

"No. I didn't plan on going."

"Remember, they know odors; they know footprints. We're going to the Mahaxay Region. If you're like me, you don't believe there are Americans held there, but we need U.S. ground operation to confirm or deny the numerous reports of sightings. The Admiral wants this done ASAP. You and I are that ground team." Mike must have had a lot of trust in whomever was calling the shots to take me with him as the only other American. I still couldn't believe I was the one the government wanted to go. *Why isn't Bo, the big famous decorated Green Beret Colonel, here?* I puzzled. *Anybody could have stayed behind to set up the rescue team. He should be here!!!* That still bothers me to this day. *Could it be the people calling the shots had always intended for me to be the one to go into Laos? Maybe this was intentional!*

While we waited, I attempted some shop talk: Who is Michael J. Baldwin, really? What's he all about? What's really going on? But he was much less talkative than I. "I've been in Asia almost since Asia was Asia," was about the only comment he gave. Evidently the border was his base area and he had known Vang Pao for many years.

While we waited to cross the muddy Mekong, we ate what I hoped was chicken - there were a lot of dogs running around - and more hot spicy foods. "I've got to have a Coke!" I gasped, holding my throat.

Mike laughed. "What you've known as food is now in the past. Come with me." We went outside and around a cluster of bushes to the river bank where a fleet of heavily loaded sampans and approximately thirty of Vang Pao's soldiers in fatigues, heavily armed and ready for battle, awaited the signal to embark. The uneasiness I had been trying to conquer only increased.

I snapped some pictures of the boats. Remembering the criticism I'd previously received for being a shutterbug, I explained, "Just want to get used to this one before I use the high tech stuff." To my surprise my urge to take pictures didn't seem to bother him much.

"No pictures of me or the equipment, and none when we reach the other side, okay?" I agreed.

I recognized some of the Laotians as ones J.D. and I had met the previous day. One had accompanied the Colonel's wife on the bus ride north but hadn't returned with us. I asked MJB how this guy might have come back down here without my seeing him. Mike merely shrugged his shoulders but certainly was not surprised. Evidently there was a communications and transportation network I didn't know about.

"What kind of physical condition are you in?" he asked me.

"I'm in pretty good shape."

"Good." He looked toward the spot where the sun had just disappeared. "It's about time to go." It didn't take me long to figure out why a guy like MJB was in charge of a ground team mission. He was knowledgeable, competent, and well-liked by the Laotians. A local in charge of communications was next in the line of command. He and Mike talked very little.

My new partner pointed toward the middle of the river. "We can use the engines until we get to that point. Then the engines will be killed and, since the river flows slowly, we will drift until we hit the other bank." The landing point had already been calculated.

It was a wide river but, because the monsoon season was now over, low at the time. Now the few scattered clouds which had been lazily floating by could scarcely be detected in the increasing grayness of dusk. The jungle and mountain range on the opposite side appeared to be more threatening as the light decreased.

I asked Mike, "Are there POWs? Would our country really have left anyone behind?"

"None. But the indigenous* continue to return with reports, so we've got orders from Admirals Tuttle and Paulson to go ground recon." Mike signaled to a group of 12 to 15 fellows standing nearest the sampans and instantly they began to climb in, not more than two or three to each boat loaded with the heavy electronic gear, munitions, medication, travel supplies and food.

Bizarre old engines with long shafts, quiet as Volkswagen engines, joined the purr of the fishing boats that already filled the river and slowly pushed the first company of indigenous forces toward Laotian jungle on the opposite bank.

We waited to leave until Mike felt the first group had already landed and were securing the area. Then without rehearsal or drill of any kind, he and I climbed into the sampan that carried the high tech radio equipment and cameras. A Laotian, chattering softly in a language I couldn't understand pushed us away from the riverbank. A dozen or so of the other locals immediately jumped into loaded boats and flanked ours. The journey across the Mekong must have taken only ten minutes or so, but seemed to me like forever.

---

*Natives.

Five or six minutes after we landed, the final group of ten or more made their way up the river bank from the sampans. After all our gear was unloaded, the Sampans were returned to the Thai side of the Mekong, one man in each.

"Here I am," I whispered to Mike as we lay quietly on the riverbank, "one of two Americans in communist territory, and at my back the muddy Mekong River, too wide to swim across. I'm scared - really scared! I could be killed!"

"You'll get over it," he replied. I wondered, *How could he stay so calm? And what had happened to the cocky Scott Barnes, so anxious to become involved in adventure and intrigue that he ignored the concern and advice of his dearest friends?*

We had been given rucksacks in which to carry food and supplies on our backs. "We've got to wear boogie bags too," Mike said softly. We tied the lightweight waterproof bags around our waists, then strapped them around one leg. "These carry the things you'll need the most. Double check them." Inside was a gun, extra ammunition, a small container of drinking water, purification tablets, dehydrated high-protein food, a small map, a compass and a few medical supplies. "If all hell breaks loose, you drop everything else, and you BOOGIE! Don't look around and don't wait for me - just GO!"

He took out a map, checking the compass as he talked to our communications man. A runner returned from the group which had gone ahead. "Pathet Lao, Pathet Lao, Pathet Lao!"

Mike turned to me. "Little people were here two days ago. We've got to avoid villages."

As we packed all our gear and equipment for travel, Mike explained that before that first group had embarked for Laos a security team had already crossed to secure and set up a perimeter. Scouts were already a half mile ahead of us, traveling in a reversed "V" formation to provide security and recon. We had a glimpse of the security elements only once. When we stopped to rest in a small clearing the following morning, we could see them in a distant clearing through the trees. The next time I saw them was at the objective area.

The local Hmongs were amazingly swift in spite of the fact each one carried 50 to 60 pounds on his back without batting an eye. As they had loaded the AR-180s equipped with silencers, night scopes, laser sightings, and teflon ammunition I became even more concerned, recalling that Ken Vest at Gem World had stressed that these were assassination weapons. Most of Vang Pao's people carried American M-1 carbines, M-16 rifles, M-79 grenade launchers, some M-203s (over/under M-16 and grenade launcher), several LAWs (light anti-tank weapons) and claymore mines. They were ready for battle. *Was this really going to become a rescue mission?* I worried and wondered if Moberg knew where I was and what I was doing.

MJB insisted that he and I keep the high tech Litton/Hughes equipment with us - the cameras and the radio equipment which we never dared risk using while we infiltrated for fear we would be monitored by Soviets. He carried a .45 caliber pistol and as much of the equipment as he could. I carried a Wingmaster 870 shotgun, cameras, a battery pack and one of the radios.

My biggest fear was snakes: vipers and cobras. MJB laughed softly. "We've got worse than snakes to worry about, man. We're worried about the communists - patrols and booby traps. That's why the indigenous are with us." It hadn't yet fully dawned on me that we were in danger of a communist attack. Constantly I felt this was all a bad dream.

Once packed and organized, we began our trek inland. Our group included a couple of translators and a radio man. We were flanked by Laotians carrying the remaining equipment - the heavy armaments, food and medical supplies and more guns. The third group always kept a thousand yards or so behind us. We traveled in no set pattern, zigging and zagging through trees and heavy brush and across small creeks, even backtracking a half mile or so a couple of times.

A few scouts frequently ran to keep ahead of the foremost V of Hmongs, exchanging places with some of the fellows in the V every few hours. Regularly this small party would send back a man - a different fellow nearly every time - to whisper in his native tongue to our key interpreter, who was never more than twenty feet away from

Mike and me, what we needed to know in order to avoid communist patrols, Pathet Lao areas and villages.

"Why does he talk so quietly?" I asked Mike after one of these fellows returned to the front. "Who's going to hear? It's the middle of the night."

"Hey, the communists may be out there listening," he reminded me.

"Yeh, and we can't even see them. No street lights," I quipped.

It seemed only a few hours until we stepped upon a hard surface highway, which Mike said was the number one highway going north and south through Laos. Other than the brief walk across that road our trip was through thicket, jungle and one mucky swamp, past some of the tallest trees I had ever seen in that area, trees unlike any just across the Mekong in Thailand.

Traveling mostly at night, we saw little wildlife. A few weird-looking birds were disturbed by our intrusion. In one area a lot of water buffalo ran as we walked by. Our biggest concern was not wildlife but keeping the village people from knowing there were roundeyes in the area.

We traveled eight or nine hours at a time, sometimes more. While we rested, mostly during daylight hours, I tried to learn more about my only roundeyed companion, asking about hometown, likes and dislikes, hobbies and such. But Mike was extremely reluctant to reveal much about himself except that he too was not Green Beret nor did he ever want to be, and hinted that he believed that violations of the biological warfare agreements were occurring, creating a lot of discord between him and some of the higher-ups. He was very fussy about the care of the equipment, always checking to see that everything was securely packed and nothing was missing. He did admit he enjoyed outdoor life, fishing in northern Idaho, wasn't married, and was totally dedicated to Vang Pao and his people and to the CIA.

I finally became used to the burning aftermath from eating the rice balls, enjoyed the fruit, but found the dried fish the women had packed was tasteless.

Only once did we come close to a little village. Mike and I remained carefully out of sight while some of the indigenous traded medication for information about sightings of communists in the area. Substantial amounts of malaria pills, atropine, potassium and penicillin were given out by Vang Pao's people along the way. Penicillin was most in demand.

Pausing in a valley, I looked up at the top of a high mountain range. "We've got to go over those?"

"Yeh." Mike pointed to one peak. "That's the 'nipple.' It got its name because it's shaped like a woman's breast. That's the safest way for us to go."

The nipple, at the lowest end of the mountain range, was minus cliffs, so we needed no ropes. Our guides knew exactly where to climb and how. This terrain was their "backyard."

By the time we had climbed a third of the way to the top I was huffing and puffing - not in as good physical condition as I had thought. "I don't think I can go it any more."

"Don't worry," Mike encouraged me. "We'll keep you going." Even after his old-fashioned pep talk I had a difficult time, but the Hmongs had no problems whatsoever.

At times we progressed faster and with more ease by following little village trails as far as we dared. At other times, the indigenous had to cut paths through dense undergrowth for us. The farther inland, the thicker the vegetation. A couple of times they did spot patrols and we'd have to lie low for a period of time.

I was so fatigued I had lost track of time. After what had seemed like two or three days after the night we'd climbed out of our sampans and on to Laotian soil one of the runners returned and announced, "We're there."

I wanna go home! I panicked. My adrenalin began to flow. After Mike talked to the scout about perimeter, security and booby traps, he sat down next to me. Leaning over he warned me in hushed tones, "Be careful. NVA/Pathet Lao patrols may be very close by."

He began to partially unwrap the equipment he had so carefully guarded throughout our trip - waterproof cameras packed in sheets of plastic-coated air bubbles - then motioned for one of the Hmong leaders to come to him. They exchanged a few brief words in Laotian and the fellow motioned to other Vang Pao forces standing nearby to follow him up the knoll in front of us to secure the area.

Mike pulled out his copy of Vang Pao's map. "This is where we are. The Mahaxay region. We've got to get pictures of the camp, but we've also got to spot for an LZ* where a helicopter can land in case there really are POWs."

I was finding it more difficult to breathe smoothly. The warm, humid air seemed heavier as minutes ticked on. All too soon Mike gave the word to proceed. "Let's go up and see what lies ahead."

*Landing Zone.

Taken from Scott's hotel window, NKP. Note the steel fence surrounding the complex.

J. D. and a courier taken just outside the NKP hotel area.

J. D. and Scott in NKP.

Scott and two of Vang Pao's guerrillas/bodyguards in Ban Pheng, eating dog meat for lunch. (He found out later.)

Along Mekong River. Laos in the background.

Scott with free Laotians along Mekong River.

Scott with two of Vang Pao's guerrillas in Ban Pheng. Both accompanied Scott and Jerry Daniels into Laos. Note "Bo" on the shirt of the man on the right. Evidently he was expecting an opportunity to welcome Bo Gritz.

Col. Soubanh's wife.

"Undercover" monk at monastery in Nong Khai.

Monk and Lt. Col. Kham Ouane inside monastery at Nong Khai. The man who gave Scott the 3 letters to be delivered stateside.

Women preparing the food for the mission, laughing at the white-skinned roundeye.

Ban Pheng. Women preparing food on left. Street number nailed on post.

Laotian hamlet.

Members of the scout team starting across the Mekong.

13

They're There!

"Gather up your equipment," Mike whispered. "We'll go up to the top." Without a watch it was hard to guess the time. It must have been late afternoon. Again perimeter security had been set up by Vang Pao's people. Scouts were out, so we could observe the camp in safety.

In less time than I had wished, we sighted one of the indigenous Mike had sent ahead. He signaled for Mike and me to come where he and the others were kneeling. Although we were well hidden by shrubs and underbrush, we could clearly see into the valley below where the thick jungle abruptly gave way to a circular clearing at least 150 yards in diameter. Even with the naked eye we could distinguish a few small buildings in the middle of the clearing approximately 600 feet away.

Mike cautioned, "We shouldn't get any closer," and began to assemble the cameras and listening devices. One had the longest lens I had ever seen. He fastened it on the swiveled top of a tripod. Next he set up electronic equipment which looked like a satellite dish that could be hand-held or mounted on a stand. From this parabolic mirror he ran wires to a battery pack connected to a recorder. "With this we can listen to what's going on down there." He tested the battery.

Another piece of our equipment looked like a one-eyed binocular or a small telescope.

The scouts who had traveled before us stationed themselves just below the crest of the knoll and those who had protected our rear were horseshoed in the back. These recon people were constantly coming and going to let the interpreter know we had not been discovered. It was obvious they were ready - and anxious - to attack on a moment's notice. But our orders were to recon only - without being detected.

Mike wasted no time in gathering information. He would look through the binocular device, then write down figures, estimating approximately how many meters from here to there...and how tall is this tree...etc. He was concerned that the area below was so wet and muddy. It would be next to impossible to safely land a helicopter, especially since there was no way of telling if there were booby traps or mines.

From our angle the camp appeared triangular in shape, surrounded by a tall fence of wood, probably bamboo, and wire with a watchtower at each of three points. We could see sandbags hanging on one of the towers and the hat of a guard moving in another. Under a big water storage tank was a large tin funnel. In another area there was a hole in the ground with wood slats covering it. One of the buildings was much larger than the others and was surrounded with what appeared to be fifty-five gallon drums.

Outside the wired-in compound were two fields, one to our left and the other facing us, where peasants worked in gardens while armed guards stood watch over them. At the farthest point the thick jungle suddenly formed a tunnel over a little dirt road that vanished into the darkness of the overgrowth. It was apparent this camp had been in existence for some time.

After we had been there several minutes, Mike dropped the camera he was using. *"My God! Look!"* I picked up the one-eyed binocular. Two men, clearly Caucasians, wearing "black pajamas," heads down, were being escorted from an outlying area on our left toward the buildings to our right. Following closely behind them were two armed guards carrying Soviet assault rifles.

"There *are* some there! And they're Caucasian!" Mike hissed in disbelief. He frantically began to tune the electronic parabolic mirror, listening to and recording everything he could pick up, in hope of verifying that they were speaking English. Then he started snapping pictures with a rapid exposure camera that didn't have to be rewound and made hardly any noise at all. Pausing only for a brief second, he nodded toward the other cameras. "Snap as fast as your finger will snap."

I moved to the long-lensed camera and began to focus the rings inside. This camera was so rapid-fire that it seemed I took whole rolls of film in thirty seconds. I adjusted the focus so that I could take mostly close shots of the two men from the navel up, but I don't think I ever got a full shot of either face, only side views.

The closest we came to getting a full view of either man was as one turned toward the other, seeming to say something. At that moment, one of the guards hit him in the arm with the butt of his rifle as if to tell him to shut up and get moving. As the guard struck him, the Caucasian momentarily turned in our direction to look back at the guard.

"Scott, now use the other camera," Mike would instruct at short intervals. "...Okay. Move to the ASA-400." "...Now put in the high-speed infrared film." He continued to listen through the device in his ear while we both snapped one picture after another. We changed focus; we changed depth, throwing one roll of exposed film after another into special moistureproof bags. We must have taken four hundred exposures.

I couldn't believe that the film we were using could take pictures in such dim lighting without a flash. (The sun was fading behind the tall jungle trees.) "You'll see," Mike said. He knew exactly what to do to get the results he wanted.

Through the lenses of those sensitive cameras we could see that the eyes of the prisoners were sunken, cheek bones prominent. They were thin and filthy and appeared to be in poor health.

Once Mike put his hand over the listening device on his ear. "They're American!" He handed the earpiece to me. They were speaking

English, but I couldn't tune the device well enough to distinguish what they were saying. We recorded and photographed until our view of the two men and their guards was obstructed as they walked behind a building.

Mike began to cry. *"They're here! We really did leave them behind!"* In anger he hit the ground with his fist. *"I DON'T BELIEVE IT! I DIDN'T EXPECT THIS!"*

I wept with him.

The interpreter gently placed his hand on Mike's shoulder. "Why not hit now? We've got enough armed men."

"We're not here to rescue," Mike insisted. "We're here to confirm."

"But we keep telling your government and they haven't done anything. We've got enough people here now to take them out."

Mike turned to me. "Let's say we're successful. Infiltration was the easy part, but exfiltration…that's hard. In their weakened condition how are we going to get them out? What if there are more than we can carry? We see only two, but there could be more. What happens if we lose and get killed?"

One of the guerrillas thought he heard something nearby, so we were silent for a few minutes. Not seeing or hearing anything unusual, Mike continued, "Those men are in no condition to walk out; they'd have to be carried. By the time we are a mile away the communists will have the border closed, gun ships, helicopters, planes and everything. No, we need our chopper ships to do the rescue."

Fervently he refocused and refigured and made notes, sometimes with a pen and sometimes with a grease pencil, on the map and another diagram he had sketched. "Let's see, helicopters could land there…snipers could take out the towers…ground guys could hit here… We've got to get back immediately."

14

Exfiltration

"Just in case, we're going to split the film." Mike handed me one of the watertight, fireproof bags that contained half the film. "Put this in your boogie bag." He kept raising one knee then the other as if he was ready to jog back to the river, he was so anxious to report our confirmation. Mike picked up the tapes encased in a heavy steel case. "We can't split this. Only the Activity can get into this. Take your film back to NKP and mail them to Daniel Arnold, 1705 Fox Run Court..."

"I already have the address," I told him, remembering the address of the Vienna, Virginia base Bo had given me for the CIA Station Chief. I had it recorded in my blue address book.

"This way we'll be double safe," Mike continued in a tone of certainty. "Yours will go out in the standard mail and I'll take mine directly to the Embassy." He checked everything. Gun, okay. Clip in place. Equipment packed, except for one radio which we left with the indigenous people for later groundburst communications, rather than risk a second patrol to see if the prisoners were still there or had been moved. With this Litton-made radio they would be able to communicate in brief split-second bursts and the rescue team would know whether the area was still hot.

Next Mike ordered the security men to sanitize the area.

"Sanitize?" I asked.

"They know what to do to get rid of all evidence of our being here. We've got sufficient proof, now let's get back so we can notify the rescue people to get this thing going." After only forty minutes or so of picture taking and high emotion, I turned to leave the same way we had come.

Mike took hold of my arm. "Doesn't work that way, Barnes." We had entered the area on an angle, but left in a straight shot. He knew what he was doing.

Fewer indigenous returned with us. Mike and our communications man rarely said much except instructions to each other. Once the communications man stopped and Mike asked, "What's going on?"

"A patrol. Wait a bit." Their eyes were constantly on the move, more security conscious than on the way in. Though anxious to get back, Mike was comfortable with caution, unwilling to sacrifice security for speed.

I guessed it must have been two-and-a-half days later, in late afternoon, when we came out of the jungle close to NKP, much farther south than where we had landed. Although I never saw anyone with us send any radio messages, one sampan was waiting. Evidently the local scout team which had traveled in advance of us had made contact somehow with their counterparts on the other side. Mike and I wasted no time boarding and starting for the Thai side of the river, pooped after 60 hours of nearly nonstop travel. Only after waving goodbye to the others did I realize we had been so occupied that I'd had no time to be scared - until now.

"I'm going to Udorn and fly down to Bangkok to get this film and the tapes to the Embassy," Mike repeated as we crossed the river. "You get back down to your guys and send the message to get those rescue boys here."

I turned for one final glance at Vang Pao's Hmong guerrillas who had been so loyal and protective. They were sitting on the river banks, guns hanging at their sides, looks of despair on their faces. Lonely young men. It seemed they were all saying, *All these years we've been telling you... Now that you've seen them, what are you going to do about the POW's you left behind?*

I got the feeling we should have hit the camp. I would have been more than willing to risk my life again to try to bring those two men out of that jungle.

Mike interrupted my thoughts, "We've got to get them out of there!"

15

My Troubles Begin

As we neared the Thai bank of the Mekong, Mike broke the tense silence with a grin. "I think we just spent Halloween 1981, in Laos." *Today I wonder if the "trick" hadn't been on us.*

Several people were on the Thai bank to meet us. Mike and I said goodbye, and he was on his way to the Udorn air base, a considerable distance to travel after all the constant on-the-move running and walking we had been doing the past few days. I wondered when or if I would see him again.

With only my boogie bag and the film, I climbed into a waiting vehicle. To my surprise I was handed the little bag containing the few personal belongings I had to leave behind. Half asleep, I rode for a couple of hours down to NKP in a not-too-fancy automobile. The face of the guy who had escorted us back to the river came to mind. He'd had "BO" printed on the front of his T-shirt. No doubt he had planned to welcome his old friend but instead had become my guide. "Finally we have confirmation from two U.S. roundeyes," he had told Mike and me. He seemed relieved. The Hmongs evidently had been reporting that particular camp and the transporting of POWs through the Mu Gia Pass from Laos to Vietnam and back to Nomsnarath, Mahaxay, and to Nape, a little south of Mahaxay for a long time.

Immediately upon my arrival in NKP I took the film MJB had placed in my care to the postal service building where it was packed in a shoebox-size container, wrapped and sent without any return address (as a double security measure in case MJB was captured) to the home of Daniel C. Arnold, CIA Station Chief in charge of overseeing *Operation Grand Eagle* for the Executive Branch. Then I went to the hotel where I hoped the other three men were still waiting. I looked down at my filthy clothes and my rash-covered skin. I was certainly in fine condition to be entering a hotel.

Deciding to contact J.D. first, I dragged up the stairs to his room and knocked on the door. When the door opened, all three of my teammates were standing there.

"Where the hell have you been? We went up to Ban Pheng and everybody there took the fifth amendment! They said they never heard of you. We knew something was fishy." Their welcome of yelling and cursing caused an explosive effect in my tired mind.

"They're there!" I tried to yell louder than they were. It shocked them into silence.

"What?"

"By God, they're there! We saw two of them. Americans."

"You're kidding!" J.D. was the only one calm enough to respond.

"No, I'm not. This guy MJB—Michael J. Baldwin..."

Mac interrupted. "You mean...Jerry Daniels?"

"Whoever. Anyway, he's on his way to the Embassy to see Eiland."

Mac shoved two pieces of paper toward me. "While you were gone we got some messages you need to know about. One from Langley, Virginia, came over our Washington DoE Telex; the other was from Eiland's people who got their orders from the Embassy. When decoded one says that Bo's been fired from the mission and Eiland has taken over, and the other says 'If merchandise confirmed, then liquidate.' "

Although I couldn't decipher the coded message he held in his hand, I had no reason to believe he was lying. "*Merchandise* is our code for POWs!" I exclaimed in disbelief.

"Orders!" Mac shouted back. "They've got to be killed!"

"No way!" No longer did I feel tired. "Is this a setup? What's going on? I'll have no part in this!"

I thought Mac was pretty angry before, but now he was furious. "You sonofabitch!" He hit me right in the face knocking me to the floor. "You weren't even supposed to go!" The other two men grabbed him and pulled him off me.

"Don't do this!" J.D. yelled at Mac. "Don't fight with him! This mission isn't complete yet!" When we had all calmed down a bit, J.D. advised us, "We'd all better get out of here. There's been a lot of firefights lately and rumor's getting around there are Caucasians in the area."

"J.D., take HIM to the Embassy," Mac ordered angrily, referring to me. "Escort him there and officially turn him over for debriefing. Whatever happens happens." I realized I hadn't experienced his hostility for several days.

Refusing to give up, I insisted, "You've got to get this message out. Get the rescue teams here!"

"Moberg's been transferred to Singapore and the helicopter's been grounded." It was as if Mac had thrown ice water in my face. I wondered if Mike had sent communications to the Embassy from Udorn: "They're there and I'm on my way down," and when the Embassy got the word, they stopped everything. I couldn't understand the intensity of Mac's anger.

My three teammates followed me to the room where we had stored all our personal and non-classified luggage. I changed into clean civilian clothes, my head swollen and throbbing, and checked to see if my money and my plane ticket were still in the bag I had left behind.

"Jim, take him to the Embassy," Mac insisted.

J.D. grabbed me by the arm and jerked me around, playing the tough guy. "Come on. Let's go." He grabbed my bags and we went downstairs.

The lady at the desk in the hotel lobby looked alarmed as we walked by. She must have sensed the tenseness and anger with which I was being escorted out.

Once outside the hotel we caught a bus to Ubon, leaving NKP by a road that goes along the border then cuts inland. It bothered me that we didn't go back to Udorn and take a plane. After about three hours of riding in uncomfortable silence, during which I tried to sleep only to awaken with a jerk time after time, I finally asked, "Okay. What's wrong? What's going on?"

"Relax. From now on you don't know me; I don't know you. You know *nothing*. Understand?" J.D. hadn't been so cold toward me since the day he had asked me why I had been selected to be part of the mission.

Dumbfounded, I nodded in agreement and for the first time in days opened my Bible. Turning to Matthew 24 I read the part about wars and rumors of wars. *Wow!*, I thought. *What am I into?* I recalled the night I had been baptized just before I'd left for Hawaii and realized I was searching for something more in my own life, but didn't know what.

Late that night we arrived in Ubon. I waited while J.D. tried unsuccessfully to get a plane. "All flights have been canceled because of sniper fire," he informed me as he returned to the bench where I was waiting; no place to run or hide now. "A lot of people are saying that communist Thais are coming in from south Laos, so people are leaving the area. They must know we're here. That could mean problems. We'll have to risk going by train."

Riding all night, we were the only two Caucasians in the slowest train in existence—double-packed with people fleeing from the area. It was comforting to feel the .45 automatic pistols each of us had tucked in the back of our pants. (J.D. felt it was okay to arm me on the way down. We needed to protect each other.)

"We're going to have to sleep with one eye open, if you know what I mean," Bath said. "You sit facing this direction and I'll face the opposite way. If anybody makes a wrong move, shoot 'em. We'll just dump them off the train. Barnes, I'll take you to the Embassy as I was told, but only to the sidewalk in front of the gates. Then you get out of here. I suggest you go to another country for a while and lay low. What may happen from here on, you'll never believe. Take your money and enjoy yourself and I'll tell the others only that I did drop you off at the Embassy." When we arrived in Bangkok at dawn J.D. disposed of our guns and we taxied to the Embassy. He ordered the driver to stop fifty feet from the gate. Both of us got out.

"Keep your mouth shut for the rest of your life. You were never here," he warned me. He said goodbye, returned to the vehicle and drove away.

At first I didn't know what to do, feeling very much like an orphan that had just been dropped off on a doorstep. There was no doubt in my mind that Eiland and the people inside would have killed me had I gone in. Deeply grateful to J.D. for having saved my life by not forcing me to enter the Embassy, I took from my bag the open return Pan Am ticket which had been paid for in cash several months earlier and hailed a cab.

"Airport - Pan Am office, please," I told the driver.

16

Sorry, Ticket No Good

"When's the next flight out?" I asked the girl at the flight desk.

"One o'clock this afternoon."

"I'll take it." I handed her my ticket and she ran a check on the computer.

Returning to her desk where I was trying to appear nonchalant, she apologized, "Sorry. This ticket no good. Canceled."

My resistance low, I lost my composure. "How can you cancel a return ticket that was paid for in cash in America? That's ridiculous!" I was also afraid of the implications.

Trying to remain polite, the girl called her supervisor to the desk. He ran a second computer check. "Sorry," he said. "Computer says this ticket canceled. Lost."

"This is crazy!" I retorted. "Something's haywire."

He spoke sharply, "Sir, all we know, this ticket number canceled." The full danger of my predicament struck. *They've pulled all the plugs! Why would they want to be so sure that I would never leave the country? What do I do now ...Obviously I can't go to American authorities.* Panic overwhelmed me. *I certainly can't go back to the hotel/embassy area either.* I decided to try JAL Airlines.

Attempting to maintain a front of confidence I asked the Japanese girl at the desk, "Do you do cross-ticketing?" and handed her my ticket.

"Yes, we cross-ticket." She checked my ticket number on her computer. "Ooooh...Sorry...This ticket no good."

I played dumb. "What do you mean? You can see it was paid for in cash months ago."

"Sorry. Ticket comes up as invalid."

"What does it cost to get a ticket?" I knew nothing else to do.

"Next plane all full."

Suspecting she was lying, I took out the cash I had left. It was all American money. "How much?" I repeated. "I *must* catch the next plane out of here. *How much?*"

She sensed that I was desperate. "Seven hundred dollars."

Without hesitation, I paid her and caught a taxi to the airport. The many military people and customs officers walking around didn't help my uneasiness. It took everything I had in me to act like a regular person, looking other Americans in the eye and casually greeting them with a "Hi, how are you?"

The guy at customs noticed that I'd "left" the country on October 24, according to my passport. *Oh, boy!* I thought. *This is where I get busted!* But to my relief, thinking this to be an error, he simply canceled it and stamped that I was leaving on November 3rd.

No sooner had I sat down on the plane than several customs officers boarded. *Oh, oh. What will I do with the three letters I'm supposed to deliver? Vang Pao just can't be disappointed again.* Quickly I tucked the letters in the crotch of my pants. The officers casually looked through some of the luggage on board, including mine, but never searched anyone.

I was awakened when the plane landed in Tokyo by hearing someone call my name. Since the authorities who had called me off the plane were speaking in Japanese, I could understand only my name and my seat number. Then in English they introduced themselves.

Osamu Iwahashi was the name of one. I asked him how to spell it so I could write it down in English in my blue address book for future reference.

"Passport, please," he asked holding out his hand. "...You Mr. Barnes?"

"Yes. But what have I done?"

"We have communication from your government to hold you. You will spend the night here at our expense." They took me into a room where they stripped me naked then searched my bag. Thank goodness I had transferred the three letters to the inside of the back leather cover on my Bible!

Satisfied that I was "safe," they took me to a fairly nice hotel where I took my first shower in days. Unable to sleep in spite of aching all over from fatigue and tension, I was still awake when my customs friends returned the following morning.

"Okay. You can leave now," I was informed to my relief.

They escorted me to the airport and I boarded the next flight to Los Angeles. How good it would be to get home!

17

Welcome Home

November 3, 1981
(One day was lost crossing the International Date Line.)

American customs really gave me the one-two when I landed at
LAX, Los Angeles. One officer at the customs gate was holding a
computer printout and carefully watched as people came through. In
compliance with their request, I gave them my passport. They huddled
together and looked it over page by page.

"Left Thailand just a few days after you arrived, huh?" I nodded.
"What's this: 'Canceled'? Is this Thai writing?"

Hoping he would buy the explanation, I said "Ah…it was a mistake."

"Now how could they have made a mistake like that?" he asked
and continued to turn pages as if he hadn't asked. "Mmm…Okay…
Come with us, please." He introduced himself as we walked toward
a closed door lettered "U.S. CUSTOMS."

"How come me?" I asked. "Must have been two hundred to two
hundred fifty people on that plane."

"We pick people's profiles at random," he snapped. …*Right!* I
thought, now suspicious of everyone.

Once inside customs, we entered a windowless room where I was
stripsearched. Thoroughly.

"You have anything illegal on you?" one of the officers asked.

"No, no. Just been on vacation."

That made him angry. "No you weren't. Where will you be staying?"

"With friends."

"Their address, please." After what seemed like a couple of hours of waiting and being questioned and waiting some more, finding no incriminating evidence or discrepancies in my answers and explanations, they gave me permission to leave. I phoned a friend who lived only nine miles away to come to the airport to pick me up.

From his home I mailed one of the letters I had somehow managed to keep out of customs' sight to Daniel Arnold, then called Randy at the church who came immediately to give me a ride home.

"Sure glad to see you," he said once we were on the highway.

"Glad to see you, too. Glad to be in America. I'm never leaving this country again." The comfort of being back in the States and on my way home again was indescribable.

"What went on over there?" he asked, interrupting my basking in a peace of mind such as I'd not experienced for many days.

"Nothing much. I'll talk about it later," I stalled. Guessing that something had gone wrong Randy was sensitive enough to wait until I was ready to talk.

It was November 4 when I finally got home. Immediately I phoned Daniel Arnold, giving my name and the code name *Bohica*.

"Give me your phone number," he responded cautiously. "I'll secure a line then call you back."

I barely had time to give my number before he hung up. Moments later my phone rang.

"Hey, how was the trip? How are you doing?" he asked, sounding as though we had been close buddies all our lives.

"I got a letter I was supposed to give you," I told him.

"Just drop it in the mail - send it right away."

"I already mailed it to 1705 Fox Run Court, the same address I sent the photos to."

Anxious to get on with reporting what MJB - or Jerry Daniels, if that's who he was - and I had seen, I began to chatter to him about the mission. "We didn't know we would be told to kill," I said. "And we were all puzzled about the sophisticated weapons provided us." Suddenly the conversation turned to ice.

Daniel C. Arnold President	
Tashkent Associates International Research Associates	1705 Fox Run Ct. Vienna, Va. 22180 (703) 938-1868

Scott —
Thank for the letter from D. I have forwarded to Chao Suouk and to Vang Pao. Best wishes
Dan

"You don't know me. You don't know anything. Just take your money and have a good time. Is that clear?" He slammed the phone down. Document 38 - A,B,C) Okay, I thought, *It was a secret mission. I'll not discuss what happened with anyone. I'll deliver the other two letters, then let the government take it from there.* He hadn't indicated that he'd received the film, but I doubted it could have arrived so soon. At that point in time, I was never suspected that the intention of the key people involved with *Bohica* would be to do nothing.

I called Vang Pao's office, making arrangements to deliver the other two letters. This would complete my assignment and I would be free from "Subject: *Bohica*" once and for all. Remembering that Theresa Glowacz, a girl I'd met at Hope Chapel, lived not far from Vang Pao's office in Orange County, I looked up her number in my little blue phone book and arranged for her to meet me at his office on November 6 so I could take her to lunch.

When I arrived at the Lao Community Center, Theresa was already there, sitting on the couch in the General's front office. Vang Pao and another General were standing beside her visiting. When Colonel Vang Yee heard my voice, he emerged from the inner office.

"Ah, how was trip? How are you?" he asked, bowing, then shaking my hand.

I pulled two wrinkled letters out of my pocket. "Here's your letters. I've already mailed a third to Daniel Arnold." The Colonel took his letter and quickly returned to the inner office. Scanning his, the General acted happy and excited, saying that Bo had been in touch with him a couple of times while I was gone.

I had revealed Arnold's involvement with Bohica! I hoped he hadn't noticed.

"Now you believe Americans there?" he asked. I nodded affirmatively.

After reading more of the letter, he asked, "You know we're going to have to kill these people?"

"Oh, God!" Theresa began to cry.

"What's the matter with her?" Her outburst had alarmed Vang Pao. Evidently he thought that somehow she had been involved as a cover for the mission. *Kill what people?* I wondered; but still suspicious of what this whole mission had been about, I didn't follow up on anything. He may have been referring to J.D. and Ben for all I knew. I tried to downplay what he had said for Theresa's sake. It was then it struck him that I had mentioned Arnold's name and he realized the mission had been connected with the Agency. I didn't like the strain this put on our relationship but had no opportunity to do anything about it before I was asked to leave.

Concerned about the General after I returned home, I decided it would be wise to inform the CIA Covert Defense Operation of his discovery. To the man who answered the phone I gave my name and the code "Subject: *Bohica*."

"Forget this thing ever happened," he ordered sharply. "Forget this phone number. Shut up and enjoy your money." He hung up.

* * * * *

I did a pretty good job of forgetting until early evening on Christmas Eve, 1981. At my parent's home in Torrance, just ready to go to the early services at Hope Chapel, I grabbed my Bible from the coffee table when a sudden movement outside the front window caught my eye. Several Torrance police cars and a couple of unmarked cars were parked in front and to the side of the house. Men in civilian clothes with badges on their suit pockets were walking up the front sidewalk and across the grass while uniformed officers with rifles and shotguns ran toward both sides of the house.

My brother, a Redondo policeman, was sleeping on the living room couch. *This must have something to do with him*, I thought, and opened the door.

"Hi!" I greeted the men who by then were at our door.

"Scott Barnes?" one queried.

"Yes." The man who had spoken jerked the screen door open and pulled me outside by my shirt.

"Don't move, Barnes. U.S. Secret Service and FBI."

"What's going on?" My head was spinning with surprise.

"Don't say a word." He searched me. "Where's your gun?"

"How do you know I even have a gun?" I was frightened.

"Don't play games with us," he ordered. "We know you carry a gun. Now where is it?"

"Hey, I'm on my way to church. I'm not going to take a gun to church! You want to get tough, go talk to my lawyer." They had begun to push me around so I began to talk back.

"What's that?" one asked, pointing to the book I was clinging to.

"My Bible." He jerked it away from me and searched through the pages.

"Come with us," the main spokesman said. "You're going downtown."

The gentlemen I rode with introduced themselves as Fred Capps, Jr., FBI Counter-Intelligence agent from Los Angeles, and David Gregg, Secret Service, Executive Branch.

"Is somebody going to tell me what this is all about?" I asked them.

"We'll talk to you later." Their silence lengthened the ride to the Torrance Police Department.

A room full of men dressed in business suits awaited us at the police station. Questions were fired at me from all directions.

"About Indochina? Tell us what you know about assassinations, about arms and drug dealings in Southeast Asia. What do you know about Bo Gritz?"

Remembering the phone warnings, I answered, "I never heard of that name. Why?"

The chief interrogator grabbed a sheet of paper off a desk. "Pan Am flight...Ben Dunakoskie...J.D. Bath...William Macris...Daniel Arnold...Vang Pao... Names sound familiar?"

"Oh, so that's Mac's last name," I interjected rudely.

"What really happened in Thailand? Who gave you such sophisticated weapons? Who provided them and why?" Obviously someone had been talking. "Bo Gritz has been picked up also, by authorities on the East Coast. We want to question both of you about your involvement in an assassination plot on the President of the United States." (Document 39 - A,B,C)

"You got to be joking!"

"No, we're not joking." Hours of interrogation followed. Finally the gentleman in charge concluded, "We're going to take you before the U.S. attorney and the Federal Grand Jury. ...Unless you want to give us the evidence and the information on this mission now. Then we'll give you immunity."

Immunity from what? I asked myself. I had done nothing illegal. I served my country honorably.

"I want to talk to my lawyer," I insisted. By this time I'd forgotten it was Christmas Eve. As luck would have it, I couldn't reach my lawyer, so I called at Hope Chapel. Since Ralph Moore was not officiating at the service in progress, the man who answered the phone called him out of the service to talk to me.

"Don't say anything," Ralph advised after I explained what had just happened. "Something fishy is going on."

One of the fellows who had taken everything I was carrying in my pockets re-entered the room. "Where did you get this congressional card?" I'd kept one of Dornan's cards as a souvenir and they'd found it in my wallet. "Sign this form." He shoved a blank form toward me.

"What is it for?" I asked.

"Sign it," he ordered, raising his voice. "Otherwise you're not going anywhere." I signed the form. A polaroid picture was taken of me. They kept Dornan's card.

"We'll be in touch," I was assured and then let go. I made it to church just in time for the late service.

When Capps later talked to Bo, Bo denied he ever knew me.

"That's funny" Capps told him. "Barnes described the inside of your home to perfection." (Document 43, page 40 of *Covert Action* article)

Congressman Dornan admitted to Kevin Cody from *Easy Reader* magazine that on December 27, 1981, he had met with President Reagan aboard Air Force-1 and had talked with him about the POWs and *Operation Grand Eagle*, but nothing specific had been decided. How could I go on pretending that *Bohica* had never taken place?

18

Bohica Goes Public

January, 1982

About a month after my detention on Christmas Eve, I was at church in the overflow room adjacent to the sanctuary watching TV with some friends. Daydreaming would be a more accurate description of what I was doing, because I hadn't noticed who was on the screen until Ralph said, "Scott, look who's on the news."

It was Bo Gritz, talking about having been terminated from a U.S. government mission to rescue prisoners of war. This was the first time I had seen Bo since we had said goodbye at the airport.

"Ooh, is he lying!" I told Ralph. (Within days news publications like the *Boston Globe*, the *Chicago Tribune*, and several California papers had picked up Bo's story about his efforts to organize a POW rescue team. None of these stories ever mentioned the order to liquidate we had received after the recon mission, nor did Bo ever make it clear that he had never actually gone on the mission. Rather these stories hinted that he had been with us on the mission.) (Document 40)

The day following Bo's TV interview my phone began to ring.

People from *Los Angeles Times*, Associated Press, UPI, ABC News, local newspapers and radio stations were asking for my version of what had happened. Finally I told Ralph, "I need advice. What shall I do?"

He had a friend in the church who knew Ted Koppel from *ABC Nightline.* "We'll make arrangements for him to come out and look into this."

Since the phone warnings to keep quiet and the Christmas Eve incident, I had been careful not to talk to anybody about *Bohica* until I heard Bo lying. I met with Ralph and his friend and learned they had already contacted Ted Koppel. He would be coming soon to interview me.

Since my return from the mission, I had been working with Randy and the Hope Chapel singles ministry once again. In late February we went to Catalina Island for a retreat, but I didn't get to stay long. The first day we were there, I received a phone message that Koppel was to arrive on the next plane, so I returned to the church as quickly as I could. I arrived around seven or eight o'clock that evening. Although a church service was in progress, I found Ralph, Ted Koppel and an associate, plus a couple of people from the church in Ralph's office.

Koppel removed his dark glasses and introduced himself. "I'm here to get more information about the mission." He'd already heard a little about it.

I felt uncomfortable about him, but decided to talk with him anyway, frequently referring to my little blue address book for names, addresses, dates, times and various bits of information. I was determined that the truth would be known about why the mission had been aborted, why the rescue did not take place. I felt it was my duty to inform the American people of the truth. Koppel was extremely interested in what I had to say.

"Bill Redecker, my confidant man, and his crew will be working with you for the next several days," he informed me. "I want to do a special on this. Our Pentagon sources have confirmed a highly secret unit did conduct an across-the-border expedition into Laos."

A cameraman who was looking at some of the photos I had taken while on mission did a double take when he saw the one of Prasit, our interpreter and guide while delivering the mysterious package into Cambodia. "Hey, I know this guy!" he exclaimed. "We used him as a courier to run news crews into south Laos and Cambodia during the war."

He was saddened when I told him that Prasit had been shot not more than a week or two after I had taken that picture. "He was a good man."

Ted entered, interrupting the conversation to tell us after conferring with ABC News president Roone Artledge, he had decided to do a three-part *Nightline* series on my story.

"Wow!" I was excited. This would be the break I needed to clear the lies and cause a Senate or Congressional investigation.

Ted continued, "Yeh, we're going to blow the socks off this country. But for our protection, would you submit to a polygraph test?"

"Sure," I said confidently. "On one condition. Get the best polygraphist in the country." I placed little confidence in polygraph tests.

He agreed. "My men will call you tomorrow. I'll keep in touch." Bill walked him downstairs and he left.

I liked Bill Redecker. We talked a lot during the hours we did the filming the next day, at a quiet secluded place in Culver City.

19

Polygraph Test #1

Late February, 1982

Late that same evening, Koppel phoned to give me the address where I was to meet his men. A fellow from the church chauffeured me the forty-five minutes or so to the Taft Building in Hollywood. Upstairs we met the ABC crewmen and a slightly heavyset man wearing what looked like a white surgical gown. He smiled and introduced himself as Dr. Chris Gugas, then introduced his wife and secretary Ann. He warned me not to talk about the mission until the test began.

"Come into the other room with me, Scott," the doctor instructed. "The rest of you will remain here. Gentlemen, where are the questions I'm supposed to ask this young man?"

Only he and I entered the beautiful office where I would submit to numerous polygraph examinations. I felt threatened by the unknown, and a bit resentful, but was quickly put at ease as Dr. Gugas began to talk with me.

One of Koppel's associates who had accompanied me in the car had assured me that this man, formerly with the CIA, was the foremost polygraphist in the world. He had tested many famous people, including James Earl Ray, Martin Luther King's assassin, and Robert Vesco, international suspect of drug and gun running in Central America. (Document 41)

Gugas talked to me for some time, asking my name, the date of my birth, my background. "Scott, do you understand how the polygraph works?" he asked as he attached the instrument to my body.

"I know of it, and know that it doesn't carry much reliability. Let's get on with the test."

"We will do some preliminary tests to assure you the instrument is reliable." He attached the gadgets which would activate the instrument to my body and spread a deck of cards on the table between us. Pick one card mentally, but don't touch it."

I selected a card as instructed. "Now write which card you chose on this paper," Dr. Gugas directed, "and put the paper under your leg."

He mixed the cards and laid them off to the side. One by one he picked up the cards, asking me if each was the card I had selected. As instructed, I answered "No" every time.

When he had asked about the last card, he looked directly into my eyes and said, "You picked the Ace of Spades. Let me see the paper."

"How did you know?" I asked, giving him the paper I had tucked under my leg. "It's a card trick!"

The doctor laughed. "Everybody thinks he can beat the polygraph." He took a handful of coins from his pants pocket. "I'm going to leave the room. You pick one coin then put it back in the pile after writing down which one you select."

Giving me sufficient time to fulfill his instructions, he returned, asked a few questions and said, "You picked the dime."

"This thing really does work!" I was amazed at its accuracy and understood why FBI, CIA, Department of Defense, National Security Council, National Security Agency and the White House are convinced the polygraph is a most useful apparatus.

"All I want is the truth, Scott," he said, moving into a more relaxed position. "Answer only yes or no to the questions. No sentences. Only yes or no." Then he explained that during the test whenever he gave the date of my birth and asked me if it was correct, I was to deliberately answer no. This was to confirm that the test was effective and accurate. Then he opened the sealed envelope containing the questions he was to ask me. Glancing through them, he became very somber. "No wonder a polygraph has been requested. This is hot stuff."

He asked me the questions, reversed them, mixed them all around - test one, test two, test three...Relax a while...test four, test five. We continued from late evening into early morning. At the completion he looked up, more serious than before.

"I've conducted over 30,000 tests for our government and for private corporations. This is probably the most significant test I've ever given, Scott." I was silent. Drained. "Now that I know what this is about, I must tell you something. As a retired military intelligence officer from the Marine Corps and a former CIA agent, this scares me. ...Scott, do you know Jesus? If you don't, you're going to need to know Him."

"Yes, I know Him," I replied, "but lately I've kind of left Him in the dust, not walking with Him as I should."

There was a twinkle in his eye. "I thought you knew. You'd better get right with Him. You're sitting on a national, if not international, time bomb." He rose, opened his office door and asked the people outside in the waiting room to come in.

"I will give you the basic results," he announced once everyone had become attentive, "but the official report will be sent directly to the ABC executives in New York. This information is too classified to be seen by everyone. I am also going to take the results of the test to other national polygraph experts to confirm the findings. But you can tell Mr. Koppel that Scott's answers were *one hundred percent accurate.*"

Bill Redecker then began the filming, asking Dr. Gugas more about his background. "Isn't it true, Dr. Gugas, you are a former CIA agent?"

"Yes."

"And you're a past president of the American Polygraph Association?"

"Yes."

"You've trained some of the country's top polygraph experts, many of whom are now working in the Executive Branch?"

"Yes." I was knocked out by his impressive background.

"And what are the findings of Mr. Barnes' test?"

"He passed with flying colors." *What a relief!* I knew if I had failed at any point, I would have been shoved right in front of the TV cameras and made a fool to the whole world.

We filmed a re-enactment to show the public how I had been tested. It would have been too much of a distraction to have filmed during the actual testing.

When the filming was finished, Bill told his cameraman to take the film to their courier and tell him to personally fly it to New York, asking the network to supply security to accompany him if the courier felt it was necessary. "What is in these steel boxes could make Watergate look like nothing," he warned him.

I went home exhausted, but relieved to know that soon the whole country would know what had really happened on the *Bohica* mission.

20

I Am Not A Flake

Late February, 1982

While investigating my story, Ted Koppel told me he'd met with Robert Inman, Deputy Director of the CIA, and mentioned he knew the Department of Energy Communication Center had been our main telecommunications contact.

"Prove it," Inman had said indignantly.

"Let's go to the Center and ask what Telex numbers were used for Subject: *Bohica* in '81," Koppel suggested.

Inman flipped his head. "How did you learn about Subject: *Bohica*?" By his response Koppel was convinced I was telling the truth, but he knew my story had to be accurate down to the smallest detail. ABC could take no chances.

The day following the polygraph, Bill Redecker phoned asking me to meet him at a pay phone in Palos Verdes. "Ted wants to talk with you," he explained when I arrived. He dialed a number, then handed the receiver to me. Koppel was very friendly and pleasant. "Scott, would you be offended if I asked you to see a psychiatrist?"

"No. You want the truth and so do I," I told him. "That wouldn't bother me at all."

"Then let's get on with it. Bill will take care of everything." He was very pleased with my willingness to cooperate.

Bill and I spent the rest of the day together talking in more detail about the mission. Late that night we took a ride to Beverly Hills.

It was nearly midnight when we stopped in front of a typical small Beverly Hills high-rise. Surprised to see so many people waiting outside the locked doors of the lobby at that hour, I asked, "What's the deal? Why couldn't we have done this during the day?"

"Security people," Bill explained. "No one is to know you are here. Let's go upstairs." Security people inside unlocked the door as we approached.

In another beautiful office, unlike any I had seen shrinks have in the movies, I was introduced to Dr. Frederick Hacker, of Hacker Institute of Psychiatric Research, Vienna, Austria, who has examined Patty Hearst as well as many top CIA and Executive Branch officials. He also worked on the Bogota, Columbia Embassy hostage case which occurred during the Nixon years.

"I understand you have a bizarre story to tell," this tall elderly, very polite gentleman said, puffing on his pipe. "Gentlemen, please wait here. Mr. Barnes, come into my office."

I looked around at this room filled with books. Shelves of books. "Do all these books bother you?" he asked.

"No," I answered as I continued to look around.

"Why are you wearing those clothes?" he asked very abruptly, to observe my reaction, I'm sure.

"What are you getting at?" The question made absolutely no sense to me.

"I've worked with terrorists and hostages under the Nixon Administration, the seizure of the U.S. Embassy in Bogota, Columbia in the seventies..." I interpreted this to mean, *in other words, you can't fool me.* "And now I'm supposed to find out whether or not you are deluded." He asked me my age, my educational background, how many children I had - all kinds of questions about all kinds of topics. Then, again very abruptly, "What God do you believe in?"

"What God?"

"Mohammed, Buddha..." He named several.

"I believe there is only One."

"Oh, you do, do you? Do you believe in the Holy Bible?" I felt he was getting pushy but forced myself to be cooperative.

"Well, yeh, but I don't necessarily practice what's in it as much as I should."

Then he asked, "Do you believe Jesus Christ walked on water?" *No wonder he's a psychiatrist!* I concluded. *He's nuts!* I didn't realize that most psychiatric tests include that question.

I thought for a moment. "Well...I believe in God. ...I believe He's coming again and..."

"Hah!" he interrupted, as if trying to intimidate me. "Excuse me. Go on." He observed my reactions closely. I wondered what was going through his mind.

Drawing leisurely on the pipe he held in his hand, he asked about my mother and dad, my brothers and sisters and friends, about sexual relationships. I took a long written yes-no-maybe test. Although I was getting angry, I tried not to show it.

After over three hours of questioning, he excused himself, saying, "I'll be back shortly. Just wait here, please." For at least 40 minutes I waited in a very comfortable plush waiting room I hadn't known existed before while Dr. Hacker evaluated my responses to his questions.

Finally the doctor returned. "Mr. Barnes, would you please come back in?" I did. "This mission. What do you think about it?"

"What do you mean?"

"Do you think this government's wrong?"

"Well, we are the government - the people. But whoever the men, the women, the people in the CIA and U.S. government are who are calling the shots - I think they've done a grave injustice by leaving people over there."

I wanted to think he was trying to keep from crying. He laid down his pipe, brushed his eyes, shook his head. "Sit back out there again, please." He gestured toward the waiting room.

I returned to the waiting room for another twenty minutes. The doctor returned and invited all who were waiting outside his office to come in.

"Mr. Redecker," Dr. Hacker began, "tell Mr. Koppel I will send a written confidential report to New York by the end of the week. Tell him also that this young man is *neither deluded nor mentally disturbed.* He is not a psychotic. He's a *normal American* who is very frustrated because of the fellow Americans he saw left behind."

I could see Redecker was relieved. "Now can we film your findings, Dr. Hacker - who you are, your background?"

After a brief film interview, Bill told two of his associates to get the material to New York immediately.

"This is becoming a regular thing with you," one teased. "Every night a shipment to New York."

Bill laughed, then turned to me. "Let's go call Ted."

"But it's late. And it's three hours later where he is."

"I want to give him a verbal report now," Bill insisted. "He'll want to know." Again we called from a phone booth. Bill assured him Dr. Hacker was satisfied that I was not a "psycho," then said, "Ted, here's Scott." Again Bill handed me the receiver so I could tell Koppel the results of the test. "Give me Bill," he said curtly.

"You heard him, Ted," Bill assured him. "He's okay." Bill took me back to Hope Chapel where Randy was waiting to drive me home. We always made sure none of the news people knew where I lived. The only way they could contact me was through the church.*

After my return from the mission, people often came to me for advice, many of the young singles as well as many who were older than I. I continued to work with Randy, helping him plan activities that would encourage the singles - divorcees, widows, drug and alcohol addicts - to stay out of the world and get into the Spirit. Often that unidentifiable feeling that had come over me at my baptism returned.

---

*Bill Redecker has quit ABC and is now working for CBS as a foreign correspondent. As is customary when news people move from one network to another, he had to sign a paper saying he would never reveal what had been discussed in news interviews.

"You're great at this," Randy told me one day when we were talking about my future plans. "You'd make a good singles pastor."

"Pastor? Never!" I told him laughing. I knew I wasn't even close to being a good Christian. I was still too easily tempted by the ways of the world. Having fallen many times, none of which I am happy about, I was fully aware of how difficult it was to be "in the world but not of it."

Several days later, out of the blue, Ralph Moore the senior pastor asked me, "Have you ever thought about going into the ministry?"

"Never!" Randy must have been talking to him.

"We have a training program called Hope Chapel Ministries Institute, you know."

"I know. I've talked to some of the people who are in it. You start new churches." We talked about this over breakfast frequently.

"God has given you a gift of ministry," he often repeated.

Through working and attending services at the church nearly every day and through taking advantage of the Hope Chapel cassette library, I knew the Bible so well that a lot of people made fun of me, asking "Is that all you know?" when I witnessed to them. Still, in my heart, I had a strong desire to remain in the law enforcement field. I was experienced and felt confident in that line of work.

"But that's the world," Ralph would argue. "You can live in the world and not be part of it." Like Moses and so many others through the ages I had truly heard the call to ministry, but was resisting, saying "I don't want to do that." However after much thought and prayer and wrestling with my fleshly desires, I decided I should train to be a minister and spent most of my time at the church studying under the pastors' direction.

A day or so after Dr. Hacker had tested me, Ted Koppel phoned to say he had put together a three-part *Nightline* special and gave me the dates it would be televised, a Thursday, Friday, and Monday. Then he phoned again saying the dates had been changed. ABC News sports president had decreed it shouldn't be concluded on a Monday because of the conflict with Monday Night Football. Some of the other top executives felt the series shouldn't be broken up by a weekend. The new plan was to air my story on a Tuesday, Dr. Hacker and some others on Wednesday, and Dr. Gugas on Thursday with me making some concluding remarks.

"This is going to bring the Administration down, I can assure you. Barnes, your life is in danger." Koppel wanted me to send him my little blue book. When I refused he became furious, calling me all kinds of four letter words. "Don't you know who you're dealing with? With this story I'm going to make Woodward and Bernstein look like nobodies!"

"Woodward and Bernstein?? Oh, the *Washington Post* guys..." Then I thought, *does he only care about himself?*

Less than a week later Koppel again phoned me at the church - this time to tell me the story had been killed and he never wanted to talk to me again. Somehow the CIA had found out what was to take place. Apparently ABC News chairman Leonard Goldenson received a personal phone call about our mission from CIA Director Casey. ABC gave the tapes of my interview to the CIA and the story was then killed.* In place of my story, Koppel had made plans to interview Bo. "I'm going to fry him," he told me.

It was during this interview that Bo challenged Koppel to suggest that Mrs. Dodge insist on an autopsy of the returned body of her husband.

Bo had already told the world on the famous attorney F. Lee Bailey's *Lie Detector Show* he could "prove he was telling the truth," but by lying he failed the polygraph examination. Then he tried through intimidation and bribery to prevent it from being aired. Next Ted wiped him out, making a total fool of him on the air.

Not long after that catastrophe, during a grossly unsuccessful POW rescue attempt called *Operation Lazarus*, Bo was arrested in Thailand and convicted in a trial in NKP for illegal possession of radio

---

*Director Casey owned the single largest amount of share holder stock in Capital City which purchased ABC later on. It was the only massive amount of stock the Director continued to hold out of his blind trust which the law required when he took office.

equipment. On March 22, 1983, Bo had to appear before the House Asian and Pacific Affairs Subcommittee to explain his bungled rescue attempts. One by one witnesses from Defense Intelligence and top Pentagon officials destroyed his testimony.

When I learned of this hearing it troubled me. Bo's talk - some of it was right and some wrong - could have had me in criminal trouble. After all, even though we had gone under orders from our government, we had crossed the border, taking in guns and high tech equipment. We had illegally taken large amounts of U.S. currency into a foreign country. Using the Western Union mailgram service, I warned Congressman Stephen Solarz, chairman of the subcommittee, that Gritz would not give the committee all the facts and suggested that all who had ever worked with Gritz on missions be subpoenaed.* (Document 42 - A,B)

Still nervous, I phoned John Stein, the CIA agent. Before we ever left the country, we were told to call if anything about the mission were to go haywire. He was puzzled that I had kept his phone number, a private direct line. (I discussed this with William Casey's secretary Betty who said the Director was also very upset to learn I would continue to use this number.) Finally Stein said, "I don't know you. Never heard of you," and hung up. I would use the number again if I had to.

---

*In late '86, Bo was arrested twice again in Southeast Asia and Hong Kong. Bo continued to lie and cover up but was indicted by a Federal Court in May, 1987.

21

The Pressure's On

I don't know how Lucette Lagnado, reporter for syndicated columnist Jack Anderson, saw the results of my polygraph because ABC refused to release them or confirm that I had passed. She called me at the church saying Anderson demanded that I cooperate with him, but I refused. Dale Van Atta and a guy named Goldberg from Anderson's office threatened, "There's a lot of disinformation flying around about *Operation Grand Eagle.* Either you help us or we do nothing to help you." Disliking to be pressured by others just so they could get what they wanted, again I refused.

Sensing that increased pressure was soon to come, again I called John Stein at CIA. Both he and Gene Wilson refused to acknowledge ever having heard of me, although Wilson did back off somewhat to voice his concern that Bo was creating a media problem and neither Bo nor I should have discussed the mission or ISA.

"You haven't seen me in the media," I tried to impress upon him, hoping for some acceptance and support.

"Still it's best that I don't know you."

I tried to talk to Daniel Arnold and received basically the same treatment, although he did say he had received the letter I mailed him and would give it to "D" and Chai Lo, whoever they were.

Kevin Cody of *Easy Reader* magazine of Hermosa Beach phoned and made arrangements to interview me at Hope Chapel. More and more I became caught up in the battle for truth and gradually reneged from my ministerial studies.

I was hired by Merrill Lynch, having applied for the position some time previously. The first morning Merrill Lynch called to say they had a desk for me a large business offer came as well.

I decided to be the rebel of the company. Everyone who worked for this prestigious firm wore three-piece business suits and drove a fancy car. The first day on the job I arrived dressed in a Hawaiian shirt, old shorts and sandals. The boss did not approve, pointing out that in order to deal with important clients it was essential I dress properly.

"Evidently I am dressed properly," I told him. "Here's an offer for a $400,000 deal I just received without a three-piece suit." It pleased me to see him so taken aback. I thought I was hot stuff. Perhaps I was rebelling against people in positions of authority as a reaction to all the disappointments I had experienced from "official" people.

This was my first job unrelated to the field of criminology and intelligence. It opened my eyes to the ways of the "legitimate" business world, otherwise I never would have believed there were so many rich people and so much graft and self interest. I learned that some of the secretaries slept with clients just to make business deals for their bosses - secretaries who were considered "happily married," with families: "Good church-going people."

"What does your husband think?" I asked one of the women who worked in our office.

"Nothing. I just tell him I'm going on a business trip for the firm. It's the way you close deals with some corporate executives. You wine them, dine them, take them on weekend sailing trips."

"That's not for me." I was appalled. I also learned that Don Regan, President Reagan's former Chief of Staff, was one of the chief executive officers of Merrill Lynch during this time.

U.S. Customs phoned the church several times wanting information about me. Once they picked me up at my parents' home and took me to the Long Beach customs office where we talked for more than an hour. I asked them what I had done that was so wrong.

"There are a couple of things. You may have violated the International Neutrality Act and the U.S. Treasury Act by taking large amounts of money out of the country without reporting it or filling out the necessary documents. You illegally took arms and top secret classified radio equipment into an unfriendly nation."

I was being incriminated for things I had been instructed to do by my government. I asked, "If I get arrested and go to jail, there's going to be a trial, right? And who's going to talk at that trial? Me! And I'm going to name names, dates, times, and places. I'm going to talk about all kinds of Agency dealings - guns, drugs, about secret codes, etc." Immediately they backed off, realizing they were talking to someone who'd also had experience in law enforcement and covert intelligence.

I decided to contact J.D. Bath to see if he knew who was talking and how Customs knew we'd had so much money. "Barnes...?" he asked in a puzzled tone. "I don't know you. Mission...? What mission?"

"That's funny," I retorted. "I've got a picture of you and me." I couldn't have done more damage had I dropped a bomb. He cursed and threatened to kill me if a picture really existed. Evidently he had forgotten that one of our guards had taken a photo of us posing together by the river and didn't realize that once I had quickly turned and snapped one of him sitting in a carriage drinking a beer. Perhaps he had been too drunk at the time. I didn't know what else to do to cool him down, so I said I was just joking about the picture.

The 1982 summer issue of *Covert Action* magazine came out with fairly accurate coverage of the mission. They had interviewed Dornan and Gritz as well as myself and had included Cody's interview from *Easy Reader*. Shortly afterwards, the April 15th issue of *Easy Reader* was available on the newsstands. Cody's "Spook or Spoof" article was the cover story. Of all the articles written about the mission, his is the most accurate. Even Mark Gladstone and Richard Meyer of the *Los Angeles Times* admit that Cody's article is the best coverage of the mission. (Document 43) Nevertheless Merrill Lynch was not pleased to see one of their employees receive such publicity.

Some time around the first of May, I was surprised to receive a phone call from Harvard University. A Dr. Matthew Meselson, world-renowned biochemist, phoned me to see if I knew Jerry Daniels (MJB) had been killed in Bangkok in April. (Dr. Meselson had been working with a biochemist at the University of Montana. Evidently when the professor began to question the Hmong people in his area and investigate Jerry's past activities, he was told of our mission and relayed the information to Dr. Meselson.) I didn't want to believe it. Reports stated that he had died of accidental carbon monoxide poisoning. The man I knew as Michael J. Baldwin had been so confident, so capable - a fifteen-year man with the CIA and State Department. How could he have died this way? The Bangkok Embassy claimed "off the record" that someone had fooled around with the pilot light on Daniel's stove during a drunken party, but refused to make further statements. Enough false information had conveniently "leaked" to the *Bangkok Post* so that no one who had been at the party was willing to talk about it.

I talked to a man at the mortuary in Montana to verify that it was Daniels' body that had been shipped back to the States. A State Department seal was on the casket. Government guards and government orders prevented the casket from being opened. Not even family members could view the body. I later learned that Colonel Mike Eiland was the one who had ordered the casket sealed and shipped the body back to the United States.

General Vang Pao, who called Jerry his white son, and his men had taken charge of the funeral. I received a copy of the funeral service I had requested from Vang Pao. Jerry was buried May 10, 1982. (Document 44) A photograph of the casket taken by a local reporter

showed a portrait of Daniels placed in front of the casket. Next to
the portrait was a wreath with a ribbon on it which read "Mr. and
Mrs. D. C. Arnold."*

On August 2, 1982, at 4:55 p.m., moments before closing the Merrill
Lynch office for the day, the secretary came into my office to tell
me that I was to call the White House. Thinking it must be a joke,
I dialed (202) 395-3576. The man on the phone identified himself
as Lieutenant Colonel Richard Childress of the National Security
Council, Southeast Asia. He warned me that because *Bohica* had been
classified I shouldn't talk about it. I asked why Stein and Arnold and
the others who were supposed to support and protect me refused to
acknowledge me or the mission, and received as a reply, "It's secret.
It's over." I took his message not as a threat, but as a very serious
warning from the Executive Branch. His call convinced me there were
deep   undercurrents   connected   with   the   mission   that

---

*UPDATE: On November 15, 1986, I received a call from a former CIA agent who had worked
in Laos with Jerry Daniels. He wanted to know about Jerry's mission and what I knew about
the details of his death, saying that certain CIA personnel and former Air America personnel
were concerned, believing that indeed he had been killed. In a January 1987 phone conversation with Carl Jenkins, retired CIA man involved in the Iran-Contra deal, I was told Jerry
probably was killed because of his drug connection with Vang Pao, Daniel Arnold and Richard
Armitage. But he would discuss it no further, saying "People who talk about such things die."

neither I nor the public was to know anything about.* The pressure for truth was on. Something had to break. I started to send telegrams, mailgrams, letters - anything to get the word out.

---

*In my last conversation with Childress, on May 3, 1985, he informed me that at one time while he was consulting with Lieutenant Colonel Oliver North, it was decided that in the best interest of national security nothing about *Bohica* should ever come out. He added he would do his best, using the power of the Executive Branch, to cause disinformation on the *Bohica* mission and make me look like a fool.

22

The Times, Sportmart and Donna

December, 1982

I was sitting in my office at Merrill Lynch with my feet propped up on my desk, wondering what to do next. The secretary directed two gentlemen she thought were business associates to my door. Seeing bulges under their coats, I figured they were packing guns and were probably Feds who had come to arrest me for some reason. I was relieved but at the same time upset to discover they were Mark Gladstone and Rick Meyer from the *Los Angeles Times*. They said they had read the *Easy Reader* article and wanted to talk with me about Operation Grand Eagle.

"No way," I told them. "Get out of my office." They left.

Late that same afternoon, the secretary came to my office door. "You know those two men who were here earlier? They're waiting outside in a car."

Disgusted with dealing with reporters and feeling spiteful, I went out, got in my car and headed down the Pacific Coast Highway toward Palos Verdes, hoping to get them lost, then double back and tail them. They followed. Fed up, I stopped near the ocean in Redondo Beach and got out of my car, walked back and leaned on theirs. "What do you want?" I demanded.

"We've got to talk to you." Meyer was the spokesman.

"Go talk to Cody."

"We're not talking to him. He scooped us."

"I don't understand." They explained they had been working on the *Bohica* story for a long time through a national security leak. A *Times* Reporter in Bangkok also filtered information about the mission to them. After I clearly told them I was not interested in talking to them and made sure they were not following me, I went home.

The following morning when I arrived at work, Gladstone and Meyer were there waiting for me. In no uncertain terms I told them to please leave me alone.

"We've got to talk to you about *Grand Eagle*," Gladstone insisted. "We may know some things you don't know about and in return we need your help.

"No."

"Let us take you to lunch."

"No." My boss was getting more and more upset about the intrusions and the publicity I was receiving.

"Who are they?" he asked after they'd gone.

"They're definitely not clients," I told him. "They're newspaper reporters."

"Because of this?" He held out *Easy Reader.* "If the home office ever saw this you'd be in a lot of trouble."

Again the *Times* reporters phoned me at work, insisting that I talk with them. Then U.S. Customs came to Merrill Lynch and searched my desk. I was getting nervous. Not wanting this kind of harassment to be the cause of my losing my job, I called the Senate Intelligence Committee and talked to Spencer Davis, telling him what was going on. He asked me to forward the information to him and to send a copy certified/return receipt to Barry Goldwater. I wrote the Senate Intelligence Committee a very long and detailed letter, telling them the story of the mission and what had been happening to me since I'd come home and, because it would be quicker, sent a mailgram to Goldwater.

After Davis received my letter he telephoned to say there were some things going on he couldn't tell me about, but that the Senate Intelligence Committee would look into the information I had sent. He admitted the Committee knew about the mission but because this type mission was directed by National Security Council, had little interest in my problem.

Later I was notified there were a lot of puppets on the Committee who were against probing. Davis subsequently left his position as spokesman for the Committee. "They're not going to do anything," he assured me.

Sometime in August Bob Simms and Mike Wheeler, staff assistants of the President, each phoned and left numbers where I could reach them: (202) 395-3044 and 395-6965. Both reminded me *Bohica* was classified as confidential and talking could harm foreign relations.

I continued to write letters, even to the President. Colonel Childress of the National Security Council contacted me again and warned that if I didn't shut up I would pay, then added Bo would pay too.

The *LA Times* reporters wouldn't give up. Remembering Bo's technique for getting rid of troublesome reporters, I decided to "take them for a ride" in order to get them off my back and told them I would talk. We met at the Velvet Turtle, Redondo Beach.

While we talked, they periodically slipped a $100 bill under my napkin. Each time another bill was added to the growing pile, they would turn off their recorder and say things like, "This is gas money, okay?" Then they would wink. Cheap yellow journalism. Reporters trying to buy a story.

Realizing they knew more than I'd expected, I backed off, making the excuse I was too tired to continue. This gave me time to do some investigating; and I learned Meyer was a well-known reporter, but Gladstone certainly was not. Wondering how he got in on this story, I did some more checking. I discovered he was the one who had contacted the FBI saying he had allegedly received an anonymous call informing him that Bo and I, as well as "the secret team" were plotting to assassinate President Reagan and that Capps, one of the men who had picked me up on Christmas Eve, was a friend of Bo's. So

I FOIA'd (Freedom of Information Act) my files and, sure enough,
there it was: "Threat to the President of the United States." (Document 39 A)

The next time we met, I confronted Meyer with what I had learned
while carefully observing their reactions. He chuckled, admitting that
Gladstone was the one who had called the FBI. I wondered if he ever
really did receive an anonymous call or if he made up the story just
to get the assignment. Meyer admitted the story had been fabricated
because Gladstone had wanted so badly to be assigned to a real investigative story and get out of his flunky position.

Several times I met with these reporters I considered to be pests.
They would pick a time and I would choose the place. Besides meeting
at the Velvet Turtle, we met at Fisherman's Wharf, Redondo Beach;
at a mall in Torrance; at Marineland in Palos Verdes and at an office
building in Santa Monica. Each time I met with Gladstone and Meyer
I filled them with all kinds of baloney. It was like - I'll answer three
questions if you answer five. They admitted they'd had a contact in
Thailand during the time of the mission. Each time I shared bits of
information with them they became more excited. But finally I pushed
my luck too far. "You're lying to us!" one of them realized.

"That's right. News reporters shouldn't pay for stories. You should
be thoroughly investigated. This is what you get for hassling and
pushing." (Gladstone was removed from the assignment, demoted and
transferred to the *Sacramento Times* office to write about small time
affairs.) I took their money anyway and returned to the office and
to additional problems.

Benaz Valiz, my little Iranian colleague in our Beverly Hills office, had direct connections in Iran. One day she phoned me. "Scottee? Bad news... I think we're in trouble."

We had been working together on a major deal involving Mideast
and Iran connections which were not pleasing the Securities Exchange
Commission or the State Department.

Then I was told the office from which I worked was closing and
I wouldn't be moving with them. Tim Shreve, a Christian brother I'd
never met personally, called from the Dallas office to say he'd heard

reports from the home office of the moving plans and although he didn't know what the outcome would be he would be praying for me.

Then my boss came in to tell me the West Coast office was soon to close and Jerry, the West Coast boss, wanted to talk to me about the Mideast-Iranian deal. Jerry returned my license and told me to return to my home office. Orders for my being terminally laid off had come from the Merrill Lynch headquarters in Connecticut. (Document 45)

Immediately I applied for a job in Redondo Beach at Sportmart of Chicago which was opening a West Coast office. On October 10, 1982, I was hired as their West Coast security manager.

Four months later, February 21, 1983, the *L.A. Times* story (Document 15) came out, at least confirming I had been part of *Operation Grand Eagle*. It was then I realized I was living by a new set of values. I had become more interested in getting the truth out than in making big money. Determined to set the record straight and let the world know what had really taken place, I held a news conference in Los Angeles, documenting that Gritz had fabricated much of his story. (Document 46 - A,B)

Some of Bo's friends contacted me asking if there wasn't some way they could help us reconcile our differences. "I respect the man and all he's done for his country," I told them, "but I don't know why he's doing so much lying or what his problems are." I never have talked to Bo.

The day after the news conference Customs came again to my home to confiscate more papers and pictures that related to the mission. Luckily I'd had foresight enough to hide many of the more pertinent documents, so I could give them some, but never everything. I was saving the best for last!

In the summer of '83 a representative for the Dr. Bill Bright Campus Crusade for Christ phoned me at the church inviting me to Campus Crusade headquarters in the San Bernadino Mountains to have lunch with Dr. Bright. Arrangements were made for a Dave Hunt to drive me up. I had no idea why Dr. Bright would want to have lunch with me.

Headquarters was an old gray hotel in the foothills of the San Bernadino Mountains. We ate in a huge banquet room. It was a beautiful place and the food was plentiful and delicious.

Bill Bright and several other gentlemen entered. He introduced himself and his lawyer/advisor, then invited me to be seated next to him. After he had offered grace and the salad had been served, Dr. Bright explained, "I asked you to come because I want to know more about this mission. I personally know General David Jones for Joint Chiefs of Staff who was also involved in *Operation Grand Eagle* and General Vessey who has now taken over for him."*

Over lunch we talked about Generals Vessey* and Jones and about *Bohica*. At the close of our visit, Dr. Bright gave me his blessing, affirming that something should be done about the POWs we had deserted and promising to do what he could to help. I have not heard from him since.

It was about that same time I heard that Congressman Stephen Solarz and the Subcommittee on Asian Affairs were planning to ask Bo to testify. And it was then I contacted Solarz who admitted they hoped to prove Bo was lying so they could state therefore everyone who had worked with him was also lying.

"But Bo wasn't on the mission," I argued. "He didn't see what I saw." He ignored my protests.

*   *   *   *   *

Some time in early 1983, I had opportunity to go to the Middle East to make arms and munitions connections as a follow up on the promise to Vang Pao. Some arms went to drug war lords in Burma and some to Vang Pao's guerrilla people in Laos, the rest to a special group of people who were working on intelligence matters in Syria.

---

*After *Operation Grand Eagle*, three very important people resigned from their positions rather quickly: Rear Admiral Bobby Inman, General David Jones, and Max Freiderdorff from the White House. In 1986, President Reagan rehired Max.

---

*Vessey was recently named to negotiate with Hanoi re POWs.

(Document 47) When I returned I became better acquainted with Donna Nevins, Operations Manager at Sportmart and the most attractive female employee there as far as I was concerned. She was one of the most intelligent women I'd ever met. Donna seemed interested in my involvement with POWs, having done a lot of reading about Vietnam because her brother had done tours there and had come home with a bronze star. She sought to understand what he'd been through.

A very quiet girl, she resisted my typical male come-ons. Finally when several of the Sportmart employees got together at a restaurant for a special celebration, Donna and I found ourselves the last two to leave. We talked for a long time about the harassment I had been experiencing. She was a kind, understanding young woman.

As we became better acquainted, Donna showed interest in the fact that I spent so much time at Hope Chapel. She started to attend church with me and I bought her a New American Bible with her name engraved on it. We began to see each other often, dating frequently and eating lunch together every day at work.

In early '83, about three months after my return from the Middle East, John Stein from the CIA phoned me to say they had a job for me in Hawaii. He thought it would be good for me in order to "patch up old wounds." Since earlier he'd refused to admit that he even knew me, I was totally shocked to now hear him say he thought maybe I could get back to business in intelligence with ISA.

"I'm always willing to help our country, but I'm not going to get involved in something where I'll get set up again, then get put out in the cold." An extremely argumentative phone conversation ensued. I relented and said I would go.

23

Back To Hawaii

September, 1983

An Investment Consultant named Ron Rewald was in jail in Hawaii, waiting trial in November. I remembered the name. His firm, *Bishop, Baldwin, Reward, Dillingham and Wong*, a front for many major illegal CIA operations, had been charged with swindling investors out of more the twenty million dollars. Rewald, the one we were to call if we needed more money or equipment for *Bohica*, was indicted by the Federal Grand Jury on one hundred counts of fraud, perjury and tax evasion. I was to assess his mental and emotional condition and make sure he didn't talk too much about his previous government dealings.

Suspicious, I said to Stein, "You guys burned me on the Bo Gritz thing. How do I know this isn't another set up?"

"No, no," he said, assuring me that in the past I had been dealing with agents who were no longer with the agency and that the Gritz mess would clear up, given enough time.

My situation had certainly not improved by staying around fighting for truth. By this time I was receiving a lot of flak because of a letter I had written to *Soldier of Fortune* magazine in an attempt to correct the misinformation in their previous article about me. They had published my letter in the September, 1983 issue. (Document 48) Perhaps it would be best for me to leave the mainland for a while.

Stein saw to it that I received my instructions, my pay and my plane ticket and that same afternoon I caught a United flight to Honolulu. Donna was not exactly pleased to discover I had suddenly terminated my job with Sportmart and flown to Hawaii without telling her why I was leaving. (Document 49 - A,B)

Upon arrival in Hawaii, I looked up my pastor/friend Ralph Moore who had gone to Kahnoe Bay a few months earlier to open another Hope Chapel. "Ralph, guess who's here?" I announced, walking into his office. It was a happy reunion.

"What are you doing here?" he asked, wide-eyed with surprise and smiling.

"I decided to come to work with you for a while. Help you start the church."

"Great!" He rose from his desk chair. "Come in and meet some of the new people." Suddenly he stopped and turned toward me. "You're not here because of the Rewald affair, are you?" Ralph knew me all too well.

"Rewald? Who's that?"

"Big CIA case here. The guy's in prison waiting trial. It's been on the front page of the paper nearly every day. ...It smells."

Upon my suggestion Joan Griffiths, church secretary (now a police dispatcher in Long Beach), agreed to allow me to use her mailing address until I had my own, then invited me to start coming to her home in Honolulu for Bible Study.

Some days later she met me at my hotel and drove me to her Honolulu residence. Before we got out of her car, she warned me, "Scott, I have a gut feeling that you're over here because of the Rewald case. If you are, please don't involve the church. I'll say no more."

In order for me to get into the prison to see Rewald, the CIA saw to it that the Department of Motor Vehicles of the State of Hawaii had marked "Christian minister" as my profession on my driver's license. I had already given them Joan's address as the "Reverend's" residence.

In the role of pastor, I had written Rewald several letters that he had answered. This helped me get in to see him successfully, although the prison staff commented that I looked too young to be a seasoned preacher. They also questioned my relationship with Rewald because he was Catholic and I was not wearing a clerical collar. But I'd had the foresight to ask Ralph to print a prayer request on Rewald's behalf in the Sunday church bulletin. Showing the prison warden a copy of the church bulletin, I explained that our church had been ministering to him for some time previous to his arrest.

This worked for a couple of weeks, but every time I signed "Rev. Barnes" on the prison register my conscience would not let me rest. I felt like a hypocrite.

"Look, it's not working," my contact agent finally admitted to me. "You'll have to get a job as a prison guard in order to make sure Rewald doesn't talk."

"One week I'm a minister, then the next a prison guard. How's that going to work?"

"Don't worry," I was told. Somehow it was arranged for me to be assigned as a guard to Module 8, Oahu Community Corrective Center, the module where Rewald was in high security protective custody. The day shift prison staff I worked with was suspicious, wondering what an American with my educational background would want with a low paying job like prison guard. Few Caucasians worked as guard in OCCC.

During my nine-to-ten week stay in Hawaii, Pulitzer Prize author Sy Hersh came to the University of Hawaii to lecture on his book about Henry Kissinger. As a result of the questions asked by some of the persons in attendance, his lecture included a discussion about Bo Gritz and confirmed that *Operation Grand Eagle* was an official government mission. After the lecture I introduced myself to him and he asked if we could talk further. We met in the oceanfront coffee shop at the Royal Hawaiian Hotel and talked about the Rewald case also. He knew the CIA was deeply involved, especially after the Nugan/Hand bank collapse when a way for channeling large quantities of money out of the Golden Triangle was needed.

All over the world press releases were implicating admirals, generals and the CIA. Millions of dollars were disappearing. David Taylor of BBC did an extensive investigative story on the Rewald exposé.

After a one-month-long career as prison guard, my contact agents met with me at the Royal Hawaiian and gave me orders, "Rewald must be killed." *Another Bo Gritz game after all! I should have known!* I hurried to my hotel room and began to pack. There was a knock at my door.

"Mr. Barnes?"

I opened the door. "Yes, sir?"

It was the Honolulu sheriff. He had come to serve a subpoena from the Attorney General of the State of Hawaii. *Now what do I do?* I wondered, realizing that if Stein had lied and this was a set-up, someone could kill Rewald, make it look as though I had done it and get me for conspiracy to commit murder.

As soon as the sheriff had left, I phoned Attorney General Tany Hong. "What's this all about?"

"We want to talk to you about your position at the prison and about the Rewald case. You were hired without any processing. Why was your photo never taken, no fingerprints or ID made? We're very concerned about this." It was true. I was the only guard who had never been processed. All I'd had to do was attend their academy for 21 days while I continued to work.

"Could I talk to you right now?" I asked, wanting to get back to the mainland as quickly as possible.

"Prior to the date stated on the subpoena? ...Come to the governor's office." I went immediately.

In the meantime, the Attorney General had been called to the prison on an emergency by the FBI, so when I arrived at the governor's offices I was questioned by Jim Dannenberg, Deputy State Attorney General about my ministerial status and my current job as prison guard. They were also concerned that without proper authorization I had engaged the County Coroner to lecture to the inmates about the procedure followed after someone dies in prison. I had also brought in an undercover narcotic agent named Chuck to talk about the penalties

STATE OF HAWAII
DEPARTMENT OF SOCIAL SERVICES AND HOUSING
CORRECTIONS DIVISION

Certificate Of Training

THIS IS TO CERTIFY THAT

S C O T T T. B A R N E S

HAS SATISFACTORILY COMPLETED

BASIC CORRECTIONAL TECHNIQUES

NOVEMBER 1983

FRANKLIN Y.X. SUNN
Director #33814

MICHAEL KAKESAKO
Administrator
Corrections Division

JANICE F. YUEN
Training Administrator
Corrections Division

for crimes committed while in prison, the use and abuse of narcotics among prisoners.*

Then Deputy Dannenberg asked, "What happened on that mission to Southeast Asia you claim to be part of?"

"Well..." I hesitated to answer.

---

*I had talked the Coroner into going to the prison one day to show pictures of autopsies and lecture under the auspices that this was a drug counseling program, telling him I was working for the Volunteers in Corrections organization, a ministerial organization.

Day after day I would visit him. "We're concerned about all the drug-related prison deaths."

"Boy, you're really interested."

"Yes, I am. I really want to help those people. Maybe we can do a scare-type program." He invited me to watch while he performed autopsies - one on a seventeen-year-old and another on a guy in his forties. I learned how they took samples, what lab they sent the samples to - I had inside knowledge of the whole process that takes place when someone dies or is killed.

On the surface, it was to look like a program designed to say to prisoners, "Look, if you take dope and die, this is what we do to you." Actually the program gave me insight into how the coroner's office dealt with deaths in the prison. This way, I felt if Rewald were to be killed in prison, reports and samples could be easily intercepted. It was the first time in Hawaii's history that a coroner or a police department narc had ever gone into the prison to lecture and show films.

Sensing my reluctance to talk to him, he said, "Oh well, I'm not even the one who is supposed to be questioning you. The Attorney General should be doing that. Go back to your hotel. I'll note on your subpoena you were here and tell the Attorney General when he returns you will appear for the Grand Jury investigation.

That same day I received a call from an irate Attorney General Tany Hong. He was upset that I had talked to anyone but him and warned I was not to talk to anyone else about the case.

"It's getting close to Thanksgiving," I told him after assuring him I would talk to no one else. "Would it be possible to postpone my hearing until a later date?"

"You will cooperate?"

"Yes, sir."

He gave me a December date for my hearing, warning, "You be here." Knowing I was under so much suspicion that even if I had done nothing wrong I could be in a lot of trouble, I left my car and belongings behind, bought a plane ticket under an assumed name and flew to LAX.

24

Give Up? Why Not!

Rewald, according to reports, attempted suicide, although he claims he doesn't remember doing it. Both of his arms were slit. The question I ask is, how could he have cut his own tendons in one arm, then pick up a knife with that arm and cut the tendons in the other?

During the trial, General Hunter Harris testified that at Rewald's approval he had given Gritz funds for *Bohica* on behalf of the CIA. John Kindschi, CIA chief in Honolulu and Jack Rardin had concurred with this Rewald/Harris decision. Rewald was found guilty of fraud, perjury and tax evasion and was sentenced to 80 years in Terminal Island Prison in California. (Document 50)

It was not easy to convince Donna that I had come back to California simply because I didn't like it over there. After all, this was my 24th trip to the Hawaiian Islands since leaving South Vietnam in '73. Neither was it easy to convince her that I missed her terribly while I was gone. Finally, our relationship renewed, we were married on Valentine's Day, 1984, in Beverly Hills on Chuck Henry's *L.A. Today* ABC/TV show. Deciding to start a new life and do nothing for the government anymore, we moved to a home I owned in Kernville; and I began working as a Kern County counselor at Camp Owen, a beautiful juvenile detention center out in the country.

Although we loved our secluded home high in the mountains, a distance from any major city, we were unable to find a church that satisfied our religious needs and beliefs. Once in a while I would read the Bible and pray, but I noticed that Donna spent much of her free time reading religious books.

"We've just got to get back with God," she would constantly say.

"Yeh," I would answer, and put her off.

We hadn't lived in Kernville two weeks when I received a certified letter that had been sent to an old address in Los Angeles with the request to forward. Thoughtlessly I had filed at that post office to have all my mail forwarded. The letter, from the Attorney General of the State of Hawaii, stated that to avoid having charges filed against me for not appearing at Grand Jury, I should call and make new arrangements. Not thinking, I called collect as the letter had directed. When he received the billing, he would know where I was living.

"Why didn't you appear?" he asked.

"I never planned to. I know nothing that will help you."

"Unfortunately, failure to appear is a minor charge in Hawaii," he lamented, "not extradictable from California. You're lucky. But if you ever come near Hawaii before your statute of limitations (five years) expires, I'll send my marshals out to get you."

I didn't care that I felt I could never again safely return to Hawaii, but I was deeply concerned that Ralph Moore was very upset because I hadn't told him about the subpoena nor notified him when I left Hawaii. I regret having disappointed such a good friend.

After I had worked as juvenile counselor at Kern County Probation Department only about six months, Peter Jennings did an ABC news story that told about my involvement in the Rewald case. The newspapers revived my connection with Gritz and the POW controversy. The CIA filed a complaint with the Federal Communications Commission against ABC. This was the first time in U.S. history any such action had occurred. During the hearings, Stanley Sporkin, General Counsel of the CIA (also counselor for the CIA who wrote up the documents on the Iran-Contra affair) admitted I had signed a secrecy agreement. It was then ABC admitted they had given the tapes of my interviews with Koppel to the CIA and the case was closed. (Document 51 - A,B,C)

All this bad publicity caused a great deal of excitement at my place of employment. My colleagues kept making comments like, "Hey, we saw you on Peter Jennings."..."Who are you really?" Our new director of Camp Owen, Jim Norton, called me to his office. "What's all this with the CIA?"

"I really can't discuss it," I told him. "Besides, it's not pertinent to my work here."

"Well, I don't like it, and I'm going to do everything in my power to get you fired."

"But I'm considered an outstanding counselor here, number one on the list of the hundreds of people who applied for the job. Soon I will be on permanent staff." I felt I was one of the few staff members who really cared more about the juveniles than about my paycheck.

"You just wait and see. I'll make sure you're out." Norton was disliked by the other personnel as well as by the man who had hired him. I had seen him sneak around in the middle of the night peaking in windows to make sure staff members on the graveyard shift were not dozing off or reading.

"But you didn't hire me," I argued ineffectively. After only a couple of days, I was informed by Norton I had been fired. The reasons included, among other things, failure to state my alleged CIA involvement, not giving explanations for leaving my law enforcement jobs in Ridgecrest and San Diego and for not giving a two-week notice when I resigned from the prison guard job in Hawaii. Someone had combed the Civil Service rules and codes. Only handbooks from years back listed these as basis for terminating an employee.

I appealed and there was a hearing in Superior Court, Bakersfield. Of course, the media were there. Judge Sarah Adler ruled against me on everything except the failure to give a two-week notice count. Following the hearing, T. Glenn Brown, chief probation officer of Kern County whom I respect and admire, came to me. "Scott, I must admit you're one of the best probation counselors I've ever had in

Kernville. I mean that. I can't reveal to you why we were forced to get rid of you but I want you to know we had no choice."

"But you've ruined my life." I was bitter. "No income. No job." Later Kern County Personnel Director Joseph Drew, Jr., a retired military officer, vowed he would keep me from ever getting a county job because I had spoken against my government about the POW issue. I talked with him several times but he would not change his mind.

I was not the only one who was deeply disappointed when I lost employment. Donna, who was expecting our second child at the time, felt if I had never pushed on for truth about why the two men I had seen in Laos and the who-knows-how-many others they represented were never rescued, we could have settled down to a peaceful normal life. I could have retained a stable nine-to-five job with a steady income.

A college had advertised for an instructor with considerable college background plus experience in security, intelligence, and investigation. Twenty-three or twenty-four people applied including myself. As I talked with these hopefuls who sat with me waiting to be interviewed, I became discouraged. The others had doctorate degrees and many more years experience than I, so I was thoroughly surprised to receive a call telling me I had been selected as top candidate for the job.

Although Donna realized my work at the college, some distance from our home, would involve considerable driving time, she was eager for relief from the financial strain we had been experiencing since my dismissal from the counseling job. The following day I began the process of setting up curriculum and selecting new and better textbooks for the law enforcement department.

Besides teaching at the college, I continued to travel in connection with further investigation in the Rewald case, making investigative visits to China Lake, Miramar Naval/Air Base in San Diego, trips to Edwards Air Force Base and to Frisco for Federal and Rewald's personally hired attorneys. Convinced Rewald was innocent of many of the accusations and having been set up once too often myself, I was anxious to clear my name and get the real story uncovered.

Although our son Joshua was born during this time I spent little time at home. My many interests continued to consume all my energy and thoughts.

All this involvement didn't stop me from continuing my quest for truth. On July 2, 1985, I phoned Congressman Solarz at his home once again about Bo's lies. He insisted that I never call him again. (Document 52 - A,B) I talked to Ed Freeman who had worked with Solarz several times in '82. I wrote to congressmen and talked to members of the Senate Intelligence Committee trying to get some-one - ANYONE - to investigate the possibility of a cover-up. Nobody wanted to do a thing. Vang Pao would no longer talk to me. I felt like my credibility and self respect had been totally cut away.

In August, 1985, I received a letter c/o Donna Nevin (my wife's maiden name) from a F.C. Brown, with no identification except a Pentagon hospital personnel phone number, asking me to call him. (Document 53) Because the letterhead had no military designation, I had no idea he was a Lieutenant Commander in the Navy. When I phoned, he claimed he had been paid to do a disinformation story about me for a Jim Shultz of *Gung Ho* magazine, explaining that Shultz was a former partner of Robert K. Brown of *Soldier of Fortune*. F.C. Brown threatened to do a smear story whether I helped him or not. He seemed to have a lot of classified information. I refused to cooperate, suspecting this was another government disinformation attempt.

In September of 1985, Donna and I argued. "Our marriage is on the rocks because of this mess," she complained. "This POW thing has obsessed you. You've run up thousands of dollars in phone bills. It's ruined your life. Why don't you just throw all your documents and letters away? If nobody else cares about you or about their fellow Americans who have been left behind, why should you?"

I thought of the long-faced Hmongs that Daniels and I had left sitting on the banks of the Mekong. They cared. I thought of the families of POWs. They cared. They cared deeply not only about their own loved ones but about everyone who had been left behind. "But you don't know what it's like, Donna. For years I've been fighting and writing trying to get an explanation why this mission was aborted, trying to find out what really happened - *Why we left Americans behind.*"

"Scott, we've got two babies to raise and a life to live."

"But what I'm doing is more important than anything else." That was wrong to say; but at the time it was the way I felt. Our disagreement gave me cause to do a lot of thinking.

Finally, after a week or more of mental anguish and turmoil, I removed two big boxes of correspondence, documents, evidence and information pertaining to *Bohica* off my closet shelf. "Okay, Donna," I yelled so she could hear me in the other room. "I'll do what you say. I'll destroy the *Bohica* documents and forget the whole mess."

Sitting down in front of our fireplace insert, I opened the door and threw in the papers one by one. One box empty and the other nearly halfway gone, I paused to allow the fire to burn down. The phone rang. I closed the fireplace door and went into the bedroom to answer.

"Scott? Chris Gugas." We had kept in touch ever since he had given me the polygraph tests. "What are you doing?"

"I'm putting this whole thing behind me. I'm burning everything."

Hearing this, he was startled. "Scotty! Don't do anything! Listen. Two Army Green Berets have just filed a class action suit against the President of the United States and you're involved. Hang on!"*

Dr. Gugas gave me the number of their attorney Mark Waple and advised me to call him. I did. The next day he had me flown to his office in McPherson Plaza, a plush professional complex near Fort Bragg in Fayetteville, North Carolina.

"I've been reading a lot about you." This slender mustached young attorney glanced toward a copy of *Soldier of Fortune* on his desk.

---

*Major Mark A. Smith, Commander of a Special Forces Intelligence Unit based in Thailand and his intelligence sergeant, SFC Melvin McIntyre, charged that the current and previous administrations have not done everything possible to bring American POWs home in accordance with the Hostage Act and the U.S. Constitution. The suit, filed September 4, 1985, in the U.S. District Court in Fayetteville, North Carolina, accuses that evidence of live Americans still held captive is beign ignored. (Document 54 - A,B,C,D,E,F,G,H,I,J)

"A lot of bad things, a lot of suspicious things, BUT ...Major Smith and Sergeant McIntyre, my clients...do you know them?"

"No, I don't think so."

"Well, they know you. They were ordered by their General to look into what your recon team was doing in 1981. Would you give me a sworn affidavit telling me the truth about everything? We're suing the President and the U.S. government over this cover-up."

Waple's quiet, sincere manner put me at ease. So although I was jetlag tired, for six or seven hours we went over every detail of the mission and the denials that had followed. Each time I shared something of value with him, he would smile and say "OHHhhh!"

"Everything's falling into place," he smiled with satisfaction. "Now I want you to meet my clients." He called Smith and McIntyre from another room.

How reassuring it was to hear Major Smith, a former POW captured and held in Cambodia, say "We believe you. We know the *Soldier of Fortune* article is disinformation. Junk."

"I told them that purposely," I explained, accustomed to defending myself. "So they'd leave me alone."

"We knew that." He informed me he had been ordered to look into *Operation Grand Eagle* and knew we were involved with ISA. Unaccustomed to so much support, I was flabbergasted. We talked most of the night, then I caught the first jet out the following morning.

One month later, Mr. Waple phoned again asking me to return to his Fayetteville office.

"I'm keeping your affidavit secret," he informed me, "and will file it at the latest moment I dare by law. Do you know what truth serum is?"

"I've heard of it. I know CIA and other intelligence organizations use it."

"Would you be willing to take it?"

"Why not? I've made it through the polygraph and a psychiatric test. I'll submit to anything to prove American prisoners of war were left behind after Vietnam."

25

Yeas and Nays

End of 1985

Many continued their efforts to discourage my quest, but, to my relief, others began listening to what I had to say. Out of the blue I received a phone call from retired army intelligence officer Colonel Earl Hopper, former director of National League of Families and father of a POW. He explained that a friend had given him my phone number, and he wanted to spend some time with me reviewing documents, names, dates, times and places. After we had set a date, he hesitated for a moment, then asked if he could bring a friend. I had a positive feeling about this man, so consented to his request.

A few days later at the appointed time, Colonel Hopper came to my home with his friend, Mrs. Charles (Marian) Shelton, wife of the only POW listed alive by the Reagan administration. Although I had never met her before, unofficially we had been "on the outs" ever since I had pressured her son to abort his plan to go to Laos and search for his father. I was stunned when the Colonel told me who his "friend" was, thinking she would still be angry. But as a plaintiff in the Smith/McIntyre case, she wanted to meet me since she knew they had checked my story and believed me. (Document 55)

For several hours we reviewed what documents were still in my possession. The Colonel was astounded. "Everything jibes!" he remarked, apologizing for speaking out against me. He wrote a letter of retraction on a League letterhead. Mrs. Shelton sent a letter in support of me to Kern County and we began a friendship that continues to this day. They invited me to speak at the Children of POW/MIA Conference in Sacramento in May, 1986. (Document 56 - A,B)

I met with David Taylor in the lobby of the Hyatt Regency, Los Angeles, to tape an interview for BBC. As far as he knew, no one was aware of his itinerary, but the next evening he phoned me from his home in the suburbs of Washington, D.C.

"Scott, guess what happened!" he began in his British accent. When he had landed at Dulles Airport outside of Washington, several drug agents apprehended him and his crew and tried to confiscate all his belongings saying they had been given anonymous information that David Taylor was a drug smuggler.

"But I'm a BBC producer," he protested. They began to read all the papers he had with him. "If you're looking for drugs, why are you looking in my personal notes? Why are you checking my film and cassettes?"

The man in charge became suspicious. "Are you working on a sensitive story involving the U.S. government?" he asked David. Taylor admitted he was working on the POW project.

"Then we have been used to intimidate you." Someone had tried to pressure David through the Drug Enforcement agents. Because he is British, he would have been deported back to England had he been caught on the most minute of drug offenses. Later we learned that undercover law enforcement men observed our whole interview in Los Angeles, several armed with automatic weapons. As David and others began to believe my story was legitimate, certain government personnel became more uneasy.

Taylor also contacted Dr. Gugas about the results of my polygraph. In his soft-spoken voice, the Doctor reported, "After doing over 30,000 polygraph tests in almost 40 years, I can assure you there's no question in my mind at all. I know he's telling the truth." (Document 57)

In spite of my falling out with Vang Pao, my relationship with the Hmong people in California continued. On September 14, 1985, shortly after noon, I met at the intersection of Highway 99 and White Lane in Bakersfield with one of the same Hmong Colonels - Vang Bee who had been involved in the initial planning of *Bohica*. Driving a late model black Cadillac, license number 1JFY256, he had come to ask me to help him get more weapons and medical supplies. He and his companion gave me a list of their needs and brought me up to date saying General Vang Pao was helping the CIA once again. He had also renewed his friendship with former Premier Ky of South Vietnam, living in Orange County to be nearer the Laotian Community

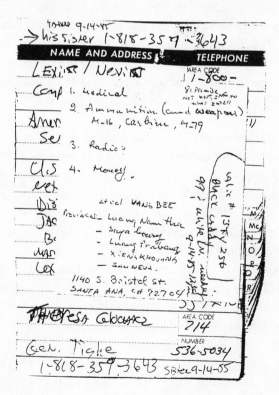

Center. Again the CIA was reneging on their promise to supply arms.
(In August '86, Carl Jenkins, retired CIA man, told me some of Vang
Pao's men had come to him wanting additional weapons in exchange
for continued contraband.)

"What about the POWs?" I asked Vang Pao's Colonel.

He bowed his head. "No come home. Bo Gritz wrong to talk. You
wrong too." It's uncanny the power Vang Pao seems to continue to
have with his people. He gets rich off drug trade while they're down
there fighting and dying.

Knowing I still receive word from Laos once in a great while and
that I am still in contact with some of Vang Pao's people, a Gene Wilson
from Litton's communications/hardware section who was taking inventory of Litton equipment phoned. He'd had a falling out with Gritz,
so called me instead to find out where the radio equipment, missing
since 1981, could be located. We had been instructed to leave the radio
with the Hmongs so the group who stayed behind to monitor the
Mahaxay area until the rescue teams arrived would have contact with
other intelligence personnel who were already set up along the river
in Nong Khai and other various locations. But no rescue teams ever
arrived.

On September 17, 1985, Lieutenant Colonel Kuckowicz of Defense
Intelligence informed me that the government had refused to investigate
the various reports of live POW sightings. I think he hoped I would
forward this on to Mark Waple - which I did - so Waple would know
someone inside DIA knew about the cover-up.

On the morning of September 21, General Eugene Tighe, commanding General of the DIA at the time *Bohica* took place, called to ask
whom I had worked under and the addresses and phone numbers and
codes I had been given. I told him in 1981 I had confirmed with Pat
Hurt and Mike Burns, Colonel John Kennedy and Colonel Robby
Robinson that the mission was legitimate. I also informed him that
I had talked with Hurt and Burns again when I returned. I gave him
the Telex numbers and the code in the Pentagon we used. He confirmed Hurt and Burns were DIA agents in '81, promising to get in
touch with me after further investigation.

When he phoned me again, he was extremely upset. Hurt and Burns did in fact work on the Laotian POW sector, but never informed the General of their activities or their findings. Neither Hurt nor Burns work for DIA any longer. (Before the House Foreign Affairs Committee, Tighe later testified that during his seven years as Defense Intelligence Director, the "human reporting on live Americans had been among the most precise and detailed intelligence he had ever seen," but that no sighting had ever been checked by any official reconnaissance group.)

I phoned General Vang Pao, hoping to discuss the POW controversy. He was very curt with me. "You lied to me."

"General, I felt I had to. The POWs are our people." He repeated how he had tried so often to convince our government to confirm Hmong sightings, but they refused. The CIA lied to him so he refused to work with them until recently. "That's why they used me to get you to do what they wanted," I said.

He agreed but insisted it was wrong for me to misinform him. "We are friends, then you stab me in the back. Never again will we talk or meet." I hated to hear this.

"I understand you gave General Tighe a Hmong tribal ring in San Nua Province in '66," I told him.

"How did you know?" he asked.

"The General phoned me not long ago and mentioned it out of the blue."

"He knows of live POWs," he said in a discouraged tone.

On about the 13th of November, Generals Peroots and Shufelt of the DIA asked Monica Jenson, CBS producer of *60 Minutes* for Mike Wallace, to meet briefly with them. Peroots indicated he was very interested in me and asked for my phone number. She phoned me to see if it was alright with me for them to call me. After hearing of their supportive interest I consented.

At noon on November 16, General Shufelt, deputy commander to three-star Lieutenant General Peroots, the commanding general of DIA, called requesting that I come to Washington immediately to talk with him "off the record" over coffee at an undisclosed location. Again on the 19th, he called to set a date for me to talk with him about the "'81 recon mission we conducted into Laos." I flew to Washington on December 12. While waiting at David Taylor's home in northern Virginia to hear an appointed time and location from Peroots, Colonel Johnson, DIA, phoned my host to tell me General Shufelt could not meet with me. The meeting had been canceled with no specific reason given. I boarded the next plane out and returned home. Once again someone had been pressured to stay away from me and ignore my testimony.

I decided to phone Ann Mills Griffiths, Executive Director of the League of Families, to ask what she was doing about the reports of live POW sightings. She mentioned that through her efforts the bones of several men had been returned to the United States. When I told her what I knew about her dealings with Bobby Schwab in Southeast Asia and her private meetings with Colonel Childress, she became very angry, threatening to destroy any remaining credibility I had.

Colonel Vang Bee recommended I call General Alexander Haig. Colonel Bee felt General Haig was supportive of what Vang Pao did for our government and was hopeful about what he could do for us in the future. I was to ask him why nothing was being done as a result of *Bohica*. I did not follow Vang Bee's advice to make this phone call.

Although Donna had been supportive of me throughout these difficult times, she was becoming very bitter because of my increased but seemingly fruitless involvement. "I thought this thing was over," she said as we relaxed together in front of the fireplace.

"It will be after this trip to talk with Waple," I promised.

"Scott, you keep telling me you're finished, but you're spending in excess of $3,000 a month - nearly all of our income - on phone calls, travel and mail. You spend little time with the children. We never go on outings anymore. And why did Camp Owen get rid of you? Get out of the limelight. Your government doesn't care!"

"Okay. After I come back from my meeting with Waple, that's it," I repeated.

How painful these difficult times must have been for someone as loving and caring as Donna.

26

The Whole Truth

December, 1985

There were other reasons why Donna wasn't happy about my number one priority. Since Dr. Gugas' phone call and my conversations with Waple, Smith and McIntyre, I had completely lost interest in my faith, shoving my Bible on the shelf to collect dust. It's funny about an immature faith. When things are going good, you don't often think about God, but when things go bad, you turn to Him seeking His advice and help. And when He fixes things, you say, "Thanks, goodbye until the next time I need you." God had miraculously kept me alive through my trips to Syria, Lebanon, Israel, Laos, China and Jordan; through my Hawaiian capers; through the whole Southeast Asia episode, letting me do my own thing. His protective hand was always on me. In my blindness I couldn't even acknowledge that fact. What a fool I was.

Besides, the college was not pleased with the publicity I was getting in the papers and on television. They were receiving a lot of negative comments about the extracurricular activities of their "famous" faculty member. It seemed as though the popular attitude toward the POW controversy was, "Let sleeping dogs lie."

Nevertheless, in order to convince my skeptics I had not been trained in, nor responded out of brainwashing techniques, here I was, in Fort Bragg, North Carolina, away from my family again, taking time off work again, to take a sodium amytal test under the administration of Dr. Robert Crummie who often administers such tests for the government. Two Federal court reporters were in the room. David Taylor of BBC, the only civilian person permitted to observe the test, was allowed to video the session for possible use in a future documentary.*

Although I did not know it at the time, the form I was asked to sign was a release in case I died during the test. I was a bit nervous.

"This isn't going to hurt me, is it?" I asked as Dr. Crummie inserted an I.V. needle and taped it to my arm.

"No," he said confidently, "because you are on no other medication. Other medical doctors and a nurse will be on hand." He explained how truth serum blocks out the functioning of the cortex of the brain. Therefore a person cannot stop himself from telling what he knows to be the truth whether he wants to or not. Sodium pentothal is now obsolete in government use, having been replaced by sodium amytal which can be fatal if a person is given too much.

As had taken place with Dr. Gugas and Dr. Hacker, Dr. Crummie had been given a list of questions. I was asked to lie down on a soft couch upholstered with a bold floral print on a dark background. He released a switch on the I.V. tube, and the serum began to flow into my arm. Later the doctor told me this was the largest dose of sodium amytal he had ever administered.

"Tell me your full name," the Dr. asked.

"Scott-t-t...Tracy-y-y...Barnes-s-s..."

"Count backward, please, starting with one hundred."

---

*Publisher's note: A DIA report claimed that this test had been arranged and paid for by David Taylor. The report also claimed that Taylor injected Barnes with water and provided the questions the psychiatrist was to ask. The DIA claims the whole examination was a theatrical device to be used by the BBC for their own gain.

"One hundr-r-r..." That's all I remember. All I know about the rest of the test is what I've seen from the edited portions televised during the 700 Club report and other documentary news specials. I am told I repeated everything I had said during the polygraph test and more, going into intricate detail, naming names, locations, files, numbers, codes, etc.

After I regained consciousness, David Taylor walked me around in the room, past a black leather chair and bookshelves several times, then out a rear door to the worn sidewalk and fresh air. My head hurt. I was nauseated. David was excited about the results.

Mark Waple offered to drive me back to my hotel room outside Fort Bragg. "Here's some paper towels in case you get sick," he said as he helped me into his car.

"Know what?" he asked as we returned to the Holiday Inn where I was staying.

"Uh?" I managed.

"I'll be honest with you. For your welfare, I was hoping you'd flunk. Then I could have let you off the hook, saying the polygraph and the psych tests had been in error."

I sat in the lobby and talked with David Taylor for a brief time. I remember hearing Waple say to me something to the effect, "This is an historic event." Unable to sit up any longer, I excused myself. "I think I'll go lie down. Boy, am I sick!"

"Let me help you." Taking hold of my arm, David helped me to my room.

"I've got to get to the bathroom," I told him. We hurried as fast as I was able, but I vomited all over the bathroom floor, then fell.

David and the others managed to get me to the bed. "Give us the key to your room. We want to check on you every hour on the hour." They were quite concerned because, according to orders, I had received maximum dosage, a rare and dangerous practice. This was done to overcome any possible training I may have had in dealing with brain-washing techniques.

I felt no better the next day. David forced me to continue to drink more water than I wanted. They insisted that I eat. Their prescription evidently helped, because on the third day I started to feel a little better, well enough to fly home.

Donna met me at the Los Angeles airport. Not having known anything about the test until I got home, she was alarmed when she saw my condition. "You're the only one who keeps taking all the polys and the psych tests. Why don't they ask anyone else?"

"I don't know why," I groaned, still in misery. I wasn't myself for several days.

27

The Hearing

January, 1986

As a result of filing my sworn federal affidavit, my name hit the news, opening Pandora's box all over again. Calls and intimidations from news people escalated, but I refused to talk. Lieutenant Commander Frank C. Brown, who had written to me c/o my wife's maiden name in August, 1985, (Document 53) phoned again saying he understood I was to testify at a Senate hearing, but if I did I would be in serious physical trouble. *If I am testifying, it's news to me,* I thought. *He must know something I don't.* I still did not understand why Commander Brown was so interested in me.

Brown sent letters and made phone calls to David Taylor, trying to convince him to kill the story about me he planned to air, insisting I never passed the polygraph test and that the sodium amytal test was a fake.

"ABC confirms he did pass," David rebutted. "And I was there for the truth serum test. I know he didn't lie."

Monica Jensen who has become deeply involved in searching for an answer to the POW controversy casually questioned a psychiatrist, "Is there any chance that people could be so psychopathic they could lie under sodium amytal?"

He replied, "No. There's no way. You simply lose control."

Further proof of the validity of the sodium amytal test came when White House Chief of Staff Donald Regan's office talked to BBC insisting that David meet Regan at the north gate of the White House and give him the original video of the test. David and I had agreed the White House should receive a copy, but Regan's people weren't satisfied. They wanted the original and wanted no one else to have a copy. "...Then you can watch it on TV," David told them and aired a special which other news organizations quickly picked up on. David agreed to keep me abreast of any new happenings as he continued to dig for the truth.

Colonel Hill from Secretary of Defense Casper Weinberger's office called me to ask if I was sure I knew what I was talking about, stressing that he had been an Air Force POW.

"I know that, Colonel," I responded. "I did a bit of checking and understand you were the healthiest POW to return - no scars or marks from beatings or torture. What did you do for them?"

"You Federal Express all your documents to me. IMMEDIATELY," he ordered, ignoring my question. I made copies of my papers and sent them to him.

"These could be very damaging," he said in a phone call after he had examined the documents. "Don't you think it would be wise to let this issue die so our country could get on with other matters?"

"All I want to do is get to the bottom of this," I told him, remembering the American soldiers who had fought for God and their country but were left behind.

"I want to see the results of your tests before I take any action." We talked several times and sent mailgrams. I got the feeling people in higher positions than his were pressuring him to cover-up. Hill admitted during one of our conversations that at one time he worked with the Deception Section, Joint Special Operations Agency of the Department of Defense. Subsequently he was promoted to full bird colonel which I interpreted as "Cover this thing up and you'll get your next promotion."

Waple called to say there was a possibility the Senate was going to hold a hearing on the POW/MIA issue. This news gave me very little encouragement. *This was the wrong committee to deal with the issue! Why the Veterans' Affairs Committee, which is responsible for paying benefits to POW families? Why not the Armed Services Committee or the Full Senate Intelligence Committee?*

I talked to Congressmen Applegate and Solomon. Solomon was adamant. "As an ex-Marine I won't believe any of this," he declared. (Document 58)

Frank Brown was right. I was notified to appear before the Senate Committee on Veterans' Affairs at a hearing "on live sighting reports of Americans still missing in action in Southeast Asia on January 28, 1986, in Washington, D.C. (Document 59) Carefully I read through the names of the Committee members listed on the letterhead: Frank H. Murkowski, Alaska, Chairman; Alan K. Simpson, Wyoming; Strom Thurmond, South Carolina; Robert T. Staffor, Vermont; Arlen Specter, Pennsylvania; Jeremiah Denton, Alabama; Rudy Boschwitz, Minnesota; Alan Cranston, California; Spark M. Matsunaga, Hawaii; Dennis DeConcini, Arizona; George J. Mitchell, Maine; John D. Rockefeller IV, West Virginia. Anthony J. Principi, Chief Counsel/Staff Director; and Jonathan R. Steinberg, Minority Chief Counsel/Staff Director.

This was an encouragement to me and to Donna too. "Finally!" she sighed in relief. "Someone is going to listen to you."

I really don't know who covered the cost of my flight. Smith and McIntyre, Jerry Mooney and Waple met me. (Prior to the hearing, Mark had called and asked me to describe everything I could remember about the coded papers Mac had guarded so carefully. I did. When I arrived in Washington, he introduced me to a Jerry Mooney, former crypto specialist of the National Security Agency, who said, "Scott, I've read your affidavit and can verify everything you said including the Telex your team used in NKP. It was wired directly to Washington. I know, I set it up.")

"You're going to be the biggest witness in this case," Mark said as he drove Mooney and me to the Senate Building. "Don't let anyone badger you."

"Senators don't threaten me," I said. "I've spoken to many senators and congressmen before, and I've been in federal court numerous times." Yet I *was* nervous. For the first time, a government body was going to listen to my testimony.

And I had good reason to be nervous. The room was packed. CIA, DIA, NSC, White House staffers and the world's major media were represented. And when I walked in with Mark and some Special Forces men, there was dead silence. Everyone - military officers, colonels, generals - looked my way. "That's him," I overheard one decorated military man whisper.

Before the actual testimonies began, Senator Murkowski announced that if there was anything of a sensitive or classified nature there would be closed, or secret hearings also. The term "in the vault" was used in reference to these possible secret hearings.

It surprised me that throughout the hearing, aides constantly entered, whispered messages in senators' ears, then left again. Frequently senators would leave and return. I think every senator left the room at least once with the exception of Senator DeConcini. At one point even Senator Murkowski was called out to the White House for some unknown reason; and not another senator, but a congressman chaired the meeting. I guess I expected everyone involved to remain to carefully listen to each testimony.

As Ann Mills Griffiths testified she was convinced there was "no conspiracy or cover-up in the present administration," I couldn't help notice a woman in a tan suit standing on the sidelines. The sign written on a rectangular piece of yellow posterboard and pinned to her lapel read, "ANN GRIFFITHS DOES NOT SPEAK FOR US. FAMILY MEMBERS."

Griffiths stated that the last thing in the world the League needed was a commission to investigate the POW situation because it would give the Vietnamese reason to stall. When questioned by Senator DeConcini about her access to classified government documents, she responded, "The entire Families have considered this at our annual meeting and have again and again supported my continued access to represent their views." (Document 60)

Following the Griffiths testimony, representatives of veterans' organizations were called to give statements: Cooper T. Holt, Executive Director of Veterans' of Foreign Wars, Washington office; Kenneth Stedman, Director of Security and National Foreign Affairs Division, Veterans of Foreign Wars; Paul S. Egan, Deputy Director of National Legislative Commission, American Legion; Harry Sullivan, Deputy Director of Foreign Relations Division, American Legion, Washington, D.C.; and Stephen Edmiston, Deputy National Legislative Director, Disabled American Veterans, Washington, D.C.

Next Major Mark Smith and SFC Melvin McIntyre told of the consequences of their efforts to carry out their orders to gain information about POWs and their abrupt removal from their posts just before an attempt to rescue three prisoners could be made.

Then I was called to testify. "Be careful what you say," Mark Waple warned. "You're under oath, this is being recorded; the world is watching." I took my oath choosing to deliberately emphasize the "under the penalty of perjury" part. (Document 61 - A,B)

As the questioning progressed during my two hour testimony, I began to feel cornered, so I started to name names. I heard someone behind me whisper, "Oh, God, no!" (The videos of the hearing show a very restless Ann Mills Griffiths seated directly behind me.)

In the midst of my testimony, Brian Bonnet entered and whispered in the ear of Murkowski who immediately announced, "Excuse me. I must go to the White House." Not long after his return, he was interrupted again, then announced, "I should advise you that unofficially we have had word that the space shuttle Challenger has blown up, and things do not look very good. I have nothing final on that but have just been advised that shortly after launching, there was an explosion. So if anybody wants to be excused, we will certainly understand." Then he continued to press me for my opinion about what the motivation for scrubbing *Bohica* might have been and who would have been responsible for such a decision. (Document 62 - A,B)

By that time most of the senators and media people had left. The hearing seemed to be over. I struggled with my mixed feelings about ending the hearing, thinking *I'm truly sorry about the seven who have perished, but we've been talking about hundreds who have been missing for years and some who are still alive.*

Asked whether I felt it would be wise for me to have security protection I agreed that it would be, at least until I boarded the plane to go home. Secret Service was instructed to provide protection for me and for Jerry Mooney. Security had been ordered for him because he had been threatened at his hotel just prior to the hearing.

When Mooney, the key communications man who had corroborated our mission, had taken the stand, the U.S. attorney stopped his testimony before he had opportunity to begin, saying that Jerry knew too much secret information to be testifying in an open hearing and that I had been talking about some activities that should only be discussed in secret. He announced further testimony would take place in a secret hearing in two days. I later learned that had Mooney been allowed to testify publicly and name the staff persons who had set up the codes and intercepted messages so the appropriate people never received them, many government officials would have been shaken.

Following the hearing, Secret Service escorted Jerry and me to the car that was to take us to our hotels in northern Virginia, normally a twenty-minute drive. For more than two hours we were driven all over northern Virginia. The driver, a local, made the excuse that he was not familiar with the highways and got lost.

Never having met until Mark introduced us at the airport, Jerry and I spent the time getting acquainted and comparing notes on our knowledge of the *Bohica* operation. We talked further about his relationship with NSA and setting up the codes we used. Again he confirmed the codes I had seen were the crypts he had set up in NKP.

Everything was finally fitting into place.

As we talked, the agent in front would innocently interject inquiries such as, "What hotel did you say?"..."Tell me a little more."..."I'm not too familiar with that area." Both Jerry and I knew he was lying.

Jerry said, "You know, Scott, after I deciphered the last coded message and left, I thought those guys would be rescued. I've been back home, innocently enjoying a life of retirement on my Montana ranch until recently."

Our conversation ended abruptly when the automobile in which we were riding stopped in front of the Holiday Inn in Arlington. "Here you are, Scott," the agent in front announced. "Jerry, we'll drop you off next, then return with security for both of you."

28

The Plumbers

January 28, 1986

Disappointed that I was unable to complete my entire testimony, yet grateful to be away from the stares and the pressure, I hurried to my hotel room to relax. Upon removing my necktie and unbuttoning my shirt collar, I sat down in the chair between the bed and the phone stand and phoned Smith and McIntyre to tell them about the "ride" Jerry and I had just experienced. They had been anxious to hear from me, wondering why I hadn't called sooner.

I also phoned David Taylor in response to a message he had left for me at the hotel desk. Our conversation was interrupted by a knock on my door. "David, wait a minute. Someone's at my door."

"Yes?" I queried in response to the knock.

"Plumbers. Is your plumbing still leaking?" I told David goodbye and hung up the phone.

"I didn't know it was broken," I said as the door I had shut was pushed open. I hadn't taken time to fasten the night latch. Apparently the "plumbers" had a master key.

Two men wearing dress suits under heavy overcoats entered without invitation. *Plumbers? Dressed like this??*

As I stood, one asked, "In the bathtub, wasn't it?" and walked to the bathroom. The other mumbled something I couldn't quite understand, then staring at me added, "You sure do a lot of talking." *Watergate?* I wondered. *This can't be real!*

"I think you guys had better leave," I ordered, then reached for the phone and dialed hotel security. Both guys split.

Hotel security had received no report of leaky plumbing, so I quickly called Mark Waple who was staying at the Marriott just across the street. "McIntyre's on his way. *Lock your door!*"

It seemed like only moments had passed before McIntyre knocked at my door and identified himself. Jerry Mooney was receiving additional phone calls threatening him if he testified in secret. It was obvious there was a security leak. No one except Waple and the Secret Service agent who dropped Mooney off knew where he was staying.

Secret Service never did arrive to protect either one of us, so for our safety Waple, Smith, and McIntyre decided Jerry and I should be shifted from place to place.

I couldn't get to sleep in my new location. Finally, in the middle of the night, I decided, *That's it!*, sneaked out and caught the first plane available - to Texas, then California. Through Waple I notified the Senate Committee I would not testify at the secret hearing. Either my story would be told full blown and out in the open with full protection or not at all. (Document 63)

The Senate Committee insisted secret or nothing. Smith, McIntyre, Mooney, and Congressional Medal of Honor winner Lieutenant Colonel Robert Howard, who had been Smith's superior officer, and the most highly decorated Vietnam veteran, testified in secret, but I did not.

Murkowski's aide Brian Bonnet called me to apologize for all the threats. He admitted the Committee would have liked to have brought charges against me if I had perjured myself, but rather than having evidence against me, the information was against high government officials they would not touch.

"I testified under oath," I told him. "If I'm lying, you'd better charge me with perjury. My affidavit, the tests I've passed, all the corroborating evidence - *Don't you want to get to the bottom of this?* General Robby Robinson committed suicide, Jerry Daniels (alias Michael J. Baldwin) died strangely by carbon monoxide poisoning. Colonel Kennedy, said to be an alcoholic, retired and moved. Why don't you subpoena everyone who was involved that is still alive, give them poly and psych and truth serum tests? Have a full-blown investigation. Get us all there, looking at each other face to face under oath. Then require the Justice Department and an independent investigative council to investigate. Then charge those who lie with perjury. ...Subpoena Lieutenant Colonel Paul Mather, government agents Jim Tully and William Wharton, and Colonel Mike Eiland. Subpoena CIA agent Daniel Arnold and helicopter pilot Robert Moberg and CIA man Gene Wilson. Subpoena CIA man John Stein and CIA Director William Casey, National Security's Dick Childress, Admiral Tuttle, General Vang Pao, Admiral Paulson - and Colonel North and Richard Armitage.

It seemed he gulped, saying that the issue did not warrant action so drastic.

"I think it does," I insisted. "American lives are at stake. We're talking about a major security problem. When the President took office, he declared the prisoner of war issue would be the highest national priority."

"What do you want me to do? Go down there and start a war?" Bonnet retorted. He said he would check with the CIA and asked if I would return to testify at my own expense.

"I can't afford it," I told him in all honesty. There were more hearings, but I did not go.

29

Bobby Garwood

During the January '86 hearing, Senator Murkowski had asked me, "You further state that you had never heard of any of these individuals before; and my question is, can the committee assume that you had never heard of Robert Garwood, though in 1979 his return from Southeast Asia received a good deal of press, and did you not know at that time that Mr. Garwood was charged with collaborating against the government?"

The Garwood story had come out in '79 at the time I was working on the Hell's Angels case, and his trial and subsequent court martial didn't start until '81 while I was in Southeast Asia. Knowing very little about POWs at the time, all I had heard about Bobby Garwood was what Colonel Mather told me when I met with him at the U.S. Embassy in Bangkok, June, 1981.

About the time the Smith/McIntyre law suit was filed, Bobby Garwood called me at my home to see if we could get together for a talk, but we did not meet until he came to Washington for the Senate hearings. He met me for lunch at the Holiday Inn where I was staying. We must have talked for three hours.

Bobby wouldn't touch a drink, so I bought him coffee and a club sandwich. It hurt me to watch him pick at his food with his fingers, painfully recalling his experiences as a POW.

A very subdued, quiet man, he asked me what I knew about his case and I shared with him what had been said at the '81 Embassy meeting. Garwood told me that in 1965, he was captured near Da Nang while sitting in a jeep smoking a cigarette, thinking about having only eleven days left before he would be going home. From that time on he was transported continuously from one location to another until after fourteen years of imprisonment he was released in '79, six years after the war had ended.

In '67, the communists had removed him and two others from the camp and had given them what they called a "liberation ceremony" but did not release him. Regularly he asked his captors why he had not been released along with the other two and was told it had not been a favorable time.

He said that in '77, he had snuck a note identifying himself as an American prisoner to a visiting businessman from Finland. One particular day there had been a lot of military movement going on. He related how hopeful he'd been, seeing a lot of communist troops surrounding the camp as if they'd had word there was going to be an attack, but nothing happened.

He was especially interested in what I thought Paul Mather had meant when he said in June '81, "we" had known about him in '77. Together we came to the conclusion that the note did reach the proper authorities at the U.S. Embassy, but they did nothing about it.

Garwood talked about the numerous POWs he had seen. Some who had died long after the war had ended, he personally helped bury. (He has publicly announced, *"I want it known for a fact that I was not and am not the last American live prisoner of war in Vietnam."*) But because upon his return he was convicted as a collaborator by the U.S., no one will listen to him. He has never been debriefed. I felt so sorry for that man, a victim of circumstances he did not create.

He admitted that he had collaborated. "I am not trying to make excuses for what I did," he told me, "but I was only a nineteen-year-old kid, tortured and starved, wanting to come home." I wondered if anybody else might not have done the same thing.

He explained the military's system of training in the '60's. Only officers were trained about interrogation and debriefing in case of capture. Enlisted men were not, so he was not prepared for what had happened to him. He had only done what the communists had tortured him into doing. He described the horrible treatment he had received as a prisoner and how he felt our government had set him up so his information about other existing POWs would not be believed. (Mark Smith later confirmed in his testimony that much of the training given enlisted men while they were stateside was of little help to them when they were captured.)

Bobby can still speak Vietnamese fluently. He won't talk to his family, won't even see them because he is so ashamed of his conviction. He pumps gas and does minor automotive repairs in northern Virginia for a living. It was the only job he could get because of who he now is known to be. Garwood still keeps in touch with his high school sweetheart. She was told he had been killed in action, so she went on with her life and finally married someone else.

While we talked I thought about his family. In November, 1985, thinking he should know what Mather had told me, I had talked by phone with Bobby's father who lives in Indiana to find out how to get in touch with Bobby. Garwood's family wishes he would let them see him to tell him that they still love him and are proud of his service and sacrifice on behalf of his country. But he will not, he's too ashamed. Bobby Garwood is deeply disturbed by his 14 years in captivity and by his country's rejection of him. He will not sleep on a bed, because he feels guilty knowing fellow Americans still sleep on the ground in Laos and Cambodia.

While I was in Washington for the Senate hearings, Brian Bonnet had confronted me during a recess, saying anyone would know about the Garwood case. I suggested that he talk to several people to see if that was correct. So following the hearing he stopped several people in the hallway, asking if they had ever heard of Bobby Garwood. I overheard one young woman respond, "Isn't he a senator?" and another agree, "Yes. I believe he's from Vermont."

I turned to Brian. "There's your proof." Bonnet, in my opinion, was one of the most uncaring persons involved with the Senate hearings. It seemed to me he could not care less about the suffering of the POWs and their families. He only wanted to prove the government was right, no matter what.

30

My Little Blue Book

As Mark Waple photocopied every page of my well-worn blue address book (Document 64), I asked him why the book was so important and why Ted Koppel had been so anxious to get his hands on it. Mark explained it was because the notes and information in it - dates, times, names, addresses and brief records of conversations - could be used as legitimate court evidence.

While I was on the mission, I carried the book with me everywhere I went, except into Laos. Each time I met someone I thought might be significant or each time I received a pertinent message, I would say, "Hang on just a minute...How do you spell that?...Repeat what you just said...Would you write that down for me?"

My little blue book includes Robert Schwab's Georgia phone number and his number in Thailand, and the phone numbers at the Nana Hotel for Norman Shimmel, contact person who works with the Laotian underground. On one page are the names of the three female agents I met at the Nana during my first trip. In their own handwriting are some of the names of people who helped the CIA and worked with General Vang Pao's resistance forces smuggling drugs with the CIA out of the Golden Triangle. Also listed are Lieutenant Colonel Kham Ouane and where he's living in Thailand; Patrick Khamvongsa, Laotian Royal Air Force officer who defected; Lieutenant Colonel Socum and the address where we stayed on the border. The name of Thai agent Sunthorn Chirayos of whom I have pictures is on the back cover.

This important little book includes a record of government and military officials who have contacted me regarding *Bohica* and brief summaries of our conversations. It includes all kinds of information which would make sense only to someone who has been involved with the mission and the controversy that followed.

The name of Ed Dietel* who works on disinformation with the CIA is listed along with Dave Gilbreath who helped spread disinformation about remains of POWs being shipped to families. Stanley Sporkin of the CIA (Chief Counsel for the recent Iranian/Contra deal) is recorded. Sporkin said I had a secrecy agreement with the CIA and that ABC was going to kill my story, which they did. Later he tried to say he'd made a mistake in making such a statement.

In the address book is recorded the notes from a conversation with FBI agent Conrad Banner from FBI headquarters Identification Division, Washington, D.C., who said, "We helped cover up files and conduct disinformation against you." Larry Hornsby, Division Director of Expunging, FBI, Washington headquarters, said they were given false information on my fingerprints and a phony FBI file regarding a threat against President Reagan.

*   *   *   *   *

SOMEONE WAS WORRIED ABOUT INFORMATION JERRY MOONEY MAY HAVE GIVEN ME

Recorded in my address book is a phone call February 25, 1986, 2:20 p.m. E.S.T., from Carolyn Johnson from National Security Agency, (301) 688-6524. She'd heard I rode in a car around Virginia for two hours discussing alleged secret NSA communications with their former analyst Jerry Mooney. I informed her that we had not discussed

---

*Dietel's name was brought up at the Iran/Contra hearings as a principal CIA attorney making the deal.

anything secret. She said that NSA security personnel and possibly FBI agents would be in touch with me.

Later I received a phone call from a gentleman identifying himself only as Mike, (301) 688-6704, who said he was looking into my conversation with former NSA crypto Jerry Mooney. I told him I had no information.

Five minutes later I received a call from (301) 688-6824. Other NSA agents were inquiring. Apparently the pressure was on.

* * * * *

RICHARD ARMITAGE'S NAME BEGINS TO SURFACE

February 24, 1986, 4:40 p.m. E.S.T., I talked to Assistant Secretary of Defense Richard Armitage on direct line, (202) 695-4351, about his alleged involvement in a house of prostitution for senior military officers, intelligence agents, and informants in Southeast Asia; about his dealing with Jerry Daniels, Carl Jenkins, Daniel Arnold; about his work with Vang Pao and drug laundering; and about how Ambassador Abramowitz had uncovered some of this information.

On February 28, 8:30 a.m., I had a phone conversation with Dave Hall, assistant special agent in charge of the Inspector General's office, Washington, D.C., field office, Department of Defense, (202) 746-0256. We discussed Richard Armitage's connection with drugs and prostitution in Southeast Asia and his continued involvement with Mr. O'Rourke of Trinidad running guns. The agent said he had heard of a possible connection, but more important, former Ambassador Phil Habib was also involved. A Major General had written a note to Intelligence revealing Armitage's and Habib's alleged involvement in prostitution in a Da Nang house of prostitution and in drug laundering out of Indochina. He said that Habib had also helped Armitage smuggle money out of Southeast Asia to the Philippines and to Sidney, Australia, using Air America, Van Pao connections and secret airlines.

(At 9:30 a.m. that same day I spoke to White House Press Secretary Del Patrovsky about the POW controversy.)

March 16 I received a message to call (213) 645-4600 and ask for Room 451. David Hall, investigator for Defense Criminal Investigative Service, answered the phone and wanted to discuss information I may have had about arms and drug dealings going on while I was on *Operation Grand Eagle*.

March 20, 4:01 p.m., I talked again with Armitage and with Jim Kelly in Armitage's office who informed me that if I continued to investigate or discuss with ANYBODY Armitage's involvement, it could become quite unhealthy for me. I also talked with Lieutenant Colonel Schneider, Steven Johnson of the State Department, and Admiral Poindexter in charge of National Security Affairs in the White House in regard to POWs. At first they denied any existed, but Poindexter did admit *Grand Eagle* may have been part of ISA, but that ISA no longer existed. (Someone in Poindexter's office informed me that at one time one of his deputies on the National Security Council had tried to work to release American prisoners of war but found it was futile. This deputy was identified as Lieutenant Colonel Oliver North.)

April 4, 1:15, Colonel Schneider called to tell me he had spoken to Colonel Howard Hill who had just met with Colonel Dick Childress at the White House National Security Council regarding my report of a POW sighting. Colonel Hill had stated firmly that information could be divulged only to families of POW/MIAs.

Agent Gutenshon, State Department Intelligence, (202) 647-2084, wanted to discuss my knowledge of Moberg's involvement with Armitage and Arnold, Carl Jenkins and with drug smuggling. Agent Joel Henderson, (202) 647-7732, phoned from Diplomatic Intelligence to ask me not to cooperate with any other agencies and to contact him if I was contacted by anybody regarding the Armitage mess.

* * * * *

SOMEONE TAMPERED WITH MY GOVERNMENT FILES

In 1982 when I had decided I had better get a copy of my files (FOIA) before it was too late, the lady at CIA Personnel who handled my contact file, Marian Braxton, said she had been told to send most of my files through Systems 57 and 59, because "files on contract operatives such as yourself were to be deleted both on computer and in manual records as though you had never existed." I phoned Max Dex, Larry Straderman, John Stein and numerous others within the Agency, but to no avail. (Document 9)

Had I gone to the Embassy to be debriefed following my trip into Laos with Jerry Daniels, I honestly believe in my heart I would have turned up as a murder victim of some drug dealer on a side street in Bangkok. Someone did not expect nor want me to leave that country. My deleted files were a safety precaution.

When these and hundreds of other messages and bits of information are gathered together, more and more my situation and the *Bohica* mission become parts of a tangled mystery of crime and coverup.

31

More Nays

January, 1986

Many key people worked very hard trying to discredit my name and the names of others who have reported there are POWs still in captivity in Southeast Asia. David Taylor in his investigations questioned Daniel Arnold about the film I had mailed to him from NKP in 1981, and was told that it never arrived and that Arnold was working in the White House on national security matters at the time. Waple was told the photos were accidentally destroyed during processing. OVER 400 PHOTOGRAPHS TAKEN WITH VARIOUS CAMERAS, VARIOUS TYPES OF FILM AND FILM SETTING, AND NOT ONE WAS GOOD?

In January of '86 as people arrived for the Senate Veterans' Affairs hearing, Colonel Howard Hill who works for Casper Weinberger, Secretary of Defense, and Ann Mills Griffiths stood in the hallway outside the Senate room distributing photo copies of the cartoon drawing of me that had appeared in *Soldier of Fortune* and telling everyone who would listen that I should not be believed. I was a liar and a flake. Before long a sergeant of arms informed them this kind of action was forbidden at Senate hearings, so Griffiths and Hill walked inside, talked to some officials and were seated.

When Lieutenant Colonel Paul Mather was called to testify at the subsequent "vault" hearing, he did admit that when he and I met in June of '81 at the U.S. Embassy, Bangkok, to his best recollection I had given him something which could have been a code book, but it had been so long ago his memory was a bit fuzzy about details. He failed to take with him to the Senate any of the documents or notes I had given him but did say he would provide these documents if the committee requested him to.*

"What does that tell you?" I asked Brian Bonnet when he called to tell me about Mather's testimony.

"I don't know what to believe," he replied. "Both the CIA and DIA deny everything, but their information conflicts." I wondered why the Senators didn't prod into Mather's remarks a little further or subpoena the others I had previously named.

After I had gone home from the hearings, a lady telephoned who would only identify herself as someone from Director of National Security Council Admiral Poindexter's office. I decided to remain silent.

"...The Admiral is Dick Childress' boss," she said as though she thought that would clarify the matter.

"AHhh...," I said and paused again. She told me the Admiral wanted any information I could give him about POWs, about the mission and who I had met in the Mideast in '83. If I would relate that information to her, she would pass it on to the Admiral. I refused, thinking she was not from Poindexter's office at all. I believe if the call were legitimate it would have been handled much differently.

I continued to be harassed by Frank C. Brown, convinced he must be working for the government, perhaps with the DIA. David Taylor also received a letter and phone calls. Even Susan Katz who was investigating the POW controversy, including my involvement, for the

---

*David Taylor, in checking on this information one year later, learned the documents and code book Mather had agreed to give to the committee had never been received and the transcripts from this hearing had never been typed. Approval for such release comes through Armitage's office.

Washington Times received a call from Brown trying to persuade her to change her mind.

After I finally filed a complaint against Brown with the Naval Investigative Service, I phoned the Service office as a follow up. The guy with whom I talked told me I wouldn't have to worry about Brown any more because he had been transferred to Subic Bay. But Brown's transfer didn't stop his harassment. I reported this and the Navy sent Senior Agent John Hopec from the Naval Investigative Service at China Lake Weapons Center to interview me at my home. "This is out of my hands," he told me. "Check with D.C." I phoned Commander Foley at the offices of the Secretary of the Navy, describing Brown's threats and the responses to my complaints. He assured me there would be an investigation.

Both Taylor and I received letters postmarked Manilla from Brown. He even wrote to Daring Books telling the publisher, Dennis Bartow, that he had thoroughly investigated me. He stated I was "a liar of the first order" and he "was nothing short of amazed" to find out Dennis was now supporting me. In a return letter Bartow challenged Brown, "Come up with evidence." (Refer to Document 65 - A,B,C,D) Brown's response was that because Dennis had already issued a letter recanting the references to me in the *"Heroes"* book he doubted if Dennis would change his mind again. Therefore, Brown felt Dennis would not accept the evidence he had against me.

David Taylor informed Brown's commander at Subic Bay that BBC would sue if Brown persisted. This action ended the harassment for David and me. In November Dennis Bartow did receive a letter from Brown expressing his concern about his name appearing in this book. Apparently someone informed him he was to be "portrayed as an 'intelligence agent' of the United States". He stated that should his name "appear in any context" in this book he will file suit against Dennis, as the publisher. Brown further added there would be a "follow-up letter from my attorney in the very near future." As of August 20, 1987 this letter from the attorney has not been received by Dennis.

In my conversations with Richard Armitage, I had been told I was hurting his delicate negotiations with the communists in Hanoi, hurting the POW issue instead of helping, that I didn't know what I was talking about. I responded that I felt no progress had been made through his negotiations and the only thing I ever saw him do with the communists was socialize. Ann Mills Griffiths of the League of Families was upset with me because she didn't want the League to hear what I was saying, accusing me of causing dissension among the Family members. Lieutenant Colonel Schneider, spokesman for public information at the Pentagon, and Colonel Howard Hill also from the Pentagon, were in conversation with me, insisting that I keep quiet. (Document 66)

More and more the name of Richard Armitage came to my attention as someone who was definitely involved with *Bohica*-connected dealings which were not to be known to the public. In addition to the many phone calls about Armitage recorded in my blue address book, there was one from a Mark McMahon, former Virginia detective now with the State Department Diplomatic Security Intelligence Sector. McMahon phoned me several times, wanting to talk with me.

"No reason for you to come out here," I told him. "We've talked sufficiently on the phone." He insisted that his boss wanted him to talk with me personally about Richard Armitage's involvement not only in the POW situation and in a Vietnamese prostitution ring, but in allegedly removing, along with the CIA, large amounts of funds from Indochina to various overseas banking entities. Finally I consented to see him, telling him to let me know when he would arrive.

The day before we met he called from Los Angeles to arrange a luncheon meeting. I told him to meet me at the college where I taught.

On February 27, 1986, after I had finished teaching a class and was in the dean's office, I saw a car pull up in front of the main building. As one of the men stepped out of the car to put on his jacket, I could see that he wore a gun.

I was just coming down the hallway as he entered the reception center. "I'm here to see Scott Barnes," he told the receptionist.

"Hi!" I greeted him before she could ask who he was. He began to introduce himself, then realizing the receptionist was listening, cut off his introduction.

"Let's go next door," he suggested. I agreed.

The hostess in the Chinese restaurant next to the college led McMahon, another agent who had accompanied him and me to a table, but Mark didn't like the location. "We prefer to sit alone in the back," he said politely. "We'll pay extra if necessary."

When the hostess left us, he introduced me to his companion, Anthony Jones. A quiet man, Jones apparently knew little about why we were meeting and was there primarily as security.

Mark ordered three Heineken beers and offered to buy lunch for Jones and me. We never did eat.

Before he would say anything, he asked to see my credentials, then questioned me about my personal background. Briefly he mentioned my testimony at the Senate hearings the previous month, then explained that he had been the senior agent in charge of the investigation into Armitage's involvement with drug laundering in Indochina, arms dealing with the Contras and a gambling ring in northern Virginia involving two Vietnamese girls. One of the girls was Patrick O'Rourke's wife.*

"Was the evidence there?" I asked McMahon about the information he shared with me.

"Of course. Armitage should have been indicted then." Eyewitnesses had revealed he had been involved and bank accounts and transfers had been discovered. He showed me some of the documents related to the case. But because Armitage was dealing with Hanoi at the time, trying to negotiate for the release of POWs and because of the pressures of the POW issue, McMahon was ordered to back off to protect him. "That's why we're here to see you, to find out what you know about this situation and what you've told others.

He wanted to talk more about some possible misdeeds that were said to have taken place in '81 at the U.S. Embassy in Thailand and about a DEA agent, Thuy, who had leaked information. We discussed

---

*O'Rourke, former CIA agent hiding in Trinidad, called me. He had been married and divorced from a Vietnamese girl who with her sister and Armitage ran a house of prostitution during the war and funneled money out of Indochina after the war. When she and her sister were arrested on gambling charges in Arlington, allegedly Armitage used his influence to help them out.

Mather and Moberg, Arnold, Jenkins and Eiland. But he was most interested in finding out what I knew about Armitage, calling him "the Wrestler."

I commented, "Nearly every time you see this man he's drinking with communists. I know he's a 'diplomat,' but isn't this a little bit strange?"

He refused to comment, saying there was so much I didn't understand about how the government must operate, it was not for him to judge such activities. He said Secretary of State Schultz called the shots.

McMahon mentioned Dave Hall, Defense Criminal Investigative Service agent, who had investigated another angle to the Armitage case involving Colonel Jack Frost of South Africa in a CIA arms deal. I informed him that Hall and I had discussed Colonel Frost's involvement in the shipment of arms to South Africa, but it was in fact an official CIA-sanctioned operation. U.S. Attorney Theodore Greenburg and a Stephen Trott kept running interference on the Armitage deal, but Jenkins, Arnold, Secord and Singlaub were also involved.

Not wanting to discuss that situation any further, McMahon hinted that too much talk about the POW issue at this time could be very damaging. Looking at me through his glasses he advised, "You're not going to make any progress with your cause until we have finished our investigation." He stood up and left without a handshake or a farewell.

Finished teaching for the day, I got in my car and drove home. The following afternoon I spoke with Eva Cam in Mike Armcost's office, (202) 647-2471, then with Habib's daughter, (202) 647-3178, about the Armitage investigation and the visit from McMahon. Both felt Dave Hall and Agent McMahon should not have shared information with me because the case was classified and supposedly had long been closed. (Document 67 - A,B,C)

Two or three days later McMahon phoned again, wanting additional information about an employee at the Embassy. I told him I had no reason to talk to him further.

In March, 1986, in Federal Court, Los Angeles, I filed a RICO*
suit (Civil Action No. 85-3719) in Washington, D.C., accusing the
CIA of becoming like the Mafia, dealing in drugs, assasinations,
murders, counterinsurgencies, and lying to Congress. (Document 68
- A,B,C) This was the first time anyone had ever sued the CIA under
the RICO statute. The U.S. attorneys successfully pleaded dismissal
on the grounds that the CIA is an organization immune from suit,
and the suit was filed under the wrong jurisdiciton; but they requested
the evidence I had. The judge refused their request. I then filed in
U.S. District Court, Washington, D.C. In a sworn affadavit, John Stein
admitted he was former director of clandestine operations.

Bob McKewen, congressman from Ohio and guest congressman
on the Senate Veterans' Affairs Committee, was making derogatory
remarks about me in response to the publicity I had received. Using
a phony name I telephoned his office as a private investigator and
said I was looking into the Scott Barnes case and wanted to tape a
conversation with him. He wouldn't talk to me; but I was able to involve a man named John, the staff person who answered the phone,
in a brief conversation during which he shared his opinion of Bo.

"Bo's living in the '60s," he admitted. "A lot of his medals are
"suspect medals."

"What are you going to do about Barnes?" I asked John.

He said that Mr. Barnes should be discredited, therefore they planned
to publicize disinformation about him. I thanked him, hung up and
immediately called him back.

"This is Scott Barnes," I said when John answered the phone. He
recognized my voice as being his previous caller. I told him I had
taped everything he had said.

He sputtered, "You can get into trouble for taping me."

"Fine!" I retorted. "Have your Congressman's attorneys file a complaint. I'd love to go to court and reveal what you've just told me."

In August of 1986, I learned McKewen was informing the Senate
Committee and various other people that I had called him using a

---

*Racketeering Influence of a Corrupt Organization.

phony name. But in order to cover his own bases his office did call back and apologize. I've left it at that.

The college finally had had enough of my publicity through media exposure. Due to this pressure I resigned my position. (Document 69) Having just been made recipient of the 1986 California Law Enforcement Officers Scholarship award, I registered as a law student with the California State Bar and enrolled in a school of law.*

I continued to work as a private investigator, doing investigative work on narcotic cases involving U.S. Embassy personnel. Deciding it would be wise to again carry a gun, I applied with the county for a gun permit. It was at this time Lieutenant Fred Ross from Kern County Sheriff's Department phoned to notify me my firearms permit would be denied because of my current stand on the POW issue and the discrediting story in *Soldier of Fortune*, adding that my private investigator's license might also be challenged. I immediately applied for and received a state permit.

---

*A letter from the university reads: "July 26, 1986. Pursuant to your response we confirm your acceptance of our scholarship offer for the next four years of formal law study. Please find enclosed the enrollment agreement..." The complete letter and the name of the school have been omitted for their protection. The card which confirms Scott's registration as a law student reads: "November 26, 1986. The Committee of Bar Examiners, State of California. State Bar. Your registration as a law student has been approved. The Committee of Bar Examiners regrets the delay in responding, but with our backlog... Your law student card will be issued to you shortly. If you need any numbers, currently use your Social Security number because that will be yor law registration number."

32

More Yeas

Late summer, 1986

Soon after my interchange with McKewen's office, Mark Waple called. "Scott? Are you sitting down? I've got good news for you."

I was more than ready for some good news. Through his diligent researching, he was now able to identify the two Caucasians MJB (Jerry Daniels) and I had observed in the Mahaxay prison camp. They have now been verified as American POWs.

"Who told you this?" I was really excited. But Mark could only reveal to me that a military intelligence officer who had been heavily involved in planning the *Grand Eagle* mission had verified my report. His affidavit will be filed with the courts when the time is right and should not now be made public. All I know now is this person's affidavit confirmed my affidavit "right down to the apostrophe." He drew a map identical to the one I had drawn for the hearing; he knows the names of the two men I watched being prodded by guards across the prison complex; and he has said that if Daniels and I had waited a while longer we probably would have seen several more American POWs enter the camp returning from a work detail.

This same witness identified the code that Jerry Mooney and I had discussed during our Virginia ride as a top secret crypto code used for only a short period of time in 1981.

"I know I couldn't decipher it," I told Mark. Then he told me that while I was under the influence of the truth serum I had revealed much more than my conscious mind remembered about the code.

This same witness confirmed that the *Bohica* team had been given a Department of Energy Telex number because the Soviets rarely have reason to monitor the communications of DoE. (David Taylor in his research also found out the Telex number we had used was a direct link to D.C. communications headquarters in '81.)

"We WILL HAVE our day in court, Scott," Mark concluded triumphantly, but suggested it would be wise for me to submit to a second polygraph so the government couldn't say the first was a staged media event.

I went to Los Angeles and again was tested by Dr. Chris Gugas. The results confirmed everything was still the same. This was a great encouragement to me, but the beginning of a stressful experience for the doctor.

He received an anonymous phone call threatening that the forthcoming promotion of his son, a Lieutenant Colonel in Air Force SAC (Strategic Air Command), would be denied if the doctor revealed the results of my latest polygraph.

David Taylor had me flown to Washington to meet a man named Mike Hearn, one of Jerry Daniels' best friends who had worked for the State Department at the Bangkok Embassy but was currently working in an office on Capitol Hill. Mike's brother was working for DEA and also at the embassy while I was there. At Mike's request I told him all I knew about MJB. He dropped his head. "That sure sounds like Jerry," he acknowledged and related how in October of '81 Jerry had disappeared then reappeared several weeks later. He recalled that before his disappearance, Jerry spent a lot of time jogging and getting in good physical condition, but refused to explain why. After Jerry's mysterious death, Mike requested a full investigation; but in spite of the fact that he was an Embassy employee his request was refused. It was painful for this man to talk about his good friend Daniels.

I can't help but wonder if Daniels, a CIA career man, hadn't squealed too loudly about our orders to liquidate rather than rescue the Americans we had seen when he returned to Bangkok after our mission. Perhaps someone had decided to quiet him. He was intimately involved in the secret drug laundering team which included Armitage, Jenkins, Vang Pao, Arnold, Moberg, Secord, Singlaub and many others. "Now he's dead," Jenkins told me in a recent phone conversation, "and dead people don't talk."

In an interview with Daniels' mother, David Taylor asked, "Tell me about your son." Mrs. Daniels replied that all she knew was he was with the CIA and involved in secret missions.

Media coverage of my story came to life once again. Shortly after the Senate hearings, Gary Lane, Washington, D.C. correspondent for CBN News, became interested in our mission and the sightings of POWs. He knew the results of my truth tests and interviews, called to his attention through various negative media reports. Wondering why so many people were going out of their way to discredit me, he phoned to talk with me several times. Convinced there was a deliberate effort to discredit me - especially by Bo and Childress - he personally interviewed Chris Gugas and talked to Brian Bonnet and concluded that the only "evidence" the government now holds is the *Soldier of Fortune* article. Lane flew to my home in mid-April to film a segment with me to be used in a two-part series about the POW issue of '86, reporting what the secular news would not. In an on-camera interview Colonel Howard Hill claimed someone told him a journalist had conducted my truth serum test, stating that the test is "just one tool. We look at the totality of a situation." If he had "looked at the totality" accurately and thoroughly, he would have known the very qualified Dr. Crummie administered the test. This series was aired in May of '86. The newsshows, ABC's *20/20*, CBS's *60 Minutes*, AP/UPI wire stories, spots on all the major network affiliate stations, *Time* magazine all began to produce evidence that live POWs still remained in captivity and question the reasons for such an injustice.

On June 19, 1986, my 32nd birthday, Federal Court Judge Boyle ruled to uphold the Smith/McIntyre case. "You're my primary witness now, Scott," Attorney Waple told me. By authority of the judge, Smith and McIntyre were removed from the case as plaintiffs and made material witnesses like myself on the basis that neither was a relative of a POW. The families of the POWs are now the plaintiffs.

The June issue of *Navy Times* included an article "The Truth About Lie Detectors - Despite the Controversy, the Pentagon is relying on them more than ever." The cover picture is of John R. Schwartz, professional polygraph examiner and faculty instructor at the Department of Defense Polygraph Institute, a man who received training from Dr. Gugas. The article explains why the poly is so reliable and why the government uses and relies on it. In the famous Arthur Walker spy trial, the government relied heavily on the polygraph. Why has my testimony not been received?

Eugene "Red" McDaniel, ex-Navy Captain who experienced extreme torture by the Vietnamese during the '60s and '70s, now the president of the American Defense Institute, wrote a general letter dated July 25, 1986, stating that in government bureaucracy there has been a "massive effort to discredit" Scott Barnes, that I have "paid a very high price" and deserve a chance to prove myself trustworthy. (Document 70) The Institute letterhead lists the names of its prestigious directors and advisors, which include Senator Jeremiah Denton, Major General Elliott Roosevelt, and General William C. Westmoreland. Many other generals, congressmen and senators are members of this institute. McDaniel believed all living prisoners of war were home until just a couple of years ago and has been pressing for their release ever since.

On August 5, 1986, H. Ross Perot, Texas billionaire appointed by President Reagan to investigate the POW situation, called me to get more information about my involvement with the BOHICA mission. He planned to be talking again with Vice President Bush and wanted to discuss this with him. Subsequently he was appointed to the Tighe Commission as was Dr. Gugas.

Shortly after Perot's meeting with Bush, in a call from the Vice President's office at the White House, Colonel Terry Mattke, USMC, insisted I back off the issue because I was going against national security and causing considerable problems. Mattke, (202) 395-4223, is a personal aide to the Vice President and works directly with him on military affairs.

"You work with the Vice President?" I asked Mattke, although I knew he did. I was told the Vice President and Colonel Mattke had already examined my testimony, had discussed it with Mr. Perot, and had decided that if they could prove additional confirmation about POW reports, they would take action at higher levels. I was angry. Additional confirmation, additional time lost. "Don't you want those guys back?"

I was reminded for the umpteenth time that the current administration had neither started the Vietnamese war nor had they ended it. The Carter administration had declared dead all who had not been returned with the exception of Colonel Charles Shelton. As far as Mattke was concerned, Smith and McIntyre had perjured themselves and should be shot as traitors and that "Mr. Big Man out of Texas" didn't run the west wing of the White House or the National Security Council.

"What about me?" I asked. He admitted neither he nor the government could disprove my testimony or my involvement, but they would continue to use the *Soldier of Fortune* article as sufficient evidence in order to consider my testimony less than correct. He added that as a major witness in a lawsuit against the President, I had been labeled as being against my country; and on that basis, they hoped my report would be dismissed. I was also told that Vice President Bush had given Mattke explicit instructions to take any action necessary for keeping the *Bohica* mission out of the picture, away from public eye.

I asked Mattke if he was keeping the Vice President informed of all facets of the issue. Receiving no satisfactory reply, I sent a mailgram (Document 71) to the Vice President saying I was convinced he was not receiving all the facts of my testimony, that I believed his advisors were preventing the right people from receiving the total information, knowing perfectly well that Colonels Mattke and North frequently discussed their activities - they were close friends, having known each other for some time and both Marine Lieutenant Colonels working on specials projects in the White House - but did not keep their supervisors fully informed.

I called David Waller, assistant to the President on national security affairs and special counselor (202) 456-2674 to confirm the fact that Colonel Mattke was working with the Vice President on the *Bohica* mission. (I learned of Waller when I had received a letter from him in response to letters I had written to Fred Felding, White House counsel who has since resigned.) (Document 72)

Mr. Perot, a fine gentleman, contacted me again to advise me to quietly back off the issue and refuse to talk about it with anyone. The Commission would now carry the ball on my behalf. (Document 73 - A,B)

Captain Mead and Colonel Alexander, (402) 294-4459, asked me for information regarding Blackbird SR-71 spy photos taken on our mission. I refused to comment. They left a call-back number, (402) 294-4459, if I decided I wanted to discuss this in detail.

The government did ask the judge to reconsider dismissal of the lawsuit against the President, but the judge refused, stating that there was more than enough evidence to proceed. The Executive Branch was worried enough to threaten to appeal, using their own hand-picked attorneys - I am told Theodore Greenberg is one - to go even to the Supreme Court if necessary to get the case dismissed. (Document 74 - A,B) I would think that if the judge hadn't found the evidence believable or sufficient, or if there were nothing to hide, the case would have been thrown out of court. The suit now awaits a trial date.

Dr. Matthew Meselson, who was the first to tell me about Jerry Daniels' death, called me this past spring (1987) to again deliver bad tidings. General Robinson, a colonel at the time *Bohica* took place and one of the persons I had originally called to verify the mission, had allegedly committed suicide. Robinson was the second main figure connected with the mission to die mysteriously. I immediately began to make inquiries and found that the title of Robinson's position at the time of his death was Executive Deputy Director for Nuclear, Chemical and Biological Warfare.

Within 24 hours after my inquiries, several from the Department of Defense called me to find out why I was making these inquiries. I explained, "I knew him in '81 during *Operation Grand Eagle*."

"What period of '81?"

"October-November."

"He was at that time Commander of the Pine Bluff Arsenal for Chemical and Biological Warfare where he worked with the National Security Agency on nerve gas problems."

I called the CID (Criminal Investigative Division) and talked to Lieutenant Colonel Robert Flatkey at Bailey's Crossroad, Virginia, (202) 756-1430, who did the investigation of Robinson's death. "Most of the report is secret," I was told. "It is an inconclusive report, having to do with nerve gas and suicide." Allegedly, in the early morning of the 14th of January, 1985, Robinson got out of bed, went down to his basement, took an army .45 automatic pistol and blew the top of his head off. No note, no indication that anything was wrong.

His death was a complete mystery to everyone, even his wife. The death was ruled as suspicious suicide. The *Lexington Kentuckian* reported "General Commits Suicide Under Cloud of Mystery." (Document 75)

Colonel McNabb of the Department of Defense, (202) 697-7589, a personal friend of the General and in charge of any inquiries regarding the General's death, called and shared that during '81 Robinson was working on something very sensitive with a chemical warfare problem in Indochina. I mentioned Jerry Daniels' death. This upset the Colonel. Jerry Daniels had been filtering information back to the unit McNabb and Robinson were working with. Sergeant Bender of the Fairfax Police Department (703) 385-1470 told me, "We began the investigation as a homicide, but it ended up reported as a suicide. This switch was not because of us."

To David Taylor, Dr. Meselson, an expert in chemical and
biological warfare, asked, "Now why do you think Scott had to take
atropine to Vang Pao's people?" Atropine is an antidote for nerve
agent GB. The month following my mysterious errand into Cambodia the United Nations' yellow rain team found yellow rain samples
in that area. It is my understanding that *Soldier of Fortune* personnel were the first to discover it. Why are so many refugees having
unidentifiable sicknesses and dying? Are the communists using this
agent? Has the U.S. experimented with chemical warfare in Southeast
Asia? Could I have been used to deliver yellow rain samples into
Cambodia?

Daniel Arnold has now admitted to David Taylor that he was working in an advisory capacity in the White House during the time *Operation Grand Eagle* took place but had no part in the mission. Arnold
said he did receive information from me. He admitted he was a friend
of Vang Pao. Having been registered as a foreign agent with the
government of Thailand with an annual salary of $50,000, Arnold
retired from the CIA in '79 to set up a private business called Tashkant
Associates and worked with Secord, Shackley and others. It was during this conversation with Taylor that he admitted receiving our
messages but denied receiving the film I had sent and asked to be
kept out of the whole controversy.

Arnold has admitted to me that FBI agents had contacted him regarding the mission and my involvement, but he had persuaded them
it was classified.

Following the sudden death of his son, a very grievous experience
for him, Arnold left the Agency, closed his private business because
it was getting too well-known within the National Security Council
and moved from Vienna, Virginia, to New Hope, Pennsylvania.
...Does anybody ever REALLY quit dealing with the Agency? Why
did the Senate refuse to subpoena such a key witness?

On August 12, Senators Frank Murkowski and Strom Thurmond
declared the Veterans' Affairs hearings officially closed. (Document
76) Shortly after that, Marian Shelton sent me a CIA report (Document 77) under FOIA that talks about the possibility of one hundred

or more American POWs still being held in the Mahaxay region alone. This report confirms where Daniels and I had gone, that there definitely are prisoners, that our reports were received by the CIA. Things were really starting to fall into place!

Just prior to my going to Ohio to begin work on this book, in a conversation with Brian Bonnet, I was told that because they can find nothing else to go on, Armitage, Colonel Hill and Ann Mills Griffiths continue to base all their opposition against me on the Spring '83 *Soldier of Fortune* smear, knowing full well this was deliberate disinformation. Griffiths calls the article an "amazing expose."

While in Ohio in August, 1986, NBC phoned wanting to know why I had given BBC an exclusive interview. Using foul four-letter words, the representative chided me for cooperating with a foreign network. I reminded him that several years ago I had often tried to give my story to the American media, but I had been told consistently the POW issue was not one to be reckoned with.

Then Jim Coyne, who had provided information for the '83 *SOF* article, called me while I was staying at Pastor Bartow's home in Canton and admitted that his story was used as disinformation but that he didn't want to risk the bad name that might go along with making a public retraction. To get his reaction, I said, "Nobody believes that magazine anyway." (Dennis Bartow and another individual happened to be present and listened to my side of this conversation).

He agreed, saying that if it was a *Time* or *Newsweek* article I should have had a problem. But since it was *SOF*, everyone should have understood the nature of the article. Then he admitted, "Unfortunately the government does believe it. That article is the only thing they have against you. They don't want anyone to believe you because they know you're right." He agreed the Senate Hearings were a complete joke. "You testified and what did they do? Nothing!"

"Tell me what you know about my wife," Coyne requested. Through our conversation I learned that Thuy, whose name had been mentioned at the Embassy on my first trip to Thailand, was Coyne's wife. It seems she recently had received a phone call asking about her relationship with Moberg, Eiland, Arnold, Armitage and others.

"No." I refused. "Not now that I know who she is," I said, and I suddenly realized that was the real reason he had called me.

Allegedly she had been leaking intelligence information to her husband about our various operations. I suspect she was actually at the Embassy when I first met Moberg. A couple of Vietnamese ladies had been working nearby. Although Moberg never talked to them, I noticed he did make significant eye contact with one. I now know that Thuy and Moberg, Thuy and Eiland were best of friends while working together at the Embassy. She was transferred back to the States a couple of years after *Operation Grand Eagle* and is now in charge of the Southeast Asia Intelligence Unit for the Drug Enforcement Administration in Washington, D.C., and allegedly she frequently feeds the Drug Enforcement Administration disinformation on narcotics trafficking. Having intimate knowledge of Southeast Asian narcotics trafficking for the CIA, she has been able to continue to provide them with sufficient information so that the DEA could never get them.

Reading the August 19, 1986, issue of *The Wall Street Journal* was a healing experience for me. An article written by Bill Paul reported that one of General Tighe's former top assistants confirmed the General's belief that POWs are still alive in Southeast Asia, stating that since 1978, the Pentagon has had "hard evidence" of Americans still imprisoned. Although the identity of this officer cannot be revealed because he is still on active duty, this is the first that any of Tighe's staff has been willing to back him up. The article, long overdue, spells out in intricate detail that the Reagan administration did launch a daring mission in 1981. (Document 78) As time goes on, more and more missing pieces to my story and the tragic POW situation are being discovered, but still Americans remain in captivity.

33

Much Time For Thought

August, 1986

Many positive breakthroughs and supportive experiences occurred during the week in August I was in Ohio: The *Wall Street* article (Refer to Document 78), an updated POW-MIA FACT BOOK report (Refer to Document 77), my phone converstion with Jim Coyne during which I learned that Thuy was his wife and received additional confirmation that the *Soldier of Fortune* article was a deliberate attempt to discredit me.

A man and woman from Malvern, a little town south of Canton, Ohio, visited me to share their endorsement of what I was trying to accomplish. The man, a Vietnam veteran, and member of the Vietnam Veterans of America said, "As long as someone is still left behind, part of me remains as well." They gave me a copy of the resolution they had presented to their church body for endorsement. (Document 79)

The prayers of Pastor Bartow and the warmth I received from the people of Pastor Bartow's church really touched my heart and revitalized my faith in God. I was among a group of people who believed in me.

Although I talked to Donna almost daily, I wished she and the children could have been there to experience with me the love and acceptance and encouragement I had found. Both Donna and I were relieved, certain that my book would finally tell my story so my long impassioned quest to be listened to, the government harassment, the negative reactions of the media would now end and our dream of being a normal family would finally become a reality.

My emotions ran high on the flight home. I was anxious to be with my family once again. Spiritual renewal, emotions beginning to heal, my mind at ease, it was time to find new employment and begin life all over again. I could hardly wait to be home sitting with Donna in front of the fireplace sharing all that had taken place while I was away.

When that long-awaited moment finally came, I described to her everything that had taken place inside me from the moment I had first arrived at Pastor Bartow's home. My faith in God at low ebb, wondering how that week would turn out, I was driven by Dennis Bartow along with his wife Patrice and their 3 sons from the airport to his parents' home where I was to stay. With the pastor and his wife out of town and not expected to return until the day after my arrival, I found myself totally alone in a town I had never been in before and an extremely quiet and serene new environment.

I spent a long time in front of the picture window which looked out on a little lake surrounded by trees, the greenery and the moist air resembling some of the peaceful spots of beauty in Laos. It occurred to me, *These people don't know me from Adam, yet although no one is around they've opened their home to me.* Not only was this a step of faith and trust, it was a depth of Christian love not often seen.

Donna and I savored our new opportunities to talk and read the Bible together. Our relationship restored, it was time for me to look for employment. Utopia didn't last long. Bills continued to pour in, financial pressure increased and tension crept back into our marriage.

Government officials continued to phone me at all hours seeking information I might have about undercurrents of possible illegal dealings at the time of *Operation Grand Eagle.* We had hoped, perhaps unrealistically, this kind of invasion into our family life was over.

Billy Graham's movie producer asked to meet with me wanting to know more about the POW issue. A friend of a POW family, he felt a personal concern. Since I had spoken at several POW-related meetings many POW family members called to ask what the two men I had seen in the Laotian prison camp looked like, hoping one of them might have been their loved one.

Determined to be a better father to my two children, I scraped up enough money to take them on an outing to Marineland. When we returned home, the house was empty. Donna and most of our belongings were gone. The following day Donna and I again argued. She decided we needed a separation.

I agreed. "This is something that will probably follow me to my grave. Mine is definitely not a normal situation." Donna took the children and left.

My two-mile walk to town to assist my brother in his daily business activities gave me much time for thought. For a couple of days I had tried riding a bike but hadn't liked pedaling up the steep hill on my way home, so I resorted to walking, especially enjoying the coolness of the flat section by the river bottom where I usually jogged.

Away from the constant interruptions of phone calls, the hour to hour-and-a-half walk to and from work provided me opportunity to assess my situation. Although I am still quite young, I'd worked long and hard to get ahead and provide a comfortable life. Suddenly everything I treasured most was gone.

I felt I'd lost every friend I had, with the exception of one person I will call M.A.J. who continuously prods me to trust in God and to look at the problems of others in order to keep from feeling sorry for myself. For a while I was in despair. For days when I entered my dark empty home, Donna and the kids gone, rooms nearly empty, little food to eat, the stack of bills piling higher and higher, I began to wonder if life was worth living. For the first time in my life loneliness caught up with me. I am grateful my having no transportation to work forced me to get away from the house and gave me time

to assess objectively "What's happening here?" Otherwise I might
have just sat at home and pulled myself deeper and deeper into a dark
pit of depression.

I realized that I'm still pro-CIA and still a member of several
prestigious intelligence organizations. I love God and my country;
I have nothing against this country. Why would my government harass
me? I thought about the suffering Donna has been inflicted with and
ache over the hurt and inconveniences she and the children have had
to experience over my problems. I wondered what the future holds
for my kids.

As I walked, I had time to look at the beauty of the world, time
to discover where I'm at with God and why I am where I am. Turning to God, I heard the reassuring words, "I will never leave thee
nor forsake thee." I knew that, yet as with most Christians, I still
have times of doubt and ask, "But, God, where are you? I'm not getting any younger. I want to raise my children, to be around them more."

But I do see that God's hand has been in all that happened to me.
So many have been killed, yet I still live. My long walks along the
banks of the river twice a day have truly been walks with God. In
spite of the difficult times I've experienced these past months, the
spiritual revitalization which began while I stayed at Pastor Bartow's
continues to grow.

I thank God for M.A.J. and for Marian Shelton who, even though
she lives far away, is now my closest friend and most loyal supporter;
for new friends like Dr. Gugas, Ross Perot, David Taylor, Congressman
Hendon and Red McDaniel. What a joy to hear the voice of one of
these fine people on the other end of the phone once in awhile instead of a bill collector or a government official. Often they call just
to see how I am doing and to remind me they are praying for me and
for the men we left behind.

One major problem continues to dominate my thoughts, something
I will probably wrestle with for the rest of my life. I wonder about
those two men. Many times I see them in my mind and wish we had
returned and tried to bring them to freedom. I review the mission
step by step, wondering what I would have done differently had I known

more of the implications. If someone else had done what I did, had seen what I saw, had come home and reported what I've reported, how would I have reacted? I began to feel grateful I did go, knowing had I heard such a report from someone else, I would have wanted to go see for myself.

Yet I do feel responsible for leaving them behind. The tug to return which I felt as Daniels and I reached the Thai side of the Mekong returns often. I was serious when I told Senators I would go right back.

I believe government officials knew all along that Bo Gritz, as gung ho as he was to rescue the POWs, would push aside all government orders to reach them. That's probably why they left him stateside.

I ponder the new information which hints at the possibility of the camp I saw being a detainment camp for smugglers. Had we gone back, would we have rescued a bunch of smugglers? It hurts me to think that what was to be a POW recon mission to set the stage for a future rescue may have become the beginning of an expose of secret drug transactions.

I wonder what my future holds. One of my close friends recently asked, "Scott, if you had to do the whole thing over again and you knew it would come out the same, would you do it?" I've thought about that. Too many POWs have died unnecessarily, but we know some are still there and alive. Have the sacrifices and the subsequent losses which have occurred been worth it? I don't know. Would they want to be rescued knowing their coming home might destroy lots of other people? Bobby Garwood told me recently, "Scott, if I had known that I would have to deal with all this resentment and animosity, I would have stayed. I don't want to cause problems."

Bohica is something I'll never get over. Every time I get a call from someone saying, "That could have been my loved one. Why couldn't you have brought him home?" I feel bad. Those two men were somebody's son, somebody's brother, somebody's husband or father. I'll always feel bad.

Yet my trust in God and the prayers and encouragement of my friends continue to see me through. It's very depressing to wake up every morning to loneliness, emptiness and bills, and wonder, is there going to be another phone call?...will I find happiness and peace of mind today?...but I know I must continue to put my faith in God and affirm, "Okay, it's another day and it's going to be tough. But we're going to make it." I can do it. It's exciting to step out in faith, then watch as the fruits of that faith come to life.

Dr. Chris Gugas questioning Scott during the first polygraph test.

Polygraph instrument.

Peter Jennings reporting on the Rewald case.

Reporter for ABC interviewing Scott regarding the Rewald case.

Prison in Hawaii where Rewald was held.

General Eugene Tighe.

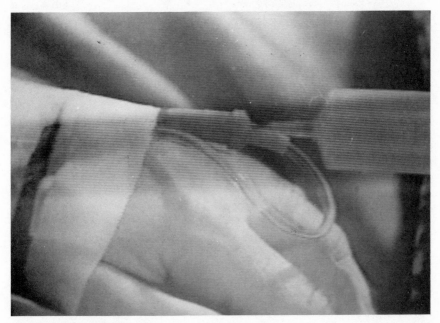

Sodium amytal injection.

Dr. Crummie examining Scott after sodium amytal has taken effect.

David Taylor guiding Scott as he begins to "walk off" the effects of the sodium amytal.

Scott being sworn in at the Senate Veterans' Affairs Committee hearing.

Scott during his testimony. An uncomfortable Ann Mills Griffiths in the background.

Scott referring to his blue address book for information.

Ann Mills Griffiths toasting with a Vietnamese official in Hanoi. Richard Armitage in the background.

Gary Lane, CBN, interviewing Scott at his California home.

Left to right: Dennis W. Bartow, publisher; Scott Barnes; Patrice Bartow.

Left to right: Scott Barnes talks to Lou Maglio on Morning Exchange, a Cleveland-based daily talk show.

Epilogue

One of the major reasons Scott Barnes will never be able to "get over" the experiences of the last five or six years is, of course, his memory of the two men he and Jerry Daniels photographed left behind in Laos and the impact and sacrifice this experience has caused. But there is another reason as well. Certain people in our government will not allow him to forget. Although he has been warned time and time again to keep his mouth shut and has been told "I don't know you...Forget this ever happened," he continues to receive calls and visitors from official governmental divisions pressing him to reveal names and information about issues he does not even want to be involved with.

On January 3, 1987, Scott received a phone call from Mike Figpan from the U.S. government office of Personnel Management Investigations, (619) 293-6170. Figpan wanted to visit and discuss various cases in connection with General Vang Pao. While with Scott, Figpan informed him someone in the government had issued an all States order that Scott Barnes was never again to be employed in any government-related job, the main source of Scott's income. (Document 80 - A,B)

When Scott related this to Ross Perot, he found it hard to believe anyone in government would do such a thing, but upon checking, found not only was it true but Figpan had lied about which branch of the government he had represented.

Within the following days, several present and former key government officials talked with Scott about the Iran/Contra affair, seeking any information he might have that would shed light on this case.

On January 28, 1987, Scott received a call from his brother Brian. Two U.S. Federal agents had entered his brother's place of business looking for Scott. Special Sr. Agent Bill Vizzard and Keith Dunkel, Federal Badge #1593, wanted to talk to him about arms smuggling from Indochina to Central America with Lieutenant Colonel Bo Gritz during the time of the mission and about CIA-Vang Pao connections. This investigation had already led to the arrest of David Scott Weekly, who was said to have been a former member of a POW rescue team. These agents believed Scott Barnes had first-hand knowledge and promised to be in touch with him.

January 29, these two U.S. agents drove into Kernville in a vehicle with license number 1G25547 and served Scott with a subpoena to U.S. Federal Court in Oklahoma City to testify in a secret grand jury hearing in regard to the alleged arms dealings.

"Remember me?" Dunkel asked. Scott told him he did not. "You and I worked together on the Hell's Angels case about ten years ago. Remember Jeff Rome?"

"Vaguely."

"He worked on the CIA Rewald case with you a couple of years ago. He's now in Vegas. I'm out of the Fresno office." He discussed with Scott many aspects of the upcoming case and possible connections with personnel in the Executive Branch.

That same day U.S. attorney Stephen Korotash called from the Federal Courthouse, Oklahoma City, to inform Scott that since he had no means of transportation, on February 4, U.S. Marshals would escort Scott to the airport and he would be flown to Oklahoma City. Korotash warned, "If you do not show up, U.S. Federal Marshals

will arrest you." (Refer to Document 12) From the day of his subpoena, government people kept in constant contact with him - phoning, stopping by, to make sure he did not skip out.

On January 30, 1987, U.S. Federal Supervising Marshal Mike Nelson
from Fresno, California, called regarding what would be expected
of him in the case. Having referred Scott back to the U.S. Attorney,
Scott spoke to Korotash once again. Basically he was told "This is
a secret criminal investigation into shipment of arms and explosives.
I am not at liberty to discuss this any further. You will be asked questions of the Federal Grand Jury in secret. If you do not appear at
9:30 a.m. on Thursday, February 5, 1987, U.S. Marshals will then
be ordered by a Federal Judge to pick you up."

Scott spoke again to Nelson, (209) 487-5205, on February 3 to ask
what the current status of his appearance was since he had not received
definite arrangements about a pick up time.

"Mr. Barnes," the Marshal responded, "we have information that
you now have a new Toyota pickup truck registered in your name.
In fact, we understand while under surveillance you have been seen
driving several vehicles in town these past several days. We are not
coming to get you, but if you do not appear at 9:30 a.m., February
5, the U.S. attorney has instructed us to arrest you and put you in
custody."

"Why didn't you call me to arrange transportation the other day
when you said you would?" Scott pressed him.

The Marshal's explanation: "I was too busy. But if you do not appear, a material witness warrant will be issued for your arrest." Scott
tried to contact the U.S. attorney in Oklahoma City, left messages
asking him to return his calls, but never received a word from him.

Expecting to be arrested, Scott was taken by surprise when he was
informed by the Marshal the trial date had been rescheduled for April
8, 1987, and they had mistakenly identified Scott as the owner of a
new truck his brother had recently purchased.

"But my brother's new truck is a Datsun, not a Toyota," Scott informed him, finding it difficult to believe such an error could be made
by professionals.

"We neglected to notice the first name when we checked the information out on the computer. Boy, you and your brother sure do look alike!"

"...And you're Federal investigators???" The hearing was canceled.

Soon David Taylor warned Scott that Frank Panessa, senior inspector for DEA Internal Security from the Office of Responsibility, would be in touch with him. Having met with Panessa for a couple of hours and feeling that he was legit, Taylor encouraged Scott to talk with him. A meeting was set up for Tuesday, April 7, 1987. Panessa and Bonneville, his associate, met Scott at the airport, drove him to a supposedly secured building in the area where they talked for nearly three hours. (Scott has since learned that the room in which they met was bugged.) This meeting with such a key governmental official, which Scott believed would be the breakthrough he had been seeking for so many years, he now feels was another set-up.

Where can he be heard? Whom can he trust? Where can an American citizen turn for protection and credibility when his government persists in attempts to destroy him? Should Scott Barnes just give up and live with the haunting memories of *Bohica*?

How will the American people respond to his story? To the POW disgrace? How will *Bohica* end?

In conclusion to this book and my involvement, I wish foremost to thank M.A.J. for everything; you'll truly be in my heart and part of my life always. To those men I left behind, I'm deeply sorry!

"Forget Me Not
For I Live
For Thee to be Free."

Scott Barnes

Index

LIST OF DOCUMENTS IN DEDICATION

LIST OF DOCUMENTS IN TEXT

LIST OF DOCUMENTS IN APPENDIX

1. Memorandum for the Secretary of Defense 8-10-79
2. Letter to Cyrus Vance 8-17-79
3. Letter from Cyrus Vance 9-17-79
4. UPI White House aid reportedly probed by FBI 10-15-87
5. Tighe report on American POWs & MIAs 10-15-86
6. MIA/POW Symposium Pamphlet 11-8-86
7. News article: Speakers press for action
8. News article: MIA Speakers say U.S. believes problem is insurmountable
9. A. Department of Justice letter 11-24-82
   B. Department of Treasury letter 12-9-82
   C. Department of Justice Letter 11-8-84
   D. Fingerprints 10-26-84
   E. Department of Justice letter 10-23-84
   F. CIA letter 4-8-86
   G. CIA letter 3-16-86
   H. CIA letter and explanation of exemptions 2-28-87
10. Scott's résumé
11. Scott's Diplomas & Certificates
    A. El Camino College
    B. Drug Enforcement Administration
    C. Miramar College
    D. Drug Enforcement Administration
    E. South Bayu Regional Reserve Academy
    F. San Diego Sheriff's Department
    G. Powers Security Training School
    H. Office of Civil Defense
    I. City of Long Beach
    J. Civil Defense & Disaster Corps.
    K. ''   ''   ''   ''   ''
    L. ''   ''   ''   ''   ''
    M. Staff College Department of Defense
    N. State of California—Department of Justice
    O. California Security Training School
    P. San Diego County Sheriff's Department
    Q. The Commmission on Peace Officers Standards & Training
12. Subpoena to testify before Grand Jury 2-5-87
13. Letter of Recommendation - David Taylor—2-27-87

U-56,245/DB-4

10 AUG 1979

MEMORANDUM FOR THE SECRETARY OF DEFENSE

SUBJECT: Prompt entry into the United States, of a Vietnamese refugee
reporting American Prisoners of War in Vietnam as late as
1978 - ACTION MEMORANDUM

A Vietnamese refugee, ░░░░░░░░░░ who is presently in a Vietnamese
refugee camp in Indonesia, has reported that he was captured in 1971 while
serving as an ARVN soldier, held in various Vietnamese prison camps, and
just prior to his release was detained in a camp from December 1977 to
July 1978 with 49 Americans.

If the substance of ░░░░░░░░ information is true, then its importance
goes without saying. However, if ░░░░░░ is not telling the truth -- if
for some reason it is a fabrication -- it raises cruel false hopes for the
families of those men still missing in Southeast Asia.

There are some difficulties with ░░░░░░ coming to this country in that
he made material misstatement of facts during his application for entry into
the United States. Additionally, during his initial interviews, he denied
to State Department officials any knowledge of U.S. prisoners or having had
any military service. Although initiatives have been taken with State
Department to have ░░░░░░ brought to this country for thorough interrogation, his status remains as "ineligible" at this time.

As reported, ░░░░░░ story of capture and confinement with Americans is
plausible. His report agrees in some instances with confirmed information
and yet there are some important discrepancies.

I feel there is an obligation on the U.S. Government to make every effort to
confirm or deny ░░░░░░ report and that this can best be done through
interrogating him in this country.

Recommend you sign the enclosed letter requesting Mr. Vance's assistance
in this matter.

SIGNED

Enclosure

EUGENE F. TIGHE, JR.
Lieutenant General, USAF
Director

Coordination:

OASD/ISA Brig Gen TC Pinckney, USAF

Prepared by Mr. CF Trowbridge, Jr., x25928

CFTrowbridge:bp:3 Aug 79:DIA/DB-4H:25928:WPE

OSD Record Copy   DIA CAO Comeback
Signer's Copy   DIA File Copy

I FORM 343 (2-73) OFFICIAL FILE COPY   (Previous Editions Obsolete)

THE SECRETARY OF DEFENSE
WASHINGTON, D.C. 20301

AUG 17 1979

Honorable Cyrus Vance
Secretary of State
Washington, D.C. 20520

Dear Cy:

I have received a report of a Vietnamese refugee in
Indonesia who claims to have been detained in the northern
part of Vietnam with 49 American prisoners of war as late
as July 1978. This former ARVN soldier, ██████████████
██████, has been interviewed and relates a consistent and
plausible story, although there are some significant discrepancies.

If his story is true, it provides important information, and if it is not it cruelly raises false hope for
the families of those still missing in Southeast Asia. I
therefore believe there is an obligation on the part of the
U.S. Government to make every effort to confirm or deny
███████████ report.

However, I understand that there are apparently some
difficulties associated with ███████████ entry into this
country--he is reported to have made material misstatements
of fact to U.S. immigration officials during his processing
for entry. Although approaches have been made to the State
Department concerning the desirability of interrogating ██
██████ in this country, his status continues to be categorized
by State as ineligible.

Could you help?

Sincerely,

EXHIBIT 9, P. 2 of 3 (9B)

THE SECRETARY OF STATE
WASHINGTON

RECEIVED IN H/S   SEP 1 8 1979

September 17, 1979

Dear Harold:

Thank you for bringing to my attention the case of
Nguyen Dac Giang, the Vietnamese refugee who claimed to
have information about US prisoners of war in Vietnam. I
share fully your desire to check the veracity of Mr. Giang's
story, and to this end our staff in Indonesia would welcome a
visit by Defense Department officials as soon as possible.
We are fully prepared to cooperate in helping you determine,
as quickly as possible, the accuracy of Mr. Giang's statement.

In view of the decision of the Immigration and Natu-
ralization Service not to admit Mr. Giang to the United States,
you might wish to consider approaching the Commissioner of
Immigration to have the decision changed. For the moment,
however, I believe the necessary interviews could be conducted
in Indonesia, with the advantage that officials who previously
interviewed Mr. Giang would be available.

Whatever venue is finally arranged for further questioning of Mr. Giang, you have our full support in your efforts.

With warm regards,

Sincerely,

The Honorable
Harold Brown,
    Secretary of Defense.

EXHIBIT 9, P. 3 of 3 (9C)

4

S B Union Sun
Mar 22, 87

White House aide reportedly probed by FBI

United Press International

WASHINGTON — The FBI is reportedly investigating allegations that a White House aide offered former Rep. John LeBoutillier, R-N.Y., $40,000 a month to discredit a former congressman who had accused the administration of concealing evidence about American prisoners of war in Southeast Asia.

Seven POW activists said LeBoutillier told them he was offered the money in late 1983 by Richard Childress, a National Security Council official in charge of Asian affairs.

According to the activists, LeBoutillier said that in return for the money, he was asked to assail Republican William Hendon, who had just alleged that the Pentagon was covering up information about POWs in Vietnam and Laos.

The activists said the incident occurred in November 1983, when Hendon was considering running for his old House seat in North Carolina. Four of the POW activists said they were interviewed individually by FBI agents last week about their conversations with LeBoutillier, who served in Congress from 1980 to 1982.

Both Childress and LeBoutillier denied the activists' charges, although LeBoutillier did say Childress pressured him to attack Hendon.

But Childress, an Army colonel who has worked at the NSC since 1981, denied he sought to smear Hendon.

LeBoutillier told a reporter that he felt pressured by Childress to discredit Hendon at the time but denied that the White House aide offered him money.

He said it was Childress's promise of Drug Enforcement Agency credentials, which would let his group travel freely in Thailand while looking for American POWs in Laos, that convinced him to discredit Hendon.

The credentials were never given.

After being pressured by Childress, witnesses said, LeBoutillier told a group of family members of U.S. servicemen missing in Vietnam that Hendon had endangered the lives of missing Americans by revealing classified information.

He also said Hendon, a former political ally, was motivated not by genuine concern but by personal and professional ambitions, some of those present said.

THE TIGHE REPORT ON AMERICAN POW's AND MIA's

HEARING AND MARKUP

BEFORE THE

SUBCOMMITTEE ON ASIAN AND PACIFIC AFFAIRS

OF THE

COMMITTEE ON FOREIGN AFFAIRS HOUSE OF REPRESENTATIVES

NINETY-NINTH CONGRESS

SECOND SESSION

ON

H. Con. Res. 129

OCTOBER 15, 1986

Printed for the use of the Committee on Foreign Affairs

U.S. GOVERNMENT PRINTING OFFICE

67-473   WASHINGTON : 1987

CONTENTS

WITNESSES

(III)

COMMITTEE ON FOREIGN AFFAIRS

DANTE B. FASCELL, Florida, *Chairman*

LEE H. HAMILTON, Indiana
GUS YATRON, Pennsylvania
STEPHEN J. SOLARZ, New York
DON BONKER, Washington
GERRY E. STUDDS, Massachusetts
DAN MICA, Florida
MICHAEL D. BARNES, Maryland
HOWARD WOLPE, Michigan
GEO. W. CROCKETT, JR., Michigan
SAM GEJDENSON, Connecticut
MERVYN M. DYMALLY, California
TOM LANTOS, California
PETER H. KOSTMAYER, Pennsylvania
ROBERT G. TORRICELLI, New Jersey
LAWRENCE J. SMITH, Florida
HOWARD L. BERMAN, California
HARRY REID, Nevada
MEL LEVINE, California
EDWARD F. FEIGHAN, Ohio
TED WEISS, New York
GARY L. ACKERMAN, New York
BUDDY MacKAY, Florida
MORRIS K. UDALL, Arizona
ROBERT GARCIA, New York

WILLIAM S. BROOMFIELD, Michigan
BENJAMIN A. GILMAN, New York
ROBERT J. LAGOMARSINO, California
JIM LEACH, Iowa
TOBY ROTH, Wisconsin
OLYMPIA J. SNOWE, Maine
HENRY J. HYDE, Illinois
GERALD B.H. SOLOMON, New York
DOUG BEREUTER, Nebraska
MARK D. SILJANDER, Michigan
ED ZSCHAU, California
ROBERT K. DORNAN, California
CHRISTOPHER H. SMITH, New Jersey
CONNIE MACK, Florida
MICHAEL DeWINE, Ohio
DAN BURTON, Indiana
JOHN McCAIN, Arizona

JOHN J. BRADY, Jr., *Chief of Staff*
MARY T. BOYLE, *Staff Assistant*

SUBCOMMITTEE ON ASIAN AND PACIFIC AFFAIRS

STEPHEN J. SOLARZ, New York, *Chairman*

MERVYN M. DYMALLY, California
ROBERT G. TORRICELLI, New Jersey
MORRIS K. UDALL, Arizona
MICHAEL D. BARNES, Maryland
SAM GEJDENSON, Connecticut

JIM LEACH, Iowa
TOBY ROTH, Wisconsin
GERALD B.H. SOLOMON, New York
DOUG BEREUTER, Nebraska

STANLEY ROTH *Subcommittee Staff Director*
CYNTHIA D. SPRUNGER, *Minority Staff Consultant*
RICHARD BUSH, *Subcommittee Staff Consultant*
DAWN CALABIA, *Subcommittee Staff Consultant*

THE TIGHE REPORT ON AMERICAN POW'S AND MIA'S

WEDNESDAY, OCTOBER 5, 1986

House of Representatives,
Committee on Foreign Affairs,
Subcommittee on Asian and Pacific Affairs,
Washington, DC.

The subcommittee met, in open markup session at 12 noon, in room 2257, Rayburn House Office Building, Hon. Stephen J. Solarz (chairman of the subcommittee) presiding.

Mr. SOLARZ. The subcommittee will come to order.

The Subcommittee on Asian and Pacific Affairs, in conjunction with its task force on American MIA's and POW's in Southeast Asia, meet today to hear formal testimony from General Eugene Tighe, who was the Director of the Defense Intelligence Agency from 1974 to 1981. At the request of General Leonard Perroots, the current Director of DIA, General Tighe, along with a panel of distinguished military and intelligence experts, examined the procedures currently employed by the DIA to account for missing Americans in Southeast Asia.

Specifically, General Tighe was asked to evaluate case files currently under review by the DIA and, upon completion, offer his conclusions with respect to the likelihood of a USG cover-up, the possibility of live Americans still being held against their will in Southeast Asia and the methods used by the DIA to evaluate pertinent information regarding POW/MIA's. Finally, General Tighe was asked to propose any recommendations, based on his extensive analysis of DIA's procedures, which would improve the manner in which the agency executes its strategy for resolving this issue.

Let me say now, as I did when General Tighe was first asked to head this Commission, that I welcome any constructive method which will facilitate the resolution of the POW/MIA question and thus am anxious to hear testimony about his findings.

I want to extend my thanks to General Tighe, who has devoted such a great deal of his time to this issue. This subcommittee has had the privilege of hearing testimony from him on numerous occasions in the past during his tenure as Director of the DIA and again as a private citizen in 1985. Time and again, he has demonstrated his deep commitment to resolving this troubling question and, in his testimony before us, has always spoken with great candor and insight, which we greatly appreciate.

I also want to commend General Perroots for his willingness, at the risk of possible criticism, to have his agency withstand the ex-

(1)

2

tensive scrutiny of this type of analysis. It is testimony to his genuine desire to see that this lingering legacy of the Indochina war—the fate of over 2,400 Americans—be resolved as quickly and in as comprehensive a manner as possible.

Indeed, it is incumbent upon not only the DIA, but the Congress to do everything in our power to attempt to heal this festering wound by achieving a satisfactory answer to the fate of those Americans who did not return from the war.

At the same time, we must remember that the statements we make and conclusions we reach reverberate in the minds and hearts of those family members who have had to endure the prolonged agony of not knowing the fate of their loved ones. Thus, we must take care not to make irresponsible statements or engage in indiscriminate actions that may unjustly raise the expectations of families and friends or—worse still—endanger any men who might remain in captivity.

Let me emphasize that this subcommittee has been, and continues to be, dedicated to ensuring that our Government sustains its commitment to achieving a satisfactory accounting of our men. It is for that reason that, as chairman of the subcommittee, I have asked General Tighe to appear before us today.

To ensure that the Congress and the American public are fully apprised of General Tighe's report, the subcommittee has asked General Tighe to elaborate on some of the statements he has made publicly about the report he gave to the DIA. While the subcommittee appreciates the fact that some of the data in this report is classified—and therefore not appropriate for discussion in open session—we nevertheless believe it is vital that the American people be made aware of any and all efforts to account for our men.

Let me say in conclusion that it is the intention of the chair at the conclusion of the hearing to bring up for consideration House Concurrent Resolution 129, which has been introduced by Mr. Hendon. Some of you may know that 275 or so of our colleagues have co-sponsored this resolution, and while I personally continue to have serious reservations about the wisdom of approving it, I think that, whenever you have a resolution cosponsored by a clear majority of the House, there is an institutional responsibility to give the sponsors of the resolution the opportunity to have their resolution brought up for a vote. It is my hope that we can do that today.

I recognize that we are approaching the end of the session, but it is possible that we will be meeting next week. I have seen other legislation move very quickly. I even see today that we will be experiencing the resurrection of at least one bill that had been consigned to the grave as recently as 1 week ago, the immigration bill, and while it is true that even Lazarus only rose from the dead once, who knows maybe in this session we will resurrect not one bill but two.

I wouldn't preclude the possibility, if it is the will of the Congress to move forward on this matter, that we will do so. Nevertheless, I do expect that we will have a serious debate on this resolution when we bring it up before the subcommittee. Before calling on General Tighe, Mr. Leach, would you care to make a statement?

3

Mr. LEACH. I have no statement. I wish that we would go right to General Tighe, but there may be other members of the minority who would like to say something.

Mr. SOLARZ. Does anyone else care to make a presentation at this point?

If not, General Tighe, if you will come to the witness table. General, I gather you have submitted for the record written responses to the questions we gave to you and those, of course, will be included in the transcript. If you would like to elaborate on any of these answer, or briefly summarize what you would like to say, feel free to do so.

STATEMENT OF GENERAL EUGENE TIGHE, FORMER DIRECTOR, DEFENSE INTELLIGENCE AGENCY

General TIGHE. I would like to start off by reminding that it was at the request of Congressman McCain that Secretary Weinberger asked General Perroots to have me head this task force and to go back and look at what had happened in the DIA procedures since I left in 1981. My report and the charter are in the possession of the Director of the Defense Intelligence Agency. He asked for the report. I submitted it to him.

I note the fact that he said there would be no unclassified release of the report for the record, so I am either bound, I suppose, to stick to my own opinions and/or to comment on those things through which I can wade between the classified parts of the report. I will do my best in both regards.

We worry about the impact and the long tenure of the problem of MIA's and POW's. I have come across recently some 1954 Congressional Records in which a young Congressman, Tip O'Neill, asked his colleagues in the House to pay attention to a resolution by the city council of Boston, MA, that begs for an accounting—this is 1954—of those MIA's/POW's who were known to have been alive after the conclusions of the truce with North Korea and had not been returned. So the question as to whether or not you can quickly resolve this issue I think is moot when you realize that the U.S. Government is reported to have gone back to Panmunjom in 1986 and asked again of their counterparts across the negotiating table there in North Korea to account for those known to have been alive at the end of the Korean war and not returned to United States custody.

I wish that I could believe that this issue then will not be an issue for a very long time. I am just afraid that ball is in Hanoi's court. It is not the United States that is dragging its feet, but it is Hanoi's reluctance to cooperate, in my judgment. It keeps us from resolving that issue until they agree to cooperate. I gathered a group of people to help me review this report that knew me, whose integrity I could count on, who knew a lot about the issue from their contacts with me or from the fact that they were involved heavily in activities in Vietnam. My report was submitted as a unanimous report, unanimous agreements on its considerations and recommendations.

I note in the press report that General Perroots has chosen to adopt the recommendations that were made in the main. I suggest

4

that there are probably a couple he will not, but that he found the report helpful.

With that, I think for time's sake and for the benefit of the people here gathered, Mr. Chairman, I will go to answering any questions that you might put before me.

[The information was subsequently submitted:]

The specific responses to the questions you suggested be ~~Tighe~~ *Tighe*

included in my statement today are as follows:

<u>1.</u> On what basis did you come to the conclusion that there is a strong possibility there are live Americans still in Indochina?

On the evaluation of reports, the clustering of several of them

in geographical areas, the sifting of those which came from responsible,

often unsolicited individuals, and those from obviously self-seeking;

and the amount of results of cross-checking which DIA had done on

6

some of the sources.

<u>2.</u> Does this conclusion distinguish between the Vietnamese and Laotian cases?

No, it does not.

<u>3.</u> Did you receive the full cooperation of all personnel at the DIA? Did you at any time feel that you were being prevented in any way from performing a thorough investigation?

Certainly many of the DIA personnel with whom my Task Force met

and on whose support of our effort we depended were not happy to

undergo another investigation of their activities. A damage-limiting

attitude, after the findings of Col. Gaines leak, had been reached,

seemed very important to most of those involved at DIA. We received

excellent cooperation from Col. Gaines and Mr. Trowbridge, and were

able to satisfy the specifics of our charter. We did not seize the

entire data base from DIA personnel for fear that work on this really

important issue might be impeded.

<u>4.</u> Even though you have stated that you believe there has been no cover-up in the Administration, do you feel there has been a level of effort dedicated to this problem to match the Administration's stated priorities?

As awareness and interest in this issue grew it was and is

almost impossible to keep up with real analysis of the problem. A

majority of the effort in DIA must, by direction, go to answering

Freedom of Information requests, responding to queries from outside

DIA and to keeping up with communications and administration of the

activities regarding POW-MIA's. Often registration of priority
need from the Director level fails to achieve the results necessary
by the time those who must actually provide resources get the word.
General Perroots has provided dramatic improvement to the support
of this effort and as long as there is positive belief and support of th
effort from all involved, results from the POW-MIA shop should improve
dramatically.

5. How do you explain the difference between the contents of your
    report and the remarks you made to the press. Namely, you spoke
    publicly about considering the possibility of normalizing
    relations with the Vietnamese as a means of securing the release
    of Americans possibly being held in Indochina? Why did you not
    address this question in your main report? Did DIA prevent you
    from making such assertions?

I have been asked by you before of my opinions on eventual
solution of the impasse between Hanoi and the U.S. on this issue
and responded as I have done so publicly in recent days that normalization seems an inevitable means involved. Although some at DIA may
have felt this and similar issues fell outside the Task Force Charter,
we included them in the report.

6. Do you feel that your position on the POW/MIA question is
    substantially different from the official position of the
    Administration?

I believe the basis for the government's assumption that "we
cannot rule out the possibility of Americans being held captive" remains
"the weight of the evidence and previous Vietnamese behaviour". As
Secretary Weinberger has stated. An examination of the reports which
have continued to flow in to DIA from all corners of the world - not
only first-hand, live sightings but second-source and beyond leads
to the "strong possibility that live American military POW's remain .

8

captive in Southeast Asia". This belief should be clearly enunciated
as the U.S. position and importantly, the position of everyone in
the Department of Defense working to bring Americans home. Unless
that certitude guides DIA's efforts the great sacrifices of all
who are working the problem may as well be brought to a halt.

7. Having had renewed access to DIA's files, how has your opinion
    changed, if it has changed at all, from your original testimony
    on this issue before this Subcommittee in 1979 and again in 1985?
    Did you come to any new conclusions in this report that you have
    not already stated publicly in the past?

Mr. Chairman, during my testimony before you on June 25, 1981,
you asked "In your view, given your personal judgement as you are

about to leave this assignment, does the weight of evidence suggest to you, taking everything into consideration, that American servicemen are still living in Indochina?

My response was "yes".

You continued."And that there are still - and this is a somewhat different question - American servicemen being held against their will in Indochina?"

I responded: "My convictions would be "yes" in answer to both questions, sir.

After the passage of five years and review of an almost entirely new, different and convincing set of reports which I recently reviewed, my opinion - my conviction on this issue has not changed, but is reinforced - stronger now, by far, than in 1981.

__8.__ Did any members of the review panel with whom you worked dissent from any of the findings in your report?

No sir - ours was a unanimous report, stated in our conveyance to General Perroots, at the request of Task Force members and

9

reiterated in strong terms by the Senior Review Panel.

__9.__ You reviewed 43 case files from a data base consisting of 5387 reports? How did you decide which files to investigate? Why did you limit the number to a small percentage of the total cases available?

I was insistent that our review be representative, starting with the overview of data available, briefed us by members of VO-POW and Col. Gaines.One case file (maintained under the title of the principal source) may contain many source reports. The files include heavy duplication "one file may have 50 reports in it." We pursued a path through relevant data we found in the report and rated ourselves on the quality of data and DIA analysis of .43.

__10.__ You submitted a draft of your report in May of this year. Why was the final version not made available until the end of September

A review of the report as I submitted it in May was conducted by DIA and the Senior Review Panel to correct typographic errors, discuss possible rearrangement of internal sections to annex status, resolve some errors in language and to assure acceptable and understandé language. Since I spent a great deal of the summer recovering from major surgery and General Perroots had to carry out the heavy burden of other responsibilities our meetings had to be sandwiched where possible.

11. One of the concerns of those who share your view that there is
the possibility of live Americans still in Indochina, has been
that false hopes will be raised among the families of those still
missing. Do you share that concern?

Certainly. I am reassured, however, by regular calls from
parents, wives and sons who tell me they are as concerned for the
fate of other mother's sons as their own. I do what I feel I must.

10

There is little likelihood we'll account for all our missing but
whatever the number, even a small one, is important.

12. Does your conclusion that there is a strong possibility of
Americans still being held in Indochina distinguish between
the Vietnamese and Laotian cases?

No, it does not.

13. In light of your report, what do you feel Congress should do?

As I recommended last year and building on your long years
of devotion for and support to this issue - continue your interest,
inquire, as I suggested to both House and Senate last year, as to the
direct U.S. human collection program attendant and continue to give
fenced financial appropriation to General Perroots and all who are
working the problem - for their support of it.

14. Although your panel made a number of recommendations to improve
government efforts in the POW/MIA issue, overall is it fair to
conclude that the Executive Branch is doing more today than it
did while under your leadership at DIA?

Most definitely. General Perroots has substantially improved the
support to the POW-MIA effort - in DIA. The challenge has increased
manyfold. DIA must do much more than analyze. Right now, a major
effort is under way to bring the DIA intelligence data base (SAFE)
to every member in the VO-POW shop. When our investigation began there
was a single, SAFE terminal available and no one in the shop had been
trained to use it. Much of the intelligence data base has scattered
to retirement - rests in depositories outside Washington. All of it must
be consolidated - automated - in the shortest possible time. The
practice of "resolving" information must continue to transition to
analyzing information. Stop trying to discredit the source and kill
the messenger and analyze and act on the valuable and believable
evidential base.

Mr. SOLARZ. Thank you very much, General.

Last night I reviewed the testimony from the hearing which we held on this issue in March of this year. I have also reviewed your testimony on previous occasions before the subcommittee and I think it is fair to say that you have consistently testified that it is your personal judgment and conviction there are in fact live Americans being held against their will in Indochina.

General TIGHE. That is correct, Mr. Chairman.

Mr. SOLARZ. Given the extent to which it remains your personal conviction that live Americans are being held against their will in Indochina, how do you account for the fact that in the report your task force submitted, you indicated in the conclusion that there was a strong possibility that there are live Americans still in Indochina. There is, as I am sure you would recognize, a significant difference between a strong possibility that there are Americans who are being held there against their will and certitude that Americans are being held there against their will.

The strong possibility language, which was used in the report, implies the possibility that they may not be there, yet you obviously believe Americans are there. So I would like to ask you why the language of the report didn't reflect your own long-held and publicly expressed view on this issue?

General TIGHE. Of course I was interested in producing a report that represented the expertise and views of everybody that worked on that report with me. I can't claim to have a stronghold on the only truth, and you negotiate words and terms and shades of difference in adjectives so as to describe a certitude. My personal certitude was considered with along that of people whose inability to prove, which has always been the major down issue in this whole thing—can you prove it.

And the United States has not been able to prove it, nor will it prove it, until it has people roaming the Earth in the nation in which these people are held, finding out for themselves and reporting directly back to their government. It is that lack of so-called proof as opposed to this weight of evidence which supports the U.S. position today that constitutes the difference in words.

I think it is only fair to say that until you can offer that proof, you have to work with adjectives and so forth to describe the varying degrees with which people are certain.

Mr. SOLARZ. Would it be fair to say that there were other members of your commission that did not share your certainty there were Americans being held there, although presumably they did believe, as the report says, that there is a strong possiblity that they are there?

General TIGHE. Our conclusion, of course, says American military prisoners of war, and if my memory serves, the only lack of certitude among any members of my review group had to do with whether or not these were actually military, had to do with, in reading these reports as to whether or not they were in captivity at the time they were sighted. My view, my certitude was that in each instance they could not have been living with military personnel attendant to them without having been guarded very closely.

Mr. SOLARZ. Are you saying that there was unanimity on the panel that there are today Americans in Indochina who have remained behind after the war but there was disagreement over whether they are being kept in captive situations?

General TIGHE. Some of the reports don't give you that certitude that they were unhappy in captivity, and therefore there may be cooperation going on between them and their captors.

Mr. SOLARZ. I thought the report says there is a strong possibility there are live Americans still in Indochina?

General TIGHE. My records show that it is American military prisoners of war remaining in captivity.

Mr. SOLARZ. That is the language of the report?

General TIGHE. Yes, sir.

Mr. SOLARZ. So, there was agreement that live Americans are there, but some doubt among members of your panel as to whether or not they are in a captive situation?

General TIGHE. And/or in discussion with the DIA whose officials discussed our iterative reports on this thing, doubted or called to our attention the shades of difference.

Mr. SOLARZ. When you were head of DIA, General, did you have any reason to believe or suspect that there was any coverup going on in your agency with respect to the facts of this situation?

General TIGHE. No; I did not. As a matter of fact, I think it is almost impossible to have a coverup on this.

Mr. SOLARZ. On the basis of the review you have just conducted, is there any reason to believe there may be any coverup or conspiracy?

General TIGHE. None whatsoever. Our task was to find out whether there was and we found no evidence whatsoever.

Mr. SOLARZ. Were you given access to all the data which you requested?

General TIGHE. As far as we know. The data base is scattered. The old records are in retirement, so I suggest that in light of the fact that we were using records that constitute day-to-day activities of the DIA, we got just about everything we wanted.

Mr. SOLARZ. The President has said that this is a matter of the highest national priority. Do you feel that the practice of the administration has reflected its pronouncements on this issue?

General TIGHE. I think, for example, a matter of the highest priority does not mean it is the highest priority. The Nation's defenses are more important. Within the priorities, I would suggest it enjoys in the President's mind the highest priority and I think that most of the people that work on the issue reflect that very well.

Mr. SOLARZ. Based on your experience with this issue, do you think there is anything significant that we could be doing as a nation to resolve this matter that we are not now doing?

General TIGHE. Yes. I have very strong feelings that this is not an intelligence issue and we have the Defense Intelligence Agency, which is a foreign intelligence organization, which is handling a lot of parts of this problem that include public policy, the answering of the Freedom of Information requests, liaison with various and sundry civilian organizations and my belief is that this activity should instead enjoy the status of a Permanent Presidential commission which would start accumulating and automating the data base from all wars; to make sure that retired records are already in the data base that is computer accessible, so that you can have a good way to check down through the years as the situation changes and new reports come in, and check the old.

I think until we get a commission that is not subject to either the extraordinarily busy regime of the Congress or with all the other distractions of a foreign intelligence organization that we will ever get the satisfaction the American public is demanding.

Mr. SOLARZ. Would this commission have any authorities that the DIA doesn't now enjoy?

General TIGHE. I would suggest that it would be wise if, for example, it had subpoena power. I would suggest that it have direct access to the President or that its periodic, appointed chief have direct access to the President so there would be no doubt of the priorities of collection against this issue, intelligence collection.

Mr. SOLARZ. It sounds as if you feel that the DIA is either not doing an adequate job of isn't in a position to do an adequate job.

Can you spell out a little bit more clearly what you think such a commission could do that the DIA hasn't already done or isn't in a position to do?

General TIGHE. I would answer that very directly and that is put all of their effort into analysis and less and less into liaison and answering all of the various and sundry other organizations of government that demand their attention, including the public.

I think it is very important that you enlarge that basis very considerably, but get it out of the foreign intelligence arena.

Second is the automation of the data base. That data base belongs to the services, DIA—a lot of records are retired that have to be reaccumulated, and I don't think that is within the capability of today's DIA task force, even though it is considerably larger, General Perroots has corrected a lot of problems in the past.

Mr. SOLARZ. Have you seen the text of House Concurrent Resolution 129?

General TIGHE. I have.

Mr. SOLARZ. Do you recommend to this subcommittee that we approve it or not?

General TIGHE. My suggestion is that your schedules would not permit the attention to this unless it were permanentized in some way and some degree of control other than appropriations over the collection priorities and the day-to-day management of intelligence activities regarding this would be available to you.

Mr. SOLARZ. What is the answer?

General TIGHE. The answer is I do not support the establishment of a Congressional Commission.

Mr. SOLARZ. Would you support the establishment of a Presidential Commission?

General TIGHE. Correct.

Mr. SOLARZ. Does the President need the authority of the Congress to appoint the commission?

General TIGHE. No; he does not.

Mr. SOLARZ. Would he need the authority of the Congress to give the commission subpoena power?

General TIGHE. I suspect that he would, but he probably would get it from Justice and the Justice people would probably have to come to you for concurrence.

Mr. SOLARZ. Would you prefer the establishment of a Presidential Commission?

General TIGHE. That is correct.

Mr. SOLARZ. Why do you prefer it that way?

General TIGHE. I think it has to be a full-time job for the people working on it.

Mr. SOLARZ. Have you made this suggestion to the President?

General TIGHE. I understand that he is knowledgeable of my suggestion. I do not have any feedback on the subject.

Mr. SOLARZ. Mr. Solomon—I will yield to Mr. Leach.

Mr. LEACH. First, let me ask Mr. Solomon, who is chair of a congressional task force do you want to say anything first?

Mr. SOLOMON. Go ahead and I will follow up.

Mr. LEACH. General Tighe, I think it has to be emphasized that you did conclude that there was no coverup in DIA.

General TIGHE. Yes, sir.

Mr. LEACH. Was that a unanimous decision of your group?

General TIGHE. Yes, sir.

Mr. LEACH. That is good news.

General TIGHE. There were two lawyers in my review group who were looking at the legal verbiage as well as the ordinary understanding of the word "coverup."

Mr. LEACH. Do you have any sense why some Americans have concluded there might have been a coverup?

General TIGHE. I think the fact that this whole issue is being held in the hands of an intelligence organization will breed suspicion as long as they have it. I think there is a great suspicion among the American public for anything that an intelligence organization is in charge of.

Mr. LEACH. You have been quoted widely as indicating you believe there are still Americans missing. Based upon your study, are your beliefs strengthened, or do you feel the same, or do you think there is a little more doubt today?

General TIGHE. I was quite surprised to find out that those kinds of reports that had been coming to me during the time I was at the DIA, and understand that I have not had access to the data base since 1981, continued to come in, that there are reports as late as 1985, 1986 citings, that is. And the continuum of that kind of evidence cannot be ignored, in my judgment, and therefore my beliefs were strengthened considerably as a result of my review.

Mr. LEACH. Other than the formation of the kind of Presidential Commission you just indicated 1 minute ago, are there other things you think the U.S. Government should be doing at this time?

General TIGHE. I would hope very much that the Congress would find it in its mind to back up and somehow or other make sure that there are fenced appropriations for the automation of the POW-MIA data base to make sure that the funds are available now. I suspect this is going to be a very large project. It cannot be done by the DIA. It has to be done outside the Agency. You have to start around the fringes and impinge yourself on the working files of the Agency and I would hope that those funds would be forthcoming.

As I said in my last appearance before the task force, Mr. Chairman, the need is great to impress upon both Houses of the Congress that direct personal human governmental intervention in the discovery process and the proving process in Southeast Asia is essential and that is difficult to do.

Mr. LEACH. Why, in your judgment, are Governments, in Indochina, particularly Vietnam, withholding information? What are they seeking from the United States? What is their hidden agenda, if it is hidden?

General TIGHE. I will make this a personal judgment and then I will refer to some of the findings of the group.

It is my view that the Vietnamese feel strongly that they should get reparations from the United States and feel somehow deprived of that.

I think there is the view that in their current economic position, they need all kinds of things, including U.S. recognition to pull them out of the chaotic economic conditions they endure and that this is one way, but I think from the very start, and here I will start to talk about some of the facts available on the record, you see evidence in the data base that they considered the economic value of prisoners of war, they had them categorized as to type, for example, a pilot was worth so much to them in terms of reward. Another type of individual captured was worth so much and so forth.

But they speak of those captives in economic terms and rewards for the Government of Vietnam.

Mr. LEACH. Mr. Chairman, I would like to conclude by asking unanimous consent that a press conference statement of General Perroots' of September 30 be placed in the record.

Mr. SOLARZ. Without objection, it will be included in the appropriate place in the record.

[The information subsequently submitted follows:]

18

pain and sorrow felt by many American families and we must take care to avoid giving false hope to those who have placed their trust in us. I assure you that the DIA is dedicating all necessary efforts and resources to supporting the President's goal of achieving the fullest accounting on this national issue.

What are your questions?

19

TIGHE Report Contributors

TIGHE TASK FORCE

MAJ GENERAL JOHN S. MURRAY, USA (RET)
Chief of U.S. Military Interest in Vietnam for the Secretary of Defense (1972-1974).

COLONEL LESTER E. MCGEE, JR., USA, (RET) - Staff Director
Army Intelligence Specialist

ARTHUR G. KLOS
Vice Assistant Deputy Director of Security and Counterintelligence, Defense Intelligence Agency.

JOHN FRANCIS MCCREARY
Senior Warning Specialist - U.S. National Strategic Warning Staff and Far East
Area Specialist, Defense Intelligence Agency

ROBERTA CARPER MAYNARD
Former Navy Personnel Officer, DIA Management Specialist, Defense Intelligence
Agency.

TIGHE REVIEW PANEL

MR. LYMAN KIRKPATRICK, CIA (RETIRED)
Former Inspector General, CIA & Brown University Professor.

GENERAL RUSSELL DOUGHERTY, USAF (RET)
Former Commander-In-Chief, Strategic Air Command.

GENERAL BOB KINGSTON, USA (RET)
Former Commander-In-Chief, United States Central Command.

BRIG GEN ROBBIE RISNER, USAF (RET)
Distinguished Air Force Fighter Pilot; former POW in Hanoi.

MR. ROSS PEROT
Chairman, Electronic Data Systems.

LT GEN JOHN PETER FLYNN, USAF (RET)
A Distinguished Air Force Fighter Pilot; former leader of U.S. POW's in Hanoi.
Former Inspector General, U.S. Air Force.

TECHNICAL ASSISTANCE

POLYGRAPH: DR. CHRIS GUGAS; "PHD, Polygraph Expert, Director "Professional
Security Consultants" - Los Angeles, CA.

SIGNAL INTELLIGENCE: MAJ GEN JOHN MORRISON, USAF (RET), Former Chief N.F.I.B.
Signal Committee.

VIETNAM INTELLIGENCE: HOANG LY - Former Chief of Vietnam Air Force
Intelligence and E.D. S. Employee.

PHOTO INTERPRETATION: MR. DINO BRUGIONI, Photo Interpretation Specialist -CIA
retired.

20

Mr. SOLARZ. The gentleman from California, Mr. Dymally.
Mr. DYMALLY. Thank you, Mr. Chairman.
General, you have read this resolution?
General TIGHE. I have.
Mr. DYMALLY. The two last lines on page 2, you are quoted as
saying that the evidence is clear that there are Americans being
held against their will in Southeast Asia.
General TIGHE. Yes.
Mr. DYMALLY. Do you have that evidence?
General TIGHE. That is my opinion today.
Mr. DYMALLY. Opinion is different from evidence.
General TIGHE. Opinions are based on very substantive data base
which is available to the Government and part of the DIA files.
Mr. DYMALLY. I think you are a nice guy, but I don't have any
evidence of it.
General TIGHE. Well, I would commend to you all of the files
that I reviewed and I suggest you read them and evaluate them for
yourselves. They are a very strong, in my judgment, evidentiary
base.
Mr. DYMALLY. On page 3, it is stated that you have called for formation of a special commission to investigate at DIA. Page 3 of the

resolution says, "has called for the formation of a special commission to investigate the work of the various agency heads citing the DIA work as showing a mindset to debunk intelligence received on our prisoners of war."

General TIGHE. That is a part of a Wall Street article written quoting me in reference to some freedom-of-information-furnished responses from the DIA to the Wall Street Journal.

Debunking I felt was a problem in the DIA and I believe before we started my investigation, General Perroots' private investigation found the same thing true.

I refer here, of course, to the Gaines report conducted by the man who now heads that shop.

Mr. DYMALLY. One final comment.

I told Mr. Hendon in our previous hearing—I have serious problems about tombstoning Mr. Perot's name as the Perot Commission. It is my own personal bias this ought to be a congressional commission, a U.S. commission.

We had a dialog on what tombstoning means. It means putting somebody's name on a bill forever. I have problems with the fact that Mr. Perot is going to nominate the members, we had taken away Presidential powers and given it to a private citizen.

I don't know the gentleman. I have read good things about him and I praise him for his work, but the notion of giving to a private citizen Presidential powers is something I opposed as a Democrat when Reagan was Governor. I said this is wrong because one day we will get that governorship. We got it and I have problems with that.

I am in opposition to the notion of taking away Presidential powers and giving it to a party or individual. In this case, we have taken the power of the President and given it to an individual.

Without those changes, I couldn't vote for this bill.

Mr. LEACH. Mr. Chairman, point of personal privilege.

21

I have never raised a point of personal privilege, but there are no cameras here. Is it possible that we could turn off these lights?

Mr. SOLARZ. That is fine with me.

Without objection, for those members who don't care about being plunged into darkness, somebody on the staff please figure out a way to turn down these lights.

The gentleman from New York, Mr. Solomon.

Mr. SOLOMON. I thank you very much and let me say thank you, Mr. Minority Leader. I suffer from eye strain and it really helps.

General Tighe, first I want to thank you very much for coming here today and I want to thank you for the job that you undertook.

I want to say that I agree with just about everything that you have said here today.

You, I think, have really hit the nail right on the head because we in the Congress do not have the time or the capability to do this job ourselves. I say that as the chairman of the task force appointed by the chairman of this subcommittee, Steve Solarz, a position that has been so time consuming for me in the last 2 years that I have really neglected other parts of my job. Based on your testimony, I think that you are on the right track and that maybe we could discuss this before we finish consideration of the legislation that is before us today.

I just want to ask a couple of questions that you have already clarified to some extent, in answering the questions, questions from

Chairman Solarz concerning an alleged coverup. I was so very, very pleased to hear you say and to read in your report that there has been no coverup, because the thing that has bothered me the most is the fact that many good, patriotic men and women who have served this country have come under criticism as if they would even take part in such a thing.

It literally broke my heart to have those kinds of things said in public about them. I know for a fact that many of those men have gone home at night and have suffered because of things that have been said about them.

You have done a lot of the good, patriotic people in our military a great service with your report. So I thank you from the bottom of my heart for that.

Can you tell me in some detail what is the basic difference, in what was being done on this issue when you left your Agency in 1981, and what has happened since then in President Reagan's efforts to make this a high priority, in other words, what is different now as far as manpower, as far as what is being done to look into the issue?

General TIGHE. The first major change is the amount of public awareness that his interest and oft-stated interest has aroused in the American public.

That, of course, brings great pressure on the DIA as all of these interested parties who share with the President, the need for resolution of the issue.

It redounds on the freedom-of-information request. It redounds on the amount of press interest which impacts on the same small group of people that are trying to do the job in the DIA.

The major impact has been to explode this into a major domestic issue, but leaving it in the foreign intelligence arena for resolution

22

and investigation which in my judgment has brought about suspicion and a lot of charlatans in the act. There are an awful lot of phonys around who cause a great deal of burden to the DIA and everybody in Government interested in this issue, but the great difference is the amount of public awareness and the reactions to that awareness.

Mr. SOLOMON. That awareness really helps, I think, in the long run.

General TIGHE. Yes, sir.

Mr. SOLOMON. One of the problems that I have had as chairman of the task force, is that we do have a great many Members of Congress who are extremely interested in this issue, and while trying to work with the Defense Intelligence Agency, it seems that sometimes the Congress has been so demanding that we really interfere with their work, and that is why I was so interested in your commentary about the need for a commission, and how that should be set up, and the fact that it should be separate from the Congress. I really agree with that, because I think I noted in your report some criticism that Congress, in its very sincere effort to try to get to the bottom of this, has in truth sometimes just interfered. In the task force, we have tried to make rules that would govern this somewhat, that would hopefully cut down on any inadvertent interference but yet still be able to respond to members' sincere interest.

With regard to the legislation to be considered today, sponsored by Mr. Hendon, the reason that I have not sponsored that legislation is the fact that it is a congressional commission that would be set up, and I also think that that would be wrong. Once again, I was very interested in your reasons for thinking that that was wrong, too, and I have thought from the beginning that if such a commission were to be established it should be established as a U.S. commission by the President and that it should be answerable to the President. I think that that is the way by which we will get results.

Finally, I would just confirm that during your period of negotiation with the Vietnamese Government they insisted that there be a government-to-government relationship, or else there would be no relationship.

If that is so, I guess a U.S. commission answerable to the President, who in many respects is viewed by the Vietnamese Government as being the Government here, would have a much greater chance of success than another type of commission, simply because that commission would be seen by the Vietnamese as being under the arm of the President.

General TIGHE. That is my view.

Mr. SOLOMON. Is that your view?

General TIGHE. That is very much my view.

Mr. SOLOMON. Mr. Chairman, I have a lot of other questions, but I know there are a lot of members here, so I am going to stop at this time, but again, General, I just want to really commend you on the fine job you have done.

You are a great American and we really appreciate your volunteering your efforts to help us get to the bottom of this.

General TIGHE. Thank you.

23

Mr. SOLARZ. I just want to say to my good friend from New York, particularly since this may well be the last time this subcommittee meets this session, how very much I appreciate the fine work he has done as chairman of the task force. He has devoted an enormous amount of effort to this undertaking, and in spite of some profound political and ideological differences between us, he has always conducted himself not only as a gentleman, but in a very cooperative fashion. Our ability to work closely together on this issue is a rather meaningful manifestation of the extent to which this is not, and has never been, a partisan issue.

It is an American issue, concerning Members on both sides of the aisle, Democrats as well as Republicans. It is one of the few, if not the only, example I know of in the Congress where a member of the minority chairs a task force appointed by a member of the majority. That has always been the tradition with respect to this subcommittee.

I see two of the previous chairmen of the task force, Mr. Dornan and Mr. Gilman, both of whom also served with great distinction, and who have maintained a very real interest in this question are here. It is certainly my hope, despite whatever may happen with this resolution today, that we are able to continue this bipartisan approach when most of us, I presume, return next year.

The gentleman from Connecticut, Mr. Gejdenson.

Mr. GEJDENSON. You have now stated that you think it is better as an executive branch commission rather than a legislative branch commission.

Do you think it makes sense to tell the President who ought to head the committee, specifically that it ought to be Mr. Perot, and that Mr. Perot should nominate the committee members?

General TIGHE. I don't know that anyone is empowered to tell the President who to name to anything. There is somewhat of a vehicle to power over on the Hill in that regard, but I think that is up to the President. I think there are a great number of very distinguished Americans, including Mr. Perot, who would do an admirable job.

Mr. GEJDENSON. You think we could do the right thing by moving forward with legislation that established an executive commission while leaving it to the administration and the others to nominate the head of the committee and so forth?

General TIGHE. I am not too sure of the legislative appropriateness of enacting legislation for the President's action.

Mr. GEJDENSON. Thank you.

General TIGHE. Recommendations to that effect are in order.

Mr. SOLOMON. Will the gentleman yield?

Mr. GEJDENSON. I will be happy to yield.

Mr. SOLOMON. The one reason I can see for enacting legislation along those lines is to show the support of the Congress for the establishment of such a commission, and that would be the only difference that I would see with General Tighe, if a bipartisan, overwhelming effort was in that area.

Mr. SOLARZ. Mr. Gejdenson, have you finished?

Mr. GEJDENSON. Yes, I have completed my questions. Thank you.

Mr. SOLARZ. Mr. Bereuter.

24

Mr. BEREUTER. Thank you, Mr. Chairman.

General Tighe, thank you for your continuing contributions to the American republic. I am pleased and proud of the work that you have done for many years.

In 1982 when I had I suppose unauthorized access to information, I was convinced that there were Americans, numerous Americans, held in captivity against their will in Southeast Asia. I have no way of knowing what the situation is today, but I am an early cosponsor of this resolution.

I have heard the arguments that you advanced about the reason why we ought to have a Presidential commission. They are sound, as offered.

Mr. Solomon made some good points in that respect, but I am also concerned about the reaction that we may see across the country if we fail to take action on the establishment of a congressional commission by whatever name, and in contrast to the fact that we have over 270 cosponsors.

There is also the question that I would ask perhaps if you want to react to as to which will have more credibility with the American people. Will the credibility of the congressional commission be stronger than the Presidential commission, or will placing all of the responsibility ultimately in one person's hand, the Chief Executive, current or future, make this report less credible to the American people, and what do you think Congress should do now at the end of our 99th Congress, in light of the fact that a Presidential commission has not yet been established, and that we have no indication that it will be established.

Those two questions, if you could respond, I would appreciate it.

General TIGHE. Let me start with the first one, and that is I think the reaction of the American people to failure of the House to act on a resolution that 270 of its members has signed should be explained in a postrecommendation that a Presidential commission be established, and I think that is important.

It may also serve to allow your constituents a little better insight into really how busy lives you live. I don't think very many outside of Washington, DC really understand the pace of your lives and the difficulty of carrying out a congressional commission's work.

The answer to the second question as to whether or not it would be more credible in that it would endure beyond administrations, bipartisan in nature, in that it would last regardless of who was in the White House. I would suggest that over the years it would have much greater credibility than the congressional commission which might change from time to time or complete its work during the one regime or another.

Mr. BEREUTER. I do recall that we have had a lot of discussion lately about disinformation, and that causes me some concern with respect to the creation of a Presidential commission.

I would also like to ask you this question, General Tighe.

What would you recommend we avoid doing that might endanger the lives of Americans held in captivity yet today in Southeast Asia?

General TIGHE. I would suggest that pinpointing specific locations in any way or insight to the origin of some of the data that is available as to sources and methods be guarded very jealously.

25

I think you should avoid that, of course, as you regularly do, I think it would be very, very unfortunate if in the process of deciding whether or not you were going to have a congressional or a Presidential commission that the powers of the presidency to collect be elaborated in any great extent?

Mr. BEREUTER. Finally—and this will be my last question, Mr. Chairman—what, General Tighe, do you think we could do in at least maintaining some incentive for the Vietnamese Government to continue to keep alive Americans that they may have in captivity yet today?

General TIGHE. I would like to make sure you understand this is a personal opinion that I am going to give in answer to that question.

Mr. BEREUTER. Yes.

General TIGHE. I spent 4 years in the South Pacific during World War II. I couldn't conceive that we would ever have diplomatic relations with Japan, and I drive a new Toyota. I would suggest that the inevitability of at least de facto recognition of the Hanoi Government would hasten our ability to resolve this issue, and it is my recommendation that we stop trying to avoid that and try to move it forward to the point where it could be a centerpiece in our resolution of the issue.

Mr. BEREUTER. And that that might be an incentive to maintain Americans alive who may be held in captivity.

General TIGHE. Absolutely.

Mr. BEREUTER. Thank you, Mr. Chairman.

Thank you, General.

Mr. SOLARZ. Thank you.

We now have a vote on the rule on the DOD conference report. The subcommittee will stand in recess for approximately 10 minutes while we vote and then we shall return, if you can bear with us.

[Recess.]

Mr. SOLARZ. The subcommittee will come back to order.

It has been customary in the past for us to extend courtesies to those of our colleagues who are not on the subcommittee, but who have taken an interest in this issue, in order to find out if they would like to ask any questions. Mr. Hendon, do you have any questions you want to ask?

Mr. HENDON. I just appreciate your holding the hearing, Mr. Chairman.

Mr. SOLARZ. Mr. Gilman, do you have any questions you would like to ask?

Mr. GILMAN. Yes, I do.

General Tighe, we are pretty clear on your thoughts of the need to have some separate entity. Can you spell out a little more clearly why DIA or some military organization could not perform the kind of responsibilities that you would have us transfer to either a commission or some other entity within the administration?

General TIGHE. Since this is a public policy issue, and is of great concern to most of the American people, I think it is terribly important that a commission be able to handle its activities in a much more open manner than an intelligence agency can, for one thing.

26

Mr. GILMAN. Can you be more specific? What is it that a commission could do that the DIA could not do?

General TIGHE. This issue can never be priority one for the Defense Intelligence Agency.

Mr. GILMAN. Hasn't the President established it as a top priority, and hasn't the National Security Council so established it?

General TIGHE. There is no way the President can do that, with all his other responsibilities, nor would he ask any institution of government to give up their primary responsibility—which is the producing of foreign military intelligence at the Defense Intelligence Agency—and substitute it, address the question of whether or not there are live Americans in Vietnam.

Mr. GILMAN. There is a separate unit within the DIA that has been assigned the responsibility for the missing in action.

General TIGHE. Yes.

Mr. GILMAN. Doesn't that unit give a top priority to this issue.

General TIGHE. As you know, it has as much priority as General Perroots can give it, with all of the other priorities that he has. As you know, he does not invest that organization with its own collection capabilities either on the ground or in any of the technical ways, and it is not appropriate that he do so. There are great responsibilities placed on collection other than this issue, so it can never enjoy an equal priority with other issues inside the organization, nor does it have within its own walls the necessary means to accomplish collection.

Mr. GILMAN. General Tighe, it is my impression that in this particular report that you made some recommendations.

General TIGHE. Yes sir.

Mr. GILMAN. Aimed at perfecting the working capability of the DIA as it carries out its responsibilities?

General TIGHE. Yes sir.

Mr. GILMAN. And General Perroots is reported to have said he has implemented a number of those recommendations?

General TIGHE. Yes.

Mr. GILMAN. With those recommendations and that implementation, doesn't DIA now have the capability of doing the kinds of things you would like to have done in a separate entity?

General TIGHE. You have more capability, but the question was put to me how better can the United States do its job in this regard?

My response is that no matter how you improve the Defense Intelligence Agency, it is an agency under one department of government which has a priority mission quite contrary to the one in which this places it.

Mr. GILMAN. Despite the fact that the President has insisted it be given a priority issue.

General TIGHE. It has not so much to do with the fact that he says this is a priority issue, but it cannot in that organization be a priority one. The requirement that we know what weapons to build, the requirement that we know what our opponents around the world are up to technologically, and so forth, are all going to enjoy the primary responsibility of General Perroots.

Mr. GILMAN. But this is a separate unit within the DIA that concentrates just on this issue.

27

General TIGHE. That has no power but to go to other units within the DIA to get its budget, to other units to get its collection, to another organization run by somebody else out in the field, to track down refugee reports in Indochina, all of which belong to somebody else.

Mr. GILMAN. General Tighe, assume you are on this new commission——

General TIGHE. Yes sir.

Mr. GILMAN [continuing]. Whether it be congressional or Presidential, and you want to track down some information.

General TIGHE. Yes sir.

Mr. GILMAN. Where are you going to go? Don't you have to go back to the Defense Intelligence or some other intelligence group to get your supportive activity?

General TIGHE. No sir. If the President empowers the head of the commission to levy collection requirements on the DCI—Mr. Casey—they go directly to him, and will enjoy in that regard the very highest priority if it has the President's signature that you develop and do this today.

Mr. GILMAN. The DIA doesn't have that authority to do that or make that request?

General TIGHE. Never will, because for one thing it has to have its briefs as far as collection measured with others, balanced for priority with others that are always gong to come out first.

Mr. GILMAN. Are you telling us then, General Tighe, if there was some request for intelligence in the unit that you commanded, and you thought that the CIA could get more information than your own unit in DIA, that you didn't have the capability of making a request of the CIA?

General TIGHE. The Defense Intelligence Agency is not largely a collection organization at all. As you know, the collection responsibilities are vested with the DCI, and mainly conducted by the Central Intelligence Agency.

Mr. GILMAN. There is no cooperation or coordination with other intelligence groups?

General TIGHE. Absolutely, but priorities are always weighed. There is almost never a time when everything can be priority one, and it is in that light that the Defense Intelligence Agency must have its requirements measured against everybody else.

Mr. GILMAN. Wasn't it possible for your unit then to go to the President and get the kind of priority that was needed?

General TIGHE. I would suggest that General Perroots can go to the National Foreign Intelligence Board on which he represents the Defense Department, and submit his requirements there, and based on all the other requirements that Mr. Casey has to accomplish, it will get what priority it can.

Mr. GILMAN. Were you ever stymied in not being able to get that kind of priority information while you headed this unit?

General TIGHE. Always balanced—my priorities were always balanced against those of making sure that we had adequate warning to protect the Nation, we had adequate knowledge of what was going on around the world in current crises and crises reduction, and a great many other things that, of course, always take priorities over this kind of an issue.

28

Mr. GILMAN. Was your work hampered, General Tighe, by this lack of priorities in your unit?

General TIGHE. I think if you are talking about the difference between what I could have had if I had the President telling his DCI to do it versus a subordinate department asking that he consider doing it, it is quite different, yes.

Mr. GILMAN. Had you made a request for priority that was denied you?

General TIGHE. Yes sir, of course, and in one of our recommendations, for example, to enlarge the human collection about refugees in this regard, and there is a very, very small capability—I understand General Perroots is surveying that now, and is taking that recommendation very seriously.

Mr. GILMAN. Would you feel that this new presidential unit should be folded in, perhaps, to the CIA?

General TIGHE. I think it should be of course empowered to have a liaison function—people from the Central Intelligence Agency working within it, people from the Defense Intelligence Agency working within it, but it should have a considerably different focus, and that is on examination of an empowered collection against all the reports that it gets.

Mr. GILMAN. Did the Tighe report include those recommendations?

General TIGHE. In the Tighe report, that would have been considered a policy recommendation, in my judgment, it is included in an annex that dealt with things outside my charter.

Mr. GILMAN. And it was not included as part of the recommendations?

General TIGHE. Not specifically that a Presidential commission be established. That an outside agency be established, yes, that is part of the report.

Mr. GILMAN. So essentially then, the reason that you feel that we need this new separate unit of either Presidential or congressional, or whatever the unit may be, is so that there could be a priority in intelligence collection, is that correct?

General TIGHE. That is one of the results of it. The first result is to make sure that you elevate this to a level that enjoys under an outside individual, someone who has absolutely no responsibilities for promotion or in any other way to the current administration or any other element of government, can act independently in judging what should be acted on, and go for priority collection.

No. two, to make sure that it has permanent ties beyond one administration so that we have a record built up for many wars and all of those wars are kept in an active data base.

And third, that it have the support of people outside of the current foreign intelligence community, which I think hampers the mission itself.

Mr. GILMAN. And yet its major responsibility is gathering intelligence that could be used in accounting for our missing?

General TIGHE. In my judgment the public polls issue has gone far beyond that today in importance. The requirement and allies. There are too many people in this country who feel very strongly about this who demand a great deal of time from the people that

29

are working the problems wherever they are, including of course yourselves, who have worked so hard on this.

Mr. GILMAN. General Tighe, were your responsibilities as head of the DIA eroded by any other responsibilities? Did you have any other outside responsibilities besides commanding the DIA?

General TIGHE. My responsibilities always went far beyond and above the responsibility for POW/MIA affairs. My first responsibility was to make sure that the Secretary of Defense was advised of any threat to the security of the United States or its Armed Forces worldwide, and then on a very large descending order of priorities, would you come across a requirement to address this one issue as a priority. But like it or not, it is going to be a lower priority than you might think if it is in an intelligence organization.

Mr. GILMAN. Thank you.

Thank you, Mr. Chairman.

Mr. SOLARZ. Mr. Smith, did you have any questions?

Mr. SMITH. No questions.

Mr. SOLARZ. Mr. Dornan?

Mr. DORNAN. Mr. Chairman, first of all, General Tighe, we have been friends now for 10 years, brought together by this issue, and I think your contribution has been most significant, particularly in the last few months. I know that what has not been brought out here is that there has been some damage to you, that lifelong friends of yours in the intelligence community somehow or other felt that there was something wrong with the conclusions of your committee, your commission, even though you had defended their honor and had taken the position that I had also taken. Everyone involved in this was as patriotic, as well meaning as possible, but ironically there is something inherent in this issue that would 'cause people with the same goal to tear at one another.

I saw this dissension at the foundation of the league in the early 1970's. I have seen pain and suffering among family members with a single purpose, one goal, the kinds of parents and brothers and sisters who come from those families that would give a young man to his country where he would lose his life or find himself in the incredible man, in the iron mask type, almost fiction situation that these men are in who I believe are alive.

So, I appreciate so much what you have done in this go-around.

Mr. Chairman, I would like to suggest, since he is in the room, another member of the commission whose hard work on this issue goes way back to the 1960's—Ross Perot is an Annapolis Naval Academy graduate. I remember the Christmas of 1969 when, at his own personal expense, he loaded a four-engine jet aircraft with food and medical supplies for our prisoners, and came to Los Angeles where we crossed paths as I helped to load some of the supplies on that airplane, begging to go with him to Laos but there was just no room to get on the airplane. This incident helped heighten my interest.

I was hosting a daily television show at the time that I ended every single day, 12,500 shows, with the expression, "Remember Rob Reisner and our other men in Southeast Asia."

For 11 honorable months I had a tag on that said, "Remember the crew of the Pueblo in North Korea," but after 500 shows and 120 dawn shows, after that 14 hours of TV time which I dedicated

30

to this issue, and over 53 radio shows solely to this issue, I feel that I have had a piece of this action, this honorable tragic action for 21 years, and I would like to move, Mr. Chairman, that we bring Mr. Ross Perot up to the front of the room here and sit at the desk to answer some of these questions.

Mr. SOLARZ. As the gentleman knows, he is not in a position to make a formal motion or request since he is not a member of the subcommittee.

Mr. DORNAN. It is not a formal motion.

Mr. SOLARZ. I will certainly entertain the suggestion.

We have always been willing to hear from anyone who has anything to contribute to our deliberation.

Before I call on Mr. Perot, however, are you finished with your questions of General Tighe?

Mr. DORNAN. No. I just wanted to ask General Tighe this.

The groups that have been most focused on live Americans have been characterized by some as a "Rambo" faction. You may not be aware, Mr. Chairman, that our delegation of nine Congressmen that went to Hanoi in mid-February has been characterized in the L.A. Times Sunday by anonymous quotes as a "Rambo delegation," attributed to high level White House people.

Now, my objection here is that those that are placed in this category have never believed in direct military action to get these people out. I never have. I have always thought it was impossible.

If our heros who conceived and activated the Sontai raid of November 20, 1970 with a hot ongoing war with 500,000 plus military personnel in Southeast Asia couldn't pull off the Sontai raid, how can we snatch anybody out?

The irony is that those that I disagree with in Defense and in State Departments really are recovery-oriented. They want to pull somebody out. They say, "Give me the hard evidence and we will go to the wall and get these guys out."

There is only one way we are going to get these men out—and that is to negotiate them out. So, what an irony that those who believe in negotiations with the enemy that we defeated on every battle field, completely crushed on the sea and in the sky with supremacy, not superiority—supremacy—would say, "Negotiate with them," and the others say, "Oh, you can't do that. We have got to get hard evidence. You get it for us and then we will go in with a Rambo raid and pull them out."

What a complete 180-degree reversal of the truth. Would you just comment on whether you believe that it is the negotiation process by which we will extract live American heros rather than any hope of finding enough hard evidence from intelligence sources to ever execute some sort of a rescue mission?

General TIGHE. I believe very firmly that the Hanoi government is very much aware of the value of prisoners. I don't think this is anything new with a Communist government. I recall that after strong denials, the Soviets released German prisoners after World War II. I can recall that an aircrew was discovered in a Chinese jail by accident after the Korean War, et cetera., et cetera., et cetera.

Mr. DORNAN. Two years after.

31

General TIGHE. I am concerned for the tendency to berate anyone that becomes involved in this issue and isn't officially involved, and that is beginning to change. As you have noted, I guess, this berating goes with the territory.

This is such an emotional issue that you can expect just about any kind of an emotional response.

The issue is the issue, however, and if everyone concerned with this can stop worrying about personalities and branding an individual that disagrees with him right off the bat as a Rambo type or whatever, and stick to the issue and see what they can contribute to that issue, then I think eventually we can, through negotiations, go our route.

I would suggest the last thing in the world is that you are going to be able to extract anyone. Hanoi has, in my view, controls the activities of everyone within its boundaries.

You are not going to be able to get at them. There is movement and they control their population so precisely it is going to be very difficult.

I have no intention to recommend to anybody that we start World War III. Then, I can only suggest that negotiation is the only way.

Mr. DORNAN. Negotiation is the only way.

General TIGHE. Yes, sir.

Mr. DORNAN. One final thought. In constantly bumping up against this request for hard evidence toward the goal of an Admiral Thout, a rescue mission—impossible though it may be. Have you encountered over the years, not just this statement that was in the Wall Street Journal about a mindset to debunk, but a mindset that says that we will never negotiate with those bastards who got a victory out of us at Paris when they never beat us on the battle-field? In other words, any discussion of normalization of relations, let alone paying the money that the Government promised them in writing—and it was confirmed by the Secretary of State—and Congress suddenly gets very tough even though they had helped to bring about the Vietnam walkaway after the war. Only afterward did they all want to get tough on Hanoi.

Have you run into this—not dishonorable—but this military attitude that we will never negotiate with those people; it has got to be hard evidence in a military mission to get them out or nothing.

General TIGHE. I don't think that that is unusual after any war. I don't know how long it is going to persist after this one, but since we had a rather inconclusive end to this one, it tends to be a little longer, I think, than a war that you won and have the capability to traverse terrain of the enemy, so this is a natural eventuality.

Mr. DORNAN. But you have run into that attitude?

General TIGHE. It is certainly very prevalent, and I don't think it is just military. I think it persists elsewhere besides the military mind if there is anything such as a military mind.

Mr. DORNAN. My final thought is, did you take note over the weekend that the Vietnamese Government had just returned over 860 boxes of bones of what the French consider their heroes.

General TIGHE. I did very much, of course. I would suggest that the French finally have decided that they have an honor to uphold also.

32

Mr. DORNAN. Do you think that those bones, boxes of heroes' bones, were warehoused somewhere, or were they all dug out of the ground and warehoused?

General TIGHE. I only know what the press had to say, but the press described them as having been taken from cemeteries where they had been identified.

Mr. DORNAN. Thank you, Mr. Chairman.

Mr. SOLARZ. The gentleman from Connecticut, Mr. Rowland, I think, had a question or two.

Mr. ROWLAND. Thank you, Mr. Chairman.

General, the only question that I had came up during the briefing that we had last week by General Perroots with regard to the comments made by your commission, and there was some great contradiction between two of the conclusions.

We first saw—and I don't have the specifics with me—we first saw a comment to the fact everyone on this commission believes there are live prisoners in Southeast Asia, period.

And then, following on with the flip charts, there was a rather long, drawn out mumbo-jumbo type of conclusion which detracted or, at the very least, contradicted the initial statement.

Would you, No. 1, make comments about that? I am not giving you specifics. I think you might know what I am making reference to.

It was a rather long, drawn out statement which detracted immediately from the initial statement that was made by the commission.

General TIGHE. I, of course, did not attend the hearing of General Perroots nor his press conference, so I have no idea what you are referring to.

When it comes to making, bringing about succinct statements of

onclusions, or all conclusions, and then, from them, drawing recommendations; a lot of the verbiage may be left out, but I don't
now of any contradictions in the report to that effect.

I would like to make one point that I hadn't made before when I
poke of how this whole thing got started, and remind the commit-
ee that General Perroots was the former Chief of Air Force Intelli-
ence and we spoke of this issue before he ever went to the Defense
ntelligence Agency.

We had long lunch time discussions of the need for investigating
his and giving it high priority and so forth, but I do not know
hat you are referring to.

Mr. ROWLAND. General, just one other quick question.

We have talked about evidence, and a number of the committee
members have been concerned about what is evidence. What do
ou feel the threshold of evidence is of live Americans, and has
hat been met?

General TIGHE. The threshold has got to be, first of all, an ap-
raisal of the believability of the report that you have. Can the
ource have had access to the area? Is it reasonable to assume that
e is not reporting for some benefit, and so forth, and then cross-
hecking as much as you can all of the things that he has to say.

Does it make sense? Is there a location that looks like this at a
lace that he reported it? Was he, indeed, there, and so forth.

A time has passed, I would like to make the point that a great many of these sources have come out of Asia and been out for a very long time, and finally, come out of the woodwork and reported, and they are already U.S. citizens or French citizens, and so forth, and so their believability should be given a little more credit in that regard.

They don't have anything to gain, or much less, to gain by coming forward. But specifically, it is that threshold where an intelligence analyst with a long time in the business answers two questions—is the data believable, and is the source believable—and that is a judgment factor.

Mr. ROWLAND. Do you feel the threshold has been met on any occasions?

General TIGHE. I think it has been met on a great many occasions, yes.

Mr. ROWLAND. Thank you, General.

Mr. SOLARZ. General, I have a few final questions.

Do you believe, based on the evidence available, that we know the precise location where any Americans are being held in Indochina?

General TIGHE. I suspect if we counted on the Vietnamese allowing us to know and then leaving them there, we would be very naive.

My answer to your question is no.

Mr. SOLARZ. You are convinced that Americans are there, and that they are being held against their will, but you are not sure exactly where they are being held.

General TIGHE. No. I think a profound study of the incarceration system out there and a little better knowledge on the grounds of what has happened to it since we were out there would allow you to have a fairly firm data base on this.

For example, I had quite a long discussion here a couple of weeks ago with a guy by the name of Schwab who was a prisoner in the Saigon area for 16 months, and he was imprisoned in a prison that we knew about when we were down there before we ever left, between Cholon, and the center of the city, in solitary confinement.

Of course, as you know, Hanoi denied that he was a captive there. It shouldn't surprise anybody that that is so. But I think it takes a great deal of in-depth study with people who are giving you current information on the ground in Hanoi to know what the imprisonment system is.

Mr. BEREUTER. Will the gentleman yield on that?

Mr. SOLARZ. Certainly.

Mr. BEREUTER. I thank the chairman for yielding.

I am afraid that question and response might be a little misleading. I want to make sure it is clear so that it is not misleading.

We may not know where Americans are being incarcerated at this point, but isn't it true—it is my opinion; I will see if it is your opinion—that we have known where Americans are incarcerated at a specific point in time in the past.

General TIGHE. Yes, and we have views regularly that we tie to the human reports that we get that they are being held in this or that or the other facility.

My only caution is that if you count on that as a location today when you picked up the information 2 years ago, it might not be good.

Mr. Solarz. General, on the question of the Vietnamese motivation for holding these men, it seems to me that if they are holding them, either they are holding them for purposes of bargaining for something in the future or they are not.

If they are not holding them for bargaining purposes, then presumably, negotiations would not be particularly productive. On what basis do you conclude that there is reason to believe they are holding them for bargaining purposes, when over the course of the last 11 years, they have never indicated directly or indirectly to the variety of emissaries, plenipotentiaries, visiting congressional committees and the like, that they might be interested in some kind of trade or bargain arrangement.

If, in fact, they are holding them for bargaining purposes, haven't they had ample opportunity to even hint that, for the right offer, they might be willing to produce some American POW's?

Mr. Childress has been there. Congressional committees have been there. Other U.S. Representatives have been there. I have been there. Almost all of us have asked the question point blank. They have consistently held to the same line—that there is nobody there, and they know of nobody there.

So my question to you is, if, in fact, they are holding these people for bargaining purposes, leaving aside what their price is or whether we would be prepared to pay, why haven't they hinted that they might be amenable to some arrangement?

General Tighe. I think there are a couple of things that need to be said on this issue.

I have not had access to the transcript of the proceedings between U.S. emissaries or Congressmen and the Hanoi Government at any time since 1981. I don't know what has been said, but I have read their public releases generally from the Foreign Minister or from the Deputy Foreign Minister.

It appears to me that at the end of each of those public statements there is always a little carrot left dangling. For example, in one of them not too long ago, I recall them saying that they may find it profitable to go out and see if, indeed, there are Americans that they don't know about out in the bush.

A second thing that I think you should take note of and which I think dangles——

Mr. Dornan. Could you repeat that, General? This is a very important point.

Mr. Solarz. I can hear.

Mr. Dornan. I am going to ask that I be allowed to divulge for the first time publicly that they said the same thing to me on my trip, so I would like him to repeat it.

General Tighe. I am just talking about the carrot that I saw dangled at the end of a statement by the Foreign Minister of Vietnam to the effect that they may find it useful to go out and see if, indeed, they could find American prisoners who may be out in the hinterland that they did not know about.

That is one of the types of these carrots that I see dangled.

The second that I see regularly dangled to make sure that we stay interested is the exchange of remains from what I consider a rather large depository of carefully identified and prepared remains which Hanoi had, and, in my judgment, doles out from time to time to make sure this Government stays interested.

If I could add one thing, the motivation thing, there may be several motivations among people still there if they are there under the control of the central government—Americans, I am talking about.

There could be maimed—mentally or physically maimed—that they were embarrassed to return, and there could be technicians who were encouraged to stay behind and maintain equipment, or there could be people who had special knowledge and were traded off to Chinese and Russians and so forth.

Mr. SOLARZ. I can think of several reasons why they may not want to divulge that Americans are being held. You have mentioned some; I imagine we could think of others.

My question, however, is a little bit different. If they are prepared to bargain for these people, why haven't they indicated any willingness to bargain?

General TIGHE. I think the bargaining comes on the basis of recognition of them as an equal entity at the bargaining table.

Mr. SOLARZ. Have they indicated that?

General TIGHE. In my judgment, they are looking for recognition by the U.S. Government as a de facto Government—and by that I mean specifically diplomatic recognition.

Mr. SOLARZ. There is no question that they want diplomatic recognition. But are you saying that if we extend diplomatic recognition to them, they will divulge——

General TIGHE. I suggest that immediately upon diplomatic recognition they would find a larger number of remains as a start to the negotiation.

Mr. SOLARZ. Are you saying they have indicated that, if we did extend diplomatic recognition, they would, in fact, divulge the existence of living Americans and begin to talk about conditions for their release?

General TIGHE. I have no way of knowing that.

Mr. SOLARZ. You are making an assumption that they would be willing to?

General TIGHE. Yes.

Mr. SOLARZ. If they would be willing to, why haven't they indicated it?

General TIGHE. I think it is a two-step affair, whether or not you are willing to recognize them as equals before you get serious negotiations.

Mr. SOLARZ. I would think, from their point of view, they would have a better chance of getting diplomatic recognition if they were prepared to indicate that recognition would result in serious talks on the return of Americans whom they have recently discovered, or whatever euphemism we use.

General TIGHE. We might break diplomatic relations right after they have returned people based on arousal of ire of the American people because of their condition, or for a lot of other reasons that were apparent after homecoming.

Mr. SOLARZ. Mr. Bilirakis.

Mr. BILIRAKIS. Thank you, Mr. Chairman, and my appreciation for your invitation to be a part of this very important hearing.

General Tighe, you have stated that we know—to use your words, I think—we know where Americans were incarcerated in the past, in response to the Congressman from Nebraska's question.

General TIGHE. Yes, sir.

Mr. BILIRAKIS. We are talking about Americans incarcerated in the past who have not been returned; is that correct?

General TIGHE. They have been reported incarcerated in Hanoi and other places, yes.

Mr. BILIRAKIS. If we say we know, we are past the report stage. Are we not confident that they are there?

General TIGHE. Not only those not returned, and with reference to Mr. Schwab's interment in Saigon—there are several categories of knowledge: one on the POW's that came back, one on the basis of reporting after they returned, and up to the recent date of Mr. Schwab's return.

Mr. BILIRAKIS. Would we still put that in the category of knowledge and fact?

General TIGHE. Yes, sir.

Mr. BILIRAKIS. Do we know that they are not there any longer?

General TIGHE. No, sir. As a matter of fact, you will never prove that until you get somebody on the ground to find out.

Mr. BILIRAKIS. So we know they were there?

General TIGHE. Mr. Schwab is not there. He is back in the United States. He was bailed out and is back with us.

The other people reported out there, of course we haven't got any of them back. We don't know where they are.

Mr. BILIRAKIS. You are a fact-finding committee. You also indicated earlier that there is unanimity among the committee that there are live Americans in Southeast Asia?

General TIGHE. Yes, sir.

Mr. SOLARZ. Will the gentleman yield? I think this is an example of the semantic confusion into which we are falling.

The language of the report that you submitted, General, does not go quite that far. The language of the report said that there was a strong possibility there were Americans being held there. It is your personal view that Americans are being held. You are convinced of it. Presumably, there were some other members of the task force of your committee that were also convinced of it, as well, but not all. You indicated in your testimony that everybody on the task force thought there were Americans there, but not everybody thought they were being held against their will.

Mr. BILIRAKIS. That is the point that I was leading up to, Mr. Chairman. Thank you for the clarification.

There apparently is unanimity that there are live Americans in Southeast Asia, not as POW's but a lot of Americans in Southeast Asia; is that correct?

General TIGHE. Yes.

When we were exploring the way you arrive at strong possibility——

Mr. BILIRAKIS. I am not at the strong possibility part. The strong possibility is I think Americans, against their will—but there is no strong possibility when it comes to live Americans in Southeast Asia. That is not a strong possibility; that is a fact.

Is that correct?

General TIGHE. That was not debated at all. That is correct.

Mr. BILIRAKIS. So what do we base that on?

General TIGHE. On the live sighting reports and the subsequent activities of agencies of this Government in exploring their validity that are on file in the Defense Intelligence Agency today.

Mr. BILIRAKIS. We are placing an awful lot of credence on the same type of reports; in other words, we say that those reports are not adequate as far as Americans held against their will. But they are adequate insofar as Americans not held against their will?

General TIGHE. I don't think that is a necessary followup to our statements. I don't think we got into that kind of debate as to what those words meant.

I would suggest in any other kind of environment the evidence that we are talking about here, which led to the certitude expressed in our report, would in any other circumstance concerning any other activity on Earth be considered very, very important evidence.

Mr. BILIRAKIS. All right, sir.

But in the minds of all of the study committee, from a unanimity standpoint, that was not adequate to cause them to believe what you believe very strongly, that there are Americans held there against their will?

General TIGHE. I would suggest you could canvass each of the members and find all agreeing with my conviction.

Mr. BILIRAKIS. All agreeing, and yet the best you could come up with was strong possibility?

General TIGHE. I have explained that when you negotiate for words, you want to make sure you don't overstate the problem and the strong requirement over and over again for proof, which has confronted me every time I have come before this House or discussed this with anybody, which is not provable. Then it is wise to be cautious in the words that you use.

As the chairman suggested, we don't want to mislead with our words.

Mr. BILIRAKIS. That is true.

Mr. Chairman, with your further indulgence, you know we represent folks back home and they look to us to explain to them what is happening here on this issue and on others.

How can we explain to them that General Tighe, in whom so many people, including us, have a lot of confidence, thinks one thing but the study commission thinks differently enough to only want to use strong possibility?

General TIGHE. All I was doing was giving the other members of my review panel and senior review group that out if they chose to make that distinction. I did not make that distinction myself.

Mr. BILIRAKIS. Time prevents me from going into it further, and I would like to.

Very quickly, if we went into these negotiations that you refer to, normalization negotiations, would the Vietnamese—would they be willing to admit that, in fact, there have been live POW's, when they have told us so many times that there are none?

General TIGHE. I find them so hardened in dialectic it wouldn't bother them one bit. As a matter of fact, I think that is the record of every Communist government that I have any experience with.

Mr. BILIRAKIS. Thank you, sir.

Mr. SOLARZ. Mr. Solomon, do you have a final question or two?

Mr. SOLOMON. Thank you, Mr. Chairman.

General, I wanted to touch on that a little bit, too, because when you start talking about normalization of relations or reparations, I want to point out that when we were there in February I think that the thing that perhaps aggravated me the most is the fact that Hoang Bicsaong, the Deputy Foreign Minister, changed the position that had been taken in the past, because, if I am not mistaken, they had always said that there were no live Americans in Vietnam under any circumstances, period, and taken the hard line that that was all that they would ever say.

Of course, Hoang Bicsaong, along with some of us here on this panel today, later attended a press conference at which there were representatives of the American press present, and made the statement that there were no live Americans under the direct control of the central government, but—and it was the first time that I had ever heard it—and I think the gentleman from California was touching on this before—he then said, that there could be Americans in the caves or in the mountains. I thought that that was very significant.

But the fact was that he was lying to us right then because Mr. Schwab was being held by the government and he certainly knew that it was a lie. So this all comes back to the question of their attitude as far as linkage of this issue to normalization and reparations are concerned, because they time and time again have told this task force, this subcommittee, the DIA and other representatives of the U.S. Government, that now there is no linkage; that they are doing it for purely humanitarian reasons.

When we were there in February you could look in the eyes of the people, official Communist government people, rank and file Communists on the streets, rank and file non-Communists on the streets, and there was nothing that I could see but total despair in the eyes of all those people. There were no jobs, no economy, and no industry. And those people, it seemed to me, had no hope of anything. And in my opinion, this is the reason that they are doing this and the reason why I have a gut feeling that there are some Americans being held against their will.

You have to ask: Why are they now showing some degree of wanting to cooperate? I think you have touched on it. The one reason is because they need recognition, not just from the United States, but they need recognition from somebody other than the Soviet Government because the Soviet Government gives them military help—but no economic help—as they don't give any of their puppet governments help other than military. So they need something to lift them up. And if they don't get recognized by the United States or their free world neighbors around them, they have no hope. That is one reason.

The second reason, when Chris Smith and I went into the refugee camps in Thailand and had an opportunity to talk to a great many people, there were more and more people defecting from the Vietnamese Government and army, and they were giving some credence to some of these reports that we have been getting, whether it is about the remains of soldiers being held in boxes or whether it is live sighting reports. And sooner or later all of this is going to come to fruition. In other words, sooner or later we are going to be able to put our hands on it.

The point I was trying to make is that, if there are Americans there, that the authorities are going to look for a way out. They are liable to take an American who has just been staying over there, for whatever reason, and they are liable to pick him up and say here is one of those live Americans or they could take Americans that have been under their central control and say they were being held, but not under our central control. This is why I think we need to get to the bottom of this thing.

Mr. Chairman, you said you wanted a motion to ask Mr. Perot to come forward. If he doesn't mind, maybe he would like to come forward because we might have a couple of questions for him.

Mr. SOLARZ. I have one final question for General Tighe, and then I would, without objection from the subcommittee like to invite Mr. Perot to address us on this question. I would also like to ask two other people who are present to come up, as well: Ann Griffiths, the executive director of the League of Families; and General Shufelt, the Deputy Director of DIA. Since we will be voting on House Concurrent Resolution 129, and since we are going to hear from Mr. Perot, I think it would be appropriate to hear from them.

I hope each of them can address themselves to the question of whether they think the establishment of such a commission would be in the interest of the country and whether it would help the effort to determine the fate of the POW's.

General Tighe, I have one final question: You would agree, I gather, the President has the authority to establish such a commission on his own should he choose to do so. The only thing that he doesn't have the authority to do, as I understand it, is to give such a commission subpoena power. That would have to be given to the commission by the Congress.

The subpoena power, as I am sure you know, is applicable within the jurisdiction of the United States and not in Vietnam or in Laos. I would love to be able to subpoena the records of the Politboro, but I rather doubt that our subpoenas would be respected there. If the President doesn't like the idea of a commission, then it is fairly obvious that even if the Congress did establish a Presidential commission, it is doubtful that it would have much success.

For such a commission to work, it would have to have the backing of the President. Since the only purpose of the subpoena power is to obtain testimony from American citizens—presumably those working for the Government in this instance—that could be done simply by a directive of the President to anybody who has worked on this issue.

I am not, I must tell you, overly comfortable with the idea of giving a blanket authority to issue subpoenas to a commission when one doesn't know exactly how it is going to be used, and when presumably the information they would be seeking could be obtained by an order of the President.

I assume if the President believed the commission were useful to establish, he would also instruct all relevant U.S. employees to co-operate with the commission.

So, I ask you: If that is the case, do you in fact see a need for giving such a commission the subpoena power? If so, why?

General TIGHE. That power is not the sine qua non of the commission, as I envision it. However, I would suggest as time passes there are a growing number of witnesses that could be very supportive of this issue who have become more and more reluctant to get involved, to share what they know, some who have occupied high positions in the governments of Southeast Asia. And I think it is very important that the man heading this commission be able to get those people to come forward.

I don't know of any other way to make sure that you are tapping all the sources possible than to have that. But, as I say, if you were establishing a permanent Presidential commission and could not get that, it is not going to fail on that basis.

Mr. SOLARZ. If there are no further questions, let me thank you once again, General, for taking time to be with us today. I think all of us deeply appreciate the interest you have shown in this issue, and your willingness, long after your retirement as the head of the DIA, to remain involved and to lend the country the benefit of your experience and wisdom.

Mr. SOLOMON. Are we not going to keep General Tighe here while we talk to the other people?

Mr. SOLARZ, General, are you in a position to remain?

General TIGHE. I can stay.

Mr. SOLARZ. Although Mr. Perot's name has been bandied about fairly frequently, let me ask him whether he would like to share his views with the committee on the desirability of establishing a commission. Mr. Perot, we would be pleased to hear from you, if you would like to make a statement.

STATEMENT OF H. ROSS PEROT

Mr. PEROT. Whatever the will of the committee is. I just came to listen to General Tighe.

Mr. SOLARZ. I think some of the members would like to ask you some questions. If you would like to answer them, we would be happy to have you come up.

Thank you very much. If there is any statement you would like to make, feel free to do so. Otherwise we will ask questions.

Mr. PEROT. It has been interesting to listen. I am sure all of you are very busy and want to get to the bottom of this and want to know the hard truth and facts. I have been intrigued by your fair questions about the difference in what you hear and the difference in what you read. That can be easily addressed. I was asked to be on this group. Couldn't be on it because of my business schedule. Asked that Gen. Robbie Risner represent me. He did. He was a prisoner of war 8 years, 5 years in solitary confinement. If you talked with a cross-section of POW's about who the most admired

Americans were in the camps because of leadership and strength, Risner comes out close to the top.

I stayed close to the commission, and then at the request of the Vice President and with the understanding of General Tighe, came in after the commission had finished its work and started my individual study because both the Vice President and the President wanted me to get to the bottom of this, come to them and tell them what I have found.

I am midflight in that study now. Every member of this commission, I believe, will come in here and under oath say what General Tighe said, only most will say it in much stronger and more colorful language, because General Tighe tends to understatement. So you are not looking at a one man minority position.

Second, in terms of what DIA can and can't do, I don't believe this committee, or at least all the members of the committee understand that. DIA sits over there and receives information. If they don't get anything, they don't study anything. So now immediately you say you have got a good group there, highly motivated, fine people. What are they getting? No problem, we have the JCRC over there. They are getting all this information out of the refugee camps. It is important to ask the right question. How many people have worked in JCRC, over the years. I have seen testimony stating 15 people. Most of those are in Hawaii. They don't go to Bangkok. It has been two people in Bangkok over the years since the war.

The refugee camps are several hours from Bangkok. The JCRC primary mission is recovering remains. Their mission says nothing about gathering information. Go talk to the refugee workers. They live in the camps. They swim in this sea of refugees; they hear this information day after day. What is the problem? Since everybody here is a person of good will, in my judgment, I have not found a villain yet, didn't expect to. What is the problem? Everybody lives in their tiny little world. That is the problem.

We are not giving them nearly the quality of information they deserve in DIA. People in Bangkok are a weak second to a high-powered team that speaks the language fluently in the refugee camps living there day after day with the refugees, because that is where the information is. That is a major problem, just the flow of information. There is a second problem, and this will come to why you need subpoena power. Any number of people in very sensitive positions have come forward that have known me for years on this issue. They feel a moral obligation to testify. but, because of their position, can only testify if subpoenaed and place under oath, and they cannot testify under any other conditions. That is where that comes from. That is why you need it. Now, what are these people saying?

Let me give you one very colorful conversation that will help put it in perspective about why the system is not working. I had a senior person in a sensitive position come to me and say, "Ross, don't you wonder how we live with ourselves?"

I said, "Yes, as a matter of fact I do.

"It is simple. We set the screens so tight that nothing can get through." Now let's talk consistency. You say, how does that happen? These people are trained in their military background to gather information to a sufficient level to rescue someone. That requires many times the order of magnitude of knowledge over, "Is there anyone there?" which is what basically I hear you asking again and again today. We have people trying to find enough information so that we can mount a rescue. Believe me, gentlemen, we cannot rescue these people with military force. There is no way to do it, and I can spend as much time as you want on that.

I have had any number of senior people in our Government say, "We will never bend, negotiate." And I say, "Then there is only one thing to do—declare them live casualties of the war and write them off". It is fundamentally important to face the issue. I think we have used the DIA and CIA as an excuse for years. I believe the only way we would have an opportunity to get these men out is through negotiation. Then the logical question is, Is there anyone there? Absolutely there is somebody there. Why do I think there is somebody there? Because in 1969, in 1970, when the CIA was running the war in Laos, and I was going back and forth, we had totally cracked the radio system. We knew everything they were doing. From the time a man hit the ground, we tracked him to the prison camps, we knew who, what, when, and how. Anybody that was around then knows exactly what happened, and again, totally facing the issue. We had the negotiations; Nixon wrote the letter; nobody got to read it; everybody thought they understood the letter; but the North Vietnamese got to read it. We didn't. Every time Henry Kissinger said, "No problem," the people from Laos are coming out through Hanoi. The Pathet Lao people said, "Not so, not until we get a treaty and the money, then you will get the prisoners back."

Why do I think Hanoi had prisoners? Because their representative told me twice. At the end of the war they told the press, "We have prisoners and will return them after the war." The prisoners come home from Hanoi. Everybody expected more prisoners. No ifs, ands, and buts. Look at what the Defense Department was saying at that point in time about more prisoners coming home. Now then, the issue on the multi-billion-dollar rebuilding plan, reparations is the wrong word, but the $3.5 billion plan hit Congress, and Congress was so angered by the treatment of the POW's that they said, "No, forget it."

We were midflight in Watergate, a military man could not wear his uniform in Washington, and after 60 or 90 days suddenly there was an article in the press from the Pentagon, all of the POW's are dead. Now, is there a villain there? Absolutely not. Who made the decision? I don't know. If you ever want to know you are going to have to give somebody subpoena power to get there, I will tell you that. I am not sure it is important because I don't think there are any villains here. That is where I am.

Now we will talk about anything you want to. I apologize if I have covered things you didn't want me to cover.

Mr. Solarz. I appreciate your willingness to come to Washington today and to share your views with us. Let me first say to the Members who are present, particularly of the subcommittee and also our guests, that we have now been in session since roughly 11:30, and we haven't had lunch. Some of us have other matters to attend to, and we also want to get to the question of the resolution.

I want to give everybody ample opportunity to ask questions but I also want people to know that it is not the intention of the Chair to keep the committee in session until midnight. Mr. Perot, I just have one thing to say and then one question to ask.

This subcommittee does have subpoena authority.

Mr. PEROT. Right.

Mr. SOLARZ. If you, or anybody else, know of individuals whose testimony could contribute to a resolution of this problem and who would only testify if subpoenaed, I certainly hope you will provide us their names and give us as much information as you can about them so we could pursue that possibility.

We have issued subpoenas in the past and I am sure we could get a majority to issue subpoenas in the future. I don't want to just issue subpoenas for the sake of issuing subpoenas. We would want to talk to people first, if we can, to see whether they are prepared to cooperate voluntarily, and to get a sense of what they would tell us should they testify. I want to make it clear that if you know people, although you don't have to give their names in public, I hope you would inform the subcommittee in some fashion so we can follow up on this.

I can tell you that for the 6 years I have been chairman of this subcommittee we have never hesitated to call anybody before the subcommittee, in public or private session, depending on what was appropriate, who had something to contribute or where somebody suggested it would be useful to hear them. I would like you to be on notice of that.

Finally, do you favor the approval of House Concurrent Resolution 129 as it is written?

Mr. PEROT. Well, that is a very narrow question. The answer has to be no, because I think the thing terminates in about 60 days, doesn't it?

Mr. SOLARZ. What do you favor?

Mr. PEROT. I favor to get them home and getting the men home. What does that take, we can talk like you have been talking today for ever, because we are talking around the issue.

Mr. SOLARZ. But——

Mr. PEROT. I am trying to tell you, but I won't if you don't want to hear.

Mr. SOLARZ. If I didn't want to hear what you have to say, I wouldn't have invited you to testify. You are convinced that there are Americans in Indochina being held against their will and that it is impossible to rescue them. You believe that the only way to get them out is through negotiation with the Vietnamese. We have a Logan Act which prohibits private citizens from engaging in negotiations on behalf of the Government. The President can appoint emissaries for the purposes of conducting such negotiations. He can even meet, himself, with Vietnamese leaders.

If your analysis is accurate that there are men being held there against their will and that it is impossible for us to rescue them and that the only way to get them out is through a process of negotiation, it is not clear to me what useful purpose the establishment of a commission would serve. A commission cannot conduct negotiations. Only the President of the United States, or his designees, can conduct negotiations. If there is a solution to the problem, it seems to me it lies not in establishing a commission, with or without subpoena power, but in having the President embark on these negotiations.

Do you want to respond to that?

Mr. PEROT. I was trying to respond when you told me the answer.

Mr. SOLARZ. Do you agree or disagree with that analysis?

Mr. PEROT. What I would like to do is give you my answer.

Mr. SOLARZ. Sure.

Mr. PEROT. This is the only thing worth doing, figure out what it takes to get them back and get them back. What is the ideal mechanism to accomplish this?

We are going to have to get a group, and I am not a student of government, you are a better man than I am on that, but I am a student of the other side and they are very sensitive to what Congress thinks. Assume that you decide that this is a good idea, you want to do it at the Presidential level.

Congress' fingerprints need to be on it in my judgment. I am talking about impact on the North Vietnamese because all of you are elected by the people and if you go back to the war, those people—the Vietnamese—were masterminds in studying this country and particularly sensitive to the House of Representatives, so I would hope your fingerprints are on it. That is your call.

The main thing is to stop talking around the issue, to stop this situation where everybody is embarrassed and where everybody is polarized and we spend all our energy fighting internally.

We need to spend our energy getting the men home.

Mr. SOLARZ. I agree that the No. 1 priority should be to bring back anybody who might be over there, particularly those who would like to return. The answer lies not in conducting additional investigations, not in subpoenaing Americans, but in inducing the President to muster the will to engage in negotiations.

That, in my judgment, would not require a commission. All it requires is the President of the United States, who has the responsibility for our foreign policy, to do it.

My impression is the President has, in fact, sent emissaries over there, and that the Vietnamese have said that they don't have anybody.

It is very difficult to negotiate something if your negotiating partner says he doesn't have the capacity to accomplish whatever it is you are asking for.

Mr. PEROT. You are from New York, right? The best traders in the world come from New York City.

I have a horse. You want to buy it, you say, "Ross, do you want to sell your horse or not?" That is where we start.

Nobody has ever come head to head with the Vietnamese in a trading situation.

Mr. SOLARZ. This is a little different, Mr. Perot.

It is not as if we have said, "We want to buy your horse. What do you want for it?" They say they have no horse to sell.

Mr. PEROT. What I would say in a trading situation, "This is a horse that is lame. I have wanted to get rid of for years, but my first reaction is, I don't want to sell it."

We go through that in the preliminaries, in these tours. You don't really get into the depth that you are going to have to get into to get this done. This has to be single purpose, focused and people are going to have to get on it and stay on it because the folks on the other side are tough as leather and resolute.

I am not looking for work, so this is not a personal campaign on my part. I have plenty to do. All I am saying is that whatever in your wisdom you conclude is the way to get it done as opposed to continuing to sort of knead the dough which is what we have been doing for years.

Over in the Defense Department there is a great apprehension about the fact that we may have to go rescue these folks some day.

How would you like to be in charge of 25 or 30 simultaneous rescues in a place where we have no military presence. Because if you don't get them all at once, they are going to move them, kill them, go into all those things you know better than I.

It is going to come as a tremendous sigh of relief in our country when we say, "Let's bite the bullet." We are not psychologically equipped to do anything, but win a war. We didn't win this war. We want to relieve Bataan and just take our people out. We can't do that, so we have with the best of intentions avoided facing the real issue.

All I am pleading with you to do today is whatever, and I don't know what that is, within the power of Congress, do everything you can. The White House and Senate should do everything they can because I am confident the American people want that.

One last thing: All this stuff that comes up about the families, I have been close to these families since the sixties. They have been through it all. You are getting really concerned and doing everything you can will not upset the families.

What upsets the families is a bad set of bones. That upsets the family. I don't know how you define coverup, but you look at the standards we require to show you that there is one live American still in Vietnam or Laos and compare that to what we send home, in caskets and we've got a double standard.

We close the books with the tiniest shred of information. I don't want anybody to be embarrassed and I don't know any villains, but I suggest, if possible, this group take the leadership today and do whatever you decide is appropriate to bring this to a conclusion.

Mr. SOLARZ. You indicated you knew some people who had information that would be very helpful.

Mr. PEROT. That is right.

Mr. SOLARZ. Could you tell us who they are?

Mr. PEROT. No. Here we go again. These people came to me in confidence. They had waited for years. For some reason I showed up on the scene and their level of trust was such they said they would talk to me informally, but they could only go public under subpoena.

Mr. SOLARZ. We are in a position to subpoena people.

Mr. PEROT. I would have to ask them.

Mr. SOLARZ. In other words, you know people who have information that could contribute to a solution to this problem. They have told you that they can only divulge that information if subpoenaed, yet you won't give us their names so we can subpoena them?

Mr. PEROT. Not without getting their approval.

Mr. SOLARZ. In other words, even if they refuse to give you their approval and you believe that what they have to say would help contribute to a solution of this problem, you would refuse to give us their names so we could subpoena them?

Mr. PEROT. I would first go to them and ask for their approval and encourage them to talk to you. Aren't we playing a game? I will do everything I can to help you. I will talk to them and do my best to get them to come talk to you.

Mr. SOLARZ. The thing you can do right now is give us their names. If you want to do it confidentially, that is fine.

Mr. PEROT. I will have to talk to them first.

Mr. SOLARZ. What if they refuse?

Mr. PEROT. I will decide what to do then based on my conversations with them one at a time.

Mr. SOLARZ. Have they told you their stories?

Mr. PEROT. In some cases, in reasonable detail. In other cases, they have said they want to be placed under oath, but they can't come forward voluntarily.

Mr. SOLARZ. Is it your view that their testimony would be helpful?

Mr. PEROT. This is like putting 18 inches of additional concrete on a road already paved. That is why I say we are off the subject. Certainly the evidence is overwhelming that people are there.

Mr. SOLARZ. Mr. Leach.

Mr. LEACH. I have one question.

Earlier today, I asked you if you would be interested in serving on a commission and you indicated only if the President so requested. Is that your position?

Mr. PEROT. Yes, sir. I am not looking for this job. If everybody wants me to do this job and if the job is real and it is not one of these slow-waltz operations, a 2-week trip to Hanoi, then I will drop everything and do it, but you could probably find a better man and that is fine with me and I will keep doing business.

Mr. LEACH. Did you tell the Chairman at GM you didn't know of computer business for sale? I think that we have found the man, and I have no complaints on that issue.

By the way, I think one of Gen. Tighe's comments is of relevance here. He said one of the major issues is a data base.

Mr. PEROT. He is dead right on that and that is strictly a matter of budget. DIA has got good people. It is a terrible analogy, but you remember the three monkeys, the monkey that had his hands over his ears? They don't have their hands over their ears, but there is not enough coming through their ears.

A handful of people sitting in Bangkok can't begin to supply the flow of information that these people deserve. You go find out exactly how many people we have on the ground and in Laos and you will have some spare fingers left over in terms of just what our intelligence gathering capability is on the ground.

We don't know. We don't have it. Why don't we have it? You now why; we dismantled it.

Mr. SOLOMON. Ross, I know you may have to go and I know we have a vote on, but I just want to take you to task for one statement you made.

Mr. PEROT. Yes, sir.

Mr. SOLOMON. You said that those guys from New York are the best horse traders. Us guys from Upstate New York; there is a difference.

Mr. PEROT. Those fellows, too, just country boys; there is a difference.

Mr. SOLOMON. Let me just say that the other day that I had the privilege of being at the United States Marine Corps Reserve Officers Association annual event, and Ross Perot got the Man of the Year Award, and, Ross, we are very happy to give that award to you. Nobody deserves it more than you do.

Let me just real quickly ask you something. We have really serious problems in the Congress itself trying to deal with the Vietnamese Government, because they insist on a government-to-government relationship. I discussed this with General Tighe before, and it was his testimony that we ought to have a Presidential commission.

We have before us today the Bill Hendon bill, which calls for a congressional commission. We have amendments to this bill that might be offered, which would establish a Presidential commission with subpoena powers, which would allow for the normal process for appointment to that commission.

Congressman Leach may offer that amendment, which would establish a Presidential commission that would go into effect at the request of the President of the United States, whoever that might be.

The reason I feel that it should be a Presidential commission is because we may not have President Reagan 2 years from now; and we can't pass a constitutional amendment to keep him there, which we would like to do. Whoever the next President is, in other words, we would like to have that Presidential commission functioning.

It would be the intent maybe of this committee and Congressman Leach to offer such an amendment, and then with a sense of Congress resolution that you be considered to be heading up that commission.

Some of us feel this is the direction we ought to go in, so that then the commission would have government-to-government authority directly with the Vietnamese Government to do exactly what you have been saying here today.

Would you have any objection to that approach?

Mr. PEROT. No, sir. I leave that to the wisdom of the Congress. It is my understanding that is where the whole thing started, that they requested, a Presidential commission, couldn't get it off the ground, and it came to this. I have just really one major suggestion here since the other side is patient, they are tougher, they are patient: For heaven sakes, don't let this thing expire when President Reagan leaves office.

Somehow Congress needs—somehow we need to keep it alive past the end of the Presidential term, or they will sit there and watch the clock tick, see who is running, see if there is a soft guy on the ballot, somebody they can make a better deal with, somebody else is going to own the horse.

Mr. SOLARZ. We are new on the second bells. It is the intention of the Chair to recess the subcommittee until 2:30. When we return, I would like to hear from Ms. Griffiths and General Shufelt. We will -return and then beginning hopefully by 3:00 o'clock at the latest take up this resolution.

[Brief recess.]

Mr. SOLARZ. The subcommittee will resume its deliberation.

Sam, did you have any questions you wanted to ask of Mr. Perot? If not, Mr. Perot, let me say I very much appreciate your willingness to come here and share your views with us. There may be some other Members who would have some questions. The subcommittee would appreciate it if you could possibly keep yourself available for further questioning. I would like to now move forward and have Ann Mills Griffiths, the Executive Director of the National League of Families, which represents the great majority of the families of the men who are missing in action and who were POW's testify; General Shufelt, the Deputy Director of the Defense Intelligence Agency, who has been dealing with this issue, will also give his views on General Tighe's report and on the desirability of establishing a congressional commission.

General, if you would like to go first.

STATEMENT OF BRIG. GEN. JAMES SHUFELT, DEPUTY DIRECTOR FOR PLANS, TRAINING, AND OPERATIONS, DEFENSE INTELLIGENCE AGENCY

General SHUFELT. I will start out by saying that this has probably been the most interesting afternoon of any of the sessions that I have attended in the last 10 months.

Let me start off by reminding you all that DIA does three things: We collect, analyze and disseminate intelligence. We are responsible for the tasking of collection entities that are part of the U.S. intelligence community. When we get information, we are responsible for the analysis of that information and then we disseminate it to the decisionmakers. Obviously, it is up to the decisionmakers both within the Department of Defense and within the White House to decide what they are going to do with that information.

As I listen to people, I get the feeling that there is a conclusion that DIA on a small island standing there by ourselves trying to juggle 47 balls in the air at one time. I want to reemphasize that we are not alone in our endeavors and that, we are, in fact, part of a team that President Reagan in effect put together.

That team is comprised of people in the White House. It is composed of the League of Families as represented by Ann Griffiths who is here today. It is also composed of people in OSD, State Department, and, of course, DIA. That team is responding to the President's priorities and his sense of direction as to how to go about resolving this issue over the long haul.

Therefore while DIA plays a very important role, it is not the totality of what tales place in the halls of Washington. Of course, the subcommittee is also a part of that team, and I don't want to neglect mentioning that fact.

Your subcommittee, the House Task Force, and the committees on the Senate side all have played a role over the past year in trying to work this issue.

Obviously, I am speaking not as a policymaker on this issue. As I said, I am the provider of information. No matter what happens, DIA will continue to bear a tremendous responsibility in providing information.

We are, in fact, the mechanism by which, as I said, you do the collection tasking, as well as the analysis and dissemination of that information. So from our perspective, we are providing a service to a customer, whoever that customer is.

But I think from a personal perspective, as Mr. Perot pointed out, the issue is negotiations. Negotiations must proceed in such a responsible way that you get certain end results. It seems to me as I think he also indicated, it is going to be a personal representative of the President at some level who is going to do the talking and negotiating on this issue. It isn't going to be a commission which will be negotiating.

So in my mind the question comes down then to what do you really want a commission to do.

You have had prior commissions, presidential as well as congressional. Is the neceessity for the Commission to restudy the issue? Is the Commission to reinvestigate DIA and how we do business? I don't think so.

Everybody feels that what they really want is to get on and resolve the issues so we can put this thing to rest. I think those are really my thoughts on the Commission.

One thing I must say from the DIA perspective, of course, is that we have discussed today the question of semantics. I think General Tighe did an excellent job of discussing the study he did for General Perroots. Concerning the question of strong possibility of prisoners, I have heard the word "evidence," and I have heard the word "fact." All I can tell you at this point in time from the Agency responsible for providing that information to the decisionmakers and people who desire it, is that we certainly don't have the facts.

We simply continue to assume that Americans are there, and we are working desperately in DIA to confirm that assumption. We are not suggesting that the purpose is to conduct some sort of a raid or do anything. We are simply to provide that information and let the policymakers decide what they are going to do with it.

Mr. SOLARZ. Thank you very much.

Ms. Griffiths?

STATEMENT OF ANN MILLS GRIFFITHS, EXECUTIVE DIRECTOR, NATIONAL LEAGUE OF FAMILIES

Ms. GRIFFITHS. Well, the position of the League we have conveyed several times to the Congress, but it is a fairly complex one.

First of all, three boards of directors have voted against it and at an annual meeting it was very narrowly defeated then the full membership voted it down by mail, so it is a solid position of the league.

The origin of the Commission proposal was basically conspiracy and coverup, which has now been investigated five times, two times in the Congress and three other investigations, including General Tighe's latest one, and is a discredited theory.

Our main objections derive from the following, and that it will set aside the solution to the POW–MIA issue, which everyone agrees is going to require negotiations.

It removes the issue from the policy mainstream, and it took us 5 years to get the POW–MIA issue into the policy mainstream, to try to get the cooperation of the Vietnamese and Lao Governments.

To have that thrown aside for any commission, which will require the resources in DIA that took us many years to build up, from the 6 or so at the time of General Tighe's departure in 1981 to 28 with more on the way at the present time, all of which resources have recently been devoted to one investigation after another. Feeding information to another commission, no matter how lofty, no matter who the chairman, no matter who directs its being established, is going to drain assets from the live prisoner issue: Collection followup and the intelligence analysis that General Shufelt mentioned, and which the policymakers need to resolve this issue.

I agree negotiations are the best way to get this issue resolved, but it did take us that long, and we, I think, are finally reaching the point you said, Mr. Chairman, the Vietnamese don't tie this to reparations or normalization.

I don't know how many times some people in this room have met with the Vietnamese, but I have met with them more times than I can count, and 9 or 10 times with the Foreign Minister of Vietnam.

Never in this administration has the Vietnamese Government raised to United States delegations reparations or normalization of relations as a precondition.

In fact, in the most recent meeting a week ago Friday, they made it very clear that they do not put normalization before cooperation on this issue. They said they seek cooperation as a way of bridging that gap, and eventually, naturally leading to improvements in the atmosphere so that once Cambodia is settled there can be serious improvement in the relationship between the two countries.

The Commission would send very mixed signals to the Vietnamese and Lao Governments. It would give them an opportunity to wait and see if perhaps there would be policy recommendations for changes, to what some have advocated, normalization of relations.

We just saw a postponement, they called it a delay, in the latest technical meeting. Nobody knows the real reason yet, and we are trying to figure it out. It could be, just possibly, for several reasons including what you mentioned, the French picking up over 800 remains, all of which the French interred in French cemeteries, a very different circumstance from ours.

It could be because General Tighe was on television advocating normalization of relations, or because they know that you all in the Congress are considering passing a congressional resolution which would take this out of the policy mainstream.

It also is very clear in the minds of the Vietnamese that if they are ever going to have serious improvement in relations, it is going to be through responsiveness to the executive branch.

They are now responding to the specific personal concern of this President and his priority as established during this administration.

Also, we are not opposed to a commission on an indefinite basis. We have made clear in the communications we have had with the Congress that if in the future there is a lessening of priorities, or if the President should decide that that is the best way to resolve this issue, then fine. We would want to talk to him about it first, and make sure it was his personal direction that was being given. But that time is not now; that is at some time in the future if we see a lessening of priority rather than a continuing increase in priority.

The President is opposed to the establishment of a commission.

Finally, I think it needs to be understood that there is no simplistic, easy solution. It is going to take those kinds of tough negotiations that I have been through for a very long time. Having known Mr. Dornan since 1969 and was on his television program during those years, I have been through several administrations. I have been through these kinds of proposals, changes in the Vietnamese leadership as well, so it is not a simple problem.

They are going to respond to the U.S. Government because that is where the eventual improvements lie and they look in the long term, not short term. It is going to require continued perseverance under the current priority.

That is why we are opposed.

Mr. SOLARZ. Ms. Griffiths, first of all, let me thank you for your testimony. I think all of us who have had the opportunity to work with you over the years on this issue have been deeply impressed by your dedication, your ability, and by your achievements in really helping to keep this issue alive and at the forefront of our national concerns. I think the families of all of the men who are missing, your own brother, and any who may be alive now in Indochina owe you an enormous debt of gratitude.

If one day anybody is returned alive, it will be due in no small measure to the hard work you have put in over the years. I have just been tremendously impressed and deeply touched by what you have done.

I gather that based on your personal discussions with the President, he is opposed to the Commission?

Ms. GRIFFITHS. Yes.

Mr. SOLARZ. General Shufelt, as a representative of the administration, is the President in favor of a commission or opposed to it?

General SHUFELT. Is the President?

Mr. SOLARZ. In favor of a commission at this time or against it?

General SHUFELT. I have no idea as far as the President is concerned.

Mr. SOLARZ. What is the position of the administration?

General SHUFELT. The administration is opposed to the Commission.

Mr. SOLARZ. Presumably the administration reflects the views of the Department.

I have no further questions.

Mr. Leach?

Mr. LEACH. First, let me echo what Congressman Solarz says about the respect for you and your work.

Second, if there were a commission, do you think it would be appropriate to make a presumption of the Commission the notion that the President approves of it?

Ms. GRIFFITHS. Well, absolutely, but the President has no reluctance to establish a commission if he sees the need, and if he feels t will better help resolve this issue. He has none whatsoever. He appreciates the congressional bipartisan interest in the issue, but if he felt that is what is necessary, he would do it.

Mr. LEACH. Second, if a commission were formed, would it be more appropriate for it to be congressional or Presidential?

Ms. GRIFFITHS. Presidential, for many of the reasons that General Tighe outlined, but also because we have lived through two commissions and committees, and many of you here in this room served on those. This issue was very nearly dealt serious death blows, and it took many years to overcome the results of both a presidential commission and a congressional select committee. They almost did in this issue totally.

Now, is not the time. The families are not gluttons for punishment. We finally have serious bipartisan priority and strategy which we never had before. Why would we want to give that up for commission that would have to learn the issue first. And that is no simple task as you all know. Why would we want to resort to that?

To me, you resort to that when or if the current priority fails. As you know, our long-held position is that Americans are alive. We were pleased with General Tighe recently coming out and saying a strong possibility." I was pleased to hear Bud McFarland say he believes prisoners are there. I believe it.

That is the league position. It has been our position; forever, but the same time, the priority has to be, allowed to work, to bring eater results. If at such time in the future there is a lessening of priorities and we have to resort to a commission, then fine, do it, then them relearn the issue. Let them press on and do it. At this int in history, if we can't get what we are looking for under this priority, then I think we are in serious trouble, and the priority is to be high enough to where it transcends a change in administration.

If that takes a Presidential commission, fine, look at it then as option, but not as a priority now.

Mr. LEACH. Thank you.

Mr. SOLARZ. Mr. Solomon, do you have any questions?

Mr. SOLOMON. Mr. Chairman, first of all, I just want to also thank Ann for all her help. Believe me, I don't know where we would have been without it over these last years Ann, you and George Brooks—I think I saw George back there someplace, too—and we really, really deeply appreciate it.

We have got a dilemma here which needs to be resolved. We have got a bill before us with 275 signatures on it, and that is significant. Many of the cosponsors of this legislation do not necessarily in my opinion, support the written legislation, but they have some concerns, the way I do, and some kind of action is going to be to be taken on this legislation. By the way I think everybody this room knows that, although some may take exception to it, I probably Ronald Reagan's greatest supporter in this Congress going all the way back to 1976 when I was a delegate over Jerry and for Ronald Reagan.

Mr. DORNAN. I was in Miami in 1968, so I have never stipulated to that.

Mr. SOLOMON. I think that at this point we are going to have to do something with the legislation, and Congressman Leach, the ranking Republican on this subcommittee, has made some suggestions to us about establishing a Presidential commission that would not go into effect unless the President approved it; in other words, unless he initiated it, with a sense of the Congress that Ross Perot be appointed head of any commission that is initiated. It seems to me that this committee today has to take some kind of action.

I don't know what the feeling of the ranking Member is at this point, but I think we are reaching the point where we are going to have to discuss the bill itself and what we are going to do with it—whether we are going to just kill the bill, whether we are going to amend it, or what.

I personally don't see anything wrong with sending this bill, as amended by Congressman Leach, to the President. It would show him the amount of support that there is in the U.S. Congress, and that there is from the American people, that we think we need to go a step further, whatever that is. I have seen one of those who have adamantly opposed reparations, who have adamantly opposed normalization, and I still am, but the highest priority has to be that if there are live Americans there, we have to bring them home, and I just believe that if we send this message on to the President, letting him use his good common sense, and he has the best of any American that I know, that he will have a choice of doing nothing as far as that legislation is concerned, and continuing with the high priority the way he is going about it, or he will appoint the Presidential commission, or he will appoint an emissary, who could be H. Ross Perot, or even Bill Hendon or Steve Solarz or Jerry Solomon or whoever, to go and negotiate.

That is going to be my recommendation to this committee, as the chairman of the task force. At the appropriate time I would hope that we would get to the bill.

Mr. SOLARZ. The appropriate time is rapidly approaching and I would like to move forward.

Are there any other members of the subcommittee who have questions?

Mr. Bereuter?

Mr. BEREUTER. Thank you.

I will limit it to one quick question, and without editorial comment.

Do you believe that the creation of a Presidential commission would, as you put it, remove this issue from the policy mainstream as compared to a congressional commission?

Ms. GRIFFITHS. I think either one, in fact, I am sure either one would. The only agency who would probably be directly involved were a commission established would be DIA, to feed them information to learn the issue, until such time as they felt sufficiently backgrounded to look at policy options or something like that. As far as initiation of activities, other than JCRC collection of information, DAO and all the other tasking intelligence wise, then it would be more or less deferred, waiting to see what the commission came up as far as any recommendation. Everything would have to slow down bureaucratically, even at Armitage's level or Sigur's or whomever to stop and see what the commission comes up with. In any event, it is harmful and will delay progress.

Mr. BEREUTER. If I can just pack up and reclaim 30 seconds of the time I said I wouldn't take, I believe that if the Members of the House of Representatives were polled, whether by one fashion or another, with a voting card or whatever, at least the majority would say that they believed there is a strong possibility that Americans are alive in Vietnam, and therefore, I am concerned, despite having respect for your opinion about what kind of reaction there will be, if we fail to take some action on an amended form, at least on some bill of which there are now 275 cosponsors, what kind of reaction is this going to cause not only here and among families, but also in Vietnam?

Ms. GRIFFITHS. Well, I think there at least are two things at work here as far as the number of cosponsors. Certainly there are many. One is that due to the priority on this issue and the visibility, the media attention on all of the activities and the policy level negotiations as well as technical meetings, massive amounts of publicity and priority have been generated. So any Member of Congress is naturally going to support and want to support something that is humanitarian. Two, how does one oppose God, motherhood, and apple pie? But the fact that they have cosponsored it is known; the Vietnamese have already counted them. They already know all the cosponsors this has.

The Vietnamese have had visits from many congressional delegations and accepted them all, so the level of support is already registered with our administration, the Vietnamese and Lao as well as the American people. If it is going to be passed at all, I still think there are severe dangers, not that I believe at all that the President would establish a commission in spite of so many cosponsors. He would consider it bipartisan congressional support which he has sought as part of the strategy.

Mr. BEREUTER. Thank you. Thank you, Mr. Chairman.

Mr. SOLARZ. Mr. Gilman.

Mr. GILMAN. Thank you, Mr. Chairman.

I too want to commend Ann Griffiths for her devotion to the National League of Families; George Brooks, its chairman; and Joel Cook of the National Human Rights Committee for POW's and MIA's, who have given so much time and dedication to this issue. Ann Griffiths stated that the President is opposed to this idea of a commission. What confirmation do you have that the President is opposed to a commission?

Ms. GRIFFITHS. This week, and January of this year.

Mr. GILMAN. This week was with an administration official who confirmed it?

Ms. GRIFFITHS. Yes.

Mr. GILMAN. General, earlier today we heard that there wasn't a high enough priority given to this issue. Has a high priority been established by the administration for this issue? What is that priority, and is that priority eroded by other responsibilites?

General SHUFELT. First of all, the priority on the POW/MIA issue is high. The manpower resources within DIA today which are directly related to the issue consists of 28 people. They are soon going to increase by another 16 people. Much of this increase is due in part to General Tighe's recommendation about increased ADP support for the effort both in terms of the ability to manipulate the data, as well as entering the data that has been in the repository or archives for a number of years now.

As you get these increased assets you have to train them. We have only half a dozen people in the POW/MIA office who have been there more than 3 years. It is not an old group and it is becoming younger all the time with the addition of new personnel. I think we have resources to do the job. As we add more people we will add those responsibilities that we have said are ours and that we need to do. The intelligence community, in general, does respond to our tasking in a very, very positive high-priority way.

Mr. GILMAN. Then there is good cooperation with the other agencies?

General SHUFELT. Absolutely.

Mr. GILMAN. Do they provide the resources to you when you need them? Are you put on the back burner?

General SHUFELT. No, sir; cooperation from all agencies continues to be excellent. That responsiveness is both at the highest levels and down at the action levels. We are getting responsive action out of the community in toto.

Mr. GILMAN. Have you been at any time denied the resources needed to fulfill your responsibilities?

General SHUFELT. I am sure that has been true in the past.

Mr. GILMAN. Since you have been in office, have you been denied any resources?

General SHUFELT. I have not been denied any resources, and our priorities are better now than when we started a year ago.

Mr. GILMAN. You know, General, for I guess as many as 3 or 4 years, each time a witness came up from DIA I always ask the question: "Do you have the resources you need? Is there anything further you need, or what more can our committee provide you with?" I think on each occasion we were told, "We have everything we need at this point."

General SHUFELT. We have the money, the dollars to do it in the budget. It is a question of hiring the people and getting them trained. Your support—and I mean this in a very positive sense—is equally as important and in many ways more important than anything else. The fact that you believe we are trying to do the best possible job with the talent and the people that we have is encouraging. As Mr. Perot indicated, we are a very dedicated bunch of people.

Mr. GILMAN. Is there recognition in your shop that the President gives this the highest priority?

General SHUFELT. Oh, yes, indeed.

Mr. SOLARZ. Mr. Dornan, a guest of the subcommittee

Mr. DORNAN. I will try to act like a guest as regards time.

It has been 18 years, almost, since you appeared on that show and fired me up to work harder; 8 years I keep reminding the military would be like after World War II in 1945 trying to work in 1963 to resolve some nagging leftover problem. If such a commission is formed—and I accept Mr. Leach's and Mr. Solomon's concept as it's evolving of how we go—would you be willing to serve on it?

Ms. GRIFFITHS. No; I couldn't in good conscience participate in a stalling action.

Mr. DORNAN. I think I see more clearly than ever why you think that is a stalling action because of the experience of the other two commissions, but keep in mind that the House commission which adjourned permanently 13 days before I was sworn in as a Congressman and turned back hundreds of thousands of dollars, was preboat people. This commission I think now would impinge on no one's honor and if Robby Reiser were on the commission other heroes from Vietnam, or Ann Griffiths, I see it as a unifying force, not this division between who is a Rambo and who isn't.

Ms. GRIFFITHS. You mentioned Rambo a while ago as those who focused on live prisoners. I was attacked by Rambos, and I have focused directly on live prisoners for 21 years.

Mr. DORNAN. I never heard you call for the U.S. Government to do it.

Ms. GRIFFITHS. For the U.S. Government to go to rescue them, good solid intelligence is required. Or it can be done through negotiations to play "Let's Make a Deal." There are only two ways.

Mr. DORNAN. You are more generous than I am. I think it is impossible.

Ms. GRIFFITHS. That is not my decision. The very highest level people decide that. But as far as the Commission itself, I still say that even if you had the most knowledgeable people in the world, George Brooks, others who have been involved for many, many years, you have taken it out of the policy mainstream. Let me give you an example.

Mr. DORNAN. But it is still under the President?

Ms. GRIFFITHS. If you take this issue out of the U.S. foreign-policy mainstream, you have taken away the incentive that attract Vietnamese cooperation and the flexibility to gain progress through negotiations.

Mr. DORNAN. It is still the President's policy.

Ms. GRIFFITHS. They used LeBoutillier's name last time and used the congressional hearings held on the Senate side, hammering us on why we are pushing the live prisoner issue so hard. They said, "Even Members of Congress don't believe this" because allegations were made that could not be substantiated. The Vietnamese used it against Armitage and Wolfowitz, when they went there.

John LeBoutillier publicly said "the problem is in Washington, not Hanoi". Guess who quoted it to us—the Vietnamese! I am telling you they look at and read and know every cosponsor, everything you advocate, every word that is said, every article that is published, the Congressional Record and every hiccup in a committee.

Mr. DORNAN. They do not think Dick Armitage or Dick Childress are high enough, or you, either. They want to see somebody at the ambassador level. The Russians are fascinated with Armand Hammer and the Vietnamese are fascinated with ambassadors, and I think you are missing a great opportunity.

Ms. GRIFFITHS. Why would the Vietnamese want a higher level? Because if they get a higher level, and we have heard people recommended sending the Vice President, do you really want the Vice President to go over and talk to the senior Vietnamese officials and be told "We hold no Americans"? Then where do you go?

Mr. DORNAN. At that level they might not say it, and yes, I would like to see the Vice President go over there.

Mr. SOLARZ. The gentleman's time has expired. I want to thank both the witnesses very much. We deeply appreciate the opportunity to get the benefit of your wisdom.

I think the time has now come, after having been in continuous session for 3½ hours, to move to the consideration of this resolution.

The CLERK. House concurrent resolution——

Mr. LEACH. Mr. Chairman, I ask unanimous consent that the resolution be considered as read and I ask to be recognized.

Mr. SOLARZ. Without objection, the resolution will be considered as read and before the subcommittee and open to amendment at any point.

[House Con. Res. 129 follows:]

IV

99TH CONGRESS
1ST SESSION

H. CON. RES. 129

To establish a congressional commission to be known as the Perot Commission on Americans Missing in Southeast Asia to determine whether or not United States prisoners of war are being held in Southeast Asia and to report to Congress appropriate action to effect the release of any prisoners of war found to be alive.

IN THE HOUSE OF REPRESENTATIVES

APRIL 24, 1985

Mr. HENDON submitted the following concurrent resolution; which was referred to the Committee on Foreign Affairs

JANUARY 10, 1986

Additional sponsors: Mr. BURTON of Indiana, Mr. SUNDQUIST, Mr. DREIER of California, Mr. SMITH of New Hampshire, Mr. HUNTER, Mr. GALLO, Mr. GINGRICH, Mr. LIGHTFOOT, Mr. MURPHY, Mr. BROWN of Colorado, Mr. LIPINSKI, Mr. BILIRAKIS, Mr. YOUNG of Florida, Mr. APPLEGATE, Mr. PORTER, Mr. MONSON, Mr. JEFFORDS, Mr. CRAIG, Mr. GREGG, Mr. MARLENEE, Mr. FROST, Mr. ROWLAND of Connecticut, Mr. HANSEN, Mr. SAVAGE, Mr. DAUB, Mr. RICHARDSON, Mr. PARRIS, Mr. JONES of North Carolina, Mr. KOLBE, Mr. McCLOSKEY, Mr. DELAY, Mr. PACKARD, Mr. SCHULZE, Mr. CRANE, Mr. BORSKI, Mr. TORRES, Mr. ANDREWS, Mr. FIELDS, Mr. HUBBARD, Mr. COBEY, Mr. RUDD, Mr. SLATTERY, Mr. WILSON, Mr. BATES, Mr. ENGLISH, Mr. GROTBERG, Mr. WHITLEY, Mr. EDWARDS of Oklahoma, Mr. REID, Mr. BLILEY, Mr. WILLIAMS, Mr. BEREUTER, Mr. COBLE, Mrs. KENNELLY, Mr. WEBER, Mr. HEFNER, Mr. DIOGUARDI, Mr. KEMP, Mr. LOEFFLER, Mr. WATKINS, Mr. OBERSTAR, Mr. WHITEHURST, Mr. DANIEL, Mr. ROBERTS, Mr. MACKAY, Mr. BARTLETT, Mr. NIELSON of Utah, Mrs. SMITH of Nebraska, Mr. WORTLEY, Mr. JONES of Oklahoma, Mr. BARTON of Texas, Mrs. BENTLEY, Mr. HORTON, Mr. MOORHEAD, Mr. CHAPPIE, Mr. SAXTON, Mr. HARTNETT, Mr. HEFTEL of Hawaii, Mr. LEATH of Texas, Mr. EDGAR, Mr. McGRATH, Mr. GLICKMAN, Mr. BEVILL, Mr. KOLTER, Mr. VALENTINE, Mr. McMILLAN, Mr. GUARINI, Mrs. MEYERS of Kansas, Mr. BEDELL, Mrs. BYRON, Mr. DORNAN of California, Mr. RITTER, Mrs. JOHNSON, Mr. STENHOLM, Mr. WHITTAKER, Mr. YOUNG of Missouri, Mr. DOWDY of Mississippi, Mr. DASCHLE, Mr. MORRISON of Connecticut, Mr. SILJANDER, Mr. McKINNEY, Mr. CHANDLER, Mr. STALLINGS, Mr. HUTTO, Mr. SPRATT, Mr. BLAZ, Mr. LELAND, Mr. ARMEY, Mr. CAMPBELL, Mr. COATS, Mr. LEWIS of California, Mr.

McCANDLESS, Mr. MOLINARI, Mr. PASHAYAN, Mr. SKEEN, Mrs. VUCANO-
VICH, Mr. STANGELAND, Mr. YATRON, and Mr. McCURDY

CONCURRENT RESOLUTION

To establish a congressional commission to be known as the
Perot Commission on Americans Missing in Southeast Asia
to determine whether or not United States prisoners of war
are being held in Southeast Asia and to report to Congress
appropriate action to effect the release of any prisoners of
war found to be alive.

Whereas over twenty-four hundred American servicemen remain
unaccounted for from the Vietnam war;

Whereas 73 per centum of the American people believe the
North Vietnamese are still holding American prisoners of
war;

Whereas even though the Montgomery and Woodcock Commissions found in the mid-1970's that no Americans remained
prisoner, hundreds of eyewitness accounts of alleged American prisoners of war have been reported to the Defense Intelligence Agency since that time;

Whereas Lieutenant General Eugene Tighe United States Air
Force (retired), former Director of the Defense Intelligence
Agency, stated in 1982 that during his tenure in the Defense Intelligence Agency, the prisoners of war-missing in
action issue was a key issue for him and of high priority, he
ordered a daily update every morning on his desk, he saw
more information daily than any man in the world, and the
evidence is clear to him that there are Americans being held
against their will in Southeast Asia;

Whereas Lieutenant General Tighe has further stated publicly
that some people involved in the United States' effort have
been disclaiming good reports about remaining American
captives for so long that it has become habit-forming, and
has called for the formation of a special Commission to investigate the work of the very agency he headed, citing the
Defense Intelligence Agency's work as showing a mind-set
to debunk intelligence received on our prisoners of war; and

Whereas H. Ross Perot, who has served as a member of the
President's Foreign Intelligence Advisory Board, is world-
renowned for his exemplary public service, humanitarian efforts, and especially for his work during the Vietnam war
on behalf of United States prisoners of war: Now, therefore,
be it

1   *Resolved by the House of Representatives (the Senate*

2 *concurring),*

3 SECTION 1. ESTABLISHMENT OF CONGRESSIONAL COMMIS-

4   SION.

5   There is established in the legislative branch of the Gov-

6 ernment a congressional commission to be known as the

7 Perot Commission on Americans Missing In Southeast Asia

8 (hereinafter in this resolution referred to as the "Commis-

9 sion").

10 SEC. 2. FUNCTIONS.

11   The Commission shall conduct a full and complete in-

12 vestigation of all information made available to the United

13 States Government and its agencies since the findings of the

1 Montgomery and Woodcock Commissions, and report their

2 findings on—

3   (1) whether or not prisoners of war are still alive

4   and being held against their will in Southeast Asia;

5   and

6   (2) the appropriate congressional action to effect

7   the release of any prisoners of war found to be alive.

8 SEC. 3. APPOINTMENT AND MEMBERSHIP.

9   (a) MEMBERS.—The Commission shall be composed of

10 fifteen members. Such members shall be selected, within

11 thirty days of the date of the adoption of this resolution, by

12 the Speaker of the House of Representatives and the Presi-

13 dent pro tempore of the Senate from a bipartisan list of not

14 less than twenty nominees submitted by H. Ross Perot, of

15 Dallas, Texas, who is hereby appointed to the Commission

16 and shall serve as its Chairman.

17   (b) VACANCY.—Any vacancy occurring in the member-

18 ship of the Commission shall be filled in the same manner in

19 which the original appointment was made.

20 SEC. 4. AUTHORITY AND PROCEDURES.

21   (a) AUTHORITY.—For purposes of carrying out this res-

22 olution, the Commission, or any subcommittee thereof au-

23 thorized to hold hearings, is authorized—

24   (1) to sit and act during the present Congress at

25   such times and places within the United States, includ-

1   ing any Commonwealth or possession thereof, or else-

2   where, whether the Congress is in session, has re-

3   cessed, or has adjourned, and to hold such hearings as

4   it deems necessary; and

5   (2) to require, by subpoena or otherwise, the at-

6   tendence and testimony of such witnesses and the pro-

7   duction of such books, records, correspondence, memo-

8   randa, papers, and documents as it deems necessary.

9   (b) ENFORCEMENT.—Compliance with any subpoena

10   issued by the Commission under subsection (a) may be en-

11   forced only as authorized or directed by the House of Repre-

12   sentatives or the Senate.

13   SEC. 5. ADMINISTRATIVE PROVISIONS.

14   (a) EXPENSES.—Subject to the adoption of expense res-

15   olutions as required by clause 5 of rule XI of the Rules of the

16   House of Representatives, the Commission may incur ex-

17   penses in connection with its duties under this resolution.

18   (b) STAFF AND TRAVEL.—In carrying out its functions

19   under this resolution, the Commission is authorized—

20   (1) to appoint, either on a permanent basis or as

21   experts or consultants, such staff as the Commission

22   considers necessary;

23   (2) to prescribe the duties and responsibilities of

24   such staff;

1   (3) to fix the compensation of such staff at a

2   single per annum gross rate which does not exceed the

3   highest rate of basic pay, as in effect from time to

4   time, of level V of the Executive Schedule in section

5   5316 of title 5, United States Code;

6   (4) to terminate the employment of any such staff

7   as the Commission considers appropriate; and

8   (5) to reimburse members of the Commission and

9   of its staff for travel, subsistence, and other necessary

10   expenses incurred by them in the performance of their

11   duties and responsibilities for the Commission, other

12   than expenses in connection with any meeting of the

13   Commission, or a subcommittee thereof, held in the

14   District of Columbia.

15 (c) EXPIRATION.—The Commission and all authority

16 granted in this resolution shall expire thirty days after the

17 filing of the report of the Commission with the Congress or

18 just prior to noon on January 3, 1987, whichever occurs

19 first.

20 SEC. 6. REPORT AND RECORDS.

21 (a) REPORT.—The Commission shall report to the Con-

22 gress as soon as practicable during the present Congress, but

23 not later than six months after the date of the adoption of this

24 resolution, the results of its investigation and study, together

25 with such recommendations as it deems advisable.

1   (b) FILING OF REPORT.—Any such report which is
2 made when the House is not in session shall be filed with the
3 Clerk of the House and any such report which is made when
4 the Senate is not in session shall be filed with the Clerk of
5 the Senate.

6   (c) REFERRAL OF REPORT.—Any such report shall be
7 referred to the committee or committees which have jurisdic-
8 tion over the subject matter thereof.

Mr. SOLARZ. The gentleman from Iowa is recognized.

Mr. LEACH. Mr. Chairman, I think there are some things the committee ought to discuss before we go right into amendments.

There are basically, as I see it, four potential approaches that could seriously be considered at this time. One is the precise bill of Mr. Hendon, which is one that has garnered so much galvanizing support. My personal sense is that it suffers from two modest disadvantages: First, it is congressional, and second, it probably should be modified in three or four ways, including receiving a request from the President before it goes forward. In addition, there are a series of kind of cleaning-up amendments that I would offer to it. I would define that modifying approach as a second approach. There is a third approach, which is largely pretty well done by the gentleman from North Dakota, Mr. Dorgan, who has a bill establishing a Presidential commission. I have looked at it and I started to write a Presidential commission approach. I thought it had some disadvantages and was too hurried. But as I looked at Dorgan's bill I concluded that it is well done. I added a couple of paragraphs asking the President to give serious consideration to naming Mr. Perot and Ms. Griffiths vice chairman. That is an approach that can be considered. The gentleman from New York has another approach calling on the President to study the issue and to report back to Congress on that study.

My own sense is that approaches 2, 3, and 4 make some sense. Approach 1 makes probably the least sense although it is, in a sense the one that deserves the most respect because it is the bill that got the committee to where it is today. But I just want to throw all three of those possibilities out and I think we ought to discuss what other members of the committee would prefer.

Mr. SOLARZ. I thank the gentleman. I think that your analysis is very helpful. I would like to respond by offering some observations of my own. First let me say that I think this has been a very productive hearing. Second, I want to pay tribute to the members of the Subcommittee, and those of our other colleagues who join us, for the way this session has been conducted. I know of few more controversial issues than this one and believe it is a tribute to the House that an issue like this can be conducted in fashion whereby disagreements are acknowledged but respected. This originates from the premise that everybody is operating from the highest and best motivations. Having said that, let me then move to the alternatives which the gentleman from Iowa has set before us.

There is one other alternative, and that is, of course, to defeat the resolution pointblank. I came into this hearing opposed to the resolution. I indicated to Mr. Hendon, when he told me that 275 Members had co-sponsored it and that he thought they were entitled to a vote, that while I disagreed with him on the merits, I found that argument, frankly, very persuasive and felt I had an institutional responsibility to permit it to come up for a vote, my despite my personal inclinations. I decided to bring it up and keep an open mind.

One of my colleagues suggested that I speak with Mr. Perot. I did, I had a long talk with him on the phone and heard him again today. Based on what I have heard today, I am more convinced than I was before that a commission, whether it is a Presidential Commission or a congressional Commission, is the wrong way to go.

I think there are two questions, basically, before us: One, do we have adequate information; are the people responsible for getting the information doing an adequate job; do we need more if we are going to effectively deal with this issue. The second question, assuming there are people there, is how do we best go about getting them out.

As far as the first is concerned, it strikes me that virutally all of us believe that no coverup has gone on, that there is no conspiracy of silence and that the DIA is doing the best job it can with the resources that are available. Indeed, as Mr. Perot said, and as General Tighe said also, they are convinced that the facts are in, that there are Americans there. They may not know exactly where they are on this particular day, but they are convinced there is sufficient evidence available to reach the conclusion that there are Americans over there.

Now, in those terms it seems clear to me that the primary purpose of a commission would be to obtain additional information. One of the problems I have with a commission is the notion that it implicitly legitimizes the perception that there is a coverup or a conspiracy at work. I don't know what more a commission can find out, with or without the subpoena power, than the DIA has already found out. If they could get more information, what would it tell us that we don't already know?

So, in terms of additional information, I don't see that the Commission is needed. If there was any suggestion whatsoever that DIA was engaged in a coverup, I would be the first to support a commission. But I don't believe that contention has been persuasively demonstrated. Then the next question comes up: What do we do to get these people out? It is on this point that I think the hearing was extremely illuminating.

All of the witnesses said to us that, to the extent there are men there, and I believe they all believe there are, the best way to get them out, is through negotiations. A commission is manifestly not the appropriate instrument for negotiations. Commissions do not negotiate. The President of the United States or his designated emissaries negotiate. Let me say that if we were to establish a commission in the hope that it might negotiate, I would ask my colleagues to think of the president that would set.

There may be differing interpretations as to who is responsible for the failure of President Reagan and Mr. Gorbachev to reach an agreement in Iceland, but I would imagine that if such a precedent were to be established, there might be a lot of Members of the House, particularly on my side of the aisle, that would like to have a commission adopted to negotiate with Gorbachev on arms control. But I would be opposed to that because it is the President who has the constitutional responsibility to conduct negotiations.

For these reasons, I don't see what a commission could accomplish. The real question before us today is not whether we want to see this issue resolved but over how best to resolve it and whether a commission is the way to go.

If the members feel that we need to encourage the President, to negotiate with Vietnam, let's get a resolution which says that. These resolutions don't.

My impression, though, is the President doesn't need encouragement. Emissaries are going over there. They are talking. He seems to feel it is on the appropriate level. Maybe we should have a meeting with the President to talk with him privately about what we think can be done to resolve this issue.

I believe the President has made this issue a matter of the highest national priority. I don't believe he needs pressure or encouragement from us. I think there are few things that are probably more important to him and that nothing would please him more than to be able to secure the release of any men who may be held against their will.

I know that some of my colleagues recognize the political sensitivities of this issue. I can't see, though, how any member would have a problem justifying a vote against a resolution that is opposed by the League of Families, which represents the men and women of our Nation who have the greatest direct interest in this; which is opposed by virtually every veterans' organization; which is opposed by the President of the U.S., DIA, DOD, the State Department, and the like, all of which have indicated that a commission is likely to make resolution of the issue more distant.

For all those reasons, I, frankly, don't see the need for a resolution and I am not sure what we gain by bucking it over to the President.

We know he is against it. He has told us through his emissaries that he is against it.

The gentleman from Nebraska.

Mr. BEREUTER. Mr. Chairman, I would like to be recognized to speak on the concept of which approach we might take. I might say first of all that I have not seen the proposed amendments discussed that the gentleman from Iowa might offer which would make the Hendon bill a Presidential commission.

But it seems to me, based upon what I understand about it, there are several things that should be said in favor of that approach.

First, there is no question about the resolve of the President and the priority he gives this, but I think there is something to be said for keeping the pot boiling here in the Congress as we move legislation and keeping the pot boiling through a commission that is established.

It is important to keep the focus of people in the National Security Council and the top Presidential advisors on this issue. The President is a human being and can not continue to give top priority day in and day out, hour after hour, to this issue.

This commission which would be established, of course, is not to secure the release of the prisoners, the Americans held in captivity. What it is to do is to give its recommendations to the Congress on if Americans are alive in captivity and how we should release them if they are there.

I see nothing in conflict on a two-track approach to permit the President to pursue the responsibilities of a chief executive officer of this country and at the same time of having a Presidential commission establishing, documenting to the point it is irrefutable evidénce that there are Americans held in captivity in Southeast Asia.

I see nothing inherent in the creation of such a commission which suggests that this is an effort to disclose some conspiracy. I don't think it is driven by some conspiracy theory. I believe that there is yet a lack of understanding and appreciation among the American people that there is the strong possibility there are Americans alive held captive in Southeast Asia.

The action of the Congress heightens the visibility and understanding of the American people that their representatives believe there are Americans alive in Vietnam and that kind of visibility and recognition puts the pressure on the administration to move ahead with negotiations which I am convinced is the only way to release Americans that are held in captivity.

So, I don't see the conflicts. I don't see how this moves it away and out of the policy track. It seems to me it is perfectly reasonable to pursue two tracks on this very important problem.

Those are the arguments I would like to advance.

Mr. SOLARZ. I thank the gentleman.

I would like to make one objection. If one of the primary purposes here is to give the issue visibility and continued attention, that is precisely what our subcommittee has done by convening numerous hearings over the years. It is precisely what the task force has done, chaired by Mr. Solomon, and before him, by Mr. Gilman and Mr. Dornan.

We will continue to do just that. The task force will be reappointed next year, and the subcommittee will continue to hold hearings. If there is ever a reason to believe that the administration is slackening off in its efforts, we will turn up the heat.

Mr. BEREUTER. If we kill the resolution here today and don't pass a substitute that is meaningful, that sends a message that is in the opposite direction.

Mr. SOLARZ. We now have the second bell. The subcommittee is in recess. We will return in 10 minutes and, hopefully, resolve this one way or the other.

[Recess.]

Mr. SOLARZ. The subcommittee will resume.

A sufficient number of members being present for the purpose of marking up the resolution, the resolution is now before the committee and open to amendment at any point. If there are amendments to be offered, now is the time to offer them.

Mr. Leach.

Mr. LEACH. Mr. Chairman, what I intend to do is offer first an amendment to clean up somewhat the approach of Mr. Hendon, and second, offer an amendment that would supercede that amendment.

Let me mention as a preface for 15 seconds in response to your very extraordinary comments which have a great deal of merit to them, that there is no intent in any of the approaches that I have seen, at least from members of this committee, to be motivated by a concern for a coverup to attempt to move in the direction of direct negotiations.

Commissions are formed all the time to advise negotiators or to advise presidents or to advise Congress. There is nothing new in that.

The only point you made that I thought was of persuasive import was your concern about what is the best way to encourage the administration, whether it be the status quo or a new approach. I think that is one that each member can have their own individual judgment on.

The first amendment I offer is one that provides that the commission will be established and commissioners appointed only if the President so requests it in writing and if Mr. Perot agrees in writing to be a member and chairman.

Mr. SOLARZ. Let the amendment be distributed and then the gentleman from Iowa can explain.

[The information follows:]

HCR129A3

[October 15, 1986]

AMENDMENTS OFFERED BY MR. ·LEACH TO H.CON.RES. 129

In the next to the last paragraph of the preamble, strike out ``, citing the Defense Intelligence Agency's work as showing a mind-set to debunk intelligence received on our prisoners of war''.

In section 1, strike out ``There is established'' and insert in lieu thereof ``Subject to section 4, there is established''.

Strike out section 3(a) and insert in lieu thereof the following:

1   (a) MEMBERSHIP.--

2   (1) NUMBER.--The Commission shall be composed of
3   fifteen members.

4   (2) APPOINTMENTS BY HOUSE AND SENATE
5   LEADERSHIP.--Subject to section 4, fourteen members of
6   the Commission shall be appointed as follows:

7   (A) Four shall be appointed by the Speaker of the
8   House of Representatives.

9   (B) Three shall be appointed by the Minority
10   Leader of the House of Representatives.

CR129A3

1   (C) Four shall be appointed by the President pro

2   tempore of the Senate.

3   (D) Three shall be appointed by the Minority

4   Leader of the Senate.

5   Not less than one member appointed under each of

6   subparagraphs (A) through (D) shall be an individual who

7   represents families of members of the Armed Forces who

8   are prisoners of war or missing in action or who

9   represents organizations that represent members of the

10 Armed Forces who are prisoners of war or missing in

11 action or the families of such members.

12   (3) H. ROSS PEROT.—Subject to section 4, H. Ross

13 Perot of Dallas, Texas, shall be a member of the

14 Commission and shall serve as its chairman.

    After section 3, insert the following new section 4 and

    redesignate subsequent sections accordingly:

15 SEC. 4. CONDITIONS ON ESTABLISHMENT OF COMMISSION AND

16   APPOINTMENT OF MEMBERS.

17 The Commission provided for in this concurrent resolution

18 shall be established, and members may be appointed to the

19 Commission pursuant to section 3, only if—

20   (1) the President has submitted to the Congress a

21 written request for the establishment of the Commission;

22 and

HCR129A3

1   (2) H. Ross Perot of Dallas, Texas, has submitted to

2   the Congress a written statement that he is willing to be

3   a member of the Commission and to serve as its Chairman.

    In subsection (a)(1) of section 5 (as so redesignated),
by striking out ``during the present Congress''.

    In subsection (c) of section 6 (as so redesignated),
strike out ``or just prior to noon on January 3, 1987,
whichever occurs first''.

    In subsection (a) of section 7 (as so redesignated ,
strike out ``during the present Congress''.

Mr. SOLARZ. Please proceed.

Mr. LEACH. Another provision of these amendment changes the manner in the original bill of Mr. Hendon's by which members would be selected. Instead of having the chairman of the commission designate 20 from which Congress would pick 15, it gives the right to the President of the Senate, and to the Speaker of the House each to designate 4 individuals to the commission and to the minority leaders of both bodies to each name 3, so a total of 14 would be selected with Mr. Perot as the chairman being the 15th member.

It designates that at least one of each of the four selections must represent families of POWs or MIAs or organizations representing POW's/MIA's and their families.

In addition, it strikes some of the preambular language which I think represents gratuitous criticism of the DIA.

That, in a nut shell, is the first amendment I am offering, and I would urge its serious consideration.

I don't want to repeat all my previous remarks, particularly since it is obvious most of them were not persuasive to my good friend. But I do want you to keep this in mind as we proceed marking up this resolution.

No matter what anybody here says, this clearly constitutes an implicit vote of no confidence in the President of the United States.

He has said after all this is a matter of the highest national priority. The DIA has told us that pursuant to that statement they have been given all the resources they have asked for. If it is a matter of the highest national priority and if the DIA has the resources which it needs, what do we need the commission for?

I don't understand what the commission will do or can do that isn't already being done, but by virtue of the commission being established, you have a separate locus of responsibility.

If it is going to serve a useful purpose, the President can do it any way. I make for those reasons and for the ones I have enumerated before, I am still opposed to it. I notice that the gentleman's amendment leaves this as a congressional resolution and Mr. Perot is chairman of the commission.

Mr. LEACH. That is why I will be offering a second resolution.

Mr. SOLOMON. Would the gentleman explain the other amendments so we will know——

Mr. LEACH. It is my hope, as I explained to the chairman, that this amendment can be accepted to lead the committee potentially to consideration of a cleaner approach if they prefer the congressional route. Then the committee can go on and consider a presidential approach which I think is preferable to congressional.

Mr. SOLOMON. Will the gentleman be offering such an amendment?

Mr. LEACH. Yes.

Mr. SOLARZ. Mr. Bereuter.

Mr. BEREUTER. Respectfully, I do not agree with the chairman's connotation that this would be a vote of no confidence in the President.

Second, to the gentleman from Iowa, just for the record, it would be your intent, I assume, that if Mr. Perot would not be able to serve as commission chairman or would choose not to do so that the commission would be able to continue with an alternate chairman?

Mr. LEACH. In this particular resolution, that would not be the case, but in terms of the Presidential approach, that would be the case.

Mr. BEREUTER. So even then you leave this commission under the revised Hendon approach, congressional commission potentially leaderless?

Mr. LEACH. Potentially, it would not go into effect unless Mr. Perot agrees to lead it.

Mr. SOLARZ. The question occurs on the amendment by the gentleman from Iowa, Mr. Leach.

All those in favor, say "aye."

All those opposed, say "nay."

The ayes appear to have it. The ayes have it, and the amendment is adopted.

Mr. LEACH. I have a second amendment and this one I am sorry to say I don't have in duplicate. It is the bill H.R. 3429 with a handwritten amendment attached to it.

[Text of amendment follows:]

I

99TH CONGRESS
1ST SESSION
H. R. 3429 *with Leadh amedment*

To establish a commission to report and make recommendations concerning the
status of members of the Armed Forces who are officially recorded as being
prisoners of war or missing in action.

IN THE HOUSE OF REPRESENTATIVES

September 26, 1985

Mr. DORGAN of North Dakota introduced the following bill; which was referred to
the Committee on Foreign Affairs

A BILL

To establish a commission to report and make recommendations
concerning the status of members of the Armed Forces who
are officially recorded as being prisoners of war or missing
in action.

1   *Be it enacted by the Senate and House of Representa-*
2 *tives of the United States of America in Congress assembled,*
3 SECTION 1. ESTABLISHMENT OF COMMISSION.
4   There is hereby established a commission to be known
5 as the National Commission on POWs and MIAs (hereinafter
6 in this Act referred to as the "Commission").
7 SEC. 2. DUTIES OF COMMISSION.
8   The Commission shall—

76

1   (1) investigate the status of members of the
2   Armed Forces who are officially recorded as being
3   prisoners of war or missing in action;
4   (2) recommend actions to secure the release of
5   members of the Armed Forces who are prisoners of
6   war; and
7   (3) recommend actions to secure the release of the
8   remains of any deceased member of the Armed Forces

9   that are within the territorial jurisdiction of any foreign

10   government.

11 **SEC. 2. MEMBERSHIP.**

12   (a) NUMBER AND APPOINTMENT.—There shall be 15

13 members of the Commission, who shall be appointed by the

14 President.

15   (b) COMPOSITION.—Not less than three members of the

16 Commission shall be individuals who represent—

17   (1) families of members of the Armed Forces who

18   are prisoners of war or missing in action; or

19   (2) organizations that represent members of the

20   Armed Forces who are prisoners of war or missing in

21   action or the families of such members.

22   (b) SECURITY CLEARANCES.—The Commission shall

23 promptly request for each member the security clearance

24 necessary to carry out the duties of a member of the Commis-

25 sion under this Act. If any member of the Commission does

77

1 not qualify for a security clearance, the member shall be ter-

2 minated as a member of the Commission.

3   (c) TERMS.—Members shall be appointed for five-year

4 terms.

5   (d) VACANCIES.—A member appointed to fill a vacancy

6 occurring before the end of the term for which the predeces-

7 sor of such member was appointed shall be appointed only for

8 the remainder of that term. A member may serve after the

9 end of the term of such member until a successor has taken

10 office.

11   (e) BASIC PAY.—

12   (1) Members of the Commission who are not offi-

13   cers or employees of the United States shall each be

14   paid at a rate equal to the rate of basic pay payable for

15   GS–14 of the General Schedule for each day

16   (including travel time) during which they are en-

17   gaged in the actual performance of the duties

18   vested in the Commission.

19   (2) Except as provided in paragraph (3), members

20   of the Commission who are officers or employees of the

21   United States shall receive no additional pay, allow-

22   ances, or benefits by reason of their service on the

23   Commission.

24   (3) While away from their homes or regular

25   places of business in the performance of services for

78

1   the Commission, each member of the Commission shall

2   be allowed travel expenses, including per diem in lieu

3   of subsistence, under section 5703 of title 5, United

4   States Code, in the same manner as persons employed

5   intermittently in the Government service.

6   (f) QUORUM.—Eight members of the Commission shall

7   constitute a quorum, but a lesser number may hold meetings.

8   (g) CHAIRMAN.—The chairman of the Commission shall

9   be appointed by the President from among the members of

10   the Commission. *It is the sense of the Congress that H. R. A*
of Dallas, Texas be given serious consideratio

11   *for appointment to the Commission as it chairman and the*
(h) MEETINGS.—The Commission shall hold its first *Ann Mills Grif*
of the National A

12   meeting before the end of the 30-day period beginning on the *of Families of Ame*
Prisoners and mi

13   date on which the last member of the Commission is appoint- *in Southeast As*
be given serious

14   ed and shall hold meetings thereafter at the call of the chair- *sideration for Vi*

15   man or a majority of its members. *Chairman.*

16   (i) DEADLINE FOR APPOINTMENTS.—The President

17   shall appoint all the members of the Commission before the

18   end of the 180-day period beginning on the date of the enact-

19   ment of this Act.

20   SEC. 4. DIRECTOR AND STAFF.

21   (a) DIRECTOR.—The Commission shall appoint a direc-

22   tor, who shall be paid at a rate to be determined by the

23   Commission.

24   (b) STAFF.—The Commission may appoint and fix the

25   pay of any additional personnel as it considers appropriate.

1   (c) STAFF OF FEDERAL AGENCIES.—Upon request of

2 the Commission, the head of any Federal agency may detail,

3 on a reimbursable basis, any of the personnel of such agency

4 to the Commission to assist the Commission in carrying out

5 its duties under this Act.

6 SEC. 5. EXPERTS AND CONSULTANTS.

7   The Commission may procure temporary and intermit-

8 tent services under section 3109(b) of title 5, United States

9 Code.

10 SEC. 6. POWERS.

11   (a) HEARINGS AND SESSIONS.—The Commission may

12 hold such hearings, sit and act at such times and places, take

13 such testimony, and receive such evidence as the Commission

14 considers appropriate.

15   (b) OBTAINING OFFICIAL DATA.—The Commission

16 may secure directly from any department or agency of the

17 United States information necessary to enable it to carry out

18 this Act. Upon request of the chairman, the head of the de-

19 partment or agency shall furnish the information to the

20 Commission.

21   (c) GIFTS.—The Commission may accept, use, and dis-

22 pose of gifts or donations of services and property.

23   (d) MAILS.—The Commission may use the United

24 States mails in the same manner and under the same condi-

25 tions as other departments and agencies of the United States.

1   (e) ADMINISTRATIVE SUPPORT SERVICES.—The Ad-

2 ministrator of General Services shall provide to the Commis-

3 sion on a reimbursable basis any administrative support serv-

4 ices the Commission may request.

5   (f) SUBPOENA POWER.—

6   (1) The Commission may issue subpoenas requir-

7   ing the attendance and testimony of witnesses and the

8   production of evidence that relates to any matter under

9   investigation by the Commission. The attendance of

10 witnesses and the production of evidence may be re-
11 quired from any place in the United States at any des-
12 ignated place of hearing in the United States.

13 (2) If a person issued a subpoena under paragraph
14 (1) refuses to obey the subpoena or is guilty of contu-
15 macy, any court of the United States in the judicial
16 district in which the hearing is conducted or in the ju-
17 dicial district in which the person is found or resides or
18 transacts business may (upon application by the Com-
19 mission) order the person to appear before the Com-
20 mission to produce evidence or to give testimony relat-
21 ing to the matter under investigation. Any failure to
22 obey the order of the court may be punished by the
23 court as a contempt.

24 (3) The subpoenas of the Commission shall be
25 served in the manner provided for subpoenas issued by

81

1 a United States district court under the Federal Rules
2 of Civil Procedure for the United States district courts.

3 (4) All process of any court to which application
4 may be made under this section may be served in the
5 judicial district in which the person required to be
6 served resides or may be found.

7 (g) IMMUNITY.—For purposes of sections 6002 and
8 6004 of title 18, United States Code, the Commission shall
9 be considered an agency of the United States.

10 SEC. 7. REPORTS.

11 (a) ANNUAL REPORT REQUIREMENT.—The Commis-
12 sion shall transmit to the President and to the Congress
13 an annual report and such other reports as it considers
14 necessary.

15 (b) CONTENT OF REPORTS.—Each annual report shall
16 contain the findings, conclusions, and recommendations of the
17 Commission with respect to the matters described in
18 section 2.

19   (c) DEADLINE FOR FIRST REPORT.—The first annual

20   report shall be transmitted to the President and to the Con-

21   gress before the end of the one-year period beginning on

22   the date on which the last member is appointed to the

23   Commission.

82

1   SEC. 8. TERMINATION.

2   The Commission shall continue in existence until termi-

                the President.

3   nated by ~~an Act of Congress~~.

83

What the bill does is establish a Presidential commission to be made up of 15 members to be designated by the President. I add a clause that says it is the sense of the Congress that H.R. Perot of Dallas, TX be given serious consideration for appointment to the commission as its chairman and that Ann Mills Griffiths of the League of Families be given serious consideration for vice chairman.

It includes authorization for subpoena power, plus all the technicalities relating to how meetings can be held, how people may be compensated. I had intended to redraft the Hendon approach with some of this approach, but, frankly, find that the resolution as introduced by Mr. Dorgan is a very complete one and far better than I had intended to craft.

Mr. SOLARZ. The gentleman's amendment would provide for the immediate establishment of a commission?

Mr. LEACH. Yes, it would.

Mr. SOLARZ. Even if the President doesn't want it?

Mr. LEACH. Yes. There is one further addition. The commission would have its existence continued until termination by the President.

Mr. SOLARZ. The amendment has been introduced. Is there anybody who cares to be heard on the amendment?

The gentleman from Nebraska.

Mr. BEREUTER. May I ask, may we have a 2-minute recess so that the members may examine this?

Mr. SOLARZ. Certainly.

[Recess.]

Mr. BEREUTER. Mr. Chairman, I thank you for the recess.

Mr. SOLARZ. The committee will resume its proceedings.

In the absence of any further debate on the gentleman from Iowa's amendment——

Mr. BEREUTER. Mr. Chairman, I have a parliamentary inquiry.

Mr. SOLARZ. The gentleman will state his inquiry.

Mr. BEREUTER. Is the intent of the motion to substitute the language of the Dorgan bill, H.R. 3429 in House Concurrent Resolution 129——

Mr. LEACH. No. This would be a substitute because of the subtlety of the distinction between a House Concurrent Resolution and an H.R. The H.R. is of stronger value.

Mr. BEREUTER. Thank you.

Mr. SOLARZ. Let me ask our legal advisor about the adoption of this resolution by the House. Wouldn't there have to be a counterpart resolution in the Senate in order to actually establish the commission?

Mr. MOHRMAN. Of course. In the case of either the concurrent resolution or Mr. Dorgan's bill, it would have to be adopted by the Senate and in the case of Mr. Dorgan's bill, it would also have to be signed by the President or passed over his veto.

Mr. SOLARZ. An H.R. has to be signed by the President or passed over his veto.

Mr. MOHRMAN. Yes.

Mr. SOLARZ. And a concurrent resolution——

Mr. MOHRMAN. Would have to be passed by the Senate, would not have to be signed by the President.

84

Mr. SOLARZ. Would it have the force of law?

Mr. MOHRMAN. No. It would not have the force of law, and it would expire at the end of this Congress.

Mr. SOLARZ. The vote occurs on the amendment to the resolution introduced by the gentleman from Iowa.

All those in favor, say "aye."

Opposed, say "nay."

The ayes appear to have it, and the amendment is adopted.

Are there any further amendments?

If there are no further amendments, I will now move to vote on final passage of the resolution, as amended.

All those in favor, say "aye."

All those opposed, say "nay."

On that I will ask for a record vote.

The Clerk will call the roll.

Ms. BOYLE. Mr. Dymally.

Mr. SOLARZ. No by proxy.

Ms. BOYLE. Mr. Torricelli.

[No response.]

Ms. BOYLE. Mr. Udall.

Mr. SOLARZ. No by proxy.

Ms. BOYLE. Mr. Barnes.

Mr. SOLARZ. No by proxy.

Ms. BOYLE. Mr. Gejdenson.

[No response.]

Ms. BOYLE. Mr. Leach.

Mr. LEACH. Aye.

Ms. BOYLE. Mr. Roth.

[No response.]

Ms. BOYLE. Mr. Solomon.

Mr. SOLOMON. Aye.

Ms. BOYLE. Mr. Bereuter.

Mr. BEREUTER. Aye.

Ms. BOYLE. Mr. Chairman.

Mr. SOLARZ. No.

Mr. SOLOMON. Mr. Chairman, before the vote is announced, I would yield to you——

Mr. LEACH. Mr. Gejdenson has left a proxy in favor, yes.

Mr. SOLOMON. I don't know how that leaves the count.

I was going to question whether or not a quorum was present. Is it necessary to have a quorum to report a bill?

Mr. SOLARZ. If somebody wants to make a point of order about it, the answer is yes.

Mr. SOLOMON. What was the vote and I will tell you.

Mr. SOLARZ. Well, we may not meet again to consider this. We are running out of time as it is.

Mr. SOLOMON. It is my understanding if we did not have a quorum, Mr. Chairman, that you would call a brief meeting tomorrow where we might have a quorum.

Mr. SOLARZ. We are having a hearing tomorrow and it might be possible at some point to bring it up then. But there is a question of members getting ample notice and the like.

If we are going to resort to technicalities, which members have a right to do, then that can be done tomorrow also.

I think the rules require sufficient notice in advance that legisla tion will be brought up and I don't know that that notice could be given in a timely fashion if someone chose to object tomorrow.

Mr. SOLOMON. Could counsel advise us now?

Mr. SOLARZ. Let me say that I think it is best to take this up now. Whatever happens, happens.

If it is defeated, that doesn't mean that it couldn't be brought up again subject to discussion among members of the committee, particularly in a new forum.

I would just as soon have it resolved given the fact we have spent a few hours here.

Mr. LEACH. I have no objection.

Mr. SOLARZ. Do you want to cast a proxy for Mr. Gejdenson?

Mr. LEACH. Yes. He votes "aye."

Mr. SOLARZ. On the motion then to report out the resolution, four voting in the affirmative and four voting in the negative. The resolution does not have a sufficient number to report out and the resolution is not reported out.

Let me say to my colleagues on the committee, and to Mr. Hendon and anyone else who is here with an interest in this, I will be more than happy to continue consultations and discussions with you on it. I think all of us share a common concern here. We have differences over how best to advance our mutual objectives, but I am hopeful that a way can be found.

Given the difficulties of enacting something in this session, we probably wouldn't have been able to do anything until next year even if we had reported it out. But I didn't want it said that we didn't bring it up for a vote.

If we don't have an opportunity to consider this again this year, which it would not be my intention to do in the absence of a consensus, members will have ample opportunity to have their legislation considered next year. In the meantime, we will all have opportunities to discuss this with the administration and to get their views on how best to proceed.

If there are no further comments, the meeting is adjourned.

[Whereupon, at 4 p.m. the subcommittee adjourned subject to the call of the Chair.]

APPENDIX

OFFICIAL POSITION PAPER

POW/MIA SPECIAL COMMISSION

The League is opposed to the establishment of such a commission based on several considered factors, including the seriously detrimental results of two previous commissions: The 1975-76 Select Committee on POW/MIA, headed by Representative G.V. "Sonny" Montgomery, (D-MS), and the 1977 Woodcock (Presidential) Commission on POW/MIA, chaired by Leonard Woodcock. The respective final reports contained conclusions and recommendations which were negative and damaging to the issue. In both instances, the League was forced to reject the final reports as being speculative and based on the word of the Vietnamese rather than facts.

The POW/MIA issue cannot afford another "conclusion" based on anything other than facts. A special commission or committee inherits the requirement to reach conclusions and make recommendations. A final conclusion on the POW/MIA issue is not yet possible, and any serious assessment would reach the position now held by the U.S. government: Information available precludes ruling out the possibility that prisoners may still be held; therefore, investigative efforts are undertaken with high priority and resources, based on the assumption that Americans are held against their will.

The League has long maintained the position that Americans are held in Southeast Asia; however, proof to support this position has as yet not been obtained, even with current raised intelligence priorities and sustained negotiations. There is now reason to expect that such evidence can be obtained due to the high priority assigned by the President and his pledge that "all intelligence assets are now focused on this issue." The President's commitment, supported by Defense Secretary Caspar Weinberger, Secretary of State George Shultz and Chairman of the Joint Chiefs of Staff Admiral William Crowe, is open-ended and will continue "until the fullest possible accounting has been achieved."

Legislation to establish a separate commission to investigate the POW/MIA issue directly undermines the only President who has given the POW/MIA issue an open-ended commitment and assigned highest national priority to resolving this humanitarian matter. The Congress is not in a position, regardless of significant bi-partisan interest, to determine whether POWs are currently held in Southeast Asia, and several committees of the Congress have looked at this question. Such a determination must be made by the intelligence community or through negotiations. Recommendations for effecting the release of POWs have been and are continuously analyzed, and the US government has previously stated that the options range from "bribery to black helicopters in the night." The President has pledged "decisive action" on any report that can be confirmed.

The elected Board of Directors is on record opposing any special POW/MIA commission, and the League's membership voted against the concept by a substantial margin. The 1985/86 Board affirmed confidence in the highest national priority emphasis assigned by the President and his Administration on the POW/MIA issue and reiterated that same confidence in the continuing oversight capacity of the Subcommittee on Asian and Pacific Affairs, House Foreign Affairs Committee, and the House Task Force on POW/MIA. Accumulated knowledge within the membership of both groups supercedes that which would reasonably be available in any newly formed commission, regardless of the membership.

Important Points Against a Commission

- Signals Vietnam of a lack of confidence in current government policy, and Vietnam could delay cooperation thinking they might gain advantage.

- Clearly demonstrates a lack of confidence in the President and the sincerity of his commitment.

- Demonstrates belief in the conspiracy and coverup theory alledged by Representative Hendon and determined to be without basis by the Subcommittee on Asian and Pacific Affairs, House POW/MIA Task Force and House Select Committee on Intelligence.

- The POW/MIA issue is now a matter of highest national priority and is being seriously implemented as a part of US foreign policy by the entire government. A special commission, regardless of the level, would take the issue out of the mainstream of US policy and into the sidelines.

- The President's commitment has been endorsed publicly by the Secretary of Defense, Secretary of State, National Security Council, Chairman of the Joint Chiefs of Staff, the military service chiefs and the entire cabinet.

- The issue is in better hands with the Reagan Administration, the first to be committed, than with unknown commission members who would have to learn the issue and obtain all data from relevant US government agencies.

- All responsible congressional committee chairmen in the Senate and House are opposed to the formation of a special commission.

- The Reagan Administration is formally on record as opposed to a special commission.

- Past committees and commissions have had a negative impact on the issue.

- A short-term requirement to reach a conclusion will be negative for the issue, especially compared to the open-ended, high priority commitment of the President and the entire Administration, supported on a bipartisan basis by the Congress.

The current League position is based upon knowledge of the way this issue has been treated by politicians, US government officials, foreign governments, the media and the public. We will not hesitate, since our relatives are at stake, to advocate a commission when we believe it is needed. Such a commission is not necessary or helpful now, and before advocating one, the League would want to discuss it personally with President Reagan.

American must portray to the Vietnamese a united concern on the POW/MIA issue. Divisiveness during the war created opportunities for Vietnam. It is imperative to current negotiations that the Vietnamese realize the majority of Americans are fully supportive of this administration's high priority policy. There is no substitute for serious government-wide effort, led by the President, to gain the release of live prisoners and those still missing. Should that effort falter, the League will be the first to announce it.

CONSPIRACY AND COVERUP

This charge has its real roots in history surrounding the unsatisfactory, incomplete and subsequently misleading results of the Paris Peace Accords, the nature of the secret war in Laos and Cambodia, the negative conclusions of the House Select Committee of the Congress and the Woodcock Commission, and US government reluctance over the years to provide the families with forthright answers to their questions. This mindset prevailed in varying degrees though three administrations (Nixon, Ford and Carter). It created a hostile and adversarial relationship between the League and the US government and built justifiable suspicion in the minds of individual families and the League, as an organization.

The policy of the Reagan Administration calls for the release of all possible information to the families. This was in recognition of the need to overcome the past and build confidence in the sincerity of current efforts. Many families received additional information as a result of this policy. Combined with the opening of serious negotiations, raising of intelligence priorities, endorsement of public awareness and integration of the POW/MIA issue into US foreign policy, most family members are convinced of the determination of this administration to overcome the "apathy and inaction of the past" (the President's terms) by exhausting all avenues to resolve the issue.

This history is quite familiar to the families but was and is new to previously uninvolved Americans and a very few politicians whose interest was aroused by successful public awareness activities. The overwhelming majority now support the current direction of efforts; however, a few have not taken the time to learn the issue in a comprehensive way, have been ill-advised or misinformed and decided to pursue their own course, often to the detriment of what the League fought years to achieve - serious efforts to resolve the fates of our missing men.

There were successive expressions of frustration and outspoken criticism during the 1970's; but ironically, the first serious charge of actual conspiracy and coverup was made against the Reagan Administration by Representative Billy Hendon of North Carolina. Mr. Hendon was elected to Congress in 1980 and brought with him an evident interest in the POW/MIA issue. The League executive director met with him at his request during his first weeks in office.

Initially, Mr. Hendon was primarily involved in efforts with the Lao to move forward the level of cooperation on accountability for nearly 600 Americans still unaccounted for in that country. Toward that objective, he and former Representative John LeBoutillier were instrumental in gaining executive branch agreement to provide, in 1981, medical disaster relief to a hospital in Vientiane, Laos. This step paved the way for cooperative acceptance of the League's delegation in 1982, a visit which was termed a "significant breakthrough" by the State Department. Sustained negotiations following these events has generated some progress in accounting for our men in Laos.

The League crashsite visit was the first of its kind and led to the official survey and subsequent joint excavation at Pakse, conducted in February, 1985, after a delay of almost one year due to the irresponsible, private cross-border foray of Bo Gritz. In the interim, Mr. Hendon was defeated in his election bid and was temporarily hired (January - July, 1983) as a consultant at the Pentagon to assist Colonel Jerry Venanzi, then Principal Advisor to the Secretary of Defense for POW/MIA Affairs. In that capacity, Hendon had access to the "raw" data reporting Americans being held captive, primarily collected from refugee sources as a result of upgraded screening procedures. Since Mr. Hendon was only cleared to view material classified at the Secret level or lower, he did not then have access to much of the detailed follow-up investigations or more highly classified data on the POW/MIA issue.

In November, 1983, apparently based on incoming reports not yet fully evaluated or analyzed and research from the past, Mr. Hendon publicly charged the Reagan Administration with conspiracy and coverup on the POW/MIA issue. His appearance before the League board of directors expressing such views resulted in the board's referral of the matter to the House Task Force on POW/MIAs, then chaired by Representative Ben Gilman (R-NY).

After a year-long investigation, the Task Force formally issued their findings in August of 1984 as follows: "After thorough review of more than eighty case files cited by Mr. Hendon as providing proof of live Americans, the Task Force concludes that there is no government coverup of information on live prisoners." The Task Force further found that in the past, "DIA was understaffed, had little direction from the top, and tried to do as best they could with their limited personnel, resources and equipment. These impediments to progress have now been corrected, and the Task Force is pleased to report that the Defense Intelligence Agency undertakes its mission seriously and is allocating proper resources to its mission."

In spite of the Task Force's findings, claims of "conspiracy and coverup" continued to surface, many of which are still generated by Mr. Hendon, to the detriment of the issue and using critical assets within the intelligence community. Another look at Mr. Hendon's theory was completed September 10, 1985, by the House Select Committee on Intelligence which reaffirmed the Task Force's conclusion that no conspiracy or coverup exists.

Hundreds of hours have been unnecessarily expended to substantiate DIA's professionalism at the expense of other priorities - namely collection, analysis and evaluation of firsthand sighting reports. Yet, in 1986, we find such allegations still being made and the media's appetite unabated for controversy and rumor. As a result, Director of DIA Lt. General Leonard Perroots invited former DIA Director Lt. General Eugene Tighe to review DIA's procedures, cases and evaluations, asking for further investigation of already discredited charges of conspiracy and coverup as well as recommendations for any improvements deemed necessary or helpful.

Those long involved are acutely aware that information was distorted or withheld in years past; however, now is not the time for those who are currently working this issue to undertake an historical investigation of past efforts - history will take care of itself. The League holds the firm conviction that efforts must focus on the present and future. Our men's lives may well depend on current decisions; they do not depend on history except in the context of policy negotiations.

The League awaits the results of the Tighe team's effort and hopes for objectivity in this report; the issue deserves it. The League has not found nor been provided with any evidence to support claims that there is currently a conspiracy or coverup on the POW/MIA issue and intends to focus on what is best for accomplishing our objectives. Our first priority is to obtain the release of POWs, secondly the repatriation of remains and the fullest possible accounting for our men.

NATIONAL LEAGUE OF FAMILIES
OF AMERICAN PRISONERS AND MISSING IN SOUTHEAST ASIA
1608 K STREET, N.W., WASHINGTON, D. C. 20006   (202) 223-6846

MISSING BUT NOT FORGOTTEN

AMERICAN PRISONERS OF WAR AND MISSING IN ACTION

"POOR IS THE NATION THAT HAS NO HEROES;

SHAMEFUL IS THE ONE THAT HAVING THEM, FORGETS."

— A KOREAN VETERAN

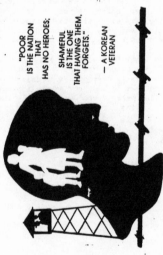

THEY HAVE SERVED LONG ENOUGH ... NEVER LET IT HAPPEN AGAIN

CO-SPONSORED BY:

COLORADO VETERANS ALLIANCE

THE CHILDREN OF MIA/POWS IN SOUTHEAST ASIA

PEACE & JUSTICE FACILIATION UNITED CAMPUS MINISTRY

NOVEMBER 13, 1986   7 P.M.

COLORADO STATE UNIVERSITY
LORY STUDENT CENTER BALLROOM
FORT COLLINS, COLORADO

INFO: 223-5272,
223-5512, 484-4113

FREE ADMISSION

COLORADO MEN STILL MISSING FROM THE VIET NAM WAR

SSGT	ANSELMO, William Frank	Denver
MAJ	APODACA, Victor Joe Jr.	Englewood
AN	BARBER, Thomas David	Aurora
CWO	BERRY, John Alvin	Naturita
COL	BOSTON, Leo Sydney	Canon City
COL	BROWNLEE, Charles Richard	Alamosa
COL	CORBITT, Gilland Wales	Denver
CAPT	DANIELSON, Mark Giles	Rangely
PFC	DE HERRERA, Benjamin David	Colorado Springs
SFC	DONOVAN, Leroy Melvin	Cedaredge
MAJ	GILCHRIST, Robert Michael	Littleton
LTJG	GREEN, Gerald	Fort Morgan
CAPT	HAMM, James Edward	Longmont
PFC	HANRATTY, Thomas Michael	Beulah
CWO	HANSEN, Lester Alan	Pueblo
CAPT	HELWIG, Roger Danny	Colorado Springs
LTC	HRDLICKA, David Louis	Littleton
CAPT	HYDE, Michael Lewis	Boulder City
PFC	JACQUES, James Joseph	Denver
MAJ	JEFFERSON, Perry Henry	Denver
AX3	KEMP, Clayton Charles Jr.	Wheatridge
AMS3	KOHLER, Delvin Lee	Kersey
CAPT	LA VOO, John Allen	Pueblo
CAPT	LADEWIG, Melvin Earl	Englewood
CWO	LEEPER, Wallace Wilson	Wellington
CAPT	MARTIN, Duane Whitney	Denver
CAPT	MC VEY, Lavoy Don	Lamar
MAJ	MITCHELL, Thomas Barry	Littleton
MAJ	MORGAN, Burke Henderson	Manitou Springs
CMS	MULLINS, Harold Eugene	Denver
CAPT	PACKARD, Ronald Lyle	Canon City
LCDR	PAWLISH, George Francis	Las Animas
MAJ	RALSTON, Frank Delzell III	Denver
SPG	SHAFER, Philip Raymond	Grand Junction
LTC	SILVA, Claude Arnold	Monte Vista
SSGT	SIMPSON, Joseph Louis	Denver
CAPT	STEADMAN, James Eugene	Fort Collins
CAPT	STEARNS, Roger Horace	Boulder
CAPT	SWANSON, Jon Edward	Denver
CAPT	TUCKER, Timothy Michael	Las Animas
CAPT	WALKER, Bruce Charles	Pueblo

SPEAKERS

MICHAEL CHARNEY, Ph.D - Forensic anthropologist - expert at identifying remains; from CSU; is involved in cases of returned, "identified," "human remains from the Vietnam war since July 1985; 25 MIA cases are in his files which the military has positively identified. Dr. Charney contends only three cases are identified.

CAPT. (Ret) EUGENE "RED" McDANIEL - USN - Former POW of six years who was one of the most brutally tortured men in the Vietnam war. He is president and founder of the American Defense Foundation, the American Defense Institute and is on the Board of Directors of the National League of POW/MIA Families.

CONGRESSMAN BOB SMITH - Representative for N.H. - A Vietnam veteran and one of the nine members of a Congressional delegation that went to Vietnam to stress the need for achieving the fullest possible accounting of POW/MIAs. The delegation found evidence that substantiated accounts of eyewitnesses' claims to have seen American POWs as late as 1982. Congressman Smith strongly believes that live American POWs are being held in Southeast Asia.

MR. SCOTT BARNES - States that he was part of a U.S. chartered activity to gather intelligence and possibly extract POWs in Laos in 1981. Two caucasians were sighted. He was informed that the U.S. Embassy communicated that if caucasians presence was confirmed that the "merchandise was to be liquidated."

DR. CHRIS GUGAS - Behavioral psychologist - An expert with 40 years experience with polygraph and security programs for the military, business, and industry. Dr. Gugas became involved in the POW issue after polygraphing Scott Barnes.

MAJOR MARK SMITH (Ret) - US Army (Special Forces) - Former POW; was with Special Forces Detachment in Korea where he established a network in Vietnam and Laos for information about sightings of POWs. When he stated he could produce three live POWs, he was told to shred the evidence, was reassigned, and then retired by the Army. He filed a lawsuit against the government for ignoring reports, compromising information, and lack of interest in POWs.

JERRY DENNIS - National Coordinator for the Smith, McIntire, Howard Foundation and a member of its Board of Directors. His brother, Mark Dennis, was listed killed in action July 15, 1966, but Mark's photograph appeared in Newsweek in November 1970. Jerry has been an activist in the POW issue since then and is a plaintiff in the pending lawsuit against the government.

COL. (Ret) EARL HOPPER - Had a full military career in the U.S. Army. He is an active member in the National League of POW/MIA Families. His son, Earl Jr., was an Air Force pilot shot down in 1968. Earl Jr.'s status was changed from MIA to "killed in action." After careful reevaluation of Earl Jr.'s case, the Justice Department concluded that Lt. Col. Earl P. Hopper, Jr. survived the crash and was captured in January 1968.

MIA/POW SYMPOSIUM AGENDA

November 13, 1986

7-8 p.m.

Introduction of Master of Ceremonies
Color Guard - CSU Army ROTC
Benediction - Father Guy Morgan, Colonel (Ret.), USAF
Pledge of Allegiance - Colonel (Ret.) Earl P. Hopper, USA
Introduction of Guest Speakers - Colonel Earl P. Hopper, MC

SPEAKERS:

Dr. Michael Charney
Captain Eugene "Red" McDaniel, USN

Break - 5 minutes

8-9 p.m.

Congressman Bob Smith, R - NH
Mr. Scott Barnes

Break - 10 minutes

9-10 p.m.

Dr. Chris Gugas
Major (Ret.) Mark Smith, US Army (Special Forces)

Break - 5 minutes

10-11 p.m.

Jerry Dennis
Panel discussion with audience participation.

The panel will be comprised of all guest speakers with Colonel Earl F. Hopper as moderator.

Joseph Devera/The Coloradoan

FORMER POW: 'When you go to war, you are prepared to die, to be captured, tortured, but you are not prepared to be abandoned,' former POW Eugene 'Red' McDaniel says.

Speakers press for action on sightings of U.S. POWs

By PATRICE WENDLING
The Coloradoan

The government should create a presidential commission or Cabinet post to investigate current reports of live American prisoners of war still held in Southeast Asia, according to POW supporters.

A panel of seven national speakers actively seeking the release of POWs, attracted more than 1,000 people Thursday night to the Lory Student Center at Colorado State University. The symposium was entitled "Missing But Not Forgotten: American Prisoners of War and Missing in Action."

Former POW Eugene "Red" McDaniel told the crowd the question is not if there are live Americans still in captivity, but how can people work for their release.

"When you go to war, you are prepared to die, to be captured, tortured, but you are not prepared to be abandoned."

A bipartisan commission must be created to investigate this problem, McDaniel said. "If there is a commission on pornography, on drugs, why not on the prisoners of war."

Smith was released from Vietnam in 1973 as part of the final negotiations at the end of the war. He spoke of six years of rope tortures and sleeping on a concrete slab, which bore the imprint of a man's body on the hard surface.

Despite years of disbelief, Smith viewed recent satellite pictures of Southeast Asia and now believes there are live prisoners. "I'm absolutely convinced, beyond a shadow of a doubt, that we

have a large number of men serving still in the traditional sense of POW."

Rep. Robert C. Smith, R-N.H., said while President Reagan declared the POW/MIA issue the nation's highest priority in 1983, little has been done to secure prisoners. "It's not a priority," Smith said. "The president of the U.S. believes it is and is working for it, but he's not getting the information he needs."

The government has received more than 5,500 reports pertaining to POWs, including 906 live sightings, Department of Defense spokesman Lt. Col. Keith Schneider said. About 61 percent of those live sightings have been resolved by the person returning to America, another 21

percent have been proven to be false by the source and approximately 18 percent, or 161 reports, are under continuing high priority investigation, Schneider said.

"We can't rule out the possibility Americans are still being held against their will. Should any report prove true, the government would take appropriate actions."

Schneider would not elaborate on what actions, but said, "The range of possibilities would be from negotiations to black helicopters in the night, if you will." There are ongoing dialogues between the Reagan administration and Southeast Asian governments to obtain an accounting as for those still missing, he said.

Smith, who agreed a commission with subpoena power should be formed, also called for a Cabinet position to be created to collect and assimilate information and work directly with the president. The government has ignored live citings by Vietnamese refugees and former POW Robert Garwood, who came out of Vietnam in 1979, he said.

"How many more live sightings do we need? Even the number two negotitator (during the Nixon administration) with (Henry) Kissinger, (Robert) McFarlane (President Reagan's former national security adviser) says there are still POWs alive in Vietnam, Laos and Cambodia."

Fort Collins forensic anthropologist Michael Charney told the crowd the Army's Central Identification Laboratory should be moved from Honolulu to Washington, D.C. The lab, which identifies the remains of Vietnam soldiers from all branches of the military, has deliberately distorted and falsified identifications, Charney says.

Other speakers included: Scott Barnes, who publicly claims to have seen live American prisoners in Laos recently; psychologist and polygraph expert Chris Gugas; retired Maj. Mark Smith, who initiated a lawsuit against President Reagan for information on POWs; and Jerry Dennis, who is searching for his brother after receiving what he believes are the wrong remains.

Professor: MIA remains misidentified

DALLAS (AP) — Very few of the remains of missing-in-action servicemen returned from Southeast Asia can be positively identified, and saying such identification is possible is cruel to their families, a researcher says.

Michael Charney, a forensic anthropologist and professor emeritus of physical anthroplogy at Colorado State University, said he had examined the remains of 19 servicemen identified by the military and concluded that the identification can be verified in only two of them.

Charney, in Dallas on Saturday to address a meeting of Vietnam veterans, said military officials "were making judgments that nobody could make. So I have been tearing at them ever since. It's not right to do this to the families. They should tell them the truth."

Charney, 74, is director of forensic science laboratory at Colorado State. He said he is an expert on bone identification and facial reconstruction and one of 34 certified forensic anthropologists in the United States and Canada.

Charney said he told a House subcommittee in September that if his sample of 19 investigations held for all returned MIA remains, 90 percent have been misidentified.

But Col. Keith Schneider, a Defense Department spokesman, said Sunday that it was "complete and total rubbish" to contend that 90 percent of MIA remains have been misidentified.

Charney said his work has changed the way the military refers to the identification process, a contention Schneider disputed.

MIA speakers say U.S. believes problem is insurmountable

By ROD SPAW
Courier staff writer

Two men who have sued the federal government to get action on the POW/MIA issue said Sunday that the Reagan administration doesn't want to face a hostage crisis that would overshadow former President Jimmy Carter's Iranian standoff of 1979 and 1980.

"It would be the biggest hostage crisis that this government has ever faced," said Mark A. Smith, a retired major in the U.S. Special Forces and a former POW in North Vietnam. "We can't get four or five hostages out of the Middle East. We're talking about hundreds scattered in four or five locations in Southeast Asia. I think they believe it is an insurmountable problem."

Smith thinks there could be more than 200 American servicemen and civilians who never got out of Vietnam, Cambodia or Laos when the United States withdrew from the Indochina War.

Jerry Dennis, retired fire chief from Largo, Fla., thinks his brother Mark may be among them.

"This administration isn't going to bring them home unless there is some public opinion that says get it done — or a court," said Dennis.

Both men now travel the country talking about captives who may be held in Southeast Asia, and the litigation against the federal government that is pending before the U.S. District Court for the Eastern District of North Carolina. They spoke Saturday at a rally in Newburgh sponsored by the local chapter of the Forget-Me-Not Association.

Smith was one of the original instigators of the court action in 1985, along with another retired Green Beret, Melvin C. McIntire, and their former commander, Lt. Col. Robert Howard, who Smith said still is on active duty.

Dennis is coordinator of the Smith-McIntire-Howard Foundation, a nonprofit organization that was formed to permit families of MIAs to join the class-action lawsuit.

Smith and Dennis said they base their belief that American captives still remain in Southeast Asia on intelligence gathered by the military since the end of the war and independent reports that have come to their organization within the past year.

Smith said he got his first, intensive look at the POW/MIA issue in 1981, when he and McIntire were assigned to investigate alleged sightings of live captives for the Defense Intelligence Agency.

For Dennis, the search began in 1970 when a picture appeared in Newsweek magazine of an "unknown POW" who the family was convinced was Mark Dennis, though he had been reported killed in a helicopter crash four years earlier.

A year later, Dennis said, the family had exhumed the remains that were returned by the U.S. Navy. He said the remains clearly were of someone other than Mark Dennis.

Dennis and Smith said it is both a "people and paperwork problem" that has hindered the government's approach to investigating whether any Americans remain captive in Southeast Asia.

Smith said the military continues to use the same team that has been checking captive reports, and dismissing them, for 15 years, while there is no central repository among the military branches for MIA/POW information.

"Military officers do not go around proving themselves wrong intentionally," said Smith, who spent a year as a captive in North Vietnam before being released in 1973 as part of Operation Homecoming. "Military officers don't have the option of being wrong on an issue of this magnitude."

Smith said most intelligence on live sightings have come from Vietnamese refugees, friendly countries in Southeast Asia and from foreigners traveling in Indochina. Smith said he continues to visit the area periodically to collect new intelligence.

Dennis   Smith

U.S. Department of Justice

Federal Bureau of Investigation

Washington, D.C. 20535

NOV 24 1982

Mr. Scott Tracy Barnes
4302 Mesa Street
Torrance, California 90505

Dear Mr. Barnes:

Reference is made to your recent letters regarding
an update of your Freedom of Information-Privacy Acts (FOIPA)
request number 83,263, for information in our files pertaining
to you. Reference is also made to your telephonic conversation
on November 9, 1982, with one of our analysts, Debra Weiszmann.

In accordance with the aforementioned conversation
a copy of our disclosure letter dated October 3, 1979,
and its 10 enclosure pages are being forwarded to you at this
time.

Please be advised that it has been ascertained
that FBI number 33905F is not a file in our central records
system, but it represents the number assigned to your FBI
arrest record. In order to obtain this arrest record, you
must comply with the instructions set forth in Attorney General
Order 556-73, a copy of which is enclosed. If, in addition,
you desire a search of National Crime Information Center
Computerized Criminal History (NCIC CCH) records, please
specifically indicate this on your request to the Identification
Division. Fingerprint impressions are needed for comparison
with records in both the Identification Division and the
Computerized Criminal History File to insure that an individual's
record is not disseminated to an unauthorized person.

Please note the 2 additional files pertaining to
your are currently being processed. As explained in the
November 9, 1982, conversation the processing of FOIPA
requests is handled in chronological order according to

date of receipt. Your request is being handled in this
manner and a release will be forwarded to you as equitably
as possible.

I sincerely hope this has served to answer any
questions you may have at this time regarding this matter.

Sincerely yours,

James K. Hall

James K. Hall, Chief
Freedom of Information-
Privacy Acts Section
Records Management Division

Enclosures (2)

DEPARTMENT OF THE TREASURY
(UNITED STATES SECRET SERVICE

WASHINGTON, D.C. 20223

DEPUTY DIRECTOR

Mr. Scott T. Barnes   .DEC 0 9 1982
4302 Mesa Street
Torrance, California 90505

Dear Mr. Barnes:

    Reference is made to your letter received November 4, 1982,
appealing a decision of Mr. Hugh P. Ward, Freedom of Information
Officer, United States Secret Service, denying you certain
information under the Freedom of Information Act. Treasury
regulations regarding administrative appeals of initial denials by
the United States Secret Service vest the review authority in the
Deputy Director of the Secret Service (31 Code of Federal
Regulations, Subtitle A, Part 1, Appendix D and 40 Federal
Register 49089, dated October 21, 1975).

    The records and correspondence pertinent to your appeal have
been reviewed. I have determined that the exemptions claimed by
Mr. Ward in his letter of October 27, 1982, were proper. The
Secret Service records contain investigatory information compiled
for law enforcement purposes. Pursuant to Title 5, United States
Code, Section 552, Subsection (b)(7)(C), (D), (E), and (F),
information is being withheld since disclosure would constitute an
unwarranted invasion of personal privacy, disclose the identity of
a confidential source and/or information furnished by a
confidential source, or disclose investigative techniques and
procedures, or endanger the life or physical safety of law
enforcement personnel.

    In addition, pursuant to Subsection (b)(5), Secret Service
information is being withheld since it contains inter-agency or
intra-agency memoranda or letters which would not be available by
law to a party other than an agency in litigation with the Secret
Service. Other deletions have been made in accordance with
subsection (b)(2) as matters relating solely to internal
proceedings. Additionally, information is being withheld in
accordance with Title 5, United States Code, Section 552(b)(1) as
data which is currently and properly classified pursuant to
Executive Order 12065 in the interest of national security. The
above cited exemptions are not to be construed as the only
exemptions which may be applicable to these documents under the
Freedom of Information Act.

    I have also determined that certain information in the files
may be properly disclosed to you. The documents containing that
information are enclosed with this letter.

You should also be aware that the Freedom of Information Act, as amended, has no provisions for the correction of any errors that you may think are present in the records disclosed to you. However, as a matter of policy and without waiving any right, a copy of your request for correction of errors will be placed in your file.

As Mr. Ward informed you in his letter to you, the Secret Service files contain National Military Record Center and Federal Bureau of Investigation information and reports. Your Freedom of Information Act request has been forwarded to the National Military Record Center and Federal Bureau of Investigation for their response to you.

Any denial on appeal is subject to judicial review in the District Court in the district where the complainant resides, has a principal place of business, or in which the agency records are situated, or in the District of Columbia.

For the purpose of appeals of initial denials under the Freedom of Information Act, the undersigned is the official making this determination for the United States Secret Service.

Sincerely,

William R. Barton
Deputy Director

Enclosures

JOHN K. VAN DE KAMP
Attorney General

State of California
DEPARTMENT OF JUSTICE

P. O. BOX 13417
SACRAMENTO 95813

November 8, 1984

Scott T. Barnes
P.O. Box 704
Kernville, CA 93238

Dear Mr. Barnes:

NO RECORD

This is in response to your inquiry concerning the existence of a
criminal history record within the files of the California Bureau
of Criminal Identification.

A search of your fingerprints in our files did not identify with
any criminal history record maintained by this Bureau.

If you have any further questions, please contact the Supervisor
of the Record Review Unit at the above address or call (916) 739-5140.

Very truly yours,

JOHN K. VAN DE KAMP
Attorney General

DOUGLAS A. SMITH, Manager
Record Control Program
Bureau of Criminal Identification

BCID 8708 (Rev. 1/83)

APPLICANT

- LEAVE BLANK

TYPE OR PRINT INFORMATION

LAST NAME	FIRST NAME	MIDDLE NAME
BARNES	SCOTT	TRACY

LEAVE BLANK

MAIDEN NAME/ALIASES

THIS DATA MAY BE COMPUTERIZED IN LOCAL, STATE AND NATIONAL FILES

ADDITIONAL INFORMATION REQUIRED ON BACK OF THIS CARD

FOI REQUEST
SEARCH AND FURNISH
RESULTS TO - RECORDING
SECTION - 11286C

NTRIBUTING AGENCY AND ADDRESS

SIGNATURE OF PERSON FINGERPRINTED
x Scott Tracy Barnes

SUBMITTING AGENCY NO.

SEX	HT.	WT.	EYE	HAIR	DATE OF BIRTH	PLACE OF BIRTH
M	6-01	85	HZL	BRN	6-19-54	BURBANK, CA.

SIGNATURE OF OFFICIAL TAKING FINGERPRINTS

K.C.S.O.

DATE FINGERPRINTED 10/26/84

CII NO.

FBI NO.

PAYMENT OF FEE REQUIRED FOR PROCESSING

LEAVE BLANK

CLASS 8 S 1 U II O 16
M 1 R I O I

SEARCHED BY:

VERIFIED BY:

DO NOT FOLD THIS CARD
(TYPE OR PRINT ALL INFORMATION REQUESTED)
APPLICATION FOR EMPLOYMENT

	EMPLOYING AGENCY AND ADDRESS:	☐ THIS EMPLOYMENT TITLE IS EXEMPT FROM THE PROVISIONS OF SECTION 432.7 OF THE CALIF. LABOR CODE. PLEASE CITE STATUTE OR OTHER REASON FOR EXEMPTION.
☐ PEACE OFFICER (830 PC) ☐ CRIMINAL JUSTICE EMPLOYEE ☐ STATE EMPLOYEE ☐ CITY/COUNTY EMPLOYEE ☐ SCHOOL EMPLOYEE ☐ OTHER EMPLOYEE	POSITION TITLE:	

APPLICATION FOR LICENSE, PERMIT OR CERTIFICATION

APPLICATION FOR:	ISSUING AGENCY AND ADDRESS:
☐ LICENSE ☐ PERMIT ☐ CERTIFICATION ☐ OTHER	NO ARREST RECORD, OCT 31 1984 IDENTIFICATION DIVISION FBI LICENSE-PERMIT-CERTIFICATION TITLE:

(THIS SECTION MUST BE COMPLETED FOR CONCEALED WEAPON LICENSE)			
REASON FOR DESIRING LICENSE:	KNOWINGLY FURNISHING FALSE INFORMATION IS A MISDEMEANOR (PENAL CODE SECTION 12051(b). I ATTEST THAT ALL OF THE STATEMENTS AND INFORMATION ON THIS CARD ARE TRUE AND CORRECT		14
	SIGNATURE:		DATE:
MAKE	TYPE	CALIBER	SERIAL NUMBER

PERSONAL INFORMATION

RESIDENCE ADDRESS (REQUIRED FOR CCW LICENSE)	BUSINESS ADDRESS (REQUIRED FOR CCW LICENSE)	DRIVERS LICENSE NUMBER
IN EMERGENCY NOTIFY—NAME	ADDRESS	SOCIAL SECURITY NUMBER (VOLUNTARY—FOR ID ONLY)

BID-7 (3-80)   OSP

1-454 (Rev. 2-14-84)

U.S. Department of Justice

Federal Bureau of Investigation

Washington, D.C. 20537

To: Bureau of Identification   Date: October 23, 1984
      Department of Justice
      Post Office Box 13417
      Sacramento, California 95813

Enclosed herewith is a copy of a communication questioning arrest data previously submitted by your agency, together with a copy of the subject's identification record, as it currently appears in our files. You are requested to verify or correct the challenged entry/entries submitted by your agency after conducting whatever administrative, judicial or other proceedings you find necessary or appropriate in order to resolve all matters in dispute.   It is requested that you respond by executing the reverse side of this form.   For your convenience in replying, a self-addressed, franked envelope which requires no postage is enclosed.

If there is another charge(s) submitted by your agency on subject's identification record which lacks a disposition(s), please submit the disposition(s) with your reply.

Sincerely yours,

this is Not Me

Assistant Director
Identification Division

please Correct

Enc.   (3)

Copy to: Mr. Scott Tracy Barnes
          Post Office Box 704
          Kernville, California   93238

As a matter of information, the number referred to in your letter "33 905 F" is the number assigned to your record maintained in the FBI Identification Division.

Our identification files do not contain any previous request from the California authorities regarding the expungement of your arrest record. Additionally, as long as arrest data remains in our files, it is available for dissemination to authorized agencies upon request. Since this Bureau does not honor any expungement request from the State of California unless it was processed by the Department of Justice, Bureau of Identification, Sacramento, California, we are corresponding with the above-named agency in an effort to clarify this matter. You will be advised of the results of our contact.

We appreciate your patience while your appeal was being processed.

FBI/DOJ

Sincerely,

Richard J. Kerr
Chairman
Information Review Committee

Central Intelligence Agency

Washington. D.C. 20505

8 April 1986

Mr. Scott Barnes
P.O. Box 704
Kernville, CA 93238

Dear Mr. Barnes:

This is in response to your letter of 14 January 1986 in which you appeal the decision of this Agency, dated 3 January 1986, to neither confirm nor deny the existence or nonexistence of records responsive to your 9 July 1979 Freedom of Information Act request for records pertaining to "Operation Delta" and "Operation Phoenix."

Your appeal has been presented to the Central Intelligence Agency Information Review Committee. Pursuant to the authority delegated under paragraph 1900.51(a) of Chapter XIX, Title 32 of the Code of Federal Regulations, Mr. Clair E. George, Deputy Director for Operations, has determined that the fact of the existence or nonexistence of any documents which would reveal a confidential or covert CIA connection with, or interest in, "Operation Delta" or "Operation Phoenix" is classified pursuant to Executive Order 12356. Further, the fact of the existence or nonexistence of such documents would relate directly to information concerning intelligence sources and methods which the Director of Central Intelligence has the responsibility to protect from unauthorized disclosure in accordance with subsection 102(d)(3) of the National Security Act of 1947 and section 6 of the Central Intelligence Agency Act of 1949. Accordingly, pursuant to the Freedom of Information Act exemptions (b)(1) and (b)(3), respectively, your appeal is denied to the extent that it concerns any such documents. By this statement we are neither confirming nor denying that any such documents exist.

In accordance with the provisions of the Freedom of Information Act, you have the right to seek judicial review of the above determinations in a United States district court.

We appreciate your patience while your appeal was being processed.

Sincerely,

Richard J. Kerr
Chairman
Information Review Committee

Scott Tracy Barnes   1 6 MAR 1987
P.O. Box 704
Kernville, CA   93238

Dear Mr. Barnes:

    your letter of 3 March 1987 was received in our office on
10 March 1987. This letter presented an appeal of the
determination made in our 20 February 1987 letter to you pertaining
to one CIA-originated document (document 2A) referred to this
Agency by the Federal Bureau of Investigation (FBI) pursuant to
your 10 September 1982 request to them for information on yourself
(P83-0196).

    Your appeal has been accepted and arrangements will be made for
its consideration by the appropriate Deputy Director or Senior
Official. You will be advised of the determinations made.

    In order to afford requesters the most equitable treatment
possible, we have adopted the policy of handling appeals on a
first-received, first-out basis. At the present time, our workload
consists of approximately 175 appeals awaiting completion. In view
of this, some delay in our reply must be expected, but I can assure
you that every reasonable effort will be made to complete a
response as soon as possible.

                                Sincerely,

                                Lee S. Strickland
                        Information and Privacy Coordinator

Central Intelligence Agency

Washington, D.C. 20505

2 0 FEB 1987

Scott Tracy Barnes
P.O. Box 704
Kernville, CA 93238

Dear Mr. Barnes:

In the course of the Federal Bureau of Investigation's search of its records in response to your Privacy Act request, the Bureau located two CIA-originated documents numbered 2A and 1B.

Upon review, we determined that document 1B is a duplicate of document 2A.

In regard to document 2A, we have completed our review and have determined that the document must be withheld in its entirety under Privacy Act exemptions (j)(1) and (k)(1). An explanation of exemptions is enclosed.

You have the right to appeal this determination by addressing your appeal to me and I will forward it to the appropriate senior officials of this agency. Should you choose to do this, please explain the basis of your appeal.

We apologize for the length of time it has taken us to complete the processing of your request. We have been faced, however, with a large number of requests over the past several years. Under the circumstances, we have done our best to be fair to all of our requesters. Thus, some years ago we established the policy of first-received, first-answered. Thank you for your patience and consideration while we were processing your request.

Sincerely,

Lee S. Strickland
Information and Privacy Coordinator

Enclosure

EXPLANATION OF EXEMPTIONS

FREEDOM OF INFORMATION ACT:

(b)(1)   applies to material which is properly classified pursuant to an Executive order in the interest of national defense or foreign policy;

(b)(2)   applies to information which pertains solely to the internal rules and practices of the Agency;

(b)(3)   applies to the Director's statutory obligations to protect from disclosure intelligence sources and methods, as well as the organization, functions, names, official titles, salaries or numbers of personnel employed by the Agency, in accord with the National Security Act of 1947 and the CIA Act of 1949, respectively;

(b)(4)   applies to information such as trade secrets and commercial or financial information obtained from a person on a privileged or confidential basis;

(b)(5)   applies to inter- and intra-agency memoranda which are advisory in nature;

(b)(6)   applies to information release of which would constitute an unwarranted invasion of the personal privacy of other individuals; and

(b)(7)   applies to investigatory records, release of which could (C) constitute an unwarranted invasion of the personal privacy of others, (D) disclose the identity of a confidential source, (E) disclose investigative techniques and procedures, or (F) endanger the life or physical safety of law enforcement personnel.

PRIVACY ACT:

(b)   applies to information concerning other individuals which may not be released without their written consent;

(j)(1)   applies to polygraph records: documents or segregable portions of documents, release of which would disclose intelligence sources and methods, including names of certain Agency employees and organizational components; and, documents or information provided by foreign governments;

(k)(1)   applies to information and material properly classified pursuant to an Executive order in the interest of national defense or foreign policy;

(k)(5)   applies to investigatory material compiled solely for the purpose of determining suitability, eligibility, or qualifications for Federal civilian employment, or access to classified information, release of which would disclose a confidential source; and

(k)(6)   testing or examination material used to determine individual qualifications for appointment or promotion in Federal Government service the release of which would compromise the testing or examination process.

My which were passed

RESUME   SCOTT T. BARNES
Personal Data: Date of birth: 6-19-54
                 Height: 6-0
                 Weight: 188
                 Hair: dark brown
                 Eyes: hazel

QUALIFICATIONS:

An extensive history of comprehensive experience in all aspects
of Law Enforcement, Security, Loss Prevention, Investigations,
Teaching, Emergency Services, Civil Defense, Counseling and
Management.

Accustomed to situations requiring prompt and appropriate action
and decision making under pressure and stress together with keen
swift reflexes and attention. Communicate clearly and concisely
with all types of people, a natural problem-solver with outstanding analytical and organizational abilities, works well with
executives, public and subordinates.

A former law enforcement officer having infiltrated an international biker gang, he has worked extensively in undercover cases
and received numerous awards from government and local law enforcement agencies for his work. He has appeared in two motion
pictures, appeared on the 700 Club; Entertainment Tonight; ABC,
CBS and NBC news and has been the subject of special reports for
ABC and BBC news. He was in part responsible for various segments
of Paramount Pictures "UNCOMMON VALOR" POW movie, has been written about in several books and magazines. His travels have taken
him to over thirty nations.

He a member and advisor to the following organizations:

UNITED STATES STRATEGIC INSTITUTE: Washington, D.C. Purpose:
to protect the interests of national security; the analysis of
the National Security Policy. Other members include: Richard
Allen; Generals Weyland, Rogers, Polk and Milton; Admiral Moorer
and Vice Admiral Libby

NATIONAL INTELLIGENCE STUDY CENTER: Washington, D.C. Purpose:
to review and analyze intelligence data. Members include: Dr.
Ray Cline, former Deputy Director, CIA; William Casey, former
Director, CIA; General Eugene Tighe, former Director, DIA

NATIONAL STRATEGY INFORMATION CENTER: Purpose: to advise NATO
Defense College, to review intelligence data in the interest of
American security. Members include: Rear Admiral Mott, General
Yudkin, Admiral Johnston, Rear Admiral Martineau, Admiral Elmo R.
Sumwalt, Jr.

SECURITY INTELLIGENCE FOUNDATION: Washington, D.C. Purpose: to
keep U.S. Internal Security and Foreign Intelligence updated.
Members are of FBI, CIA, NSA and DIA. Members include: James
Angleton, Former Chief of Counter-Intelligence CIA; Ambassador
Durbrow; General Richarson III; Admiral Anderson, Chairman of the
President's Foreign Intelligence Board and Generals Quinn and
Graham

AMERICAN PRESERVATION COUNCIL: Purpose: to educate and keep the
Congress updated on matters of international conflicts and sub-
versive activities aimed at the interests of the U.S.   Members
are comprised mainly of intelligence officials and military
advisors.

NAVAL INTELLIGENCE PROFESSIONALS: Washington, D.C. Purpose: to maintain a strong defense through intelligence activities and to provide analysis and input into Naval Intelligence operations.

AMERICAN SECURITY COUNCIL's National Advisory Board: Washington, D.C. Purpose: to review and analyze intelligence from a wide variety of sources and made recommendations for national security and foreign policies of national interest.

ARMED FORCES COMMUNICATIONS and ELECTRONICS ASSOCIATION: Washington, D.C. Purpose: C3 intelligence and security of codes. Works closely with the Defense Communications Agency and provides international assistance to allied nations in the areas of land, air and sea intelligence and operations

NATIONAL MILITARY INTELLIGENCE ASSOCIATION: Washington, D.C. Purpose: to analyze, interpret and make recommendations on intelligence matters of national security to the White House, to keep abreast of international intelligence crises. Members from every branch of the military and DoD intelligence agencies. Members include: Board of Directors: General L. Perroots, Director of DIA; General S. Weinstein, U.S. Army Intelligence; Rear Admiral W. Studeman, Director Naval Intelligence

DEPARTMENT OF JUSTICE NATIONAL INSTITUTE OF JUSTICE, TVI: Washington, D.C. Terrorism, Violence and Insurgency Group in conjunction with the Rand Corp. of Santa Monica, California. President: Dr. Brian Jenkins. Purpose: to review and gather intelligence on terrorism, insurgency world-wide; evaluate and analyze current trends and activities of international terrorism groups and who supports them. Review weapons and intelligence and low intensity conflicts and advise what action to take.

CALIFORNIA ASSOCIATION OF LICENSED INVESTIGATORS
CALIFORNIA STATE ASSOCIATION OF SHERIFFS
PEACE OFFICERS RESEARCH ASSOCIATION OF CALIFORNIA

He has been asked to participate in the 6th Annual Classified Military Space Symposium at the National Academy of Sciences to be held May 27-28, 1987 in Washington, D.C. This is restricted to NEED-TO-KNOW personnel only. Secret clearance is required. Other personnel are Admiral James Hogg, USN; General John Piotrowski, USAF; Edward C. Aldridge, Jr., Secretary of the Air Force Launch Systems.

Currently he is owner of Intravest International Investigations.

EXPERIENCE IN BRIEF:

Licensed Private Investigator: Conduct Criminal, Civil Investigations, Security Consulting and Intelligence, Surveillance, Missing Persons.

College Instructor: Taught in the fields of Law Enforcement, Security, Crisis Intervention, Human Relations, Special Weapons, Anti-Terrorism Tactics, Narcotic and Drug Abuse, Fire Prevention, Civil Rights, Thefts, Counter-Intelligence, Covert Operations, Executive Protection and Investigations.

Counselor/Corrections: Counseled convicted offenders, Security, Investigations into criminal conduct issued citations, enforced rules and regulations.

Security Manager: Director of retail Security Department, conducted employee background investigations, hired and fired Security Agents, investigated criminal violations, made arrests, filed criminal complaints, loss prevention.

Real Estate Agent: Licensed Real Estate Agent, advised on Commercial Development, Realty Investments, Contracts, Loans, Appraised Property, Sold Estates.

Police Officer: uniformed patrol, undercover investigations, narcotics, outlaw gangs, community and public relations, internal investigations, special operations, accident investigations, general law enforcement and intelligence.

Retail Business Owner: Owned and operated a retail gift and investment business, accounting, ordering, marketing, sales and payroll.

Substance Abuse Advisor/Investigator: Advised and taught on substance abuse, conducted covert investigations into employee abuse, fraud and theft of company assets and insurance fraud.

EDUCATION AND DEGREES:

State University of New York: B.S. Degree in Community and Human Services
El Camino College: A.A. Degree in Admin. of Justice
Saddleback College: D.E.A. Diploma in Dangerous Drugs and Narcotics
Miramar College: Diplomas in Law Enforcement, Emergency Services
Ft. Steilcoom College: Police Science, Sociology, Criminal Justice
Cal State/Oklahoma State University Dept. of Military Services - Terrorism
Staff College Dept. of Defense: Nuclear Accidents, Radiological Investigation
Mount Royal College: Certified Protection Officer, Management, Security
California State University: Masters Program in Humanities
Taft University Law School: State Bar Law Program

LICENSES AND CERTIFICATES:

U.S. Dept. of Justice Drug Enforcement Admin., Narcotics and Criminal Intelligence
U.S. Army: Military Police, Corrections, Special Investigations
City of Los Angeles: Civil Defense, Emergency Services, Firefighting
South Bay Police Academy: Law Enforcement, Weapons, Investigations
San Diego Sheriff's Academy: Criminal Justice, Patrol, Community Relations
California Security School: Weapons, Laws of Arrest, Search and Seizure
City of Long Beach: Nuclear Weapons, Civil Defense, Security, Radiological
State of Hawaii: Dept. of Social Services, Correctional Officer Academy
State of California Dept. of Justice: P.O.S.T. Certificate for Peace Officers
State of California Bureau of Collection and Investigative Services: P.I.
Anthony Real Estate School: Real Estate Contract, Appraisals, Laws
Powers Security School: Firearms, Executive Protection, Defensive Tactics
Canadian Security Academy: Investigations, Management, Planning and Procedures
County of Los Angeles: Certified SCUBA Diver

United States Department of Justice
Drug Enforcement Administration

This is to certify that

Scott T. Barnes

has successfully completed the course of instruction in

Basic Narcotics and Dangerous Drug Law Enforcement

conducted by the United States Drug Enforcement Training Academy Staff at

Arvine, California

UNITED S... JUSTICE

Drug Enforcement Administration

Certificate of Training

is to witness that: Through the authority vested in me by the Attorney
General of the United States of America, it is made known and attested that

Scott T. Barnes

... as well suited as to be proclaimed publicly as
... of instruction in narcotics and dangerous drug law enforcement

In testimony whereof I have
my name and affix the seal of the
Department of Justice, on this
20th day of June, 1975

San Diego Community Colleges

SAN DIEGO MIRAMAR COLLEGE

RECORD OF RECRUIT TRAINING

The Academy's program Meets the Basic Training Requirement
of the California Commission on Peace Officer Standards and Training

This is to certify that

Scott T. Barnes

... has satisfactorily completed

Criminal Justice 30	Introduction to Law Enforcement	3 Units
Criminal Justice 31	Patrol Procedures	3 Units
Criminal Justice 32	Traffic Control	3 Units
Criminal Justice 33	Community Relations	3 Units
Criminal Justice 34	Arrest & Control Techniques	1 Unit
Criminal Justice 35	Weapons	1 Unit
Criminal Justice 36	First Aid	1 Unit
Criminal Justice 37	Introduction to Investigative Techniques	3 Units

San Diego County Sheriff's Department

Issues this Award hereby certifying that

SCOTT T. BARNES

has successfully completed the Basic Law Enforcement Course
under the direction of the Sheriff's Training Academy **720 HOURS**

Issued this _____ **21st** _____ day of _____ **JULY** _____ 19 **76**

Andrew Park Jr.
Training Officer

_____
Chief of Police

_____
Sheriff

Office of Civil Defense

Pinn!t College
Battle Creek, Michigan

awards this Home Study Course certificate to

SCOTT BARNES

for the satisfactory completion of a course of instruction

Course: CIVIL DEFENSE, U.S.A.

Date: February 8, 1972

Fred W. Bowman
Director, Extension Training Dept.

_____
Director, Staff College

South Bay Regional Reserve Academy

This is to certify that

SCOTT BARNES

POLICE OFFICER · SOUTH BAY
POLICE

has completed a Basic Police course of instruction
as approved by the Commission on Peace Officer
Standards and Training conducted in conjunction
with El Camino College by the South Bay Police
Training Committee.

Given at El Camino College, California this ____ **14th** ____ day of ____ **June** ____ 19 **75**

_____
Academy Coordinator

Robert Brophy
Academy Coordinator

FIREARM CERTIFICATE

POWERS SECURITY TRAINING SCHOOL

IN REGARD TO

Scott   Tracy   Barnes

This Certificate which was earned by meeting and successfully
completing a course in Firearm Training in accordance with Chapter 7
of Title 16, of the California Administrative Code.

Dated this ____ **9th** ____ day of ____ **October** ____ 19 **85**

_____
Administrator

_____
Certified Instructor

Civil Defense and Disaster Corps
Public Works Division - Bureau of Personnel
City of Los Angeles
Presents

SCOTT T. BARNES

with this

Graduation Certificate

For the satisfactory completion of the
Course of Instruction in

Basic and Light Rescue

Date May 7-11, 1973

Ernest O. Walter
Chief of Division   *Director, Rescue Training*

Civil Defense and Disaster Corps
Public Works Division - Bureau of Personnel
City of Los Angeles
Presents

SCOTT BARNES

with this

Graduation Certificate

For the satisfactory completion of the
Course of Instruction in

Radiological Monitoring

Date July 12-13, 1973

Ernest O. Walter
Chief of Division   *Director, Rescue Training*

City of Long Beach

Certificate of Training

This is to certify that

SCOTT BARNES

has successfully completed

RADIOLOGICAL MONITORING CLASS

Long Beach, California

City Manager   Dept. of Civil Defense   Instructor

25.

Civil Defense and Disaster Corps
Public Works Division - Bureau of Personnel
City of Los Angeles
Presents

SCOTT BARNES

with this

Graduation Certificate

For the satisfactory completion of the
Course of Instruction in

Heavy Rescue Training

Date June 25-29, 1973

Ernest O. Walter
Chief of Division   *Director, Rescue Training*

State of California · Department of Justice

DIVISION OF LAW ENFORCEMENT

Certificate of Training

This is to certify that

SCOTT TRACY BARNES

has successfully completed 8 *hours of instruction in*

OFFICER SURVIVAL

as presented by the Department of Justice
Advanced Training Center

On the 19TH *Day of* JANUARY 1977.

_____
ATTORNEY GENERAL

_____
DIRECTOR, DIVISION OF
LAW ENFORCEMENT

Defense Civil Preparedness Agency

STAFF COLLEGE

BATTLE CREEK, MICHIGAN

Awards this certificate to

SCOTT BARNES

In recognition of the satisfactory completion of

INTRODUCTION TO RADIOLOGICAL
MONITORING

_____
DIRECTOR, STAFF COLLEGE
Defense Civil Preparedness Agency

January 15, 1972
DATE

_____
Defense Civil Preparedness Agency

San Diego County Sheriff's Department

Certificate of Completion of Course

This is to certify that

SCOTT T. BARNES

has satisfactorily completed a 36 *hour training course, under the*
direction of the Training Division, entitled **BATON TRAINING**

Dated this 23rd *day of* JUNE .19 76

_____
SHERIFF, SAN DIEGO COUNTY

California
Security Training School

Be It Known That

SCOTT TRACY BARNES

Has completed in a satisfactory manner the Course of Study in:

Firearms Training

Certificate

Dated this 7th day of October , 19 80 .

_____
Instructor

STATE OF CALIFORNIA
DEPARTMENT OF JUSTICE

EDMUND G. BROWN JR.
GOVERNOR

EVELLE J. YOUNGER
ATTORNEY GENERAL

The
Commission on Peace Officer Standards and Training

Hereby awards the

Basic Certificate

to

SCOTT TRACY BARNES

November 21, 1977

For having fulfilled the requirements for character, education, training, and experience
as prescribed in Title 11 of the California Administrative Code.

W. F. Gustory
CHAIRMAN

William R. Grady
EXECUTIVE DIRECTOR

88381

SUBPOENA TO TESTIFY BEFORE GRAND JURY

United States District Court

DISTRICT
WESTERN DISTRICT OF OKLAHOMA

TO:

Scott Barnes
P. O. Box 704
Kernville, California

SUBPOENA FOR

☒ Person
☐ Document or Object

YOU ARE HEREBY COMMANDED to appear in the United States District Court at the location, date and time specified below to testify before the Grand Jury in the above entitled case.

PLACE

Room 4434, Federal Bldg. & Courthouse
200 Northwest Fourth St.
Oklahoma City, Oklahoma 73102-3094

Telephone (405) 231-5281 FTS 736-5281

COURTROOM

DATE AND TIME
February 2, 5 w/c 1987
at 9:30 a.m.

YOU ARE ALSO COMMANDED to bring with you the following document(s) or object(s):(1)

None.

See attached advice of rights form.

☐ *Please see additional information on reverse*

This subpoena shall remain in effect until you are granted leave to depart by the court or by an officer acting on behalf of the court.

CLERK

ROBERT D. DENNIS, Court Clerk

DATE

1/5/87

(BY) DEPUTY CLERK

Jamie J. Youngberg

This subpoena is issued on application
of the United States of America by:

SK:dsm

NAME, ADDRESS AND PHONE NUMBER OF ASSISTANT U.S. ATTORNEY
STEPHEN KOROTASH, Assistant U. S. Attorney
Room 4434, Federal Bldg. & Courthouse
200 Northwest Fourth Street
Oklahoma City, Oklahoma 73102-3094

Telephone (405) 231-5281 FTS 736-5281

(1) If not applicable, enter "none."

To be used in lieu of AO-110

Replaces USA-178 which is obsolete

FORM UBD-
FEB 15

U.S. Department of Justice

Notice to Fact Witness Appearing on Behalf of United State
Government (or Subpoenaed on Behalf of an Indigent
Defendant)

The information on this form does not apply to Government employees (military or civilian), deportable aliens or to aliens paroled into the United Sta
for prosecution.

CHECK TO SEE IF ATTENDANCE IS REQUIRED: Telephone Number _____. If a telephone number has been inserted in the above
space, you are requested to call the number the workday before you need to leave your residence to attend court to verify that your attendance is required. The call may be made collect. You should identify yourself by stating your name and the case for which you have been subpoenaed. This call i
to prevent a wasted trip by you if the trial has been postponed or if the defendant changes his plea to guilty.

APPEARANCE IN ANOTHER CITY: If you have insufficient funds to travel to court, you should immediately contact the U.S. Marshal's office which
served the subpoena and request an advance of funds. The U.S. Marshal may advance the cost of one-way transportation—a Government Transportatic
Request if the cost of travel by common carrier exceeds $25—and the first day's attendance fee and meals and lodging allowances. You will be require
to sign a form indicating the need for and receipt of the advance. Any amount advanced will be deducted when your fees and allowances are computec
and final payment is made.

ATTENDANCE: The subpoena tells you where to appear. Before reporting to the courtroom, you must report to the Government attorney (or defense
attorney or office of the Clerk of the Court if subpoenaed on behalf of an indigent defendant), U.S. Parole Commission Hearing Examiner or U.S.
Trustee to have your attendance recorded. This should be done EACH DAY on which you are asked to be in attendance.

ALLOWANCES: Under Title 28, United States Code, Section 1821, witnesses are entitled to the following fees and allowances:

    a. FEE. $30.00 for each day's attendance and time spent traveling from place of residence to the place specified in the subpoena and return.

    b. TRANSPORTATION. Reimbursement for necessary transportation by the least expensive method available will be made according to the
       following rules:

        (1) LOCAL TRAVEL. (Within 50 miles of court.) If you reside within the local area of the court and transit buses and/or subway are available,
           you will be reimbursed as if you traveled by bus or subway. Travel by taxi or privately owned vehicle will require justification.
           If public transportation is not available, privately owned vehicle is the preferred method of travel.

        (2) INTERMEDIATE TRAVEL. (50 to 350 miles from court.) If you reside outside of the local area of the court, you will be reimbursed for
           travel to court by the MOST ECONOMICAL common carrier (bus, rail or plane) available in your area or by privately owned vehicle.

           NOTE: Short air trips are more expensive than travel by privately owned vehicles, bus or rail—you MAY be reimbursed as if you traveled b
           bus or rail even if you fly. In certain areas it is often faster and more convenient to travel by rail than to fly or drive.

        (3) LONG DISTANCE TRAVEL. (Over 350 miles from court.) Travel requiring longer than one day will be reimbursed as if you flew unless
           there is limited air service in your area or unless there is a meu, al reason for you not to fly.

COMMON CARRIER. Travel by common carrier (rail, bus, plane) will normally be reimbursed at LESS THAN FIRST CLASS RATES. If first-class
travel is required, it must be authorized in advance; this authorization will be given only in the most unusual circumstances. Reimbursement will also
allowed from necessary taxi and airport limousine fares between your home, the common carrier terminals, and court. A receipt is required for all
intercity common carrier fares and all single items costing over $15.00. Charter services ARE NOT considered common carriers for reimbursement
purposes.

PRIVATELY OWNED VEHICLES. The rates per mile for travel by privately owned vehicles are:

         Motorcycles-$0.20   **Automobiles-$0.20**   **Airplanes-$0.45**

Distances traveled are determined by odometer readings or the Rand McNally Standard Highway Mileage Guide. In addition, NECESSARY tolls, park
fees, tiedown fees, etc. will be paid. A receipt is required to support all single items costing over $15. For parking fees, a receipt is required regardless
the amount. If two or more witnesses travel in the same privately owned vehicle, only one reimbursement for mileage will be made.

Any other transportation expenses WILL NOT be reimbursed without special justification and advance approval.

EXPENSE LISTING. The reverse of this form has been designed to assist you in keeping a record of your transportation expenses. BE SURE TO SAV
YOUR RECEIPTS.

    c. MEALS AND LODGING. If you are REQUIRED to remain away from your residence OVERNIGHT, you will receive a meals allowance of
    $ _28.00_ for each day and a lodging allowance of $ _44.00_ for each night you incur a lodging expense.

PAYMENT. When you are advised that your attendance is no longer required, you should inquire as to the arrangements for payment of fees and
allowances. Before payment can be made, the Witness Attendance Certificate must be completed. The person who caused you to appear will assist you
in entering the required information. The certificate must be signed by the Government attorney, U.S. Parole Commission Hearing Examiner, U.S.
Trustee, the District Judge (if you were subpoenaed on behalf of an indigent defendant), or by the U.S. Magistrate (if you appeared before a Magistrat
The certificate must then be submitted to the U.S. Marshal's office in order to obtain payment.

    The U.S. Marshal's office will normally process the Witness Attendance Certificate and mail payment to you in accordance with the Prompt Paym
Act (Pub. L. 97-177, May 14, 1982).

TRANSPORTATION EXPENSE LISTING

TRAVEL BY PRIVATELY OWNED VEHICLE
Odometer Readings: *(Be sure to list each trip if more than one trip is made.)*

Residence	Court	Mileage

Local mileage at court if overnight stay required	Name of place where you stayed

Tolls

Date	Name of road, bridge, ferry, etc.	Amount

Parking Fees: *(Be sure to obtain receipts.)*

Date	Amount	Date	Amount	Date	Amount

TRAVEL BY COMMON CARRIER *(Be sure to obtain receipts.)*

Name of Carrier	Cost of one round trip ticket $

Local travel expenses: *(taxi, airport, limousine, subway, bus, etc.—receipt required for items over $15)*

Date	Mode of travel	From	To	Cost	Tip (15% maximum allowed)

OTHER EXPENSES: *(Explain in detail, obtain receipts for all single items over $15.00.)*

[handwritten, illegible notations]

U. S. ATTORNEY'S ADVICE TO GRAND JURY WITNESSES

The service of this form with the Grand Jury subpoena is for the purpose of providing you with some background information concerning your appearance before the Grand Jury.

The Grand Jury consists of sixteen to twenty-three persons who inquire into Federal crimes which may have been committed in this Judicial District. Only authorized persons may be present in the Grand Jury room while evidence is being presented. This means that the only persons who may be present while testimony is being given are members of the Grand Jury, attorneys for the Government, the witness under examination, an interpreter when needed, and for the purpose of taking the evidence, a stenographer or operator of a recording device.

As a Grand Jury witness, you will be asked to testify and answer questions concerning possible violations of Federal criminal law. The public through the Grand Jury has a right to every person's evidence, except where the privilege against self-incrimination would apply.

The mere fact that this form is provided to a person subpoenaed to testify before a Grand Jury should not be taken as any implication or suggestion that the person subpoenaed is likely to be charged (indicted) with the crime under investigation.

During your appearance as a witness before the Grand Jury, you will be expected to answer all questions asked of you, except to the extent that a truthful answer to a questions would tend to incriminate you. An untruthful answer to any question may be the basis for prosecuting the untruthful witness for perjury. Anything that you say may be used against you by the Grand Jury or may later be used against you in court. You may consult your attorney before testifying; you may have your attorney outside the Grand Jury room and if you desire, you will be afforded a reasonable opportunity to step outside the Grand Jury room to consult with your attorney before answering any question. If you have any question concerning the general subject matter of your appearance, or other questions, you may contact the United States Attorney's Office at (405) 231-5281.

THE BRITISH BROADCASTING CORPORATION
2030 M STREET, N. W., SUITE 607
WASHINGTON, D. C. 20036

WASHINGTON CORRESPONDENT

TELEPHONE 223-2050
CABLES: NEWSCASTS, WASHINGTON

January 27ᵗʰ 87

To Whom It May Concern.

I have known Scott Barnes for the past three years and during
that time I have found him to be an honourable and talented
individual.
I have checked into his background with numerous sources in
Washington and have come to the firm conclusion that there
are certain officials who, for their own protection, have
attempted to discredit Scott.
I have discussed Scott's case with H.Ross Perot in Dallas,
and we both feel that a disservice has been done to this man.
I think I speak for Ross when I say that we both hope that
Scott will be given the chance to apply for employment and
have that application considered on its obvious merits and
not on what an anonymous source may claim. As a result I
certainly have no hesitation in recommending him for
employment with your company, and to underscore my confidence
in Scott I would just mention that the BBC has on several
occasions enlisted Scott's help with investigations requiring
input from California.
He is a resourceful individual, with an ability to dig into
issues and produce results.
I would be only too happy to discuss my assessment of Scott
with you if you should wish to call the BBC in Washington.

Yours faithfully,

David C. Taylor
BBC Washington Producer

Considering the number of prospective agents—and, to the CIA pro, every one of those students is a potential agent until proven otherwise—the law of averages is on our side.

Cover

Carter: (The) trucks our agents had purchased would be removed from a warehouse on the outskirts of Tehran, driven to a point near the mountain hiding place, and used to carry the rescue team to the city. At a prearranged time, the rescue team would simultaneously enter the foreign-ministry building and the compound, overpower the guards, and free the American hostages . . . . (The) helicopters would land at the sites, picking up our people and carrying them to an abandoned air-strip near the city.

Communication between the Pentagon and the rescue team, using satellites and other rally facilities, would be instantaneous. I would receive telephone reports from David Jones and Harold Brown (from the Pentagon).

William Clark was the Reagan aide who found a mole in Carter's White House   Photo by Wide World

Copeland: There will be a "staging area" somewhere within helicopter range of Tehran at which brush-up training will be given the two teams.

There also will be a point . . . known as the . . . "penultimate position," from which the attack actually will be launched.

The choice of this latter is highly important. It—or they—must be near enough to the target to allow for a thrust lasting less than one minute and, at the same time, it must be part of the "peoples-cape" in the immediate area.

This (staging area) may or may not be the same as the "field headquarters" where some communication assistant will monitor the operation keep Washington informed . . . .

Safe Haven and Evacuation

Carter: From there (the abandoned air strip near Tehran), two C-141s would fly all the Americans to safety across the desert area of Saudi Arabia.

We also planned the procedure (after the mission was completed) for notifying Oman, Saudi Arabia, and Egypt, whose territories would be used or crossed during the mission.

Copeland: There are several well-stocked areas near Tehran to which our helicopters may flee in a very short time with minimum danger of being followed . . . .

This (use of foreign airspace or landing areas), or course, is a matter for our State Department. For present purposes, it need only be said that our government has more friends in the Middle East than is commonly suspected.

Anesthetization

Newsweek: There was speculation that the Americans intended to use nonlethal gas to neutralize the embassy guards.

Copeland: This step, which security considerations prevent me from describing in any detail, consists of measures to incapacitate all resistance.

(It) includes such measures as . . . the use of stunning or nauseating but otherwise harmless gases . . .

Secrecy of Mission

Carter: "On April 18, I had quite a discussion with my closest advisers about how to deal with the congressional leadership on the Iran decision. Fritz (Mondale) led the argument for minimum advance notice and maximum secrecy. Cy (Vance) took the opposite tack, maintaining that we should advise the Democratic and Republican leaders in the House and Senate. I agreed with Fritz . . . ."

Copeland: Unfortunately, this whole plan, whether executed separately or as part of an overall military assault, has a weakness . . . It is that our government can take no action which does not have the full support of the people and of Congress.

There is a sad quote in Jimmy Carter's journal for April 21st.

"We listened carefully to all news reports, but heard only one other indication of a leak. In monitoring radio broadcasts all over Iran, we heard a story from up near the Iraqi border of an attempted rescue mission. It turned out to be a repeat of a conjectural story which had run earlier in the Washington *Star*—no damage was done."

But the damage was done. Copeland dwells on CIA assets in Iraq, in his article. The Iranians have made clear that they had advance warning. That only the mechanical problems in the desert that aborted the full raid, prevented the police and military from slaughtering the American hostages, agents, diplomats, all. By Sunday, April 20th, according to Carter, Radio Iran was broadcasting Copeland's story: the "surprise" was spoiled—Iranian double agents had remained loyal to the Ayatollah as had Western-trained military men. Repeat: according to the highest Iranian sources the rescue of the hostages had been blown. Were the Iranians bluffing when they insisted that the raid never could have succeeded, was doomed in advance?

There is a final, strange piece in the puzzle. During the hostage crisis, in 1980, U.S. army intelligence set up a special unit in Iran. "Intelligence Support Activity" (ISA) was so secret that it operated virtually under an illegal status. It has since been disbanded. However, in 1980 CIA Director Stansfield Turner did *not* know of the existence of ISA, but Reagan campaign director William Casey *did*. According to a former Carter associate, the ISA "smells" like a back-channel of Casey's.

The coincidence between Copeland's version and official plans revealed by Carter, Jordan, Powell and others, is too great to let pass. Copeland and the official sources agree: disguise will be used; false communications will be employed to confuse the authorities; agents pretending to be media people would infiltrate the compound during the excitement. Further, Copeland chatters along about cover stories when, in fact, it is Copeland's *Star* piece that is ripping to shreds what Hamilton Jordan describes as "a disinformation campaign that will relax the Iranians."

There was more than mechanical problems at "Desert One," where the mission began. The commander of the operation,

NATIONAL AFFAIRS

itary expertise for the Company (page 46).

Also difficult to obtain were the wide range of secret support services and "proprietary" companies that the Company once could call on in an instant: two full-fledged commercial airlines, several banks in the United States and abroad, at least one major international arms company and a variety of cover operations in such useful fields as import-export. This shortfall explains the embarrassing details about U.S. equipment that turned up in so many early stories about the contra forces in Nicaragua. Well-placed sources told NEWSWEEK that the CIA simply could not obtain and ship to Central America the kind of untraceable matériel—Belgian, Czech, West German or captured Soviet stocks—that normally provide cover in such situations. According to these sources, the United States has now arranged for Israel to feed the CIA-supported guerrillas with equipment captured in Lebanon. Foreign intelligence services have a generally positive view of Casey's rebuilding efforts, but they are still wary of the weakened and jury-rigged state of CIA intelligence networks where they still exist.

Independent: In part to compensate for the Company's reduced resources in covert operations, the Reagan administration also has encouraged the development of a top-secret and totally independent Army Intelligence Support Activity (AISA), about which even many intelligence watchdogs in Congress were unaware until an accidental mention of it during hearings earlier this year. AISA was reportedly formed for commando-style missions and support in the wake of the disastrous joint military attempt to rescue the U.S. hostages in Iran—an effort made more difficult because the CIA did not have a single agent left on the ground in that country. Although Casey himself has refused to answer questions on

the subject, some administration officials say the CIA director has assigned the group a number of covert missions.

If the rebuilding of the CIA's own cloak-and-dagger capabilities is a long-term process, however, Casey has pressed quickly to improve the Company's ability to analyze and interpret the overwhelming flood of intelligence that pours into it from spy satellites, radio intercepts and an impressive array of other electronic and human intelligence collectors (ELINT and HUMINT in CIA parlance). "Casey has good instincts on the process of producing National Intelligence Estimates," says one administration "consumer" of these vital agency reports. "He has tried to make them shorter, blunter and more timely."

Up to Date: CIA analysts now pound out 50 NIE's a year instead of the dozen that were done before. And there is less bickering among the various agencies of the intelligence community, insiders say, because Casey has found ways to give more prominence to dissenting views. Aware of competing sources of intelligence, including the news media, Casey has also created a Weekly Watch Report and an even more up-to-the-minute "typescript memorandum" that reports unexpected developments immediately to the president and other top officials.

In general, the agency's predictions have been early and accurate on important matters: the elevation of Soviet leader Yuri Andropov and his subsequent health problems, the Libyan invasion of Chad, the resignation of Israeli Prime Minister Menachem Begin and the imposition of martial law in Poland. But one Washington official complains that the CIA predicted far greater resistance by the Polish people than actually occurred, and there was even more embarrassment when Israeli forces pressed far deeper into Lebanon than they had promised. "The analysts did write that they [the Israelis] would go further than anyone

expected," one intelligence expert recalls, but they were fairly low key.

Similarly, says one administration intelligence official, the CIA produced a fair amount of warning about the building threat to Egyptian leader Anwar Sadat, "but it never penetrated—it wasn't done forcefully enough to overcome the bosses' love affair with Sadat." Some critics fear that U.S. ties to regimes in Saudi Arabia, Jordan and the Philippines could also blind the CIA or its masters to major upheavals in those countries in the near future.

To further upgrade its analysis and reporting, the CIA has stepped up recruiting for specialists in high technology and area studies, especially the Third World—and the nation's college campuses are responding with more enthusiasm, or at least tolerance, than they have for decades. "I still don't agree with what they do, but for those people who are inclined to work for them, they should be allowed to interview," says University of Wisconsin senior Jay Todd Pinkert. Today's tight job market helps the CIA, but it often must compete for bright students with well-paying international banking firms, multinational corporations and high-tech industries.

Status Assignment: Robert Gates, 39, the agency's fast-rising deputy director for intelligence, is trying to make up with status what he cannot provide in pay envelopes. Increasingly he has let the experts who write the analyses brief the administration's top policymakers personally. "I know analysts who can walk out of here and double their salaries," says Gates. "But when one of our people goes alone to brief the secretary of state or an assistant secretary, that can last a long time."

The demand for people with technical backgrounds is prompted both by the agency's own increasingly sophisticated collection capabilities and by Casey's decision to make the prevention of high-tech espionage a top priority. The CIA has developed a

WIN SOME, LOSE SOME: A SCRAPBOOK

The new CIA, set up after World War II, drew on the men and experience of William Donovan's Office of Strategic Services.

Warnings against intervention did not stop the CIA from engineering the ouster of Guatemalan President Jacobo Arbenz in 1954. Covert action also helped depose Iran's Mohammad Mossadegh (below) in 1953.

The agency was flying high with spying missions over the Soviet Union by U-2 jets (below) until one of them—flown by Francis Gary Powers—was shot down in 1960. It was embarrassed again by the abortive 1961 Bay of Pigs assault on Fidel Castro and several futile murder plots against him.

NATIONAL AFFAIRS

massive data base on the methods by which Iron Curtain operatives obtain critical plans and equipment from U.S. firms and has used this information to raise consciousness on the issue among domestic research-and-development firms and allied intelligence services. "They responded, naturally, to their own security interests," says Casey, chortling over the expulsion from Europe and Japan of more than 100 enemy intelligence agents, most of whom were caught stealing high technology. "The biggest setback the KGB ever had," the CIA boss claims. Intelligence officials say that their increasing involvement with high-tech America—the better to entrap Soviet spies and safeguard U.S. scientific secrets—will not result in improper domestic surveillance or infiltration of American business. But some outside critics of the agency fear that excesses in this area are inevitable.

Conflicts: Casey also has volunteered the CIA and other U.S. intelligence agencies for more active duty than ever in the nation's war on narcotics, and this too may lead to conflicts. The Drug Enforcement Administration, for example, refuses to provide cover for CIA agents. Beyond that, the people best able to get sensitive military and political information out of closed countries like Iran or Afganistan are sometimes those adept at taking narcotics out as well. On several occasions in recent years, the Justice Department and Drug Enforcement Administration have pursued major drug-traffic suspects—only to learn, late in the game, that as valuable paid assets of the CIA they were virtually untouchable.

Still, Casey has concluded that the nation's drug problem is fully as serious as its national-security concerns. He even suspects that international communism vies with Mafia capitalism in mobilizing much of the world's drug trade. "We think we've identified that," says the DCI. "We can't

prove it in court." The danger in focusing the intelligence agencies on these activities is that they may be carried willy-nilly into the province of domestic operations and law enforcement.

The same danger shadows the CIA's stepped-up counterintelligence campaign. Under Casey, the agency is free of the non-productive, self-destructive mole hunting of years past—when entire careers were made or broken in the choice between which of several Soviet defectors to believe about the existence or nonexistence of a high-level Soviet agent within the CIA. Any such sleeper agent high in the Company 20 years ago would presumably be long gone today. Instead, insiders say, the CIA is now plagued by a security consciousness that some think is counterproductive and potentially unconstitutional.

Flak: NIE reports are so highly classified that almost no officials can retain them in office safes for leisurely reading; they must be perused immediately and returned to a waiting messenger. The result: quick skimming of the basic document and increasing reliance on shorter, less sophisticated digests. And after months of agonizing work—and considerable flak from Congress—Casey's CIA finally got an executive order to tighten security. It makes the use of lie detectors more widespread among intelligence employees and requires government clearance for almost any publication by employees who work with national-security information, even years after they leave their posts.

On Capitol Hill, Casey got a far more limited statute than he had wanted to bar disclosure of CIA agents' names, and nothing approaching his notion of exempting the CIA from requirements of the Freedom of Information Act. Casey also ran into opposition on his requests for more vigorous investigation of leaks by the FBI and Justice Department. "Some CIA people think that if you say something nasty about the direc-

tor, that's a leak and it has to be investigated and people have to be punished," says one lawyer who has handled many national-security cases. In the end, the number of leak investigations conducted by Justice and the FBI under Reagan has not risen markedly from the number pursued at any time during the Carter years: 15 to 20 open cases, 10 of them active.

In addition, FBI Director William Webster has fended off Casey's appeal for a special squad of FBI agents to be assigned to the CIA for in-house investigations—a questionable domestic arm for an agency otherwise barred from such activity. Still, FBI officials insist that relations between Langley and their Hoover Building headquarters have rarely been smoother. Webster, indeed, went out of his way to deny a published report that he had called Casey a "buffoon."

Relations between Casey and Congress, by contrast, are hostile enough to warrant the War Powers Act. Many Democrats were furious from the first at Reagan's nomination of a political aide to the sensitive post of DCI and at Casey's early (and short-lived) appointment of businessman Max Hugel—another campaign crony with no major intelligence background—as director of clandestine operations. The CIA chief did little to win them over with his consistent mangling of facts during congressional appearances. "You are treating this committee like it is something you would like to see go away," he was told at one point by a GOP member of the House intelligence panel, Rep. Bill Young of Florida. Most inflammatory was Casey's original description of the contra campaign as an effort to interdict arms shipments from Nicaragua to El Salvador. "He's just loose with the facts," says one disgruntled Democrat. "Truth isn't part of his vocabulary."

The CIA's more recent rationale for covert action in Nicaragua—to force an end to alleged Sandinista subversion throughout

During the war in Vietnam, CIA analysts provided a fairly accurate—if not always appreciated—assessment of enemy strength. The agency's counterinsurgency experts, meanwhile, organized the bloody Phoenix program—notorious for its murders of suspected members of the Viet Cong—and ran a secret war in neighboring Laos.

Bay of Pigs veteran Howard Hunt (below) helped to drag the agency into the Watergate scandal. Another former CIA officer, James McCord, exposed the cover-up of the White House burglary.

In 1975, a Senate panel investigated a futile CIA plot to block Salvador Allende (above) from becoming Chile's president. No CIA tie to Allende's overthrow has ever been confirmed.

Despite a long history in Iran, the CIA was largely blind-sided by Khomeini's rebellion, the takeover of the U.S. Embassy and the seizing of the hostages.

CIA Gets Billing Again in Nicaragua, as Covert Action Becomes the Norm

By James Bamford

BOSTON

Its indigo-black titanium skin begins to glow crimson as the SR-71 "Blackbird" slips through the thin air quicker than a 30.06 bullet escaping its barrel. Twenty minutes after it takes off from Beal Air Force Base near Sacramento, a faint sonic boom can be heard in San Diego as the spy plane, out over the Pacific, speeds south and then east to a secret war in Central America.

That distant boom is a subtle reminder of America's long and opaque war against the Sandinista government of Nicaragua. In a few weeks it will be five years since President Reagan signed National Security Decision Directive 17, the secret declaration of covert war against the small Latin nation. Also in a few weeks, $100 million in U.S. aid will begin joining the more than $100 million already sent to the *contra* guerrillas. Perhaps even more important, the Central Intelligence Agen-

James Bamford, author of "The Puzzle Palace," an examination of the National Security Agency, writes frequently about intelligence issues.

cy, benched by Congress for the past two years, will once again become a major player in the conflict.

Covert action and paramilitary operations, used occasionally by every President since Harry S. Truman, have become as institutionalized as formal state dinners under Reagan. Harbors are salted with deadly mines, assassination manuals are distributed and powerful surface-to-air missiles are supplied to rebels to shoot down Soviet aircraft. Reagan's raiders have waged battles in Afghanistan, Angola, Cambodia, Chad, Iran, Libya and Nicaragua thus far. Reports put the budget for these secret wars at over half a billion dollars a year. Sen. Patrick J. Leahy (D-Vt.), vice chairman of the Senate Intelligence Committee, has even speculated that the *contras* alone may receive as much as $500 million this year, with cash supplemented from the CIA director's secret contingency fund.

The CIA, however, is not the only employer of secret warriors. With such operations high in presidential prestige and low in bureaucratic restrictions, the Pentagon is also gearing up for more special warfare missions. This has led some, both in and out of government, to suggest that the burgeoning special operations capabilities of both the CIA and the Pentagon be combined into a new, separate agency dedicated solely to covert actions and paramilitary operations. However, this could cause more complications than it solves, because any bureaucracy tends to be self-perpetuating. Even Stansfield Turner, who, as CIA director, greatly enhanced the agency's technical side at the expense of its covert

side, nonetheless came to the conclusion that covert operations should be handled by the CIA.

Soon after the Reagan Administration came to power and the military budget was given a hefty boost, a highly secret unit named Intelligence Support Activity (ISA) was formed. It was an outgrowth of the Foreign Operating Group, which had supplied undercover agents in Tehran before the ill-fated rescue mission.

Little is known of the ISA except that in the past it has provided the Pentagon with a virtually unknown and unaccountable covert-action capability. It has apparently been used for conducting unspecified operations in El Salvador, collecting intelligence in support of the *contras* and supplying military equipment to foreign armies. The ISA has also been reported to have distributed, in a country that has had no diplomatic ties with the United States, arms and bulletproof vests to persons for information on military deployments. Finally, the ISA apparently also played a role in Lt. Col. James G. (Bo) Grits' search for missing POWs in Southeast Asia and the rescue of kidnaped Maj. Gen. James L. Dozier.

In addition to the ISA, the Army has beefed up its Green Berets and reactivated its 1st Special Forces Group based at Ft. Lewis, Wash. Long-remembered for their role in the Vietnam War, the Army Special Forces have worked closely with the CIA on paramilitary operations since the 1950s. In 1965, a Green Beret unit was reportedly involved in a plan to assassinate the Dominican Republic's Col. Francisco Caamano Deno, a guerrilla leader seeking to overthrow his government— but the plan was canceled at the last minute. In 1980, a group dressed as businessmen entered Tehran to collect intelligence in preparation for the rescue mission.

Two other highly secret battalions of the Army Special Forces, Delta Force and Blue Light, have been used in hostage rescue operations such as the Iranian mission and, more recently, the Achille Lauro hijacking. Still another is Task Force 160, which provides air support for Special Forces operations. According to John Prados, in his new book on covert operations, "The President's Secret War," members of Task Force 160, nicknamed "Night Stalkers," wear civilian clothes while on their missions and fly an assortment of air-commando-type helicopters. Because much of their flying is done at night in support of highly classified missions, the unit has suffered an unusually high accident rate. Almost half of all aviation fatalities admitted by the army in 1983 came from Task Force 160.

The Air Force also has a separate air

Reports 'Some ID' on Captives

Gritz Says He's on New POW Mission in Laos

By BOB SECTER, *Times Staff Writer*

BANGKOK, Thailand—Retired Green Beret Lt. Col. James G. (Bo) Gritz has told The Times that he is deep in the Laotian jungle on a new mission to rescue American prisoners of war. He said that he has come up with "some POW ID" but that he cannot confirm its authenticity.

In a handwritten message from across the Mekong River, Gritz said that another of his Laotian guerrillas has been killed—the second in as many missions. But he insisted that he will press his search for U.S. prisoners from the Vietnam War until he can tell the nation whether any Americans are being held in Laos.

"If Americans are here," he wrote, "by God, let's find out."

Whereabouts Disclosed

Gritz, 44, a Vietnam veteran from Westchester, Calif., disclosed his whereabouts in a 12-page letter dated Feb. 12 that was brought from Laos by runner. It arrived last week and was hand-delivered to The Times on Saturday by a Gritz associate. The letter was signed by Gritz and the two other Americans who are with him in Laos.

One is David Scott Weekly, 35, of Encinitas, Calif., a Vietnam War-era Navy airman with an expertise in weaponry that earned him the nickname Dr. Death. The other is Gary Goldman, 38, of Encino, Calif., described by friends as a soldier of fortune trained in anti-terrorism techniques.

State Department officials in Washington oppose Gritz's rescue missions. They say such missions could place any living American prisoners in jeopardy at the hands of their captors, might get in the way of any official rescue efforts that are using far better resources, and could harm improving U.S.-Laotian relations, which are the key to obtaining information about missing Americans.

"I have some POW ID," Gritz said in his letter. "But until I can personally confirm it, it will not be reported."

He said he had sent anti-communist Lao agents to possible prison sites with letters for any POWs to sign and to fill out, if possible, with other dossier info to ID them." Gritz said one agent carried a camera.

But Gritz said nothing more about the matter. He did not make it clear whether the "POW ID" he claimed to possess was such a letter-dossier, a photograph or something else. And he did not indicate whether it was from a living prisoner or a military man long dead.

"This report is being hastily written, from a jungle location deep in central Laos and will hopefully be delivered by messenger to you ASAP," Gritz wrote, disclosing for the first time where he has been since he returned to Southeast Asia in January. He said he was at a "northern location," apparently well above the Thai border town of Nakhon Phanom, on the banks of the Mekong River.

In his message, Gritz also:

— Hinted that he might go into Vietnam. Describing the validity of his travel papers, he added cryptically. "The only thing that has happened is that we don't have a visa for VN (Vietnam). But then, we don't have any diplomatic relations with them, either.

"Unfortunately, travel through Laos is a necessity, which I'm sure the U.S. presence in Vientiane (the Laotian capital) is—was—aware of. If not, it wasn't because we didn't inform embassy sources."

— Declared flatly for the first time that the Central Intelligence Agency and the Defense Intelligence Agency are aware of his plans.

'Knew of Our ID'

Gritz wrote, "I have 12 CIA-DIA generated targets which, through agent reports and other verification could hold U.S. POWs. . . . CIA-DIA knew of our ID, acquisition and test of state-of-the-art secure Alpha numeric-graphic code burst devices, night vision goggles, night vision cameras, etc. Some special equipment was furnished, As Rusty Capps, FBI-LA."

(At the FBI's Los Angeles field office, spokesman John Hoos said it was impossible to talk to Capps. "You won't get to him," Hoos told a reporter. "We won't even make comment on that."

(Rear Adm. Allan G. Paulson, in charge of intelligence collection for the DIA, said in Washington, "The government has no association whatever with Gritz." When asked if that included government people acting individually, Paulson replied, "DI certainly does, as far as I'm concerned."

(At the CIA, spokesman Levon Strong said, "We will have no comment on that wild allegation.")

— Denied breaking any laws. "We have (I have) never intended to conspired or acted outside the law of the United States," Gritz said.

"I did not organize (Operation Lazarus as a vigilante effort. . . . have always been dedicated to keeping the laws of our country. I do not espouse or encourage vigilantism."

In Washington, the Justice Department is reviewing information about Gritz's missions to determine whether they violate a federal law that bans any private military "expedition or enterprise" against such countries as Laos, with which the United States is at peace.

As for Thai laws, Gritz said twice in his letter that he brought no weapons into Thailand to use on his missions into Laos. "We have all the munitions needed in-country," Gritz said. The Thais have denounced Gritz's rescue efforts and have said that they will try to arrest him.

'We Are the Gladiators'

— Challenged his critics. "We are the gladiators," he said, "not the armchair critics, bureaucrats, politicians and pot-bellied has beens. . . . There may be better than us—but where are they?

The American people need to know if there are Americans alive in captivity, and if so, where they are and who they are. . . . I am not a fanatic. I may not bring home Americans, but I intend to bring home an answer."

Let them either lead, follow or get the hell out of the way.

Gritz expressed particular anger at team member Charles J. Patterson, who sold a story about Gritz's activities to Soldier of Fortune, a magazine about military adventure, for $5,000. The sale resulted in news stories disclosing Gritz's first trip into Laos last November and December.

In his letter to The Times, Gritz called Patterson "a total failure, a thief . . . a self-proclaimed coward." Gritz described the sale of Patterson's story as "criminal." He said Robert K. Brown, publisher of Soldier of Fortune, is "a phony with total disregard for POWs (and) U.S. lives."

It was disclosures by Patterson and Brown that stirred military activity against the Gritz mission in Laos, Gritz wrote. "The combined effort of Brown, his associates and Patterson have served to irrevocably damage our mission just at the precise time when we were ready to make our final efforts.

"To say that their efforts have put us in great jeopardy is to put it mildly. We were approaching the very target they disclosed."

A summary of Patterson's account, given to news reporters by Soldier of Fortune, identified the target as the Laotian village of Tchepone, also known as Sepone, about 100 miles east of the Mekong.

"Things got very animated (sic) when the 31 Jan. (publicity) bomb fell on us," Gritz wrote. "We didn't know why, at the time, but the enemy was working overtime. We had quickly and successfully infiltrated on 30 Jan. We were surrounded and engaged heavily at times. At least one of our agents keeping a target under surveillance was captured and killed eight kilometers from the objective—due, I believe, to the (unknown to us) news splash by Brown-Patterson."

The casualty is the second death of an anti-communist Laotian guerrilla during maneuvers by Gritz. The first was during his November-December mission. On that mission, which Gritz considered the initial phase of Operation Lazarus, one Laotian was killed and three were wounded. There have been no casualties among Americans.

Brown, the Soldier of Fortune

'We are the gladiators —not the arm-chair critics, bureaucrats, politicians and pot-bellied has-beens. . . . There may be better than us—but where are they? . . . Let them either lead, follow or get the hell out of the way.'

—Lt. Col. James G. (Bo) Gritz

publisher, was in Central America and unavailable for comment. But Jim Monaghan, a contributing editor, said it was Gritz who was jeopardizing POW rescue efforts. He said Brown had spent $600,000 during the last several years on his own efforts to come up with information about POWs.

Referring to Gritz's claims that Soldier of Fortune endangered lives, Monaghan declared, "I can't believe anything he says." Monaghan said Brown had refrained from making the Patterson story public until he heard that the Bangkok Post was about to publish an account of its own.

In his message, Gritz wrote that Patterson, 37, a former Army Special Forces sergeant from the Tulare County, Calif., town of Dinuba, "totally collapsed physically, mentally, emotionally" after the fire fight last fall. Patterson "was the only one to fling his boots, uniform and equipment aside before plunging into the Mekong—in his underwear," Gritz said. He said that Patterson had told him, "I have never been so afraid in my whole life."

'Kind as I Could Be'

Gritz said, "Back at NKP (Nakhon Phanom), I was as kind as I could be to Pat (Patterson). . . . Pat came down with nine reasons why he was incapable of return-

ing—I concurred on each count. Gary (Goldman) and I (re)crossed (the Mekong). I assumed (Patterson) would help at NKP. Instead, he took off with (fellow team member Dominic Zappone's) credit cards, went to Kuala Lumpur, returned to Bangkok for a few days, bought a new suit and a sapphire stone for an $18 sterling silver ring, in each case forging Zap's signature.

"An undisclosed amount of personal money was taken and then remnants left beneath the seat of an agent handler's vehicle. (He also rifled my personal briefcase and took documents that were associated with the operation. Many were outdated and merely part of the record-keeping. (Patterson) split for the States."

Patterson, reached at his home in California, acknowledged telling Gritz that he had been afraid. He said Gritz was correct in describing him as physically hurt. Patterson said he fell in the jungle, injuring his foot, and was "burning up with fever." But he denied any mental or emotional collapse. He said he swam the Mekong in a pair of shorts—and not in his underwear.

When asked about any stolen credit cards and the purchase of a suit and a stone for a silver ring, Patterson said, "There's an incident that happened, yes. But that isn't what happened. . . . I've got knowledge of it, but I'm not saying what happened." He said no personal money was taken—"not that I know of." As for Gritz's documents, Patterson said they were given to officials at the U.S. Embassy in Bangkok by another member of the Gritz team.

Patterson acknowledged that sale of his story might have jeopardized Gritz's efforts—"now that it's broke, yes." When he sold the story, Patterson said, he was not aware that Gritz was going to re-enter Laos. He said Gritz was "like a brother to me. I've got nothing bad to say about him."

In his message from Laos, Gritz told how his involvement in POW rescue missions began. He said the federal government provided the impetus.

"I did not get into this business four years ago of my own accord," Gritz said. "I was asked to look into the POW situation by executive branch officials acting through private sector."

In past interviews with The Times, Gritz has said that Harold Aaron, an Army lieutenant general who is now dead, first aroused his curiosity about POWs. He quoted Aaron as telling him, "We now have overwhelming evidence that Americans are being held against their will."

Gritz retired from the Army. By early 1979, he was traveling in Asia for Hughes Aircraft Co. Gritz contended that his job with Hughes was arranged. Hughes has said Gritz was hired through standard procedures. In his letter from Laos, Gritz said he was "using Hughes until a target was given me in January, 1981, which led to Velvet Hammer."

That was what Gritz called his first mission. He assembled a team of 23 persons, mostly former Green Berets, at the American Cheerleading Academy at Fruitland, Fla. The team included seer Karen Page, who had impressed Gritz with visions and target details known only to him, and Gil Boyne, owner of a hypnotism training center.

Gritz, one of Boyne's students, has said in an interview that he had asked Boyne to teach the team self-hypnosis "to gain a full-night's sleep in 15 minutes, be more alert, be able to suppress pain in the event of an injury and be able to move

further, eat less, whatever is required."

Some members of the Velvet Hammer team, including J. D. Bath, a former Green Beret from Lakeland, Fla., questioned "the sanity" of using seers and hypnotists—and raised other questions when Gritz included on the team a television news crew, a photographer and Washington Post reporter Art Harris.

Team members raised even more questions about operational security when Gritz provided a Florida newspaper reporter with details that were published in the Orlando Sentinel and its parent newspaper, the Chicago Tribune.

Gritz said he finally got word that the government, under newly elected President Ronald Reagan, was planning its own rescue mission. In interviews later, Gritz said he had learned that the government mission would involve The Delta Force of the Joint Special Operations Command at Ft. Bragg—the unit that tried in vain in 1980 to rescue Americans held hostage in Iran.

"So I was instructed at that point in time to stand down, to go home," Gritz said.

As he disbanded Velvet Hammer, the government sponsored at least two forays into Laos in search of POWs. The expeditions, using Southeast Asians, found no evidence of any Americans being held captive. News accounts published at the time said one patrol was fired upon.

"Then," Gritz said in his letter to The Times, "another secret intelligence activity approached me saying they wanted to pick up the action.

"So started Grand Eagle."

This second attempt by Gritz was a reconnaissance effort.

Gritz sent four men to Thailand. Bath, a retired Special Forces sergeant, Ben Dunakowski of Lancaster, Calif., also retired from the Special Forces, William Macris of Salisbury, Mass., a veteran of World War II and the Vietnam War, and Scott Barnes of Redondo Beach, Calif., a former policeman who said he was an informant against the Hell's Angels.

They went to Nakhon Phanom and other towns and villages on the

Times staff writers Mark Gladstone, Paul Dean and Richard E. Meyer and researchers Nina Green and Doug Conner contributed to this article.

Thai side of the Mekong River and questioned Lao supporters of Gen. Vang Pao, the commander of Laotian Hmong hill tribes that fought for the CIA in Laos during the Vietnam War. It was Gritz's hope that the Hmong might help him find POWs. The Gritz team said it could communicate back to the United States through a telex line at the Energy Department.

They used the code name BOHICA. Gritz said it stood for "Bend Over, Here It Comes Again."

The Energy Department denied any involvement in Grand Eagle. But Dunakowski said one or two messages were sent back to the United States using one of the department's telex numbers.

When the team returned to the United States, Barnes claimed that he had crossed the Mekong into Laos with a mysterious American who was not a team member. Barnes said they had photographed two Caucasians in a Lao prison camp. He claimed the team subsequently received a message ordering that the Caucasians be assassinated.

Gritz and all other members of his team denied Barnes' story. A check of hotel registers and telephone and telex records showed no gaps in Barnes' stay in Thailand. Vang Pao supporters in the village of Ban Don Phuong, who Barnes claimed had accompanied him into Laos, said that Barnes had not crossed the Mekong.

But his story was printed in the Covert Action Information Bulletin, a Washington-based newsletter that specializes in publicizing information about U.S. intelligence agencies. It was reprinted in some foreign newspapers. U.S. officials said it also became part of propaganda broadcast on Radio Hanoi.

At the same time, Gritz said, Grand Eagle also became snarled in a bureaucratic tangle in Washington, mainly among U.S. intelligence agencies.

"I was fired from Grand Eagle," he said in his message from Laos. "The project was put on the shelf."

"But I just couldn't quit, having worked the problem so long and having access to information that identified probable targets. I put together Operation Lazarus as a totally private sector operation to finish what the bureaucracy was too caught up in a political thicket to do.

"We are after one thing—the truth—that's all. While true, some of my personnel haven't been world-class commandos. They were there. Where are our critics?

"The American people need to know if there are Americans alive in

FLAKE

SCOTT BARNES:
MY FAVORITE FLAKE

by Alan Dawson

SCOTT Barnes says he came to Thailand to take part in a secret operation to assassinate American spooks in Laos. I suppose I'll always remember Scott Barnes most of all for his swim across the Thai-Cambodia border. The fact that there is no place to swim across the border is why I'll remember him.

He may be remembered in history, however, for a more sinister reason. In the past few months, a couple of the more unscrupulous sources of information around claim that Barnes was the main actor in what can only be called a thrilling story. Only trouble is the story doesn't stand up, exciting though it may be.

If the weirdos among us have their way, Scott Barnes will gain a reputation as the leader of a super-secret mission to Laos. These weirdos are, for now, two publications whose background, funding and past performance should — but do not always — disqualify them as legitimate sources of information. They are the *Covert Action Information Bulletin* and the New York *Daily World*.

CAIB is published by the people who gave you Philip Agee, the CIA traitor. It spends much of its time printing names, addresses and other confidential information on American CIA employees, especially those overseas. It says it is against secret intelligence operations. It is, in fact, only against American secrecy. So far as can be learned, it has never yet printed so much as a mild rebuke of a KGB operative, let alone any names.

The *Daily World* is the American Communist Party's newspaper, founded in 1968.

According to these two paragons of journalistic reporting, Scott Barnes is the hero of a story which involves the U.S. government's allegedly planting "yellow rain" samples in Laos. They also say that the second of two American-run infiltration missions in Laos in 1981 to search for prisoners of war sent to search for — and if necessary assassinate — the first.

TASS, the Vietnam News Agency and communist publications interested in denying Soviet involvement in the use of chemical-biological warfare in Indochina and Afghanistan have helped CAIB and the *Daily World* spread the story of the highly questionable Scott Barnes.

Barnes arrived in Bangkok in mid-1981 and telephoned me. He said he

If the weirdos among us have the way, Scott Barnes will gain a reputation as the leader of a supe secret mission to Laos.

was a friend of Bo Gritz, and asked if I would meet him. Gritz, I knew, had a name well-known in two circles: He was a Special Forces and special operations warfare officer, and he was a fanatical searcher for the American POWs he believes are still held by Vietnam, most probably in Laos.

Barnes asked me to meet him at the Nana Hotel, a favorite hangout of Southeast Asian adventurers for years, because he didn't have any money to come see me.

He was a friendly guy, apparently ex-military. He had the build of a Charles Atlas advertisement, the man kicking the sand, not the one getting it in the face. And he had the carriage of a man who has seen action. His beard suited him and added believability to his story that he was an ex-SEAL, the "animals" of the U.S. Navy, where beards are permitted. Later, he told two other people that he had been in SF in Vietnam, and for all I know he told others he was a Marine and an Air Force PJ man.

He pulled out — I swear it — an old Thailand-Laos-Cambodia road map, like the Esso stations used to sell.

He was going to Laos to hunt POWs, he told me in short. He asked my help in some administrative routine. And he had a fantastic story, which went on at some length.

His baggage had been stolen, which was highly plausible, but the story was odd. His scheduled hotel car did not pick him at Don Muang Airport, he said, but another car did, and the driver called him by name. As he pulled up to the hotel, two Thai soldiers ran out of its coffeeshop door, past his car, firing their MI6s in the air. At this diversion, as Barnes dove for cover, the car and driver fled with his baggage. He said $15,000 was in it.

This was obviously, Barnes sa U.S. government plot because had somehow found out about his sion and wanted to stop him.

Two major problems made me der about Scott right away. First, soldiers rarely are armed with They carry HK-33s, which look different. And second, Barnes co really explain why the $15,000 w his suitcase, while he held on t passport, customs slip, return ticket and other important paper

In fact, *Soldier of Fortune* sta Tom Reisinger and Fred Zabitosk known to Barnes, were sitting i Nana Hotel lobby when he came came in, they reported, like eve else — by getting out of the taxi, ing up his bags and walking i door. There was no shooting, no sion and no theft — but he did luggage.

It turned out Barnes had two n and telephone numbers to conta Bangkok. One was mine, at *Bangkok Post*. The other was a nant Thai desk clerk at the Nana was helpful with the routine prot of foreign guests but who, it se would not be too much help in o izing a trek of a few hundred mile Laos to search for POWs.

Barnes briefed me on his missi He said that certain intellig sources — whom he could ne course, name (fair enough) — pinpointed the location of Ame POWs in Laos. He wanted to sho where they were, however, so t might better offer advice on h reach the spot undetected f Barnes-led snatch-and-grab of o more of the Americans.

He pulled out — I swear it — a Thailand-Laos-Cambodia road like the Esso stations used to se didn't remember the pronunci spelling nor location of the place the Americans were being held, I went over the map with hi suddenly exclaimed when I got tc Neua. "That's it, Sam Neua. Ho

?"

...ined that Sam Neua was a ..., and rather a large one; that it ...ut as far from Thailand (or as ... Vietnam, if you will) as you ... and still be in Laos, and that ...'t in my wildest dreams im- ...man walking there and back. ...listing the most obvious rea- ... certain failure, I said that it ...ong distance; the mountains ...credible; the climate was

gruesome; the Vietnamese and Pathet Lao armies might take exception to his presence; all Safeway supermarkets along the way had all been closed for lack of business, and food and water could prove difficult to come by.

Well, Barnes didn't think any of those problems were insurmountable. He wanted two things from me, one at a time. He had to get to the Thai-Cambodia border to meet a Laotian who would give him the actual location of the POWs. (I still don't know what a Laotian was doing at the Cambodian border.) Could I help get him to the border, he asked.

And he wanted me to put him in touch with a CIA man.

Barnes seemed to think that getting to the Cambodian border was a clandestine matter, and when I suggested getting a hotel taxi to take him, he was somewhat taken aback. When I told him I had no special access to the

CIA, he was even more disbelieving. The fact that he still insisted that the spooks had engineered the loss of his $15,000 made his request to talk with them even more peculiar.

Eventually, I called a friend in the U.S. Embassy and said. "I don't know what to do, but there is this person who insists that he wants to talk to the CIA about walking into Laos and rescuing POWs." I learned that U.S. policy appears to be that government officials are not to talk to free-lance adventurers, and am convinced that Barnes never spoke to any U.S. Embassy officials. (He did speak to officers of the JCRC — Joint Casualty Resolution Center — who deal with POWs and who talk to anybody. They thought he was a weirdo.)

He also overheard the embassy extension that I asked for, and called it up immediately after I left him and asked to speak to a "CIA case officer." When

---

SCOTT BARNES: MAN OF MYSTERY
By Donna DuVall and Jim Graves

: In October 1982. Bo Gritz sent a five-man team to Thailand to lay the groundwork for his second POW rescue mission. Grand Eagle. Gritz and the rest of the team planned to join the advance men in November and sneak into Laos to look for POWs. Included in the five who went in October were J.D. Bath. Vinney Arnone and Scott Barnes. Grand Eagle, like its Florida-bound predecessor. Velvet Hammer, fizzled before any rescue mission could be launched.

In fact, the only memorable thing to come from Grand Eagle was the incredible web of intrigue and lies spun by one of the team members. Scott Barnes, on his return home. So incredible was Barnes' tale of CIA clandestine operations to find POWs, assassinate other operatives, plant Yellow Rain samples in Laos and terminate Libya's Mommar Khadafy that only four publications printed his story: Covert Action Information Bulletin (CAIB), a leftist journal which concentrates on exposing United States intelligence operations. the New York Daily World, the newspaper of the American Communist Party. the Hermosa Beach. Calif. Easy Reader and a Canadian newspaper The Vancouver Herald.

Upon his return to the United States. Barnes contacted several newspaper and television representatives. including Ted Koppel of ABC-TV's Nightline and Jack Anderson. whose syndicated column runs in hundreds of newspapers around the country. Because his story was so fantastic, they interviewed him extensively before determining that there was less to Scott Barnes than met the eye.

According to Barnes in his CAIB inter-

view, he was first contacted by one of Gritz's ex-SOG (Studies and Observation Group) troopers in April 1981 and told to get ready "for a secret invasion into Laos" to rescue POWs. The covert CIA operation. codenamed BOHICA (Bend Over. Here It Comes Again). had the cooperation of U.S. Representative Robert Dornan of California. chairman of the House Committee on POW/MIAs; the CIA chief in Bangkok; and former Laotian Gen. Vang Pao. In fact. Barnes said the reason he was asked to participate was because he was "close friends with both Vang Pao and Rep. Dornan" and that he later arranged a meeting in Dornan's office between Dornan, Gritz. Vang Pao and himself.

Sometime in May 1981. Soldier of Fortune Managing Editor Jim Graves took a phone call from Scott Barnes from somewhere in Hawaii. Barnes had read the articles about Operation Velvet Hammer and thought that somehow SOF was involved. Graves assured him that the fiasco was Gritz's. not SOF's. and the publicity came from the media Gritz had brought into the operation. Barnes said he did not know Gritz. but he wanted to help with the POW effort. and asked us to put him touch with "intel and communicator types."

Barnes wouldn't say much about his background. but. as best as Graves remembers. he implied that he was former Special Forces. We turned his number over to Earl Bleacher, a former Special Forces soldier who participated in the Son Tay raid. and asked him to call Barnes and find out what he wanted and what he was really up to. Earl later told Graves that the guy was a flake. and SOF forgot about Barnes.

Until June 1981 that is. when some SOF staffers in Bangkok heard from a source now forgotten that Barnes was en route to Thailand on a Pan Am flight. We assumed that he had indeed contacted Gritz and was working for him on his ongoing POW missions.

SOF staffers Tom Reisinger and Fred Zabitosky waited in the lobby of the Nana

Hotel. where we knew Barnes was planning to stay. They wanted to get a good look so they could spot him if he showed up near any SOF operations in extreme northern Thailand.

Barnes — about 28. six-foot. 190 pounds. bearded — arrived wearing a safari suit jacket and shorts. and calmly registered at the desk. Neither Reisinger nor Zabitosky heard or saw anything at all unusual. nor did Barnes appear distressed when he entered the Nana. despite his later claims. SOF did not approach Barnes. and he was unaware of their presence.

Soon after his arrival. Barnes began making the rounds with a concocted story — designed either to impress or raise money — of having his baggage stolen (with $15,000 in cash inside). As he was disembarking from the car that had brought him from the airport. Barnes claimed. two Thai soldiers ran out of the Nana coffeeshop. firing MI6s. As he dove for cover. the car sped off with his luggage and his $15,000.

Certainly having one's baggage stolen is common in Bangkok. but Barnes could not explain why he had all his cash inside his luggage. while he kept all his important papers (passport. customs slips. etc.) in his pockets. Also. both Reisinger and Zabitosky witnessed his arrival. and there was no gunfire nor speeding automobile. And Barnes walked into the lobby with luggage.

Hearing this tale. SOF Publisher Robert K. Brown and "Mekong" Jim Coyne decided to meet with Barnes later in the week by the Nana pool. After a few minutes. Brown and Coyne agreed with Bleacher's earlier diagnosis of Barnes and avoided him from then on

Barnes returned from Thailand in the summer of 1981 and sometime before August got in touch with Gritz. if he had not been in touch before. Gritz in the Easy Reader article says he first heard from Barnes before Scott left for Thailand in June: his second contact came when Barnes called him for money to get back from Thailand. which Gritz refused to give. Gritz admits he met with him in California. but hedges on the meeting with Dornan in August and denies any further contact.

According to Barnes. he attended the August meeting with Vang Pao and Gritz in Dornan's office (the record supports this) and then went to Thailand with five or six other Americans. This is also true. as BOHICA team members J.D. Bath and Vinney Arnone have stated.

From the time the Grand Eagle crew reached NKP. piecing the story together gets more difficult. Bath says their contact. presumably a Lao. never showed up. Barnes and another team member got into a fight. reportedly over a piece of camera equipment. By then. the plan was beginning to unravel. tempers were running high and morale low. so they returned to Bangkok. Soon the mission was called off and the members returned to the United States.

As Barnes tells it. he and one other man from BOHICA crossed over into Laos near Mahaxay and confirmed that there were two Americans being held in camp there. Barnes says they got a message from the CIA chief of station in Bangkok and a message from Virginia (CIA?). which when put together. directed them to kill the two Americans. Barnes says this was the reason for the fight: He refused to take part in the killing of the two Americans. while the other guy insisted that they obey their orders. Barnes claims they had AR-180 rifles with silencers. No one else on the team saw them. Barnes claims he came back separately and dropped out of sight. to avoid being terminated by the CIA. until Gritz started appearing in the press about his POW missions. at which point Barnes decided that going public was his best defense against the CIA. He surmised that the reason they were to kill the Americans is because the Americans had gone to Laos under the guise of hunting POWs. but their real mission had been to plant Yellow Rain samples to implicate the USSR of engaging in gas warfare.

How much of Scott Barnes' story is true?

Just enough to make the unknowledgeable wonder and to give the already committed a story that will stand up if one doesn't bother to check too thoroughly.

Was Barnes a part of Gritz's operation BOHICA? Answer. yes. He has too many details which are true. including the operation name which Gritz admitted in a 1982 radio interview that he coined. In addition. two BOHICA team members. Bath and Arnone. have given statements to *Soldier of Fortune* that Barnes was involved and in Thailand with them.

In several of Barnes' interviews since the fall of 1981. he has claimed — just as Gritz has — that BOHICA was connected to the United States government through an agency called "The Activity." The agency which Gritz and Barnes refer to as the "The Activity" does exist. although not under that name. It was established in the wake of the Iranian rescue mission's failure. in part because the Special Forces group (Delta). which was charged with carrying out the mission. depended upon other organizations (CIA. DIA and NSA) for its intelligence. To prevent further disasters from resulting on future such missions. an organization was created to gather and act on its intelligence. *Editor's Note: While the specific name of this organization and its home base have already been blown by one reporter with connections to Gritz. SOF declines to go any further than the explanation above.*

Was "The Activity" involved in BOHICA. or Grand Eagle — a parallel operation — or perhaps BOHICA under another name? The answer to that is no. Before the House Subcommittee on Asian and Pacific Affairs hearing on POWs. 22 March 1983. Rear Adm. Allen G. Paulson. of the Defense Intelligence Agency. was asked if Gritz ever had any official backing from the government Paulson replied that after the time of BOHICA or Grand Eagle a proposal was submitted from one intelligence agency to utilize Gritz and his organization in the POW MIA issue. Paulson stated that the

proposal was routinely brought up fo review and was rejected. Since SC learned from another independe source that any hopes Gritz had of dire government connections were squashe in December 1981. we are convince "The Activity" was not involved beyo evaluating Gritz and his associates.

Barnes has claimed in CAIB and tl Canadian newspaper that they were to to assassinate the two Americans the found in Laos because they were n American POWs from the Vietnam Wa but really two CIA agents caught plantii Yellow Rain gas samples. The Unite States reportedly planned to use tl samples to accuse Russia and Vietnam using chemicals in violation of tl Geneva Convention. In his CAIB a count. Barnes said the two men. we near Mahaxay. Laos. were in the sar area where the Yellow Rain samples cit by former Secretary of State Alexand Haig in his 1981 accusation that tl USSR was using chemical weapons we collected. In the *Vancouver Herald*. a British Columbia newspaper whi printed Barnes' story on 5 January 198 Barnes added that the area where t men were held was the same area whe *Soldier of Fortune* picked up its Yelle Rain sample. which was one of the used by Haig.

Barnes' Yellow Rain story has a ma flaw: Our sample was obtained in Th land. well over 200 miles from Mahaxa Furthermore. the Soviet attack that pr duced the sample took place in Non western Laos. not central Laos whe Mahaxay is.

The real mystery of Scott Barnes is that he was secret agent working for G and "The Activity." but how on earth was able to fool anybody. But th maybe the only ones he really foo were Bo Gritz and a few radical new papers.

Much like Allen Dawson of T *Bangkok Post*. we'll always rememb Scott Barnes as "The man who swan river that wasn't there on a trip he ne took for a government that never knew

FLAKE

Barnes is the first person in recorded history to swim across the Thai-Cambodian border if he did so. It is a land border. There is no river or creek or stream.

he was told that the number he was calling was definitely *not* the CIA, he hung up.

Barnes went to the border in a rented car, with driver, as most everyone does. Or at least he said he went to the border. When he returned he called me again and told me that he'd had a "real good trip." He had sneaked out to the frontier, he said, "and I swam across and had a look around and then came back."

Barnes is the first person in recorded history to swim across the Thai-Cambodian border if he did so. It is a land border. There is no river or creek or stream. There is an anti-tank trench a few miles long, but with all the Thai Army security there, he could hardly "sneak" up to it. In any case he couldn't swim across it since it never has much water even at the height of the rainy season. Besides it would not require more than two low strokes to cross if you were absolutely determined to get your clothes wet.

He certainly couldn't swim the *klong* (canal) a little to the south. It is almost too narrow for any meaningful jumping exercise.

That is what Barnes told me happened on his first trip to Thailand. His second trip must have been a lot more exciting; at least his story is extremely inventive. First of all, he claims he came back in October with five other American "team members." They and about 30 Hmong combatants from the former Vang Pao force clandestinely crossed the Mekong River from the Thai village of Ban Pheng to Laos, "west of Mahaxay."

This is neither a helpful nor very possible exercise. Ban Pheng, in northern Nakhon Phanom Province in the Thai northeast, and the Laotian town of Mahaxay, east of Savannakhet, may have looked close together on Barnes' Esso version of a tactical map.

In fact, they are some 120 kilometers apart, and Mahaxay is 40 klicks inland from the Mekong, which is the border between Laos and Thailand. On the map, to go from Ban Pheng to "west of Mahaxay" would mean he spent some 80 or so kilometers to cross a river less than a mile wide. That's some river crossing.

And saying that this alleged American-Laotian special warfare team crossed "from Ban Pheng to west of Mahaxay" is less geographically informative than telling someone trying to find your house for dinner that it is "in Orange County, Calif."

Barnes claims that a team similar to his had preceded him into Laos, as part of what he calls "Operation Velvet Glove" (the actual name of this operation was Operation Grand Eagle), to try to obtain photographic proof that U.S. prisoners were being held in Laos.

He told CAIB and the *Daily World* that the first team had been captured. The CIA ordered him and his team to locate the first, try to rescue them, but to kill them if necessary to keep them from talking.

The only identification he carried — or at least was able to produce later — is what the *Daily World* called an "official-looking business card, embossed with the seal of the United States Congress, identifying them as members of the staff of then U.S. Congressman Robert K. Dornan (R-Calif.)."

Asked by the newspaper why the CIA would want to kill members of the first team, Barnes *speculated* that "possibly the United States was involved in getting chemical warfare, biological stuff, over there." In other words, the first team was "seeding" false evidence which later would be picked up by Laotian resistance members or others.

Barnes also said he carried back from Thailand a letter from a Laotian to Daniel C. Arnold, a former CIA sta-

tion chief in Laos and now a private consultant based in northern Virginia, just outside the District of Columbia. Barnes said Arnold "was a major figure in the Laos infiltration operation." Why carrying a letter from a refugee to Arnold would be sinister isn't explained by the publications.

Arnold himself told the *Daily World* that he had helped several prominent Laotians escape the 1975 communist takeover (which indeed he did) and that he received — and forwarded to Vang Pao and former cabinet chief Chao Sisouk — the letter Barnes took back from Thailand.

The credibility of Barnes is somewhat strained when he identifies the Bangkok CIA station chief as Mike Eiland, or, as he spells it, "Island." Eiland, a cross-border SF operative in Vietnam, is a military officer on loan to the State Department, who has been widely praised for his work as head of the U.S. Embassy's Cambodian refugee relief program. The CIA station chief in Bangkok can be found, as at all such "open stations" in the world, by anyone with some smarts and an embassy telephone directory.

Bo Gritz, that colorful ex-SF officer who has recently come under criticism for his own role in the POW/MIA question, was unable or unwilling to confirm that Barnes played any part in the Laotian infiltration mission.

I wasn't too mystified. I made up my mind Barnes was overly excited about the idea of bringing back POWs. I also thought he was highly paranoid, and avoided contact with him.

He left Thailand after a couple of weeks. He did begin to talk to other newsmen in the United States about POWs and U.S. government actions against those committed to the cause. Most of them, it seems, took his stories with the same truckloads of salt I did. He finally had to peddle his Thailand adventures to leftist publications. 🗶

Daring Books

2020 Ninth Street, S.W. • Canton, Ohio 44706

(216) 454-7519

Dennis W. Bartow, Publisher

May 2, 1986

To Whom It May Concern:

In the book, THE HEROES WHO FELL FROM GRACE, written by Charles J. Patterson and G. Lee Tippin, (Col., U.S.Army, Ret.) and published by Daring Books (Dennis Bartow, Publisher) there is a brief but significant reference to Mr. Scott Barnes.

Recent pertinent facts have come to the attention of myself and the authors which leads us to re-evaluate this reference. We desire to publicly apologize to Mr. Barnes and to state that we feel this reference to him is inaccurate.

We are now aware of the fact that Mr. Barnes voluntarily and willingly submitted to poly-graph tests, Truth Serum, and psychological evaluation. The results from them all revealed no contradictory information and that he is a very sane and stable person.

His credibility is further enhanced by the sworn affadavit with the Federal Courts and he has witnessed under oath to the U.S. Senate Hearing as part of the Smith/McIntyre suit.

Recently I have had phone conversations with several credible individuals who have exten-sively researched Mr. Barnes as well as other matters relating to the POW/MIA issue. They all attest to his reliability and honesty.

The reference to Mr. Barnes in THE HEROES WHO FELL FROM GRACE was based in inadequate and misleading information from sources which apparantly sought to divide instead of enhance efforts to creatively and adequately address the problems surrounding the POW/MIA issue. This book should not be used as a source to descredit Mr. Barnes.

We commend Mr. Barnes on his courage and intrepid spirit in the face of many trials and tribulations. He has suffered much as a result of simply seeking to do a good job fulfilling a vital mission.

The authors and myself desire that the POW/MIA issue be resolved with the support and co-operation of the proper government authorities and all other interested individuals and organizations. All of us must unite in obtaining this worthy goal. The communists and those seeking to downplay this issue revel in our dissent. We must be resolute in our devotion to each other and this worthy cause. The MIAs must be accounted for and the POWs freed as soon as possible. Each of us will be held accountable by our nation and our God for our actions regarding this burning issue.

In conclusion I want to say Daring Books believes the complete and untarnished truth of the missions in which Mr. Barnes participated should be made known to as wide an audience as possible. We certainly shall do all in our power to assist him in this endeavor.

Sincerely,

Dennis W. Bartow
Publisher

P.S. It has been reported to me that some individuals and organizations have duplicated portions of THE HEROES WHO FELL FROM GRACE. This is a flagrant copyright infringment and will not be tolerated. Permission must be obtained from the publisher prior to the use of copyright material from this book.

ERRATA

To the Reader -

In this book there is a brief but significant reference to a Mr. Scott Barnes. Recent facts have come to the attention of the publisher and authors of this book concerning the claims of Mr. Barnes and his involvement in *Operation Grand Eagle*. We now feel the comments about Mr. Barnes are inaccurate and based on misleading information by sources that do not know the truth or are deliberately seeking to discredit Mr. Barnes for their own reasons.

We are now aware of the fact that Mr. Barnes voluntarily and willingly submitted to polygraph and truth serum tests, as well as psychological evaluations. The results in all cases revealed no contradictory information and he is a sane, stable person.

Mr. Barnes' credibility is further enhanced by the sworn affidavit with the Federal Courts, and he has been a witness under oath to the U.S. Senate hearings as part of the Smith/McIntyre suit. In addition, there are many reliable individuals who have thoroughly investigated Mr. Barnes and have found he is telling the truth about actually producing photographs of American POWs in SE Asia.

If you desire further information on his situation, contact the publisher.

THE DEPARTMENT OF THE TREASURY
BUREAU OF ALCOHOL, TOBACCO AND FIREARMS
P. O. Box 1991, Main Office
Los Angeles, CA 90053

June 6, 1973

REFER TO
W:C:LA:MGF/dlp

Mr. Scott T. Barnes
522 Susanna
Redondo Beach, CA 90277

Dear Mr. Barnes:

I would like to take this opportunity to commend you for the
outstanding assistance you rendered to our Bureau during the
months of May and June, 1972. At that time you notified us
that you had met an individual who was illegally manufacturing
numerous bombs. You then arranged a meeting with the suspect
which you later attended in the company of an undercover Special
Agent from our Bureau.

You will be happy to learn that your assistance was instrumental
in perfecting a criminal case against the suspect charging him
with unlawfully manufacturing and possessing destructive devices,
a felony. On June 14, 1972, a search warrant was executed at the
suspect's residence. At that time we seized nine fully active
pipe bombs along with various timing devices and other items used
in the manufacturing of destructive devices.

During the entire operation you acted in a manner which demonstrated
extreme good judgment and common sense. Your actions indicate that
you are an outstanding citizen of your community and one who deserves
praise for a job well done.

Respectfully,

Harry T. Morrissey
Special Agent in Charge

CONSULATE GENERAL OF VIETNAM
SUITE 353 - 361 FLOOD BLDG
870 MARKET STREET
SAN FRANCISCO, CALIFORNIA 94102

VISA APPLICATION FORM

If other persons are included on your passport specify name, birth date, place, and relationship on other side of this form.

NOTE: If any of the particulars furnished below are found to be incorrect or if any information is found to be withheld, the visa is liable to be cancelled at any time and the applicant may be subject to the penalties prescribed by law.

NAME ___BARNES___ ___SCOTT___ ___TRACY___ MARITAL STATUS ___SINGLE___
      Last   First   Middle

BIRTH ___19___ ___JUNE___ ___1954___ PRESENT ___BURBANK, CALIF.___
   Day Month   Year   Place

NATIONALITY AT BIRTH ___U.S. CITIZEN___ PRESENT ___U.S. CITIZEN___

PASSPORT NO. ___C926666___ ISSUED ON ___13 APRIL 72___ ISSUED WHERE ___LOS ANGELES CA.___ VALID UNTIL ___12 APRIL 77___

PERMANENT RESIDENCE ___522 SUSANA AVE. REDONDO BEACH CALIF.___ TEL. (Home) ___(213) 374 1889___ (Bus.)

PROFESSION ___STUDENT___ EMPLOYER (Name and address) _____

REASON FOR JOURNEY ___TOURIST___ ADDRESS IN VIETNAM ___EMBASSY, HOTEL SAIGON___

REFERENCES IN VIETNAM (Name and address) _____

DATES, PLACES AND DURATION OF PREVIOUS STAYS IN VIETNAM, if any ___MARCH 1973 SAIGON, AN LOC, MY LO, BIEN HOA.___

REFERENCES IN COUNTRY OF RESIDENCE
(Names, address of friends, relatives, or business firms.)

DATE OF DEPARTURE FROM USA ___30 APRIL 75___ DATE OF ARRIVAL IN VIETNAM ___1 MAY 75___ DATE OF DEPARTURE FROM VIETNAM ___16 MAY 75___

DURATION OF STAY ___15 DAYS___

I hereby certify that during my stay in Vietnam I will not accept employment unless under an approved contract nor try to settle there permanently, and that I will leave the territory of Vietnam upon expiration of the period of stay which has been extended to me.

___Scott Tracy Barnes___
SIGNATURE

19-B

VIỆT-NAM CỘNG-HÒA **TỜ KHAI NHẬP CẢNH** Mẫu QT-36
Republic of Việt-Nam
(Baggage and Currency Declaration: Entry)

Tên họ (Name) (1) Xin viết chữ in (Please print)	BARNES, SCOTT	Quốc tịch (2) (Nationality) U.S.A.	Thường trú nhân Resident Ngày rời Việt-Nam Left RVN (Date)
Thông hành số (3) (Passport no.) C296060	cấp tại (4) (Issued at) U.S.A.	Ngày (5) (Date) APR 2, 72	Ngoại trú nhân Non-resident Phi hành đoàn Crew member Nơi đi Port of Embarkation SINGAPORE
Địa chỉ thường xuyên (Permanent address) (6) 522 SUSANA Rekondo			Tên tàu Ship's Name SINGAPORE AIR
Địa chỉ tại Việt-Nam (Address while in Việt-Nam) (7)			

XIN XEM MẶT SAU VỀ THỂ THỨC KHAI BÁO
See reverse side for instructions to fill out this form

TIỀN TỆ – TƯ TRANG – CÁC TÀI VẬT KHÁC (CURRENCIES – JEWELRY – OTHER VALUABLES)

Chi tệ, Chi Phiếu, Tín dụng thư (Bank-notes, checks, letters of credit)	70 U.S.
Tư trang (Personal jewelry)	watch
Qui vật khác (Other valuables)	

HÀNH LÝ (BAGGAGE) Số hành lý (Pieces of baggage) 1

Chi danh vật dụng Description of articles	Số lượng Quantity	Trị giá bằng US$ Value US$	Nguyên xứ Country of origin	Cột này dành cho Q. Thuế This space for Customs use only
Sleep bag	1	85.00	U.S.	
shorts	1	2.00		
shoes	1	12.00		
shirt	3	6.00		
Shaving kit	1	5.00		

(Nếu thiếu chỗ, xin khai mặt sau)
(If additional space is needed, use reverse side)

Nhân viên Quan Thuế (Customs Officer)

Saigon, ngày (Date)
Hành khách ký tên (Passenger's Signature)

DR.9.19, 29 57 A-36

NATIONAL AGENCY CHECK REQUEST

DEPARTMENT OF DEFENSE

NACC Use Only

253 2004

REQUEST DATE: 24 AUG 73

1. LAST NAME - FIRST NAME - MIDDLE NAME: BARNES SCOTT TRACY

2. SEX: MALE

3. ALIAS(ES) AND ALL FORMER NAME(S): NONE

SEP 7 1973

4. SOCIAL SECURITY NUMBER: 550-76-8371

5. MONTH, DAY, YEAR OF BIRTH: 19 JUN 54

6. PLACE OF BIRTH: BURBANK CALIFORNIA

7. SERVICE NUMBER:

RETURN RESULTS TO: (Include ZIP Code)

DIRECTORATE OF SECURITY
HQ USATC, INF &
FORT ORD, CA. 93941
157 A-36

CONFIDENTIAL

8.A. SECURITY PROGRAM
- [X] MILITARY
- [ ] CIVILIAN
- [ ] INDUSTRIAL

b. [ ] LOCAL FILES CHECKED WITH FAVORABLE RESULTS

c. INITIATOR OF REQUEST: USARECSTA FT. ORD. CA. 93941

A 2 D F

9. RELATIVES	10. DATE AND PLACE OF BIRTH	11. PRESENT ADDRESS	12. CITIZENSHIP
a. FATHER: BARNES CHARLES	UNK	522 SUSANA Redondo Bch CA	U.S.
b. MOTHER (Full Maiden Name): Poole Stephanie	UNK	SAME	U.S.
c. SPOUSE (Full Maiden Name): NONE			

13. RESIDENCES (List all from 18th birthday or during past 15 years, whichever is shorter. If under 18, list present and most recent addresses.)

a. FROM	b. TO	c. NUMBER AND STREET	d. CITY	e. STATE
JUL 66	AUG 73	522 SUSANA	Redondo BEACH	CALIFOR

DIS NAC Center   01 OCT 1973
ENTNAC completed favorably
per DoD Dir 5210.8 Williams

14. EMPLOYMENT (List all from 18th birthday or during past 15 years, whichever is shorter. If under 18, list present and most recent employment)

a. FROM	b. TO	c. EMPLOYER	d. PLACE
APR. 72	Feb. 73	MUZICK Shoes	1012 South PACIFIC COAST HGY Redondo Bch CA.

15. LAST CIVILIAN SCHOOL

a. FROM	b. TO	c. NAME	d. PLACE
Sept. 68	JUN 72	Redondo High School	Redondo Beach California

YES	NO	16.	("Yes" answers must be explained in Item 18, below.)
	X	a.	Is the subject an alien or naturalized citizen?
	X	b.	Has the subject any foreign connections, employment or military service?
X		c.	Has the subject traveled or resided abroad other than for the U.S. Government?
	X	d.	Has the subject had employment requiring a security clearance or investigation?
	X	e.	Is the subject now or has he ever been in the Federal Civil Service or Armed Forces?
	X	f.	Has the subject qualified DD Form 398, 98, 48-1, or similar security form?
	X	g.	Has the subject ever been addicted to drugs?

17. REQUEST DATA

a. REQUESTER DESIGNATOR		b. REASON
[X] ARMY	DASA	[X] BASIC TRAINE
NAVY	DCA	PRE-COMMISS
AIR FORCE	DCAA	NUCLEAR
OSD	DIA	BI.
JCS	DSA	[X] SECRET CLEARANCE
NSA	DISCO	

18. REMARKS (If additional space is needed, continue on plain paper.)

16C   Feb. TAHITI, A: SOMOA, W: SOMOA, TONGA, ARR. FIJI,
JAN 73-APR 73 MARCH FIJI, NEW CALEDONIA, NEW ZEALAND, AUS... ...APORE, MALAYSIA, India
(DOE) --US ARMY PVI 16 JUL 73 TOURIST. Williams Howi Para 157 A-36

DD FORM 1584

REPLACES DA FORM ... 1 AUG 65, WHICH IS OBSOLETE

GPO: 1967 O 279-094

DECLARATION OF HONOUR

I .Scott.T.Barnes

The Undersigned of S22 S.aSawa Redondo Bch CaliF U.S.A.

Hereby Declare that ....

1. I will not involve myself in any Political Activities or
    break the Vietnam Current Rules and Regulations during
    my stay in the Republic of Vietnam.

2. I will leave the Territory of the Republic of Vietnam
    at expiration of the stay granted.

SIGNATURE ....

Date ...3.2.73....

It is suggested that this Declaration of Honour duly signed
by you be presented to the Vietnamese Immigration Authorities
on your arrival in Siagon.

Canberra ngày 6 thang 3 nam 1973

THI NHAN

EMBASSY
OF VIET-NAM
CANBERRA LE THE XUONG
First Secretary

Leave on 30th March 73

WARNING: ALTERATION, ADDITION OR MUTILATION OF ENTRIES IS PROHIBITED. ANY UNOFFICIAL CHANGE WILL RENDER THIS PASSPORT INVALID.

NAME
SCOTT TRACY BARNES

BIRTH DATE
JUNE 19, 1954

BIRTHPLACE
CALIFORNIA, U.S.A.

HEIGHT
6 FEET 1 INCHES

HAIR
BROWN

EYES
GREEN

WIFE
X X X

ISSUE DATE
APR. 13, 1972

MINORS
X X X

EXPIRATION DATE ➡ APR. 12, 1977

Scott Tracy Barnes
SIGNATURE OF BEARER

IMPORTANT: THIS PASSPORT IS NOT VALID UNTIL SIGNED BY THE BEARER. PERSONS INCLUDED HEREIN MAY NOT USE THIS PASSPORT FOR TRAVEL UNLESS ACCOMPANIED BY THE BEARER.

Visas

IT IS THE RESPONSIBILITY OF THE PASSPORT BEARER
TO OBTAIN NECESSARY VISAS

18 FEB 1973

HE CHASE MANHATTAN BANK, N.A.
SAIGON BRANCH
DATE **29 MAR 1973**
BANK NOTES SOLD
T/C
CHEQUE
TOTAL
EXCH. AUTHORIZATION NO
DATED

6

FRONTIERES
Calédonie
18 FEV. 1973
SORTIE

Visas

POLICE
No
15

pour

VISA FOR AUSTRALIA 319

(Subject to grant on arrival of an entry permit
under the Migration Act, 1958 - 66.)

1. Visa Number _____ H/1176/72
2. Type of Visa _____ VISITOR
3. Date of Issue _____ 18 DECEMBER, 1972
4. Date of Expiry _____ 17 DECEMBER 1976
5. Good for SEVERAL journeys to Australia
   until d t. of expiry, subject to passport
   remaining valid.
6. Period of stay in Australia which may be
   authorized by issue of entry permit on
   arrival _____ SIX MONTHS
7. Special conditions _____ "R" B2.
8. Visa Fee _____ GRATIS
9. Signature _____
10. Position CONSUL of AUSTRALIA
11. Place of Issue _____ LOS ANGELES

Visas

Immigration
Act 1966 Sec. 11
permitted to enter Western Samoa
on. (Date ___ for a
period up to ___ 12.0.73
FALEOLO AIRPORT
Immigration

1 Day

DEPARTMENT OF IMMIGRATION
PERMITTED TO ENTER
AUSTRALIA
on **22 FEB 1973**
For
SYDNEY AIRPORT

8

Visas

CONSULAT GENERAL
TAHITI-FAAA
- 2 FEV. 4.3
- ENTREE -
POLYNESIE FRAN

Immigration Dept. 30
Pago Pago, American Samoa
— ADMITTED

FEB 8 1973

CLASS
PERIOD

FIJI

Imm. Act 1971 Sect. 9
VISITOR.

14 FEB 1973

valid until 13 - 3 - 73
9 day/ month/ year

9

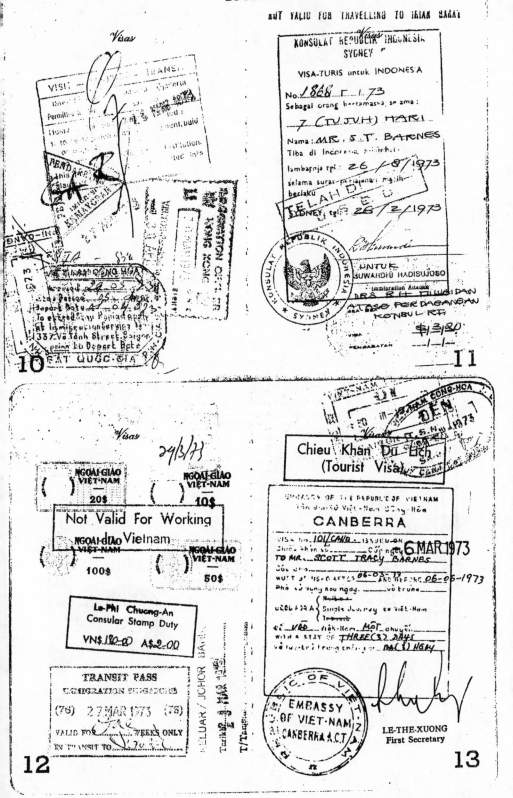

Visas

Visas

14

15

NAME—NOM

SCOTT TRACY BARNES

SEX—SEXE   DIRTHPLACE—LIEU DE NAISSANCE

M   CALIFORNIA, U.S.A.

BIRTH DATE—DATE DE NAISSANCE

JUNE 19, 1954

ISSUE DATE—DATE DE DELIVRANCE

JAN. 9, 1980

WIFE/HUSBAND—EPOUSE/EPOUX   EXPIRES ON—EXPIRE LE

X X X   JAN. 8, 1985

MINORS—ENFANTS MINEURS

X X X

SIGNATURE of BEARER—SIGNATURE DU TITULAIRE

Scott Barnes

H006298

PHOTOGRAPH ATTACHED HEREUNDER DEPICTS THE BEARER

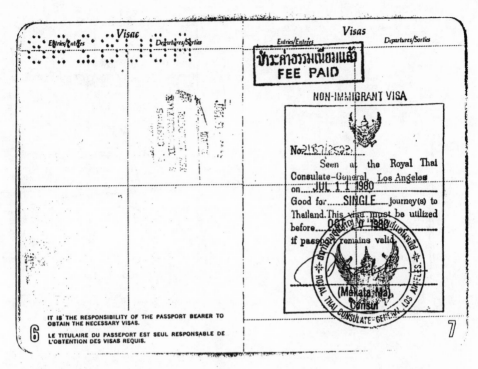

IT IS THE RESPONSIBILITY OF THE PASSPORT BEARER TO
OBTAIN THE NECESSARY VISAS.

LE TITULAIRE DU PASSEPORT EST SEUL RESPONSABLE DE
L'OBTENTION DES VISAS REQUIS.

Visas

Entries/Entrées · Departures/Sorties

FEE PAID

NON-IMMIGRANT VISA

No. 218712892

Seen at the Royal Thai
Consulate-General, Los Angeles
on JUL 1 1 1980
Good for SINGLE journey(s) to
Thailand. This visa must be utilized
before OCT 1 1980
if passport remains valid

(Malala Ma)
Consul

6

7

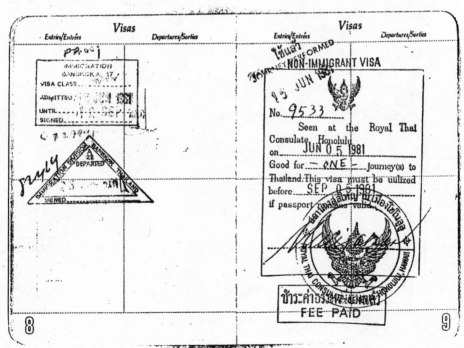

Visas

Entries/Entrées · Departures/Sorties

IMMIGRATION
BANGKOK, 17
VISA CLASS
ADMITTED
UNTIL SEP
SIGNED

DEPARTED

IMMIGRATION DIVISION BANGKOK THAILAND

SIGNED

Visas

Entries/Entrées · Departures/Sorties

NON-IMMIGRANT VISA

No. 9533

Seen at the Royal Thai
Consulate, Honolulu
on JUN 0 5 1981
Good for - ONE - journey(s) to
Thailand. This visa must be utilized
before SEP 0 5 1981
if passport remains valid

FEE PAID

8

9

Visas   PN1   *Visas*

Entries/Entrées   Departures/Sorties   Entries/Entrées   Departures/Sorties

U.S. IMMIGRATION
160 LOS ANG
JUN 26 1981
ADMITTED
UNTIL _____ (class)

IMMIGRATION
BANGKOK A. 65
VISA CLASS .... NN. 16
ADMITTED 2 1 OCT 1981
UNTIL ___ - 4 NOV 198
SIGNED ___

IMMIGRATION DIVISION BANGKOK THAILAND
A 40 DEPARTED
0 3 NOV 1981
SIGNED

POLICE NATIONALE
CHARLES DE GAULLE 1
2 2 JAN 1983
A 039 FRANCE

10   **11**

Visas   *Visas*

Entries/Entrées   Departures/Sorties   Entries/Entrées   Departures/Sorties

ADMITTED
U.S. CUSTOMS
U.S. IMMIGRATION
OC 3 10 51
HONOLULU AIRPORT
NO. _____

12   **13**

ROBERT L. HANSON
CHIEF OF POLICE

THE CITY OF SEATTLE

OUR NO.
YOUR NO.

DEPARTMENT OF

POLICE

SEATTLE WASHINGTON 98104

October 25, 1974

Attention: Special Agents Daniels and Merriman
MPIS PMO
Fort Lewis, Washington 98433

Gentlemen:

Enclosed you will find Seattle Police Department case reports concerning three arrests made the night of October 23, 1974, in Seattle. The arrests came as a direct result of assistance rendered to our Narcotics Section by your personnel. Would you extend our appreciation to Pfc. E-3 MP Officer Scott L. Barnes and C.I.D. Special Agent Delbert Richardson for the very vital information they supplied us during our investigation.

It appeared at first that Fort Lewis military personnel were involved in this group of narcotics traffickers. After the arrests were made, it was determined that no one from the military was involved; however, information obtained from your personnel enabled us to arrest James McDowell who is believed to have been trafficking in large amounts of mescaline and other dangerous drugs for the past two years. Such cooperation between military and civilian agencies strengthens the community as a whole. We sincerely appreciate your efforts.

If in the future we can be of service to you in matters relating to drug trafficking, please contact Sergeant J. Sanford of the Narcotics Section.

Yours truly,

R. L. HANSON
Chief of Police, Interim

M. D. Wilson

M. D. WILSON
Assistant Chief of Police
Investigations Bureau

MDW/JS/es
enclosure

THIS IS AN IMPORTANT RECORD
SAFEGUARD IT.

1. LAST NAME - FIRST NAME - MIDDLE NAME	2. SEX	3. SOCIAL SECURITY NUMBER	4. DATE OF BIRTH	YEAR 54	MONTH 06	DAY 19

BARNES, SCOTT TRACY — M

5. DEPARTMENT, COMPONENT AND BRANCH OR CLASS	6a. GRADE, RATE OR RANK	6b. PAY GRADE	7. DATE OF RANK	YEAR 74	MONTH 03	DAY 11

ARMY-RA

8a. SELECTIVE SERVICE NUMBER	b. SELECTIVE SERVICE LOCAL BOARD NUMBER, CITY, STATE AND ZIP CODE	c. HOME OF RECORD AT TIME OF ENTRY INTO ACTIVE SERVICE (Street, RFD, City, State and ZIP Code)
04 117 54 1338	117 Gardena, CA 90249	

9a. TYPE OF SEPARATION	b. STATION OR INSTALLATION AT WHICH EFFECTED
DISCHARGE	Ft Lewis WA

c. AUTHORITY AND REASON	d. EFFECTIVE DATE	YEAR 74	MONTH 12	DAY 19
- - -				

e. CHARACTER OF SERVICE	f. TYPE OF CERTIFICATE ISSUED	10. REENLISTMENT CODE
HONORABLE	DD FORM 256A	- - -

11. HQ OF CHIEF AND MAJOR COMMAND	12. COMMAND TO WHICH TRANSFERRED
Ft Lewis WA FORSCOM	DNA

13. TERMINAL DATE OF RESERVE/MSO OBLIGATION	14. PLACE OF ENTRY INTO CURRENT ACTIVE SERVICE (City, State and ZIP Code)	15. DATE ENTERED ACTIVE DUTY THIS PERIOD
YEAR MONTH DAY		YEAR MONTH DAY
DNA	Los Angeles, CA 90000	73 08 21

16a. PRIMARY SPECIALTY NUMBER AND TITLE	b. RELATED CIVILIAN OCCUPATION AND D.O.T. NUMBER	18. RECORD OF SERVICE	YEARS	MONTHS	DAYS
Spec 73-12-13		(a) NET ACTIVE SERVICE THIS PERIOD	1	3	29
		(b) PRIOR ACTIVE SERVICE		NONE	
17a. SECONDARY SPECIALTY NUMBER AND TITLE	b. RELATED CIVILIAN OCCUPATION AND D.O.T. NUMBER	(c) TOTAL ACTIVE SERVICE (a + b)	1	3	29
		(d) PRIOR INACTIVE SERVICE	0	1	6
DNA	DNA	(e) TOTAL SERVICE FOR PAY (c + d)	1	5	5
		(f) FOREIGN AND/OR SEA SERVICE THIS PERIOD		NONE	

19. INDOCHINA OR KOREA SERVICE SINCE AUGUST 5, 1964	20. HIGHEST EDUCATION LEVEL SUCCESSFULLY COMPLETED (In Years)
	SECONDARY/HIGH SCHOOL 12 YRS (1 - 12 grades) COLLEGE 1 YRS

21. TIME LOST (Preceding Two Yrs.)	22. DAYS ACCRUED LEAVE PAID	23. SERVICEMEN'S GROUP LIFE INSURANCE COVERAGE	24. DISABILITY SEVERANCE PAY	25. PERSONNEL SECURITY INVESTIGATION
				a. TYPE	b. DATE COMPLETED
DNA	33	☐ $15,000 ☐ $5,000 X $20,000 ☐ $10,000 ☐ NONE	☐ NO ☐ YES DNA AMOUNT	ENTNAC	73-10-01

26. DECORATIONS, MEDALS, BADGES, COMMENDATIONS, CITATIONS AND CAMPAIGN RIBBONS AWARDED OR AUTHORIZED

NDSM   SPS M-16

27. REMARKS

28. MAILING ADDRESS AFTER SEPARATION (Street, RFD, City, County, State and ZIP Code)	29. SIGNATURE OF PERSON BEING SEPARATED
Same as 8c	

30. TYPED NAME, GRADE AND TITLE OF AUTHORIZING OFFICER	31. SIGNATURE OF OFFICER AUTHORIZED TO SIGN
LARRY E. STOKKE 2LT AGC ASST AG	

DD FORM 214
1 NOV 72

PREVIOUS EDITIONS OF THIS FORM ARE OBSOLETE.

THIS IS AN IMPORTANT RECORD SAFEGUARD IT.

REPORT OF SEPARATION FROM ACTIVE DUTY

COMMANDING OFFICERS CITATION

TO: OFFICERS S.M. DOWNING

S.T. BARNES

On 9-18-77 officers S.M. Downing and S.T. Barnes were on routine patrol when they observed a set of vehicle brake lights on the darken side of the CLOTA building located in the 100 block of West Upjohn street. The officers investigated the suspicious vehicle and found a occupied automobile parked next to a apparent abandoned motorcycle. The officers contacted the occupant of the automobile and found that his story regarding the motorcycle was very questionable. Further investigation by the officers revealed that the motorcycle had just been stolen and unreported to the police. Officers Downing and Barnes arrested the suspect and then proceeded to gather physical evidence. Due to care and proper evidence collection procedures officers Downing and Branes were able to place the arrested suspect at the scene of the theft. The officers also were able to trace the suspects movements from the scene of the theft to the scene of the recovery and arrest. Officers Downing and Barnes later assisted the detective in collecting photographs of the physical evidence at the scene. The physical evidence collected by these two officers should result in a virtually uncontested case against the arrested suspect. Officers Downing and Barnes are to be commend for their observation, interogation and evidence collection procedure.

COMMANDING OFFICERS CITATION

OFFICERS: OFFICER SCOTT BARNES
              OFFICER SHIRLEY DOWNING
              DETECTIVE ALAN MITCHELL
              DETECTIVE JERRY LEFEBVRE

On 11-14-77 officers Scott Barnes and Shirley Downing investigated a residential burglary at 236 Apt-B Drummond Street, in the City of Ridgecrest. The reported loss in the burglary was in excess of $3,000 dollars, including approximately twelve rifles and pistols. Later that evening officers Barnes and Downing were contacted by an informant who advised he could arrange a buy for the stolen weapons through the suspect which had stolen them. Officers Barnes and Downing used proper departmental procedures and contacted their supervisor who authorized the transaction. Detectives Alan Mitchell and Jerry Lefebvre were summon to the scene for investigative assistance. The suspect made contact with officer Barnes who was working in a undercover capacity, and although the suspect was armed the transaction transpired, the suspect was arrested and no injurys were sustained to officers or suspect, also all the stolen weapons were recovered. Later detectives Alan Mitchell and Jerry Lefebvre after extensive interrogation with the suspect and other related partys, developed information leading to the recovery of approximately $5,000 dollars in additional stolen property, canceling six Ridgecrest burglary cases, two China Lake burglary cases and two auto theft cases from the City of Bakersfield.

Officers Barnes and Downing and Detectives Mitchell and Lefebvre are to be commended for their teamwork, safety procedures, police knowledge, and investigative abilitys.

                                              W. STULL

RIDGECREST POLICE DEPT.

March 8, 1978

TO: Officer Scott Barnes

FROM: Sgt. K. C. Vineyard

SUBJECT:' Letter of Appreciation

I would like to take this opportunity to express my appreciation for your actions leading to the arrest of four suspects; the return of approximately $2,500.00 in money and property; and the confiscation of approximately $3,500.00 worth of illegal drugs.

Through your information a PC 459 suspect was apprehended and subsequently convicted, a dealer in illegal drugs was removed from the street..

Through your direct actions and follow-up investigation, an employee of a business establishment was apprehended and convicted of stealing money from that business. Also through your actions, $500.00 taken from the business was recovered.

Also, largely through your interviewing techniques, approximately $2,000.00 worth of foreign and domestic collectors coins were returned by a juvenile offender.

Finally, through your direct actions an untold number of unlawfully possessed and illegal weapons were removed from the streets of Ridgecrest.

Again my thanks for a job well done.

K. C. Vineyard
Det. / Bureau

OFFICE OF

THE DISTRICT ATTORNEY
COUNTY OF SAN DIEGO
EDWIN L. MILLER, JR.
DISTRICT ATTORNEY

COUNTY COURTHOUSE
SAN DIEGO, CALIFORNIA 92101

March 16, 1978

To whom it may concern:

We have worked with Officer Scott Barnes
since 1976 on matters concerning outlaw
motorcyclists. These offenses have ranged
from narcotics cases to conspiracy to commit murder. Officer Barnes has rendered
invaluable assistance to our efforts. I
have found him to have performed in an
outstanding manner.

RICHARD J. LEWIS
Supervising Investigator
Special Investigations/Intelligence Unit

RJL:cjs

Subpoena to Produce Document or Object · ·   Cr. Form No. 21 (Rev. 12-73)

United States District Court
FOR THE

NORTHERN DISTRICT OF CALIFORNIA

UNITED STATES OF AMERICA		No. CR-79-0226-WHO
v.		
JAMES EZEKIEL BRANDES, ET AL.		

To Custodian of Records
U. S. Army Reserve Compoentes Personnel
and Administration Center
9700 Page Blvd.
St Louis, MO 63132

You are hereby commanded to appear in the United States District Court for the Northern
Courtroom of Judge Orrick
District of   California   at   450 Golden Gate Ave.   in the city of

San Francisco on the 13th day of January   1981 at 9:30 o'clock A.M.

to testify in the above case and bring with you any and all military records including but
not limited to the contents of the Military Personnel Records Jacket
(201 File) and DD Form 214 for SCOTT TRACY BARNES, SSN 550-76-8371,
DOB: 6-19-54.

This subpoena is issued upon application of the United States of America.

JANUARY 12, 19 81.

MARGO D. SMITH
Attorney for Plaintiff
450 Golden Gate Ave.
San Francisco, CA 94102
(415) 556-1171

WILLIAM L. WHITTAKER,
U.S. Magistrate's Clerk.
By _____
DONNA GILMOUR Clerk.

"Insert "United States," or "defendant" as the case may be.

² A subpoena shall be issued by a Magistrate in a proceeding before him, but need not be under the seal of the court.
(Rule 17(a), Federal Rules of Criminal Procedure)

RETURN

Received this subpoena at   on
and on
served it on the within named   at
by delivering a copy to   and tendering to   the fee for one day's attendance and the
age allowed by law.²

Dated:

_____, 19 _____

By _____

Seal. Fees

SPECIAL HANDLING REQUIRED / CAUTION: ... from records of ... National Personnel Records Center, St. Louis, Missouri, to be used for reference only. Do not recopy or disseminate in its original form out. ... U.S. Secret Service.

CONFIDENTIAL

1 5 JAN 1981

6NCPMA-C

Barnes, Scott T., 550-76-8371

Mr. William L. Whittaker
Clerk, United States District Court
for the Northern District
450 Golden Gate Avenue
San Francisco, CA 94102

In response to your subpoena issued January 12, 1981, enclosed is a
certificate under seal authenticating copies of the Army military
records of Scott Tracy Barnes for use in the case of the United States
of America versus James Ezekiel Brandes, ET AL, Number CR-79-0226-WHO.

This certificate is furnished with the understanding that the information
is material to the issues of the case and necessary to proper administration
of justice; furthermore, that it will be impounded and neither opened nor
inspected before the trial, except with the consent of Mr. Barnes, or his
attorney or by further court order or pre-trial hearing.

The copies of the enclosed military records may contain the names of and
certain personal information relating to individuals other than the
veteran named in the court order. Under the Privacy Act of 1974, such
personal information should be safeguarded. Further release of this
information should be in accordance with the rules and regulations
implementing the Privacy Act of 1974.

We regret some of the copies are of poor quality; however, they are the
best copies obtainable.

DEBORAH L. HAVEMAN
Chief, Army Reference Branch

Enclosures

Cert with seal

cc: Margo D. Smith
    450 Golden Gate Avenue
    San Francisco, CA 94102

cc: Scott T. Barnes
    132 Marine St.
    Manhattan Beach, CA 90266
6NCPMA-C DKENNEDY:js

AFFIDAVIT OF DANIEL P. SHEEHAN

The Christic Institute
1324 North Capitol Street, NW
Washington, DC 20002
(202)-797-8106

Filed on December 12, 1986
(Minor Revisions, 12/18/86)

This operation would give a feasible explanation for the source of the funding and supply of the Contras -- so that Congress and the press would not conclude that the CIA was still supplying the Contras.

This public organization was set up by Rob Owen by contacting General John K. Singlaub -- who, in turn, set up the United States Council on World Freedom and began publicly raising funds for the Contras.[3]

The Hull Terror-Drug Operation: A Defector's Story

43. From my late 1985 conversations with Tony Avirgan, Martha Honey and their sources, as well as from my direct personal conversations with one Carlos Rojas Chinchilla, Source #25, I next learned the following facts:

43.1.   That in early 1985, Carlos Rojas Chinchilla, a gainfully-employed professional carpenter residing in the city of San Jose, Costa Rica, was present at a public restaurant and bar named the Rendezvous Bar located a few blocks from the United States Embassy in Costa Rica.

43.2.   While present in this bar, after finishing work, Carlos Rojas Chinchilla personally witnessed three men come into the Rendezvous Bar. He saw them stop in the doorway for a short conversation and then Carlos saw two of the men leave the bar. The third man was left standing in the doorway. After a few moments of standing in the doorway, watching the two other men depart down the street in the direction of the U.S. Embassy, the man who had remained behind in the doorway of the bar turned and began surveying the persons present in the bar.

43.3.   This man's survey finally came to rest upon Carlos, and the man briskly walked from his watch at the doorway and moved into the bar to the table where Carlos sat.

---

[3] In fact, General Singlaub raised money inside the United States which was directed, by him, to be deposited by contributors in a Grand Cayman bank for use in the purchasing of weapons and explosives for the Contras. Singlaub also travelled to Central America with Robert K. Brown and personally facilitated providing one John I. W. Harper to the Contras, who trained Contras in the construction of C-4 anti-personnel bombs exactly like the one which was used to bomb the La Penca press conference. In fact, Plaintiffs' Counsel has been informed by Source #24 that Defendant Singlaub and Robert K. Brown directly provided John I. W. Harper to Defendant Amac Galil who helped Defendant Galil construct the very C-4 bomb which Galil used to blow up the May 1984 Eden Pastora press conference. Source #24 is a person with knowledge of the activities of Defendant Singlaub, Robert K. Brown and John Harper with the Contras.

17

Vietnamese free ex-soldier looking for his girlfriend

BANGKOK, Thailand (AP) — Vietnam has freed an American who went there secretly last year searching for the fiancee he left behind when the war ended in 1975. On Thursday he was in Bangkok en route to the United States.

The few friends to whom Robert Schwab III of Atlanta, Ga., revealed his plan said the Vietnam War veteran had been certain of capture but had hoped to reach Ho Chi Minh City, which was called Saigon until South Vietnam fell in April 1975.

They said his goal was to negotiate exit permits for his fiancee and a child he believed was his.

"I don't see that I have any choice," he wrote to a friend, Thomas O'Donnell, an American investment banker working in Hong Kong. "It's a little late, but now I'm going to get her out."

Richard Childress, director of Asian affairs for the U.S. National Security Council, was with Schwab in Bangkok. They could not be reached for comment.

Friends said Schwab, now 44, set sail from the Philippines in an 18-foot boat for a journey across 600 miles of water infested with pirates and regularly swept by typhoons. He carried water for about 70 days, and basic navigation and communications gear but no weapons, they reported.

The official Vietnam News Agency, monitored in Bangkok, said Thursday that Schwab was arrested April 23, 1985, for violating the communist nation's territorial waters and committing "acts "against the sovereignty and security of Vietnam."

It said the People's Committee of the province of Nghia Binh decided on Wednesday to expel Schwab. Nghia Binh is on the eastern coast facing the South China Sea.

In Washington, White House spokesman Larry Speakes said Schwab was flown to Bangkok by helicopter and was declared to be in good physical condition after a medical checkup. Speakes said it was not known when Schwab would arrive in the United States.

Schwab's stepfather said in Atlanta that he had spoken with his stepson.

"We feel absolutely wonderful that he's fine, he's healthy; he's in good shape. He says all he needs is a little suntan." Robert Davis said in an interview with radio station WGST.

The Vietnam News Agency said: "The American in

question recognized that his acts constituted an infraction of the penal code of the Socialist Republic of Vietnam. He undertook not to repeat them and asked for clemency from the Socialist Republic of Vietnam."

It made no mention of Trai, the pseudonym Schwab used for his fiancee, whom he met during army service in Vietnam in the early 1970s.

Another White House spokesman, Dan Howard, said: "He came out alone; no girlfriend."

Friends said Trai was a teen-ager when Schwab met her, from a family that lost its wealth in the war.

O'Donnell, the investment banker, said in an interview with The Associated Press late last year that his friend spent 1½ years preparing his rescue mission, talking with refugee "boat people" and sailors who had plied the South China Sea.

Schwab stayed on in South Vietnam after his army service, taking various civilian jobs. When the communists were closing in on Saigon, he was widely credited with selflessly helping evacuate Vietnamese civilians who had worked for the Americans.

He apparently was unable to take Trai's family out, and he was evacuated from the roof of the U.S. Embassy as the city was falling.

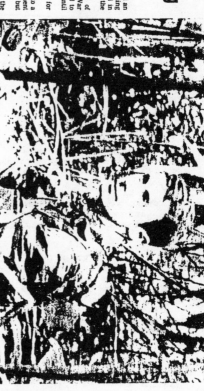

Former Green Beret Robert Schwab III shown in photo taken during his Vietnam combat duty

UNITED PRESS INTERNATIONAL

O'Donnell said Schwab re-established contact with Trai in 1981 and learned that she had been jailed twice for trying to flee Vietnam by boat. He also learned of the child.

After the war, Schwab remained in Southeast Asia and friends said he appeared tied to his experiences in Vietnam.

In Thailand, he worked on a project to eradicate opium, did research into alleged use of chemical warfare by the Vietnamese and joined anti-communist guerrillas for forays into Laos to search for Americans missing in action.

In the Philippines, he ran an ice cream and hamburger stand at Subic Bay, site of the American naval base.

U.S. officials made inquiries after he sailed from the Philippines on his search for Trai, but Vietnam initially said it knew nothing of him.

The White House said Thursday that the United States told Vietnamese officials in July 1985 the United States told Vietnamese officials in July 1985 that President Reagan was interested in the case. Childress was told to take up the case, and the Vietnamese informed him in late May of this year that Schwab was in the hands of local authorities.

Vietnam veteran begins MIA vigil in bamboo cage

MILWAUKEE (AP) — Gil La Gosh sat in a bamboo cage outside the War Memorial Center, keeping a vigil on a rainy Thursday for 37 Vietnam veterans who never came home.

"People don't remember," La Gosh said. "We were prompted to do this to catch people's attention."

La Gosh, vice president of the Wisconsin Vietnam Vets, and fellow veterans and family members plan to spend 37 days in the cage near Milwaukee's lakefront in honor of the 37 Wisconsin residents who are missing in action.

"You don't misplace 2,400 people in this day and age," said Gary Wetzel, a Medal of Honor recipient, speaking of those Americans whose whereabouts in Vietnam remain undetermined.

Wetzel is president of the Wisconsin group, which is sponsoring the demonstration, scheduled to end Sept. 19 with a rally on national POW recognition day.

"We are smart enough to realize there are not that many alive, but if one is alive, that person has a right to be here," he said. "We want people to write a letter to their congressmen and to the president and to demand, not ask, that something be done."

La Gosh, who entered the cage first Wednesday, said he conceived of the idea because he did not believe an occasional rally or vigil was keeping the MIAs in the public consciousness.

"This hardly amounts to suffering," La Gosh said. "For all we know, there are American servicemen in Southeast Asia who have been jailed for 20 years in conditions that aren't any more comfortable than this. At least I know I can get out of here in two days."

Those who are scheduled to take 24-hour shifts in the cage, which is 4 feet by 6 feet by 6 feet, include veterans of World War II and the Korean War, as well as Vietnam. Wives, parents of veterans, businessmen and police also have volunteered.

"We thought that, if just Vietnam veterans took part, people might think we're all crazy trying to do this," La Gosh said. "That is why others are taking part."

Wetzel said his group is not affiliated with any national organizations, and had about 70 members.

HEARING

BEFORE THE

SUBCOMMITTEE ON
ASIAN AND PACIFIC AFFAIRS

OF THE

COMMITTEE ON FOREIGN AFFAIRS
HOUSE OF REPRESENTATIVES

NINETY-SIXTH CONGRESS

SECOND SESSION

JUNE 27, 1980

Printed for the use of the Committee on Foreign Affairs

U.S. GOVERNMENT PRINTING OFFICE

67-214 O   WASHINGTON : 1980

So I join very closely with the views mentioned by General Tighe.

Mr. GUYER. Do people come and go in Laos? Is there very strict security?

Mr. MOSER. There is a certain amount of movement about within the country. It is not as much as we would like to see, and we hope that that can be improved. It is not totally a place——

Mr. GUYER. Not a tourist place, I am sure.

Mr. MOSER. It is not totally closed down. Mr. Dornan referred to it as the dark hole. Sort of living in a dark hole is an image that is difficult to think about. But being there, I feel that we can get some light information out of what is too dark a problem really to be acceptable.

Mr. GUYER. We thank you.

Mr. MYERS. I wonder if the general would respond to my question about sightings of live individuals, if there have been, and what conclusion might be made of those?

General PISCKNEY. Sir, as General Tighe said in his statement——

Mr. MYERS. I apologize; I wasn't here. I had a bill on the floor

CLASSIFYING REPORTS

General PISCKNEY. We keep reports of any live sightings classified because, if it became public, it could endanger anybody who is alive over there.

Mr. MYERS of Indiana. I misunderstood how you classify those sightings. I understood the fact that there have been sightings, which I didn't think were classified, but their location and their significance I understand were classified. Even the fact that there have been sightings is classified. Is that your response?

General PISCKNEY. I should defer to DIA on this.

Mr. MOSER. We are talking about reports of sightings. They have to be evaluated by the Defense Intelligence. Perhaps Admiral Tuttle——

Mr. GUYER. I think Admiral Tuttle probably has told us all within his domain to tell us. He has been here many, many times.

One of the things that has been a problem of this committee has been so many false reports from so many corners, and then the minute we call a press conference, I don't blame the press and the media for looking at us rather bluntly and saying, what is this all about—makes the fifth, sixth time you have called us in, and there is nothing you can prove.

So we are very reticent about times and dates and names and faces unless we have got corroborating evidence. However, I do think after we have had an opportunity to listen to all your testimony, we want to do some very close screening and evaluating to see what we come up with, and then return either on a classified or open session basis because this is just the beginning, not the end.

The fact everybody is scurrying today, I want to apologize. They are going to closed session at 3. There are fellows trying to catch airplanes and get home. So be it.

At the same time, we have waited a long time for some of you people to come here. The last time I saw Paul Mather was in Asia. I certainly am not going to go home—although some of you I know have appointments. (Others of us may have disappointments, but we are going to

Whenever you have to leave, we will understand, because I know this has been a long day for most of you.

Any comment on live sightings or—we have not really affirmed what our policy is on sightings anyhow, as to however we want to go before we make any announcement. We are hiding nothing from anybody, but we certainly don't want to get out here and create a furor of a lot of false hope for something that doesn't exist.

As far as the families go, let me say the League of Families, they are insensible to any kind of shock you can give them. Don't worry about them. What they have been doing, anything from here on out would be a Methodist picnic, anything you have to offer in summary.

Colonel Mather tells me he can stay a little longer. He doesn't have the same timeframe.

General PISCKNEY. Sir, there is a t me restriction in that we have buses available until 1:30 to take the group to wherever the destination is. The buses will disappear at 1:30 if they are not being boarded. I would suggest that you get Colonel Mather's statement.

Mr. GUYER. Let's get to Paul Mather. He is one of the men that went to Hanoi with us. He has been in Bangkok. He has been interviewing refugees. He was first given permission to go to Vietnam, then they turned around and, as far as I know, he didn't get back.

Colonel, would you like to get into that for us?

Mr. ARMACOST. Mr. Chairman, may I be excused?

Mr. GUYER. I understand. Thank you for staying as long as you did.

STATEMENT OF LT. COL. PAUL D. MATHER, USAF, LIAISON DIVISION, JOINT CASUALTY RESOLUTION CENTER

Colonel MATHER. I am going to abbreviate my statement.

First, I would like to point out that I am the liaison officer for the Joint Casualty Resolution Center. I would like to introduce my commander, Lt. Col. Steve Perry. He is the new commander of the Joint Casualty Resolution Center.

Mr. GUYER. Go ahead, Colonel.

Colonel MATHER. The headquarters of JCRC is located in Hawaii. Since mid-1976 I have been the organization's liaison officer in Bangkok. It is the activities of this office that I would like to report to you today.

Our office is physically located in the American Embassy in Bangkok, Thailand. It is now manned by three people. In addition to myself there is Mr. James E. Tully, a Department of Defense civilian, grade GS-13, and Gunnery Sgt. William S. Whorton, U.S. Marine Corps, grade E-7. Among the three of us we have over 18 man-years of experience with the casualty resolution issue. Both Mr. Tully and Sergeant Whorton are Vietnamese-speakers, and all of us have had prior experience in Vietnam working with Vietnamese officials in various capacities.

JCRC RESPONSIBILITIES

For the benefit of the subcommittee, I was asked to briefly describe what we do in the JCRC liaison office, and to tell how we do it.

I would like to discuss two particular areas. The first is the interviewing of Indochina refugees for POW and MIA information, and the second is our dealings with the Vietnamese Government.

With the termination of U.S. official presence in Vietnam and Cambodia in early 1975 and the isolation of the small remaining official American community in Laos from the Lao people and the countryside, our access to casualty information from within these countries came to a halt. Thus, as you are aware, we have resorted to the interviewing of refugees from these Indochinese countries in an attempt to continue the gathering of information which will hopefully assist in eventual resolution of the POW/MIA issue.

This program began in 1976, and it has now grown to the point that from our liaison office we are interviewing at all refugee camps in Thailand, Malaysia, Singapore, and Indonesia. Parenthetically, I would like to add that from JRCR Headquarters in Hawaii, interviewers are dispatched to the Philippines on a programed basis to talk to refugees there.

REFUGEE NUMBERS

Mr. Guyer. Could you tell us how many refugees you have actually talked to—I don't mean personally—that have been interrogated since the time you indicated? Has it gone into the thousands?

Colonel Mather. We have that we have actually talked to on a one-to-one basis, I could not give you a number, sir, but I can tell you a little bit about the screening process that leads us to talk to those refugees.

Mr. Guyer. Go ahead.

Colonel Mather. As I mentioned, there are hundreds of thousands of refugees in that area of the world now. We use various means to pinpoint refugees that could have information for us on this issue. Our interviewers go into the refugee camps. Some of the camps are equipped with loudspeaker systems and we announce our presence. We tell them what we are looking for.

We ask for people who have information of interest to us to come forward. In camps that don't have PA systems, we go in with posters. Recently we have incorporated a new feature, particularly in the Lao camps in Thailand, where the prescreeners, the people who are actually working with the refugee program and are gathering biodata on the refugees, ask each refugee that they talk to if they have any information of interest to us.

If they do, they make a note on their forms, which are now being put into a computer system, and we can, through the computer system, retrieve the names of all these people that answer in the affirmative. Then we go out to the camp, rather than ask the prescreeners to try to interview these people, because they have other duties to do. They turn the names over to us. Then we go out individually and interview these people.

Although there are hundreds of thousands of refugees there, we don't talk to everyone, but we do have procedures to pinpoint those individuals that would be worthwhile to talk to, and that have presented themselves——

HARDCORE CASES

Mr. Guyer. Would you want to take time just to tell the group here about the hardcore cases that you have laid on their desk. I know we referred to that before.

How many altogether were there that you took to Hanoi, and they agreed to look into every one of them? You have had it in two languages.

Colonel Mather. Referring to the case file here.

Mr. Guyer. How many were there altogether?

Colonel Mather. I believe there were 105 in the last group we turned over to Hanoi; of those 105 folders, I believe some contained more than one name.

Mr. Guyer. You gave them dates, disappearance dates, service dates, crash time dates, and you gave them photographs, identification, and no language barrier. They told you, as I recall, a table just like this one, you were welcome any time you wanted to come and they would work with you because you are an expert in this area?

Colonel Mather. Yes. These folders included a narrative of events in each case, the idea being to give them some sort of a hot trail, if you will, a place to start if they were themselves going to investigate this case.

Mr. Guyer. How many times did you get invited back into the country?

Colonel Mather. Since then, sir, the only time I have been back was in January 1980.

Mr. Guyer. And not a report on one of those cases?

Colonel Mather. Not a report, sir.

Mr. Guyer. All right. Go ahead, sir.

100 REPORTS SUBMITTED

Colonel Mather. I would like to point out that we have submitted quite a number of reports since we began this refugee interview program. Last year we submitted over 400 reports; this year we have submitted 100 thus far.

I might also point out that we are not the only ones that submit reports. The DIA gets reports from other resources. We are just one part of the whole picture.

Because we are the liaison office with a very limited staff—there are only three of us—we do not have the staff or the backup files to perform analysis on these reports. So we forward these reports through our headquarters in Hawaii, and they in turn forward them to DIA, and the analysis of these reports is done by the experts who have the assets to do this; namely, our headquarters and DIA.

Though we make no formal analysis, we cannot help forming some opinion as to the worth of what we are doing and of the results obtained. I would like to stress this point.

We do put a great deal of emphasis on the live sighting reports, and we carry on our work mindful of the possibility that there are possibly still Americans alive in Indochina.

Less publicized but also important is the compilation by JCRC of gravesite data. Additionally, with each interview we try to gather

38

detailed information about the sites of interest. Therefore, we hope to compile data which, through a cooperative effort with the Indochinese governments, could eventually lead to the recovery of the remains of those Americans who have died. This kind of information, gathered from refugee sources outside of the Indochinese countries, is unique, because it is doubtful we could get such information even if we were allowed to roam freely through the Indochinese countryside to question inhabitants.

DEALINGS WITH HANOI

I would like to mention briefly our dealings with the Vietnamese Government. One of the results of our discussions with a Vietnamese delegation to Hawaii in 1978 was the agreement that the JCRC Liaison Office in Bangkok would serve as a conduit for casualty resolution information to be passed back and forth between the United States and Vietnamese Governments. This was to be accomplished via the SRV Embassy in Bangkok.

From my perspective, our relations with the Vietnamese Embassy in Bangkok have been excellent. They willingly and faithfully pass information for us in both directions, but from the standpoint of useful results, the effort has been totally unproductive. This I attribute to conscious policy decisions made in Hanoi that cooperation will not be forthcoming until they perceive that it is in their own self-interest to cooperate.

At our level, it seems there is little that we can do to influence Vietnamese perceptions in this regard. Nevertheless, we continue to seek opportunities to keep this channel open, unproductive though it may be. For this reason, I try to meet briefly about once a month with Vietnamese Embassy officials, just to maintain this line of communication.

U.S. EMBASSY SUPPORT

Finally, I would like to add a few remarks about our liaison office support. I feel that, in carrying out our activities, we have been blessed with cooperation on the U.S. side. Ambassador Abramowitz and the Embassy staff in Bangkok have backed us completely. We get outstanding support from the officials in Kuala Lumpur, Singapore, and Jakarta. In Vientiane, Chargé Moser has embarked on a particularly aggressive campaign to encourage the Lao Government to be more forthcoming on the POW/MIA issue, and he has included us in all his planning. On the military side, support has been outstanding all the way up the chain of command.

This concludes my remarks concerning the activities of our liaison office in Bangkok. I would, again, like to thank the chairman and the subcommittee for allowing me to be here today.

Mr. GUYER. Thank you, Colonel.

One thing everybody knew but me is that you are all going to stay together and go to a panel. So any questions not asked here will likely be asked there. Since you have consented to do that, I think this is a terrific thing for all of you.

Let me say one thing before you do leave. Having visited the identification center in Honolulu, it is not true we have never had one remains of an American that we did not know who it was? Is that correct?

39

Colonel MATHER. I am not sure about that, sir. I believe we do have some—

Mr. GUYER. Even though you have examined other nationalities, we have never had an American that we could not identify, that this is the only war in which we had no unknown soldiers as such? I think that is true.

Is that right, Admiral?

Admiral TUTTLE. That is correct.

Mr. GUYER. If that is true, I think this is a tribute to the work of all of you.

With that I am going to thank you for your indulgence. You go to your buses. Remember, we are going to hold more meetings yet this year. If possible, the Lord willing, we want to go to Asia yet again this year.

[Whereupon, at 1:20 p.m., the subcommittee adjourned.]

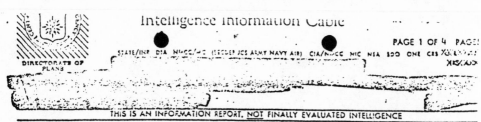

Intelligence Information Cable

DIRECTORATE OF PLANS

THIS IS AN INFORMATION REPORT, NOT FINALLY EVALUATED INTELLIGENCE

061442Z   CITE TDCS DB-315/04550-68

DIST 6 DECEMBER 1968

COUNTRY- LAOS   VH2048

DOI-   LATE 1965 - MARCH 1968   BAN LONG K

SUBJECT- AMERICAN, THAI, AND PHILIPPINE PRISONERS OF WAR

          HELD IN LAOS - LOCATIONS OF FOUR ENEMY PRISONS IN SOUTH

          LAOS

ACQ-

SOURCE-

1. DURING LATE 1967, 15 AMERICAN, FOUR THAI, AND ONE

PHILIPPINO PRISONERS OF WAR WERE INCARCERATED IN A PRISON

CAVE COMPLEX NEAR BAN LONG KOU /UNLOCATED, POSSIBLY VH 2048/,

#6

APPROVED FOR RELEASE
DATE ...2.......1978........

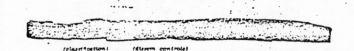

(classification)   (dissem controls)

26 KILOMETERS EAST OF SAM NEUA /VH 0358/ IN HOUA PHAN PROVINCE.
TWO OF THE AMERICAN PRISONERS WERE A MAJOR AND A LIEUTENANT
COLONEL WHO WERE SHOT DOWN WITH THEIR F105 JET NEAR BAN LONG
KOU IN LATE MARCH OR EARLY MAY 1965. THE PLANE WAS PUT ON
EXHIBITION AT LONG KOU. IN LATE 1965, FIVE OF THE ABOVE
PRISONERS WERE MOVED FROM THE LONG KOU COMPLEX TO AN UNKNOWN
LOCATION IN XIENG KHOUANG PROVINCE. COMMENT- THERE ARE
CONFIRMED REPORTS OF PRISONS AT VH 0157 AND VH 0158 IN WHICH
AMERICAN PILOTS, POSSIBLY SIX, ARE INCARCERATED.

2. ALL OF THE AMERICAN, THAI, AND PHILIPPINO PRISONERS
WERE IN GOOD PHYSICAL CONDITION. THEY RECEIVED THE SAME FOOD
RATIONS AS PATHET LAO /PL/ FIELD GRADE OFFICERS AND WERE GIVEN
BREAD TO EAT IN PLACE OF RICE.

3. ALL FLIERS SHOT DOWN IN LAOS ARE KEPT IN LAOS AND NOT
SENT TO NORTH VIETNAM. VERY FEW FLIERS HAVE BEEN DOWNED AND
CAPTURED IN SOUTH LAOS AS PL FORCES IN SOUTH LAOS HAVE
VERY LITTLE ANTIAIRCRAFT /AA/ CAPABILITY WITH WHICH TO DOWN PLANES.
COMMENT- THE ABOVE STATEMENT PROBABLY DOES NOT INCLUDE
THE CONSIDERABLE AA DEFENSES FOUND ALONG INFILTRATION
ROUTES IN SOUTH LAOS./ THE 16TH PL AA BATTALION /BN/

IN -48941

TDCS DS-315/04550-68

PAGE 3 OF 4 PAGES

WAS REPORTED TO HAVE SHOT DOWN AN F4H JET AND AN F105 JET ON THE
SAME DAY IN EARLY JANUARY 1968 NEAR THE NOW DESTROYED SE /RIVER/ BAN
HIENG/ ROUTE 23 BRIDGE AT XC 028998. THE CREWS OF BOTH PLANES WERE
KILLED.

COMMENT- THIS INFORMATION WAS OBTAINED FROM AN OFFICIAL
REPORT OF THE F4H/F105 INCIDENT AT SOUTH LAOS REGIONAL HEADQUARTERS
/HQ/. COMMENT- CURRENT ORDER OF BATTLE LISTINGS CARRY THE F
16TH AA ARTILLERY BN WITH 220 MEN AT XD 0329./

4. AS OF MARCH 1968 FOUR PRISONS IN SOUTH LAOS HOLDING MILITARY
INMATES WERE IN THE FOLLOWING AREAS. FIFTY GUERRILLA AND LAO ARMED
FORCES PRISONERS WERE INCARCERATED NEAR MAHAXAY /WE 2125/. ONE
HUNDRED AND FIFTY MILITARY INMATES WERE IN A PRISON NEAR ANG
KHAM /UNLOCATED, POSSIBLY BAN ANG KHAM XD 3047/. ONE HUNDRED
PRISONERS WERE NEAR MUONG PHINE /XD 0927/. TWENTY MILITARY
PRISONERS WERE HELD AT THE SOUTH LAOS REGIONAL HQ PRISON NORTH OF
MUONG PHINE. COMMENT- THE ABOVE FIGURES REPRESENT ONLY
MILITARY PRISONERS AND NOT CIVILIANS WHO ARE OFTEN INTERNED IN
THE SAME PRISON WITH MILITARY INMATES. THE FIGURES CAME FROM
SUPPLY REQUESTS SUBMITTED TO SOUTH LAOS REGIONAL HQ DURING MARCH
1968. COMMENT- THE PRISON NEAR MAHAXAY MAY

IN -48941

TDCS DB-315/04550-68

PAGE 4 OF 4 PAGES

(classification)   *(dissem controls)*

BE IDENTICAL TO ONE OF THE PRISONS IN THE BAN NADEN /WE 433332/-
BAN NATHAN /WE 395311/ SECTOR, WHERE PRISONS HAVE BEEN CONFIRMED A
WE 378364 AND WE 4032. A PRISON WITH MORE THAN 100 INMATES IS
CONFIRMED AT XD 3357 AS IS ANOTHER DETAINING OVER 100 FAR SOLDIERS
XD 365508. A PRISON WITH APPROXIMATELY 100 PRISONERS AND 30 PL
GUARDS IS LOCATED NEAR THE SOUTH LAOS REGIONAL PL HQS AT XD 0927./

5. ▨ DISSEM- STATE ARMY AIR USMACV 7TH AIR FORCE
CINCPAC PACFLT ARPAC PACAF

UNITED STATES DISTRICT COURT
SOUTHERN DISTRICT OF FLORIDA

CASE NO. 86-1146-CIV-KING

TONY AVIRGAN, and   )   AMENDED COMPLAINT
MARTHA HONEY,   )   FOR RICO CONSPIRACY, etc.
)
        Plaintiffs   )
)
v.   )
)
JOHN HULL, BRUCE JONES,   )
RENE CORBO,   )
FELIPE VIDAL SANTIAGO,   )
MOISES DAGOBERTO NUNEZ   )
FRANCISCO CHANES,   )
RAMON CECILIO PALACIO,   )
RICARDO GRIS, WILLIAM GRIS,)
ROGER LEE PALLAIS   )
AMAC GALIL   )
HECTOR CORNILLOT, JORGE GONZALEZ,)
ADOLFO CALERO,   )
ALVARO CRUZ, FREDERICO SAENZ,)
ROBERT W. OWEN, JOHN K. SINGLAUB,)
RONALD JOSEPH MARTIN, SR.,   )
JAMES MCCOY, THOMAS POSEY,   )
RAFAEL "CHI CHI" QUINTERO,   )
MARIO DELAMICO,   )
THOMAS CLINES,   )
THEODORE SHACKLEY,   )
ALBERT HAKIM, RICHARD SECORD)
PABLO ESCOBAR, and JORGE OCHOA,)
)
)
        Defendants   )
)

COMPLAINT FOR DAMAGES AND OTHER RELIEF

    Plaintiffs Avirgan and Honey, by their attorneys, file
this Complaint against Defendants, and in support thereof
allege as follows:

John Hull in northern Costa Rica.

24. Frederico Saenz
Frederico Saenz, on information and belief, is a citizen of Nicaragua. He resides on the ranch of Defendant John Hull in Costa Rica.

25. Robert W. Owen
Robert W. Owen is a citizen of the United States and a citizen and resident of the State of Virginia. Robert Owen is president of a private business organization, IDEA, Inc.

26. Thomas Posey
Thomas Posey is a citizen of the United States and a citizen and resident of the State of Alabama. Tom Posey is the founder and the Executive Director of Civilian Materiel Assistance ("CMA", formerly called Civilian Military Assistance), a mercenary and para-military organization doing business in the Southern District of Florida which is providing military assistance to guerrillas, known as contras, fighting to overthrow the government of Nicaragua.

27. John K. Singlaub
John K. Singlaub is a citizen of the United States and a citizen and resident of the State of Colorado. Defendant Singlaub is the Chairman of the Board of Directors of the World Anti-Communist League, President of the United States Council on World Freedom, and a former co-director of the American Security Council.

28. James McCoy
James McCoy is a citizen of the United States and a citizen and resident of the State of Florida, residing within the Southern District of Florida. Defendant McCoy is the owner and operator of R&M Equipment Co., doing business in the Southern District of Florida.

29. Ronald Joseph Martin, Sr.
Ronald Joseph Martin, Sr. is a citizen of the United States and a citizen and resident of the State of Florida, residing within the Southern District of Florida. Defendant Ronald Joseph Martin, Sr. is the owner and operator of the Tamiami Gun Shop, of Miami.

30. Rafael "Chi Chi" Quintero
Rafael "Chi Chi" Quintero is a citizen of the United States, a citizen of Cuba and a citizen and resident of the State of Florida, residing within the Southern District of Florida. Defendant Quintero is the owner and operator of the Orca Supply Co., with offices in Coral Gables, Florida.

31. Mario Delamico
Mario Delamico is a citizen of the United States, domiciled in Florida,
presently residing in Honduras. Defendant Delamico is a business associate
of Defendant Ronald Joseph Martin, Sr.

32. Thomas Clines
Thomas Clines is a citizen of the United States, a citizen and resident
of Virginia, and is a business associate of Defendants Shackley, Secord,
Hakim and Quintero in Orca Supply Co., in Stanford Technology Trading Group,
and in CSF Investments Ltd., a Bahamian corporation, the stock of which is
owned by Compagnie de Services Fiduciare with offices in Geneva,
Switzerland.

33. Theodore Shackley
Theodore Shackley is a citizen of the United States and a citizen and
resident of the State of Virginia. Shackley is associated with Orca Supply
Co., CSF Investments Ltd., and Stanford Technology Trading Group

34. Richard Secord
Richard Secord is a citizen of the United States and a citizen and
resident of the State of Virginia. Secord is associated with CSF
Investments Ltd., Orca Supply Co., and Stanford Technology Trading Group.

35. Albert Hakim
Albert Hakim, on information and belief, is a citizen of the United
States and a citizen of the State of Virginia, doing business as Stanford
Technology Trading Group, 8615 Westmoreland Dr., Vienna, Virginia. Hakim is
associated with CSF Investments Ltd. and Orca Supply Co.

36. Pablo Escobar
Pablo Escobar is a citizen of the Republic of Colombia.

37. Jorge Ochoa
Jorge Ochoa is a citizen of the Republic of Colombia and was last
reported residing in prison in Colombia. He was awaiting extradition to the
Southern District of Florida for cocaine smuggling when he escaped from the
custody of Colombian authorities.

BANGKOK POST SUNDAY APRIL 25, 1982

EXTRA

An incredible tale of duplicity

Indo-China watcher ALAN DAWSON tells of his encounter with an American ex-military man who claimed, among other things, to be on a secret mission to hunt POWs in Laos.

Mekong River seen from Nakhon Phanom Province.

AN American anti-CIA publication, the Covert Action Information Bulletin; and the New York City newspaper Daily World, quite a rare retailing in anybody's book.

... financed by Korean religious leader and businessman Sun Myung Moon, say The United ...

... only town with a similar name on ... number 120 kilometres from Vientiane. That's ...

(Later news reports identified the operational part of this plan as Operation Velvet Hammer.)

He told CAIB and the Monitor newspaper that the first team had been captured. The CIA-standard ...

tian to Daniel C. Arnold, a former CIA station chief in Laos and now a private consultant just outside Washington, DC. Barnes said Arnold was a major figure in the Lao infiltration operation.

The credibility of Barnes is ... somewhat deranged when he identifies ...

several prominent Laotians ... the 1975 Communist takeover that he received — and forwarded — to Vang Pao and former CIA chief Chao Sisouk — the ... Barnes took back from Thai ...

— Bo Gritz, a colourful Army officer who has ...

States may have planted "yellow rain" samples in Laos. They also say that the second of two missions into Laos last year was sent to search for — and if necessary assassinate — the first.

Vietnam News Agency, not surprisingly, has been a major spreader of the stories in this part of the world, and the name of Scott Barnes has suddenly grown beyond the small group of Laos-watchers who previously knew it.

Barnes (see accompanying story) has told the anti-spy CAIB, which has won its fame by printing the names of alleged CIA agents for the past several years, an incredible tale of duplicity. It's a spy novel by itself and, who knows, it could even be true, unlikely though that possibility is.

Barnes claims that last October, he and five other "team members," along with about 30 Hmong combatants from the former Vang Pao force clandestinely crossed the Mekong River from the Thai village of Ban Pheng to Laos, "west of Mahaxay."

In a straight line, Mahaxay is 40 kilometres east of the Thai border city of Nakhon Phanom. Amphoe Ban Phaeng in the northern part of Nakhon Phanom Province, the

Ban Pheng to "west of Mahaxay" is less geographically informative than telling someone trying to find your house for dinner that it is "in Bangkok."

Barnes claims that a similar team to his had preceded him into Laos, as part of what he calls "Operation Velvet Glove," to try to obtain photographic proof that US prisoners were being held in Laos.

try to rescue them, but to kill them if necessary to keep them from talking.

The only identification he carried — or was able to produce later — is what the Daily World called an official-looking business card, embossed with the seal of the United States, identifying them as members of the staff of ultra-rightist US Congressman Robert K.

the first team, Barnes speculated that "possibly the United States was involved in getting chemical warfare biological stuff over there." In other words the first team was "seeding" false evidence which later would be picked up by Laotian resistance members or others.

Barnes also said he carried back from Thailand a letter from a Lao-

somewhat strained when he'd mistles the Bangkok station chief of the CIA as Mike Eiland. Eiland, who last year was named by the pro-Hanoi Australian journalist John Pilger as US military chief of operations in Kampuchea, is head of the refugee section at the US Embassy.

Arnold admitted to the newspaper only that he had helped Laotian infiltration mission.

Beret officer who has become a primary source to some researchers on POWs. Told the newspaper that evidence brought back by the two missions launched into Laos last year was "worthless".

But even Gritz, who admits to knowing Barnes well, apparently was unable or unwilling to confirm that Barnes played any part in the Laotian infiltration mission.

Barnes claims that a similar team to his had preceded him into Laos, as part of what he calls "Operation Velvet Glove," to try to obtain photographic proof that US prisoners were being held in Laos...

The first team had been captured. The CIA ordered him and his team to locate the first, try to rescue them, but to kill them if necessary to keep them from talking.

Sunday - March 8 '87

Australian probe names several North associates

The New York Times

WASHINGTON — Several former military and intelligence officers who helped Lt. Col. Oliver L. North ship weapons to Iran and Central America were associated closely with the co-founder of an Australian financial concern that collapsed in 1980, according to an Australian government investigation.

The collapse of the financial concern came amid charges that it had laundered money earned from sales of weapons and illicit drugs.

Among those linked to the failed Sydney-based concern, Nugan Hand Bank, and its co-founder, Michael J. Hand, was Richard V. Secord, a retired Air Force major general who helped North conduct airlifts of weapons to the Middle East and Central America, according to the 4-year-old Australian investigation.

The Australian study, parts of which are secret, was conducted by the Commonwealth-New South Wales Joint Task Force on Drug Trafficking and was completed in March 1983. Although it is not new, the study is receiving scrutiny again in Washington because of the details it contains about activities and movement of weapons around the world by many of the same figures involved in the Iran-"contra" affair.

The Australian report, which has stirred U.S. congressional interest, also concluded that several former Central Intelligence Agency officials and contract operatives, among them Theodore G. Shackley, Thomas G. Clines and Rafael Quintero, were involved in military and intelligence-related activities with Hand and other top officers of the Nugan Hand concern.

The Tower Commission report on the Iran-contra affair and other published reports have linked all of these men to operations in the Middle East and Central America directed by North, the National Security Council aide dismissed in November by President Reagan.

The Australian study does not demonstrate that Secord, Shackley, Clines or Quintero smuggled weapons or narcotics. It does, however, say that these men were close to Hand, a former Army Green Beret and military intelligence officer who served in Laos during the late 1960s with a CIA-owned airline named Air America.

ROBERT J. LAGOMARSINO
19TH DISTRICT, CALIFORNIA

2332 RAYBURN BUILDING
WASHINGTON, D.C. 20515
202-225-3601

ASSISTANT REGIONAL WHIP, PLAINS AND
WESTERN STATES

Congress of the United States
House of Representatives
Washington, D.C. 20515

August 10, 1981

COMMITTEE ON
FOREIGN AFFAIRS
SUBCOMMITTEES:
INTERNATIONAL ECONOMIC POLICY
AND TRADE
RANKING MINORITY MEMBER
INTER-AMERICAN AFFAIRS

COMMITTEE ON
INTERIOR AND INSULAR
AFFAIRS
SUBCOMMITTEES:
INSULAR AFFAIRS
RANKING MINORITY MEMBER
PUBLIC LANDS AND NATIONAL PARKS

Mr. Scott Barnes
P.O. Box 863
Kernville, California 93238

Dear Mr. Barnes:

Thank you for contacting me about Captain Harley Hall.

I certainly share your grave concern about the unwillingness of the communist Vietnamese government to provide complete information about our MIA's. I visited Hanoi in August 1979 and forthrightly discussed the issue with Vietnamese government officials. They promised cooperation, including regular visits by U.S. experts. We even provided them with information on specific cases. But, to date, their pledge has not been honored. Recently they did allow members of the Joint Casualty Committee from Hawaii to visit Hanoi. The Vietnamese also said they would release three bodies. While there is great question about live prisoners, I am convinced that Hanoi is holding or has information on hundreds of remains.

The issue is still being pursued by the House Subcommittee on Asian and Pacific Affairs, and its adjunct, the Foreign Affairs Task Force on Americans Missing in Southeast Asia, of which I am a member. Additionally, an inter-agency group consisting of representatives from the Defense Department, Central Intelligence Agency, State Department, and the National League of Families has been organized to investigate reported live sightings of Americans held against their will in Southeast Asia. I am gratified by news stories that the Administration organized a daring intelligence mission to verify photographs which they thought may have indicated Americans were being held in Laos. Unfortunately, the stories indicate that no Americans were discovered.

I am confident that the new Administration will push the issue to the forefront. However, I am also sure the Vietnamese government will demand an outrageous price for information about our people. They obviously have no consideration for the anguish they are causing the families and friends of the missing.

I will certainly continue to work in Congress to see that a full accounting of our servicemen is made, and that all bodies and any live prisoners are returned.

Again, thank you for your interest.

Sincerely,

ROBERT J. LAGOMARSINO
Member of Congress

RJL:crm
Enclosure

Guests

Date	Name	Address	
8/6 2	Mr. Frederick Fenton	STREET 3571 Ocean View Ave.	397-8
Feast of the Transfiguration of Christ / Hiroshima Day		Los Angeles STATE Ca	9006
3/6/81	Maria P. Petrzyla	STREET 2743 Veteran Avenue	475
	HIROSHIMA DAY	CITY LA Ca STATE 9	9006
/6/51	LEONARD GREENBERG	STREET 766 K m M Hd	
		CITY S. M STATE	
3/6/81	PAULETTE B. DOULATSHAHE	STREET 13530 Beach Bonn Way #49B	
		CITY M. D. R STATE Ca 7081	
3/7/81	Bradley Peterson	STREET 23666 Schoenb...	
		CITY Canoga Park STATE	
3/12/81	J...il Jemn...	STREET 15467 Dickenset	
		CITY Sherman Oak STATE CA	
3/26/81	Scott Baur	STREET	
		CITY STATE	
3/26/81	L Gritz	STREET 7654 Holy Cross	
		CITY Westchester STATE CA 645-7
2/26/81	Xeuvong ...	STREET 1116 S. Bristol	
		CITY S A STATE Ca	199-2
	Genving Pov	STREET 1116 S Bristol	556
		CITY SA Ca 77474 STATE	77
3/27/51	David ...	STREET 13776 ...	
	PETE WHITNEY	CITY STATE	
		STREET	
		CITY STATE	
		STREET	
		CITY STATE	
		STREET	
		CITY STATE	
		STREET	
		CITY STATE	

ROBERT K. DORNAN
27TH DISTRICT, CALIFORNIA

FOREIGN AFFAIRS

AFRICA

ASIAN AND PACIFIC AFFAIRS

TASK FORCE ON MISSING-IN-ACTION

HUMAN RIGHTS AND INTERNATIONAL
ORGANIZATIONS

**SELECT COMMITTEE ON
AGING**

**SELECT COMMITTEE ON
NARCOTICS ABUSE
AND CONTROL**

TASK FORCE ON DRUG ABUSE IN THE
MILITARY

SPECIAL COMMITTEE ON
HOUSE RECORDING

Congress of the United States
House of Representatives
Washington, D.C. 20515

August 28, 1981

WASHINGTON OFFICE:
332 CANNON HOUSE OFFICE BUILDING
WASHINGTON, D.C. 20515
(202) 225-6451

DISTRICT OFFICES:
6151 WEST CENTURY BOULEVARD
SUITE 1018
LOS ANGELES, CALIFORNIA 90045
(213) 642-5111

1815 VIA EL PRADO
SUITE 207
REDONDO BEACH, CALIFORNIA 90277
(213) 540-2951

Mr. Scott Barnes
P.O. 863
Kernville, CA 93238

Dear Scott:

Thank you for arranging the meeting
on Wednesday. Even if I cannot arrange
any help from this end, I feel the time
was well spent.

As you are aware, I am having trouble
convincing the appropriate people that the
Congressman should get involved. Credibility
seems to be the question. I will obtain
the appropriate articles to verify this
weekend.

Enclosed is additional correspondence
that may help acquaint you with the Congressman's perspective on the issue.

I will be in touch soon.

Again, thanks for the meeting. You've
got a lot of support in this corner.

Sincerely,

STAN MULLIN

United States Department of State

Washington, D.C. 20520

September 29, 1981

Mr. Scott Barnes
Post Office Box 863
Kernville, California 93238

Dear Mr. Barnes:

I am replying to your message to President Reagan concerning
a proper accounting for the Americans still missing in Southeast
Asia. I regret the delay in this response.

The U.S. Government shares your concern and has pursued such
an accounting actively and consistently. We have raised the subject in all our contacts with Vietnamese and Lao authorities,
making clear the importance we attach to obtaining as much information as possible, as well as the return of recoverable remains.
In addition, we have sought information from Indochinese refugees
that might shed light on the fate of those Americans lost in connection with the Indochina conflict.

We are aware of numerous reports in the past year of Americans being held against their will in Indochina. Despite careful
investigation, we have thus far been unable to substantiate these
reports. Nonetheless, we continue to press the Vietnamese and
Lao authorities for all available information on our missing
servicemen. Although both governments claim to accept in principle their humanitarian duty to account for missing Americans they
are far from fulfilling that obligation. The Vietnamese and Lao
Governments assert that they are holding no Americans captive,
yet they have done little to prove that assertion.

In an effort to elicit information from the Vietnamese Government, representatives of our Joint Casualty Resolution Center
(JCRC) visited Hanoi in October 1980. When members of the JCRC
visited Hanoi again in May 1981, Vietnamese authorities offered
to return the remains of three American servicemen. These
remains were returned to us on July 7 and have now been verified
to be those of Navy Commander Ronald Dodge, Air Force Captain
Richard Van Dyke and Navy Lieutenant Stephen Musselman. We
welcome this development and hope it indicates that our efforts
may be having some success. We would like to see many more
visits to Hanoi by the JCRC, so that we might expedite the pain-
staking task of accounting for the nearly 2,500 American personnel still unaccounted for in Southeast Asia.

I assure you that the resolution of the POW/MIA issue is a
matter of high priority for this Administration. As a sign of
his concern, President Reagan proclaimed July 17, 1981 as

- 2 -

National POW/MIA Recognition Day. Ceremonies honoring American
POW/MIAs were held at the Pentagon to recognize the sacrifice
these brave men have made for their country.

Sincerely,

Francis Terry McNamara
Acting Assistant Secretary
for Public Affairs

DEFENSE INTELLIGENCE AGENCY
WASHINGTON, D.C. 20301

LTC James G. Gritz
Chief, Congressional Relations
OSD/DSAA

Bo:

Received your retirement notice. I have mixed emotions about your hanging it up to pursue this PW/MIA matter but, frankly I don't know anyother way of getting to the bottom of it all. Understand the Hughes arrangement is satisfactory. You should enjoy spending the winter in California. Your desire to put your career on hold is appreciated. Your experience in special operations can be used to best advantage. When this matter is concluded there will be strong support for your return to active duty. Depending on politics that should not be a problem.

Keep your government contacts limited to those with an absolute need to know. The word spreads fast here in Washington. I'll do what I can before checking out of the net myself. I trust you will have no problem developing a flow of information. It is too bad we have to proceed this way but the Administration will not face up to the problem. Gen Tighe is well aware of the situation but, his hands are tied. He is a true soldier in a blue suit.

Because of the politics involved, contact me only if you get in a spot with no way out. This thing is so sensitive it could result in a real inquisition if word leaked out that we were proceeding unofficially. This is a real hot potato so watch your back trail carefully. We will arrange to meet as time and circumstances allow. Of course if you uncover something critical contact me immediately. Keep the press and government offices out of it.

Bo, you have the experience and background to confirm this thing one way or another. Don't do anything to endanger your life or the lives of those we left behind. I am confident that once you prove beyond a doubt that our men are still captive the system will do the rest. Your task is not to be a one-man show but, to pull together evidence to convince political skeptics of PW existance. You will be free to do whatever is required on the outside.

Bo, destroy this and all other written communication between us.

De opresso liber!

36-A-1

WAT PHRA SI RATTANASATSADARAM

ประเทศไทย THAILAND

JANNY KROHBREL
3477 MARIOPA ST #35
TORRANCE, CALIF.
U.S.A 90503

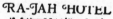

ทั้งครั้งที่ ๒ SECOND FOLD HERE →

THE ROYAL BARGE SRI SUPHANAHONG

ชื่อและตำบลที่อยู่ของผู้ฝาก SENDER'S NAME AND ADDRESS

_____

_____

_____

_____

ถ้าสกกรี่มีได้ไว้ในซอง จะส่งจดหมายอากาศนี้ไปทางถววเมา
IF ANYTHING IS ENCLOSED THIS AIR LETTER WILL BE SENT BY SURFACE MAIL

TO OPEN S

OLD HERE →

RA-JAH HOTEL
18 Sukhumvit Soi 4 (Nana South)
Bangkok, Thailand.
Tel. 2525102-7, 2518563-9
Cable: "RA-JAHOTEL BANGKOK"
450 ROOMS

ประเทศไทย THAILAND

BY AIR MAIL
PAR AVION

JANNY KROHBREL
3477 MARIOPA APT #35
TORRANCE, CALIF.
90503

USA

Dear Janny

Well I am finally back from the jungle now, so I can write you a decent letter.

So far things have been very un-easy here several americans have been killed and two days ago some surveillers killed a christian missionary the country is very unstable currently, I am in the very N/E section on the Mekong River at Laos, there's been plenty of traveling up & down the River for us all the tension is getting hard on of a couple of guys, yesterday I was up in a village handing out medicine & food when two soviet planes buzzed by us, so we left first before any communist troops came, well my job is finished here, it's now up to our Gov't to do the rest, we've located few prison camp But situation looks grim. I'm not sure what I'll do next, but I will devot my life to serving Christ, it's Been very difficult to keep in the word But I'm trusing, when keep us all in prayer I'm going to try & get out soon. Love in Christ Scott

ສຸຣິນຍະນ້ຳ ຫນວງຄຳ ທີ 25·10·1981

ຮຽນ

ທ່ານ ບຸນ ພົມ ວົງ ປ່າວ ທີ່ ເຄົາ ຣົບ ນັບ ຖື

[handwritten Lao letter text]

... Mr. BARNES ... JIM BATH ...

... Vang Yi ...

... Col Bounbayh Sisouthone ...

... U.S.A ...

... 11/7/1981 ...

... 12/8/1975 ...

... 3·1981 ...

... 1977 ...

mon adresse :

Kham Quan DOUANGPHRACHANH
570/4 PRACHACK ROAD
NONGKHAI THAILAND.

INTERNATIONAL INSTITUTE OF AKRON, INC. • 207 E. Tallmadge Ave., Akron, Ohio USA 44310-3298

Nongkhai Refugee Camp   Oct. 25, 1981   31A

Respect to Mr. General Vang Pao

I am Ex--Lt. Col. Kham Ouane Douangphrachanh, Secretary of Mr. Nachampachack Sisouk, Defense Minister of Laos. I was hoping Mr. General and your family are in good health. I went to Seminar since August 12, 1975 in Mung Vieng Say (Vieng Say City).

I got off from Seminar in March 1981. I and my family escaped from Lao Communists to Nongkhai Lao Refugee Camp in Thailand on July 11, 1981. I had heard about Mr. General with Mr. Barnes and Mr. Jim Bath. They know very well about Mr. General. Vang Yi wrote the letter to introduce me. How to come to see Lt. Col. Soubanh Sisounthone for some work. I wrote this letter to Mr. General. I am very glad. Because Mr. General worry about our country and is against the Communists. I am in agreement to fight the Communists back.

I would like to help you with anything I can do while I live in the refugee camp. In my mind I need to come to the U.S.A. for the sake of my family. Because I went to Seminar, I had worked hard with not enough food and clothing many years ago. If my family came to live in a safe place, I want to go back to fight against the Communists. I wrote a letter to Mr. Nachampachack Sisouk in French.

They had put many General Lao Army and many ministers in jail. Their names are: The General Boun Pone, Pha Souk, Ly Ratanabanlang, Chao Sinh Saysana, Thong Phanh Kanocksy, Sourith, Kane Insixiengmay, Nou Pheth and Mr. Pheng Phongsavanh, Minister. Mr. Soukanh, Minister, Phayatou Ly Fung, Minister, and Mr. Pravongviengkham, Minister.

They had many Generals and Minister killed. They left a few Generals and Ministers.

I would like to know how I and my family can come to the U.S.A. Please, Mr. General, help our family.

In 1981 the Nai Khai Refugee Camp in Thailand temporarily closed and did not receive refugees. They had sent the refugees back to Laos. But, I can't go back to Laos and I can't stay with the Communists. Because I just got off from Seminar Camp in March, 1981. The Military Officer, Police Officer and Civil Servant went to Seminar in the camp No. 3, 4, 5 and 6 in Mung Viengxay (Viengxay City) local. Now they escaped from Laos to the Nong Khai Refugee Camp in Thailand. There were about 54 persons. I myself would like to come to the U.S.A. I need Mr. General's help and please tell how I and my family can come to the U.S.

Finally, I pray that Mr. General and your family are in good health and have good luck.

My address is: Kham Ouane Douangprachanh
                570/4 Prachack Road
                Nongkhai, Thailand

I certify hereby that the foregoing is to the best of my knowledge and belief a true and correct translation of the original document in the _____Lao_____ language.

                        s/ _____
                           Translator

STATE OF OHIO)   Sworn to and subscribed before me this __25th__
)SS   day of __June_____ 19 _87___ at Akron,
SUMMIT COUNTY)   Ohio.

                    · Notary

Daniel C Arnold
1705 Fox Run Ct
Vienna, Va 22180

FIRST CLASS MAIL

Mr Scott T. Barnes
952 Calle Mirmar
Redondo Beach
California   90277

FIRST CLASS MAIL

Daniel C. Arnold

President

Tashkent Associates
International Research
Associates

1705 Fox Run Ct.
Vienna, Va. 22180
(703) 938-1868

Scott —
Thanks for the letter
from D. I have forwarded to
Chao Sirasuk and to Vang Pao.
Best wishes
Dan

AMERICA'S STRATEGIC CHALLENGE IN SOUTHEAST ASIA

By
Daniel C. Arnold
and
Michael A. Daniels

INTERNATIONAL PUBLIC POLICY FOUNDATION, INC.

THE AUTHORS

Daniel C. Arnold

Daniel C. Arnold, 56, retired in 1979 from the Central Intelligence Agency after more than 35 years of service working on and in Asia. He is President of International Research Associates, Inc., a consulting firm that specializes in Asia.

Michael A. Daniels

Michael A. Daniels is the President of the International Public Policy Foundation, Inc. and President of the International Public Policy Research Corporation. He is a specialist in foreign affairs and national security planning. He is an attorney by training with emphasis on international law.

INCIDENT REPORT

SAIC ☐
DSAIC ☐
ASAIC ___ *OPB/F*

C0286187 · DATE/TIME RECEIVED: ___ 12/23/81 194 __

R-1 ☐ DI
R-2 ☐ OP
R-3 ☐ CI
R-4 ☐ FI
FIB ☐

ION RECEIVED BY: ___ SA ▓▓▓▓▓▓▓ ___ TMF

LE OF CALLER: ___ SA ▓▓▓▓▓▓ ___ PHONE: ___ 12-30-81 A

OFFICE ADDRESS: ___ LAFO

OTHER___

****

OF INFORMATION: ☒ THREAT   ☐ INCIDENT/DEMONSTRATION   ☐ ABUSIVE LANGUAGE

FILE UPDATE ONLY   ☐ SUSPICIOUS ACTIVITY   ☐ OTHER: ___

CTION OF INTEREST: ___ President

'S NAME: ___ ▓▓▓▓▓▓▓▓▓▓ ___   ☐ NRID   ☐ NCI

☐ NCIC/CCH NEGATIVE
☐ NCIC/CCH PENDING
PHONE: ___

TION: ___

DATA: ___

****

TIVE:

▓▓▓▓▓▓▓▓▓▓▓▓▓▓▓▓▓▓▓▓▓▓▓▓▓▓▓▓▓▓

Also that Scott Barnes W/M 7/14/45 FBI # 33905F and lives with
his father in Redondo Beach CA ▓▓▓▓▓▓▓▓▓▓▓▓▓▓▓▓
▓▓▓▓ and ▓▓▓▓ and SAs of the FBI will attempt to interview him tomo
Barnes is also described as ▓▓▓▓▓▓▓▓▓▓▓▓▓▓▓▓

SA ▓▓▓ also stated that he will call FIB tomorrow after interview
Barnes.

275LAX 1250EDT 061782 USS173

//PRIORITY//

FM LOS ANGELES

TO INTELLIGENCE DIVISION - FILE:ME
   SAN DIEGO
   FRESNO RA

INFO SACRAMENTO

SUBJECT: ☐ SCOTT TRACY BARNES

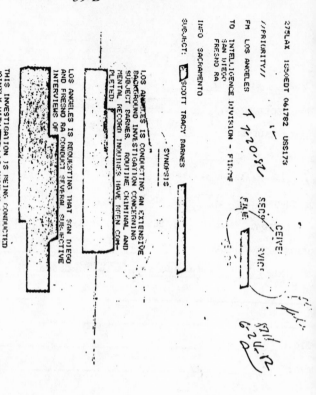

SYNOPSIS

LOS ANGELES IS CONDUCTING AN EXTENSIVE
BACKGROUND INVESTIGATION CONCERNING
SUBJECT BARNES. ROUTINE CRIMINAL AND
MENTAL RECORD INQUIRIES HAVE BEEN COM-
PLETED.

LOS ANGELES IS REQUESTING THAT SAN DIEGO
AND FRESNO RA CONDUCT SEVERAL SUBJECTIVE
INTERVIEWS OF

THIS INVESTIGATION IS BEING CONDUCTED
JOINTLY WITH THE LOS ANGELES DIVISION.

CASE CONTINUED AT LOS ANGELES PENDING
COMPLETION OF ABOVE INQUIRIES.

A) INTRODUCTION

REFERENCE IS MADE TO ALL PREVIOUS CORRESPONDENCE IN THIS CASE. THE MOST
RECENT BEING LOS ANGELES TELETYPE #252, DATED 6/16/82.

B) IDENTITY AND BACKGROUND OF SUBJECT

PAGE 2 275LAX 1250EDT 061782

- NAME   : SCOTT TRACY BARNESS
- ALIAS   : NONE KNOWN
- CURRENT/HOME ADDRESS   : 952 CALLE MIRAMAR
                                TORRANCE, CA
- TELEPHONE   : 213/540-6183
- EMPLOYMENT   : UNEMPLOYED
- PRIOR CONFINEMENT   : NONE KNOWN
- PLACE OF BIRTH   : PASADENA, CA
- DATE OF BIRTH   : 6/19/54
- RACE   : WHITE
- SEX   : MALE
- HEIGHT   : 6'0"
- WEIGHT   : 190
- HAIR   : BROWN
- EYES   : HAZEL
- COMPLEXION   : MEDIUM
- EDUCATION   : HIGH SCHOOL - 1972
- DATED PHOTO SECURED   : 12/24/81
- SCARS AND MARKS   : 4" CUT - LEFT LOWER ARM
- SOCIAL SECURITY NUMBER   : 550-76-8371
- FBI CRIMINAL NUMBER   : NONE
- VA CLAIM NUMBER   : NONE KNOWN
- MILITARY SERIAL NUMBER   : 550-76-8371
- MILITARY BRANCH   : U. S. ARMY
- CBI NUMBER   : NONE
- DRIVERS LICENSE NUMBER   : HAWAII 550-76-8371

F) DISPOSITION

FRESNO RA IS REQUESTED TO CONDUCT CHARACTER INQUIRIES CONCERNING THE
SUBJECT WITH THE RIDGECREST POLICE DEPARTMENT. SUBJECT CLAIMS THAT
HE WAS AN OFFICER WITH RIDGECREST POLICE DEPARTMENT FROM JULY 1977
TO JUNE 1978. SUBJECT FURTHER CLAIMED THAT HE QUIT THE RIDGECREST
POLICE DEPARTMENT BECAUSE HE "CAUGHT THE CHIEF OF POLICE CONDUCTING
A BOOKMAKING OPERATION."

SUBJECT ALSO CLAIMED THAT HE WAS AN OFFICER WITH THE EL CAJON POLICE
DEPARTMENT FROM MARCH 1976 TO FEBRUARY 1977. SUBJECT CLAIMED THAT
EL CAJON POLICE DEPARTMENT "FIRED HIM AS A CROOKED COP" SO THAT HE
COULD INFILTRATE THE HELLS ANGELS MOTORCYCLE CLUB. SUBJECT ALSO CLAIMED
THAT HE WORKED IN SAN DIEGO FOR THE DEA AND CALIFORNIA DEPARTMENT OF
JUSTICE, NARCOTICS DIVISION. SUBJECT CLAIMS THAT, AT THE DIRECTION
OF FEDERAL AND STATE AUTHORITIES, HE "PLANTED" NARCOTICS ON HELLS
ANGEL MEMBERS, AND HE REPEATED THIS CLAIM ON THE ABC TELEVISION
SHOW ~~20-20~~.

THEREFORE, SAN DIEGO IS REQUESTED TO CONDUCT CHARACTER INQUIRIES CON-
CERNING THE SUBJECT WITH THE FOLLOWING AGENCIES IN THEIR DISTRICT:

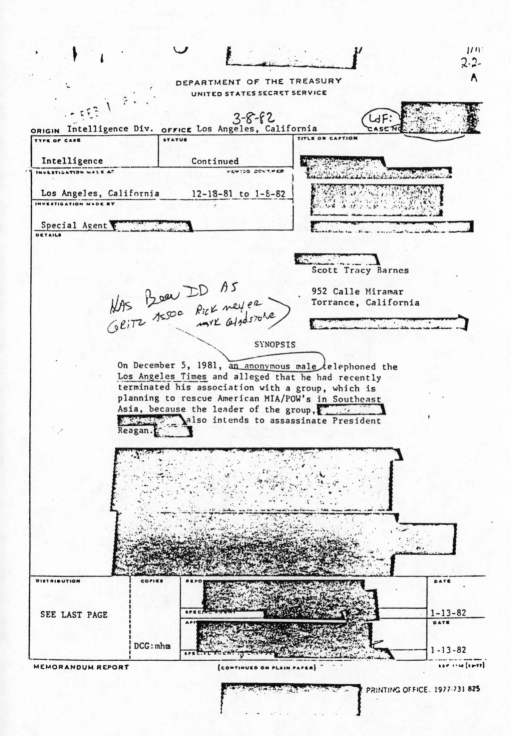

DEPARTMENT OF THE TREASURY
UNITED STATES SECRET SERVICE

3-8-82

ORIGIN Intelligence Div. OFFICE Los Angeles, California

TYPE OF CASE	STATUS	TITLE OR CAPTION
Intelligence	Continued	

INVESTIGATION MADE AT	
Los Angeles, California	12-18-81 to 1-8-82

INVESTIGATION MADE BY

Special Agent

DETAILS

Scott Tracy Barnes

952 Calle Miramar
Torrance, California

HAS BEEN DD AS
(GRITZ ASSOC RICK MEYER
MARK GLADSTONE)

SYNOPSIS

On December 5, 1981, an anonymous male telephoned the
Los Angeles Times and alleged that he had recently
terminated his association with a group, which is
planning to rescue American MIA/POW's in Southeast
Asia, because the leader of the group, _____
_____ also intends to assassinate President
Reagan.

DISTRIBUTION	COPIES	REPO		DATE
SEE LAST PAGE		SPEC		1-13-82
		APP		DATE
	DCG:mhm	SPEC		1-13-82

MEMORANDUM REPORT   (CONTINUED ON PLAIN PAPER)

PRINTING OFFICE. 1977-731 825

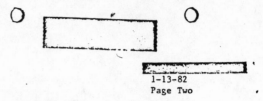

On December 24, 1981, FBI-Los Angeles SA [____] and
USSS-Los Angeles Field Office SA [____] personally
interviewed subject Barnes in Torrance, California and
he denied being the anonymous caller to the Los Angeles
Times concerning the alleged assassination plot.
Barnes claimed that he had recently terminated his
membership in Gritz' group and related that Gritz and
other members of Gritz' group of former U. S. Army
Special Forces soldiers do not like President Reagan.
Furthermore, Barnes declared that during late 1981,
in Los Angeles, he overheard Gritz state that "Reagan's
no good and he ought to be put away." Barnes added
that he did not interpret that statement as a direct
threat against the President when Gritz uttered it. [____]

FBI-SA [____] and USSS-SA [____]

(A) INTRODUCTION (U)

Reference is made to Headquarters (IS-FIB/ME) Teletype #718, dated
December 18, 1981.

(B) IDENTITY AND BACKGROUND OF [____]

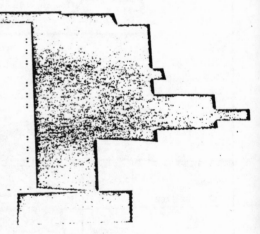

    Name   :
    Alias   :
    Current Address   :

    Telephone   :
    Home Address   :
    Employment   :

    Place of Birth   :
    Date of Birth   :
    Race   :
    Sex   :

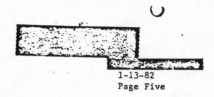

1-13-82
Page Five

(C) INTERVIEW WITH ▓▓▓▓▓▓▓▓▓▓

INTERVIEW WITH ▓▓▓▓▓▓▓▓▓▓

On 12-24-81, FBI-Los Angeles Division SA ▓▓▓▓▓▓ and USSS-
Los Angeles Field Office SA ▓▓▓▓▓▓ personally interviewed
subject Barnes. Barnes was first contacted by the Agents at the
Torrance residence of the subject's father (where the subject also
resides), and Barnes voluntarily accompanied the Agents to the
Torrance Police Department, where the interview was conducted.
Barnes permitted SA ▓▓▓ to photograph him and he voluntarily executed
SSF 1945 (on condition that he receive a copy of it-which was permitted
by ▓▓▓).

No property was taken from the subject except a business card,
which he voluntarily surrendered to SA ▓▓▓ This business card
is one for U.S. Congressman Robert K. Dornan, 27th District-California,
and also contains Scott Barnes' name on the card, listed as a
"Staff Assistant." Barnes claimed that he received 25 such cards
from subject Gritz and he does not believe that Congressman Dornan
is aware of the existence of the cards. Barnes added that Gritz
supplied each member of his "team" with similar cards and each
member had his own name on the card listed as a "Staff Assistant."

It should be noted that on 12-27-81, subject Barnes telephoned SA ▓▓▓▓
at the LAFO and declared that he desired to withdraw his consent for the
USSS to examine any of his medical files or speak to any physicians
who have treated him (thereby revoking the SSF 1945 he signed on
12-24-81). SA ▓▓▓ asked Barnes why he was revoking his consent
since he had stated that he has never had any psychiatric treatment
and therefore the USSS form seemed inapplicable in this instance.
Barnes was unable to offer a reasonable explanation ▓▓▓▓▓▓▓
▓▓▓▓▓▓▓▓▓▓▓▓▓▓ On 12-28-81, LAFO received
a handwritten letter from the subject, with a copy of his SSF 1945
attached. The correspondence, dated 12-24-81, contained a reiteration
of subject's revocation of the consent form, which he verbally did
on 12-27-81.

Subject was not advised of his SSF 1737 "Miranda" Rights.

Barnes indicated that he has been acquainted with and employed by
subject Gritz since April or May of 1981. Gritz is the leader of an
operation to locate (in Southeast Asia) and rescue POW's and

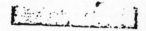

MIA's of the Vietnam War. Barnes joined Gritz' group solely to
assist in that goal. He said that Gritz displayed an interest in
Barnes because of his (Barnes') many 'contacts' throughout Southeast
Asia and the Middle East.

Barnes made at least two trips to Southeast Asia (at Gritz' expense)
and received approximately $1,000 per week when actively working for
Gritz. Although Barnes did not accuse Gritz of committing any
specific illegal acts, he formed the opinion that "something was
wrong" with Gritz' operation, that Gritz was a "bad man" and
dangerous, and in November of 1981 (in Bangkok, Thailand), Barnes
terminated his association with Gritz. Barnes mentioned that he
was a former U.S. Army soldier (military police officer), but had
never served in the Special Forces, whereas most of Gritz'
employees and friends were former S.F. soldiers.

Barnes denied being the source of the information associating Gritz
with an assassination plot against President Reagan. Furthermore,
he denied any knowledge of such a plot.

Barnes said that during one of his 1981 visits to Southeast Asia, he
illegally entered (with ease) Cambodia to verify whether or not
certain weapons had been received which would be utilized by natives
of Southeast Asia to assist Gritz' team in rescuing American MIA/POW's.
Barnes related that this entry was made at the request of Gritz
and that the weapons had been received and consisted of "M-16's
(rifles), M-60's (machine guns), M-79's (grenade launchers), AK-47's
(Russian and Chinese Communist rifles), LAWS (Light Anti-Tank Weapons -
Disposable Rocket Launchers), and other various firearms."

Barnes mentioned two meetings in Los Angeles. One of those
meetings was at the office of U.S. Congressman Dornan and consisted
of "Stan Mullin" (A member of Congressman Dornan's Staff), Gritz,
Barnes, Laotian General Vang Pao and two other foreign generals
(possibly from Thailand and the Philippines). Barnes said that
Gritz also had a private meeting in Los Angeles with Congressman
Dornan, in late August or September, 1981 (concerning the MIA/POW
rescue mission), but that he (Barnes) was not present at the meeting.

Barnes said that Gritz had access to numerous "red" (official)
U.S. Passports which his team members could use if necessary. Gritz
also supplied Barnes and other team members each with 25 of
Congressman Dornan's business cards (bearing the respective team
member's name on the card listed as a "Staff Assistant."

Barnes described other members of Gritz' team (or associates)
as follows:

It should be noted that the description of the aforementioned thirteen
persons and their relationship to Gritz are based solely upon the statements of subject Barnes,

Although Barnes denied being the original source of the assassination
plot story, he did admit speaking to three individuals/businesses concerning
Gritz' activities. Barnes said during 1981 he has spoken to Ralph
Moore (a friend of his and pastor of the non-denominational Hope
Chapel - located at Pacific Coast Highway and Artesia Boulevard
in Hermosa Beach, California), and representatives of Time and Newsweek
Magazines.

Barnes also said that while he was at the U.S. Embassy in Bangkok
in 1981, he spoke with "DIA."

Barnes said he personally believes that if Gritz had the opportunity,
he would kill President Reagan.

Barnes previously resided at 132 Marine, Manhattan Beach, California,
before moving in with his parents. While residing in Hawaii during
early 1981, he lived at 45 Nohokai Street, Kihe, Hawaii.

Barnes said he has never killed anyone, has no present desire to kill
anyone, and would only do so in self-defense. Barnes believes
that Gritz desires to kill him for reasons Barnes could not
specify clearly.

Barnes claimed that he has no present means of support although he
owns a house in the area of the Kern River in Northern California. He
said that just prior to being drafted into the U.S. Army in 1973,
he worked for a physician treating lepers in Saigon (now Ho Chi Minh
City) Vietnam, and that he also visited the PRC.

During 1975-1976, he was an Inglewood, California Police Department
Reserve Officer. During March 1976 to February, 1977, he was an
El Cajon, California Police Department Officer; and from July 1977 to
June 1978, he was a Police Officer with the Ridgecrest, California
Police Department.

Barnes' description of his undercover exploits included this brief
sample of his lengthy ramblings: El Cajon P.D. fired him as a
"crooked cop" so he could infiltrate the Hells Angels Motorcycle
Club; he quit Ridgecrest P.D. because he caught the Chief of Police

2 former Green Berets tell story of a US-aided foray into Laos

The Boston Glob

paper Co. • •   Ⓦ   WEDNESDAY, JANUARY 27, 1982   Telephon

Two tell a story of foray into Laos

Mission sought POWs, say ex-Green Berets

By Ben Bradlee
Globe Staff

JAMES G. GRITZ

In arranging the foray, Vang Pao, who today lives on a barley ranch in Montana, worked with James G. Gritz, a 43-year-old retired Green Beret lieutenant colonel and much-decorated Vietnam veteran who lives in Los Angeles.

LOS ANGELES – Two teams of Laotian resistance soldiers, organized, equipped and financed by the United States, crossed into Laos from Thailand on Nov. 15 seeking to obtain photographic evidence that American prisoners of war are still alive and being held in Laos, according to two ex-Green Berets who supported the operation.

The operation, of which the Pentagon said it had no knowledge, was at least the second such secret foray by American-backed Laotians in the last year. It is not known what happened to the reconnaissance teams dispatched in November.

The two nine-man guerrilla units, participating in what was code-named "Operation Grand Eagle," were bound for four camp sites where recently gathered intelligence reportedly showed at least 39 Americans are being held. The teams left Thailand from different locations and intended to meet in Laos.

The Laotians were made available to the United States by Vang Pao, a former Lao major general who, during the height of US involvement in Southeast Asia, commanded some 40,000 anticommunist tribesmen who served as a secret army for the CIA.

POWs, Page 2

In arranging the November foray, Vang Pao, who today lives on a barley ranch in Montana, collaborated with James G. Gritz, a 43-year-old retired Green Beret lieutenant colonel and much-decorated Vietnam veteran who lives in Los Angeles. Gritz and Vang Pao first discussed the mission last July in the Los Angeles office of Rep. Robert K. Dornan, a conservative Republican from Los Angeles who is an announced candidate for the US Senate.

Vang Pao, in a telephone interview, denied entering into an agreement with Gritz. But Gritz possesses a letter of introduction signed by the Laotian asking his followers in Thailand to cooperate with Americans sent to Thailand by Gritz on a training mission. In addition, Rep. Dornan confirmed that one of his aides was present when Gritz and Vang Pao were discussing the plan. 5 c :

Deputy CIA Director Bobby Ray Inman, who met with Gritz in December to discuss the reconnaissance plan and the prisoner-of-war issue, denied "to the best of my knowledge" that any government agency was involved in supporting the November mission. He did not deny that the mission took place, and acknowledged that government intelligence agencies have had contacts with various private groups concerning POWs over the last several years. Inman said, however, that these contacts had not yielded any "solid information."

Adm. Allan G. Paulson of the Defense Intelligence Agency (DIA), the Pentagon's intelligence arm and the group charged with official responsibility for investigating reports of missing POWs, declined through a spokesman to comment on the November mission. A Pentagon spokesman said the Department of Defense had no knowledge of it.

In a series of interviews with The Globe. Gritz said he had been contacted last June about the POW situation by a secret military intelligence agency that was created in the aftermath of the failed rescue of American hostages in Iran in 1980. Gritz would not reveal the agency's name or whom it reports to.

The elite unit, Gritz said, is patterned after the British Strategic Air Service and similar organizations in Israel and West Germany, and is designed to transcend an often-cumbersome Joint Chiefs of Staff bureaucracy and take direct action in situations where Americans abroad find themselves in life-threatening situations. The organization generates its own intelligence and has a Special Forces unit assigned to it, according to intelligence sources. Dornan, in an interview, said he knew of the group's existence but had not been told its name.

Gritz said the government agency gave him $40,000 in several cash payments over the second half of last year in order to equip Vang Pao's Laotians and send three retired Green Berets and an ex-military intelligence officer to rendezvous with the teams in Thailand and ready them for their mission. At least two of these payments were made during meetings in Tucson, Gritz said. A fourth ex-Green Beret, whose job it was to go to Bangkok and serve as a communications link with Gritz in Los Angeles, is a security consultant from Malden, Vincent W. Arnone.

Arnone said he was in Bangkok from Nov. 7 through Nov. 14. Both he and Gritz said they later received written confirmation that the two reconnaissance teams crossed over into Laos on the 15th. Arnone said he was given the code name and Telex address of an official in Washington to whom he was to send messages from Thailand.

Gritz also has two Nikon F3 cameras equipped with motor drives and long-distance telephoto lenses, a decoding machine, a portable lie-detector unit and other equipment he said was given him by the government for use on the mission.

The November mission was at least the second time in the last 12 months that US-backed Laotian soldiers have infiltrated Laos in search of American prisoners. Last May, the Washington Post reported that a group of Laotian mercenaries, apparently organized by the CIA, made an incursion into Laos but returned to Thailand with no evidence that any American prisoners were alive.

Two earlier forays

Gritz (pronounced "Grights"), relying on reports from his own Laotian intelligence network, contends that the CIA's Laotian mercenaries actually undertook two forays: the first in January 1981, when they were fired upon and forced to retreat, and the second in February or March, when they never reached their intended target.

The disclosure of the operation in November comes at a time when the POW-MIA issue seems to be gathering momentum. Tomorrow will mark the ninth anniversary of the signing of the Paris peace accord that was supposed to have repatriated all American prisoners of war. Speeches and other observances are scheduled around the nation. ABC television reported last week that the Pentagon will send a delegation to Hanoi next month for discussions on American prisoners.

By the Pentagon's current count, there are still 2456 American servicemen unaccounted for in Southeast Asia. Col. Jerry Grohowski, a spokesman for the Department of Defense, said there had been 397 reports of first-hand sightings of American prisoners since the fall of Saigon in 1975. He said some of these could be explained away, but "a significant number cannot be explained away." The official Pentagon view remains, however, that there is no evidence that any prisoners are still alive.

Gritz said Vang Pao told him he had been receiving information on American prisoners held in Laos for several years and had been passing it on to the US government. Vang Pao had hoped that Washington would help him focus attention on the plight of his Hmong tribesmen, who he says are the victims of ongoing toxic chemical attacks in violation of international agreements. Gritz said Vang Pao approached him in the belief that nonofficial efforts to free American prisoners now had a better chance of success than official efforts.

Gritz said that the use of Vang Pao's intelligence network was the basis for the official backing he received. He said he did not tell Vang Pao that he was cooperating with the government, but he felt that cooperation was necessary to ensure prompt diplomatic follow-up in the event of a successful rescue eventually.

Based on their agreement to work together, Gritz said Vang Pao ordered his tribesmen last summer to gather the best and most recent information they could on locations in Laos where American prisoners were still being held. It was after Vang Pao's agents conducted this sweep that four targets were selected and the Nov. 15 foray launched.

At these four targets, whose locations he would not disclose for the record, Gritz said there were first-hand sightings made last August, September and October of 39 American prisoners, including 17 who were being held in a cave.

Gritz said a Vietnamese agent produced reports from Laotian and Vietnamese agents, written in Lao and crude English, telling of sightings of a total of 62 American prisoners in the last year, 42 of them since November.

The most recent report Gritz received was a tape recording made Nov. 23 in Thailand by a Vietnamese agent. The tape was sent to Gritz by one of the ex-Green Berets he had sent to Thailand. Gritz said he hand-delivered it in Washington on Dec. 7th. The tape quoted the Vietnamese as saying he had seen 30 American officers earlier that month in a Laotian camp. The prisoners were reportedly being guarded by 150 Vietnamese guards, 150 Laotians and 65 armored vehichles armed with light guns.

Sighting reported

Another sighting, Gritz said, was made in early November in Vietnam by a defecting Vietnamese army officer. A written report of the interrogation given to Gritz said that 12 Americans were seen exercising in short blue pants and short-sleeved shirts with the letters "TB" on the back. The officer said this stood for "Tu Binh," Vietnamese for "prisoner of war."

On Jan. 28, 1981, Gritz said another Vietnamese agent reported seeing 20 barefoot POWs at a Laotian camp, again wearing the "TB" markings.

Gritz said he and the government group he was working with had planned to use these Vietnamese agents to launch two more photo reconnaissance missions at four other suspected POW camps: two in Laos and two in Vietnam. The planned launch date for that incursion was Dec. 10, but it never came off, according to Gritz, because the DIA declined to approve the plan fashioned by Gritz and the secret government group.

Gritz said the latter had been waging what amounted to bureaucratic warfare against the DIA in an attempt to wrest the charter – the official mandate to deal with the POW problem – away from the Pentagon's intelligence unit. In paying him $40,000 and furnishing equipment for the mission, Gritz speculated that the secret government group had exceeded its authority, betting on the hope that it would develop solid enough evidence of live American prisoners to justify winning the POW charter for itself.

The issue came to a head Dec. 8 in Washington at a closed, top-secret hearing of the congressional Task Force on American Prisoners and Missing in Southeast Asia, where several officials, including the CIA's Inman and Adm. Paulson, the man charged with overseeing POW affairs for

the Defense Intelligence Agency, were scheduled to brief members of Congress on the latest POW-related intelligence-gathering efforts.

According to sources, the officials had no new intelligence to present the panel, whereupon Rep. Dornan, with some frustration, asked Inman why the intelligence community was "stonewalling" the private option being advanced by Gritz. Inman was said to have expressed ignorance of any private plan. However, Paulson told Inman that he had known of the plan, but hadn't thought it necessary to inform the CIA.

The next day, Dec. 9, Inman called Gritz and asked to meet with him. Gritz said he had a 45-minute meeting with Inman at which Inman asked for a briefing on the semiofficial plan, saying he had been taken by surprise by the Dornan question.

Inman knew of Gritz' prior record on the POW issue: that after retiring early from the Army in 1979 he had spent the next 30 months mounting a private effort to rescue POWs, bolstered by sympathetic Pentagon officials who provided him with full access to DIA-generated intelligence from US agents, satellites and reconnaissance planes. The rescue effort never got off the ground because its planning was leaked to the press and because of a lack of funds.

Inman, in a telephone interview yesterday, said he met with Gritz at the request of Rep. Dornan, and he described the meeting as a "listening session" for him. He characterized Gritz as "a colorful guy with a lot of good stories."

Mission denied

Inman said the report that two Lao resistance groups backed by the United States had crossed into Laos Nov. 15 on a POW-related mission was "not true; from the point of view of being backed by the US government. I've done a lot of digging inside the government to see if any government entity had any part in this, and they all denied that they did. So, to the best of my knowledge, the part about the government being involved is not true."

The day after meeting with Inman, Gritz wrote him a long letter, laying out his and Vang Pao's plan for the record and arguing the merits of a private operation with tacit official support. Gritz wrote that Adm. Paulson in DIA had officially "pulled the plug" on the operation Dec. 9. He added that part of the plan had been for him to return to active duty "as the Washington, D.C., project officer and front man for the [intelligence group] working Operation Grand Eagle." Gritz provided The Globe a copy of the letter.

Inman said he received Gritz' letter and forwarded it to the Pentagon.

Dornan, who chairs the congressional POW task force, said he believed the Gritz-Vang Pao plan had been backed by the government for a time. "When I asked for clarification of this at the highest intelligence levels, no one said it was untrue," Dornan said. "I was told, 'We're going another way now, congressman.' It was indirect confirmation. They had decided that the Gritz plan was not feasible.

"Gritz is going public now because he believes the government has pulled the rug out from under him, and I don't blame him. ... Given the heart-breaking nature of the POW story, I think the government should leave no stone unturned in finding out if we still have prisoners alive over there, and that includes use of the private sector if appropriate."

Gen. Vang-Pao, then leader of an army of Meo tribesmen, calls for air support during a 1972 offensive in Laos.   AP PHOTO

REP. ROBERT K. DORNAN
"No stone unturned"

Rep. Dornan, who heads the congressional POW task force, said he believed the Gritz-Vang Pao plan had been backed by the government for a time. 'When I asked for clarification of this at the highest intelligence levels, no one said it was untrue,' Dornan said. 'I was told, "We're going another way now, congressman." It was indirect confirmation. They had decided that the Gritz plan was not feasible. Gritz is going public now because he believes the government has pulled the rug out from under him and I don't blame him ...'

Professional Security Consultants

POLYGRAPH AND SECURITY SPECIALISTS

CHRIS GUGAS, SR. - Director

~~SUITE 400 - 1680 NORTH VINE STREET~~ HOLLYWOOD, CALIFORNIA 90028 - (213) 466-3283

Suite 311   6253 Hollywood Blvd

BIOGRAPHICAL INFORMATION

NAME   :   CHRIS GUGAS, SR. Ph. D
DATE OF BIRTH :   August 12, 1921
PLACE OF BIRTH: Omaha, Nebraska

EDUCATION:

University of Southern California
University of California at Los Angeles
University of California at Northridge
University of Beverly Hills

Bachelor and Master's degrees in Public Administration
Doctor of Philosophy in Behavioral Psychology

EMPLOYMENT HISTORY:

Enlisted in January,1940. Released in December 1945 as Captain
United States Marine Corps - retired Major USMCR 1963
Recalled to USMC in 1947 through 1949 Los Angeles
Participated in World War Two in four engagements.
        Guadalcanal, Guam, Bougainsville, Iwo Jima
Assistant director of Security, Los Angeles City Schools
Central Intelligence Agency Washington D.C. and Europe
Director of Public Safety city of Omaha, Nebraska
Director of Security McKesson & Robbins Western Division
Director of Professional Security Consultants Los Angeles

Pioneered several polygraph techniques since 1942.
Established first polygraph program for the Marine Corps in 1954
Pioneered police polygraph testing in Burbank, California in 1955.

More than 25,000 + polygraph examinations have been given with several
thousands supervised.

ASSOCIATIONS AND PROFESSIONAL ORGANIZATIONS:

Past President National Board of Polygraph Examiners
Past President American Polygraph Association
Past Vice President American Polygraph Association
Past Executive Director American Polygraph Association
Charter Member California Academy of Polygraph Science
Past Executive Director California Academy of Polygraph Science
Member, California Peace Officers Association
Member, International Association of Chiefs of Police

Security Services for Legal, Industry and Business

Member Los Angeles Press Club
Life Member American Polygraph Association
Member, American Society of Criminologists
Past Commandant Marine Corps Combat Correspondents Association
Member, American Legion
Past Secretary California Governor's Investigator Advisory Board
Former Reserve Officer Los Angeles Sheriff's Department
Former Reserve Officer Los Angeles Police Department
Member American Society of Industrial Security
Past President Retail Special Agent's Association
Past President Marine Corps League Association
Member, American Society of Industrial Security

TEACHING POSITIONS:

Omaha University police science department
Instructor, Las Vegas Institute of Polygraph
Instructor, Los Angeles Institute of Polygraph
Former Instructor Gormac Polygraph School
Instructor Behavior Modification Institute Van Nuys, California

TEACHING CREDENTIALS:

California Adult Education credential, Polygraph, Investigation
Nevada Credential on Polygraph and Criminal Investigation

LECTURER ON POLYGRAPH - CRIMINAL INVESTIGATION:

American Polygraph Association
California Association of Polygraph Examiners
California Academy of Polygraph Science
Texas Polygraph Association
Oklahoma Polygraph Association
New York Polygraph Association
Washington D.C. Polygraph Association
Nebraska Polygraph Association
Canadian Security Association
Greece Gendarmarie Training Academy
Athens, Greece Police Cadet's Training Academy
Instanbul Police Training Academy
Ankara Police School
Texas Institute of Mental Health
American Society of Industrial Relations
American Society for Industrial Security
California Retail Special Agent's Association
National Jeweler's Association
National Builder's Association
Platform Exchange Washington D.C.

page three

LAW SCHOOLS: (Lecturer)

University of Southern California
Southwestern Law School
Loyola Law School
Nebraska Law School
Mid - Valley Law School Los Angeles
University of California Law School
University of Oklahoma
University of Nevada

OTHER UNIVERSITIES:

College of the Canyons, Canyon County, California
Dekalb University, Georgia Police Science Department
Omaha University Police Science
University of Nebraska Criminal Justice Department
Texas Institute of Mental Science
Northrup University, Los Angeles
University of Oklahoma Police Science Department
California State University Los Angeles

PUBLICATIONS:

Author,   The Silent Witness,published by Prentice-Hall (Book)
Co-Author, Pre-employment in the Polygraph Program (Book)
Co-Author, The polygraph in the Criminal Justice System (Book)

Columnist,   Security World Magazine
              Los Angeles Daily Legal Journal
              National Jeweler's Security Magazine

Contributor to: Beverage Bulletin Newspaper
                 Irish Digest
                 A.S.I.S Industrial Security Magazine
                 Go Magazine Transportation
                 Polygraph Magazine
                 Security Management Handbook
                 Police Magazine
                 Sheriff's Magazine
                 California Law Journal
                 Los Angeles Daily Journal

Author of more than 250 articles on polygraph, security, criminal investigation and crime.

COURT TESTIMONY:

Court qualified in municipal, superior and federal courts on the admissibility of the polygraph and expert opinion.

page four

Testified before Workman's Compensation Boards
Civil Service proceedings
Military Courts
Arbitration Hearings

MEDIA SERVICES CONSULTANT:

Los Angeles Times
Newsweek Magazine
Los Angeles Herald- Examiner
Los Angeles Daily News
Television stations, KTLA, KABC, CBS, ABC, KHJ
Radio stations, KABC, KTTC,
San Diego Union
Sacramento Bee
San Francisco Union
Omaha World Herald
Washington Post
New York Times
Baltimore Sun
South Omaha Sun
Oakland Tribune
San Francisco Chronicle
St. Louis Post-Dispatch
New York Daily News

SERVICE ORGANIZATIONS: (Lecturer).

Lions clubs   American Legion Posts
Rotary clubs   Veterans of Foreign Wars posts
Sertoma clubs   Exchange clubs
Women's clubs   Bar Associations
Masonic   Shriners
Optimists   4-H clubs
Kiwanis   Program Exchange

HONORS:

                    Who's Who in the World
Listed in: Who's Who in the West
                    Who's Who in California
                    Notables of the Bicentennial Era
                    International Biographical Center, London, England
                    National Social Register
                    Who's Who in Law Enforcement
                    Distinguished Americans

RESEARCH PROJECTS:

Co-Developed first all electronic polygraph with David Douglas, 1949
Co-Developed 1 million ohm galvanometer for polygraph use
Co-Developed Metrigraph single recording channel galvanometer

page five

Developed 300 question pre-polygraph questions for police applicants.
Originated police applicant screening via polygraph 1955.

Developed simplified pre-employment screening questions for business.
Designed coin test for Stimulation testing in specific cases.
Designed first audio-visual demonstration of polygraph for audiences.

Introduced the psychogalvanometer to local colleges for use in psy-
    chology and biofeedback experimentation in 1953.

Conducted thousands of tests with the Stoelting Plethesmograph along
    with the regular cardio-cuff unit on a Stoelting Instrument.

Researched the value of using the automatic phase of the psycho-galvan-
    ometer rather than the manual mode. Paper to be published.

Conducted research on the value to taking blood-pressure readings
    prior to a polygraph examination and upon completion.

Designed a pre-test form for all specific examinations covering a
    subject's health, medication, hypnosis, attitude physical and
    mental problems which could affect an examination.

AWARDS RENDERED:

        Military Service: National Defense medal
                        Asiatic-Pacific Defense medal
                        Good Conduct medal
                        Presidential Citation-Guam (1941)
                        Presidential Unit Citation-Guadalcanal
                            Iwo Jima
                        Navy Unit Citation- Bougainsville-Iwo Jima

        Service Groups : American Polygraph Association, Texas
                        Seminar
                        American Polygraph Association, Nevada
                        Seminar
                        American Polygraph Association, Calif
                        Seminar
                        American Polygraph Association, Washington
                        D.C. Seminar

POLYGRAPH SEMINARS: (Attended)

San Diego	Los Angeles	San Francisco	Oakland
Washington D.C	New York City	Miami	Hot Springs
Houston	Dallas	Norman	Oklahoma
Lincoln (Neb)	Chicago	St Louis	Seattle
Fort Worth (Tex)	Vancouver	Pittsburgh	Orlando (Flor)

POLYGRAPH TESTS: (Conducted Overseas)

Ankara, Turkey	Istanbul, Turkey	Athens, Greece
London, England	Londonderry, Ireland	Costa Rica
Central America	Mexico	Honolulu
Hawaii		

page six

SPECIAL TRAINING:

U.S. Marine Corps - Criminal Investigation
Fingerprinting
(3 months)   Plant Security
Officer's Academy
Police Science
Interrogation
Judo and baton use

Central Intelli- Advanced Police Science
gence Agency: Psychology
Intelligence procedures
(3 months)   Terrorist tactics

Los Angeles Police General police science
Reserve School: Interrogation
Patrol procedures
(3 months)   Crime search techniques
Polygraph use
Judo and baton use

Los Angeles   Patrol procedures
Sheriff's reserves: First Aid
Weapons use
(3 months)   Crime laboratory use
Interrogations
General police science

City of Omaha, Civil Defense procedures
Nebraska: Public Safety procedures
Budget requirements
(As Director of Fire and police procedures
Public Safety)

REFERENCES:

Will be supplied by request.

These will include:

COURTS: Municipal Court Judges
Superior Court Judges
Federal Court Judges

PROSECUTION: Attorneys in civil and criminal practice
City, County and State.

MILITARY: Army   Air Force
Navy   Coast Guard
Marines

LAW ENFORCEMENT: Police - Sheriff U. S. Narcotics
Secret Service Federal Bureau of
Investigation

SPECIAL PROJECTS DEVELOPED:

Established a four year criminal justice course for law enforcement and military security personnel at the University of Omaha while director of public safety in 1962.

Developed the first underground communications center for civil defense in 1963. Cited by the United States Government for outstanding planning in civil defense against tornados, floods and other natural or man-made disasters.

Established the first direct dialing program for calling fire, police and ambulance directly which was later developed by the Omaha telephone company for national use in all major cities. This is now known as 911.

Organized the first modern police training program for the Turkish National Police in 1951 under the American Military Aid Program.

Developed a close cooperation with all Citizen Band radio operators to assist the Omaha Police Department in all emergencies where Ham Radio operators were restricted because of immobility to move stationary equipment into disaster areas, such as floods, major fires and tornados.

Was one of two Marine Officers in 1947 to develop a news media program for the TOYS FOR TOTS Marine Corps Reserve program to give out toys to needy children. Worked on this program at Christmas time for three years.

Prepared a polygraph course for the Southern Nevada University and supplied the school with a Stoelting Instrument for use in the program. A second instrument was given that school in 1983.

POLYGRAPH TRAINING:

1942 Berkeley & Oakland, California training in polygraph with Captain C.D.Lee and Frank Waterbury. Attached to Marine Corps at Alameda Naval Air Station.

1949 Special training Central Intelligence Agency Washington D.C.

1958 Stoelting Polygraph Institute. Diploma issued.

1961 Backster-Arthur National Polygraph Institute Advanced Training.

1970 Backster Advanced Polygraph Training. San Diego, California

1955 U.S.Marine Corps Reserve training in Oceanside, California. Two
thru Weeks active duty at Provost Marshal's office in Polygraph.
1961

1976 Los Angeles Institute of Polygraph diploma issued.

MAILGRAM SERVICE CENTER
MIDDLETOWN, VA. 22645

Western Union **Mailgram**®

4-025226S076002 03/17/83 ICS IPMRNCZ CSP LSAB
1 2135427789 MGM TDRN REDONDO BEACH CA 03-17 0113P EST

SCOTT T BARNES
1401 HAWTHORNE BLVD
REDONDO BEACH CA 90278

THIS MAILGRAM IS A CONFIRMATION COPY OF THE FOLLOWING MESSAGE:

2135427789 TDRN REDONDO BEACH CA 167 03-17 0113P EST
PMS REPUBLICAN STEPHEN SOLARZ
HOUSE SUBCOMMITTEE ON ASIAN AND PACIFIC AFFAIRS RPT DLY MGM, DLR
CONGRESSIONAL HOTEL ANNEX 1 ROOM 707
WASHINGTON DC 20515
DEAR MR SOLARZ

I UNDERSTAND THAT LIEUTENANT COLONEL GRITZ WILL TESTIFY BEFORE YOUR
SUBCOMMITTEE ON POW RESCUES I WOULD LIKE TO ADVISE YOU I HAVE BEEN
TWO OPERATIONS WITH OTHER GREEN BERETS WITH GRITZ INTO LAOS AND
CAMBODIA I WOULD LIKE TO COMMENT THAT MR GRITZ IS NOT GIVING YOU AL
THE FACTS NOR IS HE GIVING THE PRESS THE ENTIRE TRUTH I WOULD URGE
YOU TO SUBPOENA ALL MEMBERS WHO HAVE EVER BEEN INVOLVED WITH GRITZ
GET TO THE TRUTH UPON MY RETURNING FROM THE LAST MISSION OPERATION
GRAND EAGLE I WAS GIVEN 5 POLYGRAPH EXAMS BY FORMER CIA AGENT CHRIS
DUGAS AND AS HE WILL CONFIRM I HAD PASSED ALL OF THEM COLONEL GRITZ
REFUSED ALL POLYGRAPH EXAMS THERE IS A CONSIDERABLE AMOUNT OF
MISINFORMATION AND DECEIT BEING PUT OUT BY GRITZ AS REPORTED 2 WEEK
AGO IN THE LOS ANGELES TIMES I WAS A MEMBER AND ASSOCIATE OF GRITZ
AND HIS OPERATION

BEST OF LUCK GETTING TO THE TRUTH THANK YOU SINCERELY
  SCOTT T BARNES 1401 HAWTHORNE BLVD REDONDO BEACH CA 90278
  2135427789
  1401 HAWTHORNE BLVD
  REDONDO BEACH CA 90278

13:14 EST

MGMCOMP

MAILGRAM SERVICE CENTER
MIDDLETOWN, VA. 22645

1-015008A076 03/17/83 ICS IPMWGWJ WSH LSAA
00560 MGMBUWASHINGTON DC 50 03-17 345P EST

SCOTT T BARNES
1401 HAWTHORNE BLVD
REDONDO BEACH CA 90278

YOUR TELEGRAM MARCH 17TH TO CONGRESSMAN STEPHEN SOLARZ
WAS DELIVERED MARCH 17TH AT 300 PM.
   WESTERN UNION.

15:56 EST

MGMCOMP

Agent Exposes Secret Mission

It was in March that *CAIB* first heard from Scott Barnes—a former police informer, undercover cop, drug enforcement agent, and military policeman. Barnes, only 28, had spent the last nine years in such marginal work, from the time he was still in high school in Redondo Beach, California, near Los Angeles. Now he had a shocking, almost unbelievable, tale to tell. He had given his story, he said, to ABC-TV and to Jack Anderson but neither had used it. After waiting weeks, on the advice of "a friend at the Pentagon" he contacted *CovertAction*.

Barnes said that in October and November 1981 he was one of a team of six Americans who were sent into Laos from Thailand by the CIA. Their mission, they thought, was to locate and if possible rescue American prisoners of war held since the final days of the Vietnam War. This mission, Barnes said, had the cooperation of a Member of Congress, was coordinated by a former war hero now working undercover for the CIA, and was directed by the CIA Chief of Station in Bangkok and his predecessor, now living in Vienna, Virginia.

As Barnes described it, the team did locate two "Caucasians," apparently Americans captured in Laos. But they appeared "recently" captured. Moreover, after the team reported their find, noting that rescue seemed difficult, they were ordered to try to kill the two captives. The team refused, disbanded the mission, and returned to the U.S. They never intended to discuss what had really happened. But the only explanation for the incredible orders, Barnes thought, was that the Americans were involved in planting false evidence of the use of yellow rain. The government was afraid the Laotions would exploit this, perhaps in a show trial.

Barnes would not have spoken out at all, he says, but for the fact that the coordinator of the mission, James "Bo" Gritz, a former Green Beret Colonel, started giving newspaper interviews in December and January, telling a very different story from what Barnes says was the truth. Barnes then decided to approach ABC—some six weeks before he called *CAIB*.

CAIB interviewed Barnes several times, at length. A transcript of a recording of one interview was prepared and, with a press release from *CAIB*, circulated to the media in April. We found it very puzzling, to say the least, that the media had not carried Barnes's story. Even if they could not prove it, even if they did not believe it, the allegations alone would be news. We later learned that the media insisted they needed more "confirmation," which did not stop them from running with the Libyan "hit squad" fabrication, nor prevent them from playing up Bo Gritz's side of the story.

CAIB's widely distributed press release moved a number of journalists to contact the key figures in Barnes's tale, as well as Pentagon and CIA sources. Most denied a lot that Barnes had to say; almost all denied the key assertions—that the mission was official, that Americans did go into Laos, and most importantly that there were assassination orders from the CIA in Virginia. But the denials were not consistent. One person, for example, denied that the mission had used phony cards identifying the team as Congressional aides; another said there was such a mission but it did not go into Laos; another said the mission did go into Laos, but it was a privately sponsored, not a CIA, operation. Bo Gritz at first denied knowing Barnes, denied giving him any support, denied meeting with him and exiled Lao General Vang Pao at a Congressman's office, all denials he later retracted. Daniel Arnold, the former CIA Chief in Bangkok—now president of Tashkent Associates in Vienna—denied any role in such a mission. As he told a *Daily World* reporter, "Because I was a former CIA officer people seem to think we are an unscrupulous bunch of rogues who would undertake such a monstrous plot . . ." But Arnold did not deny his former high Agency position, nor did he deny that he forwarded messages from Lao rebels in Thailand to Vang Pao, now living in Montana, messages brought to him by Barnes.

Arnold's name was in the news in May when stories surfaced that career diplomat Morton Abramowitz had been blocked from accepting the offer of Assistant Secretary of State for East Asian and Pacific Affairs. One of those "widely reported to be involved," according to the *Washington Post*, was Arnold, "who was CIA station chief in Bangkok for about a year during Abramowitz's tenure as ambassador." Arnold denied any friction while the two were both posted to Bangkok, but said they "quarreled in late 1980 over his return to Bangkok as a private consultant after retiring from the CIA." Arnold, in fact, is now a registered, paid agent for the Thai government.

Kevin Cody, editor of the *Easy Rider* in Hermosa Beach, California, took the *CAIB* press release seriously. His paper covers the district represented by conservative Republican Robert Dornan—the Congressman named by Barnes. Cody interviewed most of the key people and published a lengthy article, which he has given *CAIB* permission to reprint. As he notes, no one, despite all the denials, has been able to show that Scott Barnes is lying. Week by week more of Barnes's narrative is confirmed.

Early on we received a telephone call from "John," who confirmed all of Barnes's story, but who said he was afraid to go public. John - possibly John Akins, who Barnes says was one of the six on his mission—has never called back.

Shortly before going to press we received a Mailgram from Vienna, Virginia, from a name not listed by the telephone company at that address, advising us that we would never understand completely what "TF157-Bohica" was all about. "Operation Bohica" was the codename Barnes said was given to the mission. But the reference to Task Force 157, the secret Navy-CIA cover operation for which fugitive Edwin Wilson worked, was a new piece in the puzzle.

And most surprising of all has been the mysterious death of Jerry Daniels in Bangkok, described below. Daniels, who worked with Lao exiles and rebels, expressed his disbelief to journalists of the yellow rain evidence touted so much by the State Department. His mysterious death —

not, apparently, the first such strange demise at the U.S. Embassy in Bangkok—adds credence to the can of worms which Barnes seems to have opened. Moreover, as we began to hear about the Daniels case at *CAIB* we received a telephone threat, to "stay away from the Daniels investigation."

We are convinced that only the tip of the iceberg has been exposed at this time. We hope that these articles will generate further investigations and that more people with first hand information will come forward. What follows are: Excerpts from *CAIB*'s interview with Scott Barnes; Kevin Cody's *Easy Rider* article; and Ellen Ray's article on the Jerry Daniels case. ●

Excerpts from CAIB- Scott Barnes Interview

March 28, 1982

I was over in Hawaii to visit a friend who was sick. An ex-SOG [Secret Operating Group] operator got in touch with me about this proposal, which we all thought was a rescue proposal. Bo Gritz got in touch with me through the SOG guys who had told him that I knew Vang Pao. Bo Gritz was under cover, pretending to work for Hughes. He said that he was involved in Operation Velvet Hammer and that the government came in and asked him to publicly step down so they could secretly go in there [Laos] and try to verify via SR-71 photos and some reconnaissance groups, and so he did that in June of eighty-one, and then General Aaron out of the Pentagon has asked him to prepare for an "invasion into Laos."

An invasion by whom?

An invasion by American special forces. And he said it would be a three-team crossing, and he had ordered some very sophisticated weapons, contacts, and he asked for a meeting with General Vang Pao, so I arranged that, and he asked for a meeting with Congressman Bob Dornan [Rep.-Calif.] and I arranged that.

Bo wanted these meetings, because the Agency figured it'd be a good cover to use Congressman Dornan. We had some phony business cards made up with our names that we were staff aides to Congressman Dornan. That way,

ROBERT K. DORNAN
UNITED STATES CONGRESSMAN
27TH DISTRICT CALIFORNIA

SCOTT T. BARNES
STAFF ASSISTANT

6151 WEST CENTURY BLVD.
SUITE 1018
LOS ANGELES, CA 90045
(213) 642 5111

while down there, we could claim political asylum if we got caught at any of the cross-border checks.

Did Dornan know all about this?

Yeah. Oh, yeah.

And he cooperated with it?

Oh, absolutely. He set up a meeting with General David Jones, and was conferring with General Jones and President Reagan on the matter.

Do you know if other Members of Congress knew about it?

No others. Nobody else knew. Nobody. We dubbed it Operation Bohica. And then in October he arranged for some Agency aides to come out and some Green Berets, and we met in Westchester [California].

How many people were there when you met?

There were six, six Americans, and there were four others that were shadowing us to make sure we weren't followed or we didn't back out, and I never met them. I don't know who they were.

The six, were they all former Green Berets?

All but one. One was out of Ft. Meade, Maryland. He was an intelligence analyst. So then Bo said that we got the approval from the Agency to go ahead, and he said about two days' planning. He'd gotten some phony business cards made, and we were to use a Telex in the Department of Energy communications center in Washington, DC, to send overseas Telexes via a code. That way, foreign agents intercepting information would not suspect that we used a DOE Telex. We met with the station chief for the CIA at the United States Embassy in Bangkok. Prior to that I had been down at the Embassy and had met with an Agency pilot, helicopter pilot. I was at the Embassy in June to prepare the future operation of October, November. And I met with DIA people, and then I touched bases with some foreign types of agents that were helping us out through General Vang Pao.

Did Vang Pao ever leave Montana for any of these

things, or were people just in touch by phone?

No, I brought him down to California and brought him into Congressman Dornan's office, and had some meetings where he actually signed in on Congressman Dornan's personal ledger, along with Bo Gritz, myself, and another foreign intelligence agent. Then later on the Congressman's aide called me, and said, "Gosh, I made a mistake. I didn't wany any of you guys to sign in in my office." So he sent me the ledger in the mail, so I would see that it was the original, so I would destroy it. However, the way politics works, I didn't destroy it, I kept it.

You said there was a foreign intelligence person with you?

Yes. We were cooperating with another country's agent. I think he was out of China. We were trying to work something out with the Chinese people.

Taiwan or People's Republic?

People's Republic. They were going to "slap the hand of Vietnam" while a lot of guerrilla activity was going on, in Mahaxai, Gnommerat, the Mugia Pass, and Nape in Laos. Well, when we were down there the second time, we equipped a team of indigenous to take a team across the river [the Mekong] and verified that there were some Caucasians, known or unknown that they were Americans, but it was obvious that they were probably Americans.

This was across the river from where to where?

We went across at Ban Pheng, Thailand, straight across 47 km. roughly to Mahaxai, just a little bit to the west of Mahaxai.

This is in Laos?

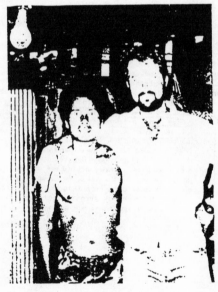

Barnes with a Lao guerrilla at camp in Ban Phang, Thailand.

Right. We verified that there were Caucasians and sent a Telex.

How many were there?

Two Caucasians.

And when you say verified, you mean somebody actually got to see them?

Yes. We had some 30-odd indigenous forces with us. And then Daniel Arnold, the former station chief for the CIA in Bangkok sent some communications and we got the message that Bo Gritz was cut off, no longer to send messages to him and no longer to trust him.

He was not with you on the mission?

No, no. He stayed in the United States. So then the Chief of Station from the U.S. Embassy brought up a coded message through some of his agents from Nakhon Phanom and we put that together with a Telex message we got back from Langley, Virginia, telling us in essence if these are in fact Americans, assassinate them. And we got in an argument, and split, and went our ways.

Did you all go back to the base in Thailand where you started out from?

Yes. We all went back to Bangkok, and one of the guys, intelligence guys, decided to go and be debriefed prior to returning to the United States. Two of the Green Berets decided that they were going to go to Hawaii and lay low for about a week before returning to the mainland, and then they were going to disappear. And the other guy decided that in the meantime he was going to go to Japan and then filter on back to the United States via Canada.

Was everybody traveling under their own individual covers at that point?

Yes. We all decided to disband quickly.

So far as you know, everybody got back their own separate ways?

Yeah, as far as I know, I only talked to one of them some time ago, and he said, "Forget we ever went, forget we ever talked to anybody."

Did you ever learn or suspect what it was that the Americans who were captured in Laos might have known or what it was they didn't want the Laotians to find out?

Two things. One is that possibly the United States was involved in getting chemical warfare, biological stuff over there.

You mean they might have been planting yellow rain stuff?

Right. That was one of the suspicions that was discussed over there. The other one was that these "guys" might have been involved in a secret operation as late as '79 or '80 and got captured. And could tell some pretty horrendous stories about what was really going on if they were forced to. And it was best that they not ever come back.

But did they have any way or reason to believe that whatever it was that they knew they would not already have revealed?

Not that I know of. They had a previous operation that had been scouting the area and setting up booby traps and stuff and there's no way of really telling except for nothing ever came out through international channels.

The area where the Americans were being held, do you know if that was anywhere near the region where evidence of yellow rain was supposedly being found?

Oh yes. It was right in that area. About which Haig himself made the accusation last year.

But you never found out any more to confirm that that is what it was?

No, I never did, I just decided it was best to leave as soon as possible.

Did you ever hear from anyone else from the mission?

The only person I heard from was John. ["John" also spoke by phone with *CAIB* and confirmed all of Barnes's story, but refused to say where he was. John said he wanted Barnes's story to come out, because he was frightened, and had heard that two of the members of the mission had met untimely deaths, one in Libya and one in Guatemala.]

How did he know how to reach you?

Well, I left a number for him that I would be at for a week, and we contacted each other and decided that for better or worse it was best we never say anything happened, and we'll keep a close eye on the local newspapers. And next thing we know, Bo Gritz is going all over the country talking.

Do you know why Bo started talking; do you have any idea?

Yes. We think it is because he was supposed to come back as a full bird colonel and was supposed to work out of DIA Section 7B as a full bird, and was turned down. I think as an insurance policy he decided to start talking. Because he got pressure from the Secret Service about the Middle East connection.

You mean he came under pressure for things unrelated to Laos?

Right.

What kind of stuff was that?

About some Special Forces guys going to Chad and Sudan, and a couple of guys he had sent down to El Salvador to start doing some training, and allegedly the United States wasn't doing any of this stuff. He was trying to get teams together for the Company to send to obscure places in El Salvador, recruiting some of the old people. I think one of the guys from our mission is there.

But this is stuff he was doing as a government employee?

Right.

This was not free lance stuff?

Right.

Who was he working for, was that CIA?

This was under the direction of the Agency. Matter of fact, I'll give you their extension number back at Langley, if you want it.

How did you have these numbers for him, and that information?

Well, he knew that I was really tight with General Vang Pao, and so he said that if anything ever happens, call area code 202, 351-1100, and ask for extension 6145. That's supposedly called CDO, which is apparently where John Stein was in charge of covert defense operations.

Did you ever call him there?

I did once.

After this mission?

Yes. The day I got back to the United States I called, asked for the extension, and that time gave the code name Bohica, and next thing the guy says okay, give me your number and let me secure a line. And he called back. He said, "Forget this thing ever existed."

But did you ask him about the bottom line, we didn't know we were going to be told to kill anybody?

Right. I asked him that and said, "You know we were all

surprised about the very sophisticated weapons that were provided," and he just said, "You don't know anything, you didn't hear anything, nobody knows anything, this number doesn't exist. Just take the money and go have a good time." And Daniel Arnold, he was a major figure in this operation. He allegedly is retired from the Agency, and he's running a private company, International Research Associates, area code 703, 938-1868, in Vienna. [The other company on the business card is Tashkent Associates.] I also have the business card that Dan sent me thanking me for a letter, a secret letter I picked up down there to be delivered to the authorities back here in the United States.

A letter you picked up where?

From Laos.

So there were other things besides looking for the Americans?

I was supposed to pick up a letter and contact some foreign indigenous agents that had been working with the Hmong previously, on chemical warfare operations.

Do you know what those things were?

They kept that real hush hush.

You never knew whether they were planting evidence?

No, it was pretty much speculated though, and we sat down one day with one of them and I brought back one of the letters and decided to make a copy of it, and keep it, which I did.

How did the journalists get in touch with you?

I got a call from a couple of guys out of the Pentagon that knew all about this that I had been dealing with, and they said, "Look, we know we were duped, this whole thing was wrong, and we're going to give you some names of people, numbers to contact and don't tell them you heard from us in the Pentagon," and I'm not going to tell anybody who they were, so they can feel safe.

Were they making the point that they thought this was a rescue mission?

They themselves all thought and Deputy Inman of the CIA, he himself thought, it was a rescue mission too, he said. He said, if this was true, that we were going to assassinate people, it had to be renegades. He said it might be people like Wilson and Terpil or Agee or Marchetti or agents like that who are no good any more. He said maybe they tried to take it on their own and just end the problem, but he would never admit it.

How could he say that? You got a telegram from Langley.

Oh, we got all kinds of Telexes.

But they couldn't very well have been from anybody like Marchetti or Agee?

Oh I know. But he was using their names as former agents being renegades, who could have used Agency communications or Agency funding to do their own secret operation.

Did you actually speak with him personally?

No, Ted Koppel did, and related that back.

But how does he justify or explain the fact that the instructions came from Langley?

He says, "Prove it." And we said, "Okay, let's go to the Department of Energy, communications center, and see all the Telexes from this date to this date under Subject Bohica." And then he flipped his head and said, "How did you guys know about Subject Bohica?" And he says that due to national security, nothing can be discussed.

You mean Koppel mentioned the name of the operation to Inman?

Yeah, then he just flipped out. He said there's a law coming to pass, if you guys start revealing agents' names you're going to be tried and prosecuted, criminally.

Basically, everybody who seems to have known anything about it is taking the position that they all thought it was an operation to rescue someone, not to kill someone?

Right.

And yet the coded messages came both from Langley and from the Chief of Station.

Right. At the U.S. Embassy.

Has anybody said to you that they've been in touch with him?

One of the guys said that he didn't know. All he was doing was taking part of the secret message and delivering it to the appropriate people. He said, "I don't know what was in it. It came over in," I think he told me, "an ERKS 53 computer."

So he was passing a message but he didn't know what it was?

Right. He said the message came from Langley to Bangkok and then he just forwarded it on from Bangkok. No, he didn't say Langley, he said Virginia.

How did you receive communications when you were in the field in Laos, by radio?

No. We took in an awful lot of radios and other equipment that Uncle Sam provided, but we didn't communicate across the river. We came across and went down to Nakhon Phanom and sent messages via Telex to the Rajah Motel in Bangkok to the Department of Energy, Com. center, Washington, DC. Attn. Subject Bohica. The following purchase items are necessary, C7, A11, and so on.

And then the messages would come back the same way?

Right.

They'd go from DOE, Washington directly to the Rajah Motel?

Right.

And then you had somebody who would pick them up there?

Right. And then filter them up to the guys at Nakhon Phanom.

And then go back across the river?

Right.

So when you were all together and got the message that was telling you that these people couldn't be rescued, to bump them off, you were back inside the Thailand side of the border then?

Right. We were back in Nakhon Phanom. Because when they told us that the Huey pilot, all of a sudden the government pulled him out of Thailand and sent back on orders to the United States, we starting getting rather suspicious. You know we had all things set up and everything was squared away, and then all of a sudden . . .

When you say all set up, you mean all set up for a rescue attempt?

Right.

Then what sort of a plan was supposed to be involved if you were killing the people instead of rescuing them? You still needed a helicopter, didn't you?

No, because they were going to go in via indigenous and if we couldn't accomplish it, then we had large sums of money and were able to purchase medicine and stuff in

Scott Barnes in Thailand.

Thailand to give to certain indigenous. One of them would carry out any orders, no matter what they were. If we couldn't accomplish it, we had to abort, then the stuff was supposed to be up to him and he would accomplish it. As far as I know, he may have accomplished it.

You never got any details from there once you left?

No. Once we left, I cut communications. I talked to General Vang Pao about three or four weeks ago, and he just said, "The thing for us to do right now is just, we never knew each other."

Have you offered to go testify before the Intelligence Committee?

Yes. I told them, I said, "Hey put me on another government polygraph exam. You guys hired the world's best one, you sent me to a shrink, I got photos, I'll bring you documentation." And he said, "But you don't understand, Scott. You don't understand what you're saying." I said, "Yeah, I know." He said, "There are a lot of problems in the Middle East, in international conflicts; we went across a sovereign nation's border. In other words we engaged in an act of war." And I said, "I know that, and it was wrong, because I wouldn't have said anything if we were going to rescue, but when I found out what the truth was, I think it's wrong." And he said, "So do I." I said, "Let's have a Senate hearing," and he said, "We're having hearings but they're secret. We don't want the public to know." I said, "I think that's wrong. Why don't you guys want the truth out?" ●

Scott Barnes:

Spook or Spoof?

By Kevin Cody

"Scott Barnes is a Walter Mitty type," says South Bay Congressman Robert K. Dornan.

Retired Green Beret Lieutenant Colonel James "Bo" Gritz, described by his General during the Vietnam War as the "best commander of special mission commandos in the United States Army," says of Scott Barnes. "If you believe anything he says you're playing with the wrong end of the stick."

Ted Koppel of ABC *Nightline* completed eight hours of taping with Scott Barnes six weeks ago and planned a three-part report about him. But *Nightline* senior producer Stew Schwartz told *Easy Reader* Monday, "We are not preparing a program (on Scott Barnes)."

Columnist Jack Anderson's office also interviewed Barnes over six weeks ago, but has yet to make mention of Barnes in print.

Monday morning *Easy Reader* received a call from a person identifying himself as Garth Williams, a *Los Angeles Times* reporter. The man said, "I've heard rumors you're planning a story about Scott Barnes. Barnes is full of lies and I advise you to really research this before printing anything about him." A check with the *Times* personnel department revealed they do not have a reporter named Garth Williams.

A brief recounting of Barnes' story is sufficient for understanding why the 28-year-old Redondo resident is viewed with suspicion and skepticism.

Barnes claims to have been part of a U.S. government supported team of ex-Green Berets who crossed the Mekong River from Thailand into northern Laos in October, 1981 to search for American prisoners of war. Upon locating and photographing two Caucasians in a prison camp. Barnes says the team received orders to assassinate the prisoners. He says the team refused to follow the orders and disbanded.

Barnes says Congressman Robert Dornan's office,

Hughes Aircraft in El Segundo, and a 'safe house' in Playa del Rey were used as covers to make the operation appear to be the work of renegade, ex-Green Berets.

Scott Barnes' Story

I first met and interviewed Scott Barnes at Hope Chapel in Hermosa, where he was recently "reborn," and where he spends much of his free time in preparation to become a minister. He is six-foot, 190 pounds, with a beard and a baby face. His dark glasses, leather jacket and grey, late model automobile, conspicuous only for its lack of even model name markings, earmark him as an undercover agent.

For the interview he had prepared copies of half a dozen of his letters of commendation, dating from a 1973 Department of Treasury letter thanking him for his assistance, while still at Redondo High School, in the arrest of a subject "illegally manufacturing numerous bombs." The most recent letter, dated March 16, 1978, from the San Diego District Attorney's office, noted, "We have worked with Officer Scott Barnes since 1976 on matters concerning outlaw motorcyclists. These offenses have ranged from narcotics to conspiracy to commit murder."

A copy of Barnes' FBI report revealed he had been in the army "attached to the 14th Military Police at Fort Lewis, Washington." But the 10 page report revealed very little else because it is almost entirely blacked out.

Of the more curious items he produced were photos he said were taken of himself and other team members on the Mekong River, copies of business cards identifying him as a staff assistant to Congressman Dornan, and a page from Dornan's office guest book.

The significance of the page from Dornan's guest book is that it lists the names of Barnes, Bo Gritz and General Vang Pao under the date of August 26. Barnes said the three men met that day in the congressman's office with Dornan aide Stan Mullin to plan an incursion into Laos.

There remain 2,456 American servicemen unaccounted for in Southeast Asia, and there have been 397 reports of first hand sightings since the fall of Saigon, the Pentagon

---

This article first appeared in the April 15, 1982 issue of the Hermosa Beach [California] *Easy Reader*. We are grateful to Kevin Cody and *Easy Reader* for their permission to reprint. Copyright © 1982 by *Easy Reader*.

reports. Of the missing, 560 were lost in Laos.

General Vang Pao was a Laotian major general during the Vietnam War. His 40,000 Hmong tribespeople were a secret army for the CIA during this period.

According to Barnes, Vang Pao was asked at the meeting in Dornan's office to provide underground assistance for the mission into Laos. "In exchange for his help," said Barnes, "we were going to equip his people with a lot of firepower so they could continue their little war—lots of automatic weapons and LAWs (Light Anti-tank Weapons). These are plastic rocket launchers about three feet long that you rest on your shoulder and use to knock out aircraft on the ground and machine gun nests."

Barnes said he was first contacted about the mission, code-named "Operation Bohica, (bend over, here it comes again)," a year ago April while he was visiting Hope Chapel's church in Maui.

"An ex-SOG (Green Beret Special Operating Group) got in touch with me and said I was to get ready for a secret invasion into Laos to rescue POWs. I'm a personal friend of General Vang Pao, and was needed to gain his cooperation because you cannot do an operation down there without the underground. There are too many factions—Pathet Lao, Free Lao, Viet Cong, NVA, Hmong.

"Vang Pao had been mad at the CIA because it failed to make good on promises to his people. So to convince him this wasn't a CIA operation I arranged for him to meet Bo Gritz at Congressman Dornan's office. The CIA has its meetings on the beach or at the Taco Bell in Hermosa, not in congressmens' offices.

"Gritz was a 'retired' Green Beret working undercover at Hughes Aircraft in El Segundo."

(A phone call to the number Barnes gave for Gritz at Hughes' Advanced Program Development, Overseas Operation revealed Gritz had been, but was no longer, employed there.)

(Until asked to stop last June by the government, Gritz had been leader of a widely-publicized program called "Operation Velvet Hammer," established to train teams of ex-Green Berets to go on POW rescue missions.)

"A few days after meeting in Dornan's office, Stan Mullin called me. 'You guys signed in Dornan's guest book. I'm taking the page out because we can't put you guys in Dornan's office.' Mullin told me. Vang Pao wouldn't have wanted it known he was in Dornan's office planning an invasion either. So I told Mullin to mail the page to me and I would destroy it. But politics being what it is, I kept it.

"In October three more special forces types joined Bo and I. The sixth guy was already in Bangkok. We spent two days together in planning at a guy named Vic's house in Playa del Rey, and then four of us took off for Bangkok. Bo, who remained in the states, gave us business cards indicating we worked for Dornan, and we carried diplomatic passports, as well as blue ones so if we were picked up we could claim diplomatic immunity.

"After we arrived, another member of the team and I went across the Mekong River at Ban Pheng to just a little bit west of Mahaxai with 30 indigenous forces. We came across a prison camp where we took photos of two Caucasian prisoners, and then crossed back into Thailand near Nakhon Panom.

"The whole time we were wondering why we had been equipped with AR 180s with silencers, night scopes, laser sightings and teflon ammunition. Because we were supposed to be on a rescue mission and these were assassination weapons. We also were concerned that our helicopter pilot was called out of the country.

"What was really going on we didn't figure out until we got two telexes delivered to us at Nakhon Phanom, which, when put together and decoded, ordered, 'If merchandise confirmed, liquidate.'

"I heard that and said I was leaving. But as I started to get up one of the guys slapped me across the face, and then J.D. Bath, our communications specialist, calmed the guy down. Bath said, "Yea, we better get out of here. There's a lot of firefights, and the rumor's getting around that there are Caucasians in the area.'

Barnes with J.D. Bath on Thai side of the Mekong River.

"So he and I returned to Bangkok together, and I flew back to the states.

"The day I got back I called the number I'd been given for the CIA Covert Defense Operation (CDO). When I gave the code named Bohica the guy answering the phone. "Forget this thing ever existed.'

"I said, 'You know we were all surprised about the very sophisticated weapons that were provided,' and he said, 'You don't know anything, you didn't hear anything, this number doesn't exist. Just take the money and go have a good time.'

"I put the operation out of my mind until Christmas Eve morning when members of the Torrance police, David Gregg of the executive branch of the Secret Service, and Fred Capps, Jr. from FBI counter-intelligence knocked on my door in Redondo.

DORNAN confirms LAOS

"They said, 'We need to talk to you about Bo Gritz and Indochina,' I said, 'I don't know what you're talking about.' And they said, 'Either you come with us now, or you can talk to a federal grand jury in Washington, D.C.'

"They questioned me for about three hours at the Torrance Police Station. They wanted to know what really happened in Thailand, why we had such sophisticated weapons. So it was obvious someone was talking, and from reading the papers a few weeks later it looked like Bo. The *Daily Breeze*, the *Boston Globe*, and the *Chicago Tribune* all did stories about Bo's efforts to organize a POW rescue team and how the government pulled the rug out from under him. But he wasn't making any mention of what we did, or the order we received to liquidate the prisoners.

"I started to get a little bit uptight because I know Bo must be passing my name around. So through a friend at Hope Chapel I got in touch with Ted Koppel of ABC *Nightline*, and the story blew him away. He said he was going to run it in three parts, but first he needed me to take a lie detector test. He hired Chris Guggis, the best there is—he did James Earl Ray, King's assassin—and I passed 100 percent. Then Koppel asked me to take a psychiatric exam, and he hired Dr. Hacker who did the examination of Patty Hearst. And he certified that I was 100 percent square.

"Next Jack Anderson's people and the Senate Intelligence Committee began looking into my story. But no one's going public with it. They're all looking for someone else to break the story first."

Barnes said he wanted his story printed as an "insurance policy." But he also stressed he has been greatly influenced by his pastor at Hope Chapel to let the truth be known. And there is the possibility that his story could be sold to Hollywood, provided it can ever be verified.

Congressman Dornan's Story

Congressman Robert K. Dornan is fighting for his political life in his underdog bid for the Republican senatorial nomination against Barry Goldwater, Jr., Maureen Reagan, Pete Wilson and Pete McClowsky. Because of the Democrats' redistricting this year he became a congressman without a district.

When I reached him by phone Friday afternoon, his mind was on the race. "We're where we hoped we'd be in the polls at this point, and the money is coming in enough so that I think we'll be competitive. If I can get one TV spot for every two of Barry's, we'll do okay," he said.

I told the congressman I was calling about Scott Barnes. "Oh yea. Did anybody move that on the wire services?" he asked.

I told him I'd heard the story on KPFK-Pacifica radio, but that was all.

Dornan replied, "Yea, they're one of the ones I couldn't get back to.

We had a little explosion yesterday. AP called. UPI called. CBS out of New York and ABC out of Washington all called. And they all accepted what I had to say.

"It was a false story. Scott Barnes is a Walter Mitty type. What he did was come to my office last August when I was in Israel fixing the F-16, and he met with a staffer, just like anybody else.

"He also asked for Stan Mullin's card (the aide Barnes met with), and had it duplicated with his name, which is probably a violation of the law. If it isn't it should be.

"Bo Gritz, the guy he came with, I rather liked—he's for real. The *Daily Breeze* did a big story on him, and I met with him later, alone.

"Gritz is upset with the government for not following through enough on the POW thing, and so am I."

I asked Dornan if he believed Barnes had gone into Laos.

"I don't think so, but I have no way of knowing. I do believe he went to Bangkok because he throws round a lot of hotel names that are correct."

"Did you talk to Gritz about an American team going into Laos?" I asked.

Dornan said he had. "It was about him gearing up to send American teams into Laos, but they (the government) jerked the rug out from under Gritz—took away their support. That would have been last November."

"Did you talk to President Reagan about Gritz's plan," I asked Dornan.

"I told Gritz I would bring this up with President Reagan, which I did December 27 aboard Air Force I. But I didn't talk to Reagan about anything specific. I told the president I didn't want him to lose interest in the POW's and he assured me he wouldn't. I said to him, 'Stay on top of those intelligence briefings, and if they get any hotter, please take the action you think is necessary. And, of course, Reagan's smarter than some people think he is. He's not going to comment even to his own congressman. He just said, 'Don't worry Bob. I won't forget the issue.'"

"Do you think the page out of your guest book and the use of your business cards indicate an effort by someone to use your office as a cover?" I asked Dornan.

"I have to assume premeditation. Barnes might have taken Stan's card and gotten that idea later, but the ripping out of the log book—that's too suspicious. There was premeditation there."

"Have you ever talked to Barnes?" I asked Dornan.

"Once, about two months ago," Dornan said. "I didn't recognize his name. Bo had never told me the name of the guy who was with him that August meeting. I was having an interview with Joe Scott of the *Political Animal* when Sally (Dornan's wife) said Barnes was on the phone and was going to go public if I didn't call him within the hour. So I called him and he gave me this big story about the CIA. Frankly, I didn't buy it.

"I knew if there had been any truth to it Bo Gritz would have told me. So I just heard Barnes out."

"Barnes claims your aide mailed him the guest book page and asked him to destroy it because you didn't want it known the CIA was plotting an invasion in your office," I told Dornan.

"Why would we have mailed it to him if we felt it should have been destroyed?" Dornan asked back.

"Bo" Gritz's Story

James "Bo" Gritz, the 43-year-old retired Green Beret lieutenant colonel and recipient of five Silver Stars for his service in Viet Nam, lives in a modest house in Westchester near Loyola University with his third wife and two young children.

He is an affable, powerfully built man with a strong handshake and a strong gaze. He was wearing leather pants, a western shirt and cowboy boots when I met him Saturday morning, the day following my conversations with Barnes and Dornan. Over the fireplace in the living room, were, as Barnes had said there would be, framed, black belt certificates for both Gritz and his wife.

Gritz's office, a small room off the garage filled with military memorabilia, was also as Barnes had described it.

"Let's start by taking a look at that page from Dornan's guest book, because I just can't imagine signing in at Dornan's office. I never sign guest books," Gritz said as we sat down.

"Here's a letter from General Vang Pao. As you can see, his signature is pretty unique."

I compared it with the signature in the guest book and there was no resemblance. vang see U.' no s, yang y

"Now here's a letter I wrote to Bobby Ray Inman (deputy director of the CIA) following our meeting on December 9. My signature is also fairly unique," Gritz said.

It too bore no resemblance to the way his name was signed in the guest book.

"Barnes is a well meaning young man, but he's on everybody's nut list," Gritz said. "And he has never done anything for the United States government. I will stake my career as a colonel with my hands on the Bible on that one.

"What I have learned about Barnes in the last year is that he has a terrible identification problem. He'll pick up on any bit of news, like the Hell's Angels thing. He called me one time, terribly excited because he was going to be on ABC *Close-Up*. He said, 'Be sure to watch it. Then you'll see who I really am, and lo and behold there was Barnes for about 10 seconds saying he was a police undercover agent who planted narcotics on the Hell's Angels so they could be arrested.

"But if you'll check with the editor in San Francisco, or with the Hell's Angels' defense attorneys you'll find out Barnes volunteered to testify on behalf of the defense, and after they checked out his story, they found it was all so much smoke.

"Check with Ron Soble at the *Los Angeles Times*. He told Soble a story that in my best day I couldn't have invented—that he had been recruited by me to work for Kadafi.

"A few weeks after that one Bill Redeker of ABC *Nightline* called me with Barnes' latest twist—that I had recruited him for an operation in which we were to locate and assassinate American POW's.

"I told Redeker basically what I'm telling you—that Barnes first contacted me after 'Velvet Hammer' went public in May, 1981.

"Barnes called me, and his first words were, 'How would you like to be a Zulu leader?' I said to him, 'What is a Zulu leader? If it means strapping a claymore (explosive) to my chest and self-destructing, no thanks.' Barnes said, 'No, we're going to rescue American POW's.' He was in Hawaii and claimed to have a group that wanted me as their leader.

"Next thing I know, Barnes is calling me collect from Thailand. He needs money because he claimed intelligence agents had stolen his passport and wallet. I told him to go to the American Embassy.

"When he came back he called and said he had secret photos showing POW camps that he wanted to show me. I agreed to meet him at a Mexican restaurant by the surfer statue at the pier in Hermosa, and I sent what he gave me through to intelligence. They informed me the photos were total fabrication."

I asked Gritz if he had seen Barnes other than that one time.

"Not that I recall," he answered.

"Has he ever been to your house?" I asked.

A full seven seconds pause elapsed before he responded. "Jesus. I don't know. We can ask my wife. It seems like she did say Barnes wanted to come over one day. He had talked to her on the phone and wanted to meet her. He thought I was such a lucky guy to have a wife like her, because his wife had walked out on him and taken his child. So I don't know if Barnes came over or not, but it's likely."

"Barnes showed me a Dornan business card with his name on it. Whose idea were those?" I asked.

"Well, I don't know what you're referring to," Gritz answered.

"The use of Dornan's business cards with agents' names listed as staff aides," I said.

"I really don't know what you're talking about," Gritz repeated. I asked him if he recalled Barnes and Mullin attending the meeting he had in Dornan's office with Vang Pao.

Gritz answered he could not recall if Mullin had been present, but he was certain Barnes wasn't.

"Barnes said you worked at Hughes as a cover," I said.

"Yea, that was arranged so I could do the things necessary to be done, and not be on the military payroll. Somebody had to pick up the tab. But I honestly prefer you not mention Hughes because they're a damn good company. If we didn't have companies like Hughes, how would we ever be able to do things?"

Gritz explained he had been asked to retire from the military in 1979 "so I could have access to the (foreign) borders without involving the United States government. Because any cross border operation, if I were a green color carrier, meaning an active duty government person, that would be an act of war."

"Who asked you to retire?" I asked.

"General Aaron, who was deputy director of the Defense Intelligence Agency (the Pentagon's intelligence arm entrusted with official responsibility for investigating reports of missing POW's). Aaron was my group commander in Viet Nam. He first brought the POW thing to me in Panama in 1976. He told me 'Bo, we've got increasing evidence that Americans are still being held captive.'

"The plan, until the morning of December 9, when Admiral Poulson (current head of the Defense Intelligence Agency) pulled the plug on Operation Grand Eagle, was for me to return to active duty as a Washington, D.C. project officer and be a front man for the Activity."

(Operation Grand Eagle was the "Activity's" plan to send special forces in to rescue POW's. The "Activity" refers to the Counter Terrorist Task Force, which was involved in the rescue of General Dozier in Italy. It is designed to transcend the cumbersome Joint Chiefs of Staff bureaucracy in situations where Americans abroad are in life-threatening situations. The organization has a Special Forces unit assigned to it.)

I asked Gritz if he was certain Barnes hadn't participated in anything similar to Operation Grand Eagle.

Gritz responded. "If Barnes had any capability I'd have probably hired him. But just look at Barnes. Does he look like an intelligence officer? I look like I was over there four years. But what skills does Barnes have? What's he good at?

Rescuing prisoners? When did he last do that?"

Sorting Out

Following my morning visit with Gritz I went to see Barnes again at Hope Chapel and told him why I thought ABC and Jack Anderson hadn't done anything with his story. Dornan and Gritz are simply more believable. I myself had no idea what to believe.

"Call J.D. Bath and ask him about 'Bohica,'" Barnes said to me. "He was our communications specialist." Barnes gave me a Florida phone number.

I made the call from the singles' pastor's office at Hope Chapel. "I'm calling about Bo Gritz and Operation Bohica," I told Bath when his wife put him on the phone.

The ensuing pause was so long I thought I'd lost Bath. But finally he said. "Bo should have been able to tell you everything there was on that."

I said I needed a second confirmation on some information, particularly about Scott Barnes.

"He's a flake. I won't go any further than to say the guy's crazier than a mutha fucker."

"Was he a problem on the operation?" I asked.

"No, not so much. He was cooperative, though we had a little dissension—he and one of the other members," Bath said.

"Are you the one who pulled Mac back after he hit Barnes?" I asked.

Bath answered. "I just told them they had to knock that bs off because we hadn't completed the mission. I wasn't in charge, but I was sort of the tie breaker when everyone got in an argument."

"Was that in Laos?"

"We didn't go into Laos, just Thailand," Bath answered.

"Did any members go into Laos?" I asked.

"No."

"When did you come back?"

"I don't remember the exact date, we were moving around so much. The first part of November, approximately."

"Why didn't you go into Laos?"

"Because we didn't have any intention to in the first place. On top of that, it would have been suicidal. The Vietnamese are using Laos as an avenue to carry supplies and ammunition and troops down into Cambodia. So to be sure nobody comes out their back side they have about three heavy Laotian divisions right along the Mekong River between Laos and Thailand. Plus they have air cover."

"Did Gritz stay in the states for the operation?" I asked.

"Yea."

"And Barnes, was he much assistance?"

"He was at first. He and I were originally together, just breaking ground over there. But he wasn't really as well versed in the area as he had claimed to be. Once we got there I found that out."

"Would you describe the operation as a success?"

"To be real truthful about it, I'm not supposed to say anything because it went to, ah . . . that's all I can tell you."

"Did you find evidence of POW's?"

"We thought there were several people in a particular location, but there was nothing we could pin down."

I asked Bath if he had spent time with Barnes and Gritz

at the "safe house" in Playa del Rey.

"Yea, we were all there for five or six days. No more than that," Bath said.

"How do you feel about the use being made of the information you brought back?" I asked.

"Well, I don't know. The Delta (a group of elite Green Berets) runs in tight circles. They really don't put out to the press everything they're doing."

"Did you also have business cards from Congressman Dornan's office?" I asked.

"Where did you get information like that?" Bath responded.

"I've been interviewing Bo and Scott," I said.

"Well, those things were made up for us. They were a piece of crap. We got rid of them".

"Did you get the cards from Bo?"

"Yes, I believe we did."

"Barnes is saying you guys were to go into Laos and liquidate any Caucasians you found. Are you familiar with that story?"

"I heard faintly about that. I never did get the full skinny on it. But Scott Barnes, I'll tell you up front, is a flake, a habitual liar. The guy tells some of the most far fetched garbage I ever heard."

"Did Bo originally contact you about the operation?"

"No, but he was involved with the people who originally contacted me."

"Do you also work through Hughes?"

"I'm gainfully unemployed."

"Do you still have Hughes radio equipment?"

"No, I sent it back."

"What's your response to Scott's insistence that you guys went across into Laos?"

"That's an absolute lie, and I'll take a polygraph test on that. I can account for everyday that we were there. Scott did want to go across, but there was no way in hell we was gonna cross."

"Can you verify that you were using DOE telexes? (to communicate stateside)"

"Yea, ah . . ."

"And this was a CIA program?"

"It was not. It was a private sector program, to my knowledge."

The conversation ended with our exchanging reports on the California and Florida weather conditions.

But shortly after hanging up I recalled Barnes had shown me a picture he said was of himself and Bath on the bank of the Mekong River, which divides Thailand and Laos. If the picture was taken there, it places Barnes, if not in Laos, at least on its border.

I called Bath back, and after apologizing for interrupting his Easter weekend again, asked where the Bohica team had spent most of its time.

"It's kind of hard to pronounce—Nakhon Phanom. We just called it NKP," Bath said.

"That's on the Mekong River?"

"Yes," he answered.

"I also wanted to ask about the dog tag you and Scott were given. Did you find out who it belonged to?"

Bath answered. "No, Scott got it on the initial contact, and I sent the information back on it. But the name wasn't being carried on the POW MIA list, or anything else."

"Did you see the letter written in Laotian with your and

Scott's names in it?" I asked.

"Oh yea. I believe that was a letter Scott was going to deliver to Vang Pao."

After this second conversation with Bath, Barnes suggested we visit the "safe house" in Playa del Rey, which he described to me as we drove. "Vic has a blue Mercedes," Barnes said. There was a blue Mercedes in the driveway when we reached Vic's address.

Barnes parked around the corner. As I walked toward the house I encountered a tall, trim, well-built man on the sidewalk.

He acknowledged he was Vic and I introduced myself.

Then I asked if he had a few minutes to talk about "Operation Bohica."

He looked very coldly at me for several seconds before finally asking, "Where did you get this address?"

I said I had interviewed Bo Gritz that morning.

'I'm going to call Bo," he said. With some relief I recalled Gritz said he would be out for the day. Vic went to a phone in his garage and made the call. He left a message on Gritz's answer phone.

"I can't talk to you until I talk to Bo," Vic said. He took my number but never called me.

The rest of the weekend was spent trying to reach some of the other people Barnes insisted could further help to verify his story. The list included ABC's Ted Koppel, a reporter in Jack Anderson's office, General Vang Pao, a girlfriend who had accompanied Barnes on a visit to Vang Pao shortly after Barnes's return, and Dornan's former aide, Stan Mullin.

Mullin was the only one I was able to reach. He returned my call Easter Sunday evening.

I asked him if Barnes, Gritz and Vang Pao had ever met together in Dornan's office.

"Yes," he said. "Barnes had called and asked if our office could be used as a meeting place for Gritz and Vang Pao. Two other Asians were with Vang Pao as well."

"Most of the meeting was devoted to discussions about 'yellow rain' in the area and about the possibility of photographing POW's imprisoned there," Mullin said.

"Whose idea was it to use Dornan's business cards?" I asked.

"I actually have no idea. We (Dornan's office) were not told about it. Scott asked for a card of mine when I first met him to verify I was who I said I was. That was the only card I gave out. The next thing I knew Scott returned from Asia and he showed me a duplicate of mine with his name on it."

"Did Congressman Dornan participate in any meetings with Gritz, Barnes and Vang Pao?" I asked.

Mullin answered, "No. The only meeting I know of between the congressman and Gritz was probably a couple of weeks following the meeting you're referring to. It was a spontaneous meeting. Gritz came by on a Sunday and happened to catch the congressman in. I think they met on one other occasion also."

"Do you recall sending Scott a page out of the congressman's guest book?" I asked.

"Yes, there were a couple pages in a normal, standard guest book. Scott had mentioned he was concerned about Vang Pao signing in, so I think he called me after the fact, and being sensitive to whatever needs he may have had, I pulled the page out and sent it to him. I didn't particularly understand, but I felt it didn't make any difference to us."

Mullin said.

I started off Monday morning with a call to Ron Soble at the *Los Angeles Times*. As Gritz had suggested, I asked Soble his views on Barnes' credibility.

Soble answered, "I don't know anything about Barnes. I worked just a few hours on a story relating to him, but was never able to reach him. Isn't Barnes the one who's supposed to be saying bad things about Gritz? Gritz should be able to tell you about Barnes."

Recalling that Gritz had said the defense attorneys for the Hell's Angels would confirm Barnes was a phony, I called Jack Palladino. Palladino was a principal attorney for the Hell's Angels in their two-and-one-half year, $15 million trial on racketeering charges in California. The trial ended in a hung jury.

Said Palladino, "Barnes was an undercover police officer with BET (Biker Enforcement Team), a State Attorney General's Office operation. He's the kind of guy who gets fervent, and may work 80 hours a week, but is difficult to control. He volunteered to testify for the defense and did so in January, 1981. We tried to use his testimony to show the police were waging a vendetta against the Hell's Angels, that they had attempted to set up Sonny Barger (leader of the Hell's Angels). But most of Barnes's testimony was blocked. The judge ruled it was too broad ranging, too far afield. We did check Barnes out, and he was who he said he was."

Monday I also talked to the girl Barnes said he had taken to meet General Vang Pao. She recalled that the meeting took place on the afternoon of Friday, November 6 (a few days after Barnes claims to have returned from Thailand).

And I talked to General Vang Pao, who chuckled at my questions, but volunteered nothing. "I don't have to talk about this thing," was the only complete sentence I got out of him.

Spencer Davis, spokesperson for the Senate Intelligence Committee, confirmed that Barnes's allegations were being looked into, but said they are "hard to swallow."

Central Intelligence Agency spokesperson Dale Peterson, in response to questions about Barnes, said, "We have never ordered Mr. Barnes to kill anyone. As a matter of fact, we've never had any relationship with Mr. Barnes."

In regards to Gritz, Peterson said, "No, we have not had any activities in relationship to him either."

"Ever?" I asked.

"That is correct," he said.

ABC *Nightline's* producer Stew Schwartz, when asked for a copy of Barnes's polygraph report, refused to release it. But Lucette Lagnado, the reporter in Jack Anderson's office working on the Barnes story, said she saw the report. Among the questions Barnes was asked, she said, were "Did you go into Laos?" and "Were you ordered to assassinate American prisoners of war?"

According to Lagnado, Barnes answered yes to both questions, and the test showed he was telling the truth.

The mind recoils at believing 28-year-old Scott Barnes passed a lie detector test administered by the foremost polygrapher in the world because Barnes was, in fact, ordered to assassinate two American POW's.

Yet, to think he passed the lie detector test, developed as much convincing evidence as he did, ensnared a Congressman and several experienced intelligence officers, all while not telling the truth may be even more frightening. ●

Mystery in Bangkok:

Yellow Rain Skeptic Found Dead

By Ellen Ray

The mysterious death of a U.S. government official attached to the State Department's refugee program in Thailand, who was also a known disbeliever of the U.S. chemical warfare propaganda, has added a new dimension to growing evidence of yellow rain fabrication—and worse—by the CIA.

Jerrold Barker Daniels, 40, of Missoula, Montana, died April 29, 1982 in his Bangkok apartment, allegedly from carbon monoxide poisoning. Journalists in Bangkok said that Daniels had been keeping copious records about "something secret," but that all his private papers were missing when authorities said they found his body—some two days after he died. A Thai university student was found unconscious in his apartment; the mother of the student apparently informed the police that her son was missing, and they learned that he was last seen with Daniels. Now

recovered from a coma, the student told a U.S. journalist that he does not remember what happened.

Information remains scant in what has become a major scandal, stretching from the remote Lao refugee camps of northern Thailand to an equally remote ranch in western Montana where the titular head of the Hmong tribespeople—General Vang Pao—resides. But according to CAIB's sources, the FBI's counter-intelligence office in Washington is investigating Daniels's death.

The Strange Death of Jerry Daniels

The U.S. Embassy initially released the unlikely story that Daniels died from a leaking gas stove. Some Embassy officials even claimed, off the record, that they had "fooled around" with the pilot on Daniels's stove while drunk at a party there a few nights before. The Embassy then clamped

Department of State *Newsletter* (June 1979) photograph of Jerry Daniels (second from right) at Nong Khai refugee center.

A rare photo of Long Cheng, Laos, CIA command post during the war.

down and refused any further statements. However, enough information was leaked to the *Bangkok Post* to make it appear there was a homosexual incident involved, limiting further inquiry.

In Washington, meanwhile, Henry B. Cushing, Director of the AID Office of Refugee Processing and Admissions, attributed Daniels's death—equally improbably—to carbon monoxide escaping from a hot water heater. In addition, Cushing confirmed what other sources told *CAIB*—that Daniels had worked for the CIA in support operations for Vang Pao in the late 1960s and early 1970s. But "he had no intelligence function" in Thailand, Cushing cautioned.

The Role of Vang Pao

When the CIA-Hmong nerve center in Long Cheng, Laos was overrun by communist forces in 1975, Vang Pao made his way to Daniels's home state of Montana, via Bangkok and West Germany. In Montana he paid cash for homes, ranches, and cars for his extended family, and dug in to continue directing his people in the CIA's secret war, now exposed. [See sidebar.]

Jerry Daniels's relationship with Vang Pao was well known. To some he appeared like a son to the General; to others, however, the relationship seemed more business-

General Vang Pao

General Vang Pao, the 53-year-old Hmong hill tribe chieftain, owes his fortunes to long service with the colonial invaders of his native country, Laos. The General's military career began at age 13 as a jungle messenger for French intelligence during World War II. He fought closely at the side of the French at Dienbienphu in 1954, but escaped capture by the Vietnamese victors by marching his Hmong troops into the mountains.

In 1959-60, the so-called Armee Clandestine (Secret Army) was founded with CIA sponsorship. As Martin Goldstein wrote in his study, *American Policy Towards Laos*, the Armee Clandestine was "armed, equipped, fed, paid, guided strategically and tactically, and often transported into and out of battle by the CIA."

Long Cheng, in north central Laos, was the base of operations for Vang Pao and the CIA. Virtually uninhabited before 1962, it grew in direct proportion to the CIA's secret war, and in profitability to the expanding opium trade in the Golden Triangle. By 1969 some 30,000 Hmong lived there, making it the second largest city in Laos. Of the 100 to 150 tons annual opium production in Laos, more than 75% was produced by the Hmong, some of that at Long Cheng in partnership with the CIA.

When Long Cheng was overrun in 1975, Vang Pao moved his family to Missoula, Montana, where he laid out almost $200,000 in cash for property including a 400-acre farm which, he said, "looks just like my country, the Plain of Jars."

Vang Pao, however, is no longer undisputed leader of the Hmong exiles in the U.S. (Their numbers are closely guarded by the State Department, but well exceed 30,000.) And though Vang Pao spends at least half his time in Orange County in southern California at what is described as a mercenary training camp for Lao resistance fighters, many Hmong are not willing to sacrifice more at the order of Vang Pao. They have lost too much already. ●

like. In 1979 American Mennonite missionaries John and Beulah Yoder visited the reception center for Lao refugees in Nong Khai, Thailand. As they picked their way through the different groups of refugees, some exhausted and wounded from raids against Lao government positions, John Yoder was approached by a young English-speaking Hmong who asked him if he knew "Jerry Hall." Yoder asked who Hall was and the Hmong explained that he had worked with Hall at Long Cheng during the war. Afterwards, and until just recently, the Hmong refugee had been fighting in the Phu Bia area of Laos, a former CIA-Hmong stronghold. Now he expected to meet Hall in Thailand.

"The Hmong people do what he says," he told Yoder. "He brings us messages from the 'big man.'" When Yoder

asked who the "big man" was, the refugee answered. "Mr. Vang Pao. When the 'big man' speaks, the Hmong listen. He will tell us if we should return to Laos and fight or if we should remain here and try to go to America." On returning to Vientiane, John Yoder asked the Charge d'Affaires at the U.S. Embassy there, George Roberts, who Jerry Hall was; he was told, "Jerrold Barker-Daniels."

It was not long after this incident that Jerry Daniels confided to a BBC reporter that he did not believe the U.S.-Hmong allegations about yellow rain. Coming from

Vang Pao (center) with CIA advisor, George Bacon (left). Bacon was later killed in Angola carrying out mercenary activities.

Credit: Harley Hettick

General Vang Pao, the CIA's man in the secret war, on his Montana ranch.

someone with Daniels's close connections with the Hmong, and his intelligence background, the reporter was understandably surprised.

The Yellow Rain Propaganda

Bangkok, with Hong Kong a close second, is the center of the yellow rain propaganda war. The *Bangkok Post* and the more prestigious *Far Eastern Economic Review* virtually parrot the U.S. charges, with little attempt to verify them. At least one of the reporters who writes often on the subject, and is picked up in the West, was formerly with Forum World Features and World Features Service [see *CAIB* Numbers 7, 10, and 12].

Given his special position with the refugees, Daniels must have interviewed Touy Manikham, the Lao pilot who defected, alleging that he had fired rockets loaded with gas on Hmong hill-tribe villages between 1977 and late 1978. Few believe the Manikham story, filled as it is with inconsistencies, not the least of which is that Manikham was American-trained, and flew five years of combat against the communist forces in Laos from the U.S. base at Udorn, Thailand. By war's end he was flying missions from Vang Pao's camp at Long Cheng, defending the very Hmong guerrillas he recently claimed to have attacked with yellow rain on orders from the Pathet Lao and the Vietnamese.

Jerry Daniels knew, if anyone did, the true story behind the dramatic media coup by Dr. Amos Townsend, who led

R. Neveu/Gamma

Former Colonel Dr. Amos Townsend, the mycotoxin mogul.

a three person ABC-TV crew by elephant through the jungle for six hours into Kampuchea to interview Khmer Rouge soldiers, alleged victims of a chemical attack by the Vietnamese. Dr. Townsend personally brought the yellow rain samples out of Kampuchea and carried them to Bangkok, whence they were rushed to Washington and slipped into the laboratory of Professor Mirocha. [See *Part I: Yellow Rain*, in this issue.]

Jerry Daniels must have known Townsend well; the doctor worked for the International Rescue Committee with all its intelligence connections [See *CAIB* Number 12], as medical director of the Nong Khai refugee camp until late 1980. Then, Townsend said, he was "approached by two American investigators" to give his assistance in investigating the poison gas reports. "Released" by IRC for full time investigating, Townsend told the *Far Eastern Economic Review* that he feels particularly "sensitive" about yellow rain because during the Korean War he worked on biological warfare at Fort Detrick. Could some of Daniels's missing notes involve Townsend?

Finally, Daniels's death coincided with a *Bangkok Post* story claiming that Lao resistance forces had captured a rocket and warhead bearing Soviet markings and believed to be armed with mycotoxin chemicals. The U.S., according to *Asia Week*, waited breathlessly for the "final, indisputable evidence they have sought so long," the smoking gun. Curiously, the Lao troops who "found" the rocket grenade took it to the Austrian Embassy in Bangkok, rather than to the U.S. Embassy. Were they afraid that Daniels might not buy their story? As it turned out later, no, one did, but this was just hours before Daniels died.

Unanswered Questions

On the evening of May 8, ten days after he died, the body of Jerrold Barker Daniels arrived at the Missoula airport—from Bangkok via New York, a strange route. The metal-lined coffin, screwed shut, varnished over and sealed, was accompanied by U.S. State Department and Thai government officials. For two days of Hmong ceremonial rituals, U.S. bodyguards watched over the sealed coffin night and day. And when the final interment ceremony commenced, with nine Hmong pallbearers, the "big man" was there to pay his last respects.

There are some postscripts to the Daniels affair. A young mortuary worker claims the State Department paid for the funeral in cash, but his boss denies it. He says that the body was putrified, suggesting a wound, but of course the coffin remained nailed shut. The *Bangkok Post* announcement was careful to mention that Daniels's body had no wounds. There were rumors in Bangkok that his hands had been bound, that there were rope burns on the wrists. Moreover, there are rumors that there have been at least two other strange deaths of U.S. Embassy personnel in Bangkok in the last year.

Daniels's mother told a Cleveland reporter that as far as she knew her son's job was to interview Hmong refugees to see if they qualified to immigrate to the U.S. The criteria, she said, were strict; they had to have served with Uncle Sam during the secret war. Vang Pao also seems to be losing influence with some of these Humong, who are challenging his leadership. Perhaps he has given too much of his people, and got too little in return. Perhaps Jerry Daniels had come to that opinion too. ●

June 11, 1941 Palo Alto, California
April 28, 1982   Bangkok, Thialand

SERVICES
9:30 A.M. Sunday, May 9, 1982
Mountain View Mortuary Chapel

HMONG RITUAL
4:00 P.M. Saturday, May 9, 1982
All Day Sunday, May 9, 1982

PALLBEARERS

Folan   Charly
General   Terrible
Ring Man   Peter Built

HONORARY PALLBEARERS

Worm   Judy
Lucky   Spider
Sancho   Glass Man

INTERMENT
11:00 A.M. Monday, May 10, 1982
Missoula Cemetery

roll 174 page 610

Kingdom of Thailand   )
)
City of Bangkok   )
)   ss:
Embassy of the United States)
)
of America, Consular Section)

      Before me, Terry R. Snell   Consul of the United States of America in and for the consular district of Bangkok, Thailand, duly commissioned and qualified, personally appeared_Mr. Veerachart Hinorn_____,
who being duly sworn, deposes and says as follows:

      My name is____Veerachart Hinorn_____, and I am_a mortician_,
at_Institute of Forensic, Police Department, Bangkok, Thailand._

      I certify that the remains of___Jerrold Barker Daniels_____,
citizen of the United States who died at_Bangkok, Thailand___on_April 29_,
_1982___, have been embalmed by me; that I witnesses the packing of the remains for shipment to the United States; that the casket and case contain nothing but the said remains together with the necessary clothing and packing; and that the outer container is marked and addressed_Mountain View Mortury,_
3035 Russell STreet, Missoula, Montana 59806.

                  Signature:_____

Subscribed and sworn to before me this_6th_day of_____May_____,1982

                  Signature:_____

I certify this to be a true and
correct copy of the document
on record in this office.
Date _____ 18. 1942 SEAL
Fern Hart, Missoula County Recorder

By_____ Deputy
I received and filed this document for record on the _ day of _ May _, 1982 _____

Terry R. Snell
Consul of the
United States of America

8205960

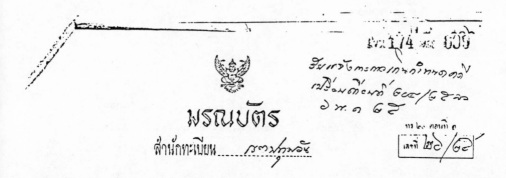

มรณบัตร

สำนักทะเบียน _____ เขตปทุมวัน

เลขที่ ๒๐/๖๙

VOL 174 PAGE 606
VOL 174 PAGE 607

KINGDOM OF THAILAND)
City of Bangkok Metropolis)
Embassy of the United States) SS:
         of America)

I, ...Terry R. Snell.................., Consul
of the United States of America, at Bangkok, Thailand,
duly commissioned and qualified, do hereby certify that
on this ...6th........ day of .....May............., 1982
before me personally appeared ...Chinda Komolviphat..... → BO GRITZ Contact
to me personally known and known to me to be the person
whose name is subscribed to the annexed translation, and
......he.... duly acknowledge to me that ....he...........
prepared the same.

IN WITNESS WHEREOF I hereunto set my hand and affixed
the seal of the Consular Section, American Embassy, at
Bangkok, Thailand this ...6th... day of ....May........., 1982.

....
                                          Terry R. Snell
                                   Consul of the United States
                                          of America

Kingdom of Thailand)
City of Bangkok)
) ss:
Embassy of the United States)
of America, Consular Section)

    I, ____Terry R. Snell____ Consul of the United States of America
in and for the consular district of __Bangkok, Thailand__
duly commissioned and qualified, hereby certify that the attached documents are to accompany the remains of __Jerrold Barker Daniels__
                                       (Name of Deceased)
citizen of the United States who died at __Bangkok, Thailand__
on /April 29, 1982_____, that the remains are to be shipped
from the Port of __BAngkok, Thailand__ on or about __May 7, 1982__,
                                                 (Date)

that the casket is encased in a strong wooden box to which is affixed a
transit lable corresponding with the attached transit permit; and that
the remains are to be entered at the port of __New York__,
arriving via __Pan American__ SS __PA 001__ on or
about ___May 7, 1982___.
           (Date)

    The following documents are attached and made a part of this
certificate: 742.   5/7   001

(1) Official Death Certificate;

(2) Translation of Death Certificate;

(3) Affidavit of __Mr. Veerachart Hinorn__, Mortician
                  (Name)   (Title, if any)

(4) Transit permit: not required by Thailand.

    IN WITNESS WHEREOF I have hereunto set my hand and official seal
this __6th__ day of __MAY__, 19__82__.

                                          Terry R. Snell
                                        Consul of the
                                        United States ofAmerica

SANVISTA INVESTMENT COMPANY, INC.

LETTER OF RECOMMENDATION

Mr. Scott T. Barnes   TO WHOM IT MAY CONCERN
4302 Mesa Street
Torrance, CA. 90505

Gentlemen:

It gives us great pleasure to recommend Mr. Scott T. Barnes with whom
we are presently involved in two multi-million dollar real estate transactions.

We found Mr. Barnes to be honest, reliable and willing to do hard work,
whenever the occasion demands it.

Respectfully yours,

SANVISTA INVESTMENT COMPANY, INC.

Peter Tinturin

PT:cv

James Gritz walks past Walter L. Fitts of Abington, Mass., at the start of a House Asian and Pacific Affairs subcommittee hearing on the possibility that Americans are being held in Southeast Asia. Fitts' son, Richard, has been missing since 1968.

Gritz accused of Laos fabrications

By John M. Bogert
Staff writer

A Redondo Beach man who claims to be a former associate of POW-hunter James "Bo" Gritz said Monday the ex-Green Beret colonel fabricated stories about missions into Laos.

At a news conference in Los Angeles, Scott Barnes, 29, said it was he, and not the highly decorated Gritz, who organized the 1981 raid into Laos that was code-named "Grand Eagle."

Furthermore, on that mission — which Gritz admitted he didn't physically take part in — Barnes says he and his five-man team were ordered by the U.S. government "to liquidate" two Caucasian prisoners they sighted.

Barnes made the assertions on the eve of Gritz's appearance before a House subcommittee in Washington, D.C., where the former Green Beret once again said he believes at least 50 American POWs are being held in Southeast Asia.

Barnes, a security guard at a Redondo Beach sporting goods store, said that on his mission — the second of two he lead into Laos for Gritz in 1981 — he got close enough to photograph the two captives. But, he said, he never found out who they were, which agency of the government wanted them killed or why.

Barnes said he and his team refused the order, received in code via a Department of Energy telex. He said they later turned over their photos of the prisoners to agents in Vienna, Va. He also said he doesn't know why a Department of Energy telex was used or the identities of the agents who received his photos.

"When you're in covert operations, you don't ask questions," says Barnes, who claims Gritz paid him $4,000 for his services.

A former policeman and stateside soldier, Barnes surmised the captives were "operatives left over from an earlier mission," not men who had been in captivity for 10 years."

Barnes' version of the story differs greatly from that of Gritz, who has called Barnes "a pathological liar." Gritz said he organized a mission into Laos executed by loyalist troops under the direction of Laotian Maj. Gen. Vang Pao, who now lives in the United States.

The mission, Gritz said, uncovered no trace of POWs, and shortly later the government withdrew support.

Barnes, who failed to give reporters promised documentation to prove his claims, also said the FBI is investigating Gritz as a possible member of the Libyan hit squad allegedly sent here last year to assassinate President Reagan.

Gritz, who lives in Westchester, laughingly denied those charges when Barnes first made them last summer, saying "he (Barnes) could be making a fortune as a fiction writer."

An FBI spokesman in Los Angeles, bound by rules prohibiting agents from discussing ongoing investigations, would not comment on the charges.

Barnes, meanwhile, remains somewhat of a mystery.

Spokesmen for the cities of El Cajon and Ridgecrest, where Barnes worked as a police officer, refused comment on his employment. The bearded young man admitted he was fired from both jobs after about a year with each.

Roy Heissner, El Cajon's personnel chief, would say only that Barnes "sued the city and at the end of the case the Superior Court judge closed the records."

"I'd like to comment on Barnes," he said. "But I'm afraid that I'd end up being sued, too."

Barnes said he could present boxes of documentation to prove his claims about Gritz if subpoenaed by the House foreign affairs subcommittee on Southeast Asia and Pacific Affairs.

Gritz told that committee today that one of the Laotians working with him had taken several photographs of a purported POW prison site.

But, he testified, "I find nothing there (in the pictures) that would provide any useful evidence." Gritz promised to provide the panel with the photos within the next several days.

He repeated his claim that U.S. government officials have been aware of his actions. Pentagon and State Department officials, however, again denied they supported Gritz.

In answer to a question from Rep. Stephen Solarz, D-N.Y., Gritz said, "I have concrete evidence, as I see it, that at least 50 Americans" are being held in Southeast Asia. He said the Pentagon has evidence that the number may be as high as 250.

Asked about the film, Gritz said the lighting in the camp was poor and the camera may have been set at the wrong shutter speed.

Solarz then asked, "Do you have any firm, hard evidence?"

"I have the same evidence that might be presented to a convention of clergymen that God exists," answered Gritz.

"Then your evidence rests exclusively on eyewitness reports?" Solarz asked.

"That's correct, sir," Gritz answered.

Last week Gritz told reporters at the Los Angeles Press Club that his belief was based more on a "skin feeling" than on any hard proof.

Though Gritz only last week said his wife would "kneecap him" (shoot him in the knees) if he went back to Laos, today he said he will go back for another rescue attempt.

"We're standing by until next called" by Laotian resistance members working with his group, Gritz said.

Gritz fabricated stories, former associate claims

By John Bogert
Staff writer

A Redondo Beach man, who claims to be a former associate of POW-hunter James "Bo" Gritz, said Monday the ex-Green Beret colonel fabricated stories about missions into Laos.

Speaking at the Los Angeles Press Club, Scott Barnes, 29, said it was he, and not the highly decorated Gritz, who organized the 1981 raid into Laos code-named "Grand Eagle."

Furthermore, on that mission — which Gritz admitted he didn't take part in — Barnes claims he and his five-man team were ordered by the government "to liquidate two Caucasian prisoners they sighted.

Though he was close enough to photograph the captives, he said he never found out who they were or why or which agency of the government wanted them killed.

Barnes said he and his team refused the order, received in code via a Department of Energy telex. He said they later turned over their photos of the prisoners to agents in Vienna, Va.

A former policeman and stateside

soldier, Barnes surmised the captives were "operatives left over from an earlier mission, not men who had been in captivity for 10 years."

Barnes' version of the story differs greatly from that of Gritz, who has called Barnes "a pathological liar." Gritz said he organized a mission into Laos executed by loyalist troops under the direction of Laotian Major General Vang Pao, who now lives in the United States.

The mission, said Gritz, uncovered no trace of POWs and shortly after the government withdrew support.

Barnes, who failed to produce promised documentation to prove his claims, also said the FBI is investigating Gritz as a possible member of the Libyan hit squad allegedly sent here last year to assassinate President Reagan.

An FBI spokesman in Los Angeles wouldn't comment on the charges.

Meanwhile, Barnes remains somewhat of a mystery.

Although he has claimed to be a Green Beret, Barnes said he only went to Vietnam as a tourist. Also, spokesmen for both the California cities where he worked as a police

officer wouldn't comment on his employment.

Barnes said he can't talk about his work in El Cajon because he still is connected with a case there involving the Hell's Angels motorcycle gang.

Roy Heissner, the city's personnel chief, said he cannot comment on the former policeman, except to say, "He sued the city and at the end of the case the Superior Court judge closed the records."

In Ridgecrest, a police spokesman offered only a terse, "I cannot comment on him."

...u hereby granted to applicant for described commodity to be permanently exported from the United States. This license may be revoked, suspended or amended by the Secretary of State without prior notice whenever the Secretary deems such action advisable. (DO NOT REPRODUCE THIS LICENSE (121.20(c))

1 91533
LICENSE NO.

LICENSE VALID FOR 24 MONTHS FROM ABOVE DATE

UNITED STATES OF AMERICA   DEPARTMENT OF STATE

APPLICATION/LICENSE FOR PERMANENT EXPORT OF UNCLASSIFIED DEFENSE ARTICLES AND RELATED UNCLASSIFIED TECHNICAL DATA

1. Date Prepared	2. PM/MC Applicant Code	3. Country of Ultimate Destination	4. Probable Port of Exit from U.S.
Feb-23-83		Burma/Syria/Laos	Los Angeles

5. Applicant's Name, Address, ZIP Code, Tel. No.

Scott Barnes
4210 Ocean dr.
Manhattan Beach, Ca. 90266

TELEPHONE NUMBER:

6. Names and telephone numbers of U.S. Government personnel (not PM/MC) familiar with the commodity

7. Name, State and telephone number of applicant contact if U.S. Government needs additional information.

8. QUANTITY	9. COMMODITY (Follow instructions carefully)	10. MUNITIONS LIST CATEGORY	11. VALUE
	⊠ Hardware ☐ Technical Data		
1. 70,000	.223 calibre ammuntion Brass, 70,000 cases	III	Unk at this date
2. 15,000	9mm calibre ammuntion Brass 15,000 cases	III	Unk at this date
3. 120	Brass wired Blasting caps and time devices 120 Boxes	IV	Unk at this date
4. 2,400	Automatic rifles, of the .223 cal. new and used 2,150 rifles and 250 Hand guns of 9mm cal.	I	Unk at this date

APPROVED

12. TOTAL VALUE: $

13. Source or Manufacturer of Commodity

Item 1. Federal Maf. 3. Source Intervest/Int,1
Item 2. Federal Maf. 4. Colt and Browning,S&W

14. Specific purpose for which the material is required, including specific program/end item   Training and Security for Ministry of Security

15. Name and address of seller in United States

To be sent

16. Name and Address of Consignor in United States

to be sent

17. Name and Address of Foreign Consignee

to be sent

18. Name and Address of Foreign end-user

to be sent

19. Name and Address of Foreign Intermediate Consignee

to be sent

20. This application represents: ⊠ONLY completely new shipment; ☐ ONLY the unshipped balance of license no. _____
NOTE: APPLICATION CAN NOT INCLUDE BOTH

21. The IDENTICAL commodity ☐ was licensed to the country in block 3 under license no. _____ ; ☐ was licensed to other countries under license no. _____ ; ☐ was denied to the country in block 3 under voided license no. _____ ; ☐ never licensed for this applicant

22. If commodity is being provided under a Foreign Military Sales (FMS) or Grant Aid (GAD) program, state which _____ and give the case no. _____

23. In this transaction, applicant is: ☐ government ☐ agent/manufacturer ☐ freight forwarder

24. LICENSE TO BE SENT TO: Name, Address, ZIP Code

Scott Barnes
4210 Ocean Dr.
Manhattan Beach. Ca. 90266

25. APPLICANT'S STATEMENT (See Instructions)
I, _____Scott Barnes_____ , hereby apply for a license to complete the transaction described above: warrant the truth of all statements made herein; and acknowledge, understand and will comply with the provisions of Title 22 CFR 121-128 and 130 and any conditions and limitations imposed.

Signature _____

FORM DSP-5
8/82 (DISCARD PREVIOUS EDITIONS)   1—APPLICATION/LICENSE   FORM APPROVED OMB NO. 47-R-0030

EDITOR'S NOTE

SINCE new developments in the James "Bo" Gritz/ POW issue have occurred between the time we sent the POW/MIA Special to press and today, we thought we should bring *Soldier of Fortune* readers up to date.

After the 22 March Congressional hearing on the POW/ MIA issue and specifically on Gritz's activities, the public has learned that the ISA or Army Intelligence Support Activity (referred to by Gritz and his supporters as "The Activity") may have lent some unsanctioned — by DIA, CIA or National Security Council — support to Gritz but, if one believes what the U.S. government says, is now back under tight control.

In an attempt to regain credibility destroyed by his disastrous appearance before Congress and the subsequent revelation by the *Washington Times* and ABC's *Nightline* that he had lied about his participation in a Vietnam battle, Gritz appeared on F. Lee Bailey's *Lie Detector* program. After the show was taped, Gritz tried unsuccessfully to prevent its airing. Two of his three responses were inconclusive, but when he answered "Yes" to this question — "In 1981, were you asked by 'Cranston' to be a principal agent of a U.S. government mission to document evidence of POWs in communist Asia?" — the polygraph results showed deception. Cranston is the code-name for an intelligence agent who was attached to "The Agency."

On 12 May, Richard T. Childress, the National Security Council adviser to President Reagan who deals with the POW/MIA issue, spoke to a group from the Vietnam Veterans of America in Richmond, Va., about the government's progress on the POW/MIA issue, specifically about a new development with the Lao government. However, he warned: "Progress with the Lao is encouraging to all of us, but the much-publicized and incredibly irresponsible actions of Lt. Col. Gritz set us back months. Our discussions indicate that he is directly responsible for stopping — and we pray only temporarily — joint crash-site searches in Laos. Relying on hearsay information, no credible operational capability and money collected from a variety of well-intentioned individuals to include family members, he managed to do the greatest damage to the government's efforts yet encountered during this administration.

"Despite his claims, he had no official backing and will never receive any. He says no one asked him to stop — tonight, I'm officially asking him to stop. If he is interested in the welfare of our missing men and their families, he will. If he craves a ticker-tape parade or the recapture of past dreams, then he won't."

EDITOR'S NOTE

Continued from page 2

Gritz went back to Thailand on 13 May, ostensibly to scout locations for a movie to be made about "Operation Lazarus," but amid speculation that this was merely a cover for another rescue attempt into Laos.

The Thais already had their hands full with three of seven Americans who had been in Nakhon Phanom since mid-April and had reportedly slipped across the border into Laos. Although the names of some of the seven were released, it is not known exactly who they are, what their purpose was or even if they had actually gone in.

Meanwhile, three Canadians beat *Soldier of Fortune's* reporter, Lian, to the IDT box left behind by Gritz's group after the November fire fight which broke up "Operation Lazarus." Capt. Lima, who had attacked the Gritz team on 30 November, attacked a guerrilla leader named Akhien (who was with Gritz on 30 November and to whom we had given the *nom de guerre* Thene Kham in our Special), who had the IDT in mid-May. Capt. Lima, who works for guerrilla chief Kham Bou, killed six of Akhien's men and recovered the box. SOF had offered a case of whiskey for it, but Lima sold it for about $10,000 to three Canadians, who SOF believes were acting on behalf of Litton Industries or the U.S. government.

In late May, Gritz team member Lance Trimmer delivered a long tape-recorded message from Gritz to the *Bangkok Post* in which Gritz stated that although he would not violate the spirit of the law he might break the letter of the law. He also referred to the "dark and evil" forces out to get him.

On 1 June, the Thai government declared Gritz and four other "Operation Lazarus" team members *persona non grata* and ordered them deported.

It would appear that the Thais have finally reacted to "the forces" — the increasingly skeptical media, the DIA, representatives of the NSC and leaders from the various POW/MIA groups — who thought Gritz was harming the cause not helping.

There may not be as much publicity in the future regarding POWs — often the best results on issues like this are obtained from quiet efforts — but here at SOF, we're convinced the search for an answer to the fate of the unaccounted-for Americans will continue. — Jim Graves 🗡

limited experience, they tended to promote on guts in the old SF, but, lordy, there was a minimum level of understanding — retires and becomes Mickey Mouse? There ought to be a good story there. Or perhaps a novel....

I did, once upon a time, get a doctorate in psychology, and I suppose I could come up with a few explanations, but I confess I am nonplused. Which is why I'd like to know a little more about his career prior to his becoming Lawrence of Indochina.

Dr. Jerry Pournelle
SOF Contributing Writer

It is unfortunate that the best journalism often results from tragic events. The POW/MIA subject certainly could be a synonym for a shameful American tragedy and your special edition on that topic was a paragon of research and investigative reporting. You and your entire staff deserve the utmost congratulations on producing a truly remarkable written perspective of a problem that demands a national priority to resolve.

Larry Wilson
Baltimore, Maryland

On a scale of zero to three, your magazine consistently rates 2.6 or better. Then along come issues like June, July and your special on the Gritz fiasco. If I could give a grade higher than 3.0 for each of those issues, I would. They were each outstand-ing. I get more straightforward, no-bullshit information and facts from SOF than all other publications combined. I'm tired of the same old biases evident in the national press and media and my own local branch of the same. They consistently give press coverage to bubble-heads such as Fonda, Asner, et al., simply because of their name appeal.

From some of the end-line hyphenations in the July issue it is obvious that your new word-processing system (or operators) still has some bugs to be ironed out. Such are the joys of modern technology.

Henry Plawer
Quincy, Illinois

I thoroughly enjoyed reading the POW/MIA special, but I have one issue to bring up. On pages 29 and 30 the printer, I assume, repeated the copy. I hope they didn't leave something out that may have been interesting. As an MI NCO for the U.S. Army, I most rightfully have a suspicious mind!

A Concerned Southeast Asia Vet

The repeated copy and the wrong end-line hyphenations along with some really strange spellings in the special issue came as a result of our new word-processing system which has some of the biggest, meanest "bugs" ever seen. The special was the first issue we put out on the system and between hardware crashes, bugs and just general wear-and-tear on the editing staff, who turned out a 72-page special while producing two regular issues, some editing snafus did slip by. In the long run our front-end computer will help us make Soldier Of Fortune a better product. — The Eds.

Not only did you bring factual and informative justice to Bo Gritz, but articles like "The Pawns of War" by Will Brownell, "The French Experience" by Milt Copulos and "Vigil for a Missing Son" by Jim Morris are each worthy of a 60 Minutes episode in themselves.

I am positive that not only is the American public misinformed on the POW/MIA issue, but most so-called journalists for our many prestigious newspapers, magazines and television stations are worse than misinformed — they don't even care.

You and your staff continue to perform a service the American people need more than they can imagine. Your dedication and loyalty to the truth sets a standard I wish more people would recognize, if not live up to.

Marty Hornstein
Los Angeles, California

After reading your special (POW/MIA) I can only say... DAMN! Not only could

Continued on page 96

FLAK

Continued from page 6

POW/MIA SPECIAL

Whether Gritz is a hero or a huckster we left up to the reader to decide. But we disagree seriously as to who has achieved what result. The thousands of hours and millions of dollars spent by the government and media running to ground the truth in the "Lazarus Affair" would have been far better spent pursuing other leads. While it did bring the issue of POWs to the public eye for a brief period of time it also did substantial damage to sincere efforts and may have the long-term effect of discrediting the issue. — The Eds.

I'd like to request an apology — or should we try a thank you? The articles in your POW/MIA special issue are very amusing to say the least; especially the one on me.

After reading it, I realized you are not professionals. So, knowing that I could expect yellow journalism, may I set some facts straight.

1) There are four small rivers on the Cambodian/Thai border. Task-force 80 sits on one. We crossed Stoeng Huoy Sei River. (See your maps.)

2) Vinney Arnone was not on Operation Grand Eagle. You should read the Los Angeles Times, 21 February 1983. They identify all of Grand Eagle's members.

3) When I arrived in Bangkok in June of '81. Your now "forgotten source" is mistaken: I didn't check into the Nana until two days later, at 0347 hours, and no one was there in the lobby. I came in with Robert Moberg.

4) Your publisher, Mr. Brown, approached me and even paid one week's stay at the Hotel Nana and meals [for me] with his American Express card, so that he and Coyne could talk to me.

5) You fail to mention I submitted, at Mr. Ted Koppel's request, to five very extensive, in-depth polygraph tests by former world-famous CIA examiner, Chris Gugas, and passed all five 100 percent. Especially questions on the "hit" order and many more. You also fail to mention that I took several psychological tests by Dr. Fredrick Hacker, Jr. He too is very well-known and respected. Again, I passed all tests 100 percent.

I'll agree on one thing. Bo is nuts. But I was there; I did the things; I passed the tests.

Many thanks to Col. Brown. I believe he is a man of honor. As for you editors,

well, not knowing you, I don't know.
Scott Barnes
P.S. Mr. Graves: I have never talked to you from Hawaii.
Scott was BOGUS

1) There is a "Stung Houei Sai" river near the Thai-Cambodian border (Southeast Asia Map Series ND 48-9, 1/250,000). Problem is that's not the place you told Dawson you crossed.

2) Vinney Arnone — according to Gritz, other Grand Eagle participants who gave us affidavits and people who were working for us — was in Bangkok just after you got into a fight with another team member over how to operate a camera. You may not have seen him or known his role but he was part of Grand Eagle or BOHICA.

3) Robert Moberg is a good friend of ours and was well known to the two individuals who were in the lobby of the Nana Hotel when you checked in. If Moberg was with you he came as Casper the ghost. But to be fair we'll ask him.

4) It is a well-known fact that SOF Publisher Robert K. Brown is sought out all around the world by "busted" adventurers and is the world's softest touch, provided one has a good enough "hard luck story." There is an unconfirmed rumor that just days before he was killed by Bolivan Rangers Ernesto "Che" Guevara hit Brown up for meal money in a cantina in Bolivia's outback. Since "Che," who called himself a Soldado de Fortuna and actually was one — but for the wrong side — had a good story I wouldn't be surprised if it's true. Brown, who, when we last talked with him, was having dinner with some scruffy-looking adventurer in a scruffier-looking restaurant in Addis Ababa, Ethiopia, denied the "Che" rumor but admits he did pay your bill for a week.

5) We had read those claims before and didn't consider them relevant and they were not worth the phone money it would have taken to check them out. As a matter of routine journalists and shrinks don't reveal the results of such tests unless they print a story. Why didn't Koppel run with the story if it's that good and you passed the tests? Could it be that the fact you passed the test and the truth have no relationship to each other?

P.S. I did talk with you from Hawaii. Somewhere in our warehouse we have the phone logs from that time period which would show your incoming call and since Earl Bleacher placed a call to you from our office our bill from Ma Bell would show a call to a number you could be reached at in Hawaii. — Jim Graves

The "classic detective novel" entitled The Maltese Falcon was penned by Dashiell Hammett and not Raymond Chandler as you state on page 2 of your special MIA/POW issue. Moreover, the detective who runs down the worthless bird is Sam Spade, and not Philip Marlowe.

As near as I can tell, you are guilty of the same sin as Gritz. By marketing a full-color, high-speed hatchet job on that fool, and charging three bucks a copy, you too are profiteering from his sojourn into Laos.

I suggest you shy away from the murky issue of POWs in Southeast Asia and concentrate on something more cut and dried, like the Rooskies in Afghanistan or the latest war movie out of Hollywood.
Don Pugsley
Los Angeles, California

To get to the bottom of this mysterious misidentification, SOF went right to the scene of the crime: Executive Editor Bob Poos's office. When confronted with the evidence, Poos replied, "Elementary, my dear fellows, elementary. While stalking the elusive Maltese author, I chanced upon a remarkable discovery. Dashiell Hammett was never seen with Raymond Chandler; nor did he ever use Philip Marlowe in any of his works. Likewise, Chandler never used Sam Spade in his. Right away, I knew that I was on to something big. Some further sleuthing confirmed my startling find: Dashiell Hammett and Raymond Chandler were the same person, and therefore, Sam Spade and Philip Marlowe are the same character and all can be used interchangeably." The mystery of the mistaken whodunit has been solved.

Seriously, Spade/Marlowe is based on a real-life, hard-nosed, ham-fisted detective who is still alive and whom Publisher Robert K. Brown is going to hire to beat up all the editors who let the mistake get through.

SOF does try to make a profit but "profiteering?" If we break even on the POW/MIA special we are going to have the wildest damn blowout anyone has ever seen in Boulder. Brown has guaranteed me that if we make a profit I get a gold star and I get to take the profits to Afghanistan to be used in a suitable manner. We did the Special because 1) the story just kept growing and growing and would not fit in our normal format, and 2) we have been considering an experiment on Special issues for a long time. If this one breaks even or even comes reasonably close we'll do more of them on other subjects we think you'll like. — Jim Graves

Congratulations on an excellent job: The POW/MIA special issue was really done well. The only thing I would like to have seen added is a very short official biography of Lt. Col. Gritz. There were hints here and there, but little to go on: Where did he get all those medals? Surely not for his work as a strategist, or even a tactician. His performance in the various "operations" described in your issue would hardly have earned a passing grade for a plebe in tactics one.

One wonders just what did happen? A presumably competent man — from my

7233 WEST DEMPSTER STREET • NILES, ILLINOIS 60648 • PHONE: (312) 966-1700

To Whom It May Concern: June-83

LETTER OF RECOMMENDATION

Scott Barnes, has been employed by Sportmart,Inc. since Oct-82 in the capacity of
Security Manager and Loss Prevention of our Redondo Beach Regional location. In that
time he has demonstrated to be a very dependable and reliable honest hardworking individual.

While employed with us he has proven his keen abilities to the highest levels of professional
service to his responsibilities, and his job assignments. Being in a supervisory position he
is superior in the handling of personnel under his control and always showed great initiative
and judgement in all decisions he made within his Dept. His investigative abilities have
saved our company many thousands of dollars and provided safety for the company and employees.

We recommend him very sincerely and with the highest regards and truly believe he will
be a tremendous asset to any company or agency who would be lucky enough to consider him.

Sincerely

Sportmart,Inc.
Western Regional Office

Donna Nevins

Operations Manager
312-572-7702

SPORTMART INC. ®

THE ■ **HOME OF NATIONALLY ADVERTISED BRANDS**

7233 WEST DEMPSTER STREET • NILES, ILLINOIS 60648 • PHONE: (312) 966-1700

July 6, 1983

To Whom It May Concern:

Scott Barnes worked as a store detective at our Redondo Beach Sportmart from October 10, 1982 until June 30, 1983. During this time Scott was promoted to security manager of that store. As a security manager Scott was responsible for the loss prevention and safty of a mass merchandiser, retail store. His duties included, apprehending shoplifters, prosecuting shoplifters, supervising 3-4 other store detectives, collecting checks, and monitering various federal, and state record keeping requirements pertaining to the sale of firearms. He was also responsible for interfacing with the store managers, the Redondo Beach P. D., the prosecutors office, and the Dept. of Justice.

I found Scott to be very knowledgable about the law, very resourcful, intelligent, and a capable leader. Scott had one of the highest statistical achievment records of any store detective in the chain. The position often called for a quick decision based on observations made by individuals, and Scott had a keen sense of the proper decision to make.

Scott will be an asset to whatever company he decides to work for. Scott represents the epitome of a well rounded, law enforcement oriented, professional.

Sincerely,

Michael R. Garvey
Western Regional Security Lieutenant

50-A-1

CLOSED CIPA HEARING

IN THE UNITED STATES DISTRICT COURT FOR THE

DISTRICT OF HAWAII

UNITED STATES OF AMERICA,)
)
Plaintiff.)
)
vs.) CRIMINAL NO. 84-02417
)
RONALD REWALD,)
)
Defendant.)
_____)

TRANSCRIPT OF PROCEEDINGS

The above-entitled matter came on for CIPA hearing

on Friday, June 14, 1985, at 9:22 a.m., at Honolulu, Hawaii,

BEFORE:

HONORABLE HAROLD M. FONG
Chief United States District Judge
District of Hawaii

APPEARANCES:

JOHN F. PEYTON, Esq.
Assistant U. S. Attorney
Department of Justice
District of Hawaii
Rm C-242 - U. S. Courthouse
300 Ala Moana Blvd.
Honolulu, Hawaii

Attorney for Plaintiff
United States of America;

MICHAEL LEVINE, Esq.
Federal Public Defender
Rm 7102
300 Ala Moana Blvd.
Honolulu, Hawaii

TERRENCE CHUN, RPR-HONOLULU, HI.

154

1 this hearing. (v)

2 MR. TANIMURA: Thank you, Your Honor. (v)

3 THE COURT: I'm getting all kinds of notices that

4 I've been taxing the personnel of the Court to a breaking

5 point. I need to get on the phone to call the east coast

6 before time runs out on me, so we'll take a 15-minute break

7 and come back and continue this hearing until we are done. (v)

8 Recess. (v)

9 (Whereupon, the proceedings recessed at 3:38 p.m

10 and reconvened at 3:56 p.m., June 5, 1985.) (v)

11 THE COURT: The next category is that relating to Bo

12 Gritts and his going over to the Vietnam, and Laos to search

13 MIA's. What -- what relevance is there? (v)

14 MR. TANIMURA: The relevance in this category, Your

15 Honor, again, are specifically the funds that Rewald alleges

16 that he provided funds to the mission for Bo Gritts and the

17 Court's concern relative to the expenditure of funds is tied

18 directly to that. Again, we argue that it's also legitimate

19 action of a proprietary organization, but specifically for the

20 Court's concern is the money that was expended, similarly the

21 money that was expended in the Pacific forum. Well, are you

22 suggesting that documents itself would relate to that -- that

23 there was any funding on the part of CIA? (v)

24 MR. TANIMURA: Again, it's corroboration. Your

25 Honor, if Rewald were to just state: I provided funds to Bo

155

Britts for the mission, the question is: What are you talking
about? But, if we have -- we have documents -- for example,
the letter which is exhibit -- that describes the government's
relationship with the mission, shows that it indeed was a
covert mission and one that would require covert funds. Now
these documents corroborate that the mission did occur, that --
that the mission occurred in a covert fashion, which would mean
that they needed funds covertly, and they're all linked
together again, showing one corroborative story. Our position
is that if Rewald just gets up without these documents and--
says: I provided funds for the So Britts mission, and he's not
entitled to show that it was a secret mission and would
necessitate secret funds, then he has very important
corroborative evidence being kept from the jury. (v)

    MR. GREENBERG: Excuse me a minute. (v)

    (Counsel conferring)

    MR. GREENBERG: Your Honor, the documents referred to
first, if I may state, with regard to Rewald's contentions, in
his confidential affidavit he stated: We did supply a few
thousand dollars to support the mission, but doubted that it
would succeed. Later I found out that the agency had abandoned
its promised support of Britts and that the mission had failed.
In the defendant's -- that's what he said in his confidential
affidavit. In his -- in his Section 5 submission he said --
changes the story and now says that Rewald assisted in funding

SECRET

the mission. So, even taking that -- the $2,000 or Rewald

funding the mission -- there's no relevance to the operation of

Bishop, Baldwin because Rewald does not assert that he spent

Bishop, Baldwin funds. He doesn't say how much, where, what,

and if you take just the $2,000 that is not in our view

relevant. It would only seek to add confusion to the issues

because of the -- because of the emotional impact of MIA's and

POW's, and all the public controversy over rescue missions, to

they authorized or unauthorized. (v)

With regard to the specific documents set forth in

defendant's submission 226, 227, 230, 33, 44, 1404, 1407, 1414

1387, these documents are classified in that they report

Rewald's submissions of information and the subsequent

briefings given by the Honolulu station officer to Lieutenant

General Braswell at the Pacific Air Forces and Admiral Robert

Long, who was then Commander-in-Chief Pacific, CINCPAC, on the

involvement of Hunter Harris in the Bo Britts mission. It's

the government's position that this is so far attenuated to the

charges in the indictment as to be confusing under 403 and not

relevant under 401. (v)

THE COURT: All right. The courts finds that most

these documents are telexes which refer to a project --

specific project -- presumably let by Bo Britts to locate POW

and MIA's in Southeast Asia. The telexes show that retired

General Harris was aware of and condoned the mission and that

TERRENCE CHUN, FPR-HONOLULU, HI

1   other military personnel were briefed regarding Baril'

2   involvement. The defendant claims that the CIA directed him to

3   assist in funding the mission. (v)

4   The document noticed here by the defendant, however,

5   does not support that claim. Take, for instance Documents 226,

6   227, 236, 1306, 1387. These documents state at its very outset

7   that the information contained therein was, quote, voluntarily

8   provided, unquote, by the defendant. There is no indication

9   that the CIA was otherwise conducting or aware of the

10   clandestine mission. Additionally, Document 1306 shows that

11   Britts requested Rewald to help finance that project. A

12   specific request, but that Rewald concluded that, quote: His

13   firm does not plan to provide the requested funds. (v)

14   The Court finds that those documents -- enumerated

15   documents I've just referred to -- specifically disclaims any

16   funding role on the part of Rewald or his company, and to the

17   extent that the other documents relate to the highly emotional

18   issues of the missing in action and prisoners of war, whatever

19   probative value there may be, the Court finds that this slight

20   potential probative value is substantially outweighed by

21   consideration of misleading the jury in violation of Rules of

22   Evidence 403. The Court will, therefore, find and likewise

23   determine all of these exhibits to be inadmissible. They

24   include 226, 227, 230, 234, 233, 1404, 1407, 1414, 1386, as

25   well as additional document 13 -- I mean -- 1387 as well as

158

additional document 1396. (v)

MR. TANAKA: Excuse me, Your Honor. The Court has separated the documents from the information itself described. As I understand the Court's ruling, the documents are not relevant because they do not support the information. If setting the information aside and ignoring the documents, if we were to submit evidence on this -- on the fact, is the Court also ruling that under 403 the information itself is excluded?

THE COURT: Yes. (v)

MR. TANAKA: The government made an assertion that Rewald funded only $2,000. Rewald's claims are substantially different. What I'd like to know from the Court is: If the expenditure of funds were the CIA invested funds and the amount was higher -- in other words, is it a de minimis ruling which makes it a 403, in which case our position is we will come forth with the actual figure, which is substantially greater than $2,000. (v)

MR. GREENBERG: Excuse me, Your Honor, so that the record is clear, what I stated was: With regard to the few thousand dollars was that I was quoting from Mr. Rewald's confidential affidavit. (v)

THE COURT: Well, I don't know how much we're talking about, but the issue itself -- the issue with respect to PCN, if it were in the figures of several or two or however many thousand dollars, does appear to be on the factor of a de

TERRENCE CHUN, RPR-HONOLULU, HI

159

minimic consideration. To the extent that you can reopen this
issue by proof of a larger amount -- that is not to suggest
that 3,000 would do the trick or whatever -- but you are free,
obviously, to make your point on this issue that if it were a
substantial amount there, then perhaps it does materially
affect the expenditure and direction of $22 million. I'm not
suggesting that you could even get close to 22 million, but to
the extent that it might be a substantial amount, the Court
will reconsider it at that time. (v)

Now, 22, Hong Kong Capital Flight study. That's the
relevance as to whether or not a Hong Kong Capital Flight study
was undertaken and perhaps may have even been written up?
Again, it's project specific, and -- (v)

MR. TANAKA: Yes, Your Honor. (v)

THE COURT: -- you know what my ruling is. (v)

MR. TANAKA: We're covering all the ground, but,
nevertheless -- the Hong Kong study itself has several
relationships to the Court's relevance distinctions. The first
relationship is one that we've been maintaining all along, it
being the traditional activities of proprietary organization
often the dissemination of misinformation or assisting through
legitimate or apparently legitimate sources -- assisting
purposes of the CIA. Fewald claims that he was given a
specific request or order by a CIA employee, and he has name
Jay Watkins as that employee, in conjunction with Station C.

Los Angeles Times

Thursday, December 13, 1984 ★

ABC RETRACTION OF CIA MURDER PLOT DETAILED

By DAVID CROOK
Times Staff Writer

ABC News moved to retract its report of a CIA murder plot two months after then Director William J. Casey made a personal phone call complaining about the charge to Leonard H. Goldenson, chairman and chief executive officer of American Broadcasting Cos. Inc., a top ABC News executive said Tuesday.

David Burke, third-ranking officer of ABC News, said that Casey's call to Goldenson shortly after ABC's Sept. 19 and 20 broadcasts led to a series of discussions between high-level network and Central Intelligence Agency officials. Those meetings, Burke said, led him to conclude that ABC could not substantiate its story that the CIA plotted to murder a Honolulu investment counselor.

Burke decided that ABC's story "could not be backed up," he said, without the CIA offering any factual refutation of the story. Burke also did not know, he said, that ABC's principal source for the charge had agreed to take a conditional lie-detector test to buttress his allegations.

CIA spokeswoman Patti Volz confirmed that there was a phone conversation between Casey and Goldenson, but declined to comment on the substance of their talk. "The director hasn't given us the authority to release any facts of his involvement in the whole thing," Volz said. "We don't quarrel with what Burke has told you."

ABC's report of the murder plan is the key issue in an unprecedented legal battle between the CIA and the network. Three weeks ago, the CIA filed a complaint with the Federal Communications Commission about the network's allegations and asked the FCC to consider its charge in determining whether ABC is fit to hold broadcast licenses.

On the day of the CIA's filing, ABC stated on the air that it could not substantiate the murder charge after former prison guard Scott T. Barnes refused a polygraph examination. Barnes, however, denies that he refused a polygraph exam.

During a two-hour tape-recorded interview, Barnes told The Times that he made a conditional offer to ABC to take a lie-detector test to back up his story that, while serving as a CIA informant in Honolulu, Barnes was told by CIA contacts that the agency intended to murder investment counselor Ronald R. Rewald, an American citizen. Barnes said that he was prepared to reiterate the story under oath to appropriate government investigators.

Barnes also recounted a two-year history of dealings with the network in other matters, which included previous ABC-financed polygraph tests and a psychological examination.

"I said, 'I'll go ahead and take another polygraph; it doesn't bother me,'" Barnes claimed during the interview at his home in Kern County.

In a telephone interview, Burke, ABC News vice president and assistant to President Roone Arledge, said that the network decided it couldn't stand by the Barnes story after a series of three meetings with Stanley Sporkin, general counsel of the intelligence agency.

The meetings with the CIA began, Burke said, after Casey called Goldenson to complain about the broadcasts. Burke said that Goldenson did not attempt to influence ABC News management on the CIA story.

Burke said that the decision to issue ABC's on-air clarification re-

---

ABC's Burke called Barnes' offer "preposterous."

---

sulted from his own "professional judgment" and not from any facts that the CIA presented refuting ABC's reporting. Burke said that the only documentation the CIA offered were newspaper clippings questioning Barnes' credibility.

"I was impressed by the vigor with which they made their case," Burke said. "I take Stanley Sporkin to be an honorable man. He was quite exercised about the story—

especially the Scott Barnes part of the story."

Until told by a Times reporter, Burke did not know that Barnes had made a conditional offer to take a polygraph exam, he said.

"The report that came back to me and all of the management at ABC News was that he (Barnes) refused to take a lie-detector test," Burke said.

According to Barnes, he told ABC, " 'Yeah, I'll go ahead and take another one. I'll name two gentlemen in the CIA. All three of us will take them publicly—none of this behind-the-closed-door stuff. It'll be filmed. It'll be on tape, and it'll be under the penalty of perjury,'" Barnes said.

ABC's Burke called Barnes' offer "preposterous. That's another way of saying no."

Burke said: "I can't imagine any reasonable man would go to the CIA and tell it to take a lie detector test."

Barnes claimed that ABC's Charles Stuart, producer of the original news reports, declined the offer because the CIA would not agree to the proposal.

"They (ABC) say, 'No, the CIA boys aren't going to take a poly,'" Barnes recalled.

Stuart confirmed Barnes' account. Stuart quoted Barnes as saying, "I'll go to the box (lie detector) if they go to the box."

However, Stuart added, Barnes made the offer to take a polygraph exam only after repeated refusals.

"I took it as an idle statement," Stuart said.

On Wednesday, Barnes said again that he is willing to take a lie-detector test, even without the CIA officials submitting to a similar exam: "Yeah, sure, unconditionally," Barnes said.

The Times also has obtained a copy of a 56-page sworn statement Barnes made repeating the allegation that there was an assassination plot. Los Angeles-based ABC News correspondent Gary Shepard made references to the statement in his initial reporting of the story on Sept. 20, but never showed the affidavit on the air or quoted from it. Shepard referred questions to ABC News executives in New York.

Barnes claims that he has a signed secrecy agreement with the CIA barring him from discussing his role in agency activities. The secrecy agreement, he believes, does not preclude him from relating his lengthy involvement with ABC News.

The CIA denies that it has such an agreement with Barnes. According to Burke and the CIA, however, agency counsel Sporkin was heard to say during one of his meetings with ABC that Barnes did have an agreement with the agency. Sporkin later denied saying it, claiming that he was referring to Rewald, not to Barnes.

ABC'S RETRACTION

On Monday, the CIA's Volz acknowledged that Rewald "did at one time have a secrecy agreement" with the agency.

Barnes has continued to stand by his claim that he was made privy to a CIA plan to kill Rewald, currently under indictment for allegedly swindling about 400 investors out of $22 million. Rewald faces 100 counts of fraud, perjury and tax-evasion charges.

According to Barnes, the intelligence agency intended to kill Rewald because the court case and the attendant publicity surrounding it endangered national security and threatened to reveal clandestine CIA activities. In response to the CIA's urgings, a federal judge in Honolulu has sealed the public records of the case for reasons of national security.

The alleged murder plot was outlined in a Sept. 20 "ABC World News Tonight" report, part of the network's two-part series about CIA involvement with the bankrupt investment firm of Bishop, Baldwin, Rewald, Dillingham and Wong.

According to official records, Rewald had only one other partner in the firm, Sunlin Wong, a Honolulu real-estate agent. Wong pleaded guilty in June to single counts of mail and securities fraud and agreed to cooperate with authorities during investigations of the company's activities. The other names associated with the firm are those of old-line Hawaii families that, according to published and official reports, had nothing to do with the company.

In April, the Wall Street Journal characterized the use of the family names as the equivalent in Hawaii of calling a New York company "Rockefeller, Roosevelt, Rewald, Vanderbilt and Mellon."

According to Wong's indictment, he and Rewald used the Bishop, Baldwin and Dillingham names to

Barnes still claims that he was made privy to plan to kill Rewald.

"reinforce their false assertion that (the company) was 'one of Hawaii's oldest and largest privately held international investment and consulting firms.'"

In addition to the murder plot, ABC alleged in its broadcasts that the CIA used the company in order to destabilize the economies of a number of foreign countries and to make illegal arms shipments to Taiwan. ABC also claimed that the investment firm was involved in secret shipments of military hardware to Syria and India.

In court in Hawaii, the CIA acknowledged limited dealings with the firm, including using it as

a mail-drop and as a telephone message center. The intelligence agency has insisted, however, that it was involved in no illegal Bishop, Baldwin activities.

After initial CIA denials of the charges in the broadcasts, ABC said on September 14 it would investigate. "On Nov. 21, however, ABC broadcast a "clarification" that said claims were unsubstantiated. Anchorman Peter Jennings said on the air: "Finally we asked Barnes to take a lie detector test, but he refused. So ABC News has now concluded that Barnes' charges cannot be substantiated, and we have no reason to doubt the CIA's denial."

The decision to issue the clarification "came from above me," said producer Stuart. "It came from the man I respect most in television— David Burke. It was a gut thing because the agency didn't offer any proof. . . . He felt in his gut that he was being told the truth (by the CIA's Sporkin)."

The CIA filed its FCC complaint the same day that ABC broadcast its clarification. In the complaint, the agency acknowledged that it

The CIA repeatedly has denied any association with Barnes.

was aware that ABC intended "to accept 'CIA's denial' limited to certain aspects of the Scott Barnes interview."

Insisting that other charges in the broadcast were also false, the agency continued to claim that ABC deliberately distorted the facts in its reports and asked the FCC to consider revoking ABC's broadcast licenses.

The CIA repeatedly has denied any association with Barnes. Kathy Pherson, another CIA spokeswoman, said: "We have never had any connection with Scott Barnes. . . . We absolutely deny that we have anything to do with him."

Despite the high-pitched battle over his remarks, Barnes said that he was prepared to tell the same story that he told ABC, under oath, to congressional investigators.

"Absolutely, under oath, with the penalty of perjury and 20 years to come!" Barnes insisted. "I've been wanting that since 1981. I'll get it someday."

Barnes is known to journalists who have reported the Bishop, Baldwin story as well as other stories about U.S. intelligence activities.

He has been identified in various published reports as, alternately, "a Walter Mitty type" (Covert Action Information Bulletin) given to tales of exploits and adventures and as a veteran of numerous clandestine operations (Soldier of Fortune magazine).

Among reporters questioned by The Times, there is considerable disagreement about Barnes' credibility.

Ira Rosen, a producer for CBS News' "60 Minutes," said that he first heard Barnes' story in June and found it "unbelievable. "I checked it out," Rosen said. "From the people I contacted I could not satisfy myself that it was true. I not only didn't go with the story, I dropped it completely. I found a number of continuing inconsistencies in what he (Barnes) was saying."

David Taylor, a producer for the British Broadcasting Corp., made one of the first televised accounts of the CIA and Bishop, Baldwin. He offered a much different picture of Barnes. "He was constantly telling me things that later transpired," Taylor said. "He seems to stand up."

A 1983 Los Angeles Times article identified Barnes as a member of a team of privately recruited commandos, led by retired Green Beret Lt. Col. James G. (Bo) Gritz, that attempted to rescue American prisoners of war in Laos. Barnes has claimed that the Laotian expedition was a CIA operation and that it was, in large part, financed by Bishop, Baldwin.

Barnes insisted that he had demonstrated his credibility to ABC with an earlier story. He passed a psychological examination and a battery of polygraph exams administered at the network's insistence and expense during a series of 1982 interviews about Barnes' exploits with Gritz in Southeast Asia.

Barnes alleged at the time that the CIA ordered murders of two Caucasians found in Laos.

ABC never broadcast the earlier interviews, and Barnes can barely contain his anger with the network over its decision not to go with the story. ABC's refusal to go ahead with the 1982 reports, Barnes said, led him to insist on the unusual conditions he attached to his offer to take a polygraph examination on the Rewald story.

"I've already done it and passed before, and the CIA refuses." Barnes said. "ABC is not man enough to stand up and say, 'We have a Catch-22 system. If so-and-so and so-and-so step forward and take a lie-detector test, Scott will also take a lie-detector test.'

"I'll voluntarily take it first. Then I want those two CIA guys to undergo psychiatric examination to see if . . . they are stable or if they're renegades. . . ."

(In The Times' interview, Barnes refused to identify the two CIA associates but claimed that he would divulge their names if given the opportunity by congressional investigators.)

Barnes' 1982 psychological examination was administered by Frederick Hacker, a Beverly Hills

psychoanalyst. The lie detector tests were conducted by Christopher Gugas, director of Professional Security Consultants in Hollywood. Gugas is a former CIA employee.

"Everything that he (Barnes) told me has checked out," Gugas said, referring to Barnes passing the lie-detector test. Regarding Barnes' story of the Laotian murder orders, Gugas said, "I found that it did check out. That's what scared me. I think it scared ABC too."

Despite Barnes' performance on the 1982 examinations, ABC "Nightline" anchor Ted Koppel decided not to go ahead with a planned broadcast on the Laos allegations when he subjectively concluded that Barnes could not be believed, according to Burke.

Koppel's objections were resisted, however, by William Lord, then executive producer of "Nightline," Burke said. There was a "strong difference of opinion" between Lord and Koppel about Barnes' credibility, Burke said.

Lord later was named executive producer of "World News Tonight" and was in charge of the nightly news program at the time of the disputed September broadcasts.

Times librarian Dan Crump contributed research to this article.

MAILGRAM SERVICE CENTER
MIDDLETOWN, VA. 22545
22P4

4-0524963022002 01/22/85 ICS IPMRNCZ CSP FS03
I 6193763249 MGM TDRN KERNVILLE CA 01-22 1058P EST

SCOTT T BARNES
619/376-3249
PO BOX 704
KERNVILLE CA 93238

THIS IS A CONFIRMATION COPY OF THE FOLLOWING MESSAGE:

6193763249 MGMS TDRN KERNVILLE CA 250 01-22 1058P EST
ZIP
PRESIDENT RONALD REAGAN
WHITE HOUSE DC 20500

HONORABLE PRESIDENT OF THE UNITED STATES OF AMERICA

RONALD WILSON REAGAN

DEAR MR PRESIDENT

AS YOU KNOW, RECENTLY THERE HAVE BEEN CONSIDERABLE CONTROVERSY WITH
MYSELF, THE CIA AND ABC NEWS. AS YOU ARE AWARE, THE CIA RECENTLY
FILED A COMPLAINT WITH THE FCC OVER AN ABC SPECIAL CONCERNING MYSELF
AND THE REWALD MATTER AND CIA. THE FCC RULED AGAINST THE CIA
COMPLAINT. HOWEVER, ANOTHER COMPLAINT WAS RECENTLY FILED AGAINST ABC
TO THE FCC BY THE AMERICAN LEGAL FOUNDATION OF WASHINGTON D.C. IN
ADDITION, THERE WAS CONSIDERABLE CONTROVERSY REGARDING THE CIA,
MYSELF AND LIEUTENANT COLONEL JAMES GORDON GRITZ REGARDING OUR
1981/82 POW RESCUE MISSIONS INTO SOUTHEAST ASIA. I'M SURE YOU'RE ALSO
AWARE YOUR FRIEND, CLINT EASTWOOD, DONATED A SUBSTANTIAL AMOUNT OF
MONEY TO THIS CAUSE. I BELIEVE THAT THE TIME HAS NOW COME THAT ALL
THE FACTS AND TRUTH REGARDING NOT ONLY THE GRITZ OPERATION AND THE
REWALD MATTER AND THE PROBLEMS CURRENTLY FACING THE CIA AND MYSELF
AND ABC NEWS BE BROUGHT TO LIGHT. I WOULD RESPECTFULLY REQUEST THAT A
HEARING EITHER OF THE EXECUTIVE NATURE, SENATE OR CONGRESSIONAL LEVEL
BE HELD AND THAT THESE BE CONDUCTED UNDER THE PENALTY OF PERJURY AND
THAT ALL PERSONS BE REQUIRED TO TESTIFY UNDER OATH AND THAT THIS
ENTIRE MATTER COME TO A CONCLUSION AS SOON AS POSSIBLE AND THAT THE
TRUTH ON THESE MATTERS BE BROUGHT TO LIGHT.

RESPECTFULLY SUBMITTED

Western Union Mailgram

SCOTT T BARNES

P.S. CONGRATULATIONS ON YOUR SECOND TERM.

SCOTT T BARNES
619/376-3249
PO BOX 704
KERNVILLE CA 93238

2301 EST

MGMCOMP MGM

THE WHITE HOUSE

WASHINGTON

April 22, 1985

Dear Mr. Barnes:

Thank you for your recent mailgram to the President suggesting the need for complete investigations of the POW rescue mission conducted by Lt. Col. Gritz and the Rewald case. I have referred a copy of your mailgram to Mr. Stephen S. Trott, the Assistant Attorney General, Criminal Division, United States Department of Justice, for his information and for whatever action, if any, he deems appropriate.

Sincerely,

Fred F. Fielding
Counsel to the President

Mr. Scott T. Barnes
Post Office Box 704
Kernville, California   93238

4-013675S202002 07/21/85 ICS IPMBNGZ CSP FSOA
1 6193763249 MGM TDBN KERNVILLE CA 07-21 1137P EST

SCOTT T BARNES
PO BOX 704
KERNVILLE CA 93238

THIS IS A CONFIRMATION COPY OF THE FOLLOWING MESSAGE:

6193763249 MGMB TDBN KERNVILLE CA 132 07-21 1137P EST
ZIP
JUDY SUTHERLAND
11705 BRIARY BRANCH
RESTON VA 22091

(THIS IS A COPY OF THE ORIGINAL MESSAGE SENT TO CONGRESSMAN STEPHEN
SOLARZ CHAIRMAN HOUSE SUBCOMMITTEE ON ASIAN PACIFIC AFFAIRS)

DEAR CONGRESSMAN
PER OUR TELEPHONE CONVERSATION THIS EVENING I WILL HAVE THE
INFORMATION AGAIN DELIVERED TO YOU TOMORROW JULY 22, 1985 REGARDING
THE MISSION IN WHICH I PARTOOK WHERE WE LOCATED OBSERVED TWO
CAUCASIAN POWS INSIDE OF LAOS. AS YOU WILL RECALL THIS INFORMATION IN
PREVIOUS MAILGRAM WAS SENT TO YOU APPROXIMATELY TWO YEARS AGO PRIOR
TO YOUR HEARING COLONEL GRITZ FRAUDULENT TESTIMONY. SINCE I WAS ON
THE MISSION I OBSERVED THESE POWS AND SUBSEQUENTLY PASSED FORMER CIA
AGENT DR. CHRIS GUGAS POLYGRAPH EXAMINATIONS I FEEL THAT MY SWORN
TESTIMONY UNDER THE PENALTY OF PERJURY AND SUBSEQUENT DOCUMENTATION
IS IMPERATIVE TO COME TO THE HARD TRUTH REGARDING AMERICANS BEING
HELD INSIDE OF LAOS.
SINCERELY
   SCOTT T BARNES
   PO BOX 704
   KERNVILLE CA 93238

2339 EST

MGMCOMP MGM

August 31, 1986

To: Bamboo Connection
From: Scott Barnes

Reference: "Solarz, you are a lying crook!"

Dear Bamboo Connection,
   In reference to the letter sent to Col. Earl Hopper from Congressman Solarz. Solarz stated: "This is ludicrous. I have never spoken with Scott Barnes, did not give him my home telephone number, as you report, and never said that the U.S. Government should not bring live Americans back home." Here is the fact: Congressman Solarz is a lying crook! Here is his home #. 702-75?-??2?, which is all over my many phone bills. Also, his Vietnamese house girl, "Chantra," can verify this. In addition, he's received 2 Western Union mailgrams from me. So, Mr. Solarz, you are a liar!

Scott Barnes

P.S. Ask his former aide, "Ed Freedman," about our many talks.

F. C. BROWN
18, Reed Avenue
Hamilton Township, NJ 08610
Tel. 609-394-0400

August 19th, 1985

Scott T. Barnes
c/o Donna Nevins
P. O. Box 704
Kernville, CA 93238

Dear Mr. Barnes,

I've heard the other side of the story; now I'd like to hear your version. It might make good copy.

Give me a call at one of the following numbers:

202-694-4786 (Mon. to Fri., 0800 - 1600)

609-394-0400 (Weekends only)

I look forward to hearing from you at your earliest convenience.

Yours truly,

F. C. Brown

SYNOPSIS OF SMITH VS. REAGAN LAWSUIT

Named Plaintiffs:

Major Mark Smith, U.S. Army, retired
Sergeant First Class Melvin McIntire, U.S. Army retired
Anne Hart, wife of MIA/possible POW
Dorothy Shelton, wife of POW
Kathryn Fanning, wife of MIA/possible POW
Jerry Dennis, brother of MIA/possible POW
All living American Prisoners of the Vietnam War

Named Defendants:

Ronald Reagan, President
Caspar Weinberger, Secretary of Defense
George Schultz, Secretary of State
James Williams, (Former) Director of Defense Intelligence
    Agency
All predecessors and successors in their official capacity

Plaintiffs' Attorney:

Mark L. Waple of the Law Firm of Hutchens & Waple, Post
Office Box 650, Fayetteville, North Carolina 28302,
(919-864-6888). Mr. Waple is a former infantry officer,
military attorney and graduate of West Point (B.S.),
University of North Carolina School of Law (J.D.) and holds
a graduate degree in International Relations from Boston
University (M.A.).

Supporting Affidavits:

Plaintiffs Smith, McIntire, Hart, Shelton, Fanning and
Dennis
Thomas Ashworth, former U.S. Marine Pilot
Jack Bailey, U.S. Air Force, retired
Scott Barnes, former U.S. Army
Robert Garwood, former POW, U.S. Marine Corps
Robert Howard, Commanding Officer, VII Corps Special Troops
Eugene McDaniel, former POW, U.S. Navy, retired
Sandra Millman, Wife of MIA/possible POW
Jerry Mooney, former NSA analyst
"John Obassy," businessman (true identity withheld)
Larry O'Daniel, former U.S. Army intelligence officer
A. L. Shinkle, former U.S. Air Force intelligence officer
John Taylor, U.S. Army, retired

AMERICAN DEFENSE INSTITUTE
214 MASSACHUSETTS AVE., N.E.
P.O. BOX 2497
WASHINGTON, D.C. 20013-2497

Page 2

Smith vs. Reagan is a class-action suit originally filed September 4, 1985, in Fayetteville, North Carolina by two former U.S. Army Green Berets and four POW/MIA family members. The suit is on behalf of all living American Prisoners of War (POWs) still being held in Southeast Asia from the Vietnam War.

The lawsuit charges that the policies of the State Department, Central Intelligence Agency and the Department of Defense are designed to suppress and discredit reports and evidence of live American POWs still in Indochina. The suit further charges the U.S. Government with failing to act to secure the release of live POWs even though it has been supplied with positive evidence of their existence by the Plaintiffs and by others.

Plaintiffs Smith and McIntire claim to still possess original reports and documents they collected which support their claim that Americans may still be alive in Southeast Asia. They allege that they were prevented from receiving three American POWs who were to be repatriated from Laos to Thailand in May 1984.

SMITH VS. REAGAN

Two former Green Berets, together with POW/MIA family members charge, in a class action lawsuit, that the State Department, Defense Department and the Central Intelligence Agency have been suppressing and discrediting reports of live U.S. POWs in Southeast Asia. In addition, they allege that the government has given them human remains which were falsely labeled as those of their missing family members, and that Plaintiffs have been misinformed regarding the circumstances surrounding their family members' disappearances.

Nineteen affidavits and multiple documents were filed in the lawsuit to support the above charges:

SUMMARIES OF AFFIDAVITS AND THEIR ALLEGATIONS

MARK SMITH (Plaintiff, highly decorated former Green Beret, returned Vietnam POW): Smith was assigned to Special Forces detachment-Korea (SFD-K) to gather intelligence information on Thai Special Forces and on American Prisoner of War (POWs). He received information from his intelligence network of Lao, Vietnamese and Thai natives which convinced him many U.S. POWs are still alive.

Page 3

In April 1984 Smith received the "code word" that three American POWs were available to be taken out of Laos. Smith reported this to his military chain of command and to the CIA. He was told to shred the evidence and to forget the incident. All SFD-K operations in Southeast Asia were immediately terminated, and Smith was told to forget what he knew of the live POWs.

MELVIN McINTIRE (Plaintiff, former Green Beret, McIntire was on active duty when the suit was originally filed. He has since retired): He was assigned to SFD-K from February 1972- August 1984. "I was assigned to...identify, locate and possibly rescue American Prisoners of War..." .

McIntire's network of sources informed him in 1983 that American POWs could be extracted from a location in Laos. McIntire's superiors told him to seek more information.

In January 1984 sources told McIntire three American POWs would be brought out of Laos in May 1984. After reporting this, McIntire's detachment was prevented from leaving Korea or making trips to Thailand. In August 1984, McIntire was prematurely sent back to the United States and told to destroy his information. He was also told that the intelligence he had already submitted had been destroyed. (Smith and McIntire had turned over copies of the information and still retain the originals.)

LT. COL. ROBERT HOWARD (Congressional Medal of Honor recipient, the most highly decorated soldier in the United States, presently commanding officer of U.S. Army VII Corps Special Forces Battalion, Stuttgart, West Germany). In September 1983 he was assigned to SFD-K. In operational control of the unit, he became convinced by January 1984 of the existence of live U.S. POWs. He personally witnessed the blatant security violation of a senior U.S. military officer who compromised one of SFD-K's sources. This "was an effort to undermine the successful intelligence gathering activity of SFD-K on the subject of living Americans in Southeast Asia." Shortly thereafter Howard was accused of participating in unauthorized cross-border operations - "something which was absolutely untrue." In May 1985 he was transferred out of Asia to West Germany.

"JOHN OBASSY" (Indochina businessman; true identity withheld): Speaking several Asian languages and having business and private connections throughout Laos, Obassy states that between 1976 and 1978 he personally saw American POWs. Obassy alleges he gave a U.S. embassy official a report and 22 photographs of POWs who, he believed, could have been rescued immediately. This information was apparently met with disinterest.

Page 4

Obassy reported to Major Mark Smith that three U.S. POWs were available to be taken out of Laos in 1984. Smith was subsequently prevented from receiving these men.

ANNE HART, KATHRYN FANNING, DOROTHY SHELTON, SANDRA MILLMAN, JERRY DENNIS (Immediate family members of missing servicemen): The above affiants have evidence and/or have seen personnel files which indicate their respective husbands and bother were all known to have been captured alive. Despite this, all are listed as killed in action (KIA) except Mrs. Shelton's husband, who is the only man still officially listed as a POW. Shelton claims to have received various reports that her husband was rescued by Laotians but later returned to captivity.

Hart, Fanning and Dennis received human remains falsely identified by the Government as those of their missing family members, one skeleton being inches shorter than the actual man, and the other set of remains consisting of bone fragments which were insufficient to be identified as those of her husband.

SCOTT BARNES (formerly employed on ground reconnaissance mission into Laos). Barnes states that in October 1981 he participated in a U.S. Government sanctioned operation to confirm the presence of and rescue American POWs in Laos. During a two to three hour meeting in the U.S. Embassy in Bangkok Barnes learned that the existence of live U.S. POWs had been confirmed and the Commander of the JCRC told him, "These are the people we are concerned with on this mission."

While on the mission, Barnes personally saw two Caucasian prisoners under heavy guard in a Laotian prison camp. Approximately 400 photographs were taken, after which Barnes returned to Thailand. There he was informed that a communication from the U.S. Embassy and a DOE telex informed his group that the "merchandise was to be liquidated." All previously arranged rescue operations were then cancelled without further explanation.

LARRY O"DANIEL (former U.S. Army Intelligence officer): O'Daniel spoke with numerous U.S. Government officials who informed him of a 1981 rescue mission for known American POWs. He was told this mission was apparently "compromised."

O'Daniel also obtained a set of fingerprints of alleged POWs, which he showed to numerous police officials, who affirmed that the prints were clear enough to be identified, whereas the DIA claimed the prints were "too fuzzy."

-COPY CONfirmation

Page 5

THOMAS ASHWORTH (Former U.S. Marine Corps pilot): Ashworth
states that between 1976 and 1984 he developed close personal
contacts with over 50 Hmong (Laotian) families, who provided him
with first and second hand live POW sightings. He reported this
information to a DIA analyst, who dismissed it as "probably not
true" and "of not consequence." Intelligence from Ashworth's
Hmong sources "documented or tended to prove that large numbers
of American Prisoners of War had been held in Laos" but never
returned. Ashworth provided DIA with other leads and human
sources, none of which, be believes "was responsibly
followed-up."

JERRY MOONEY (Former NSA analyst, U.S. Air Force, retired):
While working at NSA as a senior research and cryptology analyst
during the Vietnam War, Mooney received intercepted North
Vietnamese communications regarding captured American personnel.
By comparing these intercepts with the "operational and
collateral data from other military organizations and national
agencies" and against official U.S. MIA lists, Mooney developed
his own list of over 300 MIAs/POWs. After Operation Homecoming,
"less than five percent of those on my list known to be alive
were returned to the United States."

Mooney also analyzed enemy intercepts regarding a plane shot
down in Laos. At the time he personally reported (and DIA phone
conversations corroborated) that five to seven Americans survived
the crash, were captured alive and transported to North Vietnam.
On February 25, 1981, however, the DIA wrote the family of one of
the missing crewmembers that "no identity or nationality of the
reported prisoners was specified, and that there was no certainty
that these people were American..." . Mooney states that any
claim that the nationality was unknown is false since he
personally provided the information that this shot-down group was
American. Mooney believes DIA information "confirms my report
that certain of these crewmembers were captured alive."

JOHN TAYLOR (U.S. Army, retired): Taylor states that he
knew of a POW rescue mission into Cambodia in 1972 which had been
called off because he was told, "Henry is negotiating."

EUGENE McDANIEL (Former POW, U.S. Navy, retired): McDaniel
states that in the summer of 1985 Richard Childress, spokesman
for the National Security Council on POW/MIA Affairs telephone
him to discuss that issue. Asked if he thought U.S. POWs were
still being held in Indochina, Childress replied, "You're damn
right I do," and said he expected to get some of them back in two
to three years.

another 81 confirmation

Page 6

JACK BAILEY (U.S. Air Force, retired): In 1975 Bailey
alleges he "had information on 73 live Americans" and "10 U.S.
missionaries" being held captive in Vietnam. He briefed the
USAF about an offer by their captor, Major General Ba, to
exchange the prisoners for money and Ba's "freedom." Bailey
states, however, that he was nevertheless "unable to get any
support...to assist in this rescue mission." Bailey further
claims that "in April of 1985 I provided the [DIA] with three
photographs and one letter from a living American Prisoner of War
in Vietnam."

ROBERT GARWOOD, (Former U.S. Marine Corps POW): During his
14 years as a Prisoner of the Vietnamese, Garwood states that, on
several occasions, he personally saw American Prisoners at
specific locations in Vietnam, the last sighting occurring shortly
before his release in 1979.

MICHAEL CHARNEY (Ph.D. Forensic Anthropologist; Director of
the Center of Human Identification and Director of Forensic
Science Laboratory, Colorado State University; Deputy Coroner,
Larimer Co., Colorado; Fellow of the American Academy of Forensic
Sciences. Declaration submitted in support of Plaintiff Hart's
assertion that the Government falsely "identified" alleged
MIA/KIA remains): After examining bone fragments which the U.S.
Government "positively" identified as those of Plaintiff Hart's
husband, Charney concluded that "it is impossible to identify
said bone fragments as the mortal remains of any individual."
Nor, he states, can it be determined "whether they are from one
individual or several..." . His professional opinion is that the
Government's findings and identification "are highly speculative
and unreliable."

The Atlanta Journal

THE ATLANTA CONSTITUTION

Copyright © 1985 The Atlanta Journal and The Atlanta Constitution

SUNDAY, SEPTEMBER 29, 1985   ★★★   75 CENTS

Two soldiers battle Pentagon to prove POWs still alive

By Ron Martz
Staff Writer

FAYETTEVILLE, N.C. — Their mission seemed destined to be little more than a sweaty exercise in futility, a fruitless search through Southeast Asia's trackless jungles for the ghosts of men who died long ago.

They say they were ordered to chase down rumors that American prisoners of war still were being held in steamy, bug-infested jungle camps more than 10 years after America ended its military involvement in the region.

"When I was given the assignment in 1981, I did not believe there were any Americans still being held prisoner in Southeast Asia," says Mark Smith, then a U.S. Army Spe-

cial Forces major and a former prisoner of war in Cambodia.

"Smith and his partner in this intelligence-gathering operation, Sgt. 1st Class Melvin McIntire, soon changed their minds. The ghosts, they say, turned out to be live prisoners in Southeast Asia.

"We feel from our intelligence reports that there (are) in excess of 100 (Americans) still being held in communist areas of Southeast Asia," Smith said earlier this week.

There could be even more, they claim. Smith and McIntire say they spent 18 months trying to convince their superiors and various U.S. intelligence agencies that Americans are waiting to be rescued from bondage that for some is now in approaching 20 years. But they believe their efforts to convince the govern-

ment have fallen on deaf or uncaring ears.

Earlier this month Smith and McIntire, both highly decorated Vietnam veterans and career soldiers, filed suit in federal court, charging the U.S. government with deliberately covering up information

See POW   14/●

POW Possibility Acknowledged

By JASON BRADY
Staff Writer

The government stated in a brief Monday that it does not dispute claims in a Fayetteville federal lawsuit that Americans may still be held captive in Southeast Asia.

The statement was made in a brief supporting U.S. government efforts to win dismissal of a lawsuit filed by two former Special Forces soldiers. The brief concerns only the government motion to dismiss the suit and argues that a court is not the proper place to debate foreign policy.

But in a footnote to the brief, government lawyers said: "Although not relevant to the specific

facts as true, defendant's official position as to the existence of live POWs is not necessarily 'at odds with plaintiff's allegations'."

The government, originally denied the possibility that Americans are still being held prisoner in Vietnam, Laos or the former country of Cambodia, but have recently begun to acknowledge the possibility.

"I guess that's an admission they're there. They've (government) argued, as they have in the past, that evidence about possible POWs should not be presented until it has not been decided whether the court has jurisdiction over the issue.

Government attorneys also argue the issue of possible live POWs in Southeast Asia must be dismissed because it is a non-justiciable

issue, according to Department of Defense officials.

Smith and McIntire, along with former military policeman Scott Barnes and Air Force National Security Agency staffer Jerry Mooney, testified on Jan. 24 before the Senate subcommittee on Veterans Affairs. Barnes and Mooney supplied affidavits to Waple, which essentially support Smith and McIntire's claims.

The testimony given at the hearing, much behind closed doors, included a video tape or effort, confirming the existence of live Americans, according to a source close to the case. Waple confirmed such evidence existed but would not elaborate.

Waple did confirm that all four witnesses testifying before the Senate subcommittee have been

(Continued From Page 1B)

SFC Melvin C. McIntire, former Green Beret who sued to force the government to do all it can short of war to resolve the issue.

The brief filed Monday in U.S. District Court in Fayetteville supported its earlier motion to dismiss the suit. Waple has filed arguments against the motion, and a hearing on the motion is scheduled Feb. 18 in federal court in Elizabeth City.

The government attorneys argued, as they have in the past, that evidence about possible POWs should not be presented until it has not been decided whether the court has jurisdiction over the issue.

Government attorneys also argue the issue of possible live POWs in Southeast Asia must be dismissed because it is a non-justiciable

not, instead, for private right of action under the Hostage Act, and alleged any personal injuries or have a personal stake in the outcome of the any possible litigation, and, therefore, cannot "establish standing to assert the rights of third parties."

As of January, the U.S. government acknowledged that 2,441 servicemen are involved in the Vietnam War are still unaccounted for. It lists 700 missing in North Vietnam, 1,097 in South Vietnam, 556 in Laos, 82 in Cambodia and six in China. Of those, 916 are Air Force, 702 are Army, 490 are Navy, 299 are Marines, one is a Coast Guard member and 42 are civil-

to the airport as they left Washington. The well-being of Smith and McIntire also was threatened, Waple acknowledged. "I don't know who is doing it," Waple said.

Rep. Bill Hendon, R-N.C., a staunch believer that Americans are still in Southeast Asia, this morning left for Vietnam along with eight other members of the House Task Force on POW/MIAs, according to Chuck Lewis, a Hendon staff member.

They have a game plan. They met previously to plot their strategy," Lewis said. The congressmen Lewis said, have a list of sites they want to visit and will strongly request they be allowed to visit those sites. The primary mission of the trip is to find out whether live Americans are still in Vietnam.

MAILGRAM SERVICE CENTER
MIDDLETOWN, VA. 22645
07PM

Western Union **Mailgram**

4-048578S280002 .10/07/85 ICS IPMBNGZ CSP FSOB
1 6193763249 MGM TDBN KERNVILLE CA 10-07 1013P EST

SCOTT T. BARNES, 6193763249
PO BOX 704
KERNVILLE CA 93238

THIS IS A CONFIRMATION COPY OF THE FOLLOWING MESSAGE:

6193763249 MGMS TDBN KERNVILLE CA 96 10-07 1013P EST
ZIP
REPRESENTATIVE BILL NICHOLS
CAPITOL ONE DC 20515

DEAR CONGRESSMAN NICHOLS

I UNDERSTAND THURSDAY OF THIS WEEK THERE WILL POSSIBLY BE A HEARING
ON AMERICAN POW SERVICEMEN AND VARIOUS RESCUE ATTEMPTS TO RESCUE
THESE POWS I HAVE BEEN TRYING FOR NEARLY 4 YEARS TO GET THE FACTS OUT
REGARDING 1 RESCUE ATTEMPT I PARTOOK OF IN 1981 INTO LAOS IF IN FACT
THERE WILL BE SWORN HEARINGS AND YOU ARE SEEKING THE TRUTH OF THIS
MATTER I COULD PROVIDE YOU WITH APPROPRIATE INFORMATION IN ADDITION I
HAVE GIVEN A SWORN AFFIDAVIT IN THE SMITH-MCINTYRE LAWSUIT BEST OF
LUCK IN GETTING TO THE TRUTH

SINCERELY,

    SCOTT T. BARNES, 6193763249
    PO BOX 704
    KERNVILLE CA 93238

2216 EST

MGMCOMP MGM

ᵉNational Intelligence Study Center

SUITE 1102, 1800 K STREET, N.W.
WASHINGTON, D.C. 20006

TELEPHONE: (202) 466-6C

October 8, 1985

Mr. Scott Barnes
P.O. Box 704
Kernville, California 93238

Dear Mr. Barnes:

Thank you for your letter of September 29, 1985, regarding a 1981 attempt to rescue POWs in Laos. That mission was carried out by Lt. Col. James "Bo" Gritz, who was subsequently arrested in Thailand. There is an organization here in Washington, D.C. that maintains an extensive file on the incident. The National League of Families of American POWs and MIAs can send you more specific information on Lt. Col. Gritz. They can be reached at 1608 K Street, N.W., Suite 301, Washington, D.C., 20006 (202-223-6846). Thank you again for your letter, and good luck.

Cordially,

Ray S. Cline

RSC:sec

CUMBERLAND COUNTY

NORTH CAROLINA · · · · · · · · · A F F I D A V I T
_____

NOW COMES Thomas V. Ashworth and hereby allege and say and
declare under penalty of perjury the following:

I am a citizen and resident of the State of Arkansas and
presently reside in Fort Smith. I am 41 years of age, married
and have three children. I have completed high school, college
and hold a graduate degree in political science. I served on
active duty with the United States Marine Corps from
approximately March 1967 until approximately August 1971. During
that period of time I served in the Vietnam war for approximately
9 months. While in Vietnam I was a combat helicopter pilot and
among the missions which I flew were secret missions into Laos.
I was honorably discharged after serving my country as a captain
of Marines.

During the period of time beginning approximately August
1976 and continuing through approximately the middle of the year
of 1984 I developed a very close and trusting relationship with
many Hmong refugees both in the State of California and in the
State of Arkansas where I now live with my family. During this
period of time I have had personal contacts with more than 50
Hmong families. The nature of my contacts and relationships with

54-E-2

Page 2

these people can best be described as an informal guardian,
sponsor, friend, employer and confidant. My interest in the
Hmong largely arose out of my concern to assist them to become
integrated into American society. The Hmong families that I am
referring to are the tribal people from Laos who were resettled
in the United States and who had supported General Vang Pao's CIA
funded "secret army".

After six years of close association with these people I
first began to hear information from them concerning the
continued existence of American Prisoners of War in Laos. This
information came up in incidental conversations between myself
and certain of these Hmong. I felt obligated to provide this
information to responsible government authorities and at the time
the only way which I knew this could be done was through the
National League of Families. I then understood the "League of
Families" to be a private organization which had as one of its
objectives the close monitoring of governmental activities on the
POW/MIA issue. I began providing POW information to the League
of Families in approximately January 1983. The information which
I passed to the League of Families related to one first-hand
account and two second-hand accounts of live American Prisoners
of War held in Laos some time after 1975. This preliminary
information consisted in part of a first-hand sighting by a Hmong

Page 3

given to me in late 1982. In essence this information was that
my Hmong source saw two white prisoners in 1979 in eastern
Xiengkhouang Province and that additional American prisoners had
been seen by others who were being held with my source.

About six weeks after my conversation with the League of
Families, I was contacted by personnel working for the Defense
Intelligence Agency. After listening to my report one DIA
analyst stated that the stories were probably not true and that
the two second-hand sightings which were reported were of no
consequence. One of the second-hand sightings was from a source
who actually lived in the United States and involved the
possibility of over a hundred American Prisoners of War being
held after 1975 in Laos. My only intention at that time had been
to assist in making contact between my Hmong friends and a
responsible U.S. Government agency such as the Defense
Intelligence Agency.

By June of 1983 I learned from a former Hmong intelligence
officer who was a personal friend that he had worked on a project
to free over an estimated 200 Americans supposedly held at Nakay
Laos in the 1969 time frame. I reported this as well as the fact
that this camp at Nakay was significant because it was thought to
be the only permanent prison camp in Laos and that General Vang
Pao had been offered five million dollars in reward money by the

Page 4

Central Intelligence Agency to effect a rescue of the captive
Americans held at that location. I also reported that according
to my Hmong sources that in order to protect the American
Prisoners, the prison at Nakay which had been pinpointed by
aerial photographs was never bombed. The significance of this
information which I was attempting to pass to the Defense
Intelligence Agency from my Hmong sources was that although this
information was being reported in 1983 about facts and events
which were occurring between 1966 and 1970, it documented or
tended to evidence that large numbers of American Prisoners of
War had been held in Laos and had not been returned following the
War. No American Prisoner of War held at Nakay prior to
"Homecoming" in 1972 had ever been released from communist
captivity. Although I realized that by 1983 this information was
perhaps dated, it appeared to me that my Hmong contacts could
have been used by the Defense Intelligence Agency to develop
current information about the POW/MIA issue. To the best of my
knowledge the Defense Intelligence Agency did not act on this
potential source of information at all.

Through the summer of 1983 I continued to have contacts with
the Hmong and the DIA, but still no meaningful action was being
taken by DIA to follow-up on this information. Specifically, DIA
refused to talk to General Vang Pao who told me that he knew of a

Page 5

general location where American Prisoners of War were being held
in 1983. By late summer and early fall of 1983 I had received
two reports from former top ranking Hmong intelligence officers
which I felt were potentially very important. First, one of my
informants had stated that he had contact with senior ranking
Pathet Lao officials who where willing to participate in
anti-Communist activities in Laos. Both he and I felt that these
people might be a source for information on living POWs in Laos.
The second item was that friends of another informant lived in
Thailand and then currently knew the exact location of a Prisoner
of War camp containing a large number of Americans. All of this
information was made available by me to the Defense Intelligence
Agency directly. None of this information in my judgment was
responsibly followed-up by the Defense Intelligence Agency
representatives that I was dealing with at that time.

In sum and to my knowledge the Defense Intelligence Agency
interviewed only one of my seven informants and that informant
was the least important of my sources.

Furthermore, in approximately December of 1983 a senior
United States Air Force officer assisted me in trying to find out
why the Defense Intelligence Agency elected not to act on the
information which I had attempted to provide to them through my

Page 6

Hmong sources. As a result of this effort I learned that the United States Government knew where American Prisoners of War were being held in Laos but could not bring them home to the United States because of political considerations. I also learned that no matter how accurate or current the Hmong information was that the United States Government would not use it. I was also told that if I did not cease my efforts on behalf of the POW issue that I would be discredited and no one would believe me.

Subscribed and sworn this 13th day of September, 1985.

Thomas V. Ashworth
THOMAS V. ASHWORTH

Witnesses:

_____

_____

NORTH CAROLINA
CUMBERLAND COUNTY

I, _Charles G. Boltwood, Jr_, a Notary Public of Cumberland County, North Carolina, do hereby certify that THOMAS V. ASHWORTH, personally appeared before me this day and acknowledged the due execution of the foregoing instrument.

WITNESS my hand and notarial seal, this _13TH_ day of September, 1985.

_____
Notary Public

My Commission Expires:
_4/6/87_

CHARLES G. BOLTWOOD, JR.
NOTARY PUBLIC
My Commission
Expires
4/6/87
Cumberland County, N.C.

EXHIBIT 16, P. 6 of 6

NORTH CAROLINA

A F F I D A V I T

CUMBERLAND COUNTY

I, Larry James O'Daniel, the undersigned, being of age, do
of my own personal knowledge make the following statements and
declare them to be true under penalty of perjury. I am presently
38 years of age and am a citizen of the State of Arizona. I am a
college graduate and have completed some graduate studies. I am
married and have one son. I am a former U.S. Army officer and
was honorably discharged in December 1972. I became involved or
interested in the POW/MIA issue because while in Vietnam in late
1969 I received, as an intelligence officer, at least three
reports detailing the existence of living American POWs in U-Minh
Forest in South Vietnam. Since then I have had a continuing
interest in this issue.

I am also the author of the book MISSING IN ACTION: TRAIL OF
DECEIT (published in 1979), a former Army Intelligence Officer
from the Phoenix (Vietnamese Phung Hoang) Program, a student of
Vietnamese political, social, and military affairs since 1963,
and a former staff officer for the U.S. Army Combat Surveillance
and Electronic Warfare School trained in Electronic Warfare and
Tactical Cover and Deception for both the U.S. Doctrine and
European and Asian Communist Doctrines. The "Phoenix" program
which I refer to above had as its purpose the neutralization of
Viet Cong infrastructure. Its purpose was to identify the
political leadership of the Viet Cong insurgency at all levels.
One of the corollary functions with high priority was the
location and identification of American and allied POWs. During

the course of my research for the original book, the 1984 update, and the 1985 revised and updated book, I have had the opportunity to talk with government officials both in an official and in an unofficial "off the record" type of conversations concerning the issue of live American POWs being left behind in Southeast Asia and what was being done to facilitate an accounting for our POWs/MIAs alive or dead. In addition, I have had the opportunity to look through previously classified materials numbering in the thousands of pages, through refugee reports from Southeast Asian refugees numbering in the hundreds of reports, and I have had the opportunity to talk with the only former POW to return from Southeast Asia after 1975.

On or about March 21, 1981, I had the opportunity to travel to Washington, D.C. to attend a political conference and to concurrently brief the staff of a certain U.S. Senator, at their invitation, who was working with the staff of a certain U.S. Congressman in preparing a bill dealing with the POW-MIA issue as a Human Rights Issue.

As has been my custom over the years of researching the POW/MIA issue, I made my rounds of contacts in Washington to see if the new administration was doing anything new. During the course of conversation with my first contact, Mrs. Ann Mills Griffiths, Executive Director of the National League of Families of American Prisoners and Mission in Southeast Asia, the subject turned to new initiatives by the Reagan Administration. Prior to this, Ann had shown me bargaining positions and draft live sightings positions that she had discussed as a member of the

Page 3

POW/MIA Interagency Group. One of the proposals was a rescue mission. Since I knew that Ann had signed a DIA Secrecy Agreement (DIAR 50-2), I presumed from the beginning that she was talking about a governmentally sanctioned rescue mission. I decided to investigate further.

My next stop was the office of a certain government employee intimately familiar with the current POW situation. In the course of this conversation, I broached the subject of a possible rescue mission in light of the failure of the one we had in Iran. This individual neither confirmed that such a mission was in the works nor did he tell me I was in "left field" on the subject. The latter is significant because although this person never revealed any classified material in the past, neither did this person let me wander down dead end leads either.

My next contact was with a very Senior Administration official who was intimately familiar with not only current POW/MIA material but with current matters of other nationally significant issues. In answering a question on the POW issue, this administration official told me that the President took the questions very seriously and that because there were several options currently under consideration by the administration that he could not go too much more into detail. The tone of delivery indicated an urgent sense of protection of something that should not be discussed in the open.

Page 4

Very soon after talking with the administration official, I talked with a former very senior Intelligence official whom I knew had just recently served as an intelligence transition team member of the new administration. I asked this individual if he felt that American POWs had been left behind and were still alive. Because of both his past and then present positions, I knew that he would be in a position to know. I honestly was not prepared for his response. He said that yes, we did know of six or seven live POWs in Laos and that we were ready to do something about them.

I immediately went back to the senior administration official to make sure of what he had told me before because I now felt that I had stumbled onto a government mission that I was not supposed to know about. The senior administration official affirmed our previous conversation.

In order to confirm my suspicions about what I felt I knew, I went and sought out a government official who had an intimate knowledge of the issue and options available to the government. I told this official who I had talked with, the essence of the conversations, and asked this official if my suspicions were correct. I asked because I had briefed the staff of the Senator previously mentioned and the briefing had not gone well because of what I felt I knew. I asked point blank if such a rescue operation was planned and when so that I could act and plan

Page 5

future briefings, keeping in mind the limits I could go without compromising any ongoing plans.

Again to my surprise, I was told to be prepared to add a new chapter to my book about a rescue mission and to be prepared to have it done by Christmas 198. He paused and then reflected, "make it by the Fourth of July, Independence Day." He then told me that the rescue proposal was sitting on the President's desk.

I waited until April when I learned that the governmental plan might be compromised. By appropriate means, I informed certain senior intelligence officials of the probable compromise in security and through appropriate means let them know of what I knew. The end result was that I was told that there was no denial of what I had learned.

As a footnote to the above chain of events, an UPI article appeared on June 25, 1981, prior to the testimony of General Eugene Tighe, that Intelligence Officials believed that prisoners, thought to be Americans, had been moved from their prison site to an unknown destination in Laos because of publicity surrounding their existence in April of 1981.

Concurrent with the above chain of events, I had the opportunity to examine a set of fingerprints of alleged POWs incarcerated in Laos. During the course of possession of these fingerprints, I had the opportunity to show them to numerous police officials, at least one of whom is an expert and could be called as an expert witness. These persons agreed that the

Page 6

fingerprints, both the "fuzzy one" and the clear one, could be identified. In this case, there were six or so possible names given to be matched with the prints. Concurrently, an identical set had been furnished DIA for their evaluation. DIA's position was that the prints were too fuzzy for identification. This happened in 1981.

As a result of the above chain of events and a reading and evaluation of the thousands of refugee reports and formerly classified reports previously mentioned, I have come to the informed opinion, based upon my years of knowledge of intelligence matters, Vietnamese politics, past and present, and applying all the professional skills I possess, to the conclusion that American POWs were left behind in Southeast Asia; that some are alive today, and that in some cases, our government is cognizant of where some of the detention areas are or at the very least where they were in the very near past. My confirmation process involved the checking and crosschecking of information emanating from technical means, HUMINT means, ELINT, sworn statements, congressional testimony and my own sources.

The above is by no means exhaustive of information concerning this issue that I am in possession of. I have, prior to this, attempted to work with the government by giving information that would tend to confirm information that previously appeared. Like so many others, my efforts were explained away or discredited by DIA with an emphasis upon tiny

Page 7

inconsistencies, sometimes known to me, but with no effort to

concentrate on the areas in which the reports agreed. Based upon

my experience on this issue it is my opinion that the U.S.D.I.A.

is operating to disprove the existence of Amerinca POWs in

Southeast Asia.

_____ (SEAL)
LARRY JAMES O'DANIEL

_____ (SEAL)
Witness

NORTH CAROLINA
CUMBERLAND COUNTY

    I, Charles G. Poltwood Jr., a Notary Public of Cumberland County,
North Carolina, do hereby certify that LARRY JAMES O'DANIEL,
personally appeared before me this day and acknowledged the due
execution of the foregoing instrument.
    WITNESS my hand and notarial seal, this _11TH_ day of
October, 1985.

_____ Notary Public

My Commission Expires

_4/6/87_

CUMBERLAND COUNTY	)	
	)	AFFIDAVIT OF SANDRA E. MILLMAN
NORTH CAROLINA	)	
	)	

NOW COMES, SANDRA E. MILLMAN, first being duly sworn, deposes
and says:

My full name is SANDRA E. MILLMAN. I presently reside in
Florida. I was formerly married to an American servicemember
who served in the Armed Forces of the United States. In June, 1972, my
former husband was shot down over South Vietnam. At the time he was an
E-7 in the United States Air Force and was an same aerial gunner of the AC-130
when it went down. Three members of the crew were rescued near the site.
Initially, the government reported to me that my husband was MIA. By
June of 1972, I had been married to my former husband nearly seventeen
years. We had three children and we were very close as a family. When
we married my husband was nineteen and I was sixteen.

On 15 June, 1973, my husband's status was changed from MIA to KIA
by the United States Government, and I had no reason to dispute this.
I did not want him declared KIA that soon. From then until just recently,
I received no further information from the United States Government about
my former husband's case. Prior to Christmas of 1984, I did receive one
dog tag from the Air Force, without any explanation about where the dog
tag came from. In April, 1985, a man who I had never heard of before
came to my home and asked me if I was Mrs. _____. He explained
that he had information about my former husband. He took out three photos
of what was identified to me as a possible American POW. He asked me to
see if they could possibly be photos of my former husband. We talked
for two to three hours. He did not attempt to influence me one way or
the other. We looked at the photos and I attempted to make comparisons

AFFIDAVIT OF SANDRA E. MILLMAN
PAGE TWO

with other photos I had of my former husband, as well as my own memory.
I felt at the time that there was a strong resemblance between the
caucasian in the photograph and my former husband. When I was shown
the photograph of the caucasian which I have now marked with my initials
and today's date and number "1", I said "Oh my God, this is _____"
(I have deleted my former husband's name from this affidavit intentionally.).

Approximately four days later, I was called from Randolph Air Force
Base. I learned that the government had photos in their possession and
a letter allegedly dictated by my former husband. A month later they
came to my home with the photographs which I have marked with today's date,
my initials, and the numbers "1", "2", and "3", and the letter. I was
told by one of these men that the photos had no resemblance to my former
husband, but the second man (Atkinson) agreed with me that there were
strong resemblances. This meeting lasted approximately two hours at most.

I repeatedly asked the United States Air Force how I could contact
the sources of all of this information about my former husband. I
specifically asked how I could reach Colonel (Retired) Jack Bailey who
I understood was helping on this case. I was discouraged from contacting
anyone outside official government channels.

By July, 1985, I began receiving messages from the United States
Air Force regarding reports that my former husband was alive as a POW in
Laos. I also received, through former Congressman John LeBoutillier,
one of my former husband's dog tags and his Armed Forces Identification
Card with his photograph and signature clearly identifiable. All of the
information on these items is correct.

AFFIDAVIT OF SANDRA E. MILLMAN
PAGE THREE

At no time did the Air Force inform me that my husband was a "Category II" - according to D.I.A. I am now aware that "Category II" is the second highest reliability category. These categories range from one of "confirmed knowledge by the enemy" to one in which "the enemy has no knowledge".

Based upon all of the information and evidence I have received, as well as the reaction of my government, I have formed the opinion that my former husband, who until recently I believed to be KIA, is still alive as an American POW.

This _13_ᵗʰ day of October, 1985.

Sandra E. Millman
SANDRA E. MILLMAN

Sworn and subscribed to, before me,

this _13rd_ day of October, 1985.

_____
NOTARY PUBLIC

My Commission Expires: 4/6/87

CUMBERLAND COUNTY
)
                           AFFIDAVIT
NORTH CAROLINA   )
_____)

NOW COMES   Jerry J. Mooney, and hereby swears and affirms the following:

I am presently 46 years of age, married and have two children. I am currently a citizen and resident of the State of Montana. I have served on active duty with the United States Air Force since 28 April,1957. I retired on the 1st day of June, 1977. From approximately June,1968 to December,1974, I was assigned duties as a special research analyst and crypt analyst to include all formal reporting actions at duty locations which were Joint Sobe Processing Center (Okinawa) and the 6970th Support Group (Ft. George G. Meade,Md.) with duty to the National Security Agency (NSA).

A general description of my assigned duties was that I was a Superintendent and Section NCOIC for airborne cryptographic operations. I was also a special research analyst and fund programmer and evaluator for the B2 Group. I had responsibilities for developing , reviewing and approving plans pertaining to airborne and conventional resources (intelligence). I assisted in the planning , funding, and allocation of manpower and equipment resources in accordance with global and local requirements. I maintained a top secret security clearance during this entire period of time. //

. Specifically, on a day-to-day basis, I would receive,process,analyze, evaluate and formally report significant intelligence data in accordance with high level consumer requirements.

I have attended and graduated from the following formal training in the intelligence field: Apprentice Radio Traffic Analysis Specialist Course (AB 20230,March Air Force Base, California), Cryptanalytic Specialist Course (ALK 20130, Goodfellow Air Force Base, Texas), NCO Academy, United States Air Force Security Service. I served in an intelligence career field throughout my twenty years of service with the U.S. Air Force.

During the Vietnam conflict I was assigned to the J.S.P.C. in Sobe
Okinawa and later with the 6970th Support Group with duty assignment
to the National Security Agency. Based upon my six years of experience
in these assignments and based upon my intelligence backround, I am
presently convinced that there are living Americans who are prisoners
of the Vietnam War being held in captivity in Southeast Asia.

I base this opinion on thè following: in my job during these
assignments I received intercepted North Vietnamese communications
and messages directly relating to the command and control and military
operations of North Vietnamese units operating in North Vietnam,northern
South Vietnam and Laos. These communications were both directive and
informative in nature and contained orders to " shoot down the enemy,
shoot down the enemy and capture the pilot alive, and shoot down the
enemy and execute the pilot." These were the exact operational orders
which I   collected.

Further, other communications were received discussing the handling,
disposition and transportation of captured American personnel---both
pilots and ground forces people. These messages revealed the delivery
of captured Americans from Laos, South Vietnam through the Bankari and
Mugia passes to Vinh,North Vietnam and probably on to Hanoi. They also
revealed the execution of captured Americans and the pre-planned
execution of impending captured Americans. In my role as a senior
analyst and having access to both operational and collateral data from
other military organizations and national agencies I was able to associate North Vietnamese references to U.S. official listings of missing
U.S. personnel. I compiled a listing of over three hundred U.S. military
personnel categorized as MIA/POW. At Homecoming One less than five percent
of those on my list known to be alive were returned to the United States.

Further, as a basis for my opinion, North Vietnamese messages revealed
a high interest in selecting priority targets to include F-111 aircraft,

airborne intelligence collectors, F-4 laser bomb equipped aircraft and
electronic support aircraft. It was clear from the intelligence collected
that the Northvietnamese were particularly interested in capturing the
crew or pilots of these aircraft alive. They were considered very important
prisoners.

In approximately February,1973, while assigned with the 6970th Support
Group assigned further to the National Security Agency at Ft. Meade,
Maryland, my section received, analyzed, evaluated and formally reported
the shoot-down of an EC-47Q aircraft in Laos. Based upon the enemy messages
which we collected there were at least five to seven survivors who were
identified as Americans and transported to North Vietnam. This is an example
of their interest in an intelligence collector aircraft. Since the
aircraft was assigned to the 6994th Security Squadron (an intelligence
collection unit) and its members were trained intelligence collectors, this
confirms my earlier statement of high North Vietnamese interest in capturing
these individuals alive. This information was formally reported to interested
consumers with an add-on of "White House." I personally wrote the message
that these men had been captured alive, that they were Americans and
had been transported to North Vietnam. In secure phone conversations with
the Defense Intelligence Agency we were in total agreement that these were
the crew members of the downed EC-47Q. In this regard, the attached
correspondence from Rear Admiral Jerry O. Tuttle dated 25 February,1981,
relates to this specific incident that I reported on. The representation
that there was no identity or nationality of the reported prisoners is
completely false. I have reviewed the DIA computer print-out dated
80/02/26 under the "incident date" of 730205 which is attached hereto as
Exhibit Two. This is the same incident about which I am referring. The   -
crewmembers listed are in"category one", according to the print out which
confirms my report that certain of these crewmembers were captured alive
since I have now learned that "category one" means "confirmed knowledge"
of the presence of these men by North Vietnam.

I have given this sworn affidavit under penalty of perjury and I confirm that all of the above is true and accurate to the best of my information and belief. I have given this information also to a United States Congressman as a concerned citizen of this country. I -have made this affidavit knowing full well that it may be filed in the case of Smith, et.al. -vs- Reagan, et.al.

Subscribed and sworn this 3rd day of November,1985.

NORTH CAROLINA

CUMBERLAND COUNTY

I, CHARLES G. BOLTWOOD, JR., a Notary Public for Cumberland County, State of North Carolina, do hereby certify, that on this date, JERRY J. MOONEY, personally appeared before me, and acknowledged the due execution of the foregoing instrument.

This ⌐ᴈ𝒹 day of _Nouember_ , 1985.

NOTARY PUBLIC

My Commission Expires: 4/6,87

STATE OF NORTH CAROLINA

COUNTY OF CUMBERLAND   A F F I D A V I T

NOW COMES Captain Eugene B. McDaniel and hereby swears and affirms the following under penalty of perjury.

I am currently a citizen and resident of Alexandria, Virginia. I am employed with the American Defense Foundation in Washington, D.C. I am retired from the United States Navy and my retirement date is January 1982. I retired in the grade of Navy Captain (06). I am married and have three children.

I am a former prisoner of war of the Vietnam War where I was held in captivity in North Vietnam for 70 months. I have been actively involved in the POW/MIA issue since approximately 1979 through the present date. I have served on the Board of Directors of the National League of Families from 1983 to 1984. Additionally I was Vice President of the NAM-POW Allied POW Wing and would have been seated to the Presidency of this organization but felt that I could not get as actively involved with this issue as I could otherwise. When I was on the Board of Directors for the National League of Families I first began a professional relationship with Richard Childress who I believe was the spokesman for the National Security Council on the issue of POWs and MIAs. As a result of my position with the National League of Families and Mr. Childress' position with the National Security Council we developed a professional relationship.

EXHIBIT 24, P. 1 of 3

Page 2

I specifically recall some time during the early summer of 1985 during the evening hours receiving a telephone call from Mr. Childress at my home. The subject of the telephone conversation was directly related to the POW/MIA issue. During the course of this phone conversation which lasted approximately 1 hour, Mr. Childress and I discussed the POW/MIA problem. I specifically asked Mr. Childress if he thought we had Americans still being held in captivity in Southeast Asia. He responded by saying "your damn right I do." I recall also discussing what was being done about the problem. Mr. Childress told me that he specifically briefed the President on the POW/MIA issue.

I remember also Mr. Childress saying to me that he didn't know why he was telling me this. He didn't know why he had called. I asked Mr. Childress when we would expect to get some of the POWs back and he said in two or three years. I told him that in my opinion that was too long, that we were running out of time.

Subscribed and sworn this _11_ day of December, 1985.

Eugene B. McDaniel
EUGENE B. MCDANIEL

NORTH CAROLINA
CUMBERLAND COUNTY

I, CHARLES G. BOLTWOOD, JR, a Notary Public of Cumberland County, North Carolina, do hereby certify that EUGENE B. MCDANIEL, personally appeared before me this day and acknowledged the due execution of the foregoing instrument.

Page 3
WITNESS my hand and notarial seal, this 11th day of
December, 1985.

Notary Public

My Commission Expires:

CUMBERLAND COUNTY)
)
NORTH CAROLINA)

AFFADAVIT

Now comes Mr. John Obbasy and hereby swears and affirms the following under penalty of perjury:

My fictitious name is John Obassy. I presently reside in Southeast Asia. My experience in Southeast Asia as an entrepeneur and government contractor goes back to approximately 1967 and has continued through the present. It has largely consisted of being a businessman in this region which has included countries such as Vietnam, Laos, Cambodia,China (the People's Republic) and generally all other Asian countries. I speak a number of Asian languages and I am fully versed to most of the Asian customs. After the collapse of the Indo China War I became involved in financing, distributing and personally administering medical relief to the hungry,sick and wounded in Communist controlled areas of SE Asia. It was during this time period (1977-1978) in Laos that I was photographed by an American CIA operative as having been in Laos. This was true. I had in fact been in Laos administering medical care to the FREE Anti Communist Lao Resistance groups in the general area of central Laos and Pakse. I was recruited--or attempted to be recruited--to work for the American CIA. Supposedly this was for the purpose of re-introducing American CIA interests to the free anti-communist Laotians who at that time through the present have been abandoned. I did not accept because I did not agree with the views of CIA and American foreign policy in that region at that time. Numerous attempts were made from other intelligence agencies which I also refused. These were all American intelligence agencies including DIA and DEA. At this time I was a businessman primarily engaged in trading and imports and export of all types of consumer products. This was another reason that I did not want to get involved with the CIA. I had my own business and simply did not want to get involved.

By this time I had total access to any border and/or central region of Laos because the communists had not consolidated rural control. I traveled throghout Laos because I had many Laotian friends who asked me for assistance

-1-

EXHIBIT 25, P. 1 of 5

to help and supply food and medical aid for non-military uses—mainly to the
women and children of the abandoned of Laos. My access to this region was
partially due to the facilities offered by Thailand for the free-Laotians
and my acceptance by the free-Laotians in Laos. I also spoke the language.
Being married to a Thai from a Northeastern region of Thailand which used to
be Laos led me into the family structures of the Lao people and to enjoy
their confidence.

To continually finance the humanitarian effort which I was involved with
in Laos, I entered the business of buying precious metals and stones from the
free-Lao at very low prices which enabled me to resell for commercial prices.
These commercial prices were those set on the international market.

I was involved with this sort of activity from approximately 1976 until
the present time. During numerous occasions between 1976 and 1978 in Laos,
I encountered Americans who I presumed were doing similar activities as
mine. The usual encounters were quite hostile as they apparantly felt I was
encroaching on their sanctuaries. I now know that these Americans were former
prisoners of war because during the period of 1978, members of the American
intelligence community confronted me with photographic evidence of my presence
together with these Americans in Laos. I was informed by these intelligence
operatives that these people were in fact prisoners of war. They wanted to know
what I was doing with them. I personally spoke with these people who confirmed
to me that they had been left behind. There were approximately twenty to
thirty of these Americans in different areas which I talked to. They
were afraid to leave their sanctuary areas in Laos. I also was led and
shown by the free-Lao sites or camps which had male caucasion and asian
prisoners---some were in chains---who were heavily guarded by Vietnamese.
They were also guarded by other nationalities. I estimate that approximately
ninety of the prisoners were caucasion and that forty to fifty of this
number were north Americans. I did not have the opportunity to speak to
these people because of the extreme security measures involved. These
individuals were not in one location but were spread out over an area
which was mountainous area with a very good water shed. I was only able to
see these caucasians from a distance through telescopic lenses. The only
reason I had the opportunity to see these people was that I requested to be

- shown where the precious metals came from that I had been buying and it ·turned
out that these prisoner details were all mining for gold. Each prisoner had at
least three armed guards on them. The first time I saw this was the end of 1978
and since then I have seen such details as this one on at least twenty
occasions. The last time I saw such a detail was in October of 1985 when I
saw a work detail comprised of thirty nine men which I very strongly
believe to be Americans. I believed them to be Americans because they were
physically malnourished, looked American and not Asian. Their height was
taller and their body frame size was larger than asian and I was told by the
free-Lao that they were Americans.

In 1980 I felt it was my duty to make a full report of this issue to a US
embassy official who is personally known to me. I gave this person a seven
page report with a three page attachment consisting of twenty two photos of
people which I then believed to be prisoners of war who could be released
if an immediate extraction operation was mounted. I personally took these
photos in southern Laos and I provided specific grid locations where these
people werel located. The photos were of caucasians in chains and under
heavy guard--all in the same work gang. I gave this information thinking
that immediate action would be taken but instead I was offered immediate
employment by the CIA. However, my employment was not related to the subject
of these prisoners. Had I accepted employment I would have been brought bac k
to the United States for schooling and would have been removed from my
contacts and opportunities to travel freely throughout Laos. After reporting
this information and after declining employment by the American CIA, my
business in Thailand was greatly affected. My name and reputation were
adversely affected as well as my personal life and my economic well
being. Since 1980 I did not report any further information to the US
embassy because of the lack of interest in the information which I had
reported earlier.

Around December of 1980 I first met Major Mark Smith at my home in
Thailand where I still reside. My name had been given to him at a CINCPAC
conference when he was offered the job of the Commander of the Special
Forces Detachment in Korea, according to Major Smith. We met because I
was considered to be the only positive source with current knowledge on
the subject of live prisoners of war. Throughout the period from 1980

-3-

to 1984 I provided current information to Major Smith about what I observed
on my trips into Laos and specifically about prisoners being held there. I
specifically told Major Smith that I was to remain anonymous and that if I
was approached by any other person regardless of nationality on this
subject that I would immediately end our relationship. I gave this information
to Major Smith that he was a former American prisoner of war and would hopefully
respond. Being a source of information about border activities as well as being
a personal friend to a senior Thai general officer I asked this Thai officer if
he would agree to meet Major Smith. This was done with the hope that Major
Smith would be able to do something constructive about the information which
I had. Eventually I did introduce Major Smith to this senior Thai officer who
confirmed his own intelligence that Americans were held in Captivity in Laos.
On many occasions I was present with Major Smith and this senior Thai officer
when the subject of American POWs was discussed.

My knowledge of the opportunity for Americans to come out of Laos in the
approximate timeframe of May 1984 consists of the following: The senior Thai
officer known to me confirmed to Major Smith what I had previously reported.
This was that there were three live American prisoners of war who could
be released if the communist criteria could be met. This meant that there
had to be a set of conditions which had to be agreed upon by the American
government in written form and indorsed by a third government that an exchange
would be made possible if political asylum was given to certain members of the
Laotian communist government. It was also agreed that Major Smith would have to
be there to receive these prisoners. I was the individual who made the actual
contacts with the free-Lao.

This affadavit has been executed by me in the name of John Obassy which
is not my true identity. Because of the serious nature of the information which
I am providing and because I have reason to believe my life and the lives of
others are in danger because of this issue, I have used the name of John
Obassay. My true identity has been made known to the attorney who took
this affadavit, Mr. Mark L. Waple, and to a United States Congressman. The
conditions relating to the disclosure of my true identity are set forth in
a seperate document which is signed and notarized by me in my true identity.
I do not authorize the disclosure of my true identity by either of them
until either myself or my personal representative who's appointment shall

-4-

remain anonymous specifically authorize such disclosure in writing over my signature or the signature of my representative. Such signature shall be notarized.

Subscribed and sworn this _26_ day of December, 1985.

John O'Brien

Notary Provisions:

Sworn and subscribed to before me,

this 26th day of December, 1985.

Charles B. Boltwood
NOTARY PUBLIC

My Commission Expires: 4/6/87

-5-

MAILGRAM SERVICE CENTER
MIDDLETOWN, VA. 22645
12 AM

4-0002975193002 07/12/85 ICS IPMRNCZ CSP FSOB
1 6193763249 MGM TDRN KERNVILLE CA 07-12 1236A EST

DONNA NEVINS
PO BOX 704
KERNVILLE CA 93238

THIS IS A CONFIRMATION COPY OF THE FOLLOWING MESSAGE:

 6193763249 MGMS TDRN KERNVILLE CA 129 07-12 1236A EST
ZIP
NATIONAL LEAGUE OF FAMILIES ON POWS/MIAS
1608 K ST NW
WASHINGTON DC 20006

DEAR MEMBERS OF THE LEAGUE:

THIS EVENING I SPOKE WITH RETIRED COLONEL HOPPER WHO IS APPARENTLY
INVOLVED IN YOUR CAUSE. IT HAS COME TO MY ATTENTION THERE SEEMS TO BE
CONSIDERABLE MISINFORMATION AND DISINFORMATION REGARDING MY
INVOLVEMENT IN A POW RESCUE ATTEMPT IN 1981 INTO LAOS. SINCE YOU HAVE
NEVER HEARD MY TESTIMONY, SEEN MY DOCUMENTS, OR REVIEWED MY POLYGRAPH
EXAMS YOU ARE DOING A GRAVE INJUSTICE. THEREFORE, I WILL CONTINUE AS
OF THIS EVENING TO NO LONGER HELP OR ASSIST IN ANY WAY AND YOU MAY
CONTINUE THINKING WHAT YOU WILL ABOUT ME. AFTER ALL IT IS YOUR LOVED
ONES YOU ARE CONCERNED WITH.

RESPECTFULLY SUBMITTED,

 SCOTT T BARNES
 PO BOX 704
 KERNVILLE CA 93238

IN THE EVENT OF ANY SERVICE INQUIRIES, PLEASE DIRECT CORRESPON-
DENCE TO:

                NATIONAL CONSUMER SERVICE CENTER
                C/O WESTERN UNION TELEGRAPH COMPANY
                308 WEST ROUTE 38
                MOORESTOWN, NJ 08057

5238 Caminito Aruba
San Diego, Ca 92124
June 5, 1986

RE: Scott Barnes

Dear Sir:

My name is Marian Shelton. I am the wife of Col. Charles E. Shelton
the only man still listed officially as a Prisoner of War by the
United States Government.

For the past twenty one years I have worked consistent y with numero
individuals trying to bring our Prisoners of War home and to account
for our missing in action.

Since 1981 I have read about Scott Barnes and finally in the past ye
I was fortunate enough to meet him. Since then I have been in frequ
contact with him and hold him in the highest regard.

To my knowledge he is the only American who has seen American Prison
of War in captivity or at least is the only man who has the compassi
and integrity to testify to that fact. He has passed polygraph test
and undergone chemical analysis to prove his credibility. Scott is
true patriot of this country and should be commended for a job well
He has continued to work for what he believes and knows. Hopefully,
someday the truth will be known by all Americans.

My heart aches for Scott as he has had nothing but mental anguish an
discrimination since he returned from his mission in Laos. I am out
raged that our government officials continuously try to discredit hi

I am proud to know Scott Barnes. America needs more men like him in
every echelon of our government. It is men such as Scott and my hus
who make America such a great country.

Very truly yours,

Marian Shelton

6 June 1986

This letter is being written in regards to denials of job opportunities to Mr. Scott Barnes of Kernsville, California.

I have known and worked with Mr. Barnes on the issue of the prisoners of war (POWs) who are being held by the communist governments of Vietnam and Laos as a result of the war in Vietnam.

Mr. Barnes has been very truthful in all of his accounts of his knowledge of live POWs still being held including his account of actually seeing two in a prison camp in Laos in 1981. The authenticity of his story and his truthfulness has been verified by passing numerous polygraph tests administered by the most highly regarded polygrapher in the country, Doctor Gugas of Hollywood, California. Further, Mr. Barnes voluntarily subjected himself to a truth serum test in December, 1985, in Fayetteville, North Carolina, which again verified his truthfulness. The latter was administered by licensed doctors and in the presence of sworn court reporters.

Many individuals, because of Mr. Barnes intimate knowledge of live POWs, have been using underhanded tactics of rumors and misinformation to discredit him. Unfortunately, this includes representatives of certain US government agencies. To date, they have been unable to disprove any portion of his accounts much to their dismay. Mr. Barnes knowledge of live POWs in Laos has been corroberated by other sources and he has been proven to be telling only the truth.

I can attest to Mr. Barnes honesty, integrity and truthfulness as, at one time, I too did not place credence in his account. However, after spending several hours with him at his home, reviewing the documentation he has accumulated, and personally observing his reactions to my questions, I concluded that his story was factual and he was _not_ the "flake" some elements involved in the POW issue attempted to make him appear.

14043 North 64th Drive, Glendale, Arizona 85306

Page 2, Letter, 6 June 1986, to Mr. Brown
    RE: Mr. Scott Barnes

I closely observed and listened to Mr. Barnes testify to the
Senate Committee on Veterans Affairs in January of this year.
During this testimony, given under oath, Mr. Barnes did not
deviate in the deails of his personal information and obervations of live POWs and he stood up to every question - and
test questions - asked of him by the Senators. It is inconceiveble that Mr. Barnes would perjure himself before a Senate
Committee by lying knowing he would be facing 6 to 10 years
in prison if perjury was proven.

I am sure you are aware that the publisher of the book, THE
HEROES WHO FELL FROM GRACE, has recanted and withdrawn the
erroneous and unfavorable comments made of Mr. Barnes and has
issue a written public apology to Mr. Barnes apologizing for
his and the author's errors.

In his letter, Mr. Dennis W. Bartow, publisher states,

    "Recently I have had phone conversations with several
    credible individuals who have extensively researched
    Mr. Barnes as well as other matters relating to the
    POW/MIA issue. They all attest to his reliability and
    honesty."

Mr. Bartow also writes,

    "The reference to Mr. Barnes in the HEROES WHO FELL FROM
    GRACE was based in inadequate and misleading information
    from sources which apparently sought to divide instead
    of enhance efforts to creatively and adequately address
    the problems surrounding the POW/MIA issue."

Finally, Mr. Bartow states,

    "In conclusion I want to say Daring Books believes the
    complete and untarnished truth of the mission in which
    Mr. Barnes participated should be made known to as wide
    an audience as possible."

Mr. Bartow's unusual statements should be convincing as they
provide the highest rating to Mr. Barnes honesty, truthfulness
and character.

Mr. Barnes, in his attempts to influence US government officials
to take action to recover our live POWs, has suffered inexcusable
and unfounded attacks which has resulted in tremedous harm to
him personally and professionally. This has unjustly caused him and
his family unwarranted and unjustified problems in their personal
life. All of these personal attacks upon Mr. Barnes has gone
unproven.

Mr. Barnes personal and professional civil liberties and denial
of job opportunities have been repeatedly violated.

I would request of you to provide Mr. Barnes equal competative
opportunities for employment and not allow lies and misinformation play a part in your judgement of him.

Page 3, Letter, 6 June 1986, to Mr. Brown
    RE: Mr. Scott Barnes

I recommend to you that the honesty of Mr. Barnes is above
reproach and that he is fully qualified for any job for which
he may apply.

Sincerely

Earl P. Hopper, Sr.
Colonel, USA-Ret.

cc: Mr. Scott Barnes

Professional Security Consultants

POLYGRAPH AND SECURITY SPECIALISTS

CHRIS GUGAS, Ph.D. - Director

SUITE 311 - 6253 HOLLYWOOD BLVD. - HOLLYWOOD, CALIFORNIA 90028 - (213) 466-3283

June 9, 1986

I have been asked by Scott Barnes to comment on his background, honesty and integrity which has been questioned by
certain individuals who have never been in any position to
render any opinion pro or con about Mr. Barnes' ability,
intelligence and integrity.

A few years ago ABC Television Commentator Ted Koppel asked me to interview and then polygraph Mr. Barnes regarding
several statements he made concerning American prisoners of
war still being held in Southeast Asia. Some of the charges
made by Mr. Barnes have been verified by several government
officials as well as other sources known to be reliable.

I reviewed all the information made available to me by Mr.
Koppel's staff and then proceeded to polygraph Mr. Barnes
on two separate issues. I found all of his information
truthful and reported this to Mr. Koppel. I also learned
later that he had been sent to a nationally known psychiatrist in Beverly Hills by ABC and the doctor's report concurred that Mr. Barnes was a very rational, intelligent and
honest person who sought only to help his country by finding
out where American prisoners of the Viet Nam war were being
kept in Laos or Cambodia, or even in North Viet Nam.

Later on Mr. Barnes was examined by another nationally known
medical doctor who used sodium penthothal to induce a complete
relaxation of Mr. Barnes who then repeated the exact same information given to the government, the military, to ABC and to
other organizations with a need to know. Mr. Barnes also
testified under oath before a special legislative committee in
Washington D.C. where he again repeated, under oath, the same
information given me and others in this prisoner of war issue.

Security Services for Legal, Industry and Business

Two military writers admitted giving false and unchecked information about Mr. Barnes in a book published just recently. Mr. Barnes demanded and received an apology and a retraction of the libelous statements made against him. The publisher then offered to pull back all the books in stock and re-write that particular chapter. He has also offered a financial settlement to Mr. Barnes for this unchecked story about Mr. Barnes. I am sure Mr. Barnes will furnish you with a copy of the retraction.

Other American personnel who were with Barnes on two of his missions have also verified much of the information given by Mr. Barnes to the government and others.

I have personally checked much of the information he gave me after his polygraph examination and found no dishonest information. What he has said and testified to was 100% truthful. Mr. Barnes has lost employment because of dishonest persons attempting to blacken his name and experience because he was honest enough to tell the truth. I, along with many others know there are as many as 300-500 hundred Americans still held by enemies of America. I have been appointed on the taskforce by Lt. General Eugene F. Tighe to review government operations regarding our procedures for checking out sightings of such prisoners by many others who have come back. I spent five hours with Robert Gardwood, a former Marine who was captured on his 19th birthday and then held for 13 years by the North Vietnamese until he was returned to his home four years ago. He supplied me with a great amount of information which proves along with other information, that the enemy is still holding many of our men.

Unfortunately Garwood was found guilty by a military court of collaborating with the enemy. Yes, he admits he did work for them after he was tortured, starved and beaten throughout his early confinement.

The background of Barnes has never been proven dishonest and his motives are pure and without any financial gain to him. He has been unable to find a job where he could support his family because of unproven statements made against him. If he has lied, then why hasn't Congress or the Senate had him arrested for perjury? I think the answer is obvious. I know that my report to ABC was shown to high intelligence officials who clearly insisted that ABC NOT show the television story of what Barnes had told them. It then appears that Barnes' statements were so true that to air them would cause a severe strain upon the government for keeping quiet about the missing Americans in Southeast Asia.

If Mr. Barnes has been lying, then ask him to show you the many pages of documention he has acquired during his period of service in Southeast Asia early in the 1980's.

I hope you are an objective official who seeks the truth. Barnes needs all the help he can get. He is a Christian who fears his Lord. I think that alone is enough to show what type of individual he is. I am proud to know him and I am thankful he has shown me that we must all work toward freeing our men from the enemy. Incidently, Ross Perot, is also on the taskforce with me as are four other generals and two navy officers. Most of us know of Scott Barnes - and his testimony has yet to be proven deceitful!

Very truly yours,

CHRIS GUGAS, Ph.D
Director

Life Member: American Polygraph Association
Former Director, Public Safety, Omaha, Nebraska
Life Member: Special Agents Association, California
Member: National Association of Chief's of Police

58

4-0128093203002 07/22/85 ICS IPMRNCZ CSP FSOB
1 6193763249 MGM TDRN KERNVILLE CA 07-22 1054A EST

SCOTT T BARNES
PO BOX 704
KERNVILLE CA 93238

THIS IS A CONFIRMATION COPY OF THE FOLLOWING MESSAGE:

6193763249 MGMB TDRN KERNVILLE CA 200 07-22 1054A EST
ZIP
JUDY SUTHERLAND
11705 BRIARY BRANCHOFFICE BLDG
RESTON VA 22091

(THIS IS A COPY OF A MAILGRAM THAT WAS SENT TO TIM SECHRIST CARE OF
CONGRESSMAN DOUGLAS APPLEGATE)

DEAR MR SECHRIST,

PER OUR PHONE CONVERSATION I'VE DECIDED TO SEND A MAILGRAM TO
EXPEDITE THIS SITUATION PRIOR TO CONGRESSIONAL RECESS. I'VE ALSO
REQUESTED THAT THE MATERIAL BE DROPPED OFF AT YOUR OFFICE TODAY. LET
ME REITERATE THAT I WAS ON OPERATION GRAND EAGLE INTO SOUTHEAST ASIA
LAOS IN 1981 AND THAT WE IN FACT LOCATED A PRISON CAMP IN WHICH 2
CAUCASION MEN WERE OBSERVED. THE MISSION WAS SCRUBBED AND WE WERE
REQUESTED TO KILL THESE 2 MEN. UPON RETURNING TO THE UNITED STATES IT
APPEARS THAT THE FACTS OF THIS MISSION HAVE BEEN COVERED UP. AS I
STATED ON THE PHONE I HAVE BEEN THE ONLY ONE TO PASS ANY POLYGRAPH
EXAMINATIONS CONDUCTED BY FORMER CIA AGENT DR CHRIS GUGAS OFFICE
NUMBER 213-466-3283 I SPOKE TO CONGRESSMAN SOLARZ AGAIN LAST NIGHT
AND I HAVE SENT DOCUMENTATION TO CONGRESSMAN SOLOMANS OFFICE IN WHICH
DAVE LONIE TOLD ME THERE ARE OTHER MORE IMPORTANT ISSUES AT THIS
TIME. I WILL BE HAPPY TO REVEAL ALL THE NAMES OF THE DIA CIA AND
DELTA TEAM MEMBERS THAT WERE INVOLVED IN THIS MISSION.

SINCERELY,

SCOTT T BARNES
PO BOX 704
KERNVILLE CA 93238

TO REPLY BY MAILGRAM MESSAGE, SEE REVERSE SIDE FOR WESTERN UNION'S TOLL - FREE PHONE NUMBERS

FRANK H. MURKOWSKI, ALASKA, CHAIRMAN

ALAN K SIMPSON, WYOMING
STROM THURMOND, SOUTH CAROLINA
ROBERT T STAFFORD, VERMONT
ARLEN SPECTER, PENNSYLVANIA
JEREMIAH DENTON, ALABAMA
RUDY BOSCHWITZ, MINNESOTA

ALAN CRANSTON, CALIFORNIA
SPARK M. MATSUNAGA, HAWAII
DENNIS DECONCINI, ARIZONA
GEORGE J. MITCHELL, MAINE
JOHN D. ROCKEFELLER IV, WEST VIRGINIA

ANTHONY J. PRINCIPI, CHIEF COUNSEL/STAFF DIRECTOR
JONATHAN R. STEINBERG, MINORITY CHIEF COUNSEL/
STAFF DIRECTOR

United States Senate

COMMITTEE ON VETERANS' AFFAIRS

WASHINGTON, DC 20510
January 24, 1986

Mr. Scott Barnes
P.O. Box 704
Kernville, California 93238

Dear Mr. Barnes:

This is to confirm the invitation previously extended to you on my behalf by the staff of the Senate Committee on Veterans' Affairs to testify at oversight hearings on "live sighting" reports of Americans still missing in action in Southeast Asia. In order to provide ample opportunity for all views to be presented, it is my intention to hold hearings at 9:00 a.m., Tuesday, January 28, 1986, in room SD-138 of the Dirksen Senate Office Building, and if necessary on Thursday, January 30, 1986, in room SD-192 of the Dirksen Senate Office Building. All witnesses will be required to present testimony under oath.

The purpose of the hearing is to determine the procedures by which the United States investigates "live sighting" reports and to allow each of the government agencies involved in such investigations the opportunity to comment on the issues.

Allegations have been made which state that the United States government has suppressed information relative to "live sightings" reports and has not made a best effort to follow through on many of the reports. I request your testimony on this matter, to include any information which may be pertinent to the subject. Should certain testimony or evidence prove to be inappropriate for open session, arrangements will be made to enter into closed session.

Because of the number of witnesses scheduled to testify, and in order to allow sufficient time for questions, I am requesting that all witnesses summarize their written testimony in oral presentations of no more than five minutes. Of course, your entire written statement will be printed in full in the record of the hearing.

So that the Committee may have sufficient time to review your testimony before the hearing, I ask that you provide the Committee with 30 copies of your written testimony by January 24, 1986. Please send copies of your testimony to: Committee on Veterans' Affairs, United States Senate, Washington, D.C. 20510, Attention: Brian Bonnet. As there will be persons at the hearing who will be interested in your testimony, please bring an additional 20 copies to the hearing with you.

The Committee looks forward to receiving your testimony. If you have any questions or would like additional information, please contact Brian Bonnet at 224-9126.

Sincerely,

Frank H. Murkowski
Chairman

MY TURN

WHO IS MAKING MONEY OFF OF THE POW/MIA ISSUE?

This has been the subject of many false and libelous charges over
the past couple of years and has resulted in much misinformation,
even disinformation(lies), being distributed widely by the
executive director of the National League of Families, Ann Griffiths.

Mrs. Griffiths has repeatedly made these charges against organizations who do not agree with her and the US government failing
strategy of gaining the release of our live POWs in Southeast
Asia. She also has put these charges on a personal basis against
well known leaders of these groups, an action which discredits
the National League of Families in name and herself more
specifically. Her charges have remained unproven and ludicuous.

Among those whom Griffiths has attacked are Skyhook II and former
Congressman John LeBoutillier, Operation Rescue and Colonel Jack
Bailey, USAF-Ret., National Vietnam Veterans Coalition and attorney
Tom Burch, and the American Defense Institute and returned POW
Captain Eugene "Red" McDaniel, US Navy-Ret. There are others who
have also been targeted by Griffiths as profiteers and charlatans.

In support of charges of profiteering she continually cites "facts",
but she has never produced a shred of evidence to support her
"facts", which she can prove. She also has never provided proof
any of these organizations, or their leaders and members, are
engaged in any unethical or illegal fund raising. All of her
charges are based upon hear-say information and propaganda
provide her by her "masters" in the US government.

While the leaders and persons associated with other creditable
POW organizations are working on a non-paid voluntary basis or
for expenses only, Mrs. Griffiths is being paid $62,500.00 per
year plus expenses, plus insurance, plus her parking fee. All
of this comes from the donations made to the League by family
members, concerned citizens, veteran organizations and their
auxilleries, and more recently, from US government fund drives
such as United Way.

Consider only Mrs. Griffiths' yearly salary of $62,500.00 and not
her perks and benfits. This breaks down to $5,200.00 per month, or
to $1,200.00 per week, or to $240.00 per day. Even by the most
generous and liberal standards of wages, this has to considered
an incredible salary for one who supervises an officer staff of
only 5 or 6 people.

In 1978, when Mrs. Griffiths was first hired as an employee of
the League to be its executive director, her salary was $16,800.00
per year. In 1981, Griffiths' salary was raised to $24,960.00, a
substantial increase of 67% in 3 short years. Then, in anticipation
of the election of a new, lenient and uninformed Board of Directors
headed by George Brooks whom she could control, she proposed her
salary be increased to $47,960.00. (This was done by using a 1984
pay scale for government employees as a yardstick and insisting
she should receive 80% of the annual pay of a GS-16 whose pay is
roughly comparable to a Brigadier General.) By now, from 1978 to
1984, Griffiths' salary has jumped by nearly 300% in just 6 years.

In the next two years, 1984 to 1986, the board gave Griffiths a whopping $14,594.00 per year increase to the present $62,500.00. Thus from 1978 to 1986, Mrs. Griffiths annual salary has increased $45,700.00, an incredible 372% increase in just 8 years.

Four star Generals and Admirals on active military duty, including those who are assigned to the Joint Chiefs of Staff, have an annual salary of $68,500.000, a mere $5,000.00 per year more than Mrs. Griffiths yet with 1000 times more responsibility and authority.

A US Navy Captain of an aircraft carrier who has approximately 1,500 troops under his command and a multi-hundred million dollar warship under his feet is paid approximately $45,500.00 per year, or $17,000.00 less than the League pays its executive director, Mrs. Griffiths. The same is true in comparing the salary paid to a full Colonel on active military duty who also makes $45,500.00 or $17,000.00 less than Mrs. Griffiths. It is ironic, by making these comparisions, to learn that Griffiths is making $17,000.00 more per year than her boss, Colonel Richard Childress, who is on the White House National Security Council.

A United States Senator or Congressman has a salary of approximately $75,000.00 per year, only $12,500.00 more than Mrs. Griffiths.

Mrs. Griffiths, in August, drew up a plan to reorganize the League's staff which included the firing of Kathi Parsels, the League's outstanding National Projects and Public Awareness coordinator. One of the principal reasons given for this by the executive director was "cost effectiveness" or to save money which she claimed to be $15,000.00 per year. There can be no doubt that a large amount of these savings were to account for the 8% pay increase in "cost of living" she receive from the present uninformed ineffectual Board of Directors. Mrs. Griffiths drew up her plan for obtaining more pay from League funds and the Board obediently complied.

It is interesting to note that members of the League no longer get financial reports from the League office. Nothing is ever mentioned in newsletters or at annual meetings about the League financial status and particularly nothing is ever said about the executive director's salary and benefits. Mrs. Griffiths carefully avoids publishing her salary and benefits and even when asked specifically what her salary is, she evades answering.

Now, ask yourself - Who is making money for personal gain from the POW issue?

The answer is apparent - The one making money off of our live POWs and the POW issue is the League's executive director, Mrs. Ann Griffiths. And she is making it while working more for the US government than for the family members of the National League of Families who pay her salary.

There is only one way to describe the mercenary greed of Mrs. Griffiths. It is unethical, unscrupulous, and very obscene.

THINK ABOUT IT!!

COLONEL (RET.) EARL P. HOPPER
14043 NORTH 64th DRIVE
GLENDALE, ARIZONA 85306
(602) 979-5651

-2-

(1)

WRITTEN TESTIMONY to U.S. Senate

Committee on Veterans Affairs, Senate Hearing on POWS/MIAS

in INDOCHINA "Laos"

MY NAME IS SCOTT T. BARNES,I was recruited in early 1981 to join a United States Government
operation in which to rescue American POW's being held against their will in Laos. I was
contacted by an employee of Hughes Aircraft, CALIF. who informed me that a fellow employee
named James G. Gritz (aka, LT.COL. BO Gritz) needed to seek my assistance in aranging a meeting
with General Vang Pao former Commanding General of CIA, guriella forces in Laos during the
Viet-Nam Conflict. Mr. Gritz advised me that a special " ACTIVITY" unit needed to conduct a recon
mission into laos, and either confirm or deny the sightings of live pows, and if so,then make
a rescue mission. I was living in Hawaii when contacted and was asked by Mr. Gritz to leave
ASAP for the U.S. Embassy in Thailand,and confer with ~~with~~ other personnel on this mission.

I asked him for verification of this being an official mission, he gave me several names and
phone numbers in the DOD,DIA,CIA in which I called and confirmed this to be an official but off
the record mission, and that the members were asked to step out of active military service to
conduct this mission, and that myself a civilian knowing Vang Pao was needed to accomplish this
due to the current differences with the CIA,and Vang Pao.

Mr. Gritz asked me prior to departing from hawaii if I knew of a courier *They knew me personally* that would pick
up some documents to fly over to me to give to Lt.Col Mather,Robert Moberg, at the U.S. Embassy
in Thailand, I did and a person flew them over to me. Then June 1981 I flew to Bangkok, Thailand
went to the Embassy and had several meeting with the above named persons and several more,
I delivered the package, and at the request of Embassy officials went to the Vietnamese Embassy
nearby to pass on a message on live POW,s and to do it as a cicilian "Private Person" and report
the response back. We then discussed 4 POW,s whom at that time I had never Heard of before.

     Capt. Charles Shelton

     Maj. Albro Lundy Jr.

     PFC Robert Garwood

     Comm. Ronald Dodge

I was informed that Robert Moberg was the Helicopter pilot, that was to fly the rescue chopper into laos, if the Recon team confirmed the POWS, however that Private Carwood was causing a problem stateside and could talk, getting people to beleive him and that could cause trouble, so he had to be discredited, and that it would be in the best interest of the United States that no LIVE POW's come back. After approx. 10 days in Thailand, and Cambodia I returned to the United States, and met with Mr. Gritz for the first time in person and reported the meetings at the Embassy and that ever thing was a go, But that I was confused as to the statement of not wa LIVE POW's back, he assured me it was a mistated comment. Mr. Gritz advised me that a General Aaron had requested him to retire from the Green Berets, to secretly conducted missons to verif POW's, and that it had to be done thru the "ACTIVITY" on a quasi-unofficial channels. Mr. Gritz then gave me a large sum of U.S. cash and said he would be in touch soon , and that the Hughes nection was a cover on this mission. In early august 1981 Mr. Gritz again contacted me and said the "ACTIVITY" gave us the charter to give us the Green Light. Mr. Gritz then requested me to a nge a meeting with him and General Vang Pao, I was to convince Vang Pao that the CIA was not bel this because Vang Pao and the CIA, and his Agent Handler Daniel Arnold were at odds now.

I arranged several meeting between Gritz ,Vang Pao and several Laotain officers, Lt. Col Vang Bee, Col Yee and others. I was then asked to arrange a meeting between Vang Pao and Grit in the Congressional Offices of the Chairman of the POW/MIA task force Congressman Robert K. . Dornan, in late august 1981 myself, General Vang Pao Mr. Gritz ,congresssional aide Stan Mulli and others met in Robert K. Dornans office and discussed the mission into laos and the area of POW camp, everything was a go ahead and Mr. Gritz asked the Aide to arrange a meeting between h lf, and congressman Dornan on a Sunday, which took, place. Mr. Gritz said the reason for the met in dornans office and for him to see dornan later in person was to use him as an additiona ver if needed. Then in early Oct-1981 Mr. Gritz said it was time for me to met the team memb and prepare for the mission. I then was taken to several safe houses and introduced to severa Special Forces members and planned various details of the mission, in which we were to bring large quanties of special,communication equipment, special photo equipment, eletronic equipmer and we were given code book, and a special U.S. government Telex # directly into Washington,D

We all departed for thailand while Mr. Gritz was to stay behing and arrange the nex

(3)

Phase of the mission. Once in thailand we arranged for weapons,medicla supplies etc to be brought to our base Ban Phrang, and NKP, prior to myself and another member leaving for the base we had a visit from Col Mike Asiland from the U.S. Embassy (CIA) . I then along with another member left for NKP, then onto Nong kai to me Col Soubaun, The other member then went back to NKP to await the other members while i was to wait in Ban Phrang for the contact, while their an American Named Mike J. Baldwin showed up and said that we are ready to go into laos and photo the camp we departed along with approx. 30 indigeous forces of Vang Pao approx a two day trip into laos we came up a Guarded .Camp, after securing the area we began to monitor the camp, take phots when suddenly two white older,skinny men walked inside the camp with armed guards, Mr. Baldwin stated " o my god we did leave some behing" we listened to the electronic devices and took photos. Returned to thailand and Mr. Baldwin said report to NKP that it is confirmed and I go the the Embassy and get them advised, he told me to mail several rools of film that we took to the CIA, handler in Virginna. Upon returning to the base and meeting the other members they were angery and that a secret message came in that if the Merchandise is confirmed then to liqudate, I asked what that meant, and the Communications man said first that Bo Gritz was fired and no longer the commander and tha t Mike Aisland was in charge and the messa e, meant to kill these two POW, I started to get upnand refuse when i was struck in the head an face area and told that a green beret was to take me to the U.S. Embassy for a debriefing.

I left the country and returned to America, Later to be Questioned by the Secret Service and FBI, DIA. I was later requested by an ABC news person Ted Koppel to take a Polygraph and a Psychiatrist exam, I agreed and Retired Military officer and Former CIA Agent Dr. Chris Cugas gave me approx. 5 or 6 polygraph tests on the above and more facts of the mission and I passed, then Dr. Hacker conducted my Psychiatrist exam, and again I passed. Then recently Iwas asked to undergo a "truth Serum" Sodium Amothal test which i agred and passed. I also recently filed Sworn affadivit with the U.S. federal court in Fayetville, N.C. on the Smith/McIntyre suit.

I have been called by the Dia, General Shoulfelt, to come to Washington,D.C. and have a cup of coffee and discuss this mission when I went their, he cancelled said he was to busy. I have also been threated by several persons on not to aay anthing on this issue, in addition DIA agents in 1977, and U.S. Customs agents in 1982,1983 also discussed the fact if I talk i could ue arrested for Violation of the Neutrality Act.

I hope that this brief and to the point statement is acceptable, their is so very much more
that happened and involved it would take many hours and hundreds of pages, and some of the fa
might be secret, I can name names, dates, times ,places, and will bring all the material I st
have that has not be confieasted. I will be able to tell you much more inperson next wee .

I can state that I was a
member of operation Grand cergle
1981 and observed two U.S. Pow's
in Laos.

Signed

Scott T Barnes

1

1   I would ask the witness to rise.

2   Do you solemnly swear to tell the truth, the whole truth,

3   and nothing but the truth?

4   Mr. Barnes: I do.

5   The Chairman: Would you please be seated?

6   Mr. Scott T. Barnes, Kernville, California, would you

7   elaborate a little bit more on who you are because I am

8   sorry, I do not have a great deal of information here before

9   me.

10

11

12

13

14

15

16

17

18

19

20

21

22

23

24

25

TESTIMONY OF SCOTT T. BARNES, KERNVILLE, CALIFORNIA

ACCOMPANIED BY:

MARK L. WAPLE, ESQ., COUNSEL

Mr. Barnes: Yes, sir, Mr. Chairman. My name is Scott Barnes, former United States Army. I'm a college teacher currently at a private institution in California and hold two degrees.

The Chairman: All right, thank you.

Please proceed with your testimony.

Mr. Barnes: I, Scott T. Barnes, hereby swear and affirm under the penalty of perjury that I have experience in law enforcement and intelligence activities, both domestic and overseas.

In approximately April, 1981, while living in Hawaii, I was contacted by Hughes Aircraft on behalf of a gentleman by the name of Bo Gritz. Shortly thereafter I was contacted by Lieutenant Colonel James Gordon Gritz by telephone. I told Colonel Gritz on this occasion that I would introduce him to General Vang Pao, former commanding general of CIA Laotian forces to the United States in Laos. It was obvious to me that Colonel Gritz only assistance that I had was the introduction to General Van Pao.

Colonel Gritz asked me to take a package which he had delivered to me to United States Embassy in Bangkok, Thailand, of June of 1981. I proceeded to Thailand, made

1,

1   contact with officials at the United States Embassy, had

2   numerous meetings with United States Embassy officials,

3   including Lieutenant Colonel Paul Mather.

4   Prior to that I asked for positive proof that this would

5   be a U.S. government official mission. He gave me telephone

6   numbers and military officers in the United States Pentagon,

7   Central Intelligence Agency, and Defense Intelligence. I

8   talked to these officials. They confirmed that the

9   "activity" had given a charter for this mission.

10   Upon arriving at the United States Embassy, I was taken

11   to the third floor of the United States Embassy into a

12   secured area where several U.S. government officials were

13   present. Four files were removed from classified file

14   cabinets, and we discussed these people and of their

15   concern. I was also told that every effort was to be made to

16   discredit a man by the name of Private First Class Robert

17.   Garwood. Prior to this occasion I had never heard or met any

18   of the named of these individuals. I was informed at this

19   meeting the purpose of Gritz's operation was to send in a

20   ground recon team to confirm or deny the existence of POWs

21   inside of Laos. I learned that Gritz's operation was

22   responsible for ground confirmation.

23   Following this, I traveled back to the United States in

24   late June of 1981 and personally met with Colonel Gritz for

25   the first time. He requested a personal meeting and

1 ...

1 introduction to General Vang Pao. I introduced General Vang
2 Pao to Colonel Gritz in the congressional offices of Robert
3 K. Dornan. I was compensated financially for this. We were
4 to try to talk General Vang Pao into having Laotian
5 guerrillas help us procure information on PCWs.

6   In Congressman Robert K. Dornan's office a private
7 meeting was later set up between the Congressman and Colonel
8 Gritz which I did not attend.

9   I, along with other members of this team, traveled to
10 Bangkok carrying large quantities of military equipment from
11 both Hughes and Litton Industries, radio equipment, camera
12 equipment, recording devices, high powered binoculars, and
13 cryptographic equipment. No one in uniform, none of us were
14 in uniform. We were quickly escorted through Thai customs,
15 directly to the hotels that we had stayed in.

16   We were then met by a representative of the United States
17 Embassy who came escorted by two armed United States Marine
18 guards. We were instructed by the Embassy official, whose
19 name is known to me, to immediately depart to the northeast
20 quadrant of Thailand to U Dorn Air Base, which two of us
21 did. We traveled to NKP, Thailand. Eventually we made
22 contact with agents identified to us as agents of General
23 Vang Pao and indigenous guerrillas.

24   Myself and another individual who is known to me crossed
25 into Laos with indigenous forces. After approximately a two

1   day travel, we did in fact locate a POW camp and did in fact

2   see live American POWs. We photographed and recorded these

    POWs, confirmed the confirmation, returned to the United

4   States.

5   Upon returning, a Green Beret struck me in the face and

6   ordered me sent to the United States Embassy for debriefing.

7   I returned to the United States and subsequently picked up by

8   United States government and advised that I violated the

9   Neutrality Act, and if I continued to talk I could be

10   incarcerated and prosecuted.

11   Once a confirmation was made and we had returned, U.S.

12   Embassy officials would use U.S. government

13   telecommunications into Washington, D.C. itself. The

14   helicopter pilot and other support personnel were suddenly

15   transferred, and aircraft was in fact grounded.

16   Mr. Waple has subjected me to polygraph exams by former

17   CIA and military officer Dr. Chris Gugas, which I have

18   passed. In addition, I gave been subject to sodium amothal,

19   commonly referred to as truth serum, on these same

20   allegations and have passed that. In addition, I have been

21   subject to psychiatric review by Dr. Frederick Hacker of the

22   Vienna Institute of Austria and have passed all

23   examinations.

24   That's the end of my statement.

25   [The prepared statement of Mr. Barnes follows:]

1   The Chairman: Thank you very much, Mr. Barnes.

2   You indicated that you had received a package from

3   Colonel Bo Gritz while you were in Hawaii, and the package

4   supposedly contained, I believe, intelligence documents

5   pertaining to living American prisoners of war in Laos in

6   addition to sketches, biographical sketches on Gritz and a

7   letter from General Aaron addressed to Lieutenant Colonel

8   Gritz.

9   Might you have a copy of the letter or the letter itself

10   from General Aaron to Colonel Gritz?

11   Mr. Barnes: Yes, sir, I do.

12   The Chairman: Would you be willing to provide that for

13   the record?

14   Mr. Barnes: Yes, sir, I will.

15   [The information referred to follows:]

16   [COMMITTEE INSERT]

17

18

19

20

21

22

23

24

25

1   The Chairman: Do you know whether that is the original

2   letter or whether it is a copy?

3   Mr. Barnes: The copy I have is a copy.

4   The Chairman: Thank you.

5   Do you still have intelligence documents pertaining to

6   living American prisoners of war currently?

7   Mr. Barnes: What documents the U.S. government did not

8   remove from me upon returning, I do have bits and pieces,

9   yes.

10   The Chairman: And have these been presented to the

11   government previous to this?

12   Mr. Barnes: For the last four and a half years I've been

13   trying to present this to the United States government, and

14   have been turned down on every avenue both by Defense

15   Intelligence, Central Intelligence, and by a letter to the

16   White House in which I finally got a response from Fred

17   Fielding.

18   The Chairman: In what manner did you attempt to make

19   this material available? I believe you said you contacted

20   them, you wrote letters, and there was no response or now

21   follow-up or did they indicate any response or any

22   explanation for evidently not having any interest in the

23   material that you submitted?

24   Mr. Barnes: The agents at Defense Intelligence in late

25   '81 had informed me that the mission was highly classified

1 and it would behoove me not to discuss it outside official

2 channels. I had ascertained in regards to the information

3 the photos that were returned to the CIA in the United

4 States, and I was quickly informed that I could face

5 neutrality prosecution.

6 The Chairman: So the material that you are going to

7 submit for the record is the letter that I referred to from

8 General, I believe the pronunciation is Paren, to Colonel

9 Gritz, and you have no other material at this time?

10 Mr. Barnes: I have a letter which came from a

11 re-education camp, and I do not read Lao, so I do not know

12 what it says except other than my name in English and another

13 gentleman. I can give you a dog tag. I can give you what is

14 left of the only photos that I had.

15 The Chairman: Do you have any objection to turning over

16 to the committee the material that is in your possession

17 currently?

18 Mr. Barnes: No objection whatsoever.

19 The Chairman: Would you agree to do so, and we will make

20 it a part of the record?

21 Mr. Barnes: Yes, sir, I will.

22 The Chairman: And I would assume that that would

23 constitute all the material that you have at this time.

24 Mr. Barnes: Yes, sir. In addition, I also have

25 passports and visas. In addition, in one passport you will

124

find out where Thai intelligence had in fact cancelled one of
our exit visas to show that we were not in the country. In
addition, I understand that Dr. Jujas will make available all
polygraph exams, in addition to Dr. Hacker and I believe his
name is Crumian, in regards to the truth serum tests.

The Chairman: You've indicated you requested -- that you
were requested by Lieutenant Colonel Gritz to travel to
Thailand to make preliminary arrangements to conduct the
operation which had as its purpose the identification and
extraction of living American prisoners of war in Southeast
Asia, particularly Laos.

At that time in 1981, did you believe that Americans were
in fact held captive in Southeast Asia, and if so, what led
you to the conclusion?

Mr. Barnes: Yes, sir, Mr. Chairman. While in the
offices of the United States Embassy officials, we had
discussed files. They said they had absolute confirmation of
live POWs in a geographical location classified in Laos. In
addition, their biggest concern was this Private First Class
Garwood and people believing him that others were left
behind.

The Colonel informed me that we could not do anything
about Bobby, we knew about him in '77, but, quote unquote, we
sure as hell can do something now.

They informed me that they know of live POWs in Laos, but

1   in fact, they needed a ground confirmation of this location.

2   The Chairman: Could you tell is how you ascertained that

3   they would know if they needed ground confirmation?

4   Mr. Barnes: Yes, sir, they said via previous Thai

5   intelligence, recon information, alleged spy satellite type

6   information and bits and pieces from the refugee centers had

7   indicated American POWs in this area, but they need an

8   American on-site inspection.

9   The Chairman: You indicated that you spoke to two

10   Defense Intelligence Agency officials in Washington in order

11   that you could ascertain whether Lieutenant Colonel Gritz's

12   mission was in fact sanctioned by our government. I think

13   you further stated that the Defense Intelligence Agency

14   official confirmed that Colonel Gritz's missiuon was in fact

15   sanctioned by the United States goverament.

16   Will you name for the committee the two individuals with

17   whom you allegedly spoke regarding this matter?

18   Mr. Barnes: Yes, sir. I had spoken to Colonel John

19   Kennedy, United States --

20   The Chairman: I am sorry, Colonel?

21   Mr. Barnes: John Kennedy. I had spoken to Colonel

22   Robbie Robinson, Pat Hert, Mike Burns, in addition, personnel

23   at the Central Intelligence Agency that I cannot name

24   openly.

25   The Chairman: So the only portion that would be

12.

classified as far as your intention would be the CIA
contact.

    Mr. Barnes: Yes, sir, Mr. Chairman.

    The Chairman: You stated further that the legitimacy of
Colonel Gritz's authorization was also confirmed by two other
active duty full colonels.

    Are they included in the list of names you just gave us?

    Mr. Barnes: Yes, sir.

    The Chairman: Do you know how much money Colonel Gritz
offered to take part in the operation, offered you?

    Mr. Barnes: It was a considerable amount, sir, and --

    The Chairman: Do you have any objection to responding as
to how much?

    Mr. Barnes: I received several thousand in excess of
fifteen, in addition to --

    The Chairman: In excess of $15,000?

    Mr. Barnes: Yes. In addition --

    The Chairman: Can you tell us specifically how much you
received?

    Mr. Barnes: Counting both missions, a total of maybe
$24,000 in U.S. currency.

    The Chairman: Were these in large bills, U.S. currency
itself or was it in travelers checques or some other form
of --

    Mr. Barnes: The first initial was in relatively new $100

bills. The rest were in small envelopes of fifties and hundreds.

The Chairman: And these were two occasions?

Mr. Barnes: Yes, sir.

The Chairman: And do you recall how much on each occasion? Was it approximately half?

Mr. Barnes: The first occasion, all four members received $7500 in cash. In addition, we set up communications with Bank of America in Bangkok, Thailand in the event of additional funding was needed, it could not be procured in the country.

The Chairman: And what was your understanding specifically to be the purpose of the money that was given you?

Mr. Barnes: The money was purposely to go for the funding of us, that we were not to pay any informants or agents whatsoever, and that it would go to finance plane trips, boat trips, medical supplies that were urgently needed for General Vang Pao's people.

The Chairman: Do you recall the dates that you received these monies, approximately?

Mr. Barnes: The first part came to me in Hawaii in the early part of June of 1981 with a courier. An additional sum came to me through Bank of America, Bangkok, in June of 1981. Upon my return, approximately June 25, 1981, I

1   received additional quantities of cash, and in addition, in

2   August when we met in Congressman Dornan's office, we each

3   received additional funds, $2,000 to $3,000. And then prior

4   to leaving, or the day before we left at the safe house, we

5   all received large quantities.

6   The Chairman: Could you tell the committee how you

7   happened to know General Vang Pao?

8   Mr. Barnes: General Vang Pao, our church was helping the

9   Hmong refugee program in California.

10   The Chairman: I am sorry, I didn't hear that.

11   Mr. Barnes: Our church was helping the Hmong refugee

12   program in California.

13   The Chairman: What church was that?

14   Mr. Barnes: Hope Chapel, Hermosa Beach, California, and

15   I had gone to Lieutenant Colonel Vang Yee and Lieutenant

16   Colonel Vang Bee, and through there, I had gotten to know

17   General Vang Pao quite well.

18   The Chairman: And how did the first meeting occur? I

19   mean, it was through a church function?

20   Mr. Barnes: Through bringing clothes to the refugees and

21   discussing how we might better help them in the community to

22   relocate and settle in to the melting pot, and I went down to

23   the Lao Community Center in Orange County, California, and

24   they had introduced me to Vang Pao. Than later on we had a

25   luncheon in which Dr. Jane Hamilton Merritt was also present

1 but was excluded from the luncheon.

2 The Chairman: Did you assist Vang Pao in any operations

3 in Laos?

4 Mr. Barnes: Just in the arranging the Bo Gritz affair.

5 The Chairman: You stated that you delivered a package to

6 the Commander of the Joint Casualty Resolution Center in

7 Bangkok.

8 Did the package go to Colonel Mather?

9 Mr. Barnes: It went to Lieutenant Colonel Paul Mather.

10 The Chairman: And what were the contents of the

11 package?

12 Mr. Barnes: The letter from General Aaron, a code book

13 on codes which I do not know how to decipher, a grid

14 coordinates map on the location, some biographical

15 information on Special Forces operations and other coded

16 information that I have no idea what it meant.

17 The Chairman: Do you still have copies of the contents

18 of that package?

19 Mr. Barnes: Just the General Aaron letter. Everytning

20 else is in the hands --

21 The Chairman: I'm sorry, just the General --

22 Mr. Barnes: Aaron letter.

23 The Chairman: Which is what you have given us today.

24 Mr. Barnes: Correct.

25 The Chairman: You stated that you met with government

officials in Bangkok.

Do you have the names of those officials?

Mr. Barnes: Yes, sir, I do: Jim Tully.

The Chairman: And do you know what his capacity was?

Mr. Barnes: He said he was, I believe, a GS-14 or 15 working on the Laotian project.

Robert Moberg, Special Forces Pilot; if I pronounce the last name correctly, a William Wharton, United States Marine Corps.

The Chairman: Have you had any contact with these gentlemen since --

Mr. Barnes: Not since the affair, no.

The Chairman: We are going to probably have to go two rounds on this, and I do not -- in deference to my colleagues, I am going to ask Senator DeConcini for his questions, and then I intend to come back, because I do have some more.

Senator DeConcini, would you please proceed?

Senator DeConcini: Mr. Chairman, thank you.

I think the line of questioning you are pursuing is most important. I am interested in those answers also.

Mr. Barnes, you were recruited by Hughes Aircraft -- you were employed by Hughes Aircraft?

Mr. Barnes: No, sir, I was working for Merrill Lynch at that time.

131

Senator DeConcini: You worked for Merrill Lynch --

Mr. Barnes: Yes, sir.

Senator DeConcini: And Hughes Aircraft came and -- I didn't quite understand, how did -- what is the contact there?

Mr. Barnes: Okay. I had traveled over to Hawaii to assist on another situation. I was contacted on the Island of Maui by employees of Hughes Aircraft, El Segundo, California. They had arranged a conference with Colonel Gritz from the ADP section of Hughes, and he said that Hughes was his cover at that time.

Senator DeConcini: Why did they choose you? Did you ask them?

Mr. Barnes: Yes, because me knowing General Vang Pao and at the time, General Vang Pao's CIA agent handler, Daniel C. Arnold, was not getting along very well with the General.

Senator DeConcini: So you were a natural from their point of view. You could see that.

Mr. Barnes: Yes.

Senator DeConcini: As a result of this evidence and information and publicity, is it true you received threats on your safety and security?

Mr. Barnes: Yes, sir, that is true.

Senator DeConcini: And do you know who has threatened you?

1   Mr. Barnes: Three of them gave identification; the other
2   people did not.

3   Senator DeConcini: Can you disclose what identification
4   that was?

5   Mr. Barnes: Yes, sir. One identified himself as a
6   Colonel Johnson, one identified himself as Lieutenant Navy
7   Commander Frank C. Brown. One identified himself as Major
8   Peterson. The two others were one Secret Service agent and
9   one FBI counterintelligece agent.

10   Senator DeConcini: Do you know those names?

11   Mr. Barnes: Yes, sir, I do. Agent Capps and the Secret
12   Service Special Agent David Greggs, and Frederick Capps, Jr.,
13   FBI Counterintelligence.

14   Senator DeConcini: What was the nature of those threats,
15   Mr. Barnes?

16   Mr. Barnes: That if I continued to talk about this and
17   attempt to bring it to the attention of appropriate and
18   public authorities, that I could face violation of the
19   Neutrality Act and be prosecuted. In addition, they could
20   bring up allegations of a presidential assassination against
21   the President of the United States.

22   Senator DeConcini: You mean an allegation that you were
23   involved in such a plot?

24   Mr. Barnes: That not only was I involved, that the Bo
25   Gritz team was involved.

123

1   Senator DeConcini: And what was your response to those
2   gentlemen when they presented such?
3   Mr. Barnes: I asked that I speak to my counsel. They
4   debriefed me for approximately three hours and came to the
5   house once before and have not had any contact with them
6   since.
7   Senator DeConcini: Did you turn that information over to
8   anybody besides your counsel?
9   Mr. Barnes: Yes, sir. At the time I filed an FOIA
10   request and got some of the documents and turned those over
11   to the attorney that was representing me at the time, and
12   since there was no further contact --
13   Senator DeConcini: Have you received any other threats,
14   anonymous or otherwise?
15   Mr. Barnes: Just not to appear here this day.
16   Senator DeConcini: And what was the nature of that
17   threat?
18   Mr. Barnes: I would be sorry the day that I was born if
19   I come up on the Hill.
20   Senator DeConcini: And who made that threat to you?
21   Mr. Barnes: The gentleman identified himself as Colonel
22   Johnson.
23   Senator DeConcini: Colonel Johnson.
24   And when was that made?
25   Mr. Barnes: Approximately a week ago.

134

1   Senator DeConcini: Mr. Chairman, I hope we can call some

2 of those witnesses before this committee in due time.

3   Mr. Barnes, in your testimony you talk about identifying

4 white, older, skinny men.

5   What did you hear said by the two individuals you so

6 identified through using the electronic listening device?

7   Mr. Barnes: The State Department official that was with

8 me, or CIA official, turned and said, oh, my God, they are

9 ours. We did leave them behind. We cried briefly, and the

10 determination was made that they are in fact Americans. He

11 said they're speaking American English.

12   Senator DeConcini: You could hear them speaking American

13 English?

14   Mr. Barnes: He could, yes, on these electonic --

15   Senator DeConcini: He could.

16   Mr. Barnes: Yes.

17   Senator DeConcini: Yes. Did you listen to any of it?

18   Mr. Barnes: I tried, but I was not able to tune in, just

19 bits and pieces of garble.

20   Senator DeConcini: Did you take pictures of those men?

21   Mr. Barnes: Yes, sir, we did.

22   Senator DeConcini: And those were developed?

23   Mr. Barnes: Half of them went back to Vienna, Virginia;

24 the other half were taken to the United States Embassy,

25 Bangkok, and I --

ALDERSON REPORTING COMPANY, INC.

20 F ST., N.W., WASHINGTON, D.C. 20001 (202) 628-9300

1   Senator DeConcini: And you did not keep any copies of

2 those?

3   Mr. Barnes: No, not of those photos.

4   Senator DeConcini: Did you ever see them when they were

5 developed?

6   Mr. Barnes: No. I've been informed that they were

7 destroyed during developing.

8   Senator DeConcini: Who informed you of that?

9   Mr. Barnes: Daniel C. Arnold apparently has made it

10 known that they did not come out, and Mr. Waple, through a

11 contact, advised me that the photos did not come out.

12   Senator DeConcini: Going back to the recent threat you

13 had from Colonel Johnson, can you tell me -- was it Johnson?

14   Mr. Barnes: He identified himself as Colonel Johnson.

15   Senator DeConcini: Yes.

16 When did that happen, specifically?

17   Mr. Barnes: Approximately a week ago when I was getting

18 in touch with Mr. Bonnet.

19   Senator DeConcini: And was that by phone call?

20   Mr. Barnes: Yes, that was by phone call.

21   Senator DeConcini: Could you recognize his voice as

22 being Colonel Johnson? Had you ever talked to Colonel

23 Johnson before?

24   Mr. Barnes: Not knowing who Colonel Johnson is, sir,

25 I --

1   Senator DeConcini: You don't know a Colonel Johnson.

2   Mr. Barnes: No. I did recognize Lieutenant Commander

3   Brown's voice, though.

4   Senator DeConcini: That was on the previous threats.

5   Mr. Barnes: Yes.

6   Senator DeConcini: Did you just tell me that you did

7   know or did not know -- I am sorry, I didn't pay attention --

8   the roll of films, who it was sent to in Virginia?

9   Mr. Barnes: Yes, sir, 1705 Fox Run Court, Vienna,

10   Virginia, former CIA Station Chief of Laos Daniel C. Arnold.

11   Senator DeConcini: Arnold was the person that it was

12   supposed to be sent to.

13   Mr. Barnes: Yes, sir, in addition, I had a letter

14   written in Laotian delivered to him. He responded to me in

15   writing, thanks for the letter, Scott. I'll forward it on to

16   D, and some generals. In addition --

17   Senator DeConcini: Did he acknowledge receipt then of

18   the film in that letter?

19   Mr. Barnes: No, just the letter.

20   Senator DeConcini: Just the letter.

21   Mr. Barnes: The Laotian letter, yes, sir.

22   Senator DeConcini: But the Laotian letter went with the

23   film?

24   Mr. Barnes: No, it did not. The Laotian letter I hand

25   carried to the United States.

13.

1   Senator DeConcini: I see. So you don't know, if Arnold

2 received the files you were only told that he did.

3   Mr. Barnes: Correct.

4   Senator DeConcini: Do you know why Bo Gritz was fired?

5   Mr. Barnes: When the telecommunication came over and the

6 cryptographer deciphered it, he says Colonel Gritz has been

7 fired from the mission; he can no longer be trusted. Another

8 colonel from the Agency was not taking command, and we were

9 not to forward any information on through the agent handler,

10 and --

11   Senator DeConcini: Did you know Colonel Gritz before the

12 mission?

13   Mr. Barnes: I had never heard of him, had never known of

14 him until the Hughes contact in early '81.

15   Senator DeConcini: What was your impression of the man

16 when you worked with him?

17   Mr. Barnes: A man of immense power of stature, and

18 dedicated to freeing fellow Americans.

19   Senator DeConcini: Did you know of any other Americans

20 involved in the mission prior to your recruitment?

21   Mr. Barnes: No, sir, I did not.

22   Senator DeConcini: Mr. Chairman, I have other questions,

23 too, that I will submit for the record.

24   Thank you.

25   The Chairman: Thank you very much, Senator DeConcini.

1   Representative McEwen?

2   Mr. McEwen: Thank you, Mr. Chairman. I will submit my

3   questions for the record.

4   The Chairman: Representative Bilirakis?

5   Mr. Bilirakis: Thank you, Mr. Chairman.

6   Do you know who turned over -- who turned over the

7    $24,000 on those two occasions to you? Was it Colonel Gritz

8   in every case?

9   Mr. Barnes: Yes, sir, it was.

10   Mr. Bilirakis: And some of that money was turned over to

11   you in Congressman Dornan's office? I believe you testified

12   to that effect.

13   Mr. Barnes: Yes, sir, it was.

14   Mr. Bilirakis: And he was present?

15   Mr. Barnes: Bob wasn't there. If I could explain how

16   that situation came about, they had wanted a meeting in the

17   congressional offices with Vang Pao in hopes of convincing

18   him the Agency was not behind this. Stan Mulen, the

19   congressional aide, was present, along with some lieutenant

20   Colonels, General Vang Pao, myself, and others. Apprently

21   what had transpired is later on we received United States red

22   passports in which to claim diplomatic immunity if

23   incarcerated. In addition, Colonel Gritz had given us

24   identification that stated all of us were staff assistants

25   for the POW-MIA Task Force, and Bob had called me and said

13

1   that he wanted to know how that ended up that way. I said

2   they had come from Colonel Gritz, and that unfortunately you

3   were used as a cover, and I apologize.

4   So I think approximately a week later, on a Sunday,

5   Congressman Dornan and Colonel Gritz met. He had requested

6   that General David Jones and Bobby Inman from the CIA meet.

7   I understand that Bob met. Then Bob said that he was going

8   to meet with the President on Air Force One December 27th,

9   1981.

10   I was picked up by our government agents Christmas eve,

11   1981, and the correlation is that the meeting in Congressman

12   Dornan's office was supposed to be denied at the highest

13   levels.

14   Senator DeConcini: Excuse me. Was supposed to what?

15   Mr. Barnes: Was supposed to be denied at the highest

16   levels.

17   Senator DeConcini: Who told you that, the Agency?

18   Mr. Barnes: Colonel Gritz.

19   Senator DeConcini: Colonel Gritz. Thank you.

20   And excuse me, Congressman.

21   Mr. Bilirakis: That's all right.

22   The verification that you asked Colonel Gritz for and he

23   gave you several names and phone numbers in DOD, DIA, CIA,

24   according to your testimony, you called those people and you

25   confirmed this to be official. In other words, somebody on

140

the telephone identified themselves and told you it was an
official but off-the-record mission.

Mr. Barnes: That it was an official mission but it had
to be "unofficial" because of the activities involvement,
that Congress did not know about the existence of the
activity, and this was going to be secretly done.

Mr. Bilirakis: All right, but have you since that time,
or has your attorney -- and maybe this is something you
cannot talk about because of the litigation -- have you
confirmed that those were legitimate numbers and that those
were legitimate people you talked to?

Mr. Barnes: Yes, sir. General Eugene Tighe called me a
few months ago, and I told him the names and the locations
and the numbers, and he told me that yes, those men did in
fact work underneath me and they never, ever forwarded
information on up the chain of command, and that it was --
they were factual numbers, they were factual men, and the
physical location --

Mr. Bilirakis: Did those people acknowledge that
telephone call?

Mr. Barnes: Yes, sir, they did.

Mr. Bilirakis: They have acknowledged that telephone
call?

Mr. Barnes: Yes, sir, they have.

Mr. Bilirakis: Is there truly a Colonel Johnson?

141

1   Mr. Barnes: I have been told yes there is by Mr. Bonnet,

2   there is a Colonel Johnson working for Defense Intelligence.

3   Mr. Bilirakis: But do we know that that particular

4   individual, that live body, is really attributable to these

5   telephone calls that you received?

6   Mr. Barnes: No, sir, I do not know that. In addition, I

7   had received a telephone call from General Shoulfelt from DIA

8   requesting that I come to Washington, D.C. to meet with him

9   quietly, have a cup of coffee and discuss the mission. Last

10   month I came here to meet with him. At the last minute he

11   had called off the meeting, said he could not meet.

12   Mr. Bilirakis: Yes, that's in your testimony.

13   But Mr. Chairman, might I ask, are we going to also ask

14   this gentleman and his attorney to be part of the executive

15   session, the closed meeting?

16   Apparently there is some secret information.

17   The Chairman: I think it would be appropriate. This

18   opens up a whole new dimension, obviously, for the committee,

19   and I think that we should discuss just how we want to set an

20   agenda to accommodate that portion. It is obviously

21   classified, and I would suggest, Representative Bilirakis,

22   that it would appear that we would have to have extended

23   hearings and perhaps a hearing just to hear those witnesses

24   that had classified material. So that would be my offhand

25   response to your question.

1   Mr. Bilirakis: And you are willing to do this?

2   Mr. Barnes: Yes, sir. I might also add that the former

3   military officer and CIA gentleman who did my polygraphs has

4   gone on the record to state that he has been indirectly

5   threatened in regards to releasing the fact that I have

6   passed approximately seven to eight polygraph exams on this

7   nature.

8   Senator DeConcini: Would the Congressman yield for just

9   a short interruption?

10   Mr. Bilirakis: Certainly.

11   Senator DeConcini: Is it true that there has been a

12   cassette tape made, a videotape made of some of these tests?

13   Mr. Barnes: Yes, sir. There is a complete test of the

14   truth serum, a complete test made of the original polygraph

15   exams, or the second polygraph exams. The original polygraph

16   exams were turned over to the CIA, I am told, last year.

17   Senator DeConcini: You have no objections of that being

18   part of the record.

19   Mr. Barnes: None whatsoever.

20   Senator DeConcini: I understand that BBC has it, and I

21   have been supplied a copy.

22   Mr. Chairman, I will offer that at the appropriate time,

23   and maybe we would want to see it or at least have it as

24   evidence.

25   Thank you. Thank you for yielding.

ALDERSON REPORTING COMPANY, INC.
20 F ST., N.W., WASHINGTON, D.C. 20001   (202) 628-9300

143

1   Mr. Bilirakis: I have nothing further, sir.

2   I understand that the record will be receptive to any

3   additional questions addressed to any witnesses.

4   Is that correct, sir?

5   The Chairman: That is correct.

6   I wonder, Mr. Barnes, if you could elaborate a little bit

7   further about your communication and conversation with

8   Colonel Johnson. I gather it was from a phone call the.

9   Mr. Barnes: Yes, sir. My home telephone. I have a

10   complaint on record with my phone company, and they can

11   verify that apparently there had been problems with people

12   intercepting telephonic communications at both my business

13   and my home.

14   The phone call, I did have a typed letter from Commander

15   Brown who gave me a 202 area code number and which I

16   discussed with him, but Colonel Johnson called on the phone,

17   Major Peterson called on the phone.

18   The Chairman: Okay.

19   Now, Colonel Johnson phoned during the day not so long

20   ago, is that right?

21   Mr. Barnes: Not too long after I talked to Mr. Bonnet.

22   The Chairman: Do you know approximately what day it was

23   that you got the telephone call from Colonel Johnson?

24   Mr. Barnes: Approximately, maybe a week to nine days.

25   The Chairman: A week to nine days, when -- but you had

1   made a decision to appear before this hearing at that time?

2   I am just curious to know how Colonel Johnson knew that

3   you were appearing at the hearing nine days ago.

4   Mr. Barnes: Many things that apparently are happening in

5   this whole issue, unbeknownst to me, a lot of people in this

6   east coast area are knowing about, and I do not know how they

7   know.

8   The Chairman: And you -- when he phoned, he just said

9   this is Colonel Johnson, or you asked who it was?

10   Mr. Barnes: Yes. He was very polite at the onslaught,

11   had discussed the problems of this issue but reiterated that

12   it would be in my best interests and the interests of

13   national security that I not come to the Hill. I had had

14   brief conversation and said I told Steve Solarz several years

15   ago that I would try to come to the Hill with the evidence,

16   and that was not wise. I said --

17   The Chairman: I am interested in knowing if you have any

18   suggestions as to how we could identify if indeed there is a

19   Colonel Johnson somewhere in our military capability.

20   Are you aware of that personally?

21   Mr. Barnes: By going through personnel and what Mr.

22   Bonnet has informed me.

23   The Chairman: But he didn't indicate where he worked or

24   what office he was in?

25   Senator DeConcini: Mr. Chairman, would you yield just

1 for a point of information?

2 The Chairman: I will.

3 Senator DeConcini: I think there is testimony that there

4 is a Colonel Johnson in --

5 Mr. Barnes: The Defense Intelligence.

6 Senator DeConcini: In the Defense Intelligence. Of

7 course, we don't know whether that is the same one or not.

8 The Chairman: Yes, that is what I was approaching.

9 I wonder if you knew whether or not he -- what his

10 position was?

11 Mr. Barnes: No, I do not, sir.

12 The Chairman: and you didn't ask him, so it is purely

13 conjecture as to whether these two are the same?

14 Do you have an opinion as to whether this is the same

15 Colonel Johnson that Senator DeConcini spoke of?

16 Mr. Barnes: I believe it's the same because Colonel

17 Johnson also called and left a message in Virginia for me

18 here a few weeks back, basically not to show up and meet with

19 General Shoulfelt.

20 The Chairman: And you concluded that it was definitely a

21 threat.

22 Mr. Barnes: Oh, asolutely.

23 The Chairman: Did you indicate to him that you felt you

24 were being threatened by him?

25 Mr. Barnes: We had a few chosen words on the phone.

1   The Chairman: And did he acknowledge that he' was

2   . threatening you or dismiss it?

3   Mr. Barnes: No, I just interpreted it as a threat that I

4   would regret the day I was born.

5   The Chairman: And What do you anticipate is his

6   motivation for threatening you in some manner or form, just

7   generalizing? What -- here's one person that very recently,

8   as a consequence of your willingness to testify, has made

9   threats, what would be -- how would you conject that his

10   motivation? Obviously he has something to hide that you

11   have.

12   Mr. Barnes: The testimony, I can only assume, on the

13   Gritz mission, and what agents in DIA did not take it to

14   General Tighe.

15   The Chairman: And you do not know -- well obviously

16   there are a couple of other questions that I intend to pursue

17   here. I have highlighted, and I do not want to -- I know

18   that we marked them in red.

19   In your written testimony before the committee, you list

20   the four individuals whom you claim to have been POWs. The

21   names of those individuals were Captain Shelton, Major Lundy,

22   Private First Class Garwood and Commander Dodge. You further

23   state that you had never heard of any of these individuals

24   before, and my question is can the committee assume that you

25   had never heard of Robert Garwood, though in 1979 his return

1.

from Southeast Asia received a good deal of press, and did
you not know at that time that Mr. Garwood was charged with
collaborating against the government?

Mr. Barnes: When Colonel Mather pulled out these four
files and we discussed each of them, I did not know any one
and had never heard of any of these names.

The Chairman: Okay.

So you had not heard of the Garwood situation or case.

Mr. Barnes: No, sir, I had not.

The Chairman: Thank you.

In your written testimony you state that someone said it
would be in your best interests of the United States that no
live POWs come back.

Mr. Barnes: That is correct, sir.

The Chairman: Do you recall who made this comment?

Mr. Barnes: Yes, sir. It was Lieutenant Colonel Paul
Mather, JCRC.

The Chairman: Do you have any -- would you care to
elaborate any further as to what motivation he may have had
to make a statement like that?

Mr. Barnes: Personally, at first I thought it was a
testing question to see what my response would be. Other
than that, I, you know, conferred with Colonel Gritz that
this gentleman had said this. He said not to worry, that
things were well in hand, and it was probably a miscomment.

148

The Chairman: Since your meeting in which the four names were provided, other than Robert Garwood, have you been able to ascertain whether the names of the other three individuals are those of Americans still listed as missing in action in Southeast Asia?

Mr. Barnes: Yes, sir. The top name, sir, was one in which we had to --

The Chairman: That was Shelton?

Mr. Barnes: Yes, sir. We, prior to going down there, had to contact his son in hopes of stopping him from seeking information upon his father.

The other one, Albro, Major Lundy, and Garwood, was just basic information. Commander Dodge I was told had become a martyr, was a known live POW, and that his remains would be coming home forthwith, and I understand approximately four to five weeks later his remains did in fact come home.

The Chairman: You indicated that you were instructed, excuse me, by Colonel Mather, to travel to a Khmer Rouge camp in order to deliver a package or another package.

Do you recall what the contents of that package may have been?

Mr. Barnes: I was never privy to know what was inside the package.

The Chairman: I'm sorry.

Mr. Barnes: I was not privy to know what was inside the

149

package.

The Chairman: But you did deliver the package.

Mr. Barnes: I delivered it to Khmer Rouge.

The Chairman: Was it a small package, heavy, light? Did it appear to be something small enough to contain currency or documents or —

Mr. Barnes: It was shoe box, standard shoe box in size, maybe at the most two pounds, and both JustMAG and Task Force 80 on the Kampuchean-Thai border assisted us in crossing.

The Chairman: Who did you give the package to?

Mr. Barnes: I gave it to a Khmer Rouge translator in a Khmer Rouge camp.

The Chairman: After your return from the camp to Bangkok, and I gather you went to the Joint Casualty Resolution Center, were you debriefed there, and if so, by whom?

Mr. Barnes: Well, we had some discussions on the third floor with some Agency personnel, and in addition, I was instructed to go to the Vietnamese Embassy directly up the street from the American Embassy and as a civilian attempt to make a proposal on the possibility of some remains on POWs.

The Chairman: I wonder if you could, in view of your testimony that — I should advise you that unofficially we have had word that the spacde shuttle has blown up, and things do not look very good. I have nothing final on that

1 but have just been advised that shortly after launching,

2 there was an explosion. So if anybody wants to be excused,

3 we will certainly understand.

4   I wonder, Mr. Barnes, if you could just for us generalize

5 on what you think the motivation for scrubbing the mission

6 might have been. You proceeded, and you know, you have

7 made -- you are satisfied that you have seen living Americans

8 in Laos in one capacity or another, and then this mission was

9 planned, and then it was withdrawn, and I wonder if you have

10 any general explanation of what went wrong or why, why did

11 those, whoever was responsible, see fit to pull back of

12 cancel or scrub or --

13   Mr. Barnes: It would strictly be my opinion.

14   The Chairman: Yes. Well, I would appreciate that.

15   Mr. Barnes: Okay, I can only hypothesize and opinionize

16 that our President at that time had said all Americans are

17 back, the secret war in Laos possibly -- and I do not know

18 this for a fact -- possibly had engaged in some illicit

19 activities, and that is why things in Laos are and were as

20 they seemed.

21   The Chairman: And this date, when it was officially

22 scrubbed, your recollection, was about when?

23   Mr. Barnes: Just after Halloween, October 1981.

24   The Chairman: I hate to pursue this, but it would seem

25 even though we had assurances that everybody had been set

15

1 free and then you came up or you had information relative to

2 the fact that they weren't all free, I just wonder what would

3 be the motivation of any official to make a judgment or a

4 value judgment not to proceed with the follow-up?.

5 Mr. Barnes: Maybe it could prove to be extremely

6 embarrassing for the United States that we said they are all

7 back, they were left there, and all of a sudden they come

8 back X amount of years later. To me that would be very

9 embarrassing to our country. It would cause low morale in

10 the military services, knowing that we left some behind. An

11 all-volunteer force, that's not going to make them real

12 impressed.

13 The Chairman: Well, I know, but the humanitarian

14 responsibility of responsible officials you would assume

15 would outweigh that. But I assume that then your

16 generalizaton of the rationale is that perhaps somebody would

17 be embarrassed.

18 Mr. Barnes: Yes, sir, it is.

19 The Chairman: So they would scrub the mission rather

20 than admit that there were Americans living there.

21 And who would you suggest would be responsible ultimately

22 from the standpoint of where your participation was for this

23 kind of a decision to be made, scrubbing the mission? You

24 know, you obviously were a cog in a large wheel, and as you

25 looked up through the structured stratus of your reporting

1 officials, where would you pin the responsibility of

2 scrubbing your mission?

3 Mr. Barnes: Both on Colonel Mike Iland and Daniel C.

4 Arnold and Lieutenant Colonel Paul Mather.

5 The Chairman: Thank you.

6 I would ask Senator DeConcini to proceed.

7 Senator DeConcini: Thank you, Mr. Chairman.

8 Let me ask just a couple of quick questions.

9 No. 1, Mr. Barnes, are you now under any threat as to

10 your physical safety? Do you feel you are in any jeopardy?

11 Mr. Barnes: I don't know until I get home.

12 Senator DeConcini: Okay. But you are not -- are you

13 under any protection?

14 Mr. Barnes: No. I am authorized to be armed if need be,

15 so I --

16 Senator DeConcini: Do you feel the need of any

17 protection to get home or to leave this facility? Do you

18 feel you will be safe?

19 Mr. Barnes: I really don't know, to be honest.

20 Senator DeConcini: Would you like any assistance from

21 this body, whatever we can give, for your safe transport?

22 Mr. Barnes: I don't see any harm in it.

23 Senator DeConcini: Mr. Chairman, I would request that we

24 ask the Capitol Police to assist Mr. Barnes to wherever his

25 destination is.

15

1   The Chairman: I would so order, and I certainly agree

2   with your assessment, Senator DeConcini.

3   We would request the staff to initiate a request of the

4   Capitol Police to accompany Mr. Barnes, and I would suggest

5   strongly if you feel you need further security assistance,

6   you request it of our committee, and we will initiate

7   appropriate action.

8   But I want to be very explicit, if you do feel you need

9   it, please make sure that the request is forthcoming, becaus:

10   we would hate to feel that we had miscommunication on

11   something as significant as your personal safety.

12   Mr. Barnes: Yes, sir, I understand.

13   Senator DeConcini: So before you leave the room, if the

14   Chairman would yield, it should be very clear, I wish you

15   would contact the Chairman or the staff here, and we will --

16   The Chairman: And indicate what, if it is just home or

17   beyond.

18   Senator DeConcini: Wherever you would like.

19   The Chairman: Beyond accompanying you back to your

20   home.

21   Mr. Barnes: Accompanied home would be satisfactory

22   since I do have personal --

23   The Chairman: Now, you are going back to California, ios

24   that right?

25   Mr. Barnes: Yes, sir, I plan to.

154

1   The Chairman: So you would want somebody to accompany
2 you on the airplane?

3   Mr. Barnes: Not necessarily on the aircraft.

4   The Chairman: To the aircraft.

5   Mr. Barnes: To the aircraft would be sufficient.

6   The Chairman: Thank you, and if you need security in
7 California, why, obviously there is a capability there.

8   Mr. Bilirakis: Mr. Chairman, I wonder if the gentleman
9 would yield.

10   Senator DeConcini: I yield.

11   Mr. Bilirakis: The attorney who is also representing
12 Major Smith and Sergeant McIntire, he is not a witness, but I
13 just wonder if he has felt any pressure to not represent
14 these people.

15   The Chairman: You may direct that to the gentleman.

16   Mr. Bilirakis: If I may direct that to him, may I hear
17 his response?

18   Mr. Waple: No, sir, I can't say that I have had any
19 pressure of any kind.

20   Mr. Bilirakis: Not from the bar or any other sources?

21   Mr. Waple: Not of any sort, no, sir.

22   Senator DeConcini: Quickly, Mr. Barnes, are you still
23 employed with Merrill Lynch?

24   Mr. Barnes: No, I am a college teacher and I own a
25 private investigative agency.

155

1   Senator DeConcini: Is that what your sole source of

2   income is now?

3   Mr. Barnes: Yes, sir.

4   Senator DeConcini: One last question.

5   Ms. Griffiths testified, and I will read the testimony,

6   "I had known firsthand the President's interest and

7   commitment, but his current working knowledge of what his

8   administration is doing to resolve the POW/MIA issue renders

9   absurd any allegation that a conspiracy and coverup exists

10   under this President's administration."

11   Would you refute that in your judgment?

12   Mr. Barnes: Yes, sir. I had sent numerous

13   correspondences to the White House, to Mr. Childress, got one

14   phone call from Mr. Childress in 1932. The correspondence I

15   got from the White House was we will forward the POW

16   investigation to U.S. Attorney Stephen Trout. His office

17   informed me that if I continued the issue, that it could very

18   well lead to the prosecution.

19   Senator DeConcini: This Mr. Trout, who in Mr. Trout's

20   office?

21   Mr. Barnes: A gentleman by the name of Mark Richards.

22   Senator DeConcini: Mark Richards made that statement to

23   you? When was that, do you recall?

24   Mr. Barnes: He made that statement to me 9/20/85 at

25   approximately 2:15 p.m.

1   Senator DeConcini: Have any charges ever been brought

2 against you?

3   Mr. Barnes: No, none that I know of. I have been told

4 by the United States attorney that I could face prosecution

5 for violation of neutrality and that this presidential threat

6 could creep up.

7   Senator DeConcini: What is the nature of the

8 presidential threat? Do you have any idea what they are

9 talking about?

10   Mr. Barnes: Just from what the Bureau has informed me,

11 they have received anonymous information that Colonel Gritz's

12 team were planning to assassinate the President of the United

13 States. All team members were --

14   Senator DeConcini: Who told you that?

15   Mr. Barnes: Federal Agent Capps and a Federal Secret

16 Service Agent.

17   Senator DeConcini: And they told you you were involved n

18 that?

19   Mr. Barnes: That I was involved.

20   Senator DeConcini: But it was anonymous information.

21   Mr. Barnes: They said they got anonymous information,

22 yes, sir.

23   Senator DeConcini: Thank you, Mr. Chairman.

24   The Chairman: Thank you, Senator DeConcini.

25   In view of the hour and the complexion of the hearing, I

Homecoming II

February 7, 1986

SENATOR DECONCINI AVERTS COMMITTEE WHITEWASH

On January 28th and January 30th the Senate Veterans
Affairs Committee conducted the first Congressional
POW/MIA hearings in years which had even the appear-
ance of being a good faith search for the truth. (As we go to press a
third hearing is tentatively scheduled for Thursday, February 20). Early
optimism which resulted from discussions with Committee staff regarding
the make-up of the witness roster quickly evaporated as decisions were
made regarding who should and should not be called to testify -- then
rose again as Senator Dennis DeConcini (D-AZ) made it clear that he was
willing to _fight_ to prevent the hearings from becoming a whitewash.

You can imagine our disappointment and amazement when we discovered that
the Committee has no funds to pay the travel expenses of witnesses called
to testify. Not surprisingly, those on the witness roster who were being
called to support the government position that great progress is being
made and all is well, live in the Washington, D.C. area. The live POW
advocates are spread throughout the country, and in many cases have
already had their resources greatly depleted by their efforts on behalf
of Live POWs. Nevertheless, if a witness has not the funds to travel to
Washington to appear, the Committee will simply struggle along without
the information that witness has to give, no matter how important that
information may be to a search for the truth!

As late as Friday, January 24, just 4 days before the hearings were
scheduled to commence, the witness roster was terribly incomplete.
Worse, we were told on Friday that "today is the deadline for written
testimony" and that the sworn affidavits which had been filed by Major
Smith and SFC McIntire, as well as former NSA intelligence analyst Jerry
Mooney and former contract CIA agent Scott Barnes "are not appropriate
for submission as written testimony before this Committee". Also,
Congressional Medal of Honor recipient Lt. Col. Robert L. Howard, who had
filed an affidavit in support of the allegations of Smith and McIntire,
"is going to be on manuevers and won't be able to be here". You can
appreciate the anger and frustration felt by all involved at that point.

But good things started to happen. Someone got to someone and it was
agreed that the sworn affidavits were suitable as written testimony.
Someone got to someone and Lt. Col. Howard became available. Someone
came to the rescue and private funds were made available for the travel
expenses of two important witnesses. The picture brightened. Then...

Our high hopes for strong media interest in the hearings exploded with
the tragic loss of the space shuttle Challenger. The shuttle accident
occurred at mid-day on the first day of the hearings. Although representatives of every major media outlet were in attendance at the hearings
the video tape and the stories were shelved because of the minute-by-
minute reporting of the shuttle disaster and its aftermath. But, all was
not lost. As of this writing, the hearings have been aired three times
on C-Span. Any reader who is a student of body language should not miss
the testimonies. We have continually stated that the truth is on our

P.O. Box 8222   Shawnee Mission Kansas   66208

Page 2

side, and if gestures and facial expressions are any indication, WE HAVE
WON THIS ROUND!

One observer drew the attention of C-Span cameras as well as Live POW
advocates...none other than Third Secretary Chanthara Sayamoungkhoun of
the Lao PDR, who watched the testimonies of Mark Smith and Melvin
McIntire with great intensity. Considering that Smith and McIntire (as
do virtually all Live POW advocates) charge the Lao PDR with holding
American prisoners, it is hardly surprising that Sayamoungkhoun was
interested, and even less surprising that he entered and exited the
hearings as unobtrusively as his sense of dignity would allow!!

For those who did not have the opportunity to attend or view the
hearings, the following summaries of testimonies are provided:

Tuesday, January 28:

ANN MILLS GRIFFITHS -- Supported current USG strategy and policy.

COOPER T. HOLT -- Executive Director, Washington office, Veterans of
Foreign Wars expressed support for current strategy and policy.

HARRY SULLIVAN -- Deputy Director, Foreign Relations Division, The
American Legion. Expressed support for current strategy and policy.

STEPHEN L. EDMISTON -- Deputy Natonal Legislative Director, Disabled
American Veterans. Expressed support for current strategy and policy.

MAJOR MARK SMITH -- Revealed, in addition to the information which he has
previously provided in sworn affidavits, that he has within the past five
days, "personally viewed evidence which proves beyond any doubt that in
excess of 30 Americans and other nationalities are presently being held
as prisoners of war in Southeast Asia". He also stated that he has had a
description of the evidence and documentation delivered to the President.

SFC MELVIN MCINTIRE -- Supported and confirmed Smith's testimony.

SCOTT T. BARNES -- Explained his involvement in a "Bo" Gritz POW operation into Laos in 1981. Testified that he had taken 400 rapid exposure
pictures of two living POWs whom he believed to be American, and how it
was later reported to him by DIA that none of the pictures "came out".
He also testified as to the manner in which he was able to determine that
Gritz' operation was sanctioned and assisted by the U.S. government,
although USG later denied that fact. Repeated his allegation that he was
instructed by U.S. Embassy, Bangkok, to "liquidate the merchandise" when
he reported that two live POWs had been found.

RUTH BRELLENTHIN -- POW/MIA wife stated that her husband was declared KIA
and buried in a grave in St. Louis with the commingled remains of approximately 9 other soldiers also "KIA", in 1968. At Operation Homecoming,
one of those "KIA's" who had been on the patrol with her husband came
home alive. DOD and the Marine Corps, she says, gave her NO help in
contacting this Marine or in obtaining any other information relevant to
her husband's case, but ultimately admitted that they had erred in the
KIA classfication. However, her husband's status has not been officially
changed, and his name is not on the Missing list, and his file is
therefore not in the possession of JCRC.

Page 3

ROBERT CRESSMAN -- Provided information relating to a specific Live POW case and the apparent mishandling of that case by DIA. He provided to the committee 22 photographs of a Caucasian, allegedly taken in Laos, along with conclusive evidence that the pictures are recent, and, the statement of an American woman believed to be the former wife of the Caucasian, to the effect that she believes that the man in the pictures is indeed her former husband. When asked if he believes that a coverup of POW information exists, he responded, "There are obviously varying degrees of incompetency within the agencies handling this issue. When incompetence is condoned, it becomes a coverup."

Thursday, January 30:

RICHARD F. HEBERT -- Center of POW/MIA Accountability, Greenwich, CT Expressed support for the current strategy and policy. Was questioned about allegations that Richard Childress, National Security Council staff member, was involved in the founding of his organization, and allegation that Childress has said that the "Center" is his investigative unit. Mr Hebert denied those allegations. Hebert also stated that some of Smith and McIntire's allegations are "patently false", but when pressed for some examples of these falsehoods, the only example which he was able to present was the fact that it was "inconceivable" to him that a Major General would use his rank and authority to pressure one of his junior officers to suppress information. "What ever happened to trust and con- fidence?" he asked. Senator DeConcini said, "That's a very good questio and I'm glad you asked it!" ! !

/JERRY MOONEY -- Required to testify in Executive Session because of the potential sensitivity of the information he had to offer to the Committee. The affidavit submitted with the recent filing of the Smith/McIntire lawsuit was outlined in our last newsletter, and is a public document. The Senate Committee determined that even this affidavit was too sensitive to release at the hearings. Briefly, Mooney was an intelligence analyst for NSA and among other things, compiled a list of over 300 U.S. military personnel categorized as MIA/POW. Less than five percent of those on his list known to be alive were returned t the United States in 1973. Further, he states that he received, analyze and formally reported the shoot-down of the EC-47Q "Flying Pueblo" air- craft in February 1973 from which "at least five to seven survivors who were identified as Americans" were "transported to North Vietnam." He states that he and DIA were in full agreement that the captives were indeed the crew of that EC-47Q. In later statements, DIA representative denied having specific knowledge as to their nationality or identity.

COL. EARL P. HOPPER, SR. -- Former Chairman of the Board of the National League of Families and presently a POW/MIA consultant to Congressman Bil Hendon, Col. Hopper presented an overview of the Live POW issue since 1973, and directly addressed several areas in which there are questions to which there should be answers. He particularly noted the resentment of members of the Indochinese refugee community in the U.S. for the treatment Indochinese refugees have received at the hands of USG debriefers, or, as he said, "..more appropriately, probably, interrogators". Refugees who have said that they have information relating to American POWs seem, as a group, to feel that they have had very rude and shabby treatment at the hands of their debriefers. They have been badgered, criticized, accused of lying, and accused of being

Page 4

communists by DIA and State Department interviewers. Col. Hopper
suggested that the Committee contact some of these refugees to request
their testimony regarding their perception of that treatment.

Col. Hopper also provided documentation which proves that the CIA
knew in the early '70s that the Pathet Lao were holding American POWs at
several known locations, that several Pathet Lao officials had admitted
in the early '70s that they were holding POWs, pointed out the fact that
no American prisoner captured by the Pathet Lao has ever been returned,
and asked, "Where are those men today?"

PATRICIA B. SKELLY -- Chairman of Task Force Omega, brought evidence
that various branches collecting vital data on the missing men were not
in concert. Using computer listings from several agencies and
departments, Ms. Skelly prepared a comparison study which revealed
numerous errors and omissions. Of particular concern is that the failure
to record information correctly could prohibit the correlation of
important intelligence with an individual file. Also, because of incor-
rectly reported data, one agency may inadvertantly withhold information
from another which could provide the long-sought "actionable evidence".

LT.COL. ROBERT HOWARD -- U.S. Army, Stuttgart, W. Germany. America's
most decorated soldier, his affidavit was filed as supporting data in the
Smith/McIntire lawsuit. LtCol Howard's testimony was heard largely in
Executive Session, but he stated unequivocably that he volunteered to
testify before the Committee because Smith and McIntire were "telling the
truth" and "being honest". He also stated that it was his belief that
Americans were being held against their will in Southeast Asia, based on
specific evidence he had 19 months ago. When asked if the officer who replaced him might have the same information, Howard replied, "quite possibly, but it is my understanding that some of the information has been destroyed". Asked if he could identify locations where POWs are presently
held, he said that 19 months ago he could have marked them on a map.

MICHAEL VAN ATTA -- Editor of "The Insiders" presented a map, which Van
Atta states is currently classified, which pinpointed areas where live
Americans had been sighted. He also presented lists of known POWs, and
brief summaries of their cases, whose existence was "explained away" or
ignored by DIA and CIA.

BILL BENNETT -- Secretary of the National Vietnam Veterans Coalition
presented the testimony of National Coordinator Tom Burch, who could not
be present because of illness. Expressed disappointment that the witness
roster had been completed on such short notice and without calling
several important witnesses, specifically requesting that the Committee
make arrangements to call Tom Ashworth who has a great deal of relevant
information to provide for the Committee's consideration. Also suggested
that the inability to obtain "conclusive proof" is a significant failure
of the intelligence community and a strong indication that the
intelligence assets of the U.S. government are not "fully focused" on
this issue as alleged by USG. Bennett also referenced the problem of the
treatment of refugees during interviewing by government officials and
suggested that Ms. Le Ti Ahn be called to testify before the Committee.
Ms. Ahn is a Vietnamese translator/interpretor who has long been involved
in the effort to encourage Indochinese refugees who have information
about POWs to provide it, and has worked with the National Forget-Me-Not
Association and the National League of Families.

JOAN CARLSON -- A POW/MIA sister-in-law, appeared in the absence of Capt. Red McDaniel to detail her years of involvement in the POW issue and the basis of her conviction that Live American POWs are still held. She expressed her renewed hope that this issue can be addressed seriously and the belief that Congressman Hendon's proposal to establish an independent commission headed by Ross Perot had provided a new possibility for a successful resolution. She then presented the sworn statement of Capt. McDaniel which recounted a telephone conversation that he had with Richard Childress in the summer of 1985 in which Mr. Childress indicated his strong belief that American POWs are still held in Indochina, but that it would take two to three years to get them home.

DR. LARRY WARD -- Emeritus Food for the Hungry International -- Expressed his conviction that American POWs are still held in Vietnam, and his doubt that their freedom can be obtained in an expeditious manner. He stated his belief that the Vietnamese now see it as being in their national interest to resolve this issue, and the hope that American prisoners will be "discovered" and released.

Whatever the ultimate impact of these hearings, and we are hopeful, we do have reservations regarding the intent of the Committee Chairman, Senator Frank Murkowski (R-AK), when the hearings were initiated. We believe that he was so strongly convinced, personally, that IF there are Live POWs, which he doubted, that USG is undoubtedly doing its best to solve the problem. We believe that he wanted to take advantage of some of the limelight that has become available as a result of increasing media interest, and at the same time put to rest the "irresponsible" and "unfounded" rumors of conspiracy and coverup. We have been told that his attitude has now changed somewhat, maybe even drastically.

He has the opportunity to demonstrate that his effort is truly a good faith search for the truth by allowing some very knowledgeable members of Congress, whom he has previously denied, to join his Committee panel to question the Administration witnesses when they present their testimony on February 20. Sen. Gordon Humphrey (R-NH), Cong. Robert Smith (R-NH), Cong. Douglas Applegate (D-OH) and Cong. Bill Hendon (R-NC) all requested permission to join the Committee panel in the earlier hearings. While such requests are not always granted, it is usual and customary to do so. Murkowski refused. Why? The skeptics among us are convinced that he didn't want these four individuals, who are known to have a long-standing interest and broad knowledge of this subject, to show up his lack of knowledge and steal the limelight. They also believe that he feared that his cosmetic intent would be undermined, and that he may even have been advised by DOD and/or State to keep these men off the panel. We do not want to believe this of the Senator, and are reserving judgement. These explanations seem to make a great deal more sense than his explanation, however, which was that in the interest of time it would be necessary to limit the questioners to Committee members only. You may want to write him (especially you Alaskans) to ask whether the time of the Committee is more important than the discovery of the truth!!

PEROT COMMISSION LEGISLATION TO BE INTRODUCED IN SENATE

Senator Gordon Humphrey (R-NH) is preparing Senate legislation to propose the establishment of the Perot Commission. Write today and ask each of your Senators to contact Humphrey's office to obtain information about this extremely important legislation and to consider co-sponsoring it.

UNITY, DIVISIVENESS, MIXED SIGNALS AND OTHER FALLACIES OR THE CARROT AND THE STICK

[We do not address here the myth that, "The Vietnamese have now accepted our position that resolution of the POW/MIA issue is a humanitarian concern and should be addressed without respect to political considerations" -- Nobody believes it...some people have simply been forced into the position of having to say it.]

Administration officials, the League of Families, the American Legion and the VFW have all recently expressed the view that support of the present strategy and policy of the U.S. government on the POW issue is critical to demonstrating the unity of the American people in their resolve to obtain the freedom of living POWs and accomplish the fullest possible accounting. Often these expressions are made regarding the inadvisability of establishing an independent commission to investigate the issue and to make recommendations regarding the best course of action to reach a solution. They assert that to establish such a commission at this time would signal lack of confidence in the President (thereby weakening the Administration negotiating position and encouraging the Vietnamese to drag their feet in the hope of being offered a "better deal" by the commission) and signal the Vietnamese that the American People are divided.

Sound reasonable? Perhaps, but look again! If the President were merely negotiating for a bargain basement reparations deal with the Vietnamese, there would be two important reasons to seek "unity". The Vietnamese perception of broad support for the President would indicate to them that the President had the political strength to wait for the best possible deal (while we were waiting, their bargaining chips would be dying every day). It would also give the President the political support in the Congress which would help to obtain approval of the expenditure of funds when a settlement was reached.

The only problem with the "bargain basement theory of unity" is that anyone who hasn't had their head in the sand for the last 5 years knows that this President isn't looking for a reparations deal! He will not allow himself or this nation to be perceived as having given in to extortion. He will not allow us to be seen as rewarding the Vietnamese for the barbarous act of holding our men and the remains of those who gave their lives.

For the Vietnamese to agree to accept anything less than the "just" amount of 3.25 billion dollars they were promised in the Paris nego-tiations (leave aside the fact that they violated the terms of the agreement and disqualified themselves from any right to receive it), they will need additional motivation. Several avenues toward providing that motivation present themselves. The threat of: (1) increased covert and/or overt support for the Free Vietnamese, the Free Lao and the Cambodian Resistance to enlist their assistance to rescue American POWs or to develop intelligence about the locations where they may be held; (2) support for U.S. private sector "cross-border forays"; and (3) U.S. military rescue operations. Whatever the nature of the "stick", it is not likely that the stick alone can be the answer. The most reasonable approach to a negotiated settlement will include the judicious use of

(LAWSUIT UPDATE)

SMITH/MCINTIRE LAWSUIT -- UPDATE
(POW Videotape -- What Does it Mean?)

On Jan. 29 Maj. Mark Smith testified before
the Senate Veterans' Affairs Committee that
within the preceding 5 days he had "personally viewed evidence which proves beyond
any doubt that in excess of 30 Americans...
are presently being held as prisoners of
war in Southeast Asia".
Subsequent information has been revealed
which explains the nature of the conclusive
evidence viewed by Major Smith. An intelligence service of a foreign power friendly
to the United States showed Major Smith a
4-hour, 8 minute videotape which had been
produced from a 16mm film which was shot
over a period of 5 days in the recent past.
It was produced for the purpose of documenting certain facts which an unidentified
organization in Southeast Asia wanted to
make known to certain other political
organizations world-wide.

Smith says the videotape shows (incidental
to the purpose for which the films were
produced) 4 segments which reveal the existence of Caucasian prisoners, many of whom
are believed to be, and are reported by
other sources to be, Americans. A portion
of one of the films reveals a scene which
allows conclusive identification of the location in which it was made. A portion of
one of the films reveals conclusively that
the film was made in the recent past (2-3
years at most). Through alternative means,
it has been determined that it was probably
produced in mid-late 1985.

The four segments which show Caucasians are
as follows: (1) 20-40 individuals who appear to be Caucasians who are a part of a
much larger group of prisoners of several
nationalities; (2) 30-40 Caucasians pan-
ning gold and doing related hard labor.
These men are in chains and shackles and
under armed guard -- guards are identifiable as to their political association by
the uniforms they are wearing; (3) A
close-up of an individual thought to be
American but not yet conclusively identi-

fied; (4) A segment in which "John Obass
(one of the affiants in the lawsuit) is
shown examining male Caucasians and admi
stering medical treatment to them. Othe
portions of the film reveals informatio
which can have profound international
political consequences if it becomes pu
licly known.

Obassy showed an edited version of the
to Major Smith, SFC McIntire and attorn
Mark Waple in December, 1985. He refuse
show an unedited copy of the tape becau
some information revealed in it could p
lives in danger if that information fel
into the wrong hands. [The reason he
originally obtained the tape was to pro
certain facts contained in his affidavi
the Smith/McIntire lawsuit. DIA had
contended that he was lying about the
existence of something in a certain reg
The videotape proved that DIA was wrong

Not being able to obtain the videotape
Obassy, Maj. Smith initiated an effort
discover who else might have access to
possession of the unedited version. He
discovered that the intelligence servic
a nation friendly to the United States
a copy. Smith made contact with a memb
of that foreign intelligence service wh
was personally known to him. An opport
ity was arranged for Smith to see the
with the caveat that he not reveal publ
the most sensitive portions thereof.

Seeing the tape, Smith became aware tha
other evidence, which was even more co
sive than the tape itself, was in the
session of a particular anti-communist
group. Smith knew that Obassy had con
with that group, and asked Obassy to l
into the possibility that the other ev
dence could be obtained from that grou

After conferring with that group, Obas
returned with a list of items for whic
group would trade the "other evidence"
The list included food, clothing, medi
supplies, arms and ammunition. Smith,
McIntire and Waple attempted to estima
the cost of obtaining the listed items

YOU CLAIM TO BE
YOUR BROTHERS' KEEPER.
OUR POW/MIAs NEED TO KNOW IT.
HELP BRING THEM HOME. NOW!

Col. Charles E. Shelton has agonized as a Prisoner of War for over 21 years. He is the last Vietnam-era serviceman still officially listed as a POW. There are still over 2,400 Americans unaccounted for in Southeast Asia, and mounting evidence suggests perhaps over 100 Americans are still alive and being held against their will.

Two former Green Berets, Major (ret) Mark A. Smith, Sergeant First Class Melvin C. McIntire and four POW/ MIA families including Mrs. Anne Hart, Mr. Jerry Dennis, Mrs. Kathryn Fanning and Mrs. Dorothy Shelton have filed a federal class action lawsuit on behalf of American POWs, but they can't do it alone. Your financial assistance is greatly needed!

Our fathers, our sons, and our brothers, must not be forgotten, must not be abandoned, and must be brought home NOW. We ask on behalf of those who cannot ask for themselves.

YOU WILL MAKE THE DIFFERENCE.

The artists would like to dedicate this illustration to: Col. Charles E. Shelton and the American POWs in Southeast Asia. © 1986 Don Ohlsen/Lynn Ohlsen

Send contributions to:

Smith/McIntire/Howard Foundation
℅ Hutchens & Waple
P.O. Box 650
Fayetteville, NC 28302

☐ In addition to my donation, I would like more information from one of the POW organizations.

DISTRIBUTED BY:

NAME _____

STREET _____

CITY _____ STATE ____ ZIP _____ DONATION $_____

arrived at a figure of $4.2 million.

Waple drafted a letter to President Reagan, hoping to obtain the assistance of the President in acquiring the needed materiel. Not wanting to confuse the issue in the initial communication by including the entire list of demanded items, Waple wrote, "...required to pay the sum of $4.2 million in cash and take receipt of the original of the film and other evidence of live Americans and other allied POWs still being held in Southeast Asia." This minor misstatement of the facts for the purpose of simplicity would come back to haunt them later. Even though the whole truth was completely and exhaustively revealed to USG representatives in meetings which resulted from this letter, someone leaked the letter to the media (a possibility which should have been foreseen) and the letter itself creates the impression that someone is demanding $4.2 million as a ransom demand for the tape. Actually, the tape itself was important only in that it would prove that the "other evidence" was in the hands of the group requesting the supplies.

Subsequently, the Vice President reportedly authorized Hendon, Major Smith and Mark Waple to travel to Southeast Asia to acquire the tape and the "other evidence". Mr. Bush is said to have arranged to pay the travel costs associated with the trip, and to have caused $4.2 Million to be deposited in the Bank of America in Singapore in the name of Bill Hendon. The 3 Americans met with Obassy and told him that they had the ability to supply the $4.2 Million for the "other evidence" but that Hendon's authorization to proceed with negotiations was contingent upon his viewing the tape.

Obassy refused, saying that money was not and never had been the issue. It was the supplies themselves, and the ability to accumulate and deliver them, for which the involvement of the U.S. government was most needed. Further, because it had been revealed in the American press that Obassy was a Briton, some people in Southeast Asia were able to determine his true ident...

As a result, his life was in danger, and he had been denied authorization to show the unedited version of the tape to anyone, including Bill Hendon. He did, however, show an edited version to Hendon, and Hendon was able to confirm many of the elements of Smith's report regarding the content of the videotape.

When questioned in closed session of the Senate Veterans' Affairs Committee by Chairman Frank Murkowski about the supplies being requested, Major Smith read the list compiled by Obassy. Murkowski interrupted, "I don't want to hear a laundry list, what's the bottom line -- what will it cost us?" Major Smith responded that it appeared the cost of the materiel would be in the neighborhood of $4.2 Million. After the hearing, Murkowski claimed that Obassy was demanding $4.2 Million in ransom for the tape.

One of the conditions required by Obassy for his cooperation was that his true identity be absolutely protected. Although never told by Smith and McIntire, U.S. intelligence officials believed that they had "figured out" who he was. (He is an individual long known to the intelligence community, but not known to them as "John Obassy".) U.S. Navy Commander Frank Brown who is associated with U.S. intelligence in a manner which we have not yet determined, allegedly notified the Senate Veterans' Affairs Committee staff that "Obassy" was one Robin Gregson. A member of the Committee staff then reportedly called Washington Times reporter Susan Katz and spilled the beans. Brown also called Katz. An unknown source in Southeast Asia informed an associate of former Congressman John LeBoutillier that Obassy and Gregson were one and the same. Katz was told to confirm the story with LeBoutillier. Another person whose identity we know but cannot reveal, was informed by Brown of the alleged identity of Obassy, and Katz obtained further confirmation from that individual. On Apr. 28, The Washington Times published a story by Katz (entitled "Rumors Aplenty") in which Obassy was

identified as Gregson. On May 1, in an open, public hearing, Chairman Murkowski identified Obassy as Gregson.

On May 6, Rep. Bill Hendon wrote Murkowski, "Mr. Chairman, your identifying this critical witness is the most reprehensible action I have ever witnessed in my 5 1/2 year effort to help return U.S. military personnel from communist prisons in Southeast Asia.. here we have what appears to be the ultimate in dirty tricks: you subpoena Maj. Mark Smith to produce the Obassy videotape - and then in the same breath you virtually ensure that he cannot produce it when you divulge his source's true identity in open session. Had you asked me, I could have told you that divulging this man's identity would jeopardize not only Obassy's life but the lives of U.S. prisoners of war whom I am convinced he has direct access to."

Murkowski then wrote Hendon on May 8, defending himself by saying: (1) "Mr. Gregson's identity was revealed some time ago [3 days before the hearing] in an internationally available publication..." [An article entitled "Rumors Aplenty" hardly provides conclusive identification. Publication of a rumor article did not release Murkowski from his obligation to guard sensitive information. Murkowski had been told that efforts to obtain further cooperation and assistance from Gregson would be seriously damaged if his identity became publicly known. What did Murkowski hope to gain by confirming Katz' story?] (2) "Former Congressman John LeBoutillier, in a letter to CIA Director William Casey, also revealed Mr. Gregson's identity." [The fact that the Director of CIA knows something shouldn't automatically make that information public!]; (3) "...Mr. Obassy's true identity is contained in an unclassified document given to me by the Office of the Secretary of Defense prior to the May 1 hearing." [The "unclassified document" was reportedly a memorandum authored by Frank Brown. Why is it in the interest of the Department of Defense and/or the U.S. government to reveal this man's name? Are they so desirous of defending themselves

from the various allegations about their bad faith in pursuing live POW information that they're willing to throw away any assistance he may be able to provide?]; (4)"..identity was not 'divulged' against the wishes of the Defense Department.." [True, it was divulged over the objections of DIA Director General Leonard Perroots who has privately stated that he believes Smith and McIntire.]

Fortunately, Gregson was in Southeast Asia and did not know that his identity had been compromised. Following a series of discussions between Smith, Waple and Gregson, Gregson brought a copy of the edited version of the tape to Washington, D.C. on June 25th with the intention of taking it to the White House. Convinced that he would never "get within 100 yards of the White House" he agreed to show it in closed session to the Senate Veterans' Affairs Committee on the next day. Upon arriving in Washington, however, he discovered that his true identity had been revealed in a session of the Senate Committee by Chairman Murkowski. He was furious!

After several hours of unsuccessful attempts by Smith, McIntire and Waple to convince him to show the tape anyway, or at very minimum some extracted still pictures from it, Gregson took it and left town.

Smith was scheduled to testify before the Committee on the next day. A subpoena had been issued by the Committee demanding his presence, but upon his promise to appear, the Committee decided not to serve the subpoena. Smith, McIntire and Waple knew that the subpoena demanded evidence which they had earlier claimed to have, but exactly which of the evidence was in demand was unknown to them. Smith knew that if he went with no videotape, no Gregson and no documentary evidence, the Committee would serve him with the subpoena demanding information which he did not want to turn over to them. In a last-minute meeting, Smith decided not to testify, so those involved could have time to decide what to do next.

When Waple called the Committee to tell them Smith would not be appearing, three Committee staffers rushed to National Airport with the subpoena and an AP photographer and a newspaper reporter in tow. Smith and McIntire, not willing to participate in a media event, ducked out and returned to North Carolina. Eight days later, Waple invited Federal Marshals to his law office where Smith accepted the subpoena.

The subpoena, as written, demanded all evidence in Smith's possession. However, in a cover letter authored by Committee Counsel Anthony Principi, specific references were made to closed session testimony of Smith in which certain evidence had been mentioned. These references were to pictures of Americans left behind in 1975, and specific locations where American prisoners have been held. Unwilling to provide all evidence to the Committee, Smith chose to supply only that which was specifically demanded in the cover letter, as that information was not particularly sensitive. If the Committee were to demand additional material, he was prepared to refuse, be charged with contempt of Congress, and go to jail if necessary. When asked by the Committee why he had presented only such insubstantial material, Smith responded, "I brought exactly what you asked for." The Committee did not pursue the matter.

The primary reason that Smith is willing to pay such a price to keep information out of the hands of the Committee and its staff is his conviction that the Committee does not intend to do anything useful with any evidence he provides to them. They have been tested, and they have failed!

Perhaps the most compelling evidence that the Chairman is not interested in a good faith pursuit of the truth is his denial of Congressman Hendon's request to sit on the panel where Hendon would have the opportunity to cross-examine government witnesses if and when they are less than fully accurate in their statements. Although it is the Chairman's privilege to do so, it is unusual that he would deny participation to the

man widely known to be the most knowledgeable on Capitol Hill regarding the evidence presently in the possession of DIA.

After having been twice refused a seat on the panel, Hendon wrote Murkowski in the May 6 letter, "..if you want to see overwhelming evidence of U.S. prisoners of war being held in Southeast Asia, why don't you direct Defense Intelligence to let me and several of my colleagues show you and your Committee some of the evidence DIA already has in its possession? We don't want to show your personal staff or your Committee staff, we want to show you and your Committee along with 'Interagency Intelligence Senior Review Panel' which is now investigating the work of DIA..... If you really want to get to the bottom of this, I challenge you to arrange such a session immediately."

Murkowski wrote back in his May 8 letter, "...my earlier invitation to you to testify still stands...", but did not comment on whether he thought it would be useful to have DIA analysts bring intelligence documents and explain them in the presence of someone knowledgeable enough to make sure they keep their story straight!

Another problem with providing to the Committee all evidence in their possession, according to Smith and McIntire,-is that certain of their evidence proves their allegation that individuals within the U.S. government have destroyed files which contain evidence of living American POWs. If Smith and McIntire were to provide proof of that allegation to the Committee, it could be given to the government so that destroyed files could be "reconstituted". Additionally, it is clear that the Justice Department attorneys are much in need of advance knowledge of the evidence which they intend to produce in court, as that will give Justice the greatest opportunity to take actions and formulate plans to offset the impact of that evidence. Smith and McIntire believe that the Senate Committee could be a conduit of that information to the Justice Department. [Chairman Murkowski

has three times publicly revealed information which was given to him or his staff with the warning and the proviso that it be guarded carefully.]

The greatest difficulty faced by Smith and McIntire in deciding what to do with the evidence they possess is that it is extremely sensitive in several ways. Some of it could endanger the life of Gregson, and his assistance is much needed, not only in acquiring various kinds of information about identities and locations of American prisoners but in obtaining the cooperation of foreign organizations which can be very helpful in implementing any kind of extraction plan. Some of it, if revealed publicly could endanger the lives of some of the prisoners. Some of it, if revealed, would endanger and/ or alienate foreign organizations which have already been helpful in some ways and which can be even more helpful in the future.

Publicly revealing conclusive evidence of the existence of Live POWs could accomplish one important objective: cause the American People to DEMAND their return. However, those same revelations would destroy the best opportunity to bring some of the men home quickly, and Smith and McIntire won't throw away those opportunities until they lose all hope that necessary U.S. government cooperation can be obtained to implement actions with the greatest hope for success.

Additionally, revealing all the evidence might damage the lawsuit. Judge Boyle has made it clear that this case is not going to be "tried in the media". While the priority must remain bringing prisoners home, the lawsuit is important in that it will provide an opportunity to obtain information, in two ways, which can never be acquired outside of court: (1) Many individuals have notified Smith, McIntire ₊and Waple that if subpoenaed and placed under oath, they will provide information that they cannot supply in any other forum. These include individuals presently employed in the U.S. intelligence community, ac-

tive duty military personnel and foreign government officials; (2) If the court allows and the litigants agree upon terms which will allow "discovery", Waple will be granted access to information not otherwise accessible. Discovery is the process whereby both sides can agree to provide all evidence to the other before the case is tried It gives each the opportunity to put the adversary's evidence to the harshest test and to evaluate their own chance to win in court. If the Justice Department (Attorney for defendants) is able to predetermine, from the Senate, exactly what Smith and McIntire have, they will argue against discovery in order to deny Waple access to important Live POW information now in USG files.

On June 19, 1986, U.S. District Court Judge Terrence Boyle announced his decision on the U.S. Justice Department motion to dismiss the lawsuit. In rendering his decision, Judge Boyle issued an order denying defendants' motion to dismiss the case. A portion of the suit, the mandamus action, was dismissed on the grounds that such was a question of foreign policy and therefore under the exclusive authority of the Executive Branch.

On the declaratory judgement action, the court ruled that whether or not American Prisoners of War exist is a question of fact for decision by the court. Judge Boyle wrote,
"The government claims that the court is barred by political question considerations from entertaining any inquiry into the existence of the alleged group of persons. If there is a contested issue of fact over the existence of such persons, then the government finds itself claiming dual power. It claims the executive power to exclusively administer and execute the government and laws of the United States. This is a legitimate claim. It also claims the exclusive power to determine the facts that it will use in administering the government and executing the law as it applies to this class of persons. This claim of power is in excess

of the government's legitimate executive authority..the court is mindful of its obligation to accept the exercise of judicial power under the United States Constitution where parties seek relief and have the right to the exercise of the judicial power of the United States."

"For the reasons outlined in this opinion, the defendants' motion to dismiss the plaintiffs' claim for mandamus relief under the Hostage Act...for lack of subject matter jurisdiction is ALLOWED. The defendants' motion to dismiss the plaintiffs' action for declaratory judgement ... is DENIED."

Plaintiffs Smith and McIntire were dismissed from the case on the grounds that they have no legally recognized representative capacity regarding the rights of American POWs who may still be alive. According to attorney Waple, "...this is an inseqential development in the case... they stand ready as material and relevant witnesses on the ultimate issue."

Twenty-five POW/MIA family members who have joined the suit as plaintiffs have been allowed to continue through the court to seek declaratory judgement as to the existence of living American POWs. This is an important victory for the plaintiffs. The case may now proceed to discovery, interrogatories, and other matters which could not be accomplished prior to Boyle's ruling.

There is a possibility that the Justice Department may attempt an appeal. It is an open question whether that right exists, and even if the court should rule that appeal is permissible, then the appeal itself would have to be argued on its own merits. Whether the defendants intend to appeal will likely not be known until the time limitations approach expiration.

Whatever the outcome of this case, it is already clear that the U.S. government is feeling the pressure as a result of the victories already won by the plaintiffs. The clearest evidence of this is presented

by the outlandish attacks on the integrit and credibility of Smith and McIntire themselves. Interestingly, and wisely, t defamers have left Lt. Col. Howard alone. America's most highly decorated soldier says Smith and McIntire are telling the truth. We believe him.

This case must not be allowed to fail because of inadequate funding. If you care, and if you can, HELP NOW!

* * * *

HAVE YOU RENEWED YOUR SUBSCRIPTION ? ?

According to Rod Norberg, a Vietnam War correspondent in the early '70s, only one Vietnamese citizen ever attained "correspondent" status with Time Magazine throughout the War years. His name was Pham Xuan An.

Truong Nhu Tang, former Viet Cong Ministe of Justice, now living in France, says Ph Xuan An was well known to him during the War. It seems that Pham Xuan An was one the most valued communist agents of the Hanoi regime. Pham Xuan An now serves in the Vietnam mission to the United Nations

* * *

DID AMERICA'S "SECRET WAR" TOUCH YOU ?

Journalist Mike Reed is working on an ora history of U.S. military operations in La (and possibly Cambodia) during the Vietna War. Reed says, "I hope to include a sec tion on Americans missing in those countries, and how the U.S.Government eventua ly dealt with this problem. "My goal is t let those who served in Laos, or those wh lost relatives there, tell how the war wa fought and how it affected their lives. This was their war, and everything about it - the triumphs, the tragedy, the tears is quietly slipping into the darkness of time." Write:

Michael Reed
4229 Albemarle St., N.W.
Washington, D.C. 20016
(202) 966-2346

=================================

AM M. THOMAS
ᴴ Dɪsᴛʀɪᴄᴛ, Cᴀʟɪꜰᴏʀɴɪᴀ

COMMITTEES:
⁃ AYS AND MEANS
HC ₃E ADMINISTRATION

24 Cₐₙₙₒₙ Hₒᵤₛₑ Oꜰꜰɪᴄᴇ Bᴜɪʟᴅɪɴɢ
Wₐₛₕɪₙɢₜₒₙ, DC 20515
(202) 225-2915

ADMINISTRATIVE ASSISTANT
CATHERINE M. ABERNATHY

DISTRICT OFFICES:
1830 Tʀᴜxᴛᴜɴ Aᴠᴇɴᴜᴇ, #200
Bᴀᴋᴇʀsꜰɪᴇʟᴅ, CA 93301
(805) 327-3611

858 W. Jᴀᴄᴋᴍᴀɴ Sᴛʀᴇᴇᴛ, #115
Lᴀɴᴄᴀsᴛᴇʀ, CA 93534
(805) 948-2634

1390 Pʀɪᴄᴇ Sᴛʀᴇᴇᴛ, #203
Pɪsᴍᴏ Bᴇᴀᴄʜ, CA 93449
(805) 773-2533

Congress of the United States
House of Representatives
Washington, DC 20515

January 30, 1986

Mr. Scott Barnes
P. O. Box 704
Kernville, CA 93238

Dear Mr. Barnes:

Thank you for writing to request my support in researching the possibility of POWs and MIAs being held in Southeast Asia.

I share your concern that the full story about our servicemen in Vietnam be told, and I cosponsor legislation, House Concurrent Resolution 129, which is to establish a commission to study and investigate the issue.

I do not know whether there are any Americans being held against their will in Southeast Asia, but if there is even the smallest possibility, then every effort should be made to find them and bring them home. Your work on this matter should be commended.

Again, thank you for contacting me in this matter. I appreciate hearing from you.

Best regards,

WILLIAM M. THOMAS
Member of Congress

WMT:rcc

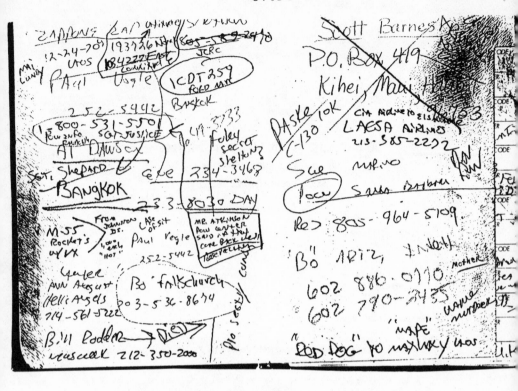

Scott Barnes
P.O. Box 419
Kihei, Maui, Hawaii

NAME AND ADDRESS — TELEPHONE

Jim West 7-12-84

John O. Akins
Finance Dept
c/o S.A.P.L.
P.O. Box 3694
Jeddah, Saudi Arabia
cy P.O. Box 2039
Anchorage, Alaska
99510 USA

Daniel C. Arnold, Assoc.
1705 Fox Run Ct Pueblo
Vienna VA 22180

Tracy Ainsworth
37 Gilwern Cres.
Llanishen, Cardiff
CF4 5AL S. Wales U.K.

Alex News
Ted Koppel Nightline
ABC 897-7777

Mike Cooper 818-881-5873

Milo Balter c/o ACLU
633 S. Shatto Pl.
L.A. 90005

*FRIEND MR ABRAHAM (CIA Chief)   LTCOL VEP   TF157 Agent   MAJ SINCLAIR

NAME AND ADDRESS	TELEPHONE	NAME AND ADDRESS	TELEPHONE
DANIEL C. ARNOLD		NIK: NIKS Fillmore BAKER	213
1705 FOX RUN CT	938-1868	22229 WAYNSIDE AVE	540
VIENNA, VA 22180		TORRANCE CA 90505	4170
MOUNG, DONNY	703	SANDY BECK	808
HANK CUSHING USCGA	938-4075	159 W. Californ.	
OR		Kihei	STERNS Schwab
Richard Ucken	213-852-1191	JIM Bates	540 813
800 6242367 EST		Inland ADA	770 858520?
ED Chris SAGAS	213-466-3285	JAN CM Rabbit CONTACT	808
Mr Robert Crummie		She'll send info to Y	536-6009
Arlin Gregs SS	213-688-4830	HUNTER HARRIS	546-512?
		w/PenSID	
BFF CA Agent Kiley	213-272-6161	SUSAN SUMMERFIELD	
NEW # 213 477-6565		20 LLANINA GROVE	
John Veld		Trewbridge Estate	
		Rumney CIRCUIT CF385	

NAME AND ADDRESS	TELEPHONE	NAME AND ADDRESS	TELEPHONE
Betsy CALKINS (Grandmother)		Debby K BARNES WIFE	213
RT #1 Box 491		9654 WESTMONT RD	699-8789
GRANT, ALABAMA 35747		WHITER CA 96601	
Philip Bailey	NEW # 1641	MARC W BARNES SON	213
NEGEV AIRBASE CONSTRUCTION		2102 #13	370-5028
APO NY 09674		Redondo Bch CA 90278	
PO Box 213		RENEE BANYE	POS
FRANKLIN, N.H. 03235		4066 NAYAN,O DR	87
		SANTA BARBARA CA 93110	2451
BETY CALKINS		Betsy CALKINS	213 4881
2693 CORTINA LN		2631 LOFTY VIEW DR	
VAIL, COLO 81657		TORRANCE CA 90505	534-2782
JOE BOCK 'Bro'		Tom BONYHON	415
59 HALE MALIA PL		STAR RTE Box 180	
LAHAINA, HI 96761		Redwood City CA 94062	747-0558
SHAUNNA BATTOMI		SANDY BECK & KAREN	808
121 Lowell ST		159 W. Ilimulani	879-4331
Klamath Falls		Kihei	
Oregon 97601			

OCCB — 1-916-739-5664 = "Chris"

Dues Hells Angels club house

NAME AND ADDRESS	TELEPHONE	NAME AND ADDRESS	TELEPHONE
"Sonny" Barger Sharon	(415) 638 ... Jack Palma	CABEEB (Danny Spitz)	AREA CODE 916 ...
7528 Golf Links Rd	NUMBER 346-9300	CIB	NUMBER 445-8555
Oakland Calif.	AREA CODE	1-916-322-6401 Crystal Gerber	AREA CODE 916 326 PF
Sherry Brehm		916-369-3066 = CIB	3360
5359 W. 118th Pl.	NUMBER	MR Pierce occib	NUMBER
Inglewood Calif 90304	AREA CODE	619 236-2441 Chief Rangers Paso	
Rebeca Bennett	NUMBER	Celeman Ple John Snook = 916-739-5666	5666
c/o Apple Travel		William Stamey	NUMBER
30232 Crown Valley		Chuck Casey occib "chief"	
Parkway Laguna	AREA CODE	P. Hells Angel P.O. Box 375	AREA CODE 1-803
Niguel CA 92677	NUMBER	Benny Nixon	991-7837
Mode Star Classic Agency		Book "Fallen Angel"	
George Brooks (N.Life)	AREA CODE 914	ATL club	1-804
16 Crest Haven Dr	NUMBER	Suzanne Smith	NUMBER 2-6000
New Windsor NY 12550	561-9419	Network Pred.	EXT 2910
N August	AREA CODE 714	Ft Heritage USA	
Bryn N.Y.	NUMBER	c/o PTL	NUMBER
	561-5222	Charlotte N.C.	
Sandy Alexander		Suzanne 28219	

NAME AND ADDRESS	TELEPHONE	NAME AND ADDRESS	TELEPHONE
"Broken Eagle" International Security Robert Murray	AREA CODE	CARLOS Rodriguez	AREA CODE
Col Robert Robinson	NUMBER	Stewart's Terr 21A M-55-A	619
Col John Kennedy		PO Box 8519	NUMBER 375-3852
S.S. Force Col	272-4762	Big Fish Calif. 93205	
Task Force "15"	AREA CODE	Diane Corsaro	NUMBER
w/ CIA/Church/Movement		66 Ocean View #58	
		Santa Barbara CA. 93103	
DR S. Watson Bic	AREA CODE	John Stein CDO	AREA CODE 202
DR Miller Meselson	NUMBER	Central Intelligence Agency	NUMBER
1-(617)-495-2264		Ale Peterson EXT 5353	351-1100
1-617-495-1000	AREA CODE	CIA Indochina	AREA CODE 202
202-224-4451		Covert Ops	NUMBER
617-495-5099		Cpt Gene Wilson	351-1100
	AREA CODE	CANDICE LYNN BOWMAN	AREA CODE
617 495-1409		805 831-4419	NUMBER
Bob Padgett CIA	202-351-2084	324-6858	
Mr Daniels 202-351-1100 ex 2084	AREA CODE	4300 Balboa Drive	AREA CODE
Jerold Baker Daniels		# A - Bakersfield CA	NUMBER
U.S. Cavalry Bangkok	NUMBER	93307	
St. Dept. CIA of Silence		John Melanson Co. CDO	
Barnes/ Ortiz			

"Broken Eagle" 4 / Internal Security Robert Murray — agent

NAME AND ADDRESS	TELEPHONE
Col Robert Robinson	AREA CODE
Col John Lenard	NUMBER 272-4962
S.S. Force Col Paul	
Task Force "157" VA	AREA CODE
w/ Libs / Chuck /	
Cheve	
DR. S. Watson "BIC"	
DR. Miller Mabeson	NUMBER
1-(615)-495-2264	
1-617-495-1000	619 495
202-224-4451	2264
617-495-5077	
NBS 3, 11R MOYNIHAN	7899
617-495-1409	
Bob Padgett CIA	202-351-2014
Mr Davis 7-25-82	202-351-1100 ext 2084
Jerrold Baker Davis	
U.S. Embassy Bangkok	NUMBER
St. Dept. CIA of course	
Barnes / Ortiz	

Agent CARLOS RODRIGUEZ CIA

NAME AND ADDRESS	TELEPHONE
Stewart Teil CIA M-55-A	AREA CODE 619
PO Box 8579	NUMBER
British CALF. 93205	375-3852
Diane Corsaro	AREA CODE
66 Ocean View #58	
Santa Barbara CA 93103	
John Stein CDO	AREA CODE 202
Central Intelligence Agency	NUMBER
Bill Peterson EXT 5353	351-1100
CIA	AREA CODE 202
Covert Ops	NUMBER 416145
Capt Gene Wilson	351-1100
CANDICE LYNN BOWMAN	AREA CODE
805 831-4419	NUMBER
- 11 324-6858	
4300 Balboa drive	AREA CODE
# A - Bakersfield - CA	NUMBER
93307	
John Mehmann CO. CDO,	

Gun owners 1-619-526-2944

NAME AND ADDRESS	TELEPHONE
Larry Sandauerman	AREA CODE 202-351-1100
CIA, Lauley	EXT 2770
	2083
CIA	2084
DAN MulQueen	AREA CODE
Case Officer	NUMBER
working on my files	
II 8-25-82	AREA CODE
1-202-351-2553	
202-351-2156	NUMBER
ARNOLD 376-2213	
CARLON Bowman	AREA CODE 619
13 Spruce St	1213
Kernville 93238	376-4258
Fred Barry	AREA CODE 714
TONY C.M.A.	NUMBER 657-1068
H Assel	
Yolis Assel "Dutchman" James Corp. Chicago	

Discard Sys

NAME AND ADDRESS	TELEPHONE
JOE SNOWDEN	AREA CODE 707
358 DARBY LN	NUMBER
Crescent City 9553 CA	464-5274
Comp of N Hora CIA	1-808
w/ round Ryder 83	536-6009
ANN Campbell (Israel)	AREA CODE
9 avenue Bordeaux	
Constantia 7800	743502
Cape Town S. AFR a	
Julie Daux 2616 Gates No. 3	213 542-5400
R.B. CA 90278	
Betsy Calkins	AREA CODE
Lee College Box 583	NUMBER
Cleveland, Tenn 37311	
Leona Cohen	AREA CODE 213
	399-8768
	325-5503

4018 Dixie Cyn. Sherman Oaks
Chris Suter 818-785-6719 CA 91433   · 604-943-3343 Meyer Han

NAME AND ADDRESS	TELEPHONE	NAME AND ADDRESS	TELEPHON
Julie Davy	AREA CODE 213	Emil Di Giacomo	202 697-05
4210 ocean Dr		405 Phelan Lane	
M. Bch 90266	NUMBER 545-3651	Redondo Bch 90278	NUMBER 374-88
John Dew III	AREA CODE 213	Philip DAIGNEAULT	213
X-white House counsel	NUMBER 851-6104	3838 Carson St. #100	NUMBER 540-2525
"ADRINA" INc		Torrance, Calif 90503	
L.A. DA's office	AREA CODE 213	Congressman Rowan: Stan Mullin	213
PDID Invest Paul Bernardo	NUMBER 974-389	6151 w century Rd 1018	NUMBER 642-5111
FRED Leon Hart		L.A. 90045	Cong-Nat'l OSB
Laura DAVY 217	AREA CODE 213	Stan Mullin	213
18th Pl. 90266		Nove III N. Glenn Dr	NUMBER 476-294
M.B	NUMBER 546-5215	CA 90049	
Rowan's Dc.	AREA CODE 202	202 694-4708	AREA CODE 202 694-4708
Private Line	NUMBER 225-6451		
Adrian			
Dan Christ Fern	AREA CODE 619	Kori Daniel	AREA CODE 808
Hon B caysan	NUMBER 571-1580	Baby Closet	NUMBER
Becky		147	
USN Frank Brown 694-4786		Brown 202-694-4786 4120	

(604-738-7683   ←

NAME AND ADDRESS	TELEPHONE	NAME AND ADDRESS	TELEPHONE
MARC W. Barnes #2	AREA CODE 213	MARY Torvetaro	AREA CODE 604
707 w 37th St	NUMBER 548-0226	6004 439-9431	
San Pedro 90731		canada	NUMBER 457-947
DAViD Taylor new #	BBC 202 703-323-2050	ARticles CBC	AREA CODE
BBC N. D.C. 378-0536	703-	Pacific	NUMBER
DiD Round Story	938-4875	Jim Lithgow CBC	
Pete RANDALL #2	AREA CODE 213		AREA CODE Brisbane CA
3929 w. 242nd St	NUMBER 373-3157	1-213-557-5261	NUMBER 1634
Torrance. 90505			CBC
Laura DAVY	AREA CODE 213 530-8178	SPortmart, INc	AREA CODE
1415 255th St	NUMBER	7233 w. Dempster	NUMBER
HARBOR City CA 90710	90710	Niles, ILL 60648	
Senate Intell comm	AREA CODE 1-202	1401 Hawthorne Blvd	AREA CODE
Eric Brondel	NUMBER 224-1700	Redondo Bch CA 90278	NUMBER
Winston Buddy		7433 Edinger Ave	
TONY marco	AREA CODE 1-704	HUNtington Bch, CA	AREA CODE
writer K.R Book	NUMBER 527-7628	92647	NUMBER
for Barry			KTB
448 Shamrew Cir. Charlotte N.C. 28210			

NAME AND ADDRESS	TELEPHONE	NAME AND ADDRESS	TELEPHO
Richard C. Webb	AREA CODE 213	ANDY ESCOBAR	AREA CODE 213
KBA movie prod	NUMBER 395 7235	13421 S. GALE AV	NUMBER 675-0
213-458-5993		HAWTHORNE CALIF 90250	
SPIN TV	AREA CODE 409-0045	Craig & Cathy Englert	AREA CODE 808
Elke willmayer	EXT 2451	224 Niwai circle	NUMBER
Nudrin sim	2453	Kailua HWI HI 96-25	
Buckingham parkway	AREA CODE NUMBER	BEVERlie ENsom	AREA CODE 213
Robert Norton	5730 Culver	3471 Maricopa St apt 6	
Media Entertainment, Inc	AREA CODE 90230 213	Torr. CALIF 90503 379-9763	
CIA bought HT	NUMBER 855-1611	Rep. Stephen Solarz DOW USA	AREA CODE 202
movie into video		202-225-2361	
PETER Ballairs	AREA CODE —	D.C. 511 freeways BAN	342-1876
	NUMBER	Bo Festing NY	
		Solarz Hotel 703 759-3326	
E.T. KTTU LA CH 11	AREA CODE 213	BEVERLY ENson	AREA CODE 213
Jack Rielo	NUMBER 468-4900	376-4098	NUMBER 526110
CIASTORY 11-20-84			

NAME AND ADDRESS	TELEPHONE	NAME AND ADDRESS	TELEPHONE
George Belkamp CIA/DEA		(2) loor INo Austria	
Jeremy C. CLARK	AREA CODE	LA PAZ office	AREA CODE 213
15N DN'L Assoc TF-157	NUMBER	Record D.V.	NUMBER 924-3546
CABLET 51 Baltica	CPT	Casey CVR w/ CCT/Bay ABC	FCC?
Robert F. DiPalma	AREA CODE	11-21-84 ABC Airs	
USN INTell w/ CM-D.C.	NUMBER	CIA Retraction Due to	
will be 7 Died 7-31-85	NTTS 9	Knows Ed. Wilson	
Herbert Scoville	AREA CODE	T.J. Gaylon Dallas M/C officer	AREA CODE
CiA + MIT my	NUMBER	Housea Shrpt	NUMBER
& enior Arms control Assc.		House com/kee on JFK HST	
Wisconsin, Milwaukee	AREA CODE 414	INDIA ATMS Dealer	AREA CODE
SA. Gary Bush	NUMBER	w/ B&B CIA	
FBI SN Record	276-4684	Abbas Ali killed in Taipei, Taiwan	
Hugh Murray DEA	AREA CODE 602	writer Nash NY	AREA CODE 602
NSSen Mero, CIA contact	NUMBER	CIA cia	NUMBER
NUked 9-5-84	629-6845	murder Tucson	792-1613
Rich	AREA CODE 21 38 18	John Drexler	AREA CODE
Ventura Blvd	NUMBER 995-4710	USA XCIA	NUMBER
Sherman Oaks CA		(Henry) (BB)	
3612 Assn w/ CMI			

NAME AND ADDRESS	TELEPHONE	NAME AND ADDRESS	TELEPHO
John Marxin Dept/Secty FBI USA Wash DC	AREA CODE 202 NUMBER 724-6913	Rich Florez classified into CSC	AREA CODE 542-62 NUMBER
Hono. Bureau Tim Miller FBI Sherry Agent Farina B.B. case	AREA CODE 1-808- NUMBER 521-1411	Ed Freedman kern sub.com DNA HRYS Rep. Stephen Solarz	AREA CODE 202 NUMBER 342-187
John Meier 360 English Bluff Rd Delta B.C. CANADA	AREA CODE 604 NUMBER 943-4561	House annex-1 Rm 707 D.C. 20575	AREA CODE NUMBER
Tasawassen V4M-2N1	943-3343	Marx Fo	AREA CODE 604
Phil Jordan Vez phoenix2,402		canada paper friend of John Meier at	NUMBER 733-328
San Bugitto CBS	1-212		AREA CODE
212-915-5431	975-3693	1-604-732-2780	NUMBER
Alison Acree Bantam Books N.Y. editor Scott Iden	AREA CODE 1-212 NUMBER 765-6500	Bob Santi case DA Tim Bodney Carlton press N.Y.	AREA CODE 212 NUMBER 243-880

2-28-06
1 5pm PS office Routland Archivist 202-649-300

NAME AND ADDRESS	TELEPHONE	NAME AND ADDRESS	TELEPHON
Audubon # of DIA 22447084709 LA D.C.-2	EC Chen was very excited	193326 North 1034227 East Xianghoang, Laos near plain of jars	MIA 2,700 ft. NUMBER
Elaine Markson N.Y. Lit Agent	AREA CODE 212 NUMBER 243-8480	10-80	AREA CODE AREA CODE NUMBER
Julie Davy 232 3rd St Manhattan Bch 90266	AREA CODE 213 NUMBER 372-1351	Dir Wey cia hands cats & block on UF CCC stock NBC	AREA CODE over
Lauer Davy Lauer 213 8178 764 W. 30th St #9 San Pedro Ca 90321	213 NUMBER 519-7508	Susan Acker Story on Cheung PANTV cia Stock Bob Jackson	272 NUMBER 377-5712
Shirley Shulhard associate w/ Andres JPM library weekly 345 N. Rockingham listed in ART in Clay (CCIA) Brett Nelly changed to 8945 w/ Greek advisor on rental	AREA CODE backumta park 44	called Hunt cia over Buying NBC stock Carl Durhman Atty for J. never	NUMBER 293-4650 AREA CODE 619 NUMBER 234-3445

~ 702-877-2565

NAME AND ADDRESS	TELEPHONE		NAME AND ADDRESS	TELEPHONE
714-89-T-3134 / (3RP 1-714-684-6280	AREA CODE / NUMBER		Col. Jim "Bo" Gritz 8C29 Holly Cross L.A. 90045	AREA CODE 213 / NUMBER 644-088 645-7577
wk. 371-001085			Penny Glowac 750 E Carson St #9 Carson CA 90745	AREA CODE 836-7472 / NUMBER 830-4440
Teresa L. Glowacz (714) 1162 Express #4 Hy Bch, Ca 92647 842-3724 714-530-5084	AREA CODE (714) / NUMBER 842-3724		Theo GRevers. underground contact with adam "Khansouk Keola" - Pachouas	AREA CODE 616 891-1937 / NUMBER 949-1790
Charles Goldberg 303 Wes "A" St S.D Caif 92101	AREA CODE -714- / NUMBER 232-6671			
Hells Angels Vago MM			Dopalysis Bouboukis B.B.	AREA CODE
John Gali 6 Sybil wheeler close Hadford, Norbk England IP24-1TG	AREA CODE / NUMBER		Kim Hancock (Mission) 1008 / Rosecrans M B	AREA CODE 545 / NUMBER 5329
6 Butchon	AREA CODE 213 / NUMBER 618-C458		Al's Gardening Box 523 Vernville 93238	AREA CODE 714 / NUMBER 376-2246 376-6924
(-3-85 Rob Bytes C14 said Sotho w/ friends				

"Key officers of Foreign service Posts" 202-783-3238

NAME AND ADDRESS	TELEPHONE		NAME AND ADDRESS	TELEPHONE
Teresa Glowacz 508 Yorktown #1 Hug Bch 6A 92648	AREA CODE / NUMBER		Kole Charello Day Phone #	AREA CODE 213 / NUMBER 374-9043
a cp Essey	AREA CODE / NUMBER		Vivan (Cia secret Covmat Aero Files (my contact)	AREA CODE 202 / NUMBER 357-7841
Kathy & Nick	AREA CODE 619 / NUMBER		A Av Huge San	AREA CODE 213 / NUMBER 822-5893
619-244-4841 244-48	AREA CODE / NUMBER		3701 Black 4th Avery Culver City CA 90230	AREA CODE / NUMBER
Col. Hill w/1 Help Disinfo w/section of operational security (SAISB) Deception section, w/JO Joint Special operations Agency	AREA CODE (SAISB) DOD / NUMBER			
Tom (Behrl) 550A 5-812 via Panero Yorba Linda CA 92686 972-1387	AREA CODE 714 / NUMBER 972-1387		1-808-536-5577 Jean Griffith Hi (contact) 1050 King St #1202	AREA CODE / NUMBER
6-714 4214 222-4548 home	AREA CODE / NUMBER		Honolulu HI 96814 U.S. State Dept "Threat Analysis Group German auto 202-632-2412	AREA CODE 702 / NUMBER 632-2412
6				

FBI Richette called 9-24-80 Sec. LT. GEN. Tyrue 103-5010

NAME AND ADDRESS	TELEPHONE	NAME AND ADDRESS	TELEPHONE
Hope's	AREA CODE	Ron Haro	AREA CODE
Dan Boyd — Clandestino	NUMBER	12231 Freeman	NUMBER
Daly Yancy — Louis Pube		Hawthorne 90260	644-64
Ted Brooks — Clandestine coerce.	AREA CODE	Shelly Hernandez	AREA CODE
on occasions	NUMBER	2301 #A Rockefeller Ln	NUMBER
missions	AREA CODE	Redondo Bch CA 90278	714
	447 Vista Day Break	Mich. Kathy John	714-866
Christian Chapel	NUMBER	Po Box 1586 work Kathy	585-4004
Honolulu		Big Bear Lake, CA 92315	846-244
Steve Hampton	AREA CODE	HOPE CHAPEL (lochin)	808
262-7359	NUMBER	PO BOX 419 office	879-385
Craig 877-0904	AREA CODE	K. hei, maui HI 96753	879-185
work	619-244-4741	Pat & chris Hamman	Six
lou	NUMBER	126 mohawk, FL	
	AREA CODE	Kihei, maui HI 96753	879-76
7623 Madera Ave	NUMBER	Mark & Sue	213
Hesperia, CA 92345		318-1021	372-82
619-244-4144			

RON Rewald 213-871

NAME AND ADDRESS	TELEPHONE	NAME AND ADDRESS	TELEPHONE
Susan Novansky "Hope"	AREA CODE	Tracy Ainsworth	AREA CODE
31 Kremer Rd	NUMBER	37 Gilwern Cres	NUMBER
Norristown, PA 19401		Llanishen	
Scott Xinkle	AREA CODE 619	Cardiff, CF4 5AL	AREA CODE
Box H	NUMBER	S. Wales, Glamorgan	NUMBER
w.lt. CA. 93285	379-3135		
	AREA CODE	Earl Birham	AREA CODE 619
To Be new	NUMBER	Merari New Ddg	NUMBER
fed. judge			234-344
Mr Sporkin, Stanley	AREA CODE 202	Don Huffaker	AREA CODE 1-215
CIA counsel	NUMBER	962 upper state Rd.	NUMBER 822
on Rewald case	351-6911	Chalfont, PA 18914	935
Ted Greenberg USA	AREA CODE 202	Henry Liu was	AREA CODE
works w/ CIA	NUMBER	Discussing BB contact	NUMBER
goes to Hono 6-4-84	552-9100	w/ Trinon Arms & Rewald CIA	
to get Gitary released	AREA CODE	Charlie Stevor	AREA CODE 212
on Row	NUMBER	ABC News	NUMBER
		N.Y.	882-400
		1-212-887-2400	

6-25-85 (8) ARRIGARD OF ANAHEIM   215-203-9835

NAME AND ADDRESS	TELEPHONE
JORI' MUAD Mel FM Hawaii	AREA CODE
N HADDY ST	NUMBER
BAT-YAN ISRAEL	AREA CODE
DAVID TANG Hong Kong Customs court cif/auto	NUMBER
"F. SLURRY BILL" CIA	AREA CODE
"Red Dog" OOPS	NUMBER
LAO #1's MALISSAY	
OSAMA NAWATA Yoshiaki	AREA CODE
OSAMU Iwahashi JACA Inoue KONI Kamano	NUMBER
Hirohito Yamazaki center	
SEN. Howard BAKER	AREA CODE 1-202
W.D.C.	NUMBER
S.J.C.	224-4944
UiCk's Mr RAE	AREA CODE 619
Det. Leonard Houston Police	376-3380
713-222-4491 INVST. Prost R, y / 15 Ann 1 mitzo	

UMU BRYANT CIA CG WENCK 72

NAME AND ADDRESS	TELEPHONE
DAWNA IDE 546-VI EF Hawaii	AREA CODE
52 TENNIS Club DR	NUMBER
DANNVille, CA 94526	AREA CODE 1-209
Agent JEFF Roehm	
ATF	875393
ALICE "DALLAS" HOYT	AREA CODE 213
Virginia Escovia	NUMBER
2702 Nelson #3	
Redondo Bch CA 90278 542-5283	
TVE SPAIN tel=428050	AREA CODE 212
Rosa Maria Chf	NUMBER
Buseau chief	371-5212
JOHN Kindschi	AREA CODE 1-808
Hono Co CIA	NUMBER
Isser Pewind	536-
JACK RARDIN CHEF	AREA CODE 600
Camp CIA Hono	NUMBER C.VT-86
Charles CONNER il Sweden pino Adults natives	
1-010 801-3013	

---

11 exo #213-396-1579

NAME AND ADDRESS	TELEPHONE
CNIN CIA MAX Den	AREA CODE
OCC1B 202-351-2083	NUMBER
LEICH MR. LiN CiA 10-25-85	AREA CODE
Scotts w/Eli's file	NUMBER
LAW enforcement intell unit	
crim-mob intell unit	
Bob Beckie	AREA CODE 202
narcotic mcyr	NUMBER
TRAEX Tenn cpr 625-1600	AREA CODE
y CHAMES BANK	NUMBER
Ron Reand	AREA CODE 213
647 June ST	NUMBER
L.A.-A 90005 939-12.84	
Evergreen Nevada	AREA CODE
NRIL air FM	NUMBER

LOYD BOONES office

NAME AND ADDRESS	TELEPHONE
JOHN NBC	AREA CODE 212
New York works	NUMBER XT 3703 664-4444 FXT 2450
for "NRA"XNR"	AREA CODE
Bohemian Club	NUMBER
NJ CALiF Henny unit meeting	AREA CODE XS.0
w/	NUMBER Annland MD 855
Jim Ann	
Dorthy Bevely	AREA CODE 212
Dan "B" cerkes	NUMBER 398-1934
N.V. authors Guild	
Mary Winfenny 877	
HERBXI investor mar	NUMBER 5665
Bill wed's Wene	
Rick underwood Producer	AREA CODE 818
Sust. Dennie Marvin	NUMBER 762-9923
NANK Cooper 1-818-881-5813	

FEB-28-86 6 PM / MBI
302-695-4355-7
Sec. Atout Deshulsen

153 MIN producer Kes 602-34X-6001
MONICA Berger PAul 805-202-457-4551

NAME AND ADDRESS	TELEPHONE	NAME AND ADDRESS	TELEPHONE
Gm + Jerry Hejecouple	AREA CODE 328-3052	JANA	AREA CODE 808
213-203-1595	NUMBER 379-1960		NUMBER 879-704
Michael Douglas	BUS	Brenda Friend	AREA CODE 714
Tom Coscia	213	JAMIS Dodge (Plow)	
Martha Anzer	NUMBER 6703	(916-446-0100)	NUMBER 546-393
FAMILN Ughan 1500' NSA	850-6200		
Caro as Reward	AREA CODE	LARRY JONES 916-629-3645	
B.B.D.W.	NUMBER	PO Box 1256 Willow Creek	NUMBER
HAND DNE mike	305-350-X503	CA 95573 (1256)	
So. East BANK Miami, FLA	AREA CODE	BEN JUSTICE	AREA CODE 213
& Barnett Bank Miami, Delores	NUMBER 305-624-444	4513 Madison	NUMBER 542-7254
		Tovy 705503	
9-24-84 9 AM TR-1	AREA CODE New used in Cent. America	JACK Alverson	AREA CODE 1-202
(Flight test, Modified to be used in Europe, Base England	NUMBER	453-1442 483-149	NUMBER
look at U-42 to be used in Europe surveillance Ha Benghazi AFB			
EL U-2/SR-71 Blkkbird	AREA CODE 1-805-	Mike Yho	AREA CODE
7 Operations Center	NUMBER 772-3393	to Robert Rogers	NUMBER
to Spy in the Sky / CIA		VKY S.F/6RITZ	
HQ LT Col EVANS			

14 MBS.
202-647-3178 philip Habib Must.
Paul Inter Dept

NAME AND ADDRESS	TELEPHONE	NAME AND ADDRESS	TELEPHONE
IRIS Bittinger	AREA CODE 213	LAURA Raux	AREA CODE
142 W. 220th ST	NUMBER 935-0588	at TUFTS	NUMBER 546-5215
CARSON CA 90745	AREA CODE	Toro - Widman	AREA CODE
Moved Paul Pompa new number to SF-8	NUMBER 5-000	18th Street Manhattan	
& Reze enterprise u		Jt One LA Divner	NUMBER
thru Lefton to Ingram			
New Area 859-9957	AREA CODE	Gay Davis	AREA CODE
1707 Harvey ST N/W	NUMBER D.C.	7-30-93 10 AM Western	NUMBER F#07
w/ Summa con		Gate 54 Summa ref J. noier	
Bob Bennett	AREA CODE 1-202	Golden Summ	AREA CODE
Re Gordon Liddy	NUMBER 452-8555	culvir city project	NUMBER
w/ Intertel in DC		for Nuclear Dev.	
Jones Golden	AREA CODE	very aware ok	AREA CODE
	NUMBER	Bill Lebo WMC	NUMBER
Chuck Berry	AREA CODE	Michael Yamanis	AREA CODE
corp sec. Invest.		Golden Associates	NUMBER
Summa in vegas	NUMBER	w/ Heberg	

202-647-3178 Philip Lab & Inst.
Daughter Dept

NAME AND ADDRESS	TELEPHONE		NAME AND ADDRESS	TELEPHONE	
CRIS BITTINGER 142 W. 220th ST CARSON CA 90745	AREA CODE 213 NUMBER 835-0588		LAURA DAUX AT TOTTERS TORU - WADMAN	AREA CODE NUMBER 546-5215	
Moved Paul PomPAN Thru LeHerro ingra NEW area 858-9957	AREA CODE 858 NUMBER 5-200		217 18th Street MAN Bcn L owe ya Dinner	AREA CODE NUMBER	
1707 Harvey ST N/W w/ Summt con D.C.			GAY DAYS 7-30-93 100 Am Leesyn Gate 54 Summ Ref J. Voier	AREA CODE NUMBER	K
Bob Bennet w/ Gordon Liddy w/ INTERTEL in DC Jones Golden	AREA CODE 1-202 NUMBER 452-8055 AREA CODE	Mc N O	Godsk Summ Culver City Project for Hughes Dev. vem alway ok	AREA CODE NUMBER AREA CODE	Mc N O
Chuck Benny corp Sec. TAWest Summ in vegas	NUMBER AREA CODE NUMBER	P Q R	Bill Lebo w/ white Michael Vannis Golden w/ Noberg	NUMBER AREA CODE NUMBER 202-872-	V W X Y Z

4) discussed Michael turkey ele on Anni's - WAIcc 'teals'

NAME AND ADDRESS	TELEPHONE		NAME AND ADDRESS	TELEPHONE	
SN. DAN INOUYE SN. SEL. Com INRU "Rahier"	AREA CODE 808 NUMBER 546-7550			AREA CODE NUMBER	
LARRY BASILE 1-93	AREA CODE 1-808-		KARIN (churn)	AREA CODE 714 NUMBER 379-4523	
HF. STATE Dept agents TONY JONES MARK McNIVEN Feb-27-86 meeting on Armitage	NUMBER 941-3913		Gary Krehbiel 34779 Maricopa St Torrance 90503	AREA CODE 213 NUMBER 542-3678	K
Keven Cscuvvi Nut Pow MIA CIA/DIA cover up	AREA CODE 703 NUMBER 534-4427	Mc N O		AREA CODE NUMBER	Mc N O
Al Haig D.C. # 7/951 Politic. Dir SEATO	AREA CODE 202 NUMBER 439-9788	P Q R	Niel Kitchen Chevy Chase Bakersfield	AREA CODE 805 NUMBER 871-6361 OFFICE 805	P Q R
Richard Helms PO BOX 821 winchester Larry Jones OR 97495 636-7657 1-503-673-3056	AREA CODE 32/703			NUMBER 323-9205	V W X Y Z

Interview w/ cooper in Husher
11 AM

Calif. Reno Utah 9-4-84 Lon no.
City Nebraska/Calif.

NAME AND ADDRESS	TELEPHONE	NAME AND ADDRESS	TELEPHONE
Regis Possino Esq 9720 Wilshire #4 B.H. CA 90212	AREA CODE 1-213 NUMBER 274-6844	Donna Neu Mus 3720 Garnet #217 Terrence CA 90503	AREA CODE 213 NUMBER 370-032
Jim Barney / 700 LA wash Latimes DC / Ron ostrow daily hotel	AREA CODE NUMBER	meet John DeGreen 2-8-85 820 Air shell Anza /10 M. Blue in Blue Station wagon	AREA CODE NUMBER
George Spackler - new P.O. Box 86544 N. Vancouver, B.C. V7K4L1	AREA CODE 604 NUMBER 985-8061	Mary Davy New Puako Beach Ar. Kamuela, HI 96743	AREA CODE 808 NUMBER 882-7327
CIA cover telex # 248923	AREA CODE NUMBER	P.O. Box 4306 Kawi Hae HI 96743	AREA CODE NUMBER
Inspector Dugan CIA Actor Insp. Gritz DCA Case Invest.	AREA CODE 1-818 NUMBER 405-1200	JCL DRC Phil Shuffn Richard Alice	AREA CODE 301 NUMBER 366-5737
Bill Harrison Esq. office / Ron Rewald 9-5-84	AREA CODE 1-805- NUMBER 523-7041	Jcl williams writer Rewald's office Po Box 181 Clearlake, CA 95	AREA CODE 707 NUMBER 743-079

General from Una
11-19-85 4:20pm DST Jim Shurfelt called

Agent of recy/CIA LAESA will fly
mission flows the covert oops in USA.

NAME AND ADDRESS	TELEPHONE	NAME AND ADDRESS	TELEPHON
Ann-Marie Llelynce 414 2nd St #123 N.B. CA 90254	AREA CODE 213 NUMBER 372-6240	Margo Lemon P.O. Box 721 Laurdale, Ca 90210	AREA CODE 213 NUMBER 679-644
Agent John Hopeck NFS 2231 3-27-86 12:30pm on 13th	AREA CODE NUMBER 325-3845	Lori Loyd PO Box 2644 Santa Bay Btra Calif 9312	AREA CODE 805 NUMBER 966-20
Hugh murray : Hazelo muse CIA censor Bells office	AREA CODE NUMBER Preview Saud	"Yellow Knife" Marina #4 Finger A Ship # 38	AREA CODE 805-48 NUMBER 805-834-251
Ron Rewald Discussion on Richard C. Smith Agency PRC 1-415-673-4736	AREA CODE NUMBER 577 4036	or 992 So Kihei Rd ESA Kihei, Maui HI 96753	AREA CODE 808 NUMBER 879-6149
4Bron Arnold 804-623-261	AREA CODE NUMBER 373-3034	(Isbeth Lundy (not sister) 28409 San Nicholas P.V. 90274 (not sister)	AREA CODE NUMBER 2-3 7154
Pete Stockton Oversight Committee Rep. Rewald CIA Probable ? Closed Hearings	AREA CODE 202 NUMBER 225-4441	Mi-chael Lee Possina 744 Hilgard Av. CA CA 90024 (UCLA) UCLA #	AREA CODE NUMBER 208-0358

I.A.A. Am. S/EAsisA 202-633-1463

--> Cao John Delorean 2-8-85 Shell

NAME AND ADDRESS	TELEPHONE
Michele Morton	AREA CODE 204
8 Glencoe Ave	NUMBER 334-4425
Winnipeg Manitoba	AREA CODE
Canada R3K OG7	
1006-595 River Ave	NUMBER
Winnipeg, Man, Canada	AREA CODE
R3L OE6	
Anna [illegible] Lelavee	NUMBER 318-2902
Fred Mathews Portland, OR	AREA CODE 916
	NUMBER 972-1835
Kayne Miles	AREA CODE 213 884-7409
29353 Hillrise Dr.	NUMBER 889-2175
Agoura, 91301 CA	AREA CODE
1-714-376-4210	
Kernville	NUMBER
1-714-376-3019 New	
1-213 889-6401	

NAME AND ADDRESS	TELEPHONE
Michele Morton	AREA CODE 213
Apt 2 101 Monterey Blvd	379-9040
Hermosa Beach, Ca	NUMBER 90254
Ralph Moore	AREA CODE 213
423 E Ave church address!	NUMBER
2420 P.C.H. Hermosa Bch 90254	379-8436
Karen Martin (5-8-81)	AREA CODE 514 684-3227
52 Clarence	NUMBER H9A2L1
Dollard Des Orneaux, Quebec Canada	AREA CODE
Karen Martin	
P.O. Box 6742	NUMBER
Jeddah, Saudi Arabia	Saj
Marti	AREA CODE 808
3414 Kilua Rd [illegible]	NUMBER
Kilua Maui HI	879-2748
Dana Fahey Munoz	AREA CODE
1662 Oakhoyne Dr.	NUMBER
Harbor City Calif.	
90710	

Arms Control Disarmament Admin 202 647-3018

Agent Joel Henderson ACDA St Dep Diplomatic 202-647-7732 647-1040

NAME AND ADDRESS	TELEPHONE
Metro/E Gida LTD	AREA CODE
142 W 83rd St N.Y.	NUMBER Mid East
Kitty Kurmisu Mexico CIA/BB	
Talked w/ Ron 3 P.M. 6-7-84	AREA CODE
At 414-257-2220	NUMBER
Michele Morton	AREA CODE 204
22-105 Roslyn Rd.	NUMBER
Winnipeg Manitoba	284-6005
Canada R3L-OG1	AREA CODE 202-647-2084
Agent Gutensohn	
St. Dept Intell Know makers & arms	NUMBER CIA secs arms deals
John Meier	AREA CODE 604
C.B.C. 700 Hamilton	943-3343
Vancouver B.C. V6B 2R5	NUMBER 943-4567
Mike Clarnask.	AREA CODE Office 604
1604 CBC Researcher	NUMBER
665 News Canada	665-6670
7454 (Meier) Home	604 685-5093

NAME AND ADDRESS	TELEPHONE
Tom McMahon	AREA CODE 805
	NUMBER
w/ Laura Robinson worked	985-2992
Control Reports	AREA CODE 1-804
S.W. DSKL	NUMBER
w/ GRU for Naval Intell	497-1863
Jeannie Hewitz	AREA CODE 213
Stanley Hatchel	NUMBER 320-6619
George Weisz CIA Ronald	AREA CODE
w/ Bob Duncan, "plan" Died	NUMBER
B.B. $ to Howe "TRI" 84	
Seymour Hersh	AREA CODE 202
Office 1-202-783-4260	NUMBER
1199 Nat Press Bld Wash D.C. 20045	244-0457
Len Greenwood	AREA CODE 601
Civil Rights Anti-CIA	NUMBER 969-2269
H. Ross Perot called 5-28 1-214 [illegible] to discuss my [illegible] [illegible] 3 P.M. mission/CIA	

CIA   Rm 418   #   · Brian TAKIGUTI (405) 746-73○ FED. Pub DEF.

NAME AND ADDRESS	TELEPHONE		NAME AND ADDRESS	TELEPHONE
CABle "ASTOR HOTEL" Company outlet 11 CARNARVON RD. Kowloon, Hong Kong Phone 3-667261	AREA CODE NUMBER RJ.5 AREA CODE NUMBER		Bob Heller Double Day ¢ Co INC 245 PARK AVE N.Y (OR PETE SYNDER) NY 10167 Christian Bro & publisher w/ Barry; "Evder Accel"	AREA CODE 1-212 NUMBER 953-448 AREA CODE NUMBER
"Al Glick" MMJ's corretl Berry's Weiper Vincent St #7 S. Diego Special DEA Invest for narcotic/anti Drug element	AREA CODE NUMBER AREA CODE 202 NUMBER 633-1369		6-25-85 sent to Tom Murray DoubleDay DoubleDay City 40er for verif 10/16 6/6 84 Called	AREA CODE 212 NUMBER 953-4288
DEA Intel Houston office S/A George FAZ S/A Bob Murphy	AREA CODE 713 NUMBER 229-2950 AREA CODE NUMBER		GRU Chronoskijki S.F. T.F. 80 thri RON KAUFMAN prod./noize/noise	AREA CODE NUMBER AREA CODE 213 NUMBER 201-0780
YAlk w/ Cen Tighe 7Pm 9-14-85 AT 818 359-342			213-827-4497	

11.3.85 Assoc/Boss of PHOUMi NOSAVAVUH died in 85○   John MERK called 5-2-85 8:30 Pm billed

NAME AND ADDRESS	TELEPHONE		NAME AND ADDRESS	TELEPHONE
NANA HOTEL SOI 4 SUKHUMVIT RD BANGKOK 11, THAILAND "CHANIDA Komoluantana" 'MARIAM Nencharoen' Miss "sorry" English way Miss 'SMAREEKIJ'	AREA CODE THAILAND NUMBER 252-4101-5 AREA CODE NUMBER		ZAC + Julie NAZARIAN 1821 Goodman Ave R.B. 90278 ANN GRIFFINS NC.F 1608 K St N.W. WASHINGTON D.C.	AREA CODE 213 NUMBER 374-8313 AREA CODE 202 NUMBER 223-6846
Salvatore Catalano new camora Galane Jerry's Monique "pancake" 2013 #A Warfield R. Bch.	AREA CODE 213 NUMBER 376-8243		Marshall Noyes 4633 Compton Blvd #212 Lawndale, CA. Sonny's Barbers Aunt MRS Nevell	AREA CODE 213 NUMBER 978-0109 AREA CODE 213 NUMBER 830-0841
BOHICA HAWAII NAVK chang office /Avo film com KGB SF CA	AREA CODE 808 NUMBER 536-6009 AREA CODE 1-808 NUMBER 548-4535		714-235-9973 St Dept ST Dept "Security" 488-7816 John Noble w/ CMPAC Ralph Rub HI# 261-4996 PRC ; BcB	AREA CODE 808 NUMBER 525-2421 AREA CODE 80 NUMBER 261-9109

Jerrie Smith   UAS Paul Capt. FD CAO BO

NAME AND ADDRESS	TELEPHONE	NAME AND ADDRESS	TELEPHONE
VAKHON Danon Hotel	AREA CODE	Col. MIKE AISLAND (JUMP)	AREA CODE
XHLAND, "Lou By"	NUMBER 571455	MAJ ED F. BROOKS	NUMBER
2:41 Bring new Tape		CAPT. ROBERT L. HAYES II	
OSSAGE Unit "E"	AREA CODE	Col. CHARLES M. HOLLAND	AREA CODE
	NUMBER	O-3 DAN G. CARR	NUMBER DELTA
	AREA CODE	E-8 GENE BELL (SOF)	AREA CODE BOYS
O-30-84	NUMBER 202 357-160x2626	E-8 VINCENT SKEEDA	NUMBER
KATHY ROBESON CIA		O-3 RICHARD HASKELL	
	AREA CODE	O-3 JOHN T. HORN	AREA CODE
he said, we have denied	NUMBER several	E-8 JOHN J. SEIF	NUMBER
any Relationship to you for	AREA CODE	E-8 EARL BLEACHER	AREA CODE
Years, we didn't send NTO	NUMBER	" WILLIAM H. BRUSHWOOD	NUMBER
to SF APT IN SEPT-83 as we	AREA CODE	O-3 VERNON W. GILLESPIE JR	AREA CODE
we drive up legrom	NUMBER	O-2 RICHARD GLAUFELTER	NUMBER
no longer ASST per Pres. order	AREA CODE	MAJ JAMES G. PRIZITZ	AREA CODE
clerk to B.B.RN	NUMBER	E-9 BILL J. NORTON	NUMBER
Kong office		E-? RON WINGO	
concerned courier		Col. JOHN FREUND	
MJC S"		DAVE G. BROWN, THOMAS CONLON	EMBASSY

JACKIE VOSS

NAME AND ADDRESS	TELEPHONE	NAME AND ADDRESS	TELEPHONE
BRAD FAULKNER	AREA CODE 212	VBB G# Sealoy	AREA CODE 213
Ed's Thy 10022	NUMBER 751-1330	M.D. FBI coverup CIA HITS	NUMBER JU5-5162
40 Madison Ny N.Y.	AREA CODE	N.Y. SUZANNA AKW	AREA CODE 212
LARRY BRYANT "CO"	NUMBER	SPAIN T.V. Reporter	NUMBER 371-5112
to acquire "Bo's"	AREA CODE	UF CBW documents	AREA CODE
VBB LIM for secret	NUMBER	TRACY AINSWORTH	Wales
Joe Flynn ASIO	AREA CODE	37 Gilwern crescent	
'Pine Gap"	NUMBER	LLAHSHON, CARDIFF CF4 SAI GBWR S. GLAME	
3-15-85		NANCY OHIZA	AREA CODE
BOB BAXOR FEC	AREA CODE 202	1040 W. CASSIDY ST	NUMBER
Wash DC	NUMBER 632-9586	GARDENA, CA 90348	
Buster	AREA CODE 213	MARCIA WAGNER	AREA CODE 213 547-1496
JIM Goode "FLINT PAKistan" 2029 Cent Park East #3800		519 crenshaw	NUMBER
L.A. 90067	NUMBER 556-9200	DR. PHILLIPS	213
JASON EPSTEIN private	AREA CODE 212	RON VAUGHN	AREA CODE
Random House	NUMBER		NUMBER
201 E 50 ST	572-2268	AL TO, CA	3 26 1612
NY 10022			

NSA Internal Intelligence 688-6824 Soviet US. Russia/USSR 1-301 50 office VUAM Office designator A305

NAME AND ADDRESS	TELEPHONE
Personnel Records CIA Security/Security Disposition Section	MARIAN BRAXTON (AREA CODE)
System 57-59 Destroy all known info on subject	S.T.P. (NUMBER)
Current employee sector 3-6-85 419pm talked	NSA (AREA CODE)
at S.A.-OFF Honolulu on record case/ no abuse	NSA CRYPTO (NUMBER)
Sergeant NSO 29	(AREA CODE)
talked w/ATF Berlin group ATF	
Asked him why he sent cables	
No Hawaii Section who ox	
Mario's Supervised I knew he said	(NUMBER)
he needed to delete	N50
" "	(AREA CODE)
Zuebel ALyAh	A305
Soto Grande AIMA-205	(NUMBER) AIMA305
Project /NS 301-688-6824 X	
NSA Office A305 Soviet DIV. A305	

VUAM postfach 13 A-2651 Reichenau/Rax AUSTRIA

Middle-east VUAM 50 PRINS Hendrikkade 1012 AC Amsterdam/Holland

FAR EAST Evangelism team 10 Borrett RD. G/F Hong Kong

VUAM Relief Services GPO. Box 177, BANGKOK Thailand 051 (AREA CODE) SILAS HONG CIA JGA (NUMBER)

JOHN JGA CIA (Russid) 722 Montgomery ST S.F. 9411 at Bell's office 1-415 398-2434

TYLIE DAVIS 213 342 5100   Moore K

NAME AND ADDRESS	TELEPHONE
ARASIT SAENGRUNGRUANG #25 SUWANSORN RD	037 (AREA CODE)
ARANYAPRVTHET, Thailand	231134'r 231234 (NUMBER)
3-5-85 12pm Paul Schrade called about CIA Destabilization and Stanley Sheinbaum UK Board	Rudy the U.S. Universe Grasso Mas activist Helen AN Drus (NUMBER)
pilot Burt Pfeifer UUN visit	406 Greene (AREA CODE) 213-0510 Res 213-41682 WUAL (NUMBER)
CCP "CONS 3-8-85 5:35pm 4 corners mall	415 (AREA CODE) 922-1662 (NUMBER)
RON Ack 011-441 113-115 Roman RD Bethnal Green London E-2	011-441 (AREA CODE) 981-3720 (NUMBER)
D.E.A. Agent Drug	916 (AREA CODE) 978-4205 (NUMBER)
on terror case w/ Keller Gold/Carter	

Paul York 12532 Cranbrook Ave #6 Hawthorne, Calif. 90250 213 644-0807

PAT CRIVELLO (Luis's friend sister in law) 1037 Pikake St. Wailuku, Maui 96793 HI yor 244-460?

Sheri (376-2797) USN cook ou E10 714 379-4752

John Pierce 6777 Del Play 7 ESN Lista, CA 93117

PTL Club (Barry Mason) 1-704 Suzanne Smith Network productions 542-6000

Robert Smith ATH 233 Bishop St 2615 Honolulu, HI. 96813 Res HD ATH 808- 523-6411 2310

NAME AND ADDRESS	TELEPHONE	NAME AND ADDRESS	TELEPHONE
Hal & Ginger Roberts	AREA CODE 213	APT Dist Cinma	AREA CODE
14125 Doty Ave	NUMBER 973-8554	4 - minute to M-East 11	NUMBER
Hawthorne CA. 90250	AREA CODE	X Asoc Critz Gerald J. Tarnaslo	AREA CODE
Information Acess Asoc Balcourt		"EL Kanas" Co. LTD	selli cegni
Luton DC. 39 watkins Cir	NUMBER	mass Newsl System	NUMBER uns cia
		Leon Kopyt 215-665-1800 offic	
Arthur Peabody FBI	NUMBER 222 6090	Bill Luthe	AREA CODE C1/mel
D.C. 1-202-222-6060	AREA CODE	Civ course/order	NUMBER
Special Litigation Section	NUMBER	Sen. w/ Vernon walters	
Mickell Dale USA		Thurmond office	AREA CODE 202
3-14-85 5:30 p.m. DC.	AREA CODE	mel Goodwin D.C.	NUMBER 224-7730
	NUMBER		
Max Felstein	AREA CODE 212	Isu Nita	AREA CODE
NBC news	NUMBER 887-3994	Sap. Intelligence	NUMBER
887-3994	AREA CODE 818	Caml Richison	AREA CODE Kauffler
Brent Carruth		Cal Ois B.11	
7120 Havenhurst #320	NUMBER 787-7609	w/ Smith agent, B:B	up
Van Nuys			

NAME AND ADDRESS	TELEPHONE	NAME AND ADDRESS	TELEPHONE
Gen Tighe called 9-21-85 9:50pm		702-871-2505 R	
Conkel CIA	AREA CODE 1-202	FBI RN	AREA CODE over Revald
oops STAN OTCD	NUMBER 357-6111	John white	NUMBER
center B:B Lawyer	AREA CODE 213	CIA Dir Chief invited to more	AREA CODE 1-808
Ron Reyold CIA.	NUMBER 739-1284	Hawaii Investor	NUMBER 326-1391
Admiral		Bill Wood	
Tom Valeu, ne Rewald	AREA CODE 619	808-524-7900	AREA CODE 1-414
writer for	NUMBER 255-2072	Wiscsn	NUMBER 628-4135
Spotlight W.D.C.		Richard Copnen	
Ean 1X4Sap CIA # 213-505-3-3345			
Austria Ch 7 Referal	3-17-85 Reysald	Ron Rewald	AREA CODE 414
called aunt interview	NUMBER	called 6-7-84	NUMBER 257-2220
George Joannides	AREA CODE 202	To Discuss CIA p.	AREA CODE
CIA w/ BB	NUMBER 351-6832	Says I have accounts	NUMBER
Gene Welly CIA		& money.	
Walter Nash	AREA CODE 602	Jeffery	AREA CODE
W Mitre CIA	NUMBER 792-4810	Cathy Sheppard Home 213	NUMBER
Methex Div. Milcary	Here	459-6382	

"BUNDESWEHR" J. MATKINS CIA

NAME AND ADDRESS	TELEPHONE		NAME AND ADDRESS	TELEPHONE
BOB SIMON	AREA CODE 202		IRA ROSEN producer	AREA CODE 202
CBS News	NUMBER		CBS 60 M.W.	NUMBER
(wsh. D.C)	457-4385		Doc. mike wallace	457-4495
202-457-4650 W.D.C.			202-338-5871	AREA CODE
Danuth? Jimmy News	NUMBER		ICA home #1	
212-84 CIA/ABC stinger w/no			Duck soap 70 w Hit	NUMBER
producer Janet			K40 Behiot	AREA CODE
Donald Jo? TA.man	NUMBER		Rainbow Guy CIA/ sponsored	NUMBER
Ha Yi-man ...jle	AREA CODE		Bob Swallow	AREA CODE NRC
Chen Hu-man B5 Arm	NUMBER		Dennis wilson CIA	NUMBER BB #1
			212-887-2400 Gren	AREA CODE Gren intell
	AREA CODE			NUMBER UN.T
	NUMBER		Gary Shepard ABC news	AREA CODE 1-213
	AREA CODE		CIA	NUMBER
Arrested Libya	NUMBER		Ref. B. Bene	557-524
Mdell Chris BILL			212-887-4040	

US K K WIEX MEUER?

NAME AND ADDRESS	TELEPHONE		NAME AND ADDRESS	TELEPHONE
SAL RUOCCO	AREA CODE 213		Carole Richelicu (AM)	AREA CODE 808
2845 S. MANSFIELD AVE	NUMBER		345-Quan ST #800	NUMBER
L.A. Ca 90016	936-3921		Honolulu HI (author 5-16-87)	531-6211
John Kelley CBS/60 M.W	AREA CODE 202		man Hyman's	AREA CODE 378-7088
B.B.C. Contempt stores	NUMBER		Col Dave Lambert	NUMBER Comp
Broadcase Reporter	328-0178		U.S-St. Dept chemical	
Kent Russell S.F.	AREA CODE 415		Ray & Carol little kandle	AREA CODE
Sonny's AM RICO	NUMBER 929-9361		2737 S. Kihei RD	NUMBER
			Kihei, Maui HI 96753	
May-21-84 Yankee	AREA CODE CIA		Bob Randall RBPD	AREA CODE 213
w/ Reugid At Bob Smith	BSB			NUMBER 373-3157
office Honolulu 6252	AREA CODE		Craig Barnes 213-442	AREA CODE 213
Ron Rewald & Nancy			RBPD 4.994	NUMBER 424-4474
OCCC Investment HI	NUMBER			
CM-I YOUR	AREA CODE		Randy & Gloria	AREA CODE 213
Hot	NUMBER			NUMBER 372-0247
Greek 4 "Firepower"			1-808-536-6963 B.B. CIA	

MORI(BOS) DAVID YA//1967 (CUARE · MAJ APODACA
US ARMY OR DOW 1-800-257-1333

NAME AND ADDRESS	TELEPHONE
LUANG PHO Phay Phachan	AREA CODE 703-896-1357
1068 WAT HAISOKE	NUMBER
NONG KHAi, XHAiLND	
(Rev/Hextlick)	AREA CODE 320
Cii Sup, John/Rosemarie	NUMBER 5035
Kny Airport (wiunk list	
Steve Werman So.Der	AREA CODE 305 school 284-2209
University of MiAMi	305 620.0
P.O. Box 24948, Govt anti FLA 284-3973
Apece Aluorin w/ 23124	AREA CODE 305-4"
Scot Bradley cell Be AAA	284
to Emily write out	NUMBER 3447
D150 (DDD. Hiro)	AREA CODE 5Steve
1-305-666-5607 Steve	NUMBER
Steve Werman 305 84	
012 305-284-360	AREA CODE 305
Hone	NUMBER
305-75-9833	
+ 1new 554-4452	

NAME AND ADDRESS	TELEPHONE
STeve WERMAN	AREA CODE 213
3323 ScADLOCK LN	NUMBER 91403
SilverMAN OAK, CA	
BARRY WAiNE	AREA CODE
3141 Second XUR/ 360 Ajave xvd	NUMBER
CHULA VISTA CHIF 92010	
Donis Ries (CHVRCH SEE)	AREA CODE
1336 P.O. Box	NUMBER
Kihei, MAui HI 96353	
MARK williams	AREA CODE 808
45 nohoKAi ST	NUMBER
Kihei MAui HI 96353	879-6069
FRANK & Joy 758-0966	AREA CODE -213-
7820 AiRPort BIVD	NUMBER
WESTCHESTER CA. 90025 649-3759	
MRS WATAN Rm 344 A	AREA CODE 24619
PO BOX CASE LB newar	376-6152
WH. CA 73205	W/Y/Z
595-231	

1-805-521-8229. Behist w/BB couer · SAC LtCol. 402-294- 5656

NAME AND ADDRESS	TELEPHONE
Sunthorn Chirayos	AREA CODE
338 Apidal RoAD	NUMBER
AMper Muns	AREA CODE
NAKon Phanom (NKP)	NUMBER
x Thailand + nuke wpn	
CIA/KGB Intell Agent	
Bob Gambino CiA	AREA CODE (USO) NED/X Dismto
SSFui Security J/V	NUMBER
BB/to V.V.in Pstches KGB/CiA	AREA CODE
Sue wilson	
NSA "Behice" w/John K	NUMBER
Uichny nelson Jau	AREA CODE 1-805
Jeka Gilcrest	NUMBER 968-8648
Senive Acq Ed. Ycc.	AREA CODE 1-202
Central Intelligence Agency	NUMBER 351-2028
1820 FT. Myer DR.	
ARLington VA. 22209	

NAME AND, ADDRESS	TELEPHONE
Cynthia Young	AREA CODE Solli T.Sgnt
Box 70 Petersburg	NUMBER MR-1 into
Alaska 99833	
OFFutt AFB (A.S.D)	AREA CODE 402 spy anmr g-2
U-2, SR-71, TR-1	NUMBER 294-4459
Spy Plane (CAPt. MEAD)	
PAVY HOng #821 mike Lily	AREA CODE 1-808
Hawaii's A.G. wd	NUMBER 548-4740
Jim Dannenberg, mike Lily	
MARCur Bape Sdr	AREA CODE 213
S. PORO CA	NUMBER 548-0226
Lily WORK 648-4595	AREA CODE
1377 W. 2nd ST	NUMBER
SAn Pedro, cA 90731	
NATIONAL SecuriTY Agency	AREA CODE 1-301
FT. George MeAde	NUMBER 796-6444
MARYLAND 20755	

JOHN HART } Bet
left Esen ... Lewis

"SUE" c/o/Hoc w/ STAN Co.

NAME AND ADDRESS	TELEPHONE
	AREA CODE
Petrina TAYLOR	
BBC T.V.	NUMBER
Konsington House RM# 5038	
Richmond way, London	AREA CODE
W14, OAX England	NUMBER
OPERATION'S	AREA CODE
Eagle to Replace	NUMBER
CONDOR W Mexico	
Hugh Murray fed.	AREA CODE
Voyager Conn.	213
Re. Venture w/ Busd	NUMBER
	201-0780
ED Diehl (Spook)	AREA CODE
works on Desalt w/ CIA	NUMBER
Navy Closeal Ave Col Davel	AREA CODE
J. Famil	NUMBER
Rafael E. Van	
Israel + Hell	

NAME AND ADDRESS	TELEPHONE
CARL Thomas	AREA CODE
Avs ont corp Vegas	NUMBER
BOX 1925 DEPT A	AREA CODE
WASH. D.C. RM 603	NUMBER
CIA Personnel, 20013	
BB/Arm V.A	AREA CODE
DS at KNXX	NUMBER
in BULGARIA	
GOV. Cuvao's	212
OFFice NY	NUMBER
	587-210
OPERATION "Coldwaters"	AREA CODE
London	NUMBER
	AREA CODE SAID
67-84	TED
TED Cessabers not	NUMBER TO HEAR
w/ NEWSPAPER AT CIA	
ON Raw Case. JAY at CIA HQ	

3rd Am Agent Wayne Hall IG: 101-202-746-0256 JAY:F TALKED 2-6-85 12 sour Rec
Feb 28-84 and they had Well from + several Hi said he got

NAME AND ADDRESS	TELEPHONE	NAME AND ADDRESS	TELEPHON
Ron R. Chatter	213	Telex # 295263 ALS UZ	AREA CODE
9(gun 9-21-84 notes	NUMBER 939-1284	JAY WALKER 619-942-999	NUMBER
Ref navy Daisy Equit life		1-714-754-5433 JAY 2-6-85 12	
Bruce Solie SYS5 → CIA HQ		J. Well case No Talk about	AREA CODE
	NUMBER	ASSOC Legal Security	NUMBER
Ron Kutema #15 326-4612		about CIA, DON NIXON, Surrey	
Voyager Enter w/ Rewald	AREA CODE	J. never 2-6-85 12	AREA CODE
Century City	NUMBER	Talked About D.NIXON + Richard	
Voyager communications 1-213-201-0780		fitteus CM, 3 to Casey Director	
Harold E. Daniels JR.	AREA CODE NSA	"Betty" CIA HQ	1-802
said to NSA Comm chief	NUMBER	william Casey office	NUMBER
Belfast will give to CIA		EXT 7676 Pers Covert Secty	351-710
GEN Lee CW done	S/E	March-23-84 15 m	AREA CODE
DICK, RICHARD, DANIEL Jack	NUMBER dope in ASIA	"PAT VOLZ" CIA.	NUMBER
JAY Sullivan	AREA CODE US	Robert B. Oakley Hell	AREA CODE
CIA ESQ	NUMBER	US. ST. Dept covert Hell w/CIA	NUMBER
works on Socret			
covert coup w/ X Agents		IRIS Ha. Oakland President	
Israel Hell		to Reagan	
Silsok			

12-9-86 free records   net w/ congressmen   X-ref chat Rod McDaniels off 202-
Vis Rush of poor Crawl eagle   Hacker Smith   A review Defense fund 544-4704
                                                       205-780-0430

NAME AND ADDRESS	TELEPHONE	NAME AND ADDRESS	TELEPHONE
George CHRISTY	AREA CODE 1-805	DANAH TAYMAN Issa/Glick	AREA CODE
Hells Angel pres.		Page w/ mase II	
Venture-camp	NUMBER 649-9531	fairchild	NUMBER 602-979-5651
Called 1-7-85 11 am	AREA CODE P.O. Box	foreign service	AREA CODE 1-202
XO MYK Hout, H.A	NUMBER 93	Dept. of STATE	
Movie, Book, Media		Wash. D.C. 20520	NUMBER 632-9438
Lawsuit, HO Dea,	OAK View	Kevin Donoghue CIA	AREA CODE
CIA problems	93072	OPS Cent CDO	NUMBER
works w/ Richard Chase			
Lyle Stuart Publ.	AREA CODE 1-201-	Brian Jarlett	AREA CODE 1-6-84
120 Enterprise Ave.	NUMBER 866-0490	NBC CBS NY	NUMBER
Secaucus N.J. 07094	AREA CODE	westmorland case, called Gietz	
Aug-84 FBI agents		11-15-84 1:25pm DMN never (Summ)	
Checked on my	NUMBER	called YAKed about court chamber	
payrolls saying w/ Ridgeways		Bremeray/CIA Summ Ly via	
YARRIS PALCHIN	AREA CODE	11-21-84 12:30pm called	AREA CODE
direct # 213-558-	NUMBER	Kathy Pherson void	NUMBER
6168		her that ABC am Air	
		a reaction this evening on NYSE)	

6-84   Workers who today have need to call   1-213 456-2162   6-9-84
                                                                      — view constituto

NAME AND ADDRESS	TELEPHONE	NAME AND ADDRESS	TELEPHONE
Charles Srove	AREA CODE 1-213	12-28-83 AT Resis place	AREA CODE
meeting 3-11-84 #1	NUMBER 933-1159	45 pm Recorded conversation	NUMBER
335 S. Rixal LA	933-9291	w/ michael Bremer DA office	
Paul Schrader # 213-658-5623	AREA CODE	686-1010 about	AREA CODE
Ref PFK Assumption	NUMBER 703-379-6347	Meir case said	
Virginia Calling state	AREA CODE	he knew about my meeting	
they got Hoover	PRIVATE #	w/Summ : winte on case	NUMBER
JOHN PEYTON	805-546-3126	(how would he know? if was also w/Summ)	
FBI office 805-546-2900	546-9170	he's been talking w/Summ officials CIA	
MAJ JOHN PEYTON	1-206	6-8-84 8:32	AREA CODE
J leclig CIA #	NUMBER 962-8226	talked w/ peyton in	NUMBER making Deal
X-CIA Now USA in	AREA CODE 1-805-	CIA Round one he found Devel phone #	
Honolulu Assoc Gietz	NUMBER	FBI said this good private	AREA CODE
Home 1241 Kaelepulu	396-0216	... this secret	NUMBER may be we
note is a lear peyton	1-206	1GN JF834 CALic	AREA CODE 93, 7 m.l
5-29-84 maj peyton working	NUMBER 962-8226	FBI hdrs	NUMBER
operation " YAMA SAKURA"		BILL BRUN	
on a series of computer		w/ Richard?	
was operations of Japan w/ LT. Gen Alexander Weyand			826 7040
Maj Gen Tahiro Kurosa			

US Customs GARWOOD file
JUNE-81 Box cut Pinather

FEB-25-86 TOP secret info on [illegible]
[illegible] CAROLYN TOHN

NAME AND ADDRESS	TELEPHONE
JUNE-7-84	AREA CODE
745 pm Ronald	
called Ret. Peyton,	NUMBER
Greenberg, G. Bush,	AREA CODE
etc CIA AND [illegible]	
NEXT week	NUMBER
9-7-84 He call [illegible]	AREA CODE
that [illegible] agent Hugh Murray	NUMBER
will take Stand to say He doesn't no.	
COL, CONG Soc Huy NH	AREA CODE
OORS phones? VC,	
Pavels	NUMBER
[illegible]	AREA CODE
G.S.E w/ [illegible] Pilot	
Cy.S.E	NUMBER
BKL [illegible]	
Craig Fuller [illegible]	AREA CODE
Stapleton [illegible] CIA	NUMBER
818/ / DEA	

NAME AND ADDRESS	TELEPHONE
Bernard Hockel/	AREA CODE 203
265 college st #3E	
New Heaven, Conn 06510	NUMBER 562-401
Brent Carruth Atty.	AREA CODE 1-818-
Atty. for Richard craig	
espionage caio Smith	NUMBER 782-760
Ross ochney [illegible]	AREA CODE 1-805
LT. Col KUCKowicz	
of DiA got [illegible] WA	NUMBER 643-67
Jett McKay [illegible]	AREA CODE
1202 Keleuina St	
Kailua, Oahu HI	NUMBER 761-39
96734	AREA CODE
chris	NUMBER
Richardsman in House	
w/ B&B chief [illegible] CIA course	
Stanley Sporkin 202 357 611

[bottom left table]

father is Fed. Judge

NAME AND ADDRESS	TELEPHONE
American Housing Guild	AREA CODE
Alan Glick & Thomas Baxxyack	NUMBER
Saratoga Devp corp.	AREA CODE
CARL Thomas	
Allan Glick w/	NUMBER
mary Cornell [illegible]	AREA CODE
Benny dePhillps	
Thomas Barrack w/ [illegible]	NUMBER
DNAH FA/[illegible]	AREA CODE
Edwin G[illegible]	
JOHN Duff	NUMBER
LA COSTA	
Butcher shop	AREA CODE
APriL-13-84 5½ pm	NUMBER
FBI agent Tour White	
Bakersfield, [illegible] Menneo	AREA CODE
re Ref Ed moose	NUMBER
Inquiry on there are	
Stein atty investigation more	

NAME AND ADDRESS	TELEPHONE
Samuel P. King JR.	AREA CODE 1-808
Pacific trade Center	
#1360 Honolulu	NUMBER 521-693
HANK wong	AREA CODE 1-808
HI film comm	
	NUMBER 548-45
DEA Glenco Ga	AREA CODE 1-912-
Hugh Shannon	
Gil mora	NUMBER 267-278
LA office. 213-688-2650	AREA CODE
Operation "Condor"	NUMBER
Eisler found.	
Richard C Smith	AREA CODE
Dick C. Smith	
works Atlens CIA intell	NUMBER
for K&B. "82	AREA CODE
ASSoc of B&B	
George Lauder new PR CIA Dis	NUMBER

Received to Give GRITZ & CIA

NAME AND ADDRESS	TELEPHONE
Summit Corp Gospd Pus Cal - Cry	AREA CODE 213
	NUMBER 641-0641
1-702-733-0123 EXT 4290 & Ray Sec'rity D.V. OR chuck Betty CALIF Section	AREA CODE
Vac for Center tper 1-800-531-5803 Nestley Bestwishon	NUMBER
DAVID BROWN CIA w/ B&B	AREA CODE 702
Brussels Detroit Cub to Summa Vegas Security	NUMBER 369-4290
MR LEVVY for Meier MR GAY & MR DAVIS	AREA CODE
7-for 83' meeting Cox w/ C. Berry	NUMBER
RMM arrive home	AREA CODE 1-22
3654 Porcrest C12 South Motel L. Vegas J-Aug-2-83	NUMBER 45-1-5805

NAME AND ADDRESS	TELEPHONE
JOHN MEIER "Had F$ on stified Neha B.H. w/ 4 Thousand Circled co. "PLO CONTACT"	AREA CODE 1-604
	NUMBER 943-4561
Larry Cester & Lt Gritz Brenner, mike D.A. Set up Meier 1891c Robbie Robertson EXT 271 U.S. Marshalls	AREA CODE B.H. P.D. 213
	NUMBER 868-9711
CIAP George agency Circles BR Rigal MR Schuman Co MRS Smally Rockefeller pers secy & agent	AREA CODE
	NUMBER
LARRY FLYNT "Rebel" 1st issue Story on me 8509 Sunset Blvd #1 L.A. 90069	AREA CODE 1213-
	NUMBER 657-4224

ATF Agent Jeff Realing 5393

Jerry Jenkins 212-987-4025

NAME AND ADDRESS	TELEPHONE
ANTON KOSCHANY Asso. of MR Chernaski C 1-604-662-6000	AREA CODE 1-604
	NUMBER 432-6980
MR CHERNASKI CAÑADA News T.V. Steve DENN, R.F. phillipines	AREA CODE 1-604
	NUMBER 665-7454
CBW "Batman" writers CIA Hit Spec. for Overseas Agency Plots	AREA CODE summer 81
	NUMBER Plots
JOHN KWITNEY WALL ST. Journal Called 12-30-83 Re? 2Ritz, Reuho etc.?	AREA CODE 1-212 285-5000
	NUMBER 285-5141
JACK Father 213 LIZ ANDERSON 463-4400 E.T. NUSON Shelly NANCE 1723 WALNUT Ave Manhattan Beach CA. 90266	AREA CODE NUMBER

NAME AND ADDRESS	TELEPHONE
WESTERN Intelligence MR WALTER "WESTENTEL" FX 6704824 Charlie Stewart Called	AREA CODE 808
	NUMBER 946-6763
From ABC News N.Y. for CIA 11-13-84 8am PST republic Bill Colby & Harper TF-157 Africa for "BKK"	AREA CODE
	NUMBER
Defense indst. Security Inst. c/o DGSC Richmond VA. 23297	AREA CODE
	NUMBER
X-FBI Pete Jorgensen Los Angeles chief counsel Security Jive Bob Ingram John Hilton SI Cement former monitor	AREA CODE 1-213
	NUMBER 305-7011
	AREA CODE 212
	NUMBER 664-4444

MARK
TIM
fohlobel 1- 808-523-7412   202-456-1414
item# &LAST is from U.S. AFFAIRS CSC-1414

NAME AND ADDRESS	TELEPHONE	NAME AND ADDRESS	TELEPHO
TED SUTTER P.I.	AREA CODE 714 619	White House	1711 MESSAGE TO 1-202-456-
Diego IXA case Home	NUMBER 275-3905	D.C. President "Mike Wheeler" staff	1-202-395- SEC. NO.
5131 GARDENA ST. SAN DIEGO CA 92110	AREA CODE NUMBER	"BOB Simms"	2-395-69 NUMBER 3-85
Philiph Habib 202-647-3148		Rick Childress	AREA CODE
DAGO CONTRACT completed CA.	COFER BARN	NSC S.E. ASIA 202-395-3576	NUMBER
TERMO CIA DRUG BUST Home #	AREA CODE 1-808- NUMBER 254-1741		AREA CODE 808-5 NUMBER
Robert Smith esq 733 Bishop #2685 Honolulu 96817	AREA CODE 1-808- NUMBER 523-6411	1-404-434-4835 M.Gerry MAX Pohlabel Michael Sudberg HONG KONG Sticking BANK	AREA CODE NUMBER
Samual King TR SON of tewinst Judge in Hawaii also representing court ID	AREA CODE NUMBER	John Mayhew Hy. TEX Youbell Dev. BOB CIA #404 1111 Gerkist ST.	10-28 -60 682-0

NAME AND ADDRESS	TELEPHONE	NAME AND ADDRESS	TELEPHON
BARRY MAYSON PO BOX 375 West columbia, S.C. 29171	AREA CODE NUMBER AREA CODE NUMBER 602	Al Shinkle Hilo HI w/ INtel AF Red Shakley CRIT/CIA vegan in CALU BuenA CAPt. Cooper	AREA CODE General NUMBER AREA CODE 11-16-85 NUMBER 02-6
CIA 573-4111 Bob "Robert" Guccione owner penthouse world work on "Do" Hit Sq. Fox Clives CDO w/ Stein Marian Shelton 619-569-7435	AREA CODE NUMBER AREA CODE NUMBER LAPD AREA CODE	American TRAN AIR covert cargo thru-out S/Pacific region William Weaver	NUMBER AREA CODE 213 NUMBER 472-171 463-200
western Goals Mendell, VA. Pro-Right Dir. info corp. w/Dick CD Moose III Info Exp. R. Smith CIA B/PDID	LT. Rigo NUMBER-CIA SAC office Chief CD	Seymour Kersh office < Home 1199 NATIONAL Press Bldg. wash. D.C. 20045	AREA CODE 1-202- NUMBER 883-426 244-045 AREA CODE NUMBER

Professor Burt Pfeifer

NAME AND ADDRESS	TELEPHONE
Thomas O'Connor (206) university	243-4682 Disconnected
Denny "Bird" Dot Prosser	
Dresser Foundation INTERPOL DC	AREA CODE 1-212
McGolrick Bob Bennett called office	NUMBER 254-1061
Mike Wallace 3-29-82	AREA CODE 212
Bill 202-265-3413 (DC)	NUMBER 975-2991
Bill 212-674-3303 (W)	
Bill 202-265-3904	AREA CODE 212 503-0241
Coy 213-828-8852 Bill in NY	
Bill 212-724-5607	
FBI Debbie Wicherm	AREA CODE 202
she must classify my files under T.S. code	NUMBER 324-5534
Barry Mayson Youth Ministry P.O. Box 315 west columbia X. HeA. S.C. 29171	AREA CODE 803-791-7829

NAME AND ADDRESS	TELEPHONE
Robert Schwab c/o Davis	AREA CODE 204
1390 West Westly RD N.W.	NUMBER
Atlanta, GA 30327	351-1738
OR in thailand	AREA CODE Thail
Norman - Chano	NUMBER 391-2201 234-9753 234-8082
of NANA - Hotel	
"LAO UNDERGROUND"	AREA CODE 941-2211
WAYNE PARSONS 1-808-	NUMBER
-202-285-5407	
"GEN WORLD" BKK	AREA CODE 1-805-277
SUKHUMVIT ZEN	NUMBER 1(C) 4-11-86
"ATROPINE TO GIV."	AREA CODE
Vic ATF cover	ASD
8113 B. Houston OR	NUMBER ATF
Naya Bed Nui ct Kyle Nance	AREA CODE
Penny Lernoux CIA	NUMBER 212-556-5600
INAL Creative NY.NY.	

Gen Tighe home 203-569-6941

NAME AND ADDRESS	TELEPHONE
1-202-224-5225	AREA CODE
W, DC. Sen Judiciary	NUMBER
1-202-224-8248	
Duke Short	
Chief Invst	202- 329-9788
Larry Beck Fire	AREA CODE 1-916
tech Dru Bus Yes knew CIA	NUMBER 252-4171
Michael Bland G/B w/ CIA Vios & Cont	AREA CODE
Corita / Dennis	NUMBER
Robert Kelly fire & tech, ct oct-83 CIA	AREA CODE
Agent Slemy KBI Honolulu on Rewald case.	AREA CODE
Richard caught is cover	

NAME AND ADDRESS	TELEPHONE
LEXIS / NEXIS	AREA CODE 1-800-
Computer Data info	NUMBER 223-2437
American Data Bank Search files Debbie	AREA CODE 213-
U.S. Gov't info Bank network & public info Disinformation group	AREA CODE
JACK Gerwood SR 74-85 Bobby's DAD Mary Bobbys Aunt	812 818-966-4148 663-6260
Lexis Corp LA	AREA CODE 213 557-4790
THERESA Glocuster	AREA CODE 214
Gen. Tighe 1-818-359-3643	NUMBER 536-5034

two dozen ... Ronald # OR 8711 8.14.34

DOUG BALDWIN ... N04-9-82 ...

NAME AND ADDRESS	TELEPHONE
SONNY'S #1-415	AREA CODE
638-1-0352	NUMBER
AUNT MRS Newell	AREA CODE
213-830-0841	NUMBER
PAUL Scherdo 3-11-80	AREA CODE 213
ref with Case, also Hit	NUMBER
Shot in Head when Debris Kills	656-5623
Melvin Belli, 1w	AREA CODE 415
Attney for TCU Ridged	NUMBER
1-213-277-3612 Belli Office	981-1849
ted FRigaRD movie	AREA CODE 808
Hi 300,000-BB	NUMBER 734-3618
	808
SONNY church Hi	AREA CODE 1-808
mui church paStor	NUMBER 261-7715

NAME AND ADDRESS	TELEPHONE
DOUG STRATTON	AREA CODE 714
PO Bx	NUMBER 396-380
Kernville 93238	AREA CODE
HE cAReL 1-805-395	
REWARD/NUMBER 9377	NUMBER
Della Torre # to BKK	AREA CODE
GOLDEN "T"	
DAVE Norman M MEIH CA. Office	NUMBER
NAVEL COMM. 408-984-6045	AREA CODE 916
+ RD Mathews	NUMBER 973-05
RANDY SANFORD	AREA CODE 28
372-0247	NUMBER 705
AARON'S Steph Surgan	AREA CODE 1808
	NUMBER 263-456
LIZA BERNARD CCB	

Mike ACKERMAN CIA operative

MERI NICIAD

NAME AND ADDRESS	TELEPHONE
Athy Slobodin	AREA CODE 212
7 BC News 77 West 66th	NUMBER
ST New York NY	887-7777
MR & MRS HARRY SCHWARTFEGER	AREA CODE CA 92307
18710 OTONIAN RD Apple Valley	NUMBER 241-242
Kathys parons	4516
JANIT SAongrums PrANG	AREA CODE 05
K 25 SuWANSORN RD	NUMBER 221134
AYANYAO (ALWEST, thAILANO	231224
PAUL's Home 252-5442 (thAILANO)	AREA CODE
#5702	NUMBER 98204
1304 BRushwood RD Everett WT	
JASON-TON Slave	AREA CODE 808
50 WAIOHULIST #M	NUMBER
Kihei, MAUi, 96953	879-9188
TONY SerrA	AREA CODE 415
HT Atty. 3rd FLOOR	NUMBER
473 JACKSON ST	986-5591
SAN FRANCISCO, CA 94111	

NAME AND ADDRESS	TELEPHONE
Schurbrock Jane : Sharry	AREA CODE 213
445 hermosa Ave	374-4825
hermosa Bch CA 90254	NUMBER
Ron Schurbrock	AREA CODE
RFR #	NUMBER
Centerville, Indiana 47330	
Randy Sanford (372-0247)	AREA CODE 13
	NUMBER 206-355
CA 90249 (anthson)	
LOR. Simpson 1304 Brushwood Everett wa	206-355-712
104 116th PL S.E. 98204	206-355-5413
Everett WA 98204	206-553-1629
Kathy Shelton CSU3	AREA CODE 1
4020 W. 234th PL	NUMBER
Torrance CA 90505	
Sharon (work)	AREA CODE 808
E walipula 3RD news	NUMBER 879 847

Secret Consl. Brian Jenkin
Belisca

NAME AND ADDRESS	TELEPHONE
Ron Toly	AREA CODE 213 324-4130
2403 Tomlee	
Torrance, Ca. 90503	NUMBER 316-2797
Winter Skiles (Dausler Skiio)	AREA CODE
O BOX AT	
Aihia, Kona HI 96740	NUMBER
Melis Saldana	AREA CODE 808
PO Box 301	
Swi, Maui Hi 96753	NUMBER 879-8462
Toni ; Jason Spons	AREA CODE 808 (868)
97 Mohan St Kihei	
	NUMBER 879-9198
Joe 'N Stewart	AREA CODE 1808
1241 Nanamuki St	NUMBER 879 596.2
Kihei Maui HI 96753	
Ron Stratton	AREA CODE 1-805
PO Box 250 (900)	NUMBER 582-2970
Hornville, Ca 93235	
Booth: Bunny ro.	

LA COSTA "Songy"
(800-542-6200)

NAME AND ADDRESS	TELEPHONE
Len, Sno thurber	AREA CODE
18804 Pat Ronella Ave	NUMBER 526 Sautos 97
Torrance CA 90504	
cousin Steve Ross	AREA CODE 714 371
Cawshy Bros Cassy cost	NUMBER 540-2943
Haii, thrills 7-3-85 shut	
A Melis Saldana	AREA CODE 201
71 Jackson St	NUMBER 47-9896
Passic NJ 07055	
Norm Khang/Bonnie/Sue 2()	
	NUMBER 377-7731
Irish 3422 marengo #123	AREA CODE (213) 371-6694
to 15.	NUMBER 615-9368
parents	378-5422
Linda Tongo	AREA CODE 213
2049 Rockinhorse VR	NUMBER
San Pedro CA 90732	832-6541

NAME AND ADDRESS	TELEPHONE
Toni: Jo Anderson	AREA CODE
Inn & Naturalist Ser.	NUMBER
Terminal Is. S. Pedro	
CA. 90731	AREA CODE
Roper: Feru	NUMBER
"Do not open in mail Run"	AREA CODE
BBC London England	
01-743-1272 T.V. "Horizon"	NUMBER
011-441 Jochim Taylor 01-705-5578	
Melichman	AREA CODE 213
Cevegy & Lorie Costick 90278	NUMBER
1613 Herkin St. RB cd	374-4736
Kato West end	AREA CODE 214 Hell's Angel Co.
Bearflag Oasis Co. 3	NUMBER 954-0233
Fine Gem Project "Alliance"	
Australia	NUMBER
Dan Arnold c/o Univ Bonica	
Laos c/ U.P. to Phoun, Nasavan	

NAME AND ADDRESS	TELEPHONE
Stylo "D"	AREA CODE 213
7-2-85 Ron called	NUMBER 271-6356
New #	526
Jill ; Terry Mayo	AREA CODE 808 97
333 N. Kanalu	NUMBER 263-4287
Kailua, oahu Hi	371
David Crook	AREA CODE 213 66-1547
LA Times Reforma	NUMBER 223-1988
1-800-LA Tms	
David Toma	AREA CODE V. cop Christian
Box 854	NUMBER
Clark New Jersey 07066	AREA CODE
C/c Paul Nick	
Duscoy Drow Ceward	NUMBER
I cliah climare (N.J.)	
Def goobs's	AREA CODE
Bill Rove II/D	NUMBER

Top Left Card

mikhail Gorbachev — *not by 8-27-85 on Point*

NAME AND ADDRESS	TELEPHONE
Li'l Col Kham Ouane DOUANGPHRACHANH 57014 PRACHACK Road Nongkhai THAILAND	AREA CODE
PATRICK P. KHAMVONGSA Royal Laos A. Force 1140 S. Bristol S.AA.	NUMBER ←
maj Chu mo 1-714-551-9520	AREA CODE
KAYSONE Phanvihan on POW 714-848-5590 (POS)	NUMBER w PNSR on POW AREA CODE POW?
Col Vang Yee 3 Bus. 714-539-1184	NUMBER
Li'l col Soukan 3 SOUNTTHONE 204 Amphun B ANTHENG NAISI NIPHANOM THAILAND	AREA CODE
JERRY DANIEL UP LBO Buddy 4LB3OR	NUMBER

Top Right Card

Kyckouya?... SARS ; Do Km

NAME AND ADDRESS	TELEPHONE
Gen VAN PAO 134 LAST CONFERENCE Laos UNDERGROUND 9-13-85	AREA CODE 714-556- NUMBER
Gen VANG TRUE	406-961-
Gen PATHAMMEVONG Laos underground or Gen Pheng Xhao	AREA CODE 714 NUMBER 546 539-118
Laos Family center	AREA CODE 714
Col Vangee 14095 Euclid underground. Garden Grove	NUMBER 556-95
Gen Private LA. Line 406-961-4397	AREA CODE 714
DIA Personnel 202 393-2677	546-43
STAN Mullin X MARAL Wasch Congressman DORNAN's office	AREA CODE 213 NUMBER 642-511
Vanpho Office 14095 Euclid Garden Grove (Gen Hmm HSO)	AREA CODE Co mill NUMBER CIA 1985 515-231

Bottom Left Card

nonil(Bos) *DAVID MAY/187 (Course)*

NAME AND ADDRESS	TELEPHONE
LUANG PHO Phay Phachon 1068 WAT NAISOKE NONG Khai, THAILAND	AREA CODE 703-896-1357 NUMBER
(Rev/Heather) Cii Sue John, Reserve	AREA CODE 320 NUMBER 5035 #
Steve WERMAN 1-305-284-2204 50 post University of miami P.O. Box 248248, cova FLA 284-3973	AREA CODE 305 School 305 1200
(Bruce Alvaren w 33124 Scot Bradley will be AAA to Emily urmi au ?	AREA CODE 305 NUMBER 284 3977 STEVE
also DDD Huro 1-305-646-5607 Steve WERMAN Steve WERMAN 305 84	AREA CODE NUMBER
012 305 Steve ORZ Home 305-375-98355 + new 551- UH 4LB3OR	AREA CODE NUMBER

Bottom Right Card

maj APODACA US ARMY on POW — *CT N 1-800-257-133*

NAME AND ADDRESS	TELEPHONE
STEVE WERMAN 3323 SCADLOCK LN SHERMAN OAKS CA 91403	AREA CODE 213 NUMBER
BARRY WAINE 3141 Second AVE 360 A1 Ave Chula VISTA CA 92010	AREA CODE NUMBER
Doris RIes (Church Sister) 1336 P.O. Box Kihei, maui HI 96353	AREA CODE NUMBER
MARK Williams 45 Nohokai ST Kihei maui HI 96753	AREA CODE 808 NUMBER 879-606
FRANK & JOY 758-0966 7820 AIRPORT BLVD WESTCHESTER CA. 90045	AREA CODE -213- NUMBER 649-375
MRS WATU Rm 344 A PO Box Lwa CA 73285	AREA CODE 4 619 NUMBER 376-6152
595-231	

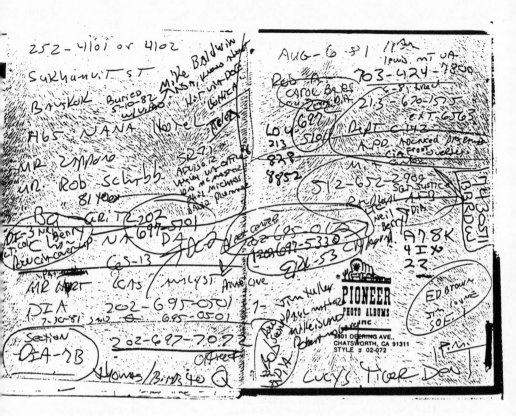

May 31st, 1986

Dennis W. Bartow, Publisher
Daring Books
2020 Ninth St., S.W.
Canton, Ohio 44706

Dear Mr. Bartow,

As a long-standing activist in MIA matters, I was nothing short of amazed to see a copy of your May 2nd letter defending Scott Barnes. I don't know who you talked to or what pressures were brought to bear, but I can tell you from personal involvement that Mr. Barnes is nothing more than a scam artist and charlatan of the first order.

Mr. Barnes (and "Akuna Jack" Bailey, I might add) were accurately portrayed in "Heroes Who Fell From Grace" and, as you undoubtably know, the book has played to good reviews. For you to now do a turn-about and attempt to portray Scott Barnes as a committed activist will only further confuse the issue.

I have done considerable background research on Mr. Barnes and have had a number of personal conversations with him. I'm familiar with all of the "landmarks" his defenders point out - the positive polygraph, truth serum, etc. I would invite your attention to the fact that the polygraph is not a definitive measurement of truth, and in fact is prohibited in many states. "Truth serum," as most familiar with the drug will tell you, is shaky at best. His affadavit, if you've seen it, speaks for itself, as does his testimony at the Senate Hearing.

Undoubtably one of the people you've heard from is one David Taylor, a BBC representative in Washington, D.C. Mr. Taylor himself has been the source of considerable disinformation with regard to the MIA issue - which I know from personal involvement with him. My guess is that his journalistic instincts got the better of him, and the truth be damned.

In short, I found Scott Barnes to be a liar of the first order, who can supply no substantiation for his allegations. The missions in which Barnes alleges he participated never happened - it's pure fantasy. Please do not allow this individual to continue to obfuscate the MIA issue by endorsing his ever-changing allegations.

I would be happy to discuss this matter with you further.

Yours truly,

F. C. BROWN

Nov 31st. 1986

Daring Books

(216) 454-7519

2020 Ninth Street, S.W. • Canton, Ohio 44706

Dennis W. Bartow, Publisher

6 June 1986

F.C. Brown
U.S.N.H., Subic Bay Box 15
FPO San Francisco 96652-1600

Dear Mr. Brown,

Thank you for your letter concerning your opinion of Mr. Scott Barnes.

The turn about in the authors and my opinion was based on conversations with many credible people, not just a few, and their verification of the position on Scott Barnes is far greater than what is available to disprove him.

The reference to Scott Barnes in THE HEROES WHO FELL FROM GRACE is but a small part and we did not feel it was appropriate to try and fight for something that could not be easily supported.

I do not seek to confuse the issue, there are enough other people making their contributions over the years to do this, but I seek truth where and with whom it seems to be.

The information you shared in your letter presents nothing new to me. If you have examples of Mr. Barnes contradicting himself from first hand experience I would be very interested in it. I do not want hear say or third party information, this has already caused me to much trouble.

I sincerely appreciate your involvement in this issue and I hope that each of us can have a part in enhancing the release and accountability of our fighting men as soon as possible.

Sincerely,

Dennis W. Bartow
Publosher

June 17th, 1986

Dennis M. Bartow, Publisher
Daring Books
2030 Ninth Street, S.W.
Canton, Ohio 44706

Dear Mr. Bartow,

Thank you for your letter of June 6th.

I presume you passed a copy of my previous letter along to David Taylor of WJW. He called me on June 10th, and left the following message:

"I have received your letter regarding the work on MIA question. The WJW resents the criticism in this matter and is very concerned if anyone else was info'd about the letter? If so, the WJW will sue for slander. A copy of the letter was forwarded to Naval Intelligence in Washington. In regards to the letter, the WJW report on Scott Barnes Affair has been supported by three government services."

Unfortunately, I was not in when Taylor called, but his message was passed along to me. He knows he is on very shaky ground with Barnes, hence his veiled threat to "sue for slander." I react poorly to threats. If he thinks he has a case, he should go for it.

My first contact with Taylor was last summer, at my initiation. I was advised that he had "checked Barnes out" and was a believer in his story. I called him up, we chatted for an hour or so, and ended on the note that, since we were only located across the river from one another, perhaps we might pursue the discussion over lunch one day soon.

Several months later, he passed along to several members of the "Bambo Faction" the information that I was a DIA agent. He even went so far as to give them a telephone number, which he said was to my office in the Pentagon. What prompted that, I'm not sure, but it was totally untrue, and at that point I started having second thoughts about Taylor. He has continued the charade in recent months, stating that his "sources" had checked me out and that I worked for U.S. intelligence.

What is Taylor's motivation? Good question. Possibly he smells a good story. As you can appreciate, people in the media not only report the news, sometimes they create it as well. I have a copy of the film he shot on Scott Barnes. It is ludicrous, and, should it appear, it will be laughed off the screen.

I have had personal dealings with Scott Barnes, and can cite numerous examples - not only of him contradicting himself, but of outright fabrication. However, at this point I find myself asking, what good would it do if I presented it to you? You have already sent out a letter saying you believe Barnes, and that he was maligned in the book. If I succeed in convincing you, will you then put out another letter saying that the book is correct, afterall? I think not. However, it's very possible I might be back Stateside soon, and would be happy to discuss the matter with you at that time.

In conclusion, let me say that I can appreciate the problems you've had thus far over the Barnes entry. His supporters tend to be very vocal, with threats to sue, etc. What they don't realize is that they have turned the MIA issue on its head, making the U.S. government the bad guy, instead of the Vietnamese. While I'll be the first to agree that the U.S. government is not blameless in this matter, they certainly have not sent "hit teams" out to gun down POWs still in Viet hands, as Barnes alleges. As they say, the proof is in the pudding. I challenge you to meet with Barnes for a half hour and let him spin his tale of intrigue and derring-do. Then tell me if you'd hire him to mow your lawn, let alone rescue POWs.

Kindest regards,

J. C. Brown

F. C. BROWN
~~48. Reed Avenue~~
~~Hamilton Township, NJ 08610~~
~~Tel. 609-394-0400~~

November 10th, 1986

Dennis W. Bartow, Publisher
Daring Books
2020 Ninth St., S.W.
Canton, Ohio 44706

Dear Mr. Bartow,

It has come to my attention that Daring Books is in the process of publishing a book by Scott T. Barnes. Further, I am informed that I will appear in the book, portrayed as an "intelligence agent" of the United States government.

I attempted to put these nonsensical rumors to rest in my letter of June 17th, 1986, but apparently you have chosen to ignore my letter. I therefore am writing to tell you that, should I appear in any context in Mr. Barnes' forthcoming book, I intend to file suit against you, the publisher.

You will be receiving a follow-up letter from my attorney in the very near future.

Yours truly,

F. C. BROWN

F. C. BROWN
U.S.N.H., SUBIC BAY
BOX ▪ 5
FPO SAN FRANCISCO
96652-1600

MAILGRAM SERVICE CENTER
MIDDLETOWN, VA. 22645
23AM

4-041346S204002 07/23/85 ICS IPMRNCZ CSP FSOC
1 6193763249 MGM TDRN KERNVILLE CA 07-23 0558P EST

SCOTT T BARNES
PO BOX 704
KERNVILLE CA 93238

THIS IS A CONFIRMATION COPY OF THE FOLLOWING MESSAGE:

6193763249 MGMB TDRN KERNVILLE CA 142 07-23 0558P EST
ZIP
LIEUT. COLONEL HOWARD HILL
OFFICE OF THE ASSISTANT SECRETARY OF DEFENSE
FOR INTERNATIONAL SECURITY AFFAIRS
THE PENAGON ROOM 4-C839
WASHINGTON DC 20301-2400

DEAR COLONEL HILL

THANK YOU FOR AT LEAST TRYING TO LOOK INTO THE FACTS SURROUNDING THE
POW SITUATION YOU AND I DISCUSSED ON THE TELEPHONE YESTERDAY. AS I
INDICATED TO YOU. THERE WOULD BE MUCH DISINFORMATION SURROUNDING
MYSELF ON THIS MATTER AND THAT YOU WOULD RUN INTO PEOPLE MORE
POWERFUL THAN YOURSELF. I REGRET THAT YOUR NOT MAN ENOUGH TO STAND UP
FOR HONESTY AND INTEGRITY ON THIS ISSUE. I WISH YOU THE BEST IN YOUR
CAREER MY ONLY MOTIVES ARE THE RELEASE OF U.S. PERSONNEL BEING HELD
IN SOUTHEAST ASIA.

RESPECTFULLY SUBMITTED.

SCOTT T BARNES

P.S. SOLDIER OF FORTUNE MAGAZINE IS NOTORIOUS FOR DECENTFUL
INFORMATION. AFTER ALL I'M THE ONLY ONE THAT HAS PASSED POLYGRAPH AND
HAVE OTHER EVIDENCE.

1801 EST

MGMCOMP MGM

4-0528185059002 02/28/86 ICS IPMRNCZ CSP ESOC
1 6193766091 MGM TDRN KERNVILLE CA 02-28 0803P EST

SCOTT T. BARNES
PO BOX 704
KERNVILLE CA 93238

THIS IS A CONFIRMATION COPY OF THE FOLLOWING MESSAGE:

6193766091 MGMB TDRN KERNVILLE CA 148 02-28 0803P EST
ZIP
DAVID TAYLOR
BBC, 2030 M STREET NW SUITE 607
WASHINGTON DC 20036

DAVID
THIS WILL PRECEED THE WRITTEN LETTER. THIS IS TO CONFIRM SPECIAL
AGENT DAVE HALL US DEPARTMENT OF DEFENSE IG 202-746-0256 CONFIRMS
THAT PHILLIP HABIB WAS UNDER INVESTIGATION FOR NARCOTICS AND
PROSTITUTION INVOLVEMENT. IN ADDITION THERE WAS A CLASSIFIED MEMO
FROM A US MILITARY GENERAL WHO ALSO CONFIRMED THIS. SECRETARY
ARMITAGE PLAYED A KEY ROLE ALONG WITH OTHERS WE KNOW ABOUT.
US STATE DEPT SPECIAL AGENT MARK MCMANON US STATE DEPT 202-647-3192
TOLD ME IN PERSON FEBRUARY 27, 1986, AT APPROXIMATELY 4:40PM PST
ASSISTANT SECRETARY TO DEFENSE RICHARD ARMITAGE WAS UNDER
INVESTIGATION. THEY HAD CONFIRMED HE WAS DEEPLY INVOLVED IN THE
SOUTHEAST ASIAN PROSTITUTION RING. HOWEVER, ALL EFFORTS TO BRING
JUSTICE HAD BEEN CURTAILED AT THE HIGHEST LEVELS.
OTHERS DISCUSSED AT THE MEETING WERE ARNOLD, M DANIELS, D DANIELS,
MOBERG, MATHER, CUTENZHON, DONOVAN, SHOUP.
SINCERELY
  SCOTT T. BARNES

2005 EST

MGMCOMP MGM

TO REPLY BY MAILGRAM MESSAGE, SEE REVERSE SIDE FOR WESTERN UNION'S TOLL - FREE PHONE NUMBERS

INTRAVEST INTERNATIONAL INVESTIGATIONS
P.O. BOX 704 - KERNVILLE, CA 93238
619-376-6091

UC #AA011290

AMSTERDAM

ATHENS

BANGKOK

BRUSSELS

CAIRO

LONDON

PARIS

ROME

TEL AVIV

TOKYO

ZURICH

Office of The General Counsel
Dept. of Defense
Pentagon, Washington, D.C. 20301

March-4-86

Chapman B. Cox

Dear General Counsel

I spoke with Col. Venzi from Asst. Sect. of Defense of The Defense Dept. f
Asst. Scet. Richard Armitage office at approx 4:30 P.M. PST today March 4-86
g an investigation into Mr. armitage involvement in a prostitution ring with
viet namese sisters, and this col. recommended I write to you.

Last week I met with some U.S. State Dept. Special Agents one whom said he
ated mr. Armitage involvement in this ring, and in fact confirmed it but th
criminal case was coming due to the Bureau in Washington D.C. I d like to
why if a U.S. ASST. SECT. of Defense was involved in criminal conduct was it
being covered up.?????

Sincerely,

Investigator, Scott T. Barnes

1-800 - 325-600

MAILGRAM SERVICE CENTER
MIDDLETOWN, VA. 22645
04PM

4-0487855063002 03/04/86 ICS IPMRNCZ CSP FSOC
1 6193766001 MGM TDRN KERNVILLE CA 03-04 0842P EST

SCOTT T BARNES INVESTIGATOR INTRAVEST
INTERNATIONAL INVESTIGATIONS
PO BOX 704
KERNVILLE CA 93238

THIS IS A CONFIRMATION COPY OF THE FOLLOWING MESSAGE:

6193766001 MGMB TDRN KERNVILLE CA 121 03-04 0842P EST
ZIP
OFFICE OF THE GENERAL COUNSEL
DEPT OF DEFENSE
ATTN CHAPMAN B COX
PENTAGON
WASHINGTON DC 20301

DEAR GENERAL COUNSEL

I WAS RECOMMENDED TO WRITE TO YOU BY COLONELVENZI FROM ASSISTANT
SECRETARY OF DEFENSE RICHARD ARMITAGE'S OFFICE TODAY REGARDING THE
UNITED STATES STATE DEPARTMENT INVESTIGATION INTO HIS INVOLVEMENT
WITH TWO VIETNAMESE SISTERS WHO ARE INVOLVED IN A PROSTITUTION RING.
I WAS VISITED LAST WEEK BY U.S STATE DEPARTMENT PERSONNEL WHO
CONFIRMED SECRETARY ARMITAGE WAS IN FACT INVOLVED IN A PROSTITUTION
RING WITH THE VIETNAMESE SISTERS. I WOULD LIKE TO INQUIRE AS TO WHY
SECRETARY ARMITAGE HAS NOT BEEN INDICTED AND IF THERE IS ANY SORT OF
GOVERNMENT COVERUP. SINCERELY
        SCOTT T BARNES INVESTIGATOR INTRAVEST INTERNATIONAL INVESTIGATIONS
        PO BOX 704
        KERNVILLE CA 93238

2045 EST

MGMCOMP MGM

TO REPLY BY MAILGRAM MESSAGE, SEE REVERSE SIDE FOR WESTERN UNION'S TOLL - FREE PHONE NUMBERS

𝒯𝒽e District of Columbia Bar
OFFICE OF PUBLIC SERVICE ACTIVITIES
1707 L Street, N.W., Sixth Floor
Washington, D.C. 20036-4202
(202) 331-4365

Pro Bono Progr

February 28, 1986

Leslie Gielow
Law Clerk to
  Judge Oberdorfer
U.S. District Court for the
  District of Columbia
Washington, D.C. 20001

✓
FILED

MAR 27 1986

CLERK, U.S. DISTRICT COURT
DISTRICT OF COLUMBIA

Re: Scott Barnes
CA. No. 85-3719

Dear Ms. Gielow:

From time to time, this office is unable to find legal counsel willing to get involved in a particular case. Unfortunately, we have not been able to locate an attorney to represent the plaintiff in the above referenced action.

I am sorry that we have been unable to assist the Court in this matter. The only suggestion that I can make is that the Court migh appoint someone.

Sincerely,

Leslie Henriquez
Pro Bono Legal Assistant

ATTACHMENT

UNITED STATES DISTRICT COURT
FOR THE DISTRICT OF COLUMBIA

FILED

MAR 2 7 1986

CLERK, U.S. DISTRICT COURT
DISTRICT OF COLUMBIA

SCOTT T. BARNES,)
)
Plaintiff,)
)
v.)   Civil Action No. 85-3719
)
WILLIAM J. CASEY, et al.,)
)
Defendants.)

ORDER

On March 13, 1986, this Court issued an Order advising
plaintiff Scott Barnes that he had failed to effect proper
service on defendants and directing him to effect such service
within 15 days or to advise the Court as to why service had not
been made. In a letter dated March 15, plaintiff stated that he
lacked the funds necessary to serve defendants, and that he had
previously been informed by the Court that the case would be
handled on a pro bono basis. Judge Oberdorfer attempted, through
the Lawyer's Referral Service, to have counsel appointed for
plaintiff, without success. See attached letter of Leslie
Henriquez, Pro Bono Legal Assistant, District of Columbia Bar.
This Court appreciates that plaintiff wishes to prosecute this
action and that he apparently lacks the financial ability to do
so. Nevertheless, it declines to force local counsel to represent plaintiff in this matter. Accordingly, plaintiff must
promptly obtain counsel (or be prepared to fully and appropriately represent himself pro se). Proper service as to each
defendant must be affected within thirty (30) days of this Order,
or this case shall stand dismissed without prejudice.
SO ORDERED this 27th day of March, 1986.

JOYCE HENS GREEN
United States District Judge

68-C

Scott T. Barnes
13 Spruce Street
P.O. Box 704
Kernville, California 93238

SCOTT T. BARNES
_____

vs.

WILLIAM J. CASEY, et al.
_____

Case No. Civil Action No. 85-3719

Please be advised that the above entitled case in which you are counsel has, by direction of the Calendar Committee, been reassigned to Judge   Joyce Hens Green
_____
for all purposes.

Sincerely yours,

JAMES F. DAVEY, Clerk

By: Joe A. Wood, Jr.
_____
Deputy Clerk

cc: Case File

CO-310
Rev.6/79

College

July 1986

To Whom It May Concern:

Scott Barnes has been an excellent member of our staff for over the past year. Scott's ability to communicate ideas, as well as initiate productive changes within the program, has made him an invaluable instructor at   College. We will miss his efforts.

I truly believe that the excellence that Scott brought to the Security Program at   College will be found in any endeavor that Scott desires to do.

Sincerely,

William R. Petty
Supervisor Law Enforcement/Private Security

July 25, 1986

To Whom It May Concern:

At the request of Scott Barnes, I am writing to express my personal admiration for the courageous stand he has taken in regards to the issue of American prisoners of war who are still held in Southeast Asia.

Scott Barnes appears to me to be a dedicated young man who is honestly attempting to help free the men left behind after the Vietnam War. I have seen a massive effort to discredit Mr. Barnes by some one in the government bureaucracy who does not want him to talk publicly about his belief that the government knows of the existence of these POW's.

It seems to me that Mr. Barnes has paid a very high price for his courage and that he deserves a chance to prove himself trustworthy.

Eugene B. McDaniel
President

4-013205D217-013 08/05/86 ICS IPMMTZZ CSP FOSB
SUSPECTED DUPLICATE: 4-0389345217002 ICS IPMMTZZ CSP
1 6193763249 MGM TDMT KEARNVILLE CA 08-05 0522P EST

SCOTT T BARNES
PO BOX 704
KEARNVILLE CA 93238

THIS IS A CONFIRMATION COPY OF THE FOLLOWING MESSAGE:

 6193763249 MGMS TDMT KEARNVILLE CA 174 08-05 0522P EST
ZIP
VICE-PRESIDENT GEORGE BUSH
WHITE HOUSE, WEST WING
WASHINGTON DC 20500
DEAR MR. VICE-PRESIDENT,
AFTER A LENGTHY CONVERSATION WITH YOUR OFFICE TODAY REGARDING THE
CURRENT POW/MIA AFFAIR, I AM NOW MORE CONVINCED THAT YOU PERSONALLY
ARE NOT RECEIVING THE ENTIRE FACTS OR TRUTH ON MY INVOLVEMENT ON AN
'81 RESCUE MISSION AND MY SWORN TESTIMONY BEFORE THE U.S. SENATE
COMMITTEE. IN ALL DUE RESPECT, I WOULD ASK THAT YOU EXECUTE YOUR
POWER AND AUTHORITY TO BRING ALL MEMBERS INVOLVED IN THIS MISSION TO
TESTIFY UNDER OATH AND THOSE THAT LIE BE FULLY PROSECUTED. AS YOU ARE
WELL AWARE, I HAVE TAKEN AND PASSED NUMEROUS POLYGRAPH EXAMINATIONS
CONDUCTED BY A MEMBER OF THE GENERAL TIGHE AND H. ROSS PEROT POW
COMMISSION. IN ADDITION, I HAVE BEEN SUBJECTED TO SODIUM AMOTHAL
(TRUTH SERUM), WHICH WAS WITNESSED BY FEDERAL COURT REPORTERS, AND
PASSED THAT. MY CONVERSATION ON TODAY WITH YOUR OFFICE CERTAINLY
INDICATES YOUR AIDES AND MILITARY ADVISORS ARE NOT INFORMING YOU OF
THE TRUE FACTS. IN GOD'S NAME, WILL YOU PLEASE RESOLVE THIS ISSUE.
SINCERELY,
  SCOTT T. BARNES

22:04 EST

MGMCOMP

THE WHITE HOUSE

WASHINGTON

September 17, 1985

Dear Mr. Barnes:

Your September 9, 1985 letter to Fred Fielding regarding your
request for an investigation of the POW rescue mission conducted
by Lt. Col. Gritz and the Rewald case has been referred to me for
response.

As in the case of your earlier correspondence, your letter has
been forwarded to the Assistant Attorney General, Criminal
Division, U.S. Department of Justice, for whatever action, if
any, he deems appropriate.

Sincerely,

David B. Waller
Senior Associate Counsel
to the President

Mr. Scott T. Barnes
Post Office Box 704
Kernville, CA 93238

NATIONAL BRIEFS

Reagan asks Dallas billionaire to assess POW situation in Asia

DALLAS — President Reagan has asked Dallas billionaire H. Ross Perot to find out if any U.S. servicemen still are held captive in Southeast Asia, and if so, to recommend a way to bring them home safely.

"The president and the vice president asked me to dig into this issue — go all the way to the bottom of it and figure out what the situation was — then come see them and give them my recommendations," Perot told the *Dallas Morning News* yesterday.

Perot, who has said in the past that he believes some Americans remain prisoner in Southeast Asia, refused to elaborate.

"I'm just working away," he said. "I really can't talk about it."

Perot also declined to say whether he might act on his own to free any of the remaining POWs or if he was limited solely to recommending a course of action to the White House.

Those working with him say Perot has brought together an informal group of experts that includes at least two retired generals and some former Vietnam-era prisoners of war.

A6 Thurs., Sept. 4, 1986   The Bakersfield Californian

Tycoon offered to pay to prove MIAs in Laos

WASHINGTON (AP) — Texas billionaire H. Ross Perot, after conferring with Vice President George Bush, pledged $4.2 million in a futile effort to obtain a videotape purporting to show American prisoners of war alive in Laos.

"I was asked by our government to pursue this thing, to get the tape if it existed," Perot said in a recent telephone interview. "I said fine, it's a long shot, but I'll be glad to do it."

The tape was never produced and the money was never paid.

Perot refused to identify who in the government asked him to pursue the matter.

Marlin Fitzwater, spokesman for Bush, said Wednesday that the vice president discussed the tape with Perot and asked him to "take a look at the issues there and see if he thought they were legitimate."

But Fitzwater added that "I'm sure he (Bush) didn't ask him to make payments."

Also involved in the effort was Rep. Bill Hendon, R-N.C., who said Wednesday that he discussed the videotape matter with Bush and that later "the vice president called me and, based on our discussion, I tried to assist Mr. Perot in any way I could."

According to a former Army major who first told the story of the tape, the money was on deposit in the Bank of America in Singapore last April when he attempted to obtain photographic evidence that Americans were still being held prisoner.

Retired Maj. Mark Smith told the Senate Veterans Affairs Committee last June that he and Hendon went to Singapore with instructions from the Defense Intelligence Agency to offer $4.2 million to Robin Gregson, a British citizen who claimed to have the videotape.

Smith told the committee that Gregson, who also uses the name John Obassy, rejected the offer.

Smith testified that Gregson told him, "I didn't ask you for $4.2 million in cash. I asked you for support for these people in Laos. I have never asked for money."

The people in Laos were rebel forces fighting the communist government.

The major also told the committee he had seen the tape and that it showed Caucasians being held prisoner and forced to work in timber and mining operations in northern Laos.

The Defense Department lists 2,441 Americans who did not return

H. Ross Perot
...videotape "will-o'-the-wisp"

from the conflict in Southeast Asia.

In its monthly tally of reports pertaining to possible POWs, the Defense Intelligence Agency lists 881 cases of alleged sightings of live Americans being held prisoner since the fall of Saigon in 1975.

The latest Defense Intelligence tally lists 136 of that total as currently unresolved. The agency said the remainder were disproven.

Perot said of the videotape: "Like everything else around the POW-MIA thing, it's a will-o'-the-wisp."

The Dallas computer magnate first became involved in the POW issue in 1969 when he attempted to fly to Hanoi to deliver medical supplies and Christmas dinners to American POWs. He also financed a successful 1979 rescue mission to Iran to free two of his employees from a Tehran prison.

"The fact that we have one American, a Special Forces major, who says he has seen the tape, makes it more than just some bogus thing floating out there in Asia," Perot said.

"The basic steps involved were to produce the tape, see the tape and if in fact the tape was what it was purported to be, at that point, pay for the tape and have it available to our government," he added. "So it was a kind of reasonably fail-safe process, in that you got (a chance) to look before you leaped."

Jurisdiction Challenged

2B   THE FAYETTEVILLE OBSERVER, Thursday, November 6, 1986

Judge Considers Ruling In POW Suit

By JASON BRADY
Staff writer

A U.S. district judge again will consider whether the federal court system has jurisdiction in a lawsuit accusing the federal government of not doing enough to seek the release of Americans who may be prisoners in Southeast Asia.

U.S. District Judge Terrence W. Boyle ruled in June that parts of a suit filed against the Reagan administration by former Special Forces Intelligence operatives Mark A. Smith and Melvin C. McIntire have merit in federal court. Ggovernment prosecutors argued that the issue deals with foreign policy and should be handled in that realm.

Government attorneys asked Boyle to reconsider his rulings during 2½ hours of arguments Wednesday in Elizabeth City.

According to Fayetteville attorney Mark Waple, who represents the plaintiffs in the case, Boyle made no ruling, but asked that both sides provide more information within five days before he again rules.

Waple said that for the first time, U.S. attorneys expressed concern about where plaintiffs would be allowed to review information now in the possession of the government. "The government expressed concern about privileged and classified information," Waple said.

And for "prudential" reasons, U.S. Attorney Virginia Strasser also asked Boyle that the court abstain from the issue, Waple said. Efforts to reach U.S. attorneys failed.

Retired Maj. Smith is a former prisoner of war captured in Cambodia, and along with retired SFC McIntire, claims that Americans are still held in Vietnam, Laos and Cambodia. Their allegations are based on information they gathered during intelligence operations in Southeast Asia.

Smith and McIntire, since their initial filing of the suit in September 1985, have testified before numerous congressional committees.

Boyle in his first decision ruled that Smith and McIntire did not have standing to sue and dismissed them from the action. Since the suit was filed, however, about 25 relatives of Americans missing in action in Southeast Asia have joined as plaintiffs.

The lawsuit, seeking to represent all alleged U.S. prisoners of war remaining in Southeast Asia as a result of the Vietnam war, accuses the government of violating the Hostage Act by not seeking the release of those prisoners. Boyle initially ruled that the remaining plaintiffs are entitled to pursue a judgment because Americans missing in action are protected under the Constitution and the Hostage Act.

But U.S. attorneys appealed his ruling, arguing on Wednesday that the Hostge Act had no private right of enforcement.

"Now it's another wait-and-see game," Waple said.

Government attorneys also asked — since the issue is so extraordinary — that his initial ruling and the arguments be presented before the 4th Circuit Court of Appeals in Richmond, Va.

"Our response to that is that we don't have time any more," Waple said. "The time it would take to appeal would forever moot the question," Waple said of the possibility many prisoners will perish before any action would come out of the drawn-out judicial process.

HUTCHENS & WAPLE
ATTORNEYS AND COUNSELORS AT LAW
McPHERSON SQUARE

H. TERRY HUTCHENS
MARK L WAPLE
FRED L FLORA, JR.
NED M. BARNES
TODD C. CONORMON

201 SOUTH McPHERSON CHURCH ROAD
FAYETTEVILLE, NORTH CAROLINA 28303

(919) 864-6888

CAROLINA BEACH OFFICE:
A-3 PLEASURE ISLAND PLAZA
CAROLINA BEACH, NORTH CAROLINA 28428
(919) 458-4466

November 6, 1986

PLEASE REPLY TO:
P.O. Box 650
Fayetteville, NC 28302

Mr. Scott Barnes
Post Office Box 704
Kearnville, California 93238

Dear Scott:

Yesterday, in U.S. District Court for the Eastern District of North Carolina hearings were held for the second time on the U.S. Government's motions to dismiss Smith, et al v. Reagan, et al, or in the alternative for the case to be sent directly to the United States Court of Appeals for the Fourth Circuit.

Government attorneys argued that the case failed to involve a Fifth Amendment deprivation since any prisoners of war that were being held were by foreign governments and not by the United States Government and that at best the only thing which the United States Government could do was to negotiate for the release of our American POWs. The second argument raised by the Government was that the Hostage Act fails to provide a private right of enforcement. Third, the Government argued that the Court should abstain from considering the case, saying that the facts necessary to resolve whether American Prisoners of War are alive and in captivity are not manageable by the judicial branch of government since that evidence was in the hands of unfriendly foreign governments. They also argued that judicial intervention would interfere with an alleged delicate dialogue between the United States Government and foreign governments. The Government also argued that the issue was best left to the legislative and the executive branches of the government. Finally the Government contended that the Court should certify the extraordinary legal issues for review by the Fourth Circuit Court of Appeals before proceeding further.

Our response to the first argument was that the Government has already conceded a moral and legal responsibility to resolve the issue and that the Government has conceded its duty to faithfully execute the laws of the United States, which should of course include the Hostage Act. We made the Court aware that our concern was not with information in the hands of unfriendly foreign governments but rather our concern was with information in the hands of our own Government. In response to the argument that our Government could only negotiate for the release of American POWs, we argued that it was impossible to negotiate for the return of any one if our declared policy was that they do not exist or that our Government was able to prove that they existed. We pointed out to the Court our position that the U.S. Government or an internal agency had taken affirmative action to misinform the American people and American MIA Families about the status of their loved ones, making particular reference to the fraudulent identification of remains issue.

In response to the issue of whether the Hostage Act confers a private right of action, several federal cases have been referred for the Court's consideration where other federal courts have found a duty to examine the basis for the incarcerations of Americans in foreign countries.

In response to the argument that the Court should abstain for "prudential" reasons, our arguments pointed out that judicial intervention was the only hope that our American POWs have and that since the U.S. Government had already released classified information to private citizens such as the Director of the National League of Families and private American businessmen, as well as the Hanoi government, that surely such information could be considered by a United States District Court.

Responding to the suggestion that the legislative and executive branches were the proper forums, we argued that the legislative branch has been unable to get the information requested and in the alternative, that the legislative branch has failed to utilize its powers of subpoena and information collection because of political considerations.

Finally, with regards to the Governments suggestion that the case should be certified for immediate consideration by the Fourth Circuit Court of Appeals, we referred the Court to the recent testimony of former DIA Director, General Tighe, where he identified twelve first-hand live sightings occurring between 1982 and 1985. Thus, any further delays in this litigation such as an interim appeal would severely prejudice the case and the livelihood of these individuals.

The Court made no ruling and requested additional legal and factual information from both the U.S. Government and ourselves. My best estimate is that some ruling will be provided within the next 30 to 45 days. We are very optimistic, particularly since the Court has already once refused to dismiss the case.

I attempted to reach you by phone to give you this information personally but thought that a letter would be the best way to get the information to you.

Sincerely,

HUTCHENS & WAPLE

Mark L. Waple

MLW/hf

COMMONWEALTH OF VIRGINIA
DEPARTMENT OF HEALTH
OFFICE OF THE CHIEF EXAMINER

NORTHERN VA. DISTRICT
THE FAIRFAX HOSPITAL
3300 GALLOWS RD.
FALLS CHURCH, VIRGINIA 22046
PHONE (703) 573-5008

REPORT OF INVESTIGATION BY MEDICAL EXAMINER

Resident ☐
Non-resident ☐

DECEDENT Bobby   Charles   Robinson   DOB 12/11/32   RACE: W   SEX: M
First Name   Middle Name   Last Name

ADDRESS: 4906 Uvcliff Lane
Number and Street

Fairfax, VA   22030   SSN: M W S D   OCCUPATION: Military   EMPLOYER: U S Army
City or County   Zip Code

CIRCUMSTANCES OF DEATH:

TYPE OF DEATH: (Check one only)
Sudden in apparent health ☐
Unwitnessed by physician ☐
in prison, jail, or police custody ☐

	NAME	Shows This if Commit	ADDRESS
FOUND DEAD BY	Mrs. Barbara Robinson	wife	4906 Uvcliff Lane
LAST SEEN ALIVE BY	same		same
WITNESSES TO INJURY OR ILLNESS			
NO DEATH			

DATE	1/13/85	1-14-85				Visitant or Unnatural ☐		If Motor Vehicle Accident Check One of the Following
TIME	p.m.	8:40 a.m.	9:30 a.m.	12:15 pm.		gun		☐ DRIVER
								☐ PASSENGER
								☐ PEDESTRIAN

| | Last Seen Alive | Injury or Illness | Death | Advised Examiner Notified | Visit of Body | Period Notified | |

NOTIFICATION BY: Invest. Dooley

Address Fairfax Police Dept.

INJURY OR ONSET OF ILLNESS	LOCATION	CITY OR COUNTY	TYPE OF PREMISES (I.E. HIGHWAY ETC)
	4906 Uvcliff Lane	Fairfax	residence

DEATH			
	Pronounced at Fairfax Hospital	Fairfax	Emergency Dept.

VIEWING OF BODY BY MEDICAL EXAMINER   Fairfax Hospital

DESCRIPTION OF BODY

FATAL WOUNDS (GUNSHOT, STAB, ETC.)   SIZE   SHAPE   LOCATION   PLANE, LINE OR DIRECTION

CAUSE OF DEATH:

MANNER OF DEATH: (check one only)
☐ Accident   ☒ Suicide   ☐ Homicide
☐ Natural   ☐ Undetermined   ☐ Pending

AUTOPSY: ☒ Yes ☐ No

AUTHORIZED BY:
Pathologist
Autopsy No.

I hereby declare that after receiving notice of the death described herein I took charge of the body and made inquiries regarding the cause and manner of death in accordance with the Code of Virginia as amended; and that the information contained herein regarding such death is correct to the best of my knowledge and belief.

Date   Signature of Medical Examiner

City or County of Appointment

NARRATIVE SUMMARY OF CIRCUMSTANCES SURROUNDING DEATH:

The decedent and his wife went to bed on the evening of January 13. At 2:00 a.m. the wife saw her husband get up and go down stairs. The alarm went off at 5:30 a.m. and wife awoke alone. She found her husband on the floor of garage.

EDICAL ATTENTION AND HOSPITAL OR INSTITUTIONAL CARE.

NAME OF PHYSICIAN OR INSTITUTION	ADDRESS	DIAGNOSIS	DATE

Sen. Murkowski refuses to investigate harrassment and security violations

Senator Frank Murkowski, Chairman of the Senate Veterans Affairs Committee, has held several hearings allegedly delving into the mystery of Vietnam veterans left behind after the Vietnam war.

Unfortunately, the Murkowski hearings have become nothing more than a "dog and pony show" controlled by Reagan administration infiuence with purpose to discredit anyone who claims live American prisoners were left behind.

Only a handfull of Veterans Affairs Committee members bother to attend the POW hearings. Most drop in, congratulate themselves for showing up, get their name entered in the record, then leave to carry on "other more important duties."

Scott Barnes testified before the Murkowski Committee that certain government employees had threatened to injure Barnes if he showed up to testify. Murkowski offered Barnes an escort to the airport but refused to ask for a FBI investigation of the threats. which the escort got lost ?

Highest decorated Vietnam veteran, Lt. Col. Robert Howard gave Murkowski testimony allegeding that Lt. Col. Paul Mather, assigned to the Joint Casualty Resolution Center at the U.S. Embassy in Bangkok, Thailand, had committd a major security violation.

Col. Howard stated in a sworn affidavit "I witnessed the compromise of a source of information by LTC Mather and COL. Alpern concerning the working relationship which had been developed between Special Forces Detachment Korea and these Senior Thai military officers. Specifically, LTC Mather and COL. Alpern openly revealed this relationship and that the Thai General Officer had been providing information concerning living American prisoners. The significance of this compromise was that it was a blatant security violation by a senior U.S. military officer and it was an effort to undermine the successful intelligence gathering activity of Special Forces Detachment Korea on the subject of living Americans in South East Asia."

Murkowski has shown no interest in investigating these serious allegations.

Senator, when are you going to do your job?

POW-MIA FACT BOOK

DEPARTMENT OF DEFENSE

1 JULY 1986

Updated for the Seventeenth Annual
Meeting of the National League of
Families of American Prisoners and
Missing in Southeast Asia

TABLE OF CONTENTS

OFFICE OF THE SECRETARY OF DEFENSE

WASHINGTON, D.C. 20301

INTRODUCTION

This Fact Book has been prepared in support of the U.S. Government's effort to ensure that public awareness on the POW/MIA issue is based on current, factual information. It outlines the extent of the problem and summarizes U.S. Government efforts to resolve the matter.

President Reagan and his entire Administration are deeply committed to obtaining the fullest possible accounting for our POWs/MIAs, supported by a strong bipartisan consensus in the Congress. Few issues enjoy such widespread, bipartisan support. The question of resolving the fates of these Americans is a matter of the highest national priority. In his remarks on May 28, 1984, at a ceremony honoring the Vietnam Unknown Soldier, the President said:

...For the war in Southeast Asia still haunts a small but brave group of Americans -- the families of those still missing in the Vietnam conflict. Well, today, then one way to honor those who served or may still be serving in Vietnam is to gather here and rededicate ourselves to securing the answers for the families of those missing in action. I ask the members of Congress, the leaders of Veteran's Groups and the citizens of an entire nation present or listening to give these families your help and support, for they still sacrifice and suffer. We write no last chapters. We close no books. We put away no final memories. An end to American's involvement in Vietnam cannot come before we've achieved the fullest possible accounting of those missing in action.

All involved government agencies are fully dedicated to re-solving the fates of 2,434 Americans still missing in Indochina as a result of the Vietnam War. The Department of Defense feels a very special commitment and a deep debt of gratitude to these Americans for serving our country in difficult times. But, just as importantly, those currently serving and those who will do so in the future must know they will never be abandoned, regardless of trying and difficult circumstances. Our efforts will continue until we have reached this goal.

GENERAL SUMMARY

During the five years of this Administration, the United States Government has accelerated negotiations with the communist governments of Indochina in an effort to obtain the fullest possible accounting for Americans lost during the military conflict there. Although there has been a significant increase in cooperation, the Indochinese governments' response to us has been minimal in comparison to what they are capable of doing.

A great deal of evidence exists that the governments of Vietnam and Laos hold information which could resolve the status of many unaccounted for Americans.

Despite the difficulties involved, the United States Government is deeply committed to resolving the POW/MIA issue. This issue is a humanitarian matter of such importance that it is pursued without linkage to other issues which separate the U.S. and the Indochinese governments, an agreement reached through policy-level negotiations.

It is a moral and legal responsibility of the U.S. Government to place such a high priority on resolving the status of missing and unaccounted for Americans. In an address before the National League of POW/MIA Families, Vice President George Bush stated:

"The return of all POWs, the fullest possible accounting for those still missing and repatriation of the remains of those who died serving our nation -- these goals are the highest national priority.

"In the area of diplomacy, it means that all parties understand the importance of the POW and MIA issue to the American people. Every government involved understands that, as a practical matter, the American people would not allow normalized relations with the United States until we have the fullest possible accounting for our men.

"And, finally, top priority means that we do not rule out the possibility that Americans are still alive and held captive in Indochina.

"Well, if we can get hard evidence that Americans are still held in Vietnamese prisons, we're pledged to do whatever's necessary to get them out."

		77-A-4
Army	702	
Air Force	913	
Navy	486	
Marines	290	
Coast Guard	1	
Civilians	42	
Total	2,434	

U.S. SERVICEMEN UNACCOUNTED FOR BY STATE

Alabama - 42	Nebraska - 24
Alaska - 3	Nevada - 10
Arizona - 24	New Hampshire - 10
Arkansas - 27	New Jersey - 63
California - 244	New Mexico - 17
Colorado - 41	New York - 157
Connecticut - 39	North Carolina - 61
Delaware - 5	North Dakota - 17
District of Columbia - 9	Ohio - 128
Florida - 80	Oklahoma - 49
Georgia - 48	Oregon - 46
Hawaii - 11	Pennsylvania - 119
Idaho - 12	Rhode Island - 10
Illinois - 100	South Carolina - 30
Indiana - 70	South Dakota - 9
Iowa - 39	Tennessee - 44
Kansas - 38	Texas - 158
Kentucky - 22	Utah - 23
Louisiana - 34	Vermont - 4
Maine - 17	Virginia - 61
Maryland - 37	Washington - 60
Massachusetts - 59	West Virginia - 26
Michigan - 75	Wisconsin - 37
Minnesota - 47	Wyoming - 6
Mississippi - 18	Puerto Rico - 2
Missouri - 51	Virgin Islands - 1
Montana - 21	Other - 7

U.S. GOVERNMENT EFFORTS TO OBTAIN

THE FULLEST POSSIBLE ACCOUNTING

United States Government policy regarding the POW/MIA problem is coordinated through the POW/MIA Interagency Group. Membership in this group includes the State and Defense Departments, the White House National Security Council (NSC) staff, representatives of the Joint Chiefs of Staff, Defense Intelligence Agency (DIA), the National League of POW/MIA Families, and House and Senate staff members from the respective Foreign Affairs and Foreign Relations Committees. The Group addresses policy considerations concerning the POW/MIA issue and evaluates current efforts, always seeking new initiatives and approaches to enhance resolution of the question.

Most Americans felt that with the signing of the agreements ending the war in Indochina, accounting for our missing countrymen would finally occur. It was expected in 1973 that the then Democratic Republic of Vietnam (DRV) --North Vietnam-- would honor Article 8 of the Paris Peace Agreement, the article dealing with those missing and killed in action. This article specifically provided for repatriating POWs from both sides as well as exchanging information about the missing and return of remains of those who died. These points were conditional only on the withdrawal of U.S. and allied forces from Vietnam. The agreement ending the war in Laos had less specific articles pertaining to POWs and MIAs of all nations. However, because of the intransigence of the Indochinese governments, the POW/MIA issue has yet to be resolved.

Prior to the fall of the Republic of Vietnam in 1975, teams from the Joint Casualty Resolution Center (JCRC) searched the jungles and mountains of South Vietnam for remains of U.S. personnel, under the auspices of the Four Party Joint Military Team (FPJMT) established by the Paris Accords. Despite a lack of cooperation from the Vietnamese communists and at times at great personal risk, the JCRC recovery teams achieved noteworthy success in their efforts.

U.S. efforts in North Vietnam were limited to negotiations with the Vietnamese concerning the fate of our servicemen and the repatriation of remains. Between April 1973 and April 1975, North Vietnam returned the remains of 23 U.S. personnel.

In the first six years after the fall of the Republic of Vietnam, several U.S. Congressional Delegations, as well as missions from both the State and Defense Departments, met with the Vietnamese specifically regarding this issue. In addition, JCRC representatives met in Hawaii with Vietnamese officials in July 1978 and travelled to Hanoi in October 1980 and May 1981. These three meetings dealt with technical aspects of the accounting process.

In February 1982, a policy-level delegation led by then Deputy Assistant Secretary of Defense Richard L. Armitage traveled to Hanoi to discuss the POW/MIA question with the Vietnamese and impress upon the Vietnamese the high priority the United States Government attaches to resolution. During the ensuing discussions, Mr. Armitage stressed the President's commitment to resolving this issue as well as the deep concern of the American people regarding our missing personnel. As a result of this visit, the Vietnamese accepted a U.S. Government invitation to visit the U.S. POW/MIA facilities in Hawaii. These facilities include the JCRC and the U.S. Army Central Identification Laboratory (CIL). The visit took place in August 1982 and continued the dialogue between the two countries.

Following a visit to Hanoi by the National League of Families, on September 30, 1982, the Vietnamese agreed to a longstanding U.S. proposal that technical experts from both sides meet on a regularly scheduled basis to discuss the POW/MIA question. The Vietnamese agreed to four technical meetings per year, the first of which was held in December 1982, the second in March 1983, and the third in June 1983, at which time the remains of nine individuals were returned, eight of which were identified as Americans. The Vietnamese then interrupted the schedule.

In October, 1983, Mr. Richard Childress, Director of Asian Affairs, National Security Council, and Mrs. Ann Mills Griffiths, Executive Director of the National League of Families, met in New York with Vietnamese Foreign Minister Nguyen Co Thach. Discussions focused on overcoming obstacles to advance serious, high-level negotiations between the two governments and laid the groundwork for future discussions.

In February 1984, a U.S. delegation visited Hanoi in an attempt to increase the pace of cooperation. Led again by Richard Armitage, Assistant Secretary of Defense, the delegation included Mrs. Griffiths, Mr. Childress and Mr. Lyall Breckon, State Department's Director of Vietnam, Laos and Cambodia. This meeting resulted in a Vietnamese offer to accelerate cooperation (concentrating initially on the most accessible cases in the Hanoi/Haiphong area and those listed as having died in captivity in the south) and to resume the quarterly technical meetings as well as a pledge by the Vietnamese to turn over the remains of eight missing servicemen. These remains were repatriated on July 17, 1984. Six of the eight remains were identified as missing American servicemen and returned to their next of kin. A technical level meeting was again held in mid-August.

In October 1984, Mr. Childress and Mrs. Griffiths met with Vietnamese Foreign Minister Nguyen Co Thach. During their discussions in New York, the Vietnamese Foreign Minister renewed and strengthened the February 1984 commitments and agreed to set an early date for the next technical meeting (subsequently held later that month).

The October technical meeting was reported as the most cooperative and positive to date and general agreement was reached to hold. the next regular meeting in early 1985.

The next meeting took place February 6-9, 1985. During this meeting, the Vietnamese announced they would soon be returning five remains. Also, during this meeting, the Vietnamese took the American team to visit a U.S. aircraft crash site in Vietnam.

Mr. Childress and Mrs. Griffiths met with Foreign Minister Thach and other high-level Vietnamese officials in Hanoi, March 3-5, to discuss continuing cooperation on the POW/MIA issue. All aspects of critical importance to the POW/MIA issued were raised, and'the U.S. and Vietnamese sides agreed to several specific points to further accelerate cooperation:

     - Meetings between technical personnel will be increased from four to a minimum of six per year, depending on the need and information available.

     - Remains mentioned during the February technical meeting were agreed to be returned in March. (Six remains were subsequently turned over to the U.S. on March 20th, identified, and returned to their next-of-kin. Of note was the fact that the names of two of these Americans appeared on the Provisional Revolutionary Government's - Viet Cong - "died-in-captivity" list, representing the first time efforts had been made by the Vietnamese to account for Americans on this list, the initial step in fulfilling a specific pledge of the Vietnamese Foreign Minister.)

     - There was an exchange of views on other methods to accelerate progress on the POW/MIA issue, to include joint efforts to excavate crash site locations.

At the technical meeting held April 17-20, 1985, in line with the agreement to hold six or more meetings per year, the Vietnamese agreed in principle to conduct a preliminary survey of a U.S. crash site in Vietnam. The U.S. Government discussed with the Vietnamese the details of such a survey, proposing a crash site to be visited.

On July 1, 1985, the Vietnamese announced their intention to work toward resolving the POW/MIA issue within a two-year timeframe. This decision, conveyed through Indonesian Foreign Minister Mochtar Kusumaatmajda, was welcomed by the U.S. government as a serious policy commitment by the government of Vietnam.

The technical meeting held July 2-6, 1985, in Hanoi resulted in an announcement by the Vietnamese of information regarding 32 Americans (26 remains and information/material evidence on 6 others). On August 14, 1985, the SRV returned 26 sets of remains (2 sets subsequently identified as not American and returned to SRV). The U.S. team also conducted a preliminary site survey of a U.S. crash site near Hanoi.

The U.S. developed and provided to SRV officials in August 1985 a full bilateral plan to resolve the issue within the pledged two-year time frame. Later that month, White House representative Richard Childress, League of Families Executive Director Ann Mills Griffiths, State Department official Lyall Breckon and JCRC representative LTC Paul Mather met in Hanoi with Vietnamese Acting Foreign Minister Vo Dong Giang and Deputy Foreign Minister Hoang Bich Son for the most substantive and constructive meeting yet held on the issue. Without responding specifically to the U.S. workplan proposal, Vietnam presented an implementation plan to resolve the issue within the two-year time frame committed to in early July. No preconditions were stated and both sides agreed the U.S. and Vietnamese workplans had many common elements. Although the Vietnamese again denied that American are held in captivity, they stated willingness to continue investigating sighting reports which come to their attention.

In mid-September 1985, meetings were held in New York with Vietnamese Minister Vo Dong Giang and Assistant Minister Le Mai. White House representative Richard Childress, National League of Families Executive Director Ann Mills Griffiths and State Department official Lyall Breckon again comprised the U.S. delegation and provided the Vietnamese delegation with U.S. input on Vietnam's two-year work plan. This included detailed U.S. cooperative actions that would be undertaken in support of the Vietnamese plan. Minister Giang reiterated recent pledges, committed to a joint excavation near Hanoi and stated he expected additional American remains to be turned over very soon. Again there was no linkage to other issues.

The September 25-28, 1985 technical meeting continued discussions on logistics regarding joint excavations. Agreement led to the first joint excavation of a crash site conducted with the SRV. The U.S.-SRV excavated what was reported to be a B-52 crash site near Hanoi. The U.S.-Vietnamese team excavated an area of 25 feet by 50 feet to a depth of 36 feet. While the results of the effort were disappointing in terms of the limited remains recovered, the willingness of the SRV to permit a joint effort and their excellent cooperation are hopeful signs for the future. The U.S. team also visited a B-52 crash site in Ngoc Ha.

During the November 13-16, 1985 technical meeting, the SRV agreed to turn over seven sets of remains, which subsequently turned out to be remains of eight individuals. Actual return date was December 4, 1985. Seven sets were identified by CIL as Americans and returned to their next of kin. One set is still undergoing analysis. The Vietnamese also provided information on seven sets of unrecoverable remains as well as personal data/effects on three other service members.

The highest level U.S. Government delegation to visit Vietnam since the end of the war met with the Vietnamese in January 1986. Assistant Secretary of Defense Richard Armitage led the U.S. contingent which included Assistant Secretary of State Paul Wolfowitz, White House Representative Richard Childress, and National League of Families Executive Director Ann Mills Griffiths. Vietnamese Foreign Minister Nguyen Co Thach agreed the POW/MIA issue is a humanitarian one and reiterated the Vietnamese pledge to resolve the issue within two years. The Vietnamese also agreed to investigate any POW live-sighting information that the U.S. might present.

During the technical talks held February 27-28, 1986 in Hanoi, the SRV presented a list of 49 cases on which the populace had reported information to Vietnamese government officials. Of the 49 cases, 21 resulted in remains being recovered and subsequently repatriated on April 10, 1986. The SRV accepted in principle the U.S. invitation to send a delegation to Hawaii for a "technical exchange" with the CIL and JCRC.

In April 1986, Mrs. Griffiths met with the Vietnamese Ambassador at their mission in New York (at their request) and was informed that statements by various USG officials were not helpful in setting the right atmosphere to resolve the issue and that the U.S. had not demonstrated commitment to the Vietnamese two-year plan.

The April 11-14, 1986, technical meeting in Hanoi was postponed by Vietnam, to be rescheduled at a mutually agreeable later date. Postponement was linked to USG retaliatory actions against Libya to counter international terrorism. Within the U.S. Government, the postponement was seen more as posturing by Hanoi rather than as a serious breakdown on the issue between the two sides. The delayed technical talks were subsequently held in Hanoi June 11-14. The Vietnamese presentation was generally critical of U.S. actions since the January 1986 high level meeting and again criticized the U.S. for failing to respond formally to their two year plan. The SRV also gave a brief update on the cases under investigation. It is anticipated that future technical meetings will be more productive with less rhetoric, thus allowing increased progress on the issue.

On July 1-2, 1986, a U.S. delegation consisting of Mr. Childress Mrs. Griffiths, Mr. Breckon and Colonel Howard Hill, Principal Adviso to the Secretary of Defense on POW/MIA Affairs, met in Hanoi with Vietamese Foreign Minister Nguyen Co Thach, Deputy Foreign Minister Hoang Bich Son and other officials for very productive discussions. Responding to media reports of Vietnam's perception that the U.S. lacked commitment to the two-year Vietnamese plan, White House representative Richard Childress delivered an official letter with attachment from Assistant Secretary of Defense Richard Armitage which outlined specific oral and written agreements previously reached. Agreement was reached with the Vietnamese on the following:

a. We and the Vietnamese will meet at the technical level in
August and again in October, confirming the agreed pattern of at
least six such meetings per year. Vietnamese officials said these
meetings would be especially productive.

b. Vietnamese and American forensic specialists will meet in
Vietnam for consultations.

c. Vietnam will provide us with the results in writing of its
investigation of reports of live prisoner sightings.

d. Vietnam will permit American experts to accompany its
officials on investigations in accessible areas.

e. Vietnamese officials agreed to discuss specific crash
sites for further excavation in the next technical meeting.

f. The Vietnamese accepted our invitation for another visit,
with the date to be determined, to U.S. technical facilities (JCRC
and CIL) in Hawaii.

Regarding Laos, our sustained effort to obtain the cooperation
of the Lao Government has met with some success. A visit by the
National League of Families in September, 1982, was followed by
several high level U.S./Lao meetings in 1983/84. These discussions
resulted in two visits by the JCRC to Laos, the first since 1975.
During the second visit, JCRC representatives surveyed the requirements to excavate a crash site in southern Laos. This eventually
led to the most encouraging development yet - an unprecedented
joint crash site excavation which took place February 10-22, 1985.
A U.S./Lao team conducted a full-scale excavation of a U.S. Air
Force AC-130 aircraft shot down near Pakse, Laos. During the excavation, the team recovered partial human remains and some personal
effects.

The remains and personal effects were taken to the U.S. Army
Central Identification Laboratory in Hawaii, where forensic specialists, using the latest in analytical techniques, identified the
remains of all 13 men lost aboard the aircraft. This excavation was
considered to be a major step in developing a sustained pattern of
cooperation with the Lao government on the POW/MIA issue. The
first of what is hoped will be of many such excavations to resolve
the fates of many of over 550 Americans still missing in Laos was
conducted with excellent cooperation by Lao officials.

Additional high-level meetings on the POW/MIA issue with the
Lao have occurred, including discussions in New York between U.S.
Assistant Secretary of State Paul Wolfowitz and Lao Foreign Minister
Phoun Sipaseut. During March 1985 meetings in Vientiane, Laos,
between Mr. Childress, Mrs. Griffiths and Lao Vice Foreign Minister
Soubanh, the Lao government agreed to continue and increase coopera-
tion with the U.S., to pursue accountability on a unilateral basis

and to meet with U.S. officials as frequently as necessary to enhance the process. They also agreed in principle to visiting the
JCRC and CIL facilities in Hawaii.

In July 1985, Laos announced agreement in principle to a
second excavation during the 1985-86 dry season and acceptance of
a U.S. Government invitation to send a delegation to the Joint
Casualty Resolution Center and the U.S. Army Central Identification
Laboratory, both in Hawaii. In September 1985, Lao experts traveled
to Hawaii for consultations with the Department of Defense, Joint
Casualty Resolution Center and the Central Identification Laboratory.
Assistant Secretary of State Paul Wolfowitz and Mr. Childress also
visited Vientiane in December, 1985, to discuss the issue.

A joint U.S.-Lao crash site survey was conducted in January of
1986 and was followed by the second joint U.S.-Lao excavation in
February, 1986. An AC-130 aircraft which crashed in March 1972 in
Savannakhet province of Southern Laos was the excavation site. The
aircraft had a crew of 14 on board. Although this crash site had
obviously been disturbed by private groups seeking remains and
material evidence from the site, a significant quantity of remains
and personal effects was recovered. The remains are currently
undergoing examination at the CIL for possible identification and
subsequent notification of next of kin.

The July 4, 1986, policy-level discussions in Vientiane, Laos,
resulted in Lao government agreements to provide written reports on
discrepancy cases of missing Americans and seriously consider a
unilateral survey, possibly accompanied by an American official,
plus added unilateral efforts by the Lao government. The delegation,
led by Mr. Childress of the NSC staff, and including Mrs. Griffiths,
Mr. Breckon and Defense Department representative Colonel Howard Hill,
stressed the need to accelerate cooperation and to resume the joint
excavation process as quickly as weather permits before the end of
1986.

In summary, significant strides have been made over the past
two years in our negotiations. More remains were returned in the
past year than any time since the end of the war. The atmosphere
has never been better for making substantial progress on the issue.
Though all involved are frustrated with the pace, we are pursuing
every available avenue to resolve this issue in the shortest time
frame possible and are determined to achieve success.

U.S. PERSONNEL

WITH EVIDENCE OF CAPTURE

The following list provides examples of U.S. personnel on whom the Indochinese governments should have information. The individuals mentioned herein are those on whom there is "hard evidence" (e.g. post-capture photography, U.S. or indigenous eyewitnesses to capture or detention, intelligence reports) that they were captured and detained by communist forces. These cases represent only a sampling of those individuals for which the Indochinese should be able to provide an accounting.

ROBERT ANDERSON
USAF
NORTH VIETNAM

COL Anderson went down over North Vietnam on October 6, 1972. He and his back seater both parachuted and talked with rescue planes. Anderson said, "I have a good parachute, am in good shape and can see no enemy forces on the ground." His back seater was immediately captured. Radio Hanoi reported that a number of U.S. pilots were captured the same day, however, Anderson's plane was the only one lost that day. The back seater was repatriated in 1973.

RICHARD L. BOWERS
USA
SOUTH VIETNAM

CAPT Bowers and SFC Arroyo-Baez were captured together. One Vietnamese captured with them escaped the same day and reported their capture. Another Vietnamese also was captured with them, escaped later and reported that Arroyo-Baez was alive but that Bowers had been shot the same day of capture. The Provisional Revolutionary Government (PRG) indicated that Arroyo-Baez died in captivity; his remains were returned in March, 1985. But the Vietnamese have never provided information on Bowers.

CHARLES DEAN
CIVILIAN
LAOS

Charles Dean and his Australian companion Neil Sharman were aboard a boat enroute to Thakhek, Laos, in early September 1974 when they were captured by the Pathet Lao at Ban Pak Hin Boun. Numerous reports indicated that they were subsequently held in the Kham Keut area of central Laos. Reliable information indicated they were alive in that area as of February 1975. Captured after the cessation of hostilities in Laos, the Lao government should have information on Charles Dean.

12

EUGENE H. DEBRUIN
CIVILIAN
LAOS

A photo of Eugene DeBruin and his surviving crewmembers in captivity was obtained from a Pathet Lao publication. LTJG Dieter Dengler, USN and one of the Thai nationals who was a member of the DeBruin crew and held with DeBruin successfully escaped from the Pathet Lao and provided information on DeBruin. In 1982, the Lao Government indicated that he was killed in an escape attempt but provided no further information or clarification.

JACK ERSKINE
CIVILIAN
SOUTH VIETNAM

A Filipino with Jack Erskine escaped from the VC ambush and reported Erskine's capture. Three months later a VC rallier who had participated in Mr. Erskine's capture reported on the incident. About one year later sketches showing Erskine in captivity were captured; however, he was not identified on any lists furnished by the Vietnamese.

SEAN FLYNN
CIVILIAN
CAMBODIA

Sean Flynn, a photographer for TIME Magazine accompanied by Dana Stone, a cameraman for CBS, rented Honda motorbikes and left Phnom Penh on April 6, 1970, travelling southeast on Route One. Villagers in the area said that two Westerners on motor scooters were captured by combined Viet Cong/North Vietnamese forces in Svay Rieng Province. Reports received after January 1973 indicate Flynn and Stone were shot to death in mid-1971 in Kampong Cham Province.

SOLOMON GODWIN
USMC
SOUTH VIETNAM

A U.S. trained Vietnamese intelligence agent who was held with WO Godwin escaped three weeks after capture and reported on Godwin's status. U.S. returnees confirmed Godwin's capture and reported his death in captivity. Godwin's name did not appear on any lists furnished by PRG.

DAVID HRDLICKA
USAF
LAOS

COL Hrdlicka's chute was observed opening and he was seen on the ground. One flight member believed he saw Hrdlicka being supported or led away by natives. A helicopter pilot landed at a nearby village and was told Hrdlicka had been picked up by the Pathet Lao. Rallier reports indicated he was a prisoner. A post capture photo of Hrdlicka was obtained from several sources. A recording allegedly made by

him was broadcast in May 1966 and the
text appeared in Foreign Broadcast
Information Service documents.

TERRY REYNOLDS
CIVILIAN
CAMBODIA

Terry Reynolds, a UPI reporter, and
Alan Hirons, an Australian UPI photographer, were reported missing on April 26,
1972. The automobile in which they were
driving was found at the site of an enemy
road block on Route 1 in Prey Veng Province,
Cambodia. Their photo equipment was found
in the abandoned car. According to
villagers in the area, both journalists
were captured and led away by communist
forces. In early May 1972, a Viet Cong
rallier reported observing two Caucasians,
equating to Reynolds and Hirons, who had
recently been captured. Another report
equating to Reynolds indicated that he
was being held in Sampan Loeu Hamlet, about
40 kilometers southeast of Phnom Penh in
June 1972.

CHARLES SHELTON
USAF
LAOS

Voice contact was made with COL Shelton on
the ground and he indicated he was in good
condition. A villager witnessed the crash
and observed the capture and arrest of
Shelton by Pathet Lao forces. Rallier
reports indicated he was a prisoner.

DONALD SPARKS
USA
SOUTH VIETNAM

Letters written by PFC Sparks while a POW
were captured. Subsequent intelligence
indicated Sparks possibly died. No
information has been furnished on Sparks.

PHILIP TERRILL
USA
SOUTH VIETNAM

There is a high degree of correlation
between VC and Hanoi radio broadcasts
describing capture of two Americans and
the circumstances surrounding the loss
of SP5 Terrill and MSGT J. Salley. Several
sighting reports correlated well to the
two men. Capture status was confirmed by
U.S. returnees who said both men died after
capture. Salley was on the PRG died in
captivity list, but Terrill was not.

DEGREE OF KNOWLEDGEABILITY POSSESSED BY

THE INDOCHINESE GOVERNMENTS REGARDING

U.S. UNACCOUNTED FOR PERSONNEL

give

well

The U.S. Government has repeatedly urged the Indochinese governments to meet their humanitarian obligation to provide the fullest possible accounting for Americans missing in their countries. These governments assert that no Americans are held captive, but they have not done enough to substantiate the assertion. It is clear that the governments of Indochina have available to them considerably more information on missing Americans than they have given to the United States. The United States is fully committed to repatriating any Americans who may still be held captive, and to obtaining the fullest possible accounting for those Americans still missing in Southeast Asia.

Cambodia

The communists in Cambodia recently claimed that they have some knowledge of U.S. personnel missing in that country. It is known that during the War, some U.S. personnel now listed as missing were captured in Cambodia, mostly in areas which were under Vietnamese control. Appeals through the Vietnamese government and other channels have not resulted thus far in information to U.S. authorities.

Lao People's Democratic Republic

With regard to Laos, an agreement was signed with that country to end the hostilities there around the time of the repatriation of U.S. prisoners from Vietnam. The United States is not a signator to that agreement; however, similar to the Vietnam Agreement, the Laos Agreement specified conditions and provisions for the exchange of prisoners of war, regardless of nationality and information on the missing. The Lao have provided little information on unaccounted for U.S. personnel. The nine American prisoners released by the Vietnamese in early 1973 during Operation Homecoming were not, as was claimed at the time, captured by the Pathet Lao. They were, in reality, captured by North Vietnamese forces operating in Laos and moved as expeditiously as possible to North Vietnam for detention. After signing the peace agreement ending the war in Laos, the Pathet Lao claimed to hold only one prisoner, Mr. Emmet Kay, a U.S. civilian, captured on May 7, 1973. He was subsequently released on September 18, 1974. This statement was in contradiction to earlier public statements by high ranking Laos officials that many prisoners were being held. A Pathet Lao official commented that the Pathet Lao Central Committee had been gathering information on U.S. missing in action personnel, but he warned that they would probably only be able to provide information on a "feeble percentage." On August 24, 1978, the Lao government provided the remains of four persons to a U.S. Congressional delegation. Two of these were determined to be indigenous Southeast Asian. One of the remaining two individuals was identified as a USAF pilot who was shot down on the Lao/Vietnam border, and the other is still unidentified. As the cases presented in this Fact Book demonstrate, the Lao should have considerably more knowledge of missing U.S. personnel than they have thus far been willing to provide.

Socialist Republic of Vietnam (SRV)

There is much evidence to indicate that the Vietnamese have knowledge concerning the fate of many U.S. personnel lost over North Vietnam. A wealth of information on specific aircraft downings was published throughout the war in the North Vietnamese press. A communist source interrogated during the Vietnam War stated that the SRV Ministry of Defense, Enemy Proselyting Department, maintained central listings of all U.S. POWs detained in the SRV. This source also reported that in the SRV, all data pertaining to the death and/or burial of an American prisoner, whether in the north or south, was to be forwarded to Hanoi as quickly as possible together with sketches of the burial site. In 1980, a Vietnamese mortician of Chinese ancestry told U.S. officials that the remains of approximately 400 Americans were warehoused in Hanoi. He also said he had seen 3 Caucasians whom he believed to be Americans. U.S. intelligence personnel conducted intensive interviews with the sources, and the U.S. Government judged the information he provided to be very credible.

In the south, representatives of the former Provisional Revolutionary Government (PRG) should have information on many unaccounted for U.S. personnel. For example, after signing the Paris Peace Agreement, the PRG provided the U.S. a list of 37 missing Americans who had died in captivity. Prior to the March 78, 1985 repatriation of remains, the Vietnamese had taken no action to return the remains of anyone on this list or to otherwise account for them. In addition, it is known that the South Vietnamese communists captured a number of U.S. personnel whose names have not appeared on any lists provided to the U.S. by either the former PRG or present Vietnamese Government.

Based on the above information, and the known communist proclivity for detailed reporting, it is believed that the SRV still holds a significant amount of specific information on missing American servicemen and civilians.

U.S. GOVERNMENT POSITION
ON AMERICANS STILL BEING HELD
CAPTIVE IN INDOCHINA

Since the fall of Saigon in 1975, the United States Government has acquired more than 5,000 reports bearing on the POW/MIA problem. Of the total reported, 861 are firsthand live-sighting reports with 542 resolved through a determination that they correlate with individuals since accounted for. Additionally, 191 of the reports are known or suspectd to be fabrications by the source while 128 are as yet unverified and are under continuing investigation in an attempt to confirm the information. The remaining reports pertain to hearsay sightings and to crash site and grave site information.

Given the above circumstances, it would be irresponsible to rule out the possibility that live Americans are being held. Thus, the U.S. Government's position since 1982 is:

LIVE-SIGHTING POSITION STATEMENT

ALTHOUGH WE HAVE THUS FAR BEEN UNABLE TO PROVE THAT AMERICANS ARE STILL DETAINED AGAINST THEIR WILL, THE INFORMATION AVAILABLE TO US PRECLUDES RULING OUT THAT POSSIBILITY. ACTIONS TO INVESTIGATE LIVE-SIGHTING REPORTS RECEIVE AND WILL CONTINUE TO RECEIVE NECESSARY PRIORITY AND RESOURCES BASED ON THE ASSUMPTION THAT AT LEAST SOME AMERICANS ARE STILL HELD CAPTIVE. SHOULD ANY REPORT PROVE TRUE, WE WILL TAKE APPROPRIATE ACTION TO ENSURE THE RETURN OF THOSE INVOLVED.

TO MELVA

INTELLIGENCE ACTIVITIES

ON THE POW/MIA ISSUE

Background

With the buildup of U.S. forces in Southeast Asia during 1964, intelligence acquisition capabilities concerning POW/MIAs were enhanced. A regular flow of captured documents as well as enemy POWs, ralliers, and refugee interrogation reports developed.

In April 1966, the intelligence community increased the emphasis on collection of information on POWs and MIAs. DoD's highest priority was assigned and CIA and DoD collectors were immediately notified of this increased emphasis, and expanded formal collection requirements were published and disseminated. U.S. Government installations and organizations worldwide were involved in obtaining information about POWs and the missing.

Past Efforts

Following the Hanoi announcement in June 1966 that captured airmen would be tried for war crimes, the entire system of collecting, disseminating and processing information on missing personnel was reviewed and intensified. A network of debriefing and interrogation centers was developed in liaison with local government intelligence agencies in Vietnam and Laos. Sources were debriefed or interrogated in depth on the information they possessed. Indigenous teams checked out, where possible, crash sites, detention sites, and reported sightings of Americans. The scope of the worldwide collection effort was expanded to include all overt media coverage and photography of POWs. Communist radio broadcasts were carefully monitored for information about POW/MIAs. The major elements of the Executive Department focusing on POW/MIA problems were the DoD (Defense Intelligence Agency, the Intelligence branches of the Military Services), the Central Intelligence Agency, and the Department of State.

The Defense Intelligence Agency (DIA), established in late 1961, was assigned a limited responsibility for POW/MIA analysis until mid-1966. After that time, DIA's role expanded. During 1967, DIA assumed chairmanship of the Interagency POW Intelligence Ad Hoc Committee. In December of 1971, DIA chaired the DoD Intelligence Task Force which was established to supervise the intelligence aspects of the POW/MIA problems and to provide more rapid and effective communication between policymakers and intelligence officials.

Following the repatriation of the POWs in 1973, the intelligence community's efforts focused on the nearly 2,500 Americans still missing. The withdrawal of U.S. forces from Vietnam in 1973 and the fall of Saigon in April 1975 resulted in a mammoth reduction in the level of field assets, the opportunity to access geographic locations as well as indigenous sources.

Current Efforts

Increased policy level emphasis on the POW/MIA issue in 1981 resulted in the raising of intelligence priorities. The entire intelligence community now affords top priority to collecting and analyzing information which would lead to an accounting for Americans who are missing in Indochina. Strong command attention is being placed on this issue. The DIA POW/MIA Division was increased in strength from 12 personnel in 1981 to 28 personnel today.

At the present time, the principal but not the only source of POW/MIA information available to the U.S. Government is Indochinese refugees. The continued absence of political stability and dismal economic conditions in the Southeast Asian region has resulted in an unabating flow of refugees from one or more of the three countries of primary concern. Interviews have been conducted with many of these refugees by both government and private individuals. Reported sightings of Americans by these sources continue to reach the USG from any number of different sources. The USG has an established program for follow-up action which is taken on each such report received.

Active collection efforts are conducted by the entire intelligence community using a wide variety of disciplines. As stated by the President, "intelligence assets of the United States are fully focused on this issue." DIA has primary responsibility for evaluating reported POW/MIA related sightings. Necessary follow-up action is conducted through the Defense Attache System, the Joint Casualty Resolution Center Liaison Office in Bangkok, the Department of State through U.S. Embassies, and by DIA or other military assets within the United States. Due to numerous refugee movements between camps, onward settlement in other countries, and temporary accommodations provided by sponsor organizations, follow-up action for clarification or amplification of reported information consumes many manhours and at times can require months to complete, but the time required is reduced to the minimum amount possible.

POW/MIA intelligence information, regardless of the source, is channeled into DIA for analysis. Through close coordination with the military services, all correlated information relating to POWs is provided to the Services; the POW/MIA's parent service Casualty Branch then transmits the information to the POW/MIA's next-of-kin. Additionally, DIA keeps the Government decisionmakers apprised of POW/MIA intelligence information.

Future Efforts

When evidence becomes convincing that one or more Americans are still detained in Indochina, the highest level U.S. Government officials will be immediately notified in order to determine appropriate action to gain their release.

An obvious question arising is - what amount of evidence is required to be "convincing." First, the evidence will have to satisfy certain criteria such as currency and specificity. It is unrealistic to assume that a single refugee report without additional verification will justify decisive action. One hope is that a report can be strengthened and supported through technical means. Another is that more than one report will be specific and similar as to time, place and circumstance, and hopefully, at least one source's credibility will be enhanced by polygraph examination. Despite the many reports we have received and the technical means available to us, no single report or combination of reports and technical sensors has thus far been specific enough to be "convincing." What continues to condition our thinking and motivate out efforts is the "weight of evidence" theory: The many reports, the limited information provided by the governments in Indochina, and the fact that some of the missing initially survived the incident in which they were lost, preclude ruling out the possibility that Americans may be alive in communist controlled Southeast Asia.

JOINT CASUALTY RESOLUTION CENTER

The Joint Casualty Resolution Center (JCRC) is a United States·
military task force designated to assist in the recovery or status
resolution of unaccounted for U.S. personnel from the Southeast
Asian conflict. Presently, JCRC maintains active case files on
all U.S. military personnel and civilians who were captured, are
missing or who died but their remains were not recovered. JCRC's
role has expanded through the years, as priority efforts increased
and particularly since 1982.

JCRC was established as a joint service, humanitarian organization,
by direction of the Joint Chiefs of Staff in January 1973 in Saigon,
Republic of Vietnam. In February 1973, with the approval of the
Royal Thai government, the JCRC relocated to Nakhon Phanom Royal
Thai Air Force Base in northeast Thailand. JCRC later moved to
Camp Samae San and U-Tapao Royal Thai Navy Base, Thailand. In
May 1976, the organization was moved to Naval Air Station, Barbers
Point, Hawaii.

Initially JCRC's mission placed almost total emphasis on American
field recoveries. For the first year, its primary activity was
conducting recovery operations in South Vietnam while negotiating
for access to sites in other Indochina countries. During the
summer of 1973, undersea recovery attempts were conducted, 142
dives were made in 82 days but the limited evidence recovered
resulted in no identifications. In December 1973, a JCRC field
team was ambushed while conducting recovery operations at a site
south of Saigon. One American officer was killed and several
team members were wounded.

This loss forced JCRC to take a more cautious approach with the
major revisions being made in recovery techniques. The "Safe
Haven" concept was developed in which U.S. recovery personnel,
remaining in secure areas, assisted and directed the operations
of U.S.-trained Vietnamese recovery teams. Complementing the
"Safe Haven" concept with Area Desk Officers in each of the
military regions, JCRC continued its activities in South Vietnam
until that country, Laos, and Cambodia fell under communist control.

JCRC efforts after cessation of field operations were concentrated
on information refinement, analytical investigations, and contin-
gency planning in anticipation of agreement which might reopen
field operations. Over 150,000 documents have been assembled,
correlated, analyzed, and processed through automated data
processing to develop the most accurate information possible concerning the fate of U.S. military and civilian personnel. It has
refined the probable location of more than 600 recovery sites.

Case files, prepared for discussions with the Indochinese, contain a description of the incident, a photo of the missing person, and a map of the most likely recovery area. Additionally, translations of the folders in the Vietnamese, Khmer and Lao language have been made and passed to the Vietnamese and Lao governments. This process has become increasingly important as cooperation with the governments of Laos and Vietnam has accelerated to recover U.S. personnel missing in those countries.

JCRC personnel conduct an extensive program to interview Indochinese refugees in an attempt to obtain POW/MIA information. Command interviewers travel to refugee camps in Thailand, Malaysia, Indonesia, Singapore, Hong Kong, and the Philippines, and produce approximately 900 interview reports per year. These reports receive careful and thorough evaluation by DIA and JCRC analysts, and if found to correlate or possibly correlate to active cases, are incorporated into the appropriate individual file and provided to the next-of-kin by the Service Casualty Office. Uncorrelated reports are continuously compared with each other in an effort to establish patterns and correlations which may not at first be evident.

While the majority of JCRC's activity is devoted to interviewing refugees, analytical investigation, and records updating, it continues to serve as the primary agency for receiving and repatriating remains of U.S. personnel. Whenever remains are recovered or returned, they are delivered to the Central Identification Laboratory (CIL), a Department of the Army activity in Honolulu, for official identification. JCRC analysts compare information provided by the returning country with data in their files to prepare a list of candidate identifications. Laboratory professionals then compare recorded physiological characteristics of the candidates with the actual remains to arrive at a tentative identification. This tentative identification is reviewed by forensic anthropoligists and the Armed Forces Institute of Pathology prior to review by the Armed Services Graves Registration Office in Washington, D.C. and before being submitted to the appropriate military service Secretary for final approval.

Though increasing cooperation of the Socialist Republic of Vietnam (SRV), JCRC has established working level dialogue on Americans. Officials of the Vietnamese Office for Seeking Missing Persons (VNOSMP) visited the JCRC during July 1978, and August 1982, and were given briefings on the U.S. casualty resolution effort, as well as detailed instruction on the physical identification of remains from the Central Identification Laboratory, Hawaii. The Lao government also visited the CIL in September 1985. The JCRC liaison office in Bangkok has been used extensively and has proven both useful and effective in exchanging information of a technical or working-level nature. Through the years, frequency of meetings between the U.S. and Vietnamese officials has increased, and a minimum of six technical meetings per year is now agreed upon.

THE WALL STREET JOURNAL.

TUESDAY, AUGUST 19, 1986

Pay for U.S. Prisoners in Communist Hands

By Bill Paul

Call them the legion of lost souls—hundreds of American prisoners of war who today are scattered throughout the Communist world: Russia, North Korea, Vietnam and Laos.

The U.S. government knows they're there but it doesn't want the American people to know because they might demand their return, even if it meant paying for them. The U.S. can't afford to be blackmailed, the Reagan administration says.

I say pay: In hard currency, if absolutely necessary; otherwise, in economic assistance or medical aid. There's precedent. The French quietly paid to get back men taken in its Indochina conflict. We paid to get back Bay of Pigs invaders.

Vietnam is desperate to cut a deal. At least that's how Washington observers view Hanoi's decision last Wednesday to release an American civilian it previously denied knowing anything about. The American, Robert Schwab, disappeared after sailing into Vietnamese waters a year ago. He was let go, apparently for a reason.

What's needed now is for President Reagan to seize this initiative and buy the men back. The American people can't allow their government to continue lying that there is no proof these prisoners exist. They do exist, and here's more evidence that Washington knows they do.

In March 1984, John Noble, an American author and lecturer who rotted in the Gulag between 1945 and 1956, introduced himself to Secretary of State George Shultz at a banquet at a Washington hotel.

Mr. Noble, who now lives in Muncy, Pa., is living proof that when a government really tries, it can save anyone. Mr. Noble was originally imprisoned by the Germans in 1938 (Michigan born and bred, he was working in one of his father's German factories.) In 1945, when the Soviets moved in, he was imprisoned by them at Dresden. In 1950, he was shipped to a Siberian prison camp.

For years the State Department sent notes to Moscow asking that Mr. Noble be released. Each time the Russians denied holding him. Then, in 1954, Mr. Noble smuggled out a postcard to relatives in Germany signed, "Your noble nephew."

"The bottom line is that until the North Koreans get to a position and they want to release the prisoners and the remains that are up there. [Pause.] They will do it when they feel it is to their advantage."

A careful listening to the 16-minute tape leaves no doubt that Col. Land is knowingly differentiating between live prisoners and remains, and that he is telling Mr. Dumas that both are still in Korea.

Contacted yesterday, Col. Land said he has "no recollection" of what he told Mr. Dumas. He also said, contrary to what is on the tape, "We honestly don't know." If American POWs remain in North Korea.

While Gen. Eugene Tighe, who retired in September 1981 as head of the Pentagon's Defense Intelligence Agency, has frequently stated that he believes American POWs are still alive in Southeast Asia, none of his staff has ever publicly backed him up. However, in a recent interview, one of Gen. Tighe's former top assistants, who because he is still on active duty asked not to be named, backed him up unequivocally.

Indeed, this officer told me that when he reviewed the U.S.'s POW intelligence in 1981, he found that, as of 1978, the Pentagon had "hard evidence" of Americans still imprisoned in Southeast Asia. He wouldn't tell me what this evidence was, just that, "I came to the conclusion that [POWs] were there."

He added that, in his opinion, the Pentagon hadn't acted on this hard evidence because it was afraid that military morale would suffer if the troops learned that fighting men had been left behind when the U.S. pulled out of Vietnam.

In 1981, just weeks after President Reagan took office, the new administration learned that Vietnam wanted to sell to the U.S. an unspecified number of live POWs still in Southeast Asia for the sum of $4 billion (less than the U.S. had promised Hanoi in postwar rebuilding aid).

It's unclear whether the offer was made to Mr. Reagan or that he inherited it from President Carter. The proposal was discussed by Mr. Reagan and his advisers at a general meeting on security matters, according to one person who says he was in the room, and whose story is supported by another attendee.

During the discussion, it was first decided that the offer was indeed genuine. Then, a number of the president's advisers said they opposed paying for POWs on the ground that it would appear as if the U.S. could be blackmailed. Mr. Reagan concurred. At that point, the president's men were prepared to let the matter drop.

To his credit, however, Mr. Reagan told William Casey, director of the Central Intelligence Agency, and Richard Allen, then the national security adviser, to try to find another way to get the men home.

Mr. Allen subsequently proposed a reconnaissance mission into Laos which, if successful, would lead to a military rescue of prisoners presumed held at a jungle prison camp. The secret mission failed and word of the failure leaked to the press.

After that, the administration went to work to make sure there would be no more publicized violations of another country's sovereignty. A new POW policy was concocted by the State Department and the Pentagon. It maintained that POWs in the U.S. can neither confirm nor deny that POWs remain in Southeast Asia, but operates on the assumption that they are there.

Through this turn of phrase, the U.S. government is now able to appear straightfastly committed to getting the men home—without having to take any decisive action.

Mr. Noble again denied holding Mr. Noble's release. At first Malenkov again denied holding Mr. Noble, but as publicity surrounding the case grew, the Russians suddenly released him—and his two American cellmates.

Mr. Noble says that when he told Mr. Shultz that many Americans remain in Russian prison camps, the secretary replied, "I know that they're there."

Then Mr. Shultz indicated that the State Department knows the names of American imprisoned in the Soviet Union. He said that occasionally the State Department sends notes to the Kremlin demanding the return of these Americans and that the Soviets, in Mr. Shultz's words, "throw [the list] back in our face." When Mr. Noble then asked what else the U.S. does besides send notes, Mr. Noble says Mr. Shultz replied, "That's all we can do."

(Calls to the State Department yesterday yielded no official comment on the matter.)

Mr. Noble didn't ask Mr. Shultz how many Americans are in the Gulag, but the New York Times once reported, on Jan. 5, 1954, that the State Department says more than 5,000 American prisoners in the hands of the Soviets and their European satellites.

While publicly the Pentagon hasn't ever admitted leaving men behind after the Korean and Vietnam wars, a few weeks ago Col. Henry Land, the number two man in the Secretary of Defense's POW office, acknowledged to Robert Dumas, the brother of a Korean War soldier still unaccounted for, that American soldiers are still imprisoned in North Korea.

Col. Land discussed the continued presence of U.S. POWs in Korea during a telephone conversation that Mr. Dumas recorded without Col. Land's knowledge. On the tape, Col. Land is heard to say.

Mr. Paul, a Journal staffer in New York, has written previously on POWs.

Resolutions Committee recommendation: For:9 Against:2 Abstention:2

Rationale: "Although the final portion of this Resolution would seem to give a blanket
endorsement to legislation without considering its consequenses, the Resolution does
address a major problem in our society today which is of concern to many of our members.
This Resolution is supported by Paragraphy 72k of the Social Principles found on page 95
of the 1984 Discipline, as well as a Resolution on Agricultural and Rural Life Issues,
pages 261-272 of the 1984 Book of Resolutions."

RESOLUTION 1986-2

Title: Prisoners of War/Missing in Action

Submitted by: Rev. James B. Jesty,
              Flat Rock Ebenezer United Methodist Church

Whereas: Over 2,000 American Prisoners of War and Missing in Action from the Vietnam
          War remain unaccounted for; and

810

Whereas: The Governments of the United States of America and the Peoples Republic of
          Vietnam continue attempts to account for those still missing; and

Whereas: Movies such as "Rambo" have renewed interest in the Prisoners of War/Missing
          in Action issue; and

Whereas: Reports continue of live sightings of Americans in detention in Kampuchea and
          Laos as well as Vietnam,

THEREFORE BE IT RESOLVED that
          the East Ohio Conference of the United Methodist Church supports any surviving
          Prisoners of War/Missing in Action and their families in the following ways:

          1. By keeping the unaccounted-for and their families in our prayers,

          2. By discouraging any support of "Rambo" type or any other violent solutions
              to the Prisoner of War/Missing in Action situation,

          3. By asking the Conference Secretary to notify the State Department in
              Washington and the Peoples Republic of Vietnam's Mission to the United
              Nations of the Conference's support of their efforts to account for those
              still missing, and

          4. By asking the Conference Secretary to notify the Peoples Republic of
              Vietnam's Mission to the United Nations, the Republic of Kampuchea's
              Mission to the United Nations, and the Kingdom of Laos' Ambassador to
              the United States of the Conference's concern that more of the missing
              be accounted-for and that live sightings of Americans in detention be
              allowed to be investigated by appropriate international organizations.

Resolutions Committee recommendation: For:13 Against:0 Absentions:0

Rationale: "The Resolution addresses a humanitarian issue of concern to persons throughout the United States and is supported by such Scriptural passages as Hebrews 13:3 and
the Social Principles of the Discipline, Paragraph 74a and 75a.

RESOLUTION 1986-3

Title: P.O.W.'s and M.I.A.'s

Submitted by: Sue Jeffers, Sandy Valley Community Center
              Jim Yeagley, member of Sandy Valley Viet Nam Veterans Organization

Whereas: Hebrews 13:3 says, "Don't forget those in jail. Suffer with them as though
          you were there yourself. Share the sorrow of those being mistreated, for you
          know what they are going through"; and

Whereas: The United States government has failed to gain release or full confirmation
          of all our P.O.W.'s and M.I.A.'s in the last thirteen years; and

Whereas: Statistics show we still have approximately 2,000 P.O.W.'s and M.I.A.'s un-
          accounted for in Vietnam and surrounding countries; and

Whereas: Some of these are from the State of Ohio, directly affecting our area;

THEREFORE BE IT RESOLVED that
          we hold the governments of the United States and Viet Nam responsible for
          the return of all P.O.W.'s and M.I.A.'s of the Viet Nam War, whether they
          be held in Vietnam or neighboring countries. We encourage the United States
          government to support all valid efforts and operations by private individuals
          or organizations that are working to secure the release of information or the
          whereabouts of the P.O.W./M.I.A.'s. Amnesty should be available as an option
          for any of the survivors who might be afraid to return home.

BE IT FURTHER RESOLVED that
          a copy of this Resolution be sent to the President of the United States, the

East Ohio Conference -- 1986

Speaker of the House of Representatives, the Ohio General Assembly, the Governor of the State of Ohio, and our Senators and Representatives from the East Ohio Conference area. We encourage this Annual Conference to remember these people and their families in their prayers, and to support, as our conscience directs, efforts to bring the P.O.W./M.I.A.'s home.

This Resolution to be implemented by Sue Jeffers and Jim Yeagley, Sandy Valley Community Center.

Resolutions Committee recommendation: FOR:11 Against:2 Abstention:0

Rationale: "This Resolution is supported by Paragraphy 74a and 75a of the Social Principles, pages 99 and 102 of the 1984 Discipline."

RESOLUTION 1986-4

Title: Hazardous Waste

Submitted by: Ben Weber

Whereas: "As for you my sheep ... not content to graze in good pastures, you trample down the rest; not content to drink clear water, you muddy the rest with your feet. Any my sheep must graze on what your feet have trampled, drink what your feet have muddied ... Since you have butted all the weak sheep with your rump and shoulders and horns, until you have chased them away. I am going to come and rescue my sheep from being cheated; I will judge between sheep and sheep." (Ezekiel 34:17-22), and;

Whereas: The United Methodist Book of Resolutions advocates that governments discourage and clean-up the hazardous waste dumps in existence (p. 536); and;

Whereas: Technological developments in modern industry and business ahve produced many good things that have made way for a better life for all, and;

Whereas: From many of these developments has come the by-product of hazardous waste, which must be disposed-of, by efficient, effective, and proper procedures which will better our environment so as to protect the health, safety, and welfare of all life on earth,

THEREFORE BE IT RESOLVED that
we, the East Ohio Annual Conference of the United Methodist Church:

1. Encourage government agencies and private industry to continue to research and develop technology which will dispose effectively and safely all hazardous waste.

2. Encourage government and private industry to allocate more funds to continue prompt clean-up of known sites.

3. Encourage government agencies and our court system to develop more efficient and less time consuming procedures for handling and issuing permits required by law, for the operation of hazardous waste facilities.

BE IT FURTHER RESOLVED that
we authorize and encourage the East Ohio Annual Conference Board of Church and Society, through its Division of Environmental Justice and Survival, within its established budget, and through all of the churches in the Conference and their members, to communicate this Resolution to everyone concerned.

This Resolution is to be implemented by the Board of Church and Society through the Division of Environmental Justice and Survival.

Resolutions Committee recommendation: For:0 Against:11 Abstentions:2

UNITED STATES OFFICE OF PERSONNEL MANAGEMENT

AUTHORITY FOR RELEASE OF INFORMATION

To Whom It May Concern

I hereby authorize any Investigator or duly accredited representative of the United States Office of Personnel Management bearing this release, or a copy thereof, within one year of its date, to obtain any information from schools, residential management agents, employers, criminal justice agencies, or individuals, relating to my activities. This information may include, but is not limited to, academic, residential, achievement, performance, attendance, personal history, disciplinary, arrest and conviction records. I hereby direct you to release such information upon request of the bearer. I understand that the information released is for official use by the Office of Personnel Management and may be disclosed to such third parties as necessary in the fulfillment of official responsibilities.

I hereby release any individual, including record custodians, from any and all liability for damages of whatever kind or nature which may at any time result to me on account of compliance, or any attempts to comply, with this authorization. Should there be any question as to the validity of this release, you may contact me as indicated below.

Signature (Full Name): _Scott Tracy Barnes_

Full Name: _Scott Tracy Barnes_

Other Names Used: _None_

Parent or Guardian: (If required) _____

Date: _Sept-19- 1986_

Current Address: _P.C. Box 704_

Kernville, CA. 93238

Telephone Number: _619- 376-3349_

PRIVACY ACT NOTICE

Authority for Collecting Information
E.O. 10450; 5 USC 1303-1305; 42 USC 2165 and 2455; 22 USC 2585 and 2519; and 5 USC 3301.

Purposes and Uses
Information provided on this form will be furnished to individuals in order to obtain information regarding your activities in connection with an investigation to determine (1) fitness for Federal employment, (2) clearance to perform contractual service for the Federal government, (3) security clearance or access. The information obtained may be furnished to third parties as necessary in the fulfillment of official responsibilities.

Effects of Nondisclosures
Furnishing the requested information is voluntary, but failure to provide all or part of the information may result in a lack of further consideration for employment, clearance or access, or in the termination of your employment.

Previous edition is usable

OPM Form 329-A
(Rev. 12/79)

NOTICE TO INDIVIDUALS COMPLETING
FEDERAL INVESTIGATIVE FORMS

PRIVACY ACT STATEMENT

Solicitation of this information is authorized by sections 1303 (Investigations), and 1304 (Loyalty Investigations), of Title 5, United States Code, and by Executive Order 10450 (Security Requirements for Government Employment).

This information will be used primarily to determine your fitness for employment, including the granting of a security clearance and evaluating your qualifications, suitability, and loyalty to the United States. Where appropriate, it will be used in determining suitability and qualifications for performing contractual services to the Federal Government.

This information may be disclosed to various sources in and out of the Federal Government in order to obtain information from their sources regarding you and may also, along with the results of the investigation, be furnished to other Federal agencies for the same purpose the Office (OPM) intends to use the data or for other criminal or civil law or regulatory enforcement purposes.

Solicitation of your Social Security Number (SSN) is authorized by Executive Order 9397, which requires Federal agencies to use the SSN as the means of identifying individuals in Federal personnel record systems.

Furnishing your SSN or any of the other requested information is voluntary. However, failure to furnish the information may result in our being unable to complete your investigation and could result in you not being considered further for employment or in termination based on available, perhaps incomplete information. A false answer to any question on this form is punishable by law (Title 18, U.S. Code, Section 1001).

STANDARD FORM 85
REVISED FEBRUARY 1966
U.S. CIVIL SERVICE COMMISSION
F.P.M. CHAPTER 736

DATA FOR NONSENSITIVE OR NONCRITICAL-SENSITIVE POSITION

IMPORTANT
Particular care must be used in completing the items numbered 1 through 9. READ THE INSTRUCTIONS ON THE BACK OF THIS FORM BEFORE ANSWERING ANY OF THESE ITEMS.

1. A. FULL NAME (LAST, FIRST, MIDDLE)
BARNES SCOTT TRACY

B. OTHER NAMES USED
NONE

2. ARMED SERVICES SERIAL NO., AND DATES AND BRANCH OF SERVICE
550268371
US ARMY
16 JUL 73 to 19 Dec 74

3. SOCIAL SECURITY NO.
550 76 8371

4. DATE AND PLACE (CITY, STATE) OF BIRTH
6-19-54 BURBANK, CALIF.

5. POSITION

6. AGENCY NAME AND ADDRESS

7. DATES & PLACES OF RESIDENCE

From (Mo./Yr.)	To (Mo./Yr.)	No. and Street Address	City and State	ZIP Code
12-83	Presently	PO BOX 704	Kernville CA.	93238
10-83	12-83	129 PAOAKALNI;	Honolulu, Hawaii	
11-82	10-83	4302 MESA ST	Torrance, CA	90505
11-81	11-82	952 Calle Miramar	Torrance CA	90505
6-81	11-81	13 Spruce ST	Kernville CA	93235

8. DATE OF THIS REQUEST

9. (CHECK ONE)
☐ NONSENSITIVE
☐ NONCRITICAL-SENSITIVE

10. (CHECK ONE)
☒ MARRIED ☐ SINGLE
☐ WIDOW(ER)
☐ DIVORCED

11. IF MARRIED, WIDOWED, OR DIVORCED, GIVE FULL NAME AND DATE AND PLACE OF BIRTH OF SPOUSE OR FORMER SPOUSE. INCLUDE WIFE'S MAIDEN NAME, GIVE DATE AND PLACE OF MARRIAGE OR DIVORCE. (GIVE SAME INFORMATION REGARDING ALL PREVIOUS MARRIAGES AND DIVORCES.)
DONNA M. (NEVINS) BARNES MARRIED 2-14-84
Vickie L. (Felton) MARRIED 5-76 Divorced 11-79 TORRANCE CA.

12. IDENTIFYING NUMBERS (OTHER THAN SOCIAL SECURITY OR ARMED SERVICES SERIAL, SUCH AS PASSPORT NO., ALIEN REGISTRATION NO., SEAMAN'S CERTIFICATE OF IDENTIFICATION, ETC. GIVE ALL, SPECIFYING WHICH.)
NONE

13. ORGANIZATIONS WITH WHICH AFFILIATED (PAST AND PRESENT) OTHER THAN RELIGIOUS OR POLITICAL ORGANIZATIONS OR THOSE WHICH SHOW RELIGIOUS OR POLITICAL AFFILIATIONS (IF "NONE," SO STATE).
1 NATIONAL Military Intelligence ASSOC, 3 NAVAL Intelligence Professionals
2 AMERICAN SECURITY COUNCIL 4 CALIF ASSOC OF Licensed Investigators

14. DATES, NAMES AND ADDRESSES OF EMPLOYERS (BEGIN WITH PRESENT AND GO BACK TO JANUARY 1, 1937. CONTINUE UNDER ITEM 21 ON OTHER SIDE IF NECESSARY.)

From (Mo./Yr.)	To (Mo./Yr.)	Employer	No., Street, City, State	ZIP Code
10-85	Current	INTRAQUEST INVESTIGATIONS	PO Box 704 Kernville CA	
5-85	7-86	Watterson College 5337 Truxton Ave Bakersfield 933		
6-84	1-85	Kern County Probation Dept 2000 Ridge Rd Bakersfield, CA		
1-84	6-84	Kern County Parks Dept Lake Isabella, CA 92040		
10-83	11-83	State of Hawaii Dept of Social Service PoBox 339		
9-83	10-83	FSEC INS. CO 1400 Kapakalni Ave. Honolulu, HF 93397		
10-82	7-83	Spottmart INC. 1401 Hawthorne Blvd. Redondo Bch CA 90277		
1-81	10-82	Merrill Lynch Realty 1415 Pacific Coast Hwy Redondo Bch		

CERTIFICATION
FALSE STATEMENT ON THIS FORM IS PUNISHABLE BY LAW.

I CERTIFY THAT THE ABOVE STATEMENTS ARE TRUE, COMPLETE, AND CORRECT TO THE BEST OF MY KNOWLEDGE AND BELIEF, AND ARE MADE IN GOOD FAITH.

DATE Sept 19-86

SIGNATURE (SIGN ORIGINAL AND FIRST CARBON COPY) Scott D Barnes

15. DATE OF APPOINTMENT

16. PLACE OF DUTY (IF DIFFERENT FROM ADDRESS IN ITEM 6)

17. TYPE OF APPOINTMENT
☐ EXCEPTED ☐ COMPETITIVE
INCLUDES INDEFINITE AND TEMPORARY TYPES OF COMPETITIVE APPOINTMENT.

18. CIVIL SERVICE REGULATION NUMBER OR OTHER APPOINTMENT AUTHORITY

19. THIS SPACE FOR FBI USE (SEE ALSO ITEM 22)

20. NAME AND FULL MAILING ADDRESS OF AGENCY OFFICIAL TO WHOM RESULTS OF INVESTIGATION SHOULD BE SENT. INCLUDE ZIP CODE.
OPM-NACI CENTER
ATTN:
BOYERS, PA 16018
SAB

107

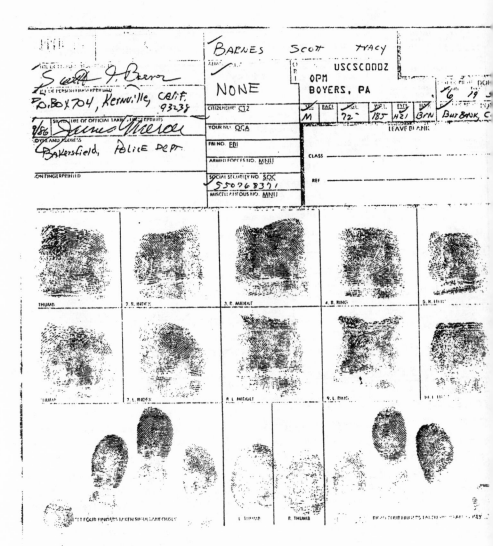

THE DAILY OKLAHOMAN

OKLAHOMA CITY, OK

The State Newspaper Since 1907

THURSDAY, FEBRUARY 5, 1987

Jury Seeks Adventurer's Testimony

By Ray Robinson

A shadowy California adventurer, who twice has claimed to have uncovered government murder plots, has been subpoenaed by federal prosecutors to testify before a grand jury investigating the connections of a mercenary implicated in the illegal shipment of 200 pounds of explosives from Oklahoma City to Las Vegas last year.

Scott Barnes of Kernville, Calif., confirmed in a series of telephone interviews over the last five days that federal prosecutors in Oklahoma City had subpoenaed him to testify today before the grand jury investigating the connections of David Scott Weekly, who pleaded guilty to explosives charges in December. It appeared doubtful, however, that Barnes would appear before the grand jury.

Weekly, known to acquaintances as "Dr. Death," is an associate of retired Army Special Forces officer James G. "Bo" Gritz, who has led several controversial and privately funded military missions aimed at rescuing the U.S. prisoners of war he believes are still being held in Laos.

After entering his guilty plea, Weekly agreed to cooperate in an ongoing investigation of the case by agents of the U.S. Bureau of Alcohol, Tobacco and Firearms.

"I think he's trying to plea-bargain and drop a dime on somebody," Barnes said of Weekly, whom he later described as a "soldier-of-fortune" mercenary and veteran with no direction.

Barnes, who also was associated with one of the Gritz missions, said

two federal agents served him with the grand jury subpoena last week despite his claims that he was completely unaware of Weekly's activities. "We know you know things," he quoted an agent as saying.

Barnes, who characterizes himself as a "counter-intelligence consultant," said he probably would not honor the subpoena and that if he does appear before the grand jury, he will refuse to answer any "incriminating" questions put to him by prosecutors.

Barnes was scheduled to appear before the grand jury this morning, but was still in California as of Wednesday afternoon. In a latter conversation, Barnes said the government had dismissed the subpoena, but there was no independent confirmation of that.

Assistant U.S. Attorney Steve Koro-

tash, who is prosecuting the Weekly case and issued the subpoena for Barnes, refused to comment on the matter. If Barnes does not appear today, prosecutors will be left with the options of dropping the subpoena or asking a judge to find Barnes in contempt of court and order his arrest.

In 1984, Barnes claimed in an interview on ABC's "World News Tonight" that the CIA had asked him to kill Honolulu financier Ronald Rewald, who had formerly operated a CIA front company and was being tried for fraud. After the CIA, in an unprecedented move, filed a complaint against ABC with the Federal Communications Commission, the network acknowledged that it could not confirm Barnes' allegations.

Last year, in an affidavit filed in federal court in North Carolina, Bar-

See JURY, Page 2

From Page 1

nes claimed that on one mission into Laos, he learned that the U.S. Embassy in Bangkok, Thailand, had issued instructions that if any U.S. prisoners were located, "the merchandise was to be liquidated."

Weekly, 39, of San Diego, was described by two former members of the Gritz missions as a one-time gun dealer who frequently claimed to have been a member of the Navy's elite SEAL (Sea, Air and Land) commando teams. They said he also had claimed to have done occasional work for the U.S. Customs Service and the Drug Enforcement Administration.

"I take some of that with a grain of salt," one of the former Gritz associates said. "He insinuates to me all the time that he's got a lot of government contacts."

In 1982, Weekly, Gritz and three other people were arrested in Thailand after staging an unsuccessful mission in search of U.S. prisoners. That mission, named "Operation Lazarus" by Gritz, was financed in part with money Gritz obtained from actors William Shatner

Publisher's Update

Since the completion of the main text of this book there have been numerous interesting events occurring in Scott's life. There have also been many events revealed through the media that support what Scott has been proclaiming over the years. This UPDATE is an attempt to briefly describe these events up to the day this book went to press.

• Towards the end of May 1987, Scott received a Notice Of Rating from the Defense Investigative Service. His rating of 105 points once again allows him to perform government-related investigations. He now has a Top-Secret clearance. Shortly after this notice arrived, he received letters from several intelligence organizations. Apparently a number of influential people feel Scott is not the flake and pathological liar he has been portrayed as being.

• Scott received a request for biographical information for the *Who's Who* in California.

• There were two New York *Times* articles concerning the Contra-related lawsuit sponsored by the Christic Institute. (See Document 27)

• Bo Gritz has made recent allegations towards high-level government officials about their involvement with drugs in Southeast Asia. Gritz has been indicted for passport fraud.

• Gritz's attorney, Lamond Mills, has been in contact with Scott to request his assistance in verifying the names, dates, codes, locations, etc. on the CIA and ISA. Scott's response was he will help when Bo starts telling the truth.

• Scott received a final response to his FOIA request. The contents were sent to his parents' address. A few days later, someone from the Agency phoned to say they released this information in error and requested that Scott return the documents immediately. The contents of Tab A is very interesting. Examine it closely starting with the date of the letter. One can only speculate who the individuals are where the names have been blocked out, but it would be reasonable to assume they are some key game players in the Iran/Contra affair. It is important to note that Scott has never been to Costa Rica. The signator of the letter, John McMahon, has been involved in the Iran/Contra hearings and other clandestine related news stories.

• On June 9 at 9:10 a.m., Scott received a phone call from Senator Tribble's office wanting some information about Gritz and his involvement in the Iran situation, funding of contraband and other allegations. Apparently this senator has been involved in the hearings.

• Mark Waple recently informed me that the funds used to fly Scott to the hearings in January 1986 were from money received for Mark Smith, Melvin McIntyre, Red McDaniel and Congressman LeBoutillier appearing on the Phil Donahue Show in 1985.

• Scott has received several calls from CIA personnel wanting him to get in touch with General Vang Pao for them. They are interested in secret information about the drug operations in Southeast Asia.

• Scott received a call from Agent Sjue of the U.S. State Department Security Section on June 6 at 2:30 p.m. He told Scott, "There was legitimacy on *Operation Grand Eagle* in 1981 by the CIA for a time period."

• The State Department, represented by U.S. Attorney Steve Wolsson, has offered Scott limited immunity if he provides information concerning drug and gun smuggling operations involving Bo Gritz and CIA personnel. The immunity would be from the Justice Department.

• Daniel P. Sheehan of the Christic Institute informed Scott on June 26, 1987 that he found evidence proving Jerry Daniels used the alias of Michael J. Baldwin on numerous occasions.

• Recently, David Taylor has found out that Paul Mather provided documents to the Senate Committee as he promised in 1986. However, many of the documents were handwritten and Scott does not recall any being in this format.

• General Vessey has been appointed by the President as a special emissary to Vietnam. There has been extensive media coverage on this envoy. Results have been nominal, at best, so far.

• There are several sources of excellent information about the POW/MIA issue. Each one represents worthwhile efforts for the cause. In addition, each needs financial support, large or small, at any time.

American Defense Institute
POW Policy Center
P.O. Box 2497
Washington, DC 20013-2497

Homecoming II Newsletter
P.O. Box 8222
Shawnee Mission, KS 66208

Bamboo Connection
P.O. Box 1713
Kinston, NC 18501

Smith/McIntyre/Howard Foundation
P.O. Box 650
Fayetteville, NC 28302

• You are encouraged to write your representative and senators to urge them to put pressure on the current administration to resolve the POW/MIA issue promptly.

(Name of Representative)
House of Representatives
Washington, DC 20515

(Name of Senator)
U.S. Senate
Washington, DC 20510

- The Hanoi delegation address is SRU Representative to the United Nations, 20 Waterside Plaza, New York City, NY 10010. The Laotian Embassy address is 2222 S Street N.W., Washington, DC.
- On August 12, 1987, Scott was scheduled to fly east for a job interview. He called his brother, Brian, from the LA Airport and received some disturbing news. Scott's home had been raided by DA Investigators, as well as agents from other federal and local law agencies. They informed Brian there was a warrant for Scott's arrest.

Scott contacted Daniel Sheehan from the Christic Institute and then flew to Washington DC to provide information to assist the Institute's lawsuit. Scott provided over 10 hours of interviews to various staff attorneys of the Institute.

Mr. Sheehan filed a complaint to the proper authorities in California and protested the search and seizure operation was illegal because Scott is a federal witness.

Scott returned home on August 19 to find the inside of his house a total shambles. The officers who conducted the raid literally tore his house apart . . . ripping phones out of the wall, cutting up carpet, tearing up books, knocking over furniture, and emptying all drawers. They seized all of Scott's PI files, 11 cassette tapes, a number of video tapes, all telephone recording equipment and answering machines, some photos of his Southeast Asia trips plus the negatives, and his passport. Brian's girlfriend was physically pushed around when she arrived on the scene during the raid.

- Daniel Sheehan has worked with the local judge to see that all items seized have been sealed in a box. Mr. Sheehan and his staff are aggressively pursuing all avenues to protect Scott. However, shortly after Scott returned home, he was arrested by the local authorities. As of this moment, August 20, 1987, he is in the Kern County Jail awaiting someone to post his bail of $15.000.
The charge: WIRETAPPING.

NOTICE OF RATING

Mr. Scott T. Barnes
P.O. Box
Kernville, CA

ID NUMBER
01369

POSITION *(Title, Series, and Grade)*

INVESTIGATOR, GS-1810- 5/7

ANNOUNCEMENT NO.	DATE
EXM-CE-120-86	04-28-87

THIS IS NOT A NOTICE OF APPOINTMENT. IT IS A RECORD OF YOUR RATING. IT IS IMPORTANT THAT YOU KEEP IT.

ELIGIBILITY
(ONLY THE SECTION(S) CHECKED BELOW REFERS TO YOUR RATING. DISREGARD SECTION(S) NOT CHECKED.)

[X] You have been rated eligible for consideration for the above position(s) with the DIS.

Your numerical score is ___105 TP___. This includes:

_____ No veterans preference (NP)
__X__ 5-point veterans preference (TP)
_____ 10-point veterans preference (XP)
_____ 10-point veterans preference (CP, CPS)

Your rating is eligible until ___03-31-88___ (Be sure to read the important message on the back)

[ ] Your qualifications statement has been carefully reviewed, and we regret that we cannot refer your name to the Regional Office for employment consideration under the above announcement. Reasons are checked in the appropriate boxes below:

1. [ ] You indicated that you would not accept the minimum salary for this grade.

2. [ ] Your qualifications statement does not show that you meet the basic requirements as to experience or education as specified in the announcement.

3. [ ] You did not indicate your geographic availability for employment consideration in accordance with instructions outlined in "How to Apply" on the attached announcement.

[ ] Information regarding veterans preference is checked in the appropriate boxes below:

1. [ ] In accordance with Public Law 95-454, members of the armed forces who retire at the rank of Major or above are not entitled to veterans preference.

2. [ ] In accordance with Public Law 94-502, veterans entering active duty after October 14, 1976, are not eligible for veterans preference unless they have served in a campaign or meet the definition of disabled veteran.

3. [ ] A completed SF 15, "Claim for 10-Point Veteran Preference," required letter from a Veterans Administration Office dated within the last year, and your latest DD 214, "Certificate of Release or Discharge from Active Duty," reflecting your honorable discharge or retirement, are needed in order to credit you with 10% veterans preference.

[X] **REMARKS:** CLEARANCE: TOP SECRET

A. JEAN WHITAKER
Personnel Staffing Specialist

DIS Form 35
May 81

Replaces DIS PERSONNEL & SECURITY OFF. FORM 2, May 66, which is obsolete.

UNITED STATES STRATEGIC INSTITUTE
WASHINGTON, D.C.

PUBLISHING OFFICE
265 WINTER STREET
WALTHAM, MA 02154
(617) 890 – 5030

May 27, 1987

Dear USSI Member:

The United States Strategic Institute is proud to announce a new book, <u>Central America and the Reagan Doctrine</u>, published by University Press of America.

The volume is a joint project of USSI and the Center for International Relations at Boston University. With an Introduction by Ambassador Jeane J. Kirkpatrick, it brings together, in updated form, the salient coverage extended in <u>Strategic Review</u> to the crisis in Central America and to the U.S. policy issues relevant to that crisis.

What makes the book unique is that the contributions of fifteen outstanding authors -- regional experts, policy-makers and strategists -- blend into a comprehensive analysis and a coherent strategic view. As the book's jacket proclaims: "The composite message is as challenging to U.S. policymakers as it is enlightening to public understanding of the fundamental issues at stake for the United States on its turbulent strategic doorstep."

We have arranged with the publisher to make the book available to USSI members at a 40 per cent discount. We hope that you will avail yourself of this offer. And we thank you, in any event, for your continued support of the work of our Institute.

Sincerely,

Walter F. Hahn

777 FOURTEENTH STREET, N.W. • SUITE 747 • WASHINGTON, D.C. 20005 • TELEPHONE 202-331-1776

Armed Forces Communications
and Electronics Association
AFCEA International Headquarters
4400 Fair Lakes Court • Fairfax, Virginia 22033-3899, USA
Telephone (U.S.) 703-631-6100 • (International) 001-703-631-6100
Facsimile (U.S.) 703-631-4693 • (International) 001-703-631-4693
Telex 90 1114 AFCEA FFX

May 29, 1987

Mr. Scott Barnes
Intravest International Investigations
P.O. Box
Kernville, CA

AFCEA is soliciting industry papers for presentation at
their annual intelligency symposium that will be held at THE
SECRET (NOFORN) level this fall in the Washington area.
This conference provides you the opportunity to respond to the
issues and challenges that will be presented at the Seventh
Defense Intelligence Forum (DITFOR VII) on the subject
of "Intelligence Support for Military Operations".

You are encouraged to seize this opportunity to make
presentations at this important national level symposium. This
year's conference will address the full spectrum of national and
tactical intelligence support for military operations. With
emphasis on emerging technologies, every essential element of
the{transmission of the final report will be covered. Sessions
are planned which will address the following areas:

Collection - collection platforms, sensors, RPV'S, stand
off capabilities is a key element.

Processing and Analysis - multilevel security, automated
tactical fusion systems, integration of heterogeneous
intelligence data bases.

Dissemination/Communications - Intelligence
Communications Architecture (INCA) Initiatives, meteor burst
communications, low probability of intercept communications,
secure networking.

Future Technologies - expert system applications, super
computer support.

The International Association of C³I •

You are invited to propose a paper for presentation at the Fall Symposium. Please submit to AFCEA a titled 100-word abstract (unclassified) of your proposed paper by 15 June 1987. The authors of papers selected will be asked to develop each subject into a formal paper for a 20-25 minute presentation at the symposium. The papers and presentations can be, classified SECRET or below. The final deadline for these papers will be 1 August 1987. A review group with DoD participation will select the papers to be presented. Papers presented will be included in the proceedings. Details regarding handling of the proceedings will be announced later.

I look forward to hearing from you, and to your company's participation. If there are any questions, please don't hesitate to call, (703) 631-6238.

Sincerely,

J. B. Pozza
Colonel, USMC (Ret)
Director, Intelligence/
Special Projects

SECURITY and INTELLIGENCE FOUNDATIC

Suite 1020, 1010 Vermont Avenue, NW, Washington, D.C. 20005 Phone: (202) 393-0883

June 2, 1987

Mr. Scott Barnes
Intravest Intl. Investigations
P.O. Box
Kernville, CA

Dear Mr. Barnes:

The Intelligence Community faces an imminent crisis.

Former CIA Director William Casey struggled tirelessly to rebuild an agency almost destroyed by the Church and Pike Committee hearings. His untimely passing deprived the Agency of his strong hand and inspired leadership at precisely the moment when they are most needed.

Judge William Webster's appointment to assume Mr. Casey's post was an inspired choice. Yet it has resulted in severe problems for the FBI--to date, no comparable successor has been found to fill this critically important position.

Finally, the Iran/Contra hearings have provided the "liberal" opponents of the Intelligence Community--I consider them extremists--with yet another opportunity for "intelligence bashing."

Whatever the merits of the Administration's policy toward Central America and Iran, one thing is certain: the self-styled "liberals" will attempt to exploit these hearings to reverse the hard won gains of the past 7 years.

As the self-anointed guardians of civil liberties, it is all but certain that they will try to repeal the legislation that has only now begun to restore our national intelligence capabilities. Another round of hearings like those of the Church committee is not out of the question. An election year is fast approaching and politicians of this sort are not adverse to grandstanding in front of the TV cameras...

Under any circumstances this would be serious. Under the current circumstances it might well prove disastrous. Given the "climate of treason" that prevails, we need more intelligence and counterintelligence, not less.

6/15/87

Who's Who in California

"California's Leading
Biographical Reference
Publisher — For
Over Half A
Century"

2 WINSLOW WAY • P.O. BOX 11410 • BAINBRIDGE ISLAND, WA 98110

(206) 842-8759

1928 – 1987
Our Fifty-Ninth Year

Scott T. Barnes

Dear Who's Who Nominee,

It is my pleasure to inform you that your name has
come to our attention for consideration for inclusion
in the 17th Edition of WHO'S WHO IN CALIFORNIA.

WHO'S WHO IN CALIFORNIA is the only biographical
reference work featuring up-to-date information solely
on Californians of significant achievement.

The new edition will include biographies of
eminent Californians from all fields of endeavor--
including business, the arts, science, education and
government.

In order to ensure data that are accurate
and current, we ask that you complete and
return the enclosed biographical data form
as soon as possible.

After we receive your data, it will be evaluated
on criteria established 59 years ago with the publication
of the first edition of WHO'S WHO IN CALIFORNIA. If
your biography is eligible for inclusion, you will be
notified promptly.

We extend our congratulations on your accomplishments
and look forward to receiving your completed biographical
data form. Thank you.

Sincerely yours,

Sarah Vitale
Editor-in-Chief

P.S. In the course of their work our researchers
      consult many sources; your name may appear
      in more than one. Please forgive any duplicate
      invitations.

The institute has also established relationships with 43 national religious, feminist, public interest and political organizations that are either based or maintain offices in Washington. These groups include the Union of American Hebrew Congregations, the Methodist Board of Global Ministries, the National Organization for Women and Americans for Democratic Action. Mr. Sheehan said leaders of these groups see the lawsuit as a tool for influencing public opinion and changing national policies.

The Christic Institute was founded in January 1980, by lawyers and investigators who six months earlier had won a $10.5 million judgment against the Oklahoma-based Kerr-McGee Corporation for the family of Karen Silkwood. A settlement of $1.38 million was eventually reached in that suit, which said Miss Silkwood and her home had become contaminated with plutonium because of negligence and inadequate safety procedures at the Kerr-McGee plant where she worked.

A Concept of Harmony

The institute takes its name from the "Christic force," a concept pioneered by a Jesuit priest that is said to be the harmony that bonds all things together and overpowers manmade destructive forces. The institute's leaders say the theory is the basis of a progressive political viewpoint that is pursued through legal actions.

Although the institute is not a religious organization, faith plays an important role in its communal culture. Eight staff members live in a group home owned by the institute and enjoy subsidized rent. Almost every staff member is paid $15,000 annually, including the top executives.

Ms. Nelson, a native of North Dakota, considered herself a conservative Republican before she attended the University of California at Berkeley in the mid-1960's and her outlook changed.

Mr. Sheehan, who grew up in Lake George, N.Y., as the son of a prison guard, attended Harvard College on a full scholarship and later graduated from Harvard Law School. He comes out of a tradition on the American left that believes in using lawsuits to change politics and culture. The Silkwood suit against Kerr-McGee was one of many celebrated public-interest cases Mr. Sheehan worked on in the 1970's.

As chief counsel of the Christic Institute, he has pursued his social-action agenda through similarly complex and weighty cases. Two years ago he won $400,000 in damages against the City of Greensboro, N.C., two Greensboro police officers and members of the Ku Klux Klan and American Nazi Party for the families of five people killed in 1979 at a demonstration in Greensboro. The victory came despite the failure of state and Federal trials to establish responsibility for the killings.

Mr. Sheehan has also challenged Judge Robert H. Bork, President Reagan's nominee to the Supreme Court, on an issue of particular vul-

The New York Times/Paul Hosefros
Daniel P. Sheehan, chief counsel to the Christic Institute.

'We're baking a cake, nice and slowly.'

nerability. In 1984, when a request by the institute for a special prosecutor in the Greensboro civil rights case came before an appellate panel headed by Judge Bork, Mr. Sheehan questioned the judge's fitness to rule in the case in light of his public opposition to such appointments. The questions about Judge Bork's failure to disqualify himself could well be raised by those who oppose the judge's confirmation.

Mr. Sheehan stumbled into the contra investigation while defending a woman in Texas who was charged with violating immigration laws by providing sanctuary to illegal aliens. During the trial, he learned of a secret program by the Reagan Administration to ship arms to the contras.

The contra investigation, he says, has been difficult, but the case will be ready to go to trial in Miami sometime next year. "We're baking a cake, nice and slowly," he said.

Based on the bombing incident, Mr. Sheehan has woven an elaborate web of conspiracy and drawn into it 29 defendants.

General Second is among those named in the suit, along with Adolfo Calero, a contra leader, and Robert Owen, Colonel North's emissary to the contras. All three have denied accusations against them.

Federal agents, United States prosecutors and spokesmen for the C.I.A. have characterized the suit as a political fantasy. Other investigators, including reporters from major news organizations, have tried without success to find proof of aspects of the case, particularly the allegations that military supplies for the contras may have been paid for with profits from drug trafficking.

Nevertheless, a few disclosures have helped convince several lawmakers and Congressional investigators that some charges may be valid.

Last month, an ex-C.I.A. agent, Glenn A. Robinette, testified before the Iran-contra committees that General Secord paid him more than $100,000 to develop derogatory information about the participants in the Christic lawsuit. The testimony came a month after General Secord had told the committees that the suit was "a minor threat."

Burmese drug kingpin links U.S. officials to trafficking

Asst. Defense Secretary Armitage involved in 1970s, warlord says

By DAVID E. HENDRIX
©1987, The Press-Enterprise

A drug warlord in Burma has accused Assistant U.S. Secretary of Defense Richard L. Armitage and former American officials of trafficking in drugs to raise money for anti-Communist operations.

In a three-hour videotape interview smuggled out of Southeast Asia within the past week and given to The Press-Enterprise yesterday, Khun Sa said high-ranking American officials were involved in drug trafficking between 1965 and at least 1979.

The alleged drug network was used to finance covert operations during the Vietnam War and continued after America's military withdrawal as a means of financing anti-Communist activities in Laos, Khun Sa said.

One of those allegedly involved in the trafficking, former CIA official Theodore Shackley, is a major participant in the Iran-Contra controversy. Shackley is a former deputy director of the CIA in charge of covert operations.

Armitage was in London yesterday for a conference and unavailable for comment, an aide said, Armitage has denied previous allegations of being involved in drug operations, calling such assertions "ludicrous and baseless."

Khun Sa, who says he directs an army of 40,000 attempting to form an independent nation from part of Burma, said Armitage controlled the finances of the alleged American drug operations.

"After the Vietnam War,

Richard Armitage was a prominent trafficker in Bangkok," a Khun Sa aide said. "Between 1975 and 1979 he was a very prominent trafficker. He was one of the embassy employees."

The aide said Armitage established the Far East Trading Co. after leaving the embassy, and used the company as a cover for drug traffic.

In an official statement responding to January allegations of involvement in drug trafficking, Armitage said he was never assigned to the U.S. Embassy in Bangkok in any capacity, nor was he ever involved with a firm named Far East Trading Co.

Who's Who in America cites Armitage's work with the Defense Attache Office in Saigon, 1973-75; a consultant with the Department of Defense in Washington, D.C., 1975-76; a partner and "Agi.-Export, Bangkok," 1976-78; and an aide to U.S. Senator Robert Dole 1978-79.

Armitage's office has said his Department of Defense work in 1975-76 concerned Iran naval programs.

The videotapes allegedly were made in Burma last month during extensive interviews of Khun Sa and his staff by James G. "Bo" Gritz, a retired Army Green Beret lieutenant colonel who has staged several expeditions to Southeast Asia in search of missing American servicemen.

Gritz said last night that he was asked "by the White House" to contact Khun Sa in October 1986 to investigate reports that his

Assistant Defense Secretary Richard Armitage, in 1986 during visit to Southeast Asia.

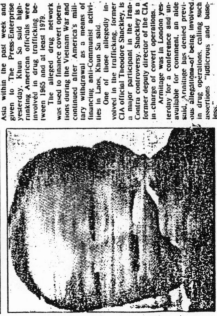
The Associated Press

forces, which are supported by drug profits, had control of or knowledge about missing American servicemen.

Gritz, who declined to identify who in the White House allegedly asked him to contact Khun Sa, yesterday turned himself in to federal authorities in Las Vegas on charges of passport violations and was released on his own recognizance.

Ben Jarratt, assistant White House press secretary, said last night that he had no knowledge of the tapes, or Gritz's allegations of

(See TAPE, Page A-9)

(From Page A-1)

going to Burma at the White House's behest.

Defense Department spokesman Maj. Randy Morger last night said the department had not seen the tapes and was in no position to comment about their contents.

"These are old allegations, but without having viewed the videotape. It's hard to address these current allegations," Morger said. "Regarding the old allegations, they have been looked into and have been found to have no substance."

Morger said Secretary of Defense (Casper) Weinberger "has complete trust in Mr. Armitage."

Khun Sa's staff said former CIA official Shackley was the central figure in the alleged American-controlled drug operations between 1965 and 1975.

Shackley, who was once viewed as a possible CIA director, is believed to have first brought up with Iran the possibility of ransoming American hostages held in Lebanon.

According to published reports, Shackley met with Iranian middleman Manucher Ghorbanifar in West Germany in late 1984. While the discussions dealt with buying the hostages' freedom, a possible arms-for-hostages deal was hinted at, according to those reports.

Copies of the videotapes were distributed yesterday to the Washington, D.C. offices of nine members of Congress, said Elvus Sasseen of Yukon, Okla.

Sasseen, a relative of an American serviceman still missing from the Vietnam War, helped copy and distribute the videotapes and made them available to The Press-Enterprise.

Representatives for congressmen named by Sasseen, including

The Press-Enterprise

Photographs made from videotape show former U.S. Army Green Beret Lt. Col. James G. "Bo" Gritz (top) and Burmese drug trade kingpin Khun Sa during a conversation that Gritz claims took place in Burma last month.

Investigations

A Liberal Group Makes Waves With Its Contra Lawsuit

By KEITH SCHNEIDER

Special to The New York Times

WASHINGTON, July 11 — In a drab row house within sight of Capitol Hill, a team of lawyers and researchers are conducting another investigation of clandestine pro-contra activities that is attracting its own share of publicity.

The work is being done by the Christic Institute, whose lawsuit filed 14 months ago in Miami substantially raised the group's influence among liberal political organizations that seek an end to the Reagan Administration's support of the Nicaraguan contras.

The institute, directed and staffed by people who were influenced by the anti-war and civil rights movements of the 1960's, alleges in its lawsuit that a terrorist bombing three years ago in Nicaragua was planned by former United States intelligence agents and military officers, financed by profits from narcotics sales and assisted by Government officials.

Although most of its main charges are unverified, enough details have been confirmed to strike a responsive chord in Congress, where two subcommittees are investigating related allegations.

The institute's suit seeks $20 million in damages on behalf of two American freelance journalists: Tony Avirgan, a television cameraman, and Martha Honey, who has been a stringer for several newspapers, including The New York Times. The two, based in Costa Rica, investigated the bombing at a news conference in May 1984 that was apparently meant to assassinate Edén Pastora Gómez, then the leader of the contra forces in Costa Rica. Mr. Avirgan was wounded in the incident.

When it filed the suit in May 1986, the institute was one of hundreds of small and largely unknown liberal groups clamoring to be noticed in a capital smitten by a popular President and his conservative policies.

But the initial disclosure last November of the Iran-contra affair confirmed one of the suit's principal contentions — that Lieut. Col. Oliver L. North, Maj. Gen. Richard V. Secord and a number of current and former operatives for the Central Intelli-

The Christic Institute says donations are pouring in and it has tripled its staff.

gence Agency were secretly directing the contras in a war against the Sandinista government of Nicaragua.

Nothing at the institute's headquarters on North Capitol Street has been the same since. Private donations are pouring in, enough to provide half of the nearly $40,000 needed each week to finance the investigation. The other half comes from public-interest and religious groups like the Unitarian Veatch Program on Long Island, the National Methodist Programs in New York, the J. Roderick MacArthur Foundation in Illinois, the C. S. Fund in Los Angeles.

The institute's chief counsel, Daniel P. Sheehan, 42 years old, and his wife, Sara Nelson, 44, the executive director, have recruited a staff of 35, triple the number of a year ago, and hired 11 private investigators.

CON'T NEXT PAGE

The Contras in Costa Rica: A Tangled Tale Is Told in Lawsuit

7/13/87

By JAMES LeMOYNE

Special to The New York Times

SAN JOSE, Costa Rica, July 4 — Two American freelance journalists living here are at the heart of an unresolved lawsuit charging that a broad conspiracy surrounded Nicaraguan rebel activities in Costa Rica, including an assassination attempt, drug-dealing and gun-running.

The two journalists, Tony Avirgan and Martha Honey, claim that the conspiracy was carried out by a network of active and former C.I.A. operatives, right-wing Cubans, contras and American mercenaries who operated here in support of the contras.

Even though a range of investigations by Government agencies and news organizations have failed to validate the lawsuit's central claims, the two journalists and the Christic Institute, a liberal Washington-based organization that has taken up their case, have doggedly pressed the suit in public for more than a year, attracting attention.

Several of the central figures in the Iran-contra affair who are also defendants in the case say they have have spent an extraordinary amount of time and effort fighting the suit. And references to the allegations have been made during the Congressional Iran-contra hearings.

American officials and several of those accused of illegal activity by the two journalists have repeatedly denied the accusations. Some American officials contend that the two reporters are political activists who have created a conspiracy theory to press their opposition to American policy in Central America.

Mr. Avirgan and Ms. Honey, who are husband and wife, deny that they are biased. They base their assertions on their investigation of a bombing that almost killed rebel leader Edén Pastora in 1984 as he spoke to a crowded news conference. The blast killed at least four people and wounded more than 20, including Mr. Avirgan.

The suit, which the Christic Institute filed on behalf of Ms. Honey and Mr. Avirgan in Miami last year before the Iran-contra scandal was disclosed, charges that 29 men conspired to run guns, deal drugs and kill Mr. Pastora in an illegal effort to press the contra war from Costa Rica.

The lawsuit does not charge that the C.I.A. was involved but does name some former senior officials of the agency. Drugs were sold, the suit charges, to buy guns for the rebels, though it is not clear who was in charge of the shipments.

Iran-Contra Figures Are Named

Those named in the suit include Richard V. Secord, the retired general who was the point man in setting up a secret supply network for the contras overseen by former White House aide Lieut. Col. Oliver L. North. Also named are contra leader Adolfo Calero and Robert Owen, Mr. North's emissary to the contras.

Mr. Secord, Mr. Calero and Mr. Owen have denied the accusations against them.

Several news organizations, as well as Congressional investigators, have looked into the allegation that drugs were sold to buy weapons for the contras, and have so far been unable to prove it.

Mr. Avirgan is a television cameraman who has worked for ABC, CBS and the BBC in England. Ms. Honey has been a stringer for several newspapers, including The New York Times and now writes for the Times of London and the Sunday Times of London.

Journalists Got Too Close

Their investigations apparently worried members of Mr. North's secret contra supply network. An ex-C.I.A. agent, Glenn A. Robinette, told Congressional investigators that Mr. Secord paid him $100,000 last year to investigate Mr. Avirgan and Ms. Honey in order to develop "derogatory" information about them.

Mr. Robinette said he came to Costa Rica and paid people for information. Mr. Secord has said he paid Mr. Robinette to investigate the two reporters only because they were close to revealing Mr. North's secret contra supply network.

Mr. Secord has denied involvement with any conspiracy that involved drug-dealing or the attempt to kill Mr. Pastora.

In the last year, Mr. Avirgan and Ms. Honey say they have received numerous anonymous death threats, and their lawyers and friends have been detained and harassed by the Costa Rican narcotics police, who have received training and funding from the American Embassy here. In addition, the two reporters, who have lived here for four years, say their house has been burglarized three times.

Targets of a Setup

Last month, they were the targets of what one Costa Rican official called a clumsy setup that involved mailing a package of cocaine to Mr. Avirgan, supposedly sent by Nicaraguan Interior Minister Tomás Borge. Two weeks ago, a rightist political group unsuccessfully demanded that the two reporters be expelled as "spies."

A senior Costa Rican official said a review had shown that Mr. Avirgan and Ms. Honey had broken no laws.

Three drug-traffickers now imprisoned in the United States have told reporters and Congressional investigators that some drug planes were allowed to land in the area in northern Costa Rica from which the contras operated. Guns were also run to the rebels, according to several ex-contras and mercenaries. In addition, someone built and planted a very professional bomb that almost killed Mr. Pastora.

But American officials say the drug trafficking, gun-running and the bombing are separate events that do not, as the two reporters contend, form part of a conspiracy.

Theory on Assassination

The man who tried to kill Mr. Pastora has never been found. American officials assert he was an agent of the Sandinistas, a claim they have not proved. In their investigation, Mr. Avirgan and Ms. Honey concluded that Mr. Pastora's rightist opponents within the contra movement hired a Libyan assassin named Amac Galil to plant the bomb.

The two journalists have a witness, a former contra adviser named Jack Terrell, who told a Costa Rican court last year that he was in a meeting where the bomb attack and other plans to kill Mr. Pastora were discussed with senior contra officials, including Mr. Calero, and an American rancher here named John Hull.

Mr. Calero and Mr. Hull have denied ever discussing killing Mr. Pastora.

Mr. Avirgan and Ms. Honey contend that the contras killed a key source of theirs' to keep him from talking. The two say they never met their source, but they communicated with him through a Costa Rican carpenter.

Victims of a Hoax?

Critics of the two journalists say they are victims of a hoax or have created a tale conveniently based on a witness who cannot be produced.

The journalists also charged that American Embassy officials here obstructed their investigative efforts on two occasions.

Two mercenaries arrested while aiding the contras here, Steven Carr and Robert Thompson, told reporters that American Embassy officials helped them jump bail last year and escape from Costa Rica. Mr. Carr, a principal source for Mr. Avirgan and Ms. Honey, died of a cocaine overdose after reaching the United States.

An embassy spokesman confirmed that embassy officials had met the two mercenaries, but denied they helped them leave Costa Rica.

The one sustained official investigation here of the bombing foundered when the Costa Rican policeman in charge of the case dropped the inquiry in 1985. Mr. Avirgan and Ms. Honey contend that the American Embassy offered the policeman a chance to continue his study in the United States on the condition that he leave immediately, forcing him to drop the investigation.

The American Embassy spokesman said that while the policeman had been sent to study in the United States, the trip had been approved in advance.

life, and answering Gritz's questions about their knowledge of alleged American involvement in drug trafficking.

"In 1965 to 1975 there is (was) one CIA agent in Lao,' said a man identified as Khun Sa's secretary, speaking through an interpreter. "His name is Shackley."

Khun Sa's staff then interrupted the narrative to discuss in Burmese how to spell Shackley's name correctly.

"He was involved in the narcotic business with Liu Si Han,' one said of Shackley.

Khun Sa called Liu Si Han "the most famous person in Burma who traffics — is involved in trafficking narcotics."

Khun Sa, who is leading the Shan State insurgents in a bid to gain independence from Burma, acknowledged in the tape interview that he had controlled major portions of the drug trafficking in Southeast Asia for more than 15 years. He said he didn't remember every American's name involved but that his aides did and that they had records of their dealings.

According to news reports and interviews published in several Southeast Asian newspapers, Khun Sa collects money from opium growers and shippers for the rights to cross Shan territory. In a January interview with the Bangkok Post, he claimed that, of the expected 900 tons of opium to be produced in Burma this year, his forces controlled 500 tons.

"We know that Shackley used one civilian to organize the (1965-75) trafficking," said Khun Sa's secretary. "And this civilian was named Santo Trafficante, who was the organizer."

Trafficante, 72, was the reputed boss of Florida's organized crime for 33 years. He died March 17 in his sleep three hours after undergoing triple-bypass surgery in Houston.

Upper map locates area of Burma near the border with Thailand in which Khun Sa, a leading drug trafficker and guerrilla leader, operates.

California Sen. Alan Cranston and Sen. David Boren of the Senate Intelligence Committee, said late yesterday the senators and representatives either had not received the videotapes or had not yet reviewed them.

In a jungle setting with a soft breeze blowing wind chimes in the background, the videotape showed Khun Sa, his staff of about 10 advisers, and about 20 members of his Shan United Army, talking, smoking cigarettes, laughing about physical threats to their

The key figures

● **Khun Sa**, leader of a well-armed insurgent Burmese group called Shan United Army, is regarded as the region's prime opium drug "war lord" by U.S. and Asian drug enforcement authorities. Burmese and Thai armies have battled Khun Sa's troops in recent months, pushing Khun Sa from his Thai mountain stronghold back into Burma. He and his men control much of the opium trafficking from the "Golden Triangle" in Burma and Thailand.

● **Richard L. Armitage**, a Navy veteran, is Defense Secretary Caspar Weinberger's assistant secretary for international security affairs. His official biography includes work with the Defense Attache Office in Saigon from 1973-75, a Defense Department consultant, an export agent in Bangkok, and an aide to Sen. Robert Dole of Kansas.

● Retired Army Lt. Col. **James G. "Bo" Gritz** is a decorated Special Forces veteran during the Vietnam War. He has made frequent trips to Southeast Asia to gather information about missing American servicemen from the Vietnam War.

● **Santo Trafficante**, 72, died March 17 in Houston after undergoing heart bypass surgery. He was the reputed Mafia crime boss for 33 years. He testified before a congressional committee in 1978 that he helped the CIA in a botched attempt to assassinate Cuban President Fidel Castro.

● **Theodore Shackley**, a retired Central Intelligence Agency officer, once headed the agency's operations in Vietnam and Laos. He was viewed at one time as a possible candidate for CIA director. He left the agency, however, in 1979 under a cloud over his association with convicted gunrunner and former CIA agent Edwin P. Wilson.

Trafficante told a congressional committee in 1978 that he was part of a failed CIA attempt to assassinate Cuban dictator Fidel Castro.

'Shackley could not be reached for comment last night.

Kuhn Sa's aides said the profits from the alleged American drug trafficking supported Laotian' anti-Communist troops and CIA operations in Laos until 1973.

'Jerry Daniels, a former CIA official in Laos and Thailand, organized the trafficking for Armitage, Kuhn Sa's aides said. Daniels died in his sleep in his Bangkok apartment in April 1982.

Daniel Arnold, the former CIA chief station in Thailand and Laos, purchased ammunition and arms for the anti-Communist

troops financed by the alleged drug trafficking, Kuhn Sa's aides said knowing Daniels. He also has denied being involved in arms deals with Arnold.

Khun Sa said, through an interpreter, that he was talking to Gritz because he wanted to blot out the opium drug trade. He accused American officials of not wanting "in their heart" to eradicate the illegal drug trade.

"The only two persons who want eradication are parents of the (addicted) child," Khun Sa said.

The drug warlord said he wanted to exchange the opium crop for other cash crops but said he needed American help to learn what to grow and train the Shan

people. He said he also wanted American help in creating a separate country for the Shan people.

Khun Sa said that for "one-tenth" of what America paid the Burmese and Thais for eradicating tons of opium, used to make heroin, he could guarantee none would pass through Shan territory.

Gritz said he was asked to visit Burma after the White House received a letter from a businessman asserting that Kuhn Sa had one American POW in his custody and control of four others. The story, Gritz said, turned out to be a fabrication by the businessman interested in opening American trade with the Shan people, who control vast teak forests.

Gritz said he and an associate, David Scott Weekly, reached Khun Sa in late November and were told by Khun Sa that he had no POWs. But Khun Sa said he would help look for them, Gritz said.

Khun Sa said in the videotape that a search in Laos for American POWs between December and May had proved fruitless.

Gritz said he was excited about Khun Sa's offer to cut off drug traffic and took a videotape of that offer to the same unnamed White House aide on Gritz's return to the United States.

The retired Green Beret officer, who has said for years that his forays were at the request of the government, said Weekly was subsequently arrested. He said the American government also denounced the Thais and Burmese for not taking action against Khun Sa.

Weekly pleaded guilty to transporting 200 pounds of plastic explosives to Las Vegas from Oklahoma City and was sentenced to five years in federal prison.

Gritz was indicted May 20 — while in Burma — by a Las Vegas federal grand jury for passport violations. Gritz turned himself in to federal authorities in Las Vegas yesterday, after making his videotapes available to Oklahoma associates, and was released on his own recognizance.

Gritz's attorney, Lamond Mills, called the indictment against Gritz "a misunderstanding that we hope can be worked out.

"If it cannot be worked out, and the United States government tries Col. Bo Gritz, believe me, he won't be the only one tried," said Mills, the former U.S. attorney for Nevada. "I'm not going to stand there and let him take the fall on a technical violation when all he was doing was acting for the American government in trying to find POWs. He's a genuine American hero.

"I've got three hours of videotape I'm going to use," Mills said.

Staff writers Marlow Chur-

POW Hunter Surrenders on Charge of Passport Violation

LAS VEGAS (AP)—Retired Army Green Beret Col. James G. (Bo) Gritz, who has staged several expeditions to Southeast Asia in search of missing American servicemen, turned himself in to federal authorities Wednesday on a charge of violating passport laws.

Gritz was freed on a personal recognizance bond after an appearance before U.S. Magistrate Elliott Sattler. He will be arraigned on Friday.

Gritz, 48, was indicted May 20 after a six-month investigation by the State Department. He reportedly was in Thailand when the indictment was returned.

The indictment charged Gritz with using a passport in the name of Patrick Richard Clark in Vancouver, Canada, on Dec. 17. Officials said Gritz was returning to the United States via Vancouver from one of his forays into Southeast Asia.

"I'd like to say to my friends and neighbors that everything done has been for the right reasons," said Gritz, who said he had proper authorization for his travels.

Gritz's attorney, Lamond Mills, also hinted that Gritz may have been involved in a mission for the government at the time he used the passport.

"At worst we have a colonel in the Special Forces who has been engaged in the last eight years in attempting to free POWs from Southeast Asia," Mills said. "At best we have a man acting under the auspices of the U.S. government."

Gritz, whose last known home was in Sandy Valley, about 30 miles southwest of Las Vegas, claims to have retrieved possessions of missing soldiers in his missions, although he has failed to rescue any POWs.

Gritz faces a maximum penalty of five years in prison if convicted on the charge.

Central Intelligence Agency

Washington, D.C. 20505

Mr. Scott T. Barnes   2 3 JUN 1987

Reference:

Dear Mr. Barnes:

This is a final response to your 10 September 1982 Privacy
Act request for an updated search for records from 4 September
1979 up through 8 October 1982.

We have completed our search for records indexed or
maintained under your name and were able to locate one
document, a memorandum dated 10 May 1982, which we have
determined may be released to you in segregable form.
Deletions were made pursuant to Privacy Act exemptions (b) and
(j)(1). A copy of the document is enclosed at Tab A and an
explanation of exemptions is enclosed at Tab B.

An additional two documents were located which we have
determined must be withheld in their entirety. They are listed
below.

Documents	Exemptions
2. Memorandum, 11 May 1982	(b), (j)(1), (k)(1)
3. Memorandum, 24 December 1981	(j)(1), (k)(1)

You may appeal these decisions by addressing your appeal to
me, and I will forward it to the appropriate senior officials
of this agency. Should you choose to do this, please explain
the basis of your appeal.

During our searches we located United States Government
material that was not originated by the CIA. This material
appears to be relevant to your request and has been referred to
its originating agency for review and direct response to you.

In addition, there is one document that has been sent to
another agency for coordination and has not yet been returned.
When it is returned, final disposition will be made and you
will be notified of our determination.

                                  Sincerely,

                                  Lee S. Strickland
                         Information and Privacy Coordinator

Enclosures - Tabs A & B

10 May 1982

SUBJECT: ███████████████

On 30 April 1982 ████████████ a lawyer representing Lacsa Airlines,
called to say that a gentleman by the name of Scott Barnes, who claimed
to be a former Agency employee, held a press conference in Costa Rica
and said that CIA had sent two or three shipments of arms by way of
Lacsa Airlines to San Salvador. The shipments included small arms,
napalm and chemicals. The person arranging these shipments, according
to ██████ was ███████████ I told ████████ that we did not ship
any arms, napalm or chemicals by way of Lacsa Airlines ████████
████████ that ██████ Barnes or ████████ were former Agency employees.

John N. McMahon
Executive Director

cc Chief ███████████
    Chief, OEA/PAD ██

EXPLANATION OF EXEMPTIONS

FREEDOM OF INFORMATION ACT:

(b)(1) applies to material which is properly classified pursuant to an Executive order in the interest of national defense or foreign policy;

(b)(2) applies to information which pertains solely to the internal rules and practices of the Agency;

(b)(3) applies to the Director's statutory obligations to protect from disclosure intelligence sources and methods, as well as the organization, functions, names, official titles, salaries or numbers of personnel employed by the Agency, in accord with the National Security Act of 1947 and the CIA Act of 1949, respectively;

(b)(4) applies to information such as trade secrets and commercial or financial information obtained from a person on a privileged or confidential basis;

(b)(5) applies to inter- and intra-agency memoranda which are advisory in nature;

(b)(6) applies to information release of which would constitute an unwarranted invasion of the personal privacy of other individuals; and

(b)(7) applies to investigatory records, release of which could (C) constitute an unwarranted invasion of the personal privacy of others, (D) disclose the identity of a confidential source, (E) disclose investigative techniques and procedures, or (F) endanger the life or physical safety of law enforcement personnel.

PRIVACY ACT:

(b) applies to information concerning other individuals which may not be released without their written consent;

(j)(1) applies to polygraph records; documents or segregable portions of documents, release of which would disclose intelligence sources and methods, including names of certain Agency employees and organizational components; and, documents or information provided by foreign governments;

(k)(1) applies to information and material properly classified pursuant to an Executive order in the interest of national defense or foreign policy;

(k)(5) applies to investigatory material compiled solely for the purpose of determining suitability, eligibility, or qualifications for Federal civilian employment, or access to classified information, release of which would disclose a confidential source; and

(k)(6) testing or examination material used to determine individual qualifications for appointment or promotion in Federal Government service the release of which would compromise the testing or examination process.

Hanoi Must Account for MIAs, and if Any Survive

By HARRY G. SUMMERS JR.   *LA Times*

Earlier this week Gen. John Vessey, the President's special envoy on POW-MIA affairs, met with Vietnamese officials in Hanoi, 14½ years after the January, 1973, Paris "peace" accords ended American involvement in the Vietnam War, Vessey, former chairman of the Joint Chiefs of Staff, was attempting to resolve the long-standing issue of American servicemen still missing in Vietnam.

As the Tomb of the Unknowns in Arlington National Cemetery attests, it is not uncommon in war that soldiers disappear in battle. In World War II and Korea they represented 22% of battlefield losses. There are still 78,751 Americans missing from World War II and 8,177 from the Korean War. In Vietnam, by comparison, the 2,413 still missing represent only 4% of battlefield losses.

Why then are the Vietnam War missing still an issue when the others, generally speaking, are not? First, the prisoner-of-war (POW) and missing-in-action (MIA) issue was politicized from the very beginning. Following the example that was set during the Korean War, the enemy saw American concern for the sanctity of human life as a vulnerability that could be exploited, and the POWs became hostages to the negotiating process. Enormous public pressure was put on the U.S. government to come to terms and "bring our POWs home."

And the U.S. government is not without blame. After the return of nearly 600 American POWs following the Paris accords, the Nixon Administration seized on the almost 2,500 Americans who were still unaccounted for and launched a nationwide POW-MIA campaign to catch public attention in order to gain support for continued military assistance to South Vietnam.

Responding in kind, the North Vietnamese linked repatriation of American remains under Article 8 of the Paris accords with Article 21, which promised American aid to rebuild Vietnam. Even though they made a mockery of the Paris accords with their 22-division cross-border blitzkrieg that overran South Vietnam in the spring of 1975, they are still using these bodies as bargaining chips to gain U.S. economic assistance.

There is another factor that makes the Vietnam experience unique. As many as 300 of the POW-MIAs still unrepatriated were positively identified as being in North Vietnamese hands. Pictures of them while in captivity were published in newspapers and magazines both in Vietnam and abroad. Still others were seen being taken into captivity or otherwise identified as POWs. Yet the Vietnamese claim no knowledge of their existence.

And then there is the question of Laos. As a former POW, retired Navy Capt. "Red" McDaniels said in a recent interview, "During the Vietnam War we lost 569 airmen over Laos. Over North Vietnam . . . 39% of us who were shot down survived. My logic tells me that in Laos there were the same anti-aircraft guns, the same terrain and the same aircraft . . . . Yet not one of those pilots has ever returned."

But those who have been there on the ground do not agree. "Laos is not at all like North Vietnam," says Army Col. Rod Paschall, who served in Laos with the Army Special Forces in the early 1960s. "The terrain is unbelievably rugged, and, unlike North Vietnam, most of it is uninhabited. There are no villagers to take injured pilots into custody and turn them over to the authorities. And even if they did fall into enemy hands, the Communist Pathet Lao were not above brutally beating their prisoners to death, as they did with Army Special Forces Capt. Walter Moon in 1961."

Finally there is the issue of live sightings. Since 1975 there have been 965 such reports. Of these, 624 reports were correlated with known individuals and 205 were judged to be untrue. Of the remaining 136 reported sightings that remain to be resolved, more than half of which occurred more than 10 years ago, 94 involve American POWs and 42 involve Americans in non-prisoner status.

Two conventions were held in Washington to call attention to this issue—one by the National League of Families of American Prisoners and Missing in Southeast Asia (whose director, Sue Mills Griffiths, accompanied Vessey to Hanoi) and another by the newer POW Policy Center, which offered a $2.4-million reward to any Vietnamese, Laotian or Cambodian who defects and brings along an American POW.

The sad truth is that the chances that there are still Americans being held against their will in Indochina are slim indeed. Only Hanoi knows for sure, but, as the Vessey commission rediscovered, Vietnam is still more interested in playing politics than in resolving this tragic issue.

Col. Harry G. Summers Jr., who is currently a contributing editor for U.S. News & World Report, was the chief of the team that negotiated with the North Vietnamese concerning the POW-MIA issue in 1974-75.

July 17, 1987

ROBERT SMITH

Denying the truth about our MIAs?

For most people, the Vietnam War is an event of the past, something you remember when watching "Platoon," or "Coming Home," or the "Deer Hunter." Or maybe you know a friend of a friend's brother who did a tour of duty.

But for over 2,400 American families, the war that officially ended 15 years ago is not yet over. Those families have fathers, brothers, uncles, and sons still listed as missing in Southeast Asia, relatives who did not come home to American soil in 1973 during "Operation Homecoming."

When our negotiators went to Paris to sign the Paris Peace Accords, they brought with them a longer list of POWs and MIAs than the Vietnamese list. They returned without a full accounting of those on our list.

This "long list/short list" controversy was further exacerbated by the fact that, even though we were bombing Laos and were at war with Laos, that country never signed the Paris Peace Accords. Contemporary news reports, however, referred to comments by Laotian and U.S. officials — including then Secretary of State Henry Kissinger and President Richard Nixon — alluding to prisoners held captive in Laos. Messrs. Kissinger and Nixon said the United States would not leave Southeast Asia until these men were accounted for. The fact is, they were not accounted for.

At the termination of this tragic era, the government of Vietnam said, "We have no more live Americans here." An executive commission, the Woodcock Commission, and a congressional commission. The Montgomery Commission, essentially confirmed that statement upon visits to Southeast Asia.

Both the Vietnamese and the commissions were proved wrong when, in 1979, Marine Pvt. Robert Garwood walked out of Vietnam. Pvt. Garwood allegedly had "collaborated with the enemy," and when he returned to the States he was immediately court-martialed and found guilty. But whether he is a "collaborator" or not is another issue. What is crucial is that he claims to have seen live men, our men, still being held captive in Southeast Asia.

Incredibly, the U.S. Government has not thoroughly debriefed Garwood. For that matter, key officials in the Vietnam negotiations — like Messrs. Kissinger and Nixon — have never been asked to testify before any congressional committee on this matter.

Former Defense Intelligence Agency Director Gen. Eugene Tighe

---

Robert C. Smith, a Republican member of the House from New Hampshire, is a Vietnam veteran.

> It is our moral obligation to sanctify the dignity of those men who risked life and limb to protect American freedoms, who may still be alive in a Vietnamese prison camp.

and former National Security Council Adviser Robert McFarlane have also both said they believe there are live American men in Southeast Asia.

Instead of thoroughly investigating reports of live men, the trend of our government agencies on POWs is to debunk and debase rather than debrief and deliver. The families of both the deceased and the missing have been denied the full truth for too many years. Although I am not one that has alleged a cover-up, it is understandable how that term could come into focus in this situation.

Last January, former Rep. Bill Hendon, North Carolina Republican, and I met personally with President Reagan on what we felt were major concerns regarding the POW MIA issue. The president was genuinely sympathetic, maybe more so than any administration in the past 10 years — but he is not receiving complete information on the reports currently held in the DIA files.

Can we honestly say that returning our missing Americans is a national priority? In rhetoric only.

For too long, there has been a pattern of mismanagement and "old blood" working to resolve this issue, in the area of both live men and remains. It is a time for a serious change — for the sake of American pride, dignity, and honor to those men who served our country with distinction. The families of our POWs MIAs deserve better than the treatment they have been given by the U.S. government.

On April 30 of this year, I introduced H.R. 2260 to declassify all live sighting case files and make available to the families information about their loved ones. The names of POWs and their families, and the sources, and methods of intelligence collection in these reports would not be released for public consumption, to protect the privacy of the families and government intelligence.

During the past several years, I and a number of my colleagues have read overwhelming numbers of these reports — currently classified as secret in the DIA files. Upon thorough review, it is my conclusion that there is evidence to substantiate that

we left men behind. The facts are staggering.

Although many of these reports have been determined by the DIA to be false, there are over 100 that have not been proved inaccurate despite the toughest scrutiny. Some of the live sighting information has been turned over to the communist government of Vietnam, yet the American public and the families of these men cannot see it! Until 1978, this live sighting information was not classified as secret. The DIA maintains "that it has no substantive evidence to prove the existence of American POWs." Why not allow the American people to decide for themselves?

It seems to me that we are in a gridlock. The DIA says the information is not valid; many of us who have seen the reports believe the opposite. We must let the public break this gridlock by declassifying the reports. There is no one more deserving of reviewing that information

than the 2,400 families of our American MIAs. No departmental bureaucrat should have knowledge that the families do not.

The bill currently has 66 cosponsors and has been referred to the three House committees on armed services, intelligence, and foreign affairs. Thus far, none has scheduled hearings. Regrettably, the DIA and other government officials are working to discredit and defeat this bill.

It is our moral obligation to sanctify and respect the dignity of those men who risked life and limb to protect American freedoms, who may still be alive in a Vietnamese prison camp. The efforts thus far have reflected the epitome of ineffectiveness, ineptitude, and bureaucratic bungling.

The nation this week has been rallying around Lt. Col. Oliver North for the great patriot that he is. I now ask Americans to rally around our POWs, MIAs, and their families, as they, too, are great patriots.

Blurred photos like this one, declassified from government files, lend credence to claims that American POWs still are held in Southeast Asia.

U.S. to Discuss MIAs and Some Aid to Hanoi

LA Times

By NICK B. WILLIAMS Jr.,
Times Staff Writer   6/4/87

HANOI—A White House-appointed delegation agreed Monday to discuss humanitarian aid for Vietnam in return for a resumption of talks aimed at accounting for American servicemen reported as missing in action or held prisoners of war during the Vietnam conflict.

In a brief statement issued at the end of three days of meetings here, the two sides declared that the discussions were limited to humanitarian concerns, including the MIA-POW issue, and were not linked to questions of diplomatic relations or U.S. economic aid.

Washington provides no aid of any kind to the pro-Soviet government of Vietnam, victors in the war of the 1960s and early 1970s over the U.S.-backed South Vietnamese regime.

New Meetings Due

The 107-word statement said two sets of meetings will take place in the near future, "one to discuss next steps to resolve MIA issues and one to discuss urgent Vietnamese humanitarian concerns."

Gen. John W. Vessey Jr., the former chairman of the Joint Chiefs of Staff who is President Reagan's hand-picked emissary, refused to answer questions after the statement was read to a crowded room of reporters and diplomats. A European diplomat told a handful of reporters earlier that the Americans were talking about such humanitarian aid as artificial arms and legs for Vietnamese who were wounded during the war.

Foreign Minister Nguyen Co Thach, head of the Vietnamese delegation, also refused to answer questions, other than replying "Many" when asked to describe his government's humanitarian concerns.

Vessey's professed goal in coming here was to achieve a resumption of technical talks on resolving the fate of nearly 1,800 American servicemen, still unaccounted for in Vietnam since the end of the war in April, 1975. The talks were broken off last fall by the Vietnamese, who at first blamed conflicts with their domestic political schedule but more recently have indicated that they wanted something in return for continuing the talks.

What the Vessey mission did achieve was a resumption of the talks, but with no apparent set timetable. In January, 1986, an American delegation headed by Assistant Defense Secretary Richard L. Armitage left Hanoi with a schedule on technical talks on the MIA issue. Six meetings a year were planned, and in a session that April, the Vietnamese turned over what were said to be the remains of 21 American servicemen.

Later that month, however, Hanoi canceled the scheduled meeting to protest the U.S. bombing of Libya. There have been no talks since last October.

'Urgent Concerns'

Now, according to the Vessey-Thach statement, "specific measures" have been agreed upon "to accelerate progress toward accounting for Americans missing in Vietnam and to address certain urgent humanitarian concerns of Vietnam. . . . The two sides have undertaken to work methodically and seriously on these humanitarian issues."

Vessey was accompanied here by a party of five, including Richard Childress, the National Security Council official who has spearheaded U.S. efforts on the MIA-POW issue, and Ann Mills Griffiths, head of the League of Families, an MIA support group, which has worked with conservative congressmen to keep MIAs as a priority issue for the Reagan Administration.

Vietnam to resume talks on missing U.S. soldiers

HANOI, Vietnam (AP) — The government agreed in three days of talks with U.S. envoy John W. Vessey to end months of deadlock and resume efforts to account for American servicemen still missing from the Vietnam War.

A joint statement issued Monday said: "Specific measures were agreed upon to accelerate progress toward accounting for Americans missing in Vietnam and to address certain humanitarian concerns of Vietnam."

Vessey, a retired general who is President Reagan's personal envoy, met with Nguyen Co Thach, foreign minister and deputy premier. The former chairman of the Joint Chiefs of Staff was the highest-ranking American official to visit Vietnam in a decade.

He flew to Bangkok on Monday for meetings with Thai officials before he returns to Washington on Wednesday.

The five-sentence statement issued in Hanoi said the two sides had "detailed, candid and constructive" talks on humanitarian issues arising from the war, which ended with a Communist victory in April 1975.

For the past several months, Vietnam has not returned any remains of U.S. servicemen and has refused meetings with American technical experts.

U.S. offficials had feared Hanoi would demand U.S. aid and renewed relations as the price of its help in accounting for 1,776 Americans still listed as missing in action.

Officials in Washington said they have no evidence that American prisoners still are detained in Vietnam but cannot discount the possibility. American forces withdrew from Vietnam in 1973, and North Vietnamese forces overran South Vietnam two years later.

Washington has said it will not consider diplomatic relations or aid until Vietnam gives "the fullest possible accounting" of the MIAs and withdraws its troops from Cambodia.

Envoy: Viets deny holding MIAs

WASHINGTON (AP) — Vietnam insists it does not have any Americans missing in action from the war but suggests it is possible there are some elsewhere in Southeast Asia, presidential envoy John W. Vessey Jr. said Monday.

Vessey, a four-star general and former chairman of the Joint Chiefs of Staff, said he would not speculate on whether there are Americans being held against their will in Vietnam.

"I don't know whether there are any there. There are certainly all sorts of evidence to show that some might be there, but yet it has been a long time since the end of the war," Vessey said.

Vessey talked with reporters at the White House after briefing President Reagan on his three days of talks in Hanoi with Vietnamese officials on the POW-MIA issue.

He said the United States and Vietnam agreed that Hanoi will accelerate its efforts to find missing Americans or their remains, and Washington will send experts to Hanoi to look into "humanitarian concerns that the Vietnamese have" — such as war orphans and people crippled by the fighting.

"We agreed that we wo address these as humanitar concerns and not link them broader political issues, such normalization of diplomatic lations, resumption of trade economic aid," he said.

More meetings will be held Hanoi at the end of the mo on the POW-MIA issue and humanitarian issues, he said.

Vessey said the Vietnam insisted "there are no American prisoners under control of the Vietnamese g ernment. The Vietnamese h acknowledged that there some wild parts of their co try...."

Hanoi Agrees to Speed MIA Hunt, Vessey Says

By MICHAEL WINES, *Times Staff Writer*

WASHINGTON—Vietnam has agreed to step up its search for American servicemen killed or captured during the Indochina war in exchange for a U.S. pledge to study "humanitarian concerns" stemming from the war, President Reagan's emissary on the issue said Monday.

Retired Army Gen. John W. Vessey Jr. said that two teams of U.S. experts will visit Vietnam in late August to discuss the prisoner of war-missing in action issue and an unspecified Vietnamese concern related to the former military presence of the United States in Vietnam.

Vessey, back from three days of talks in Hanoi with Vietnamese officials led by Foreign Minister Nguyen Co Thach, did not say how the Vietnamese plan to accelerate their search for living Americans or the remains of servicemen killed in action.

"We have an agreement to act," Vessey said. "We'll see what the actions are."

Belated Progress

The agreement reached by Vessey is the first progress seen in laborious talks over Vietnam War issues since last November, when Vietnam returned three sets of remains, two of which have been identified as American servicemen.

The Vietnamese had promised in 1985 to resolve POW-MIA questions within two years, but halted technical discussions early this year, expressing displeasure with the progress of the talks. U.S. offers to resume discussions were rejected until Reagan appointed Vessey, a former chairman of the Joint Chiefs of Staff, to pursue the POW issue in April.

Speaking at a White House briefing Monday, Vessey said that Vietnam has been given a list of 220 discrepancy cases in which the United States questions the fates of servicemen who disappeared in action during the war.

Seventy are "urgent" matters in which Vessey said there is "a compelling case to believe that a man is still alive" somewhere in Vietnam. Among them are well-publicized instances in which U.S. servicemen were photographed in the captivity of Vietnamese soldiers or seen parachuting into enemy territory and subsequently were not heard from.

Vessey declined to discuss prospects that Vietnam would find or return Americans still held prisoner there. The Vietnamese have repeatedly denied that they hold any U.S. soldiers captive, Vessey said, but they also have agreed that there are "some wild parts of their country" where Americans could be privately held.

"I just wouldn't care to speculate on that thing," he said. "I don't know whether there are any there. There are certainly all sorts of evidence to show that some might be there, but yet it has been a long time since the end of the war."

Greater Number Returned

He said, however, that a greater number of remains of American soldiers has been returned from Vietnam in the last two years than in any period since U.S. military involvement in Vietnam ended in 1974.

Vessey would not discuss in detail the war-related concerns that Vietnam is raising with the United States, except to say that they range from disabled Vietnamese veterans and war orphans to Amerasian children fathered by U.S. servicemen.

Economic aid or the payment of war reparations to Vietnam are not being considered, he said. Both sides have agreed that future discussions of the POW issue will not be tied to political issues such as the resumption of diplomatic relations.

Vessey headed a U.S. team that included State Department, Pentagon and National Security Council officials and Anne Mills-Griffith, a representative of the National League of Families of POWs-MIAs.

U.S. Aide in Laos

The NSC official, Asian affairs expert Richard K. Childress, was in Laos on Monday for an opening round of talks on 549 Americans missing in action there since the war ended. Most Americans missing in Laos are pilots who were shot down over the Ho Chi Minh Trail, the route used by Viet Cong rebels to funnel war supplies to the south during the Vietnam War.

Childress, contacted by the Associated Press in the Laotian capital of Vientiane, said that Laotian officials are "very hospitable," but he would not detail the discussions. He will return to Thailand on Wednesday.

A total of 2,413 American servicemen still are listed as missing in action in Southeast Asia.

Vietnam insists no U.S. soldiers under its control

AUG -11- 87

WASHINGTON (AP) — The Vietnamese government says it is not holding any Americans missing in action from the war but suggests it is possible there are some in Southeast Asia, presidential envoy John W. Vessey Jr. said Monday.

Vessey, a four-star general and former chairman of the Joint Chiefs of Staff, said he would not speculate on whether there are Americans being held against their will in Vietnam.

"I don't know whether there are any there. There are certainly all sorts of evidence to show that some might be there, but yet it has been a long time since the end of the war," Vessey said.

Vessey talked with reporters at the White House after briefing President Reagan on his three days of talks in Hanoi with Vietnamese officials on the POW-MIA issue. Vessey was appointed Reagan's special envoy on the matter in January.

He said the United States and Vietnam agreed that Hanoi would accelerate its efforts to find missing Americans or their remains, and Washington will send experts to Hanoi to look into "humanitarian concerns that the Vietnamese have" — such as war orphans and people crippled by the fighting.

"We agreed that we would address these as humanitarian concerns and not link them to broader political issues, such as normalization of diplomatic relations, resumption of trade or economic aid," he said.

More meetings will be held in Hanoi at the end of the month on the POW-MIA issue and the humanitarian issues, he said.

Vessey said the Vietnamese insisted "there are no live American prisoners under the control of the Vietnamese government. The Vietnamese have acknowledged that there are some wild parts of their country."

There are 2,413 Americans missing in action in Indochina, 1,776 of them in Vietnam.

Reprinted by permission: Spotlight Publication,
300 Independence, SE, Washington, DC 20003

FBI Investigating Allegations

EXCLUSIVE TO THE SPOTLIGHT
By Crowell Berrey

A ranking member of the National Security Council (NSC) is being investigated by the FBI. Allegedly he pressured a then-congressman into slandering an ex-congressman for claiming an administration cover-up of live Americans being held in southeast Asia by communists.

In several sworn affidavits, Col. Richard L. Childress is accused of pushing former Rep. John LeBoutillier (R-N.Y.) into denouncing ex-Rep. William Hendon (R-N.C.).

Both former congressmen have long maintained that the communists are still holding Americans against their will in Vietnam and Laos. Witnesses said, in sworn statements in late March of this year, that the incident occurred in November of 1983, when Hendon was considering running again for his old House seat.

Childress, a National Security Council official in charge of Asian affairs, allegedly offered LeBoutillier $40,000 a month to finance forays into Thailand to look for evidence of missing Americans, plus Drug Enforcement Administration (DEA) credentials to give LeBoutillier's associates access, in exchange for discrediting Hendon. Childress, who has been at the NSC since 1981, dismissed

The FBI is investigating allegations that (former Rep. John LeBoutillier (R-N.Y., left) was offered a bribe by Richard Childress (right).

the charges as an "absolute lie."

The sworn statements indicate that Childress was angry over Hendon's claims that the administration is "covering up" evidence that live Americans are still being held, although all involved agree that a substantial number of the nearly 2,500 unaccounted-for U.S. fighting men left in southeast Asia may still be prisoners.

PAPERS FILED

Papers were filed in a federal court in Fayetteville, North Carolina on March 30 in a legal action against the U.S. government brought by the National League of Families of Prisoners of War in Laos (NLFPOWL), an activist group maintaining that government efforts to help the missing men are inadequate. NLFPOWL is at odds with the widely known National League of Families of Prisoners and Missing in Southeast Asia, contending the latter group is accepting cover-ups by the government.

The activists' suit is an attempt to force the government to be more aggressive in pursuing the issue.

During President Jimmy Carter's years, when The SPOTLIGHT was the first in the national media to raise the POW-MIA issue, the official government position was that none had survived. By 1980, it had become a major campaign issue and candidate Ronald Reagan pledged to make rescuing the men his top priority.

Reagan has, many times—twice in public speeches to families of missing men—vowed that the government is doing everything in its power to resolve the issue.

Hendon, in an affidavit in the case on March 17, said LeBoutillier told him, in his congressional office, that Richard Childress "had arranged for LeBoutillier to receive $40,000 per month in Drug Enforcement Agency funds, plus DEA IDs," to assist in the POW recovery program.

ATTACK CHARACTER

Continued the affidavit: "LeBoutillier stated how Childress had informed him that to receive the DEA funds and IDs, LeBoutillier would have to come before the board of the National League of Families in Washington and attack my character—in Childress's words, as told to me by LeBoutillier, 'to get Hendon, to trash him, to really take him out.'

"'LeBoutillier later told me that Childress had asked him to do this because I had spoken out forcefully, against the government's handling of the POW matter.''

# of Bribery in POW-MIA Effort

Hendon's sworn statement also claimed that LeBoutillier said that, after "trashing" him, he (LeBoutillier) went back to Childress to obtain the promised funds. There, according to the affidavit, Childress told LeBoutillier that he would have to first write a letter stating that the "trashing" of Hendon was not under duress but of his own free will.

LeBoutillier, according to Hendon's affidavit, said he complied and was then told no funding or other assistance in his POW rescue program would be forthcoming.

"During the conversation," the Hendon affidavit says, "LeBoutillier repeatedly cursed Lt. Col. Childress and Ms. Ann Mills Griffiths for their having, in LeBoutillier's words, 'set me up and doublecrossed me'."

REPRISAL

The effort to destroy Hendon's credibility was, the sworn statements indicate, in reprisal for Hendon's having publicly stated that, while working in the Defense Department, he had seen reports, documents and other evidence that convinced him that Americans were being held in southeast Asia.

Hendon had also said that the evidence was known and in the files of U.S. government agencies but was not being provided to President Reagan. Furthermore such evidence had earlier been withheld from then-President Carter, he said.

According to Col. Earl P. Hopper's sworn statement, arrangements were made for Hendon to address the league's board in Washington on November 19, 1983. It was to be a joint appearance with LeBoutillier, whom Hendon regarded as a friend and fellow champion of the POWs, according to the Hopper statement. (Hopper is now retired from the Army.)

Hendon said he found no sign of LeBoutillier. After addressing the group, he took his leave, Hopper added. Then LeBoutillier and Childress appeared, he said.

Hendon was denounced by LeBoutillier for using the POW issue for "personal gain" and "publicity," and for endangering the POWs by revealing classified information, Hopper said.

Hopper was then chairman of the board but the arrangements for Hendon to be denounced after his departure had been unknown to him, he said. "They could not prove such a claim" about Hendon, Hopper added.

SMITH STATEMENT

Mark A. Smith, a retired Army major and original plaintiff in the suit to force Reagan to act on behalf of the POWs, submitted an affidavit saying LeBoutillier had told him, too, that Childress prompted LeBoutillier to denounce Hendon in exchange for $40,000 monthly for the "Skyhook II" rescue operations in southeast Asia.

Dorothy M. Shelton of San Diego swore, in a March 19 affidavit, that LeBoutillier had visited her home on a Sunday in August, 1984 and told her and other POW-MIA survivors and a former

POW about discrediting Hendon for a Childress promise of $40,000 monthly.

"I was shocked at the $40,000 figure and that is why I remember it so well," she said.

In a letter to Army Chief of Staff Gen. John Wickham Jr., dated March 29, Jerry Kiley, who served in the Army in Vietnam in 1967-68, asked Wickham to investigate Childress's alleged actions in the Hendon incident as a violation of the Hatch Act prohibition against political activity.

LeBoutillier defended his actions in a memo to the league's board dated January 23, 1984 on grounds that Hendon was implicating him in a "criminal act" for revealing "classified material."

He was referring to Hendon's public comments that, as a Defense Department official, Hendon had examined documents that convinced him POWs were being held.

The federal action in the court at Fayetteville is expected to be pending for several months, sources said.

CONGRESSMEN SPEAK OUT

Meanwhile, two congressmen told United Press International on April 5 that Pentagon and National Security Council officials have for years failed to provide Reagan important information indicating that Americans are being held.

"The Defense Intelligence Agency [DIA] just automatically tries to refute refugee reports," said Rep. John Rowland (R-Conn.).

He has examined classified reports of live POWs and been briefed often by the DIA.

Rep. Robert Smith (R-N.H.) called it "a pattern of poor management" at the White House. "NSC officials have felt the president didn't need to know important details," Smith said.

•

May 24, 87

Commentary

My Charles

Mike Shelton-The Register

America's call to action is missing

Don Feder

ast month — 12 years from the day our flag was lowered for the last time over the American embassy in Saigon — was the 55th birthday of Col. Charles E. Shelton.

People who never met the man thought of him on April 29 — and think of him still because they have joined in the national effort on behalf of U.S. military people not yet fully accounted for. Shelton, a captive of Communist forces in Southeast Asia 22 years ago, typifies the plight of our POW/MIAs.

It was on his 33rd birthday in 1965 that then-Capt. Shelton's "Voodoo" aircraft was shot down over Laos. Through voice contact made on the ground, Shelton reported his condition was good.

Villagers who observed the crash also communicated his capture by the Pathet Lao. He was last seen, by several sources, inside Laos in 1967. Thereafter, the jungles of Indochina seemingly swallowed up the brave aviator.

Col. Shelton is the sole American serviceman officially listed as a prisoner of war by the U.S. government. Not that we have more evidence of his existence than that of many others; essentially it is normality, one designed to keep the books open on our military heroes.

Shelton is one of nearly 2,400 servicemen from the Vietnam War who must be accounted for. As of Jan. 1, there were more than 100 first-hand sighting reports of Americans in captivity which have yet to be resolved.

The intelligence typically comes from refugees, who, granted, have a vested interest in peddling such information in hopes of obtaining entry to this country.

That year, the North Vietnamese swore they'd freed all prisoners. Yet, in the late 60s and early 70s (nearly 20 years after the cessation of hostilities), they released hundreds of non-French foreign legionnaires.

Yet, many of the accounts have the ring of truth. For instance, a former South Vietnamese paratrooper, who spent 15 years in Communist prisons, says he saw a number of American POWs in Thanh Hoa in 1978, three years after the war ended.

He offers a chilling description of their condition: "The POWs I saw were very thin, they were covered with scabies; there was just skin and bones left on them. They could hardly walk, yet they were forced to carry wood from the forests distant about 150 meters. They often fell down. Sometimes they were beaten by guards."

Is it unreasonable to suppose these men are still alive? The 1954 Geneva Accords, which ended French involvement in the region, provided for the repatriation of combatants.

That year, the North Vietnamese swore they'd freed all prisoners. Yet, in the late 60s and early 70s (nearly 20 years after the cessation of hostilities), they released hundreds of non-French foreign legionnaires. The moral: trust not the solemn declarations of tyrants.

What does the Hanoi politburo have to gain from such inhuman behavior? Oh, ransom (at the appropriate time, when they're desperate enough for foreign exchange), or perhaps just the on-going opportunity to satiate the pure hatred Communists harbor for their foes.

Whatever the reason, while Jane Fonda continues to make millions off her exercise tapes, and hubby Tom Hayden plots his political future, and Abbie Hoffman glories in publicity from his radical exploits, and Ramsey Clark earns fat fees representing Libyan "victims" of our bombing raid (veterans all of Ho Chi Minh's American Brigade), these courageous soldiers — who epitomize the best of our civilization — rot in tropical gulags.

When Charles Shelton entered his long night of imprisonment, his five children ranged in age from 13 to 1. Unlike much of the nation, afflicted with amnesia on the matter, they have not forgotten.

His oldest son, Charles Jr., now 32 and a Catholic priest, recently completed service as an active duty chaplain in the U.S. Air Force. John, an entertainer, will take part in Memorial Day services at the Fort Rosecrans National Cemetery in San Diego, where he'll sing "Don't Forget The Eagles," a POW/MIA anthem.

Mrs. Charles — Marian — Shelton says (with a slight, self-deprecating laugh) she devotes 12 hours a day to the cause. In June, she'll be in Louisville, Ky., to meet the Freedom Train, en-route from Memphis to Baltimore, from which popular performers will conduct a series of concerts to raise funds for POW/MIA organizations.

Few of us can care as much as the Shelton family. But we all should care, more than a little. Charles Shelton and his comrades served and suffered for us and the cause of freedom. (In all likelihood, they still do.) Our concern, our prayers, and unstinting efforts to bring them home are the very least we owe them.

Feder writes for the Boston Herald.

THE WHITE HOUSE

WASHINGTON

July 18, 1987

As you gather once again in Washington for the 18th Annual Meeting of the National League of Families, Nancy and I want you to know that our long-standing commitment to you and to our mutual quest is undiminished.

I have asked General John Vessey, a man of unquestioned integrity and commitment to your cause, to serve as my special emissary to Hanoi. I am pleased to let you know tonight that we have proposed a visit by General Vessey to Hanoi in early August.

General Vessey will go with my hopes and prayers that firm agreements can be reached that will provide the answers we all seek. I am confident that the Vietnamese will know of your unified support of this important mission.

The responsible, persistent and patriotic voice of the National League of Families has been heard throughout this great land -- a voice of urgency, reason and remembrance. Your tireless efforts in the face of political indifference, Communist intransigence and unfair attacks have been central to the progress made thus far.

Tonight, I reaffirm our unwavering commitment to resolving the POW/MIA issue as a matter of highest priority. Together, we can be proud of overcoming past challenges, knowing that more lie ahead of us. Together, we can be proud of countering apathy, remaining alert to the possibility it could reassert itself. Together, we can be proud that history will record we did what was right, certain that whoever follows us in office cannot ignore what we have started and accomplished.

Nancy and I are with you tonight in thought and prayer. God bless you, and God bless America.

Ronald Reagan